COLONIES

CANADA TO 1867

COLONIES

CANADA TO 1867

DAVID J. BERCUSON
University of Calgary

KERRY ABEL
Carleton University

DONALD HARMAN AKENSON
Queen's University

PETER A. BASKERVILLE
University of Victoria

J. M. BUMSTED
University of Manitoba

JOHN G. REID
Saint Mary's University

MCGRAW-HILL RYERSON LIMITED
Toronto Montreal New York Auckland Bogotá Caracas
Lisbon London Madrid Mexico Milan New Delhi Paris
San Juan Singapore Sydney Tokyo

COLONIES: CANADA TO 1867

1 2 3 4 5 6 7 8 9 D 1 0 9 8 7 6 5 4 3 2

Printed and bound in Canada

Care has been taken to trace ownership of copyright material contained in this text. The publishers will gladly accept any information that will enable them to rectify any reference or credit in subsequent editions.

SPONSORING EDITOR: CATHERINE A. O'TOOLE
SENIOR SUPERVISING EDITOR: ROSALYN STEINER
PERMISSIONS EDITOR: NORMA CHRISTENSEN
COVER DESIGN AND TEXT: SHARON MATTHEWS/MATTHEWS COMMUNICATIONS DESIGN

Canadian Cataloguing in Publication Data
Bercuson, David Jay, 1945–
    Colonies : Canada to 1867

Includes index.
ISBN 0-07-551013-8

1. Canada–History–To 1763 (New France).
2. Canada–History–1763–1867. I. Title.

FC161.B47 1992   971   C91-095469-0
F1026.B47 1992

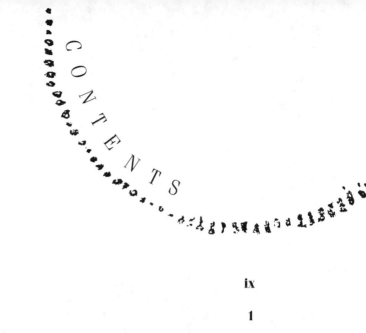

PREFACE ix

INTRODUCTION 1

CHAPTER **I** Early History to 1663 7

CHAPTER **II** Colonial Experiments, 1663–1763 41

CHAPTER **III** The Fur Trade 77

CHAPTER **IV** British North America, 1763–1791 117

CHAPTER **V** The Origins of Colonial Society and Culture 157

CHAPTER **VI** British North America, 1791–1841 197

CHAPTER **VII** The Business Cultures of Pre-Confederation Canada 265

CHAPTER **VIII** British North America , 1841–1864 309

CHAPTER **IX** The Pre-Confederation Roots of Canadian 371
Regionalism

CHAPTER **X** The Confederation Question, 1864–1867 419

CHAPTER **XI** Pre-Confederation Canada as a European Society 477

CONCLUSION 519

CREDITS 525

INDEX 529

MAPS

First Nations at the Time of European Contact: Language Groups and
    Peoples   **8**

North America, 1697   **42**

North America, 1713   **42**

Northeastern North America, 1755   **43**

Western Fur Trade   **78**

North America, 1763   **118**

North America, 1774   **118**

Ethnic Diversity in the Atlantic Colonies, 1800   **158**

Settlement in Upper Canada, 1800 to 1850   **198**

Settlement in Lower Canada and the Maritime Provinces, about 1800   **198**

Trade and Economy of Mid-19th Century British North America   **266**

British North American Railways on the Eve of Confederation   **310**

The Maritimes as an Economic Region, 1800   **372**

Canada at Confederation   **420**

Origins of Immigrants to New France, 1608–1759   **478**

Origins of Irish-Catholic Migrants Married in Toronto in the 1850s   **479**

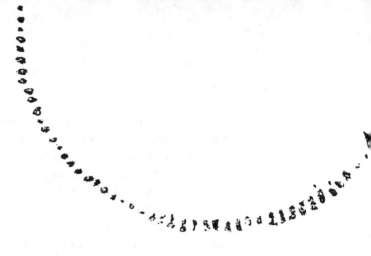

PREFACE

Although much of the world considers Canada a
rather dull place and Canadians even-tempered, the truth is more exciting.
Canada has always been a precarious thing. The aboriginal people fought a
continual battle to survive and, at the same time, developed a unique
culture that has sustained them through harrowing challenges right up to
the present. The Europeans, who arrived on this continent over 400 years
ago, also faced adversity. Clinging to the narrow band of cultivable land
that lies astride the St. Lawrence River or to the rocky coasts of the Atlantic
Ocean, they tried to build new societies that preserved their heritage but
that also reflected the realities of the singular environment they had
adopted. This was no less true even after they had spanned the continent
with steel and telegraph wire and had built a political structure and an
economy that was and is one of the freest and most prosperous on earth.

The precariousness of Canadian existence has created a mercurial
temperament among Canadians. Throughout its history, optimism and
hope have given way to pessimism and despair, which, in turn, have
changed into optimism and hope again. Since Canada brings together
people of widely varying backgrounds, interests, and aspirations in a
nation divided by geography and climate, the belief that Canada would
endure as a united nation has often been balanced by the fear that Canada
could not possibly survive. The history of Canada is, therefore, the history
of diverse peoples struggling for stability and trying, sometimes unsuccessfully, to live together in one country by one set of rules.

This book describes that struggle from the time of early human habitation in what is now Canada to the era of Confederation. The authors of this
text have used an approach that differs from the usual one that relates the

history of colonial Canada. They have been careful to show that Canada's native peoples have a unique history of their own, one that did not end with white settlement. They have told the story not only of the politicians and businesspeople, but also of the farmers, workers, fur traders, and other "ordinary" colonists whose labours moulded Canada as much as did the work of governors and bishops. They have emphasized the importance of family and the central role of women in Canada's colonial past. They have been careful to demonstrate that colonial history happened every-where, from Newfoundland to Vancouver Island, and not only in, or even primarily in, Ontario and Quebec. And they have demonstrated that Confederation was never inevitable, not a logical outcome of colonial history but a reflection of the rather narrow outlook of the men who made the Confederation agreements, and added little to existing Canadian society.

Anyone who digests this book will see that the major issues facing Canada today—the place of First Nations in Canadian society, the role of women, the balance between regionalism and national unity, the unique-ness of Quebec—have all had their roots in colonial history. They will also see that colonial Canada was a complex and vibrant place, no less than the Canada of today.

Although this book stands alone in telling the story of Canada up to Confederation, it is also the first of two volumes that span all of Canadian history. Its companion, *Nation: Canada Since Confederation*, is concerned with the post-Confederation time frame. In both books, historians who are experts in their fields have written about Canada with a view to emphasiz-ing those trends that they believe have shaped the contours of Canada's development. They have offered lively interpretations, interesting insights, and solid scholarship based on detailed research. Not everyone will agree with the emphases, with the points of view, with the perspective of the authors, but no one will call these books dull!

D.J.B.
December 1991

INTRODUCTION

On 23 June 1990 at the stroke of midnight, the Meech Lake Accord died. It had been drafted three years earlier by Prime Minister Brian Mulroney, representing the federal government and the premiers of all ten provinces. The accord had been designed to bring Quebec back into the constitutional process from which that province had bowed out in 1982. At that time, Ottawa and nine provinces agreed to a formula by which the Canadian Constitution could be brought to Canada from Britain, an amending formula attached, and a Charter of Rights and Freedoms added. Although Quebec had refused to agree with the others, the new Constitution Act was proclaimed anyway, and the government of Quebec resolved not to take part in any future constitutional discussions until its conditions were accepted. The most important of those was a demand that the Constitution recognize Quebec's special status within Canada and that the government of Quebec be acknowledged as having a special responsibility to preserve that distinct status. The Meech Lake Accord had been designed to meet those demands. According to the Constitution Act, it was to become effective three years after first ratification by either Ottawa or any of the provincial legislatures, provided that all eleven governments ratified it within that three-year time span.

Although Ottawa and eight provinces did adopt the accord, two provinces—Manitoba and New Brunswick—balked after their governments changed following provincial elections. Then opposition to the accord mounted across English-speaking Canada after Quebec passed Bill 178,

1

prohibiting the use of any language other than French on outdoor commercial signs within the province. Women's groups and native people were especially opposed. They (and others) feared that Quebec's special status would supplant individual rights if it believed that the collective identity of francophone Quebecers was in danger. Finally, the government of Newfoundland rescinded the approval it had already given after a new premier came to power who opposed special status in principle. Amid predictions that the death of the accord would doom Canada, the prime minister called a meeting of first ministers in early June 1990 to attempt a salvage operation. It failed. Although New Brunswick decided to approve the accord, the legislatures of Newfoundland and Manitoba failed to take action before the deadline ran out. In Manitoba, Elijah Harper, an aboriginal member of the legislative assembly, with the support of native peoples across Canada, succeeded in using procedural tactics to prevent legislative approval.

Although the Meech Lake affair took place 123 years after Confederation, all the elements that led both to its creation and to its destruction were present in Canada before 1867. The battle for native survival started shortly after European explorers and traders began to interact with Canada's aboriginal people. The struggle of Quebecers to build and maintain a distinct society began long before Confederation, even before the Conquest of New France by the British toward the end of the Seven Years' War. The regional differences that undermined most efforts of English-speaking Canadians to unite behind a common set of constitutional principles in 1990 are rooted in ethnic, cultural, religious, and occupational differences that marked pre-Confederation Canada. Those differences were exacerbated then, as they are now, by the distance and isolation that results from geography and climate. Finally, the role played by women in society was as crucial in pre-Confederation Canada as it is today, even if that role has been all but ignored in most Canadian texts up to the present time.

Canadian history, like all history, is a continuity. Historical events blend into each other. Cause and effect are never neatly laid out. Historians need to impose arbitrary divisions on history so that they can break it up into easily digestible portions that can be taught or written about. But the human events that history is supposed to explain are never so conveniently packaged. Thus, Canadian history is often broken down into "pre-Confederation" and "post-Confederation" eras, but the division hides much more than it reveals.

Although this textbook ends roughly at Confederation (and its companion volume *Nation: Canada Since Confederation* begins at about the same point), Confederation itself is really only important for the potential it created for British North Americans to try to build a country in the decades that followed. Confederation did not, in and of itself, do very much at all. For example, the political events from 1864 to 1867 did not have as immediate and dramatic an impact on Canadian history as did the Conquest of New France by the British or the First World War. The Confederation process consisted primarily of the establishment of a new layer of government (the federal one) between the governments of the individual colonies (later the provinces, for the most part) and the imperial government in London. After Confederation, Canada remained a colony; it had no more self-government than British North America had had before 1867. Greater Canadian self-government did not follow for many decades; Canada still had no right to conduct its own foreign policy until the First World War, more than 45 years later.

When we examine the immediate impact of Confederation, we find that few of the major problems plaguing colonial Canada were resolved and that nothing fundamental was re-arranged by it. The white, Christian, middle-class males who hammered out Confederation were interested in fiscal and political questions, but in little else. Thus, Confederation created a *potential* for something more; it was not something more of itself. At Confederation, Canada was a disunited, diverse, physically separated, and very complex society. It was from the very beginning. It is now.

Therefore, it is very much a mistake to think about two Canadian histories—the story of the colonial peoples who joined together beginning in 1867, and the story of the people of Canada after Confederation. This text ends roughly at Confederation only because it is convenient (and traditional) to divide Canadian history at that point. A good argument could also be made that 1914—Canada's entry into the First World War—is just as good a dividing point.

Probably the greatest misconception about pre-Confederation Canada is believing that it was a simpler place than Canada is now. That error is often compounded by the impression that Canada later changed fundamentally as it expanded across the continent, welcomed millions of immigrants, fought two world wars, and met the challenges of a nuclear and technologically advanced world. Of course, some things did change dramatically, but the basic characteristics that have shaped Canadian development were present from the earliest days of colonial Canada. Those who comprehend pre-Confederation Canada will understand the Canada of the 1990s because many of the major issues that colonial Canadians wrestled with are still unresolved and challenging our survival as a viable national entity.

The basic fact about Canada is that climate and geography have always divided it. The St. Lawrence, Canada's major river system, which links the Gulf of St. Lawrence with the continental interior, was not a natural highway as was, for example, the Ohio-Missouri-Mississippi river system in the United States. Many obstacles blocked upriver navigation on the St. Lawrence in the days of wind and sail; much early financial activity in colonial Canada was directed toward marshalling the capital to improve the system and make it a viable commerce route for intra-British-American trade.

There was, thus, no easy way for colonists to communicate with each other except by building costly and difficult overland roads. Even this was not practical when it came to communication with the West, which was virtually blocked by the Precambrian Shield until the advent of railways, telecommunications, and air travel. In the severe winter that grips the northern half of the continent for about half the year, what water transport there was between the Atlantic colonies and those in the interior was suspended. If colonists were removed from each other in the warm part of the year, during the winter, they were almost totally isolated.

Geography, and to a lesser degree climate, guaranteed regional differences. Not only were people separated from each other by time and space, they did different things and therefore had differing concerns and aspirations. In Upper Canada, wheat and cash crops dominated agriculture. In the Atlantic colonies, lumbering, coal mining, and fishing shared importance with agriculture. In the port cities (towns, really) of the Atlantic colonies and Quebec, seaborne commerce provided livelihoods for those who sailed, those who built ships, wharfs, and warehouses, those who provisioned, those who bought and sold cargoes.

Other major differences added to those imposed by geography and occupation. The people of the colonies were neither united by language nor by culture. European settlers first worked in cooperation with native peoples to establish trade networks or to subdue their enemies—they had little choice but to work with the native peoples at first—but then relegated them to smaller and smaller areas of the country as white settlement expanded. The structures of European society were built atop the ruins of native society. But native people did not cease to exist; they were simply ignored by historians. They had played their role in history, it was assumed, and then others came along to take up the vanguard of human progress.

Although various groups of white settlers acted alike in dealing with native people, they were themselves very different from each other in origin, background, language, religion, and culture. To proclaim, as some modern politicians, academics, and journalists do, that Canada was the creation of "two founding peoples" is to totally ignore the facts of Canadian history. Although it is true that, after the Conquest of New France, colonists largely spoke either English or French—and even that was not done without significant differences in style, accent, vocabulary, at least in the English-speaking colonies—they had little else in common. The divisions and rivalries of language, ethnicity, and religion were many and deep. Thus, even if they could have communicated with each other more easily, it is not clear that they really wanted or needed to.

The diversity of colonial society reflected a variety and richness of life that is not often understood today. Religion was deeply important to colonial peoples. Family life was the foundation of colonial society and was strengthened by religious values. Women played a vital and active role in colonial society from its inception. There was nothing inherently masculine about pioneering or fur trading. Women are missing from pre-Confederation history only because they have been ignored. When Canadians take a good look at their society today, they see a country with many diverse people, with women playing a full role in social and economic life, and with little homogeneity of aspiration or view. That description would have fit colonial society perfectly.

Just as cultural, religious, and political life was vibrant, complex, and diverse, so too was commercial and economic life. The North West Company's continent-spanning fur trade network would be the envy of any major corporation today. The Hudson's Bay Company's commercial and organizational structures were a forerunner of the major retail establishments of the twentieth century. Colonists engaged in a wide variety of occupations, commercial pursuits, and economic activities. They aspired to improve their position and their standard of living. Their political and social structures were a reflection of their economic aspirations. So too were their relationships to each other. That would describe most Canadians in the 1990s as well.

The amount of diversity was mirrored in the extent of disunity. As this textbook shows time and again, regionalism was a basic fact of Canadian life long before the death of the Meech Lake Accord, long before the emergence of the Maritime Rights Movement of the 1920s, long before the rise of western protest groups in the 1880s, long before Confederation itself. Thus, in some fundamental ways, Confederation was an "unnatural" act that brought together groups that had lived separate and distinct lives for decades, even centuries, and that had been perfectly happy doing so.

There was, therefore, nothing inevitable about it. Canadians today, following the demise of the Meech Lake Accord, are beginning to see that the continuation of Confederation is not inevitable either, at least not in the form it has taken since 1867.

Colonial history did not take place in a vacuum. The events that marked the European discovery and settlement of the continent were part of a larger trend in Western Europe involving the expansion of both the physical frontiers of Western European living space and the psychological frontiers of the Western European mind. Thus, the great changes that moulded European society in the last 350 years were reflected in developments in North America. The struggles of religion, politics, ideology, and for domination of the European continent, which changed the course of human development so profoundly in Western Europe and which so affected the rest of the world, were played out in microcosm in colonial North America. Colonial Canada was a unique society—collection of societies would better describe it—but it was also very much a reflection of its varied European and native origins.

Early Canadian history must also be viewed within the context of the French-British-American struggle for mastery over North America. The contours of that struggle were shaped by geography, by the existing native cultures, by the settlement and migration of European peoples, by commerce, and by military necessity. The outcome of that struggle was determined far from North America in the case of the Conquest of New France. As the French and then the British colonies developed around the Bay of Fundy, the Gulf of St. Lawrence, and the St. Lawrence River, the course of developments in the colonies to the South were a constant factor. "America" was as dominant in colonial days as it is now.

Thus, colonial Canada was two things simultaneously: a unique collection of communities loosely linked by commerce, a common political tradition, and fear of those to the South; and an amorphous group divided by geography, language, ethnicity, and occupation. It was also a North American reflection of European culture, religion, and values. Colonial Canada was the meeting point of Europeans with the North American environment—its vastness, its natural riches, its potential—with each other, and, of course, with the indigenous peoples. The story of Canada from its origins is the story of those interactions. It begins with the First Nations.

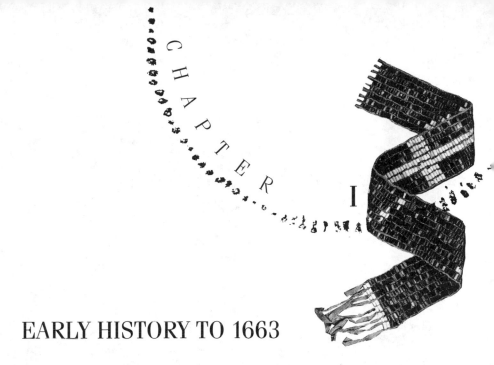

CHAPTER I

EARLY HISTORY TO 1663

It may be commonplace to refer to the lands of the western hemisphere as the "New World," but the term is misleading in many ways. Human habitation of North and South America has a long and complex history. It is a story of competition and cooperation, of international politics and family networks, of ordinary men and women as well as community leaders. Above all, it is the story of human beings adapting to changing circumstances. Perhaps the most dramatic change was not a sudden event but the slow process of encounter between the original populations and brash, aggressive newcomers from Europe. As these newcomers attempted to establish their political and economic systems in a new setting, the patterns of life both for them and for the aboriginal populations were slowly and irrevocably changed.

Land was the focus of the encounter—land and the resources that it sustained or guarded. The European newcomers assumed that they were entitled to help themselves, and the native peoples were initially willing to share. But soon competition for land and resources was raging across the continent. European nations battled each other and the native population for control. In what would become Canada, the British eventually succeeded in driving out French administrative control, but most ordinary men and women whose ancestors had come as settlers chose to remain, finding their family ties in their new homes stronger than the pull of European politics. Nevertheless, they were still essentially European people, and their ideas about government, economics, family life, and

7

FIRST NATIONS AT THE TIME OF EUROPEAN CONTACT: LANGUAGE GROUPS AND PEOPLES

BEOTHUK 12

MICMAC 1

MALECITE 1

ABENAKI 1

MOHAWK 2

IROQUOIS

ONEIDA 2

ONONDAGA

CAYUGA

SENECA

NASKAPI 1

MONTAGNAIS

ALGONQUIN 2

HURON

TOBACCO

NEUTRAL

POTAWATOMI (OJIBWA) 1

LABRADOR INUIT 11

CENTRAL INUIT 11

HUDSON BAY

CREE 1

OJIBWA

SALK 1

FOX

CARIBOO INUIT 11

CHIPEWYAN

CHIPEWYAN

PLAINS CREE 1

ASSINIBOINE 3

COPPER INUIT

DOGRIB

MACKENZIE INUIT

HARE

SLAVE

BEAVER

SARCEE

BLACKFOOT

BLOOD

PEIGAN

GROS VENTRE

KUTENAI

KUTCHIN

NAHANI

TAHLTAN 4

TSETSAUT

SEKANI

CARRIER

BELLA COOLA 6

CHILCOTIN 7

INTERIOR SALISH

KWAKIUTL

NOOTKA

HAIDA 9

TLINGIT 10

TSIMSHIAN 8

1 cm = 312 km

1	ALGONQUIAN	7	WAKASHAN
2	IROQUOIAN	8	TSIMSHIAN
3	SIOUAN	9	HAIDAN
4	ATHAPASKAN	10	TLINGIT
5	KOOTENAIAN	11	INUKTITUK
6	SALISHAN	12	BEOTHUKAN

even relations between men and women would come to shape the core of Canadian society.

The process by which these foreigners established themselves in Canada is the theme of this chapter. It was neither automatic nor inevitable that they should dominate the aboriginal people of the continent. Indeed, at first, they were forced to rely on the knowledge of the native peoples and to adapt European political and economic goals to their agendas. When the European populations in Canada were still small, as they were before 1763, and the British and the French were competing with one another on several fronts, the native peoples found themselves in relatively advantageous positions. This chapter examines this period of multifaceted jostling for position in the lands that would become Canada, ending with a crisis for the French colony in the mid-seventeenth century.

Ancient History

When the King in Lewis Carroll's *Alice's Adventures in Wonderland* suggests to a befuddled subject that the sensible approach to telling a story is to begin at the beginning, young readers always chuckle at the self-evident simplicity of the observation. But it is not always such a simple task to agree upon a beginning. Debate still rages over scientific and religious theories about the origins of the human species, and a similar disagreement exists about the ancient history of North America. Many aboriginal people argue that their ancestors have lived on the continent since the beginning of time; archaeologists and other social scientists believe that human habitation in North America dates from a more recent period in global history. For aboriginal people, the question is more than an abstract debate. Faced with the necessity of demonstrating their use of land "from time immemorial" in contemporary land claims cases, they fear that any suggestion that limits the time period in which they occupied those lands might undermine their claims. The issue of origins can thus be very emotionally charged indeed.

The First Nations tell many different versions of the beginnings of human habitation in North America. Iroquoian-speaking people tell of Aataentsic, daughter of the Great Sky Chief, who was sent down to a world covered in water. The animals and birds dove deeply to find earth to save her from drowning and built an island for her on Turtle's back. She bore twin sons, one good and one evil, and the world was shaped by their efforts. The Ojibwa tell a similar story about the creation of the earth from a ball of mud but explain that the Great Spirit or Creator made people by breathing life into a handful of earth. For the Blackfoot, it was Napi or Old Man who travelled through the world establishing the mountains, lakes, and forests and who moulded a woman and her son from clay. Some groups tell of a time when all was harmony among peoples, but a disaster of one form or another introduced dissension and scattered the nations into different territories, speaking different languages. Many of the origin stories are very specific about geographic location, describing how the people were placed on their particular lands at the beginning and how every convenience for life was available to them there.

Europeans have taken quite a different approach to explaining the origins of human societies in the Americas. At the time of the earliest contact, they debated who these people were and how they came to be living in the western hemisphere. Initially, the question was even raised as to whether the inhabitants of the Americas were, in fact, human beings at all or some strange new species hitherto unimagined. Once that issue was settled, theologians attempted to fit their new knowledge into their own traditions about the origins of humankind. Since the Book of Genesis in the Bible explained that all humans were descendants of Adam and Eve, the question was raised as to how some of those descendants ended up in Europe, while others were found in Asia and now the Americas. By the nineteenth century, one theory suggested that native peoples were descendants of one of the lost tribes of Israel. How they reached the Americas became the topic of a new debate. Some proposed that they had wandered across Asia and crossed to North America through Siberia to Alaska. Others suggested that people had travelled across the South Pacific to South America, or across the Atlantic from Ireland, or from the fabled lost continent of Atlantis.

Most social scientists today prefer the theory that human habitation of North America probably dates from about 20 000 to 40 000 years ago, about the same time that biologically modern human beings (*Homo sapiens sapiens*) were appearing in what is now Europe. At that time, the planet was experiencing the most recent in a series of ice ages, and much of North America was covered by glaciers. However, certain areas of exposed land were habitable. Because much of the ocean water was locked in glacier ice, sea levels were lower than they are today, and the continents of Asia and America were joined by a strip of land now called Beringia. Parts of Alaska and the Yukon interior were also free of ice, although a number of large glacial lakes covered areas of what is now dry land. Grasses and shrubs eventually invaded these lands, along with animal populations, so human habitation was possible at least in theory. However, no conclusive evidence of settlement at this very early date has been found. A caribou bone worked into a fleshing tool was discovered at Old Crow, Yukon, and dated at an age of 23 000 to 28 000 years, but questions have been raised recently about the accuracy of the dating. It is less controversial to suggest that people were able to move into areas of Canada that were ice free beginning about 14 000 years ago. The massive eastern Laurentide ice sheet met the western Cordilleran sheet, and as the climate fluctuated, the ice sheets coalesced and then separated periodically along the western mountain ranges so that from time to time an ice-free corridor existed between Beringia and the southern regions of North America, which were also free of ice. It is believed that people moved into these southern regions first, then as the climate warmed and the glaciers retreated, populations were able to expand northward. The process was a gradual one, occurring over thousands of years. Even after Beringia had been flooded by the rising oceans, people could still cross between continents on foot over the ice in winter and by boat across the narrow waterway in summer. Approximately four thousand years ago, at about the same time as the development of the so-called New Stone Age cultures in Europe, the last large migration to North America occurred, bringing into the Arctic regions people who were probably the ancestors of today's Inuit.

Meanwhile, important changes were occurring throughout the continent. About nine thousand years ago, the people of Middle America (Mexico and Central America) had developed a sophisticated economy based on the cultivation of beans, squash, and maize and the harvesting of wild resources. Those regions that were particularly favoured with good climates, rich soils, and abundant resources evolved gradually into large and complex societies with sufficient leisure time to produce fine works of art and develop scientific and mathematical knowledge. About the time of the birth of Christ, the Mexican and Mayan civilizations had formed large cities and towns, were building great pyramids, and were manufacturing a wide range of goods for home consumption and for trade. It was probably along their trade routes that knowledge of agriculture and a variety of religious practices spread northward. Squash and maize were being grown in what is now the southeastern United States four thousand years ago and in more northerly areas some three thousand years later. Elsewhere, people were also adapting to local conditions and opportunities, evolving a variety of cultures across the continent. Today we tend to forget that the original inhabitants of North America did not form a single population but made up hundreds of different societies, speaking different languages and developing unique religious, economic, and political preferences.

About a thousand years ago, the population of North America had probably reached its largest size and geographical distribution to that point in history. For purposes of convenience, anthropologists have developed various methods of classifying the populations, using language, economy, religious beliefs, and material goods as traits to define culture groups. These classifications are in common use today because of their convenience, although it must be remembered that native people did not identify with these categories themselves. Rather, they recognized local and regional bands, communities, and nations as their kin. In the geographic area now known as Canada, dozens of different languages were spoken. Some of these were as dissimilar as English and Greek, while others were as related as are Spanish and French. For convenience, linguists have classified similar languages into families. Hence in Canada, the language families include Algonquian, Iroquoian, Athapaskan, Siouan, Haida, Kutenai, Salishan, Tlingit, Tsimshian, and Wakashan as well as Eskimo-Aleut. When native peoples are classified according to socio-economic indicators, anthropologists speak of the Arctic, Subarctic, Northeastern Woodlands, Plains, Plateau, and Northwest Coastal groups.

The people of the Northeastern Woodlands include the Micmac, Maliseet, and Abenaki of the eastern coastal areas; the members of the Iroquois Confederacy (Mohawk, Oneida, Onondaga, Cayuga, Seneca, and later, Tuscarora); members of the Huron Confederacy and their neighbours the Petun and Neutral nations; and the Algonquian-speaking Ottawa and Algonquin nations. All made use of game and fish resources, while, in many areas, agriculture was also practised. The men were responsible for large game hunting and clearing the fields for planting, while the women manufactured pottery, planted and tilled the crops, and collected and distributed the harvest. The Iroquoian-speaking people lived in large villages, housing two thousand or more people before the arrival of European diseases. The Iroquois and Huron confederacies had also evolved complex political and religious systems, aspects of which still exist today. The Iroquois Confederacy, for example, was proposed and arranged by Deganawida some years before the arrival of Europeans as a means to establish a lasting peace among the original five-member nations. A grand council of fifty sachems or chiefs chosen by the clan mothers met regularly to discuss issues of mutual concern. They followed an elaborate procedure to reach a consensus regarding appropriate collective action.

Subarctic peoples did not enjoy as comfortable an environment as the Woodland peoples and so were forced to develop sophisticated survival strategies. In the eastern regions, the Montagnais, Naskapi, Beothuk, Cree, Ojibwa and other Algonquian-speaking nations hunted, fished, and, in some areas, collected wild rice and maple syrup. Some also traded their meat and animal products (like leather) to agricultural groups such as the Huron for corn and squash. In the western Subarctic, groups like the Chipewyan and Dogrib relied on gathering, fishing, and hunting large herds of caribou for most of their needs. Others like the Beaver, Carrier, Hare, Kaska, Kutchin (or Loucheux), Sarcee, Sekani, Slavey, Tagish, Tahltan, and Tutchone hunted other large game animals to supplement diets of fish, small game, and gathered plants. People lived in small bands linked by family ties, moving back and forth to recognized hunting territories according to the seasons. The bands would occasionally congregate in large groups for social, religious, or political purposes.

Plains groups like the Dakota, Assiniboine, and three Blackfoot tribes hunted the massive herds of plains bison and traded with more southerly neighbours for agricultural products. When Spanish colonists introduced horses into what is now the southwestern United States early in the sixteenth century, the Plains people quickly learned the skills of horse

Bison hunting was an exciting undertaking into which the Plains people quickly incorporated the horse.   NATIONAL ARCHIVES OF CANADA/C403

breeding and riding, and a socio-economic system based on the use and trading of the horse spread rapidly north throughout the interior. The horse was useful in driving the bison herds into pounds (or corrals) or over cliffs known as buffalo jumps, a variant on older techniques that required more human energy.

The Salish, Lillooet, Okanagan, and Kutenai peoples lived in the interior plateau regions of what is now British Columbia. Like many other groups, their economy was based on a mix of gathering, hunting, and fishing, with salmon providing an important part of the resource base.

The many nations of the northwest coast were able to make use of an environment rich in natural resources to provide a comfortable base from which to establish a sophisticated social, ceremonial, and artistic life. The major resources were land and sea mammals, and, above all, salmon. Communities were organized through kin groups, membership in which was matrilineal in northern groups and patrilineal in the southern regions. Leadership positions were hereditary, with a society structured through a complex system of rank and class. Slavery was also practised.

The Inuit of the Arctic lived in coastal and inland communities, harvesting the resources of the land and sea. The band, structured around family units, formed the basis of social organization. Because of the harsh environment, the Inuit had developed a range of unique tools and techniques including the igloo and the kayak, which made use of local supplies without disrupting the sensitive ecosystem. In many areas, there appears to have been relatively little trade or contact between the Inuit and their Indian neighbours.

While archaeology can help in the reconstruction of the physical materials of people's lives in very ancient times, far less can be reconstructed about social organization and religious beliefs. Oral traditions allow us to understand a little about these intangibles during such periods as that immediately prior to contact with Europeans. Across the continent, people enjoyed a variety of religious beliefs that enabled them to make sense of their world and provide guidelines for everyday living. While it is misleading to think that all native peoples shared the same religious system, there were common elements. All believed that there was an unseen world: a world of spirits and power that had a direct role to play in the ordinary, physical world. People could travel in the unseen world in dreams or other altered states of consciousness. Those who were particularly skilled in accessing the powers of the unseen world or communicating with the spirits would be recognized by the community as spiritual advisers or healers. Some First Nations had organized societies of such people, and the secrets of spirit travel and medicine would be passed on from one generation to the next through these societies. Among other groups, such powers were recognized and developed in more individualistic and private ways such as the dream quest experience for young people. Both men and women could become spiritual advisers or shamans; women were deemed to be particularly powerful during menstruation, and many societies developed special rituals to recognize that tremendous power.

Religious observances and beliefs generated systems of rules for personal and social behaviour. Because each individual had the potential to acquire spiritual power, the individual was valued and respected. Children were rarely punished or coerced into following rules; instead they learned for themselves by experimenting or were guided to see moral codes through indirect means like the fireside tales of a grandparent. But at the same time, individualism had its limits, and people were expected to sustain the community as a whole through a willingness to share and a profound respect for others. The value placed upon hospitality by most native peoples helped encourage social harmony; it also proved to be dangerous in their contacts with Europeans.

Respect and reciprocity were vital. While there were no written codes of law in the sense understood by Europeans, people nonetheless learned that the world operated through a network of rules that had to be followed, or personal and community disaster might strike. If a hunter did not demonstrate respect for his prey, that animal's spirit might retaliate and cause his arrows to miss their mark in a future hunt. If the proper rituals were not observed at harvest time, women might find that their next crop would fail. People, animals, and their lands all lived in an interrelated mingling of time and space.[1]

It would be incorrect to conclude that the history of North America before the arrival of Europeans was relatively uneventful, lacking in much

---

[1] There are few general works on the ancient history of native peoples. The best survey is contained in the Prehistory section of R. Cole Harris (ed.), *Historical Atlas of Canada*, Vol. 1 (Toronto, 1987). See also Jesse Jennings (ed.), *Ancient Native Americans* (San Francisco, 1978) or relevant chapters in the *Handbook of North American Indians* series from the Smithsonian Institute in Washington. For anthropological descriptions of culture groups, see Alan McMillan, *Native Peoples and Cultures of Canada* (Vancouver, 1988); R. Bruce Morrison and C. Roderick Wilson (eds), *Native Peoples. The Canadian Experience* (Toronto, 1986).

change or conflict. Although we will probably never know much about the details of that very ancient history, we do know that change was a constant fact of life. Some changes were caused by long-term shifts in climate conditions, such as a great drought that occurred in the interior of the continent between 6000 and 7500 years ago, forcing the Plains people to move out to moister parkland areas and abandon the semidesert that formed in their original homelands. Other changes were the result of trade and contact between societies. New ideas, new products, and new beliefs were shared and transferred. Other contacts were less peaceful and political differences or economic conflicts might lead to war. It is important to remember that most areas of what is now Canada have enjoyed some ten thousand years of human history but it is not until about one thousand years ago that details of events begin to appear a little more clearly.

The Norse

At the beginning of the ninth century, armies of Scandinavian soldiers began an expansionist campaign that soon brought them across the North Atlantic. Norse invasions of Britain, Ireland, and northern Europe extended the power, wealth, and prestige of the people sometimes known as the Vikings. Their skills at sea brought them to Ireland in the mid-ninth century; in the 980s, Eirikr Thorvaldson (Eric the Red) visited the land he called Greenland and established two colonies there. Shortly thereafter, Bjarni Herjolfsson lost his way en route to Greenland and sighted a wooded and hilly land now believed to have been the coasts of Newfoundland and Labrador. About 1000, Eric the Red's son Leif visited these lands, naming them Helluland, Markland, and Vinland. A number of explorations followed, among them one by Thorfinnr Karlsefni Thordarson who led a group of settlers to a site possibly located in what is now Labrador or Newfoundland. Disputes among the colonists and problems with the local people eventually led to the abandonment of the community. One confirmed site of Norse occupation in Canada is located at L'Anse aux Meadows on the tip of Newfoundland's northern peninsula, now deemed to be a UNESCO world heritage site. Besides these attempts at settlement, the Norse apparently developed regular trading relations with the people whom they called Skraelings. Whales, seals, and narwhals were valued for various products, eider duck down was collected for export to Europe, and wood was supplied to Greenland. By the fourteenth century, however,

Norse influence in both Europe and North America was waning for reasons that are not entirely clear. The spread of bubonic plague in Europe in the 1340s was undoubtedly a factor in putting an end to expansionist energies. The Greenland colonies disappeared and were not replaced for many generations, while the European balance of power shifted to the British, French, Portuguese, and Spanish.[2]

European Expansionism

It was almost a century before northern Europeans had recovered sufficiently from the devastation of the Black Death to develop an interest in offshore activities. Regular fishing voyages were undertaken in search of food resources for a growing population, and the development of better navigation instruments and knowledge of navigation techniques enabled travel across greater ocean expanses. A desire to increase wealth at home through international trade or, if need be, through piracy and plunder encouraged Europeans to wander farther and farther abroad in an ever-widening spiral of competition among nations. Overland trade with Asia was generating enormous wealth for its commercial participants who at the same time became concerned with finding more direct and less expensive trade routes. In 1488, the Portuguese explorer Diaz succeeded in sailing south of the African continent, but the distance and dangers far exceeded those of the well-known overland route. A native of Genoa named Christopher Columbus, building on ancient Greek theories that a sea was all that separated Europe from Asia to the West, was sponsored by the Spanish to undertake a voyage across the Atlantic. He reached land in October 1492. Concluding erroneously that he had reached the Indies, he named the people he found there "los Indios," the Indians. Portugal and Spain both laid claim to these lands and appealed to the pope for support. Pope Alexander VI settled the issue by drawing a line on the map and

---

[2] For a controversial approach to the early Norse voyages and settlements, see Trygvi Oleson, *Early Voyages and Northern Approaches, 1000–1632* (Toronto, 1963). More moderate views are recorded in T.J. Oleson and W.L. Morton's introductory essay to the *Dictionary of Canadian Biography*, Vol. 1 (Toronto, 1966), pp. 16–21. That volume also contains biographies of the major Norse figures. See also David Quinn, *North America from Earliest Discovery to First Settlements: The Norse Voyages to 1612* (Toronto, 1977); "Norse Voyages and Settlement," in R. Cole Harris (ed.), *Historical Atlas of Canada*, Vol. 1 (Toronto, 1987).

declaring that lands to the East of it belonged to Portugal and lands to the West of it belonged to Spain. Little was known about the real extent of these lands, and, of course, no thought was given to the idea that the original inhabitants might actually be better entitled to claim them.

England viewed these developments with concern. Henry VII solicited the assistance of an Italian navigator, Giovanni Caboto (known to the English as John Cabot), to undertake an Atlantic crossing to Asia to lay a rival claim. In 1497, Cabot and his three sons set sail from Bristol and apparently reached land across the North Atlantic, although the disappearance of his map and account of his voyage has made the details unclear and somewhat suspect. The following year, he returned with a much larger expedition to explore the coasts of Newfoundland, Labrador, and possibly Nova Scotia. It appears that he died during this voyage. Two expeditions were undertaken by the Portuguese brothers Gaspar and Miguel Corte-Real into these waters shortly afterward. None, of course, succeeded in finding Asia, but each did serve to confirm what was becoming increasingly well known in Europe: the waters of these new shores were teeming with fish.

Indeed, it was fish rather than spices or gold that brought the next phase of regular visits of Europeans to North America. In particular it was cod, a stocky, spotted staple that encouraged and sustained European expansionism into colonialism. Fish was an important food source for those areas in Europe with a large Roman Catholic population or more limited agricultural potential. Dried or salted, cod was also light and easily transported— an ideal food for naval forces or trade and exploration expeditions. Through the first decades of the sixteenth century, Spanish, Portuguese, and French fishing boats were drawn increasingly to the south and east coasts of what is now Newfoundland, setting their nets in the shallow coastal waters and farther out on the Grand Banks.

Initially the British showed little interest in these fisheries. During the reign of Elizabeth I, however, the potential value of North American resources became the focus of numerous discussions. It was proposed, for instance, that an enlarged fishery would help generate wealth for England and assist in her struggles against the Spaniards in particular. During the 1580s, the Danes took a series of measures to exclude the British from the rich Icelandic fishery so the alternative of Newfoundland became increasingly attractive. Merchants from a region known as the West Country (the counties of Dorset, Devon, and, to a lesser extent, Cornwall, Hampshire, and Somerset) began to organize regular expeditions. In 1583, Sir Humphrey Gilbert laid claim to the lands around St. John's harbour, ostensibly for the purposes of settlement but more probably to establish a base from which the British could raid the Spanish fishery. With the defeat of the first Spanish Armada in 1588, the British could feel more secure in their control of the northern seas, and there seemed little need for the promotion of a colony in Newfoundland. Indeed, the Spanish gradually withdrew from their participation in the northern fishery, leaving the resource largely to the French and British by the beginning of the seventeenth century. The

An on-shore fish-drying station in Newfoundland.   NATIONAL ARCHIVES OF CANADA/C3686

French fished along the south and west coasts of the island where French place names attest to their presence to this day, while the British interests lay primarily along the southeastern shores of the Avalon Peninsula. Basque whalers scoured the waters of the Strait of Belle Isle to the North.

Fishing was seasonal work. Each winter crews would organize, departing from the ports of Devon, Dorset, and Brittany in late winter or early spring. The North Atlantic crossing generally required a month or a little more, permitting three to four months of fishing before a return home in the fall. Once a favourable fishing site had been found, the crews would split up into small boats operated by three to five men while their ship anchored in a sheltered harbour. The French had access to extensive supplies of salt at home and so were able to pack the catch directly into salt on board ship. French vessels nonetheless had to land periodically to take on supplies of fresh water and to augment on-board diets with eggs and fresh meat. Among the most popular stopping places were the Fogo and Funk islands where thousands of birds were known to nest. The great awk was particularly prized for both food and bait; by the 1840s this ducklike bird had been hunted to extinction as a result. Unlike the French, the British did not have major salt resources and so were forced to take their catches on shore for a lengthy drying process in which the fish were cleaned, split, and boned, then lightly salted and stacked in sheds for several weeks. It was a tricky and labour-intensive process in which boys and perhaps some women apparently participated, although the men formed the fishing crews. These crews might be paid in money, shares in the company, or with a portion of the catch; the precarious nature of the enterprise meant that earnings were not guaranteed, but the investors and crews alike did not seem to have been deterred. By the turn of the century, perhaps as many as three hundred ships were making their way across the Atlantic for each fishing season.

The North Atlantic cod fishery permitted a number of important developments in Europe. Employment opportunities in ship construction and fishing itself stimulated the economies of port cities, while investment opportunities contributed to the organization of financial institutions and an increasingly complex commercial economy. It was also believed at the time that the fisheries served as "nurseries" for the naval forces of Europe, although the connection is a tenuous one. Certainly the products of the fishery provided a light and durable source of protein for the sailors, enabling longer sea voyages, which permitted Europeans to press their interests around the globe.

Interest in the fish resources of the North Atlantic also brought Europeans into regular contact with the original inhabitants of North America. When vessels landed to take on fresh water and supplies or to dry the season's catch, the crews met the local inhabitants, and a small trade eventually developed along the coast. Members of the coastal nations were initially quite perplexed about the nature and motives of the strange pale creatures covered in hair who arrived on what appeared to be floating islands. It is scarcely surprising that they reacted with both uncertainty and fear, much as did the Europeans. The coastal people gradually discovered that the newcomers were human like themselves, even if they did not appear to have women, and brought with them a range of interesting gifts. The newcomers could also be uncivil and even dangerous, particularly where women were concerned. In many places, contacts for the purpose of trade became brief and anxious encounters with the women safely hidden away. There were more devastating effects of this early contact as well. Diseases to which the people of North America had no immunity were introduced through the visits of the Europeans and spread rapidly throughout the coastal populations. Contagion was passed farther inland along trade routes. While there is no way of knowing with any certainty the actual extent of the devastation, there have been estimates that up to nine-tenths of some communities may have died even before Europeans established permanent settlements. Entire villages and even societies may have been eradicated.[3]

Cartier in the "New" World

Reports from fishers about the resources and wonders of the so-called New World began to filter back to France and Spain through informal channels,

[3] For a study of early attitudes of the Europeans toward native people, see Olive Dickason, *The Myth of the Savage* (University of Alberta Press, 1984). Indian views from a slightly later date are examined in Cornelius Jaenen, "Amerindian Views of French Culture in the Seventeenth Century," *Canadian Historical Review* (September 1974), pp. 261–291. For the cod fisheries, see the classic by H.A. Innis, *The Cod Fisheries* (Toronto, 1940, 1978) and the relevant sections in R. Cole Harris (ed.), *Historical Atlas of Canada*, Vol. 1 (Toronto, 1987).

generating a good deal of interest in the potential wealth of the continent. In 1534, a navigator from St. Malo named Jacques Cartier was commissioned to visit the shores around the fishing regions and report to King François I on the existence of gold and a potential water route to Asia. During his first voyage, he mapped the coasts of the Gulf of St. Lawrence. At one of his stops on the Gaspé Peninsula, he visited a settlement of Iroquoian-speaking people and erected a large cross, claiming the territory in the name of the king of France. Alarmed, Chief Donnacona put together a band of warriors and confronted Cartier, demanding to know whether the French were attempting to seize his people's lands. Cartier made peace with a deception and a promise. He told them that the cross was intended as a navigation marker only and offered to form an alliance with the Iroquois against their enemies. The ruse worked and Donnacona's band offered Cartier's men a feast to mark the occasion. Cartier's next action seems almost incomprehensible as a result. He kidnapped Donnacona's sons Domagaya and Taignoagny, dressed them as Frenchmen, and carted them off to France for display.

The following year, Cartier returned to North America with the two young men who guided him up the St. Lawrence to the lands that their people inhabited when they were not fishing on the sea coast. At Stadacona, Donnacona's village, Cartier was received politely, but tension was thick in the air, particularly when Cartier insisted that he wanted to continue to sail up the St. Lawrence beyond Stadaconan lands to visit their neighbours. Afraid that Cartier would abandon his promises of alliance, Donnacona offered Cartier a precious gift of three children for his adoption, according to the Iroquois custom of forming alliances. Cartier refused to accede to his wishes, however, and proceeded up the St. Lawrence to the village of Hochelaga, probably located near the modern site of Montreal. Here he was greeted enthusiastically by Chief Achelacy who attempted to form an alliance of his own with Cartier. That winter, Cartier stayed with the Stadaconans amid increasing tension. He returned to France in the spring of 1536 with Donnacona, his two sons, and two principal men of the community, all of whom were apparently put on board ship against their will.

Cartier's reports to the French court stimulated François I to devise a scheme whereby France could contend with Spain and Portugal for land across the Atlantic without incurring the wrath of the papacy. Jean-François de La Rocque de Roberval was put in charge of a plan to establish a sizable colony on the shores of the St. Lawrence, the purpose of which was declared to be a missionary one. Clearly, however, the plan was also intended to consolidate a French claim to the potential resources of the continent and to provide an outlet for the Huguenots, French Protestants whose increasing wealth and power were proving problematic to the state. Unfortunately, the artisans and labourers of France did not share their sovereign's enthusiasm for colonizing the New World, and Roberval was forced to turn to the prisons for recruits. The first ships of the expedition set off from St. Malo in the spring of 1541 under Cartier's command. Roberval was to embark later, when all his supplies had arrived.

Upon his return to Stadacona, Cartier was received first as a friend, but the Iroquois became wary when they realized that their kinsmen had not returned with Cartier. The Frenchmen admitted that Donnacona was dead, but lied about the others and claimed that they were living so well in France that they preferred not to return to their homes. Perhaps because of their suspicion to his reply and his motives in bringing shiploads of his countrymen, Cartier decided to establish his colony at a distance from the Iroquois town. A site was chosen at Cap-aux-Diaments, and the men set to work building two forts and ploughing the earth in preparation for planting. Two ships were sent back to France to report on progress, while Cartier undertook a small expedition up the St. Lawrence in search of a river that was rumoured to lead to a land of great riches. He travelled as far as the Island of Montreal where he met a large gathering of natives to whom he offered gifts before turning back.

Although Cartier reported that his meeting with these natives was friendly, the Iroquois clearly had become gravely concerned about the growing French presence on their lands and had begun a campaign of harassment and intimidation in an attempt to maintain the upper hand. Indian visitors on board a Spanish ship in the Gulf of St. Lawrence boasted that they had killed a number of Cartier's men, and Cartier himself later admitted that they were persistent in their pressure on his party. Perhaps for that reason or for others that are unclear, Cartier decided to uproot the colony and return to France in the spring of 1542, carrying with him a load that he believed was precious minerals but that turned out to be nothing more than quartz and "fool's gold" (iron pyrites).

In the gulf, Cartier met Roberval, who had been delayed a full year in his departure from France because of financial and supply problems. Roberval instructed Cartier to return to the colony with him, but Cartier fled under cover of darkness, intent on reaping the glory for his discoveries in the New World. Roberval sailed up the St. Lawrence to the same site that

Cartier had just vacated. A disastrous winter followed. Some 50 colonists died of scurvy, Roberval attempted to maintain discipline with an iron hand, and the harsh winter conditions tried the stamina of everyone. Above all, the natives apparently refused to trade with the colonists, so food was in short supply. The venture was abandoned in the spring of 1543, and the survivors sailed back to France. Although no Frenchman would admit it, the Iroquois strategy had worked, and, for 35 years, the French turned their backs on the St. Lawrence in favour of a Brazilian trade where relations with the indigenous people had not yet soured.

The next official French interest in colonizing the New World was expressed in rather different terms. In 1577, a Breton nobleman, the Marquis de La Roche-Mesgouez, convinced Henry III to permit him to grant him lands in New France that he would administer as seigneur as well as governor; significantly, the king also commissioned La Roche to seize from the native people any lands required for settlement. We do not know what came of La Roche's sweeping commission, but it signifies both a renewal of official French interest in colonizing the northern part of the continent and a change in attitude toward the role of the Indians in the process: if they would not cooperate, they would have to be crushed.

Origins of the Fur Trade

Meanwhile, on other fronts, European interest in the New World continued. Almost 80 years after the failure of Cabot to find a northern route to Asia, the British reopened their search. Martin Frobisher sailed three times to Baffin Island between 1576 and 1578; John Davis returned in 1585 and mapped the strait that now bears his name. Colonizing expeditions were also attempted, but there were few successes during the sixteenth century. It seemed as if the cod fishery was to be the prime resource exploited by Europeans in North America. However, in their sporadic contacts with the coastal populations around the Gulf of St. Lawrence, some fishers were delighted to discover that the natives possessed quantities of marten pelts, which were a rarity in Europe and so were worn only by nobility. The origins of the fur trade are impossible to trace with any certainty, but by the time of Cartier's 1534 voyage, the coastal nations were already well aware of the foreigners' interest in their furs and were eager to participate in exchanges for European goods.

People developed a clear preference for items like metal knives and fish hooks. Red and blue beads were popular because of their symbolic meaning for religious purposes, not (as some commentators later claimed) because the natives were naive and gullible, accepting "trinkets" for valuable furs. In fact, many clearly believed that they were getting the better end of the exchange. As one Montagnais man observed, "The English have no sense; they give us 20 knives like this for one Beaver skin."[4] The Indians were happy to receive useful goods but less certain about the desirability of hosting strangers with dubious motives in their midst. As improved language skills began to enable real communication on both sides, the North Americans heard the Europeans extol the virtues of overseas homelands and way of life, and urged the North Americans to adopt aspects of that life. The Americans could see only hypocrisy in these statements. "For if France, as thou sayest, is a little terrestrial paradise," asked one Gaspé Indian, "art thou sensible to leave it? And why abandon wives, children, relatives, and friends?"[5] They concluded logically that Europeans must be poor indeed if they valued the common beaver pelt so highly and were forced to travel so far in search of fish to eat.

By the 1580s, significant numbers of furs and hides were reaching Europe through this trade, which was really no more than an adjunct to the fishery. Merchants were becoming interested in specializing as fur traders, however, and in 1588 two of Cartier's nephews were granted a monopoly right for trading furs in Canada. An objection was raised immediately by a number of St. Malo merchants anxious to make their own fortunes, and the king revoked the monopoly guarantee. The strength of the opposition to trade limitations indicates the degree of interest that had been generated quickly among the merchants of Brittany. The fur trade was well on its way to becoming an important part of the economy of northern France.

For their part, most of the natives with whom these first contacts had been made were also keenly interested in the trade. Women appreciated the convenience and durability of domestic utensils like metal pots, kettles, and knives, freeing them from the necessity of manufacturing their

---

[4] R.G. Thwaites (ed.), *The Jesuit Relations and Allied Documents* (Cleveland: The Burrows Brothers Company, 1896–1901. Reprinted New York: Pageant Book Company, 1959). Vol. 6 (1633–34), p. 299.

[5] Chrestien Le Clerq, *New Relation of Gaspesia (1691)*, translated and edited by William F. Ganong (Toronto: Champlain Society, 1910). Vol 5, p 104

own. Woollen blankets and European clothing were also popular, although the clothing was impractical for bush use and so was reserved for ceremonial occasions. Among many groups, men were interested in European firearms, although the utility of these guns has often been overestimated. Requiring a constant supply of imported powder and shot, prone to mechanical failure at crucial moments, and particularly unreliable in winter, they did not replace indigenous hunting methods but became an important accompaniment to weapons of warfare. At least one group, the Beothuk of Newfoundland, apparently decided against adopting European firearms for either war or hunting.

Interest in acquiring items of European manufacture had a number of consequences for native people. In order to meet the constant demand, coastal communities increasingly had to turn to their inland trade partners for pelts. New alliances and animosities followed as groups competed for advantages in the trade or for use of rich hunting territories. Among the most dramatic changes were those that occurred along the shores of the St. Lawrence. By the beginning of the seventeenth century, the Iroquois towns along the river that Cartier had visited were gone and their cornfields abandoned. There has been considerable debate about the reasons for their withdrawal, but the most likely theory is that the Algonquin of the Ottawa River, the Montagnais of the Saguenay country, and perhaps others formed an alliance against the Iroquois in order to obtain control of the fur trade. Whether this animosity predated contact with the French is unknown, but the settled Iroquois farmers were clearly a barrier to the Algonquin hunters who wanted to bring their furs to trade directly with the French on the shores of the St. Lawrence. A regular trade centre emerged at Tadoussac; European goods obtained there were then carried along standard routes north and west where Indian traders passed them on to other interior nations, including the members of the Huron Confederacy in what is now central Ontario.

As the trade in furs became increasingly profitable to French merchants and a peace was obtained in the long series of religious wars in France, several new attempts were made to organize colonizing ventures linked to the fur trade. La Roche obtained a commission as the king's lieutenant-general for the lands of Canada, Newfoundland, Labrador, and the Gulf of St. Lawrence and tried to establish a colony on Sable Island in 1598. The experiment collapsed by 1603 because of internal problems. Pierre Chauvin de Tonnetuit obtained a trade monopoly for lands along the St. Lawrence in 1600 and undertook the largest expedition to date in an attempt to establish a permanent trade base at Tadoussac. Again, however, illness, an inability to cope with Canadian winters, and financial problems led to the demise of the project.

Champlain, Settlement, and Trade

In 1603, a French Protestant named Pierre du Gua, Sieur de Monts was granted a trade monopoly and administrative jurisdiction over a vast area of the Atlantic coast and St. Lawrence on the condition (yet again) that he establish a colony to assist French interests in the New World. De Monts chose an island near the Bay of Fundy close to the mouth of what was later to be called the St. Croix River. His assistant, Samuel de Champlain, was instrumental in negotiating an agreement of peace and friendship with area Micmac and Maliseet chiefs, and so the colonists settled in for the winter of 1604–5. After a disastrous experience, de Monts decided to move the settlement across the bay to a site that Champlain had named Port Royal, until such time as a more favourable southern location could be found. A series of mishaps, the removal of de Monts's trade monopoly, and an apparent loss of interest in the trade among area Indians forced the French to abandon the experiment, and in 1607, the settlers departed for home, turning the site over to Chief Membertou and his people.

Champlain was not convinced that all settlement and trade schemes were doomed, however. He argued convincingly that de Monts should try again along the St. Lawrence, a project that seemed all the more urgent for French interests because the British were having some success at their own version of trade and colonization. In 1606, two trading companies known as the London Company and the Plymouth Company had been formed and granted the Atlantic seaboard almost in its entirety. Colonies at Jamestown, Virginia, and at the mouth of the Kennebec River were established the following year. The French were more convinced than ever that they had to make their presence known before it was too late. The St. Lawrence might provide a key to a water route to Asia, and its fur trade might generate sufficient profit to make up for the losses on the Bay of Fundy.

In 1608, de Monts sponsored another expedition, this time with Champlain in full command. At Tadoussac, the party was surprised to discover a group of Basque entrepreneurs carrying on a brisk trade. Shots were fired and Champlain realized that it would not be a simple task to open a lucrative trade in the region. He decided to proceed farther up the St. Lawrence and constructed a base for his operations at Quebec. The site

Champlain depicted as the founder of Quebec City. Perhaps he should be better known for his political and trade strategies with native peoples.   NATIONAL ARCHIVES OF CANADA/C13204

that Champlain chose may have been on Donnacona's lands, but when Champlain arrived, there was no trace of the Iroquois village and farms. Instead, the lands were merely being visited occasionally by hunters from the interior forests coming to meet European ships for the purpose of trade. Champlain appraised the situation and concluded that his next step was to begin the process of negotiating alliances with the Montagnais and Algonquin people who now made use of the region. The bands of these nations who were particularly interested in trading with the French had for some time been engaged in warfare with the Iroquois Confederacy. Periodic Iroquois raids into the St. Lawrence valley made the Algonquin reluctant to venture far from their homelands to trade, so Champlain quickly agreed when his new trade partners asked that the French ally with them against the Iroquois. Not only would such an alliance help to prevent the Iroquois from interfering in the trade but it would also signal to the Algonquin that the French could be trusted as trade partners. In 1609, Champlain undertook his first war raid with the Algonquin up the Richelieu River to Lake Champlain. Warriors of the Huron Confederacy, trade partners of the Algonquin, also participated.

The Iroquois suffered heavy losses under the combined firepower of muskets and traditional weapons. The experience convinced them of the utility of European contacts. The following year, when Dutch trading parties visited the Mahicans, neighbours of the Mohawks (the most eastern member of the Iroquois Confederacy) the Mohawks turned their energies to raiding Mahican bands in order to obtain European trade goods for themselves. Then in 1624, the Mohawk negotiated a peace with the French in order to obtain a direct supply of trade goods. Thus reinforced, they escalated their attacks on the Mahican and succeeded in driving the Mahican out of their homelands. The Mohawk then established their own trade directly with the Dutch.

Meanwhile, Champlain's contact with the Huron warriors in 1609 encouraged him to think that an even more lucrative trade for his company could be obtained if he traded directly with the Huron, rather than indirectly through the Algonquin intermediaries. Aware of Champlain's plans, the Algonquin traders attempted various strategies to prevent him from meeting with the Huron again. Finally in 1615, Champlain convinced them that he had to travel to Huron country to assist them in their war against the Oneida, and during the following winter, Champlain reached an agreement with the principal Huron chiefs despite Algonquin opposition.

Relations between Champlain and the Algonquin eventually began to sour. Increasingly, he approached his partners as if they were French subjects, an assumption that no native shared. He interfered in Montagnais politics and attempted to convince a number of Montagnais families to become French-speaking Christian farmers and form the core of his colony. The natives also resented the demands of the Recollet missionaries whom Champlain had brought to Quebec in 1615. These missionaries were not well received by the Huron either, since they quickly realized that the Recollet had no respect for their culture and refused to accommodate their practices and values. The first Jesuits, who arrived in 1625, had a more flexible approach to their work and a greater tolerance for indigenous customs, but even they were tolerated by the Huron only because of the trade relations between the confederacy and Champlain. There seemed to be little reason to pay attention to the fumbling attempts of these clergymen to explain a distant and culturally irrelevant religion.[6]

Acadia

While Champlain was pursuing French trading interests among the nations of the lower Great Lakes and St. Lawrence River regions, the idea of settlement along the east coast had not been abandoned. Not only was the climate more moderate and thus more likely suited to known agricultural practices, it was also hoped that permanent communities would reinforce French claims to the fishery and serve to provide necessary supplies and services to visiting fishing crews. Although the fledgling

---

[6] For discussions of the relations between the French and the natives, see Bruce Trigger, *Natives and Newcomers: Canada's "Heroic Age" Reconsidered* (Montreal, 1985); Cornelius Janen, *Friend and Foe; Aspects of French-Amerindian Cultural Contact in the Sixteenth and Seventeenth Centuries* (Toronto, 1976); Bruce Trigger, "Champlain Judged by his Indian Policy: A Different View of Early Canadian History," *Anthropologica* (1971), pp. 85–114. The experience of the maritime peoples is explored in A.G. Bailey, *Conflict of the European and Eastern Algonkian Cultures, 1504–1700*, second edition, (Toronto, 1969). A useful source is Helen Hornbeck Tanner (ed.), *Atlas of Great Lakes Indian History* (Newberry Library, 1987).

Opposite page:

The Recollets depict themselves as holy men bringing the light of Christianity to the "savages" of Huronia.   NATIONAL ARCHIVES OF CANADA/C113480

settlement at Port Royal had been abandoned in 1607 when de Monts had lost his grants and trade monopoly, his associate Jean de Biencourt de Poutrincourt had not given up. He obtained a seigneurial grant of his own and in 1610 returned with a small group of men to lay the groundwork for a new settlement in the same region. The following year he brought two Jesuit missionaries.

The Jesuits were also involved in another colonizing project, one that took shape under the guiding hand of a woman. The Marquise de Guercheville and a group of associates obtained seigneurial rights to a large but ill-defined region outside of Poutrincourt's seigneury and sent the first group of settlers to establish themselves on Mount Desert Island across the Bay of Fundy in 1613. Within a few months, a privateer from the newly founded British colony at Jamestown, Virginia, had looted both the Port Royal and Mount Desert settlements. It was the first of a long history of such episodes in Acadia.

When Poutrincourt died in 1615, his son Biencourt took over the family interests in the Port Royal settlement and set about establishing a mixed economy of subsistence agriculture, fur trading, and service to the fisheries. In 1623, Biencourt died and the affairs of the seigneury were taken over by Charles de Saint-Etienne de la Tour. Little detailed information has survived regarding the history of this period, but we do know that at least two fur trade posts were established at the mouths of major rivers and a small trade begun. Only limited agriculture seems to have been practised during these years; doubtless it was easier to obtain fish and game from one's trading partners, both native and European.

The French were not the only foreigners with an eye on Acadia. In 1603, James VI of Scotland became James I when he ascended the English throne, uniting the kingdoms of England, Ireland, and Scotland and bringing to the London court a retinue of Scottish supporters and hangers-on. One of that retinue was Sir William Alexander who had an interest in overseas colonization on behalf of Scottish interests. In 1621, James I granted the lands of Acadia to Alexander who called it New Scotland (later Nova Scotia). A group of settlers was sent out the following year but was forced to winter en route in Newfoundland during which time a number of them apparently found the prospects of the Newfoundland fishery more enticing and decamped from the New Scotland project. A second group, sent out in 1623, apparently was not much more successful. Alexander was not prepared to give up, however, and began to wait for a more propitious moment to pursue his ambitions across the Atlantic.

The Company of One Hundred Associates

Meanwhile in Europe new ideas about the role of the state in directing the economy were becoming fashionable. Limited resources in Europe encouraged nations to look elsewhere for sources of raw materials and markets for their products. Close links for mutual advantage could be forged between the state and commercial interests, while colonies were increasingly considered as necessary generators for the wealth that would aggrandize the position of the European monarch. To that end, the British had formed the East India Company in 1600 and the Dutch had followed suit with a company of their own in 1602. France lagged behind these initiatives, but they gained a powerful advocate in 1624 when Armand-Jean du Plessis, Cardinal Richelieu, became chief of the royal council for Louis XIII and began an energetic program of rebuilding the king's position and (not incidentally) his own powers. Almost single-handedly, he was responsible for programs intended to suppress the power of the Huguenots and the French nobility and to snatch the European balance of power from the Habsburgs. In 1627 he authorized the formation of a powerful new company modelled on the British East India Company. Its official name was the Compagnie de la Nouvelle-France, although it is usually known as the Company of One Hundred Associates. Each of its shareholders contributed 3000 livres to finance the venture. All of the lands claimed by New France from Florida to the Arctic were granted as a seigneury to the company, which was also to hold a monopoly over all business conducted on these lands for a period of 15 years, after which time the company would retain a more limited monopoly on trade in furs and skins. In return for the massive profits that everyone anticipated would accrue from these privileges, the company agreed to establish a settlement of 4000 people within the first 15 years and to maintain Roman Catholic clergy throughout the settlement. No Protestant settlers were to be permitted. Although a number of the investors had already been associated with commercial ventures in New France (including Champlain), most others were government officials and Paris merchants, so that the company is sometimes seen as a Parisian intervention in what had hitherto been primarily the business interests of Brittany and Normandy.

Almost immediately, the company found itself in serious difficulty. The Kirke family, originally of Dieppe, was organizing in London to form a company of its own. Its first action was to sponsor a privateering raid intended to seize the trade of the St. Lawrence. Their ships sailed up the St. Lawrence in 1628, capturing the small French establishments at Miscou, Tadoussac, and Cap Tourmente. They captured the advance supply ship of the Company of One Hundred Associates, then defeated the main fleet near Tadoussac. The following year, the Kirke expedition returned again, forcing the capitulation of the fort at Quebec.

With Canada in British hands, Sir William Alexander and his son were able to pursue their interests in Acadia and finally established their own settlements near Port Royal and at Gaspé. At the same time, another Scottish colonial promoter named James Stewart established a third settlement at Port Baleine on Cape Breton. This community was attacked shortly after its founding by a French privateer and the site abandoned, but elsewhere, chaos seemed to reign. For two years in a row, the Company of One Hundred Associates suffered the loss of its entire investment.

Negotiations between France and Britain to sort out what had occurred dragged on for some time. Finally in 1632, Britain agreed to return the lands of New France and to evacuate the Scottish settlers from Port Royal. The Company of One Hundred Associates could reorganize to begin its ventures in earnest. The native traders also did some reorganizing of their own. A Mohawk-Algonguin peace treaty was negotiated to give the parties opportunities to trade with both the French and the Dutch. The Huron sent a contingent of 500 people to negotiate a renewed alliance with the French at Quebec in 1633; Champlain agreed only on the condition that the Huron permit Jesuit missionaries to live in their villages.

The following year, the Company of One Hundred Associates began its first real colonizing effort on the St. Lawrence. A number of seigneuries were laid out along the river; each seigneur was then given responsibility for populating his land. In 1640, the island at Montreal was granted to an organization known as les messieurs et dames de la société de Notre-Dame de Montréal pour la conversion des sauvages de la Nouvelle France. Here, a small community of pious lay men and women developed what became the most successful settlement of the period under the leadership of retired soldier Paul Chomedy de Maisonneuve and Jeanne Mance.

The other settlement experiments of the Company of One Hundred Associates in the colony of Canada were not particularly successful. Once they had received their land grants, the seigneurs seemed no more capable of bringing out settlers than had the earlier companies. A devastating epidemic was imported from Europe, swept inland from the coastal ports, and reached at least as far as Huronia in 1634. It was the first of a long series of epidemics that decimated the Indian population, disrupting not only the fur trade but also the society and politics of all the natives affected. The Iroquois continued their raids up the St. Lawrence, shattering trade and harassing the handful of settlers. Enthusiasm for colonizing waned in France so that, by 1645, there were fewer than 300 French souls living along the St. Lawrence.

Settlement and commercial plans for Acadia were slightly more successful. The Company of One Hundred Associates made seigneurial grants here much as they had done in Canada (that is, in the lands along the St. Lawrence River), leaving to the seigneurs the responsibility of bringing settlers. The company hoped to derive its profits from the fur trade and fisheries, while the French court was no doubt interested in developing Acadia as a bulwark against the rapidly expanding New England settlements to the South. The most successful project was organized by Isaac de Razilly, a cousin of the powerful Richelieu, who arrived with a group of about three hundred men and a few women in 1632 to settle at La Have on the Atlantic coast. After the Scots had abandoned Port Royal, a number of the colonists moved from La Have to that site. The company also gave Charles de La Tour responsibility for extensive lands on Cape Sable, at the mouth of the St. John River and along the Pentagouet River. When de Razilly died in 1635, his assistant Charles de Menoir d'Aulnay was put in charge of his interests. D'Aulnay expelled Nicholas Denys, another de Razilly lieutenant, and a lengthy period of conflict ensued among d'Aulnay, La Tour, and Denys over control of the fur trade, lands, and other commercial activities. Finally in 1650, d'Aulnay died and his widow married La Tour, resolving at least one angle of the triangle. Just four years later, however, a British force commanded by Robert Sedgewick captured Port Royal, La Have, and the St. John River settlement, giving control of most of Acadia back to the British.

All of the internal conflict in Acadia doubtless hampered the settlement process, for by the mid-1640s, the non-native population was only slightly larger than that of the St. Lawrence settlement, with between 300 and 400 people. However, between 1632 and 1654, the foundations were laid for the future development of Acadian society. More women arrived to join the handful already in residence, and in some areas (such as La Have), intermarriage with the Micmac helped to establish families, giving the settlements an aura of greater permanency. Thus, even though de Razilly and his associates were more interested in the profits of the fisheries and the fur trade, they did succeed in rooting a European population in Acadian soil.[7]

The Newfoundland Colonies

While European interests were struggling to establish competing claims to the eastern seaboard of North America, the island of Newfoundland had not been forgotten. Its strategic importance to the cod fishery and potential northern routes to Asia convinced several British investors that a permanent settlement should be established there. In 1610, a royal charter was issued to John Guy and a group of merchants from Bristol and London, giving them the right to settle the coast of the Avalon Peninsula and develop its resources, including any furs, iron, and timber that they might obtain. Above all, however, Guy and his associates clearly had their eyes on the potential of the fishery and hoped that a stable, year-round base would secure British interests by giving their fishers an advantage over seasonal visitors.

The first 40 British settlers arrived in the summer of 1610, building houses, storage and work facilities, and a number of boats in preparation for the arrival of women and other colonists. In 1612, the first contacts were made with the Beothuk, the aboriginal people of the island, in hopes of initiating a fur trade. Problems soon arose. Raids from competing fishing interests, disease, death of the settlers' livestock, and a failure to establish regular contacts with the Beothuk were all serious setbacks. Guy himself returned to England in 1613 and broke off his connection with the company the following year. Many of the settlers also drifted away, either returning to England or settling elsewhere on the island. In 1616, the company began to sell its lands. Among the purchasers was Sir William Vaughan, who attempted to establish settlements in 1617 and 1618 under the governorship of Sir Richard Whitbourne. After these experiments also failed, Vaughan sold his interests to Lord Falkland and Sir George Calvert

---

[7] For the early history of Acadia, see Naomi Griffiths, "The Acadians," *Dictionary of Canadian Biography*, Vol. IV (Toronto, 1979) pp xvii-xxxi; Griffiths, *The Acadians: Creation of a People* (Toronto, 1973); Andrew H. Clark, *Acadia: The Geography of Early Nova Scotia to 1760* (Wisconsin, 1968); "Acadian Marshland Settlement," in R. Cole Harris (ed.), *Historical Atlas of Canada*, Vol. 1 (Toronto, 1987). On Indian relations see L.F.S. Upton, *Micmacs and Colonists: Indian-White Relations in the Maritimes*, 1713-1867 (Vancouver, 1979).

(later Lord Baltimore). Neither of these gentlemen could succeed where their predecessors had failed.

In 1638, Sir David Kirke, who had fought against the French at Quebec, decided to try his hand at colonization in Newfoundland and obtained a charter from Charles I, which purported to cover the entire island. Among other things, the charter gave Kirke the right to collect a 5 percent fee from ships using the island's harbours for drying fish. Kirke's subsequent activity in Newfoundland generated controversy at home and, not surprisingly, precipitated international complaint when he attempted to collect his harbour fees. While Kirke's colony lasted longer than its predecessors, it did not succeed in giving the British claim to Newfoundland a secure footing. In 1651, Kirke returned to England to face charges relating to the nonpayment of taxes, and his colonists appear to have been left to pursue their own interests. By then, about 350 British families were living on the southeastern shore.

Among other things, they faced an increasing insistence by the French that Newfoundland was rightly French territory. In 1624, the French had announced that they, and not the British, were entitled to the island, and during the 1660s, they founded a year-round settlement at Plaisance on Placentia Bay to serve as the headquarters for French interests on land and at sea. By 1698, 40 families had established themselves as permanent residents at Plaisance. Competition in the cod fishery had evolved into competition for a land base as well.

The French had now laid claim to lands in several parts of North America. Collectively, these French colonies are referred to as New France. Individually, they included the areas known as Canada, along the St. Lawrence and extending into the lower Great Lakes region; Acadia, consisting of parts of the present provinces of Nova Scotia and New Brunswick (although sometimes broadened to include Cape Breton and Prince Edward Island); parts of the Newfoundland shores; and after 1681, the region known as Louisiana, which the explorer La Salle claimed and which included the entire Mississippi River to its mouth in the Gulf of Mexico.

Problems on the St. Lawrence

By 1645, the Company of One Hundred Associates was deeply in debt, and the affairs of New France as a whole were in disarray. As a means of extricating itself from the overwhelming difficulties, the company agreed to give up most of its privileges to a new organization called the Community of Habitants of New France. The One Hundred Associates retained the right to appoint the governor and judiciary and continued to hold the title to the land, but the Community of Habitants received the fur trade monopoly as well as the settlement obligations that the associates had been unable to meet. Perhaps the most significant aspect of the change was the fact that the community was composed of businesspeople resident in New France. Two years later, colonial input was increased with the establishment of the first limited local government. A council was created that consisted of the governor of Montreal, the governor of Quebec, and the Jesuit superior. The three communities at Montreal, Trois Rivières, and Quebec were to elect one representative each who would participate in the discussions of the council, although the elected delegates had no real power. While the council was really only a mechanism for overseeing the affairs of the Community of Habitants, it did provide the first local outlet for settlers' grievances.

It was hoped that these new administrative arrangements would put an end to the problems of the old colonization schemes, but events beyond the control of the French soon ensured that their hopes were in vain. After a brief truce in the Iroquois raiding, the five Iroquois nations regrouped, and, heavily armed with Dutch weaponry, began attacks in earnest throughout New France and Huronia. They were running out of furs to trade in their own lands and resolved to seize furs from the trading partners of the French, if not to force the Huron into submission and ally with them in the trade. The Huron villages, severely weakened by disease and internally divided between Christian and traditionalist factions, succumbed to superior Iroquois forces one by one. In 1649, the Huron Confederacy was finally broken. Jesuit missionaries Jean de Brébeuf and Gabriel Lalemant were captured and tortured to death in the process. The victorious Iroquois then turned on the Algonquin, Petun, and Neutral nations, neighbours of the Huron, so that by the early 1650s, the Iroquois were in control of the hunting territories and trade routes to the north and west of their homelands. It looked as though the French had been cut out of the North American fur trade almost entirely.[8]

---

[8] On the destruction of Huronia, see Bruce Trigger, *The Children of Aataentsic: A History of the Huron People to 1660*, 2 vols. (Montreal, 1976). Also Helen Hornbeck Tanner, *Atlas of Great Lakes Indian History* (Newberry Library, 1987).

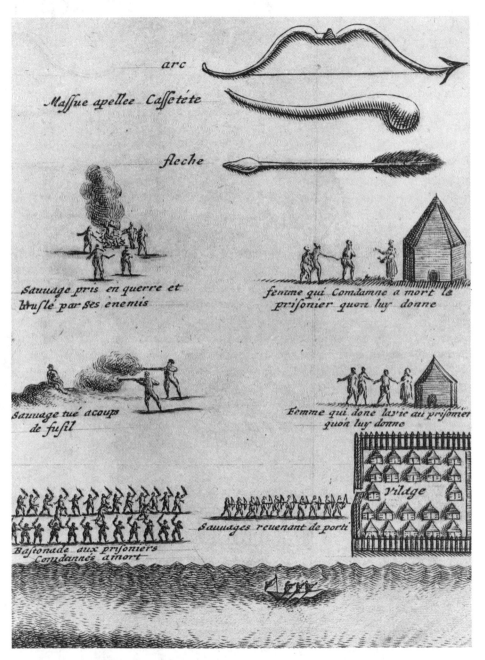

arc

Massue apellee Cassetete

fleche

Sauuage pris en querre et bruslé par ses enemis

femme qui Comdamne a mort le prisonier quon luy donne

Sauuage tué a coups de fusil

Femme qui done la vie au prisonier quon luy donne

Bastonade aux prisoniers Comdannés a mort

Sauuages reuenant de porti

Vildge

Native warfare methods as depicted in stylized form in a French publication of 1706.
NATIONAL ARCHIVES OF CANADA/C99243

The Iroquois then made a move that surprised and pleased the French. An invitation was extended to the Jesuits and to French traders to come and live in Onondaga country in the hope of initiating peaceful political relations and laying the groundwork for a new trade partnership. The Iroquois wanted to manipulate trade to their advantage by playing their two European trade contacts against each other. They were also concerned about the 1654 visit to Canada of a large trading expedition of Ottawas from the Upper Great Lakes. The French were encouraged by this visit, which had been facilitated through the work of two explorer brothers-in-law, Pierre-Esprit Radisson and Médard Chouart, Sieur des Groseilliers, in an effort to generate new trade contacts after the fall of Huronia. In response, the Iroquois attempted first to arrange a trade partnership with the French; when that agreement failed to prevent French trade with the Great Lakes nations, the Iroquois returned to their old strategy of attacking trade expeditions and attempting to control the access routes to the St. Lawrence. One of the most famous of these raids occurred in 1660 at the Long Sault rapids on the Ottawa River. A recently arrived soldier named Dollard des Ormeaux and 17 men travelled up the Ottawa with the intention of intercepting Iroquois raiding parties. To his horror, he encountered a large force of Onondaga warriors, and inevitable defeat followed. Dollard became a hero and a symbol to generations of French Canadians who saw him as the "saviour of New France"; a martyr who had sacrificed his life to prevent the Iroquois "hordes" from massacring his countrymen and women. Clearly that version of the story was a myth, but it served a useful purpose to later generations of Québécois nationalists.

Renewed warfare with the Iroquois dealt the final blow for the Company of One Hundred Associates and the Community of Habitants. The terrified colonists clamoured for proper military defences, the fur trade profits continued to decline, and the Jesuits petitioned the French court to intervene and prevent total catastrophe.[9]

---

[9] For more on the problems of early colonization, see Marcel Trudel, *The Beginnings of New France, 1524-1663* (Toronto, 1973); Marcel Trudel, *Montréal: la formation d'une société, 1642-1663* (Montreal, 1976). Useful for settlement patterns and development is R. Cole Harris, *Historical Atlas of Canada*, Vol 1 (Toronto, 1987).

CHAPTER II

COLONIAL EXPERIMENTS, 1663–1763

The Royal Colony

The calls for help from the colony of Canada came at a propitious moment. The new king, Louis XIV, and his minister of the marine, Jean-Baptiste Colbert, recognized an opportunity when one presented itself. Instead of leaving the affairs of Canada in private hands, the state would intervene and carefully direct the colony's development as part of an overall strategy designed to make France into a major imperial power in Europe, using the colonial system to strengthen the economy of France and establish the strength and authority of its monarch.

Accordingly, the privileges of the Company of One Hundred Associates were revoked and the settlement along the St. Lawrence was reorganized as a royal province like those of old France. (Because Acadia remained in British hands it was not included in these arrangements.) A new commercial company called the Compagnie des Indes Occidentales was organized essentially as a crown agency to take over all colonial trade in North America, South America, and West Africa. A governor was appointed to take charge of military and external affairs for the colony, while an intendant was appointed to direct justice, finance, and the internal administrative affairs. The colony was declared subject to the legal system then in

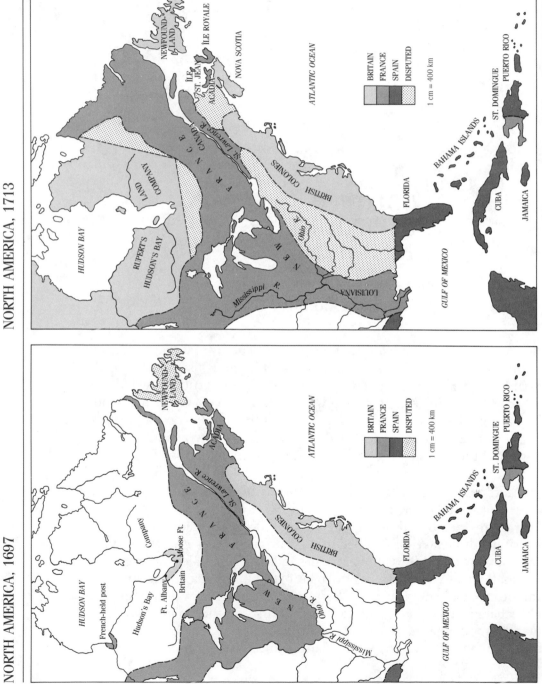

NORTH AMERICA, 1713

NORTH AMERICA, 1697

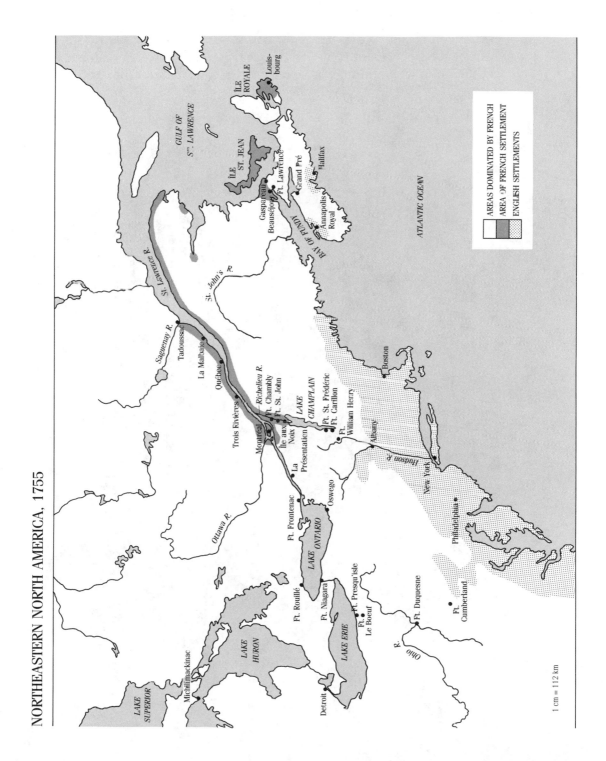

NORTHEASTERN NORTH AMERICA, 1755

1 cm = 112 km

AREAS DOMINATED BY FRENCH
AREA OF FRENCH SETTLEMENT
ENGLISH SETTLEMENTS

force in Paris (the "Custom of Paris"). A contingent of regular troops was sent from France, and the men of the local population were organized into militia units. The church was also intended to form an important part of

Jean-Baptiste Colbert, Minister of the Marine to Louis XIV. NATIONAL ARCHIVES OF CANADA/C6325

the social and administrative structure of the revitalized colony. The tithing system was introduced to pay for parish priests and the seminary at Quebec, but the power of the bishop in governmental affairs was reduced. Land was seized from owners who had done little to settle or develop it and redistributed in a reorganized seigneurial system.

Jean Talon, one of the most influential of the intendants of New France.

Colbert's next series of reforms dealt with the colonial economy. The French colonies in North America were to become part of a transatlantic system, providing timber and furs to France, and wheat, fish, and timber to the West Indies. Colbert hoped initially that Canada would become self-sufficient in food as well as a supplier of goods to France and her other colonies. With the appointment of Jean Talon as intendant, a series of measures was introduced to undertake the massive economic transformation that was needed to achieve these goals. The most urgent requirement was to increase the population base along the St. Lawrence. At a time when the British colonies had expanded to almost 100 000 people, only about 3000 French colonists made their homes in Canada, and only about one percent of the land claimed by France was being used. An aggressive immigration policy was adopted and coupled with a series of incentives to encourage marriage and child bearing. Young women known as "les filles du roi" were brought from France at state expense, dowries were provided to girls who could not afford their own, penalties and rewards were levied to encourage early marriage, and large families were rewarded through the payment of an annual gratuity of up to 400 livres for a family of 12. Marriages between French and Indians were also encouraged. An extensive agricultural experiment was undertaken to find breeds of horses, cattle, and sheep as well as grain that would thrive in the harsh climate. Talon gathered information about timber and fish resources in an attempt to lay the groundwork for a shipbuilding industry and a more efficient fishery. He attempted to establish a brewery to broaden the markets for local grain and a tannery to make use of local cattle.

Talon's energetic initiatives were short-lived for a variety of reasons. The lack of skilled workers drove up wages and made the cost of production relatively high. Few potential emigrants were convinced that the St. Lawrence was a desirable new home. Not every woman could be convinced to bear children constantly for the sake of a few sous. And furthermore, Colbert decided in 1704 upon a singular mercantile policy: the colony must exist solely for the benefit of the motherland and not develop manufacturing or commercial activities that would compete with those of France. There would be no further state support for industrial development.[1]

---

[1] For more on the Royal Colony, see W.J. Eccles, *Canada Under Louis XIV, 1669-1701* (Toronto, 1964); Gustav Lanctot, *History of Canada*, Vol 2, 1663-1713 (Harvard, 1964). For more on the conflict over colonial development, see W.J. Eccles, *Frontenac: The Courtier Governor* (Toronto, 1959).

Colbert's colonial plans also had a strategic component. Instead of encouraging development throughout the lands claimed by France, his ministry argued in favour of the concept of a "compact colony" along the St. Lawrence because of concerns that the mother country would be depopulated in an attempt to settle the huge area it claimed. Furthermore, Colbert argued that such a vast empire would be impossible to defend. Hence, he opposed western expansion and attempted to prevent independent traders from travelling beyond the borders of the settlements. On this point, Colbert and Talon conducted an extended argument. Talon's interest in expansion found an ally in Governor Frontenac, who had a personal as well as a strategic interest in seeing the fur trade grow. Without Colbert's assent, Frontenac constructed a new post at the east end of Lake Ontario and began his own trade activities in direct competition with established and state-sanctioned Montreal firms.

Also with Frontenac's encouragement, a number of expeditions set out to find new mineral and fur resources, to obtain native allies, and to find convenient water routes to the Pacific and Gulf of Mexico. In 1671, Daumont de Saint-Lusson visited Lake Superior and claimed the entire region for France. In 1673, Louis Jolliet and the Jesuit Jacques Marquette reported that the Mississippi River must flow into the Gulf of Mexico; a decade later, René-Robert Cavelier, Sieur de La Salle, and Henri Tonty followed the great river for its entire length and claimed all of its extensive basin for France. These aggressive claims led to a new stage in the contest of imperial powers in North America.

French traders and adventurers Radisson and Groseilliers had become convinced by the mid-1660s that the lands to the north of the Great Lakes were the next great source of furs for the French market. Unable to generate any French sponsorship for a fur trade expedition, they travelled to London where they found British entrepreneurs more amenable to their ideas. In 1668, they set off in the *Eaglet* and the *Nonsuch* for Hudson Bay, returning at the end of the season with a rich cargo. The investors organized themselves into a joint stock company and in 1670 obtained a royal charter as The Governor and Company of Adventurers of England Trading into Hudson's Bay. The charter granted a trade monopoly to the Hudson's Bay Company on all lands draining into Hudson Bay, the extent of which was quite unknown in England at the time. Clearly, the new company was not only a commercial opportunity but a means by which the British could claim more territory in North America. And just as clearly, the aboriginal inhabitants of the land had not the least inkling of what the British king believed he had done with their lands.

The new company proved to be highly successful in attracting the Cree people of the northern interior to its posts along the bay coast. Instead of trading with Algonquin intermediaries, the Cree could now obtain goods directly. Some opted to become intermediaries themselves in the trade with nations to the south and west of their lands. Traders at Quebec soon realized what was happening and in 1682 attempted to counter the growing trade of the HBC with the establishment of the Compagnie-française de la Baie d'Hudson, sometimes known as the Compagnie du Nord. Their single post at the Nelson River was seized by the British in 1684, however, so two years later a military expedition sponsored by a Quebec merchant was sent overland to retaliate. Their successful undertaking was followed by a series of land and sea raids against the British posts along the bay in which the commercial interests of Aubert de la Chesnay and the Le Moyne brothers were triumphant.

Meanwhile to the South, the Iroquois were pursuing a major military offensive in the Illinois River valley, which had begun in 1680. The defeated western Indians called on their French allies for assistance, and war parties were sent against the Seneca villages in 1687. Other raids succeeded in driving the Iroquois off the north shore of Lake Ontario. In retaliation, fifteen hundred Iroquois warriors descended on Lachine in August 1689; farm buildings and crops were destroyed while over one hundred Canadians were killed or captured. Fear of Iroquois attack became part of the daily reality of life in the St. Lawrence colony.[2]

To the East, French settlers in Acadia were experiencing problems of their own. In 1667, the British had returned the region to France in the Treaty of Breda, although it was not actually until 1670 that the British finally withdrew. For the next 30 years, repeated raids and harassment by New England privateers caused considerable damage and an unknown number of deaths. These attacks may have been motivated in part by a desire for retaliation for raids by the French and their Indian allies on New

---

[2] On the wars of the Iroquois, see R.A. Goldstein, *French-Iroquois Diplomatic and Military Relations*, 1609–1701 (The Hague, 1969); K.F. Otterbein, "Why the Iroquois Won: An Analysis of Iroquois Military Tactics," *Ethnohistory* (1964); Helen Tanner (ed.), *Atlas of Great Lakes Indian History* (Newberry Library, 1987); Leroy Eid, "The Ojibwa-Iroquois War: The War the Five Nations did not Win," *Ethnohistory* (Fall 1979), pp. 297–324. An old but still useful source is Cadwallader Colden, *The History of the Five Indian Nations of Canada* (1747, Coles Canadiana Reprint, 1972).

England settlements, but they were also largely individual initiatives carried out by profit-seeking "pirates." None succeeded in capturing any of the major settlements, but the situation called for constant vigilance from the population.

In Europe, the French and the British were pursuing agendas of their own. In May 1689, England joined Spain, the Netherlands, and the Habsburg empire in their war against France. The war soon spread to the North American colonies. Sir William Phips led an expedition from New England and captured Port Royal in 1690, his men running wild on a looting spree after their victory. A joint New England–British assault on Quebec was then attempted, but ended in disaster for the Anglo-American troops. Indian allies on both sides were drawn into the conflict. For their part, the French were unable to organize any major expeditions, and the war deteriorated into a series of small-scale raids. Initially, the Iroquois clearly held the advantage, but the Canadian militia soon learned the techniques of what would now be called guerrilla warfare. In 1696, Governor Frontenac led an expedition against the Oneida and Onondaga, destroying their towns and crops, while Indian allies of the French repeatedly harassed the western Iroquois.

Even Newfoundland was drawn into the war. In 1692, the British unsuccessfully attacked the French settlement at Placentia Bay; in 1694 and 1696, the French retaliated with equally unsuccessful attacks on the British settlements. The French then launched a dual attack by sea and by land in a determined effort to remove the British entirely from the island. The sea assault was forced back in bad weather, but Pierre Le Moyne D'Iberville led an army of militiamen, French troops, and Micmac warriors on an orgy of destruction through the British fishery stations, leaving the French in temporary possession of the island.

When the European war ended in 1697, the Iroquois also decided to seek peace. The European Treaty of Ryswick gave Acadia and Hudson Bay to the French while the British obtained Newfoundland. Negotiations with the Iroquois and the native allies of the French were more difficult, and an agreement was not reached until 1701. Under its terms, the Ottawa and Iroquois were to be permitted to travel unmolested through each other's lands, and the Iroquois agreed to remain neutral in any future conflict between the French and the British. Neutrality for the Iroquois Confederacy did not mean passive nonparticipation, however. While the French were anxious to prevent Iroquois attacks on French settlements and allies, the Iroquois had motives of their own for consenting to neutrality. That

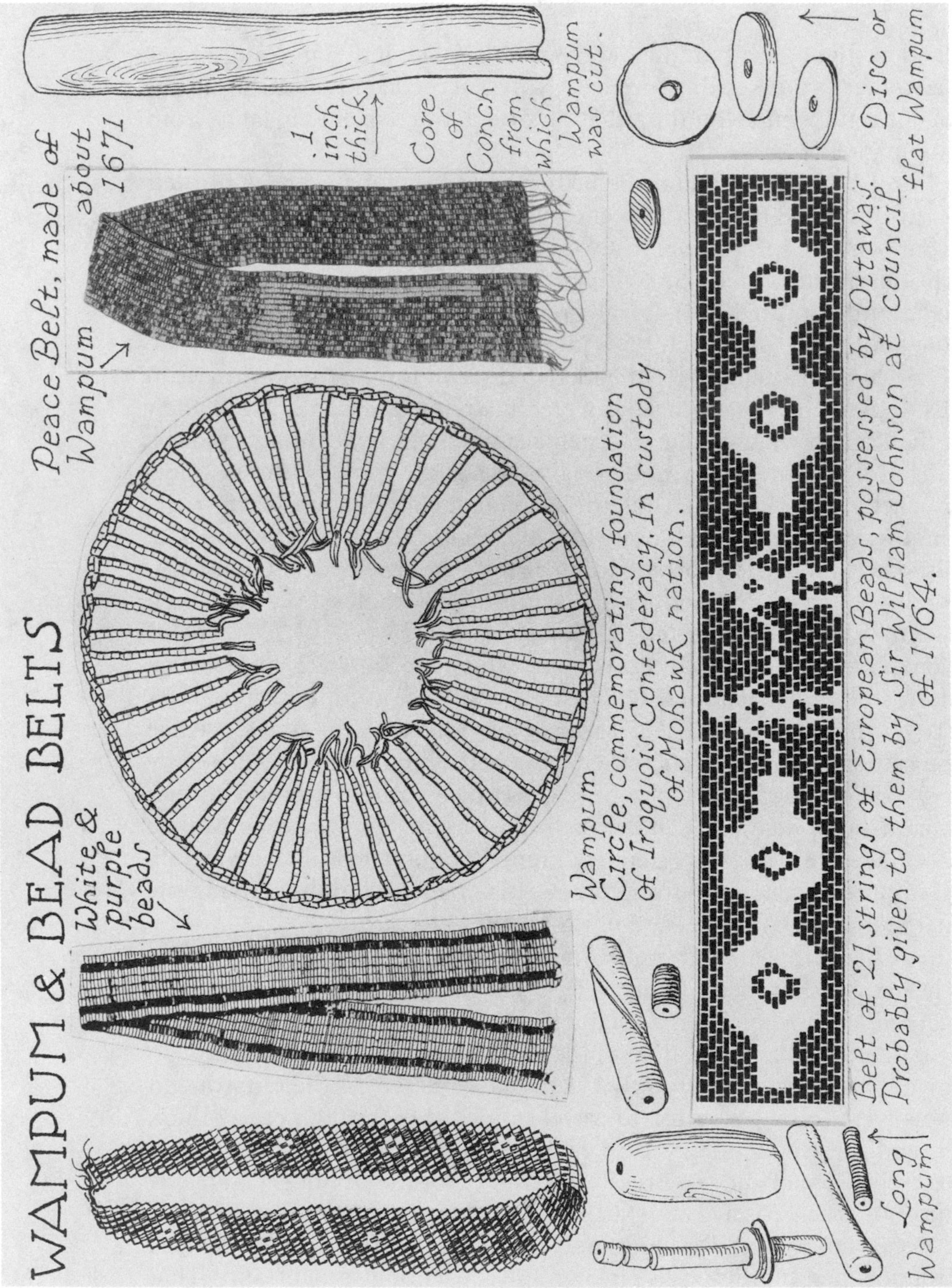
WAMPUM & BEAD BELTS
White & purple beads
Peace Belt, made of Wampum about 1671
1 inch thick
Core of Conch from which Wampum was cut.
Wampum Circle, commemorating foundation of Iroquois Confederacy. In custody of Mohawk nation.
Belt of 21 strings of European Beads, possessed by Ottawas. Probably given to them by Sir William Johnson at council of 1764.
Disc or flat Wampum
Long Wampum

Types of wampum, from the archives of some northeastern First Nations (drawn by C.W. Jefferys).

NATIONAL ARCHIVES OF CANADA/C69114

same year, the Iroquois met with the British at Albany, agreeing to permit Protestant missionaries to live among their villages as a sign of good faith and promising to maintain cordial relations with the British. In part, it would seem that the agreements of 1701 marked a decision by the confederacy to revive its policy of playing the British and the French against each other to maximize Iroquois benefits from their geographically strategic position. It has also been suggested that the Iroquois were attempting to extend their influence over the western nations who were trading partners of the French. The Iroquois needed both French friendship and access to the British trading goods to do so.

The Iroquois-French agreement of 1701 was tested sooner than anyone expected. In the spring of 1702, Great Britain declared war on France and Spain in a conflict that has become known as the War of the Spanish Succession. In North America, the Iroquois held to their agreement, in no small way keeping Canada relatively free from the effects of this new war. Two Anglo-American expeditions were sent to attempt to invade Canada via the Lake Champlain route, but these came to nothing. Acadia was not similarly spared, however. Raiders from New England had been harassing coastal settlements for years; in 1710 a combined force of New England militiamen and British troops seized Port Royal. The French captured the British town of St. John's, Newfoundland, and held it for a brief time in 1709. They also managed to hang on to the lands that they claimed elsewhere: Louisiana, the Mississippi, Detroit, and the Great Lakes. Thus when the war ended in 1712, the French empire in North America was at its largest in terms of territorial claims despite the loss of Acadia. On the European battlefields, however, France had not fared so well, and by the Treaty of Utrecht (1713), Louis XIV was forced to surrender Hudson Bay, Newfoundland, and Acadia and to recognize the legitimacy of Iroquois trade with the British. France was left with the valleys of the St. Lawrence and Mississippi rivers, separated by British and Iroquois territory.

The years following the war were difficult for everyone who had an interest in the lands and resources of North America. For those who participated in the fur trade, not only did war interrupt the business, but a decline in demand in the European market severely undercut the profits of Indian and French traders alike. As the market recovered in the 1720s, the activity of the trade shifted away from the St. Lawrence and into the interior, while an illegal trade through Albany sprang up as French independents took their cargoes there to British merchants who offered better prices than could be obtained in Canada. The economy of Canada in particular was on the verge of collapse. Wartime expenses had led to an accumulation of bills that the French government could not pay, while lack of funds made it difficult just to meet the regular expenses of maintaining the colonial administration. Although the population continued to grow slowly and land was increasingly brought under cultivation, many of Colbert's plans for development failed to materialize. Lack of skilled labour, lack of investment capital, navigation difficulties on the St. Lawrence, and an unforgiving climate all contributed to the slow diversification of the economy even under the control and planning of the monarch.

For the various Indian nations, the postwar period was a time of difficult decisions. Governor Robert Hunter of New York began a campaign among the Iroquois to encourage an alliance. The Iroquois eventually agreed to the construction of Fort Oswego on their lands. To the West, Fox bands were raiding the native allies of the French; Governor Vaudreuil sent two war parties in 1715 and 1716 to invade Fox lands along Green Bay on Lake Michigan. The Fox capitulated and agreed to hold the peace. A few years later, however, the Fox went to war against the Ojibwa and the Illinois, while farther west, the Dakota continued to battle the Assiniboine. Concerned that these wars were interfering with trade profits, the French attempted to intervene on a number of occasions. One of the most disastrous encounters occurred in 1730, when three hundred Fox men, women, and children were killed by a large force of Canadians, Louisiana men, and their Indian allies near the Illinois River. To the East, a number of Abenaki refugees from New England who had been living in Canada were distressed at what they saw as French abandonment of their interests in postwar negotiations with the British. Deciding that the Abenaki and their Maliseet neighbours would be valuable allies against the British, Vaudreuil set about bettering relations with gifts and an agreement to recognize Abenaki who resettled their lands in Acadia as allies rather than French subjects. Secret military aid was also offered to encourage the Abenaki in any war that they might undertake against New England. Nevertheless, the Abenaki were badly divided among themselves about whether to support the French or the British. Amid the tension, war finally erupted in 1722. By the time a treaty brought hostilities to an end in 1726–27, the military and political issues were rapidly becoming irrelevant. Massachusetts settlers had begun helping themselves to the Abenaki lands, thereby destroying the Abenaki economy and seriously challenging the once-powerful nation.

• Île Royale

Although the French had lost Acadia and Newfoundland in the Treaty of Utrecht, they remained anxious to protect their interests in the North Atlantic fisheries and looked to Île Royale (Cape Breton Island) as a strategically located base. In 1713, they founded a community called Louisbourg to which the Newfoundland fishing interests from Plaisance were moved. Here construction was begun on a massive fortification that would be the largest in North America. Because it was designed according to the latest military theories in Europe, the French hoped that the fort would be able to withstand prolonged attacks from the sea. By 1734, a small community was established within its walls. Men were drawn from France, Acadia, and Canada to fish, trade, and provide the necessary services for the garrison stationed there. Other villages grew up along the coast of the island as the French re-established their position in the fishery. The European newcomers met women from Canada and Acadia, married and established new homes and businesses. Unlike the colonies of Acadia and Canada, agriculture never became a significant part of the economy on Île Royale. Food, other than fish, had to be imported. Initially much of it came from Canada; by the 1740s, a considerable trade had developed with New England for the supply of necessary provisions. These trade networks also included important links with the Caribbean. Sugar, molasses, and rum were obtained in return for the fish required to feed the growing population of slaves on the West Indian plantations. By 1740, some two thousand people had made Louisbourg their home.

Meanwhile, beyond the borders of Île Royale, the British were attempting to deal with their newly gained colony of Acadia. A suggestion was raised that the small French population be expelled from the territory, but the idea was rejected, partly on the grounds that the new garrison at Port Royal (now called Annapolis Royal) required food supplies and partly because of fears that the Acadians might simply move to Île Royale and strengthen the French presence there. So the Acadians were asked to swear an oath of allegience to the British king as a condition for remaining on their lands. The Acadians were badly torn, unwilling to swear an oath that could very well require them to fight against their French cousins should another war erupt, but afraid that if they refused to swear, they would be sent from their homes and lands. In the end, the British did not force the issue, and for the next 30 years left the population fairly well on its own. A council was established to administer the colony, and a system of deputies was put in place to represent the districts, but there seems to have been little official intervention in people's lives.

The French kept a careful eye on developments in Acadia, clearly hoping that one day the territory would be returned to them. At one point, the governor at Quebec proposed that the Acadians could be moved to Île Royale, but the rocky highlands of that place were ill-suited to their farming economy. Others argued that it would be better for the Acadians to remain on their lands in anticipation of the eventual return of Acadia to France.

Life in Canada

By the 1730s, the colony on the St. Lawrence was taking on a more established appearance. The population had grown slowly but steadily, and farms could now be found continuously along the river from Montreal to south of Quebec. Montreal, Trois Rivières, and Quebec had emerged as major town centres, each with a unique function and social cross-section. Although Colbert's immigration schemes had soon petered out, the population had increased primarily because of a high birth rate and low death rate; by the 1730s there were several generations of Canadian-born settlers who had few ties with France. They shared the colony with soldiers, clergy, and merchants, who maintained closer links with Europe, as well as several communities of native people who had migrated to the upper St. Lawrence for political and economic reasons.

To what extent did this new society resemble its various parent societies in Europe, and to what extent had it been changed by the circumstances of North America? The question has been debated by historians at some length. Certainly many institutions, ideas, building styles, and social conventions crossed the Atlantic with the emigrants, but people also learned to adapt to new conditions. First, it should be noted that most settlers came to the banks of the St. Lawrence from the provinces of Île-de-France, Normandy, and other regions of the northwest. Two-thirds of the women and a majority of the men came from urban centres. Hence, the settlers came from a particular segment of French society and it is scarcely surprising that observers commented on the similarities between the towns of Canada and those of the northwestern regions of France.

The physical appearance of the St. Lawrence countryside was somewhat different. Instead of central villages surrounded by farmlands, a pattern of long, narrow lots fronting on the river evolved. As in France, the crown claimed title to the land and granted it in parcels to seigneurs who, in turn, brought in tenants to manage individual lots. The tenants, who preferred to be called habitants rather than peasants, paid regular dues to the seigneur and might also be required to send their grain to the seigneur's mill or to permit the seigneur access to timber on their lots. In other respects, however, each habitant family managed its own land and could pass on the farming rights and obligations to its children. Because the system was similar to that of France, a number of historians have argued that New France was essentially a feudal society. The habitants, they suggest, were like Old World peasants in that they were small family farmers who did not own the land that they worked and who were

A view of Quebec in 1722. The Europeans shape their landscape to remind them of home.
NATIONAL ARCHIVES OF CANADA/C4696

exploited by the privileged classes because the latter required that the peasantry supply them with portions of what they had produced. Other historians have argued that the burdens of tithing and seigneurial dues that fell to the habitants were significantly less onerous than those that fell on the shoulders of the French peasantry. As well, because of the problems inherent in the pioneering settlement process, many of the seigneurs of New France were scarcely better off than their tenants. Social class was less clearly defined as a result. It has also been argued that the fur trade provided an alternative activity for those who disliked the restrictions of the seigneurial system. Thus, since they had more options open to them, the habitants of New France were less likely to submit to the demands of the privileged classes. These historians depict the population of New France as independent minded and materially well off, enjoying a freedom and degree of comfort unavailable in the villages of France. Was New France a feudal society? The answer really depends on how one defines the term "feudal," and the question will doubtless continue to generate a lively debate for some time.

Farms along the St. Lawrence provided the habitant families with the necessitites of life as well as a small surplus. Wheat was the major crop, but each farm also had a large vegetable garden and kept a variety of livestock. Nowhere were farm families entirely self-sufficient. Merchants from the towns provided contact with the wider world of commerce. Manufactured tools, household utensils, and readymade clothing were much preferred to the homemade alternatives, and those who could afford them were quick to purchase them. A chronic shortage of cash in the economy, however, necessitated payment in goods. Businesspeople, in turn, marketed the wheat and other farm products that they obtained from these sales, either locally or on the transatlantic market. Skilled craftsmen and women produced goods on a small scale for local manufacture; Canadian silversmiths and woodcarvers became particularly renowned for their fine work. Other economic activities, of course, included timber cutting and the fur trade. Although it has been estimated that two-thirds or more of the fur trade revenue accrued to European participants, there is no doubt that it was a lucrative activity for New France as well. Fur trade profits provided a number of Montreal families with the opportunity to rise on the social ladder and to display their wealth in substantial homes, imported clothing, and fine horses.

The military also provided an important source of revenue for the economy through the salaries of soldiers and the necessity of purchasing supplies to maintain the not-insignificant military presence. The military also provided an important component in the social structure of Canada. Jean-Baptiste Colbert had created a new force of regular troops for colonial duties, known as the Troupes de la Marine, under the control of his ministry. Unlike the practice in the French military, officers of these troops were commissioned on merit rather than through the purchase of rank, and the men were organized in local companies rather than regiments. The system encouraged young men born in the colonies to join as cadets and to work hard to display their qualifications for commissioned rank. By the mid-eighteenth century, there were 30 companies of these troops in Canada and 20 in Louisbourg. Most of the officers were Canadians (generally the sons of seigneurs) drawn to the life of adventure and action.

Historian W. J. Eccles has argued that the military ethic encouraged by this system became part of a wider community ethic throughout New France. Rather than seeking social status through business or entrepreneurship, Eccles argued, the young men of New France looked to the military for opportunities. The public display of a dashing uniform and a fine high-spirited horse would make its owner the envy of other young men, producing an interest in fashion and style that sometimes surprised foreign visitors to the French colonies. Public taste may have had unexpected economic ramifications, as well, according to Eccles's thesis. People insisted on imported high fashion from France rather than clothing made in the colony, thus limiting the incentive for the development of local production. Young men preferred to invest their salaries in visual and social displays rather than investing in business development, hence limiting the potential for economic diversification in the French colonies of North America. Perhaps, then, the limited development of the economy of Canada, in particular, was in part the result of popular attitudes and not entirely the result of the heavy-handed application of mercantilist policies designed to benefit France.

Certainly the fact remains that in spite of early programs to encourage manufacturing, the French colony of Canada never developed an extensive industrial sector. Some analysts have attributed this failure to the mercantilist policies of the Crown, while others have suggested that local considerations like high wages, lengthy transportation routes, and lack of necessary materials were more significant factors. Nevertheless, manufacturing was not entirely absent from the economy. Shipbuilding to supply the navy and commercial shipping developed at Quebec under the direction of the Ministry of the Marine. A group of private businesspeople established an ironworks plant at St. Maurice near Trois Rivières but quickly encountered serious financial problems; in 1741 the government took over the business and eventually turned it into a profit-making venture. Although it was never as productive as European smelters, St. Maurice iron was reputed to be as good as the best produced in Europe. Because of a shortage of skilled labour, workers could command wages that were higher than those of France and that were high enough to ensure a much better standard of living. A Canadian carpenter, for example, received a higher salary than a member of the governing council. There were constant labour problems, including strikes, as the workers took advantage of their position to demand the best possible terms.

Religious zeal was an important factor in the founding of the St. Lawrence colony, and the Roman Catholic church continued to have a visible presence in the evolving society, although the nature of that presence has been a matter of some debate. Certainly the same tensions regarding church-state relations and areas of jurisdiction arose in the colonies just as they did in France. Perhaps the least controversial role of the church was in its educational work and social services. In 1635, the Jesuits established a college at Quebec for the education of middle- and upper-class boys. Senior courses for the training of surveyors and navigators were eventually developed there. Other religious orders and congregations established schools for native and French children throughout Canada, while a seminary at Quebec prepared young men for the priesthood. The Ursuline order of nuns was particularly successful in its large program of education for girls of all social classes. Rural children, and particularly girls, were also able to attend the schools of a secular community founded by Marguerite Bourgeoys, known as the Sisters of the Congregation. With widely available educational opportunities, the women of New France were probably better educated as a whole than their sisters in Europe, and furthermore, they tended to be better educated than men who had grown up beside them in New France. It was also women who were primarily responsible for founding and running the several hospitals and charitable institutions that developed in the large towns. Services for the sick, elderly, mentally ill, or physically disabled were provided by women through these institutions.

The church also attempted to play a role in regulating the moral and spiritual life of the population, but here it was clearly less successful. Attempts were made to discourage drinking and dancing and to censor literature, but the people do not appear to have been much affected by these pronouncements. There were constant complaints that parishoners were refusing to pay tithes to the church, and the amazing range of church ordinances prohibiting a variety of activities suggests that the church may have attempted to control, but people simply found no real need to comply. New France was scarcely under the dominating thumb of the church as some historians once suggested.

At the centre of the entire social, political, and economic system of Canada was the family. Farms, fur trade partnerships, manufacturing, and retail establishments all developed as family businesses. Marriages were considered economic as well as personal arrangements, with property laws to protect women's rights regardless of their marriage status. Women were particularly involved in the business of the fur trade. With their partners away for extended periods, they managed the supplies and the bookkeeping at home, or developed business interests of their own. Farm women, who had greater educational opportunities than their sisters in France, were able to make use of their education to manage the business side of the farm operation. Because labour was in short supply, few rural households had servants, so most of the work was probably done by family members, and wage labour was relatively unimportant in the rural economy.

Families tended to be large because people married at a slightly younger age than in France, and more children survived the difficult first year after birth, probably because of better nutrition and health enjoyed by their mothers. By far the majority of households was composed of married couples with their children; the extended family that was once believed to characterize pre-industrial society was a rarity. Children lived at home until they married, at about age 28 for men and 21 for women. In order to provide for newly married couples in rural areas, parents might give their child a piece of their land or arrange a partnership to farm it jointly. Land was more often given to sons on the assumption that daughters would obtain property through their husbands, but there was no legal impediment to women owning land. As family farms were divided into smaller and smaller strips over time, it became common practice to give the land to only one child (usually a son), and offer gifts of "movable" property to the remaining children. Children of business families in town might learn the business from their parents or be apprenticed to a family friend's business for a period of three years.

Because the family was so integral to the functioning of the Canadian economy, it is not surprising that most children grew up to fill similar economic roles as those of their parents. Nevertheless, social mobility was possible, and the strictly defined class divisions of the Old World were somewhat less focused in the new. There were no members of the high nobility in Canada, and members of the lesser nobility may have held titles, but they often lived in a manner indistinguishable from the middle class. Seigneurs could be nobility or commoners, and the possession of a seigneury was no guarantee for improving one's position in life. Merchants, on the other hand, were much more likely to be able to rise on the social scale as their businesses grew, and they invested the profits in putting on a show of social respectability. In fact, it has been noted that commercial profits were not always reinvested in the business to the extent that is common today; people preferred to spend their money on consumer goods that created a favourable display. A common route to improved social standing both in town and on the farm was, of course, a good marriage. Apparently much official and private energy was devoted to the problems of arranging mutually advantageous unions. Social mobility could also work the other way, of course. There are dozens of stories of merchants who worked an initial investment into a large fortune only to lose it all in the sudden sinking of a supply ship or similar misfortune.

Other important social groups were the clergy and the military. Senior church officials and senior officers participated in the social and political leadership of the colonies alongside the lesser nobility and the leading merchants of the fur trade. Positions in this upper stratum of society were really not accessible to outsiders, so it would be misleading to suggest that social mobility was truly extensive. It was more a matter of improving one's position within the middle ranks. Furthermore, there was always a social "underclass" consisting of the very poor, the mentally ill, and the unemployable about whom we know very little except through glimpses of them as clients of the social service network in the major towns. The existence of an "underclass" is not restricted to societies with a capitalist, industrial economy.

One important social division was that which defined the roles of men and women. A number of factors combined to give women a relatively favourable status in Canada. Women had been in short supply during the early years of the colonizing venture, and as was the case with most settler societies, their role in building the new community was recognized and valued for several generations. The Parisian legal system (the Custom of Paris) decreed that married couples owned all property jointly, so when women married, they did not lose their rights to own property, as was the case in many other European legal traditions. A number of women owned businesses in their own right, ranging from the large lumber business maintained by Louise de Ramezay along the Richelieu River to the many small taverns and hostelries run by women in the towns. Women also had the option of making their perpetual vows in the church and devoting their lives to service. These communities of women, whether lay or religious, provided a respectable option for those who did not wish to marry or bear children and gave women an opportunity to take on positions of leadership and authority. Nevertheless, it would be a mistake to characterize mid-eighteenth century Canadian society as egalitarian. Men held the major positions of public authority, and within the household, they were considered the legal masters of their wives and children. Women who owned businesses were usually either widows or wives of absent fur traders; if there was a husband resident in the household, it was his work that defined the family's role in society. By the 1730s, then, Canada was developing a social system that largely reflected Old World patterns but that did represent some adaptations to the circumstances of the New World. A hierarchical and patriarchal social system, a state-controlled land distribution system, and a dependent economy all reflected the relationship between New France and France. Nevertheless, people seemed to have enjoyed a healthy and satisfying existence with a degree of independence from forces of social control and an element of choice about their lives that they may not have enjoyed in Europe.[3]

Life in Acadia/Nova Scotia

By the mid-eighteenth century, the descendants of de Razilly's settlers in Acadia had been joined by a variety of others, including Basques, Scots,

---

[3] On the social history of New France, see Louise Dechêne, *Habitants et marchands de Montréal au XVIIe siécle* (Paris, 1974); Guy Fregault, Canadian Society in the French Regime (Canadian Historical Association Booklet No. 3, 1954); Allan Greer, *Peasant, Lord and Merchant. Rural Society in Three Quebec Parishes, 1740–1840* (Toronto, 1985); Roberta Hamilton, *Feudal Society and Colonization: The Historiography of New France* (Gananoque, Ont, 1988); Cornelius Janen, *The Role of the Church in New France* (Toronto, 1976); R. Colebrook Harris, *The Seigneurial System in Early Canada* (Montreal, 1966, 1984); Dale Miquelon, *Society and Conquest. The Debate on the Bourgeoisie and Social Change in French Canada, 1700–1850* (Copp Clark, 1977); Peter Moogk, "'Thieving Buggers' and 'Stupid Sluts': Insults and Popular Culture in New France," *William and Mary Quarterly* (October 1971), pp. 524–547; Marcel Trudel, *The Seigneurial Regime in Canada* (Canadian Historical Association Booklet No. 6, 1956). Much useful information is contained in R. Cole Harris (ed.), *Historical Atlas of Canada*, Vol.1 (Toronto, 1987).

English, and Canadians. That diversity of origins, coupled with the unique circumstances of Acadian history, contributed to the development of a society that differed in some intriguing ways from that just described in Canada. Statistics are unreliable, but geographer A.H. Clark has argued that there may have been as many as ten to fifteen thousand people living in Acadia/Nova Scotia by 1750. They supported themselves in a variety of activities, raising livestock, growing wheat and other grains, fishing, trading with fishing crews, and even dabbling in the fur trade. In spite of the insecurity of raiding by New England "pirates" and the ongoing international dispute about their lands, the period from 1730 to 1748 is sometimes idealized as a sort of "golden age" in which Acadian society flourished. People attempted to maintain their distance from the competing political interests and pursue their lives in peace.

Most historians have commented in passing on the excellent relationship that developed between the Acadians and their Micmac neighbours, although there has not been much detailed research on the subject. In part, that amiable relationship was no doubt related to the fact that there was little conflict between Acadians and Micmac for land or resources. The Acadians preferred to settle on the coastal flood plain, dyking the tidal marshes for farming purposes rather than moving inland to clear forest lands. While the Micmac had made use of coastal resources, at the time of contact, their numbers appear to have been sufficiently small that there was plenty of coastal land left. Indeed, the Micmac provided essential assistance to the early settlers in the form of instruction regarding hunting and fishing techniques and the location of local resources of other kinds. The Acadians adopted Micmac methods of sewing clothing, constructing canoes, and insulating walls for dwellings. Their language eventually incorporated Micmac words and structures. Some intermarriage apparently took place, notably at La Have, although the extent of these connections is still a matter of some debate. Historian Naomi Griffiths has suggested that most communities had at least one family that had intermarried with the Micmac. Certainly such kinship networks were important parts of native-European trade and political alliances elsewhere in the French sphere of influence in North America. While it is possible to trace the lives of native women who came to live in the Acadian settlements, we may never know the stories of the men who chose to abandon the settlements to live with their wives' families in the interior.

Before 1632, experiments in agriculture had not proven particularly successful in Acadia, in part because the main interests of the first settlers lay in the fisheries and in trade. By the beginning of the eighteenth century, however, settlers at the major sites around the Bay of Fundy had developed a system of log dykes and sluice gates that enabled them to flush the coastal marshlands of salt water and prepare a fertile soil for growing grain. After a few years preparation, dyked fields could be highly productive. The Acadians also used the "uplands," which had to be cleared, but seemed to favour the marsh lands. They also discovered that fruit trees (and particularly apples) did well in the vicinity of Port Royal; apple orchards have been an important part of Annapolis Basin agriculture ever since. Most families also kept a few head of cattle and sheep. Farming was primarily a subsistence activity, although wheat and some other products were provided to fishing crews and, for a time, to the garrison at Louisbourg.

It would be a mistake to conclude that Acadian households were entirely self-sufficient. Goods were imported from New England or manufactured locally by the artisans who had been encouraged to join the colony. Trade became particularly important after 1710; much to official British dismay, a thriving illicit connection to Louisbourg was pursued despite demands from the governor that it be stopped. It was through this trade that the Acadians obtained goods from the West Indies and France. Many farming families found it necessary to send their young men off to work in the fishery during the summer.

The family was very much at the centre of Acadian social structure. Because there was relatively little population growth through immigration in the formative years of the seventeenth century, marriage created important connections within each village as well as between villages. Connections among a number of early settlers already had existed in France, and these networks were extended and reinforced over the years in Acadia. People married in their early twenties and tended to raise large families: infant mortality rates were substantially lower than those of France. Marriage brought "outsiders" and newcomers into the kinship networks. For example, one of Charles de La Tour's sons married a woman of Scottish ancestry, and one of their daughters married a British soldier, thus reflecting the changing situations of Acadia as well as demonstrating the flexibility of the community. People also lived relatively long lives, indicating a degree of good health and superior nutrition.

There has been considerable debate over the role of the Roman Catholic church in Acadia, reflecting in part some of the questions that have already been discussed regarding the role of the church in the St. Lawrence settlement. Representatives of a number of different orders, including the

Jesuits, Recollets, and Sulpicians pursued mission work among the Micmac and Maliseet and provided service to the non-native parishes. During the period of British rule, their presence was problematic for officials who feared that the priests provided an ongoing link with the Bishop of Quebec and believed that they were conducting a sort of local government and justice system in opposition to the British administration. The activities of one priest in particular, the Abbé Jean-Louis Le Loutre, generated tremendous controversy in the mid-1740s regarding assistance he provided to French expeditions attempting to drive the British from Acadia and for his role in encouraging the Micmac to attack the British to discourage the expansion of their interests in Acadia. The Acadians themselves seem to have been rather reluctant to accept the Roman Catholic church as an agent of social authority and apparently felt free to complain about any priests who interfered in their lives too extensively or who failed to live up to parish expectations.

Historians have also been intrigued by the question of the degree of authority exerted over the Acadians through other channels. It has been argued that prior to the British occupation, the seigneurial system was only incompletely implemented in Acadia and certainly not even to the extent it was applied in the St. Lawrence valley. While a number of seigneuries apparently existed in theory in the official papers, there seems little evidence that they were developed in reality, and even then only in the agricultural settlement at Port Royal and environs does there seem to have been an attempt to collect the *cens et rentes*, or seigneurial dues, from the settlers. After 1713, the British administration of Acadia seems to have been somewhat haphazard. Structures were put in place for a governor and council, but the governor was absent more often than not, and there were insufficient numbers of British officials to form a civilian administration independent of the military garrison. By the late 1740s, a system of local deputies was in place through which community concerns could be expressed to the governor. The system had its problems, however, as the deputies found themselves in the middle of often conflicting interests. As a result, the British administrators appear to have had little direct impact on people's lives. Historian Naomi Griffiths has called it a "phantom rule."

In the mid-nineteenth century, American poet Henry Wadsworth Longfellow composed a lengthy poem about the Acadian experience entitled "Evangeline." In it, he presented a romanticized vision of an almost utopian society, a vision that has permeated the historical consciousness of many, including the Acadians themselves. Clearly Longfellow's descriptions are misleading in many ways, but they did tap into a growing consciousness among the Acadian people that they constituted a unique society, unlike that of both France and Quebec. While it is easy to overstate the extent of that uniqueness, it is also important not to forget that New France was by no means a homogeneous society.

Life in Newfoundland

The population of Newfoundland had grown very slowly following the setbacks of war before 1713, but after 1730 the pace of settlement began to quicken and the coastal villages started to take on an aura of permanence. Significant numbers of Irish immigrants were arriving while British fishers expanded north of Cape Bonavista into areas that were considered to be reserved for the French. French settlements in the southwest continued their slow growth; by the mid-eighteenth century the total non-native population of Newfoundland was approximately 7000. The British settlements did not yet constitute a formally organized colony, however. Informal local arrangements emerged from one fishing season to the next to ensure social order, and the system seemed satisfactory until the 1720s. In 1729, the British government agreed to nominate the leader of the annual naval convoy as the official governor of Newfoundland with authority to select men as justices of the peace to act as authorities during the winter. It was a curious system, but for the time being it seemed to suit the needs of both settlers and fishing crews.

One of the most important new elements in the economy of the British settlements was a growing trade with the British colonies on the mainland, and in particular, New England. The Newfoundlanders provided fish to New Englanders in return for agricultural products and manufactured goods. The New Englanders, in turn, were delivering the fish to the West Indies to feed the plantation slaves. From the West Indies, the Anglo-Americans obtained sugar, molasses and, of course, rum, all of which also found their way to Newfoundland. The West Country merchants and fishing companies eyed this expanding trade with alarm. Not only did the trade provide competition for the fish resources, but it appears that some of their own ships were joining in a secret trade with the New Englanders for personal profit. Smuggling activities became an important economic activity as well as a major element in the folk traditions of the coastal villages. In turn, a strong commercial base in New England was encouraged, forming the basis for later expansionist energies which would come to play an important part in the history of North America.

In many ways it would be quite misleading to characterize the emerging society in Newfoundland as a community. Distinctions among French, British, and native settlements as well as significant differences among the British themselves meant that there was no single development pattern. The scattered coastal villages of the West Country and Irish settlements developed independently of one another, although conflict between Protestants and Roman Catholics surfaced occasionally. Under the terms of the Treaty of Utrecht, the French were granted the right to catch fish and dry them on shore in the region between Cape Bonavista on the north shore and Pointe Riche on the west coast. The French settlement on Placentia Bay was ordered abandoned, but the first British governor offered the population the choice of remaining if they agreed to swear an oath of allegiance to the British Crown. While part of the community did move to Louisbourg, as has been described, others chose to remain, and the French presence on the island continued in spite of the slow expansion of the British settlements into the so-called French Shore. The Beothuk decided to avoid contact with all Europeans and retreated from the coastal settlements, which forced them to make use of a more limited resource base in the interior along the Exploits River. They continued to make seasonal sorties to coastal sites in between the French and British fisheries. Sporadic island populations could scarcely be characterized as a cohesive community.

Certainly the social structures of these settlements were significantly different from those that people had left behind. Everywhere among the non-natives, the population was overwhelmingly male, even in the larger communities like St. John's and Bonavista where women constituted only 8 to 16 percent of the population. In 1750, there were approximately one thousand women of British ancestry in the settlements within a total of about seven thousand "winter" or permanent residents. The population also changed dramatically with the season as thousands of men made their way in summer to participate in the fishery. During the mid-eighteenth century, the British population more than doubled in the summer months to some 16 000 people. The ratio of men to women was obviously even larger in the summer. At Trinity Bay in the 1740s, for example, there were 13 men for every woman at the height of the fishing season. Given the seasonal fluctuations and limited permanent population, it is not surprising that social structures from home were not extensively reproduced in eighteenth-century Newfoundland. Priests appear to have accompanied the French founders of Plaisance, but they do not seem to have remained after 1713. No clergy were permanently stationed in the British settlements until 1701; after 1703 the Society for the Propagation of the Gospel funded a missionary in St. John's more or less regularly. The first church, erected by the Church of England, was located there. None of the Anglican clergy appear to have been received enthusiastically—a scarcely surprising observation given the fact that the majority of families in St. John's by the 1750s were either Roman Catholics or non-Anglican Protestants. Outside St. John's similar statistics arise but only Church of England clergy were available and even they did not begin arriving until well into the eighteenth century. The practice of Roman Catholicism was discouraged through both open and subtle pressures, in part because of official British attitudes of the day and in part because of fears regarding the loyalty of the Irish Roman Catholic settlers.

With the slow increase in the number of women, family life gradually became a reality for a minority of Newfoundlanders. Little is known about eighteenth-century educational arrangements although it seems that small family or community schools met occasionally in the villages, probably under direction of the women. The first formal school was opened apparently in the early 1720s at Bonavista under the sponsorship of the Society for the Propagation of the Gospel, but it was not duplicated elsewhere for some 20 years. The SPG schools were essentially missions for lower-class children; the handful of upper-class children in St. John's were doubtless tutored at home as was standard practice of the day.

Given the lack of permanent social systems and limited formal authority in Newfoundland, it is not surprising that people who were not governed by terms of service in the fishery found themselves able to lead much more independent lives than they would have in the villages of the West Country or Ireland. This independence was lamented by upper-class visitors on numerous occasions and interpreted as lawlessness and vice. As one observer recorded in 1764, "Seven months in the year there is not employment for a tenth part of these inhabitants and. . .consequently they spend that time in idleness and subsist for the greatest part by robbery, theft and every species of violence and wickedness."[4] Drinking was a

---

[4] Quoted in H.A. Innis, *The Cod Fisheries* (Toronto, 2nd edition, 1954), p. 154. Original source: Testimony of Palliser, recorded in the Privy Council in the Matter of the Boundary between the Dominion of Canada and the Colony of Newfoundland in the Labrador Peninsula, Vol. IV of the Joint Appendix, p. 1852. For more on the history of Newfoundland, see Innis and Frederick W. Rowe, *A History of Newfoundland and Labrador* (Toronto, 1980); G.M. Story (ed.), *Early European Settlement and Exploitation in Atlantic Canada* (St. John's, 1982).

popular pastime in Newfoundland as it was throughout the European colonies; by 1750 there were over 120 taverns on the island.

In spite of divisions into French and English, Irish and West Country, Protestant and Roman Catholic, people in the scattered outports were not entirely divided from one another. A common orientation toward the sea and international trade coupled with an integration into a complex network of credit and provisioning provided an element of shared experience. Between 1713 and 1756, sheltered briefly from international conflict, the European settlers and fishers in Newfoundland worked to establish their place in the growing transatlantic trade.

Imperial Conflicts

Away from the relative peace of eastern regions in the 1720s and 1730s, territorial expansion in the interior of the continent and competition in the fur trade continued to ensure conflict between the French and the British. Both to the south and to the northwest, French traders moved into new and richer fur-trading regions as the prime fur-bearing animals of the original trading regions became scarce and the demand for furs in Europe increased. With the failure of the Iroquois Confederacy to dominate the nations to the West in the Ohio country, the French were able to extend their influence there, much to the concern of both the British and the Anglo-Americans in the seaboard colonies, who continued to fear encirclement by a French-speaking, Roman Catholic enemy.

In 1725, the French constructed a stone fort on the banks of the Niagara River to oversee one of the major routes into the Ohio fur country; the British retaliated two years later with the construction of a fort at Oswego to oversee traffic on Lake Ontario. In 1733, the French added a fort south of Lake Champlain and distributed seigneuries along the Richelieu to officers of the Carignan-Salières regiment in the hopes of securing the old invasion route to Canada. Farther west, Pierre Gaultier de Varennes et de La Vérendrye was taking a more aggressive approach to protecting French interests. With the backing of a group of Montreal merchants, he and his family travelled through the Assiniboine and Ojibwa lands beyond Lake Superior, establishing a string of posts designed to attract the inland natives and persuade them to trade with his company instead of travelling the lengthy trade routes to meet the Hudson's Bay Company to the North. La Vérendrye's travels were not purely in the interests of commerce, however. In 1731, Governor Beauharnois provided him with gifts for negotiating Indian alliances and instructions to seek a route to the western sea. Like Champlain before him, La Vérendrye was part adventurer, part businessman, and part imperial agent. And while he and his sons ultimately failed to find the western sea, they did provide the French with considerable knowledge of the western interior of the continent and established relationships with a number of Indian nations hitherto unknown to Canadians.[5]

Once again a combination of economic competition, native politics, and European rivalries brought an end to the uneasy peace that had held since 1713. In 1739, Great Britain and Spain had gone to war over Spanish claims in America; five years later, France declared war on Great Britain in a conflict that would become known as the War of the Austrian Succession. That same year (1744), an enterprising group of Americans founded the Ohio Company of Virginia and laid claim to half a million acres (200 000 ha) in the region west of the Appalachians, which the French had always considered their sphere of influence. Conflict seemed inevitable.

However, it was not in the Ohio country that the opening salvo in the North American war was fired. When Du Quesnel, governor of Île Royale, learned of the outbreak of war in Europe, he determined to do his part to assist in the recovery of Acadia for France. He organized a group of soldiers and opportunists who succeeded in capturing an American fishing station at Canso. The British troops stationed there were unaware that war had been declared and found themselves carted off to Louisbourg as prisoners. The attack was followed by a number of small raids that might better be described as privateering.

Governor William Shirley of Massachusetts had grander plans. He convinced a number of New England businesspeople to sponsor an expedition that would take over Cape Breton so that the Americans could then assert control over the entire fishery. In 1745, 3400 militia from Massachusetts, Connecticut, New Hampshire, and Rhode Island under the leadership of William Pepperell joined with a regular naval force under the command of British officer Peter Warren and succeeded in capturing

---

[5] For more on La Vérendrye and early French exploration and trade in the western interior, see Yves Zoltvany's entry on him in the *Dictionary of Canadian Biography*, Vol. III (Toronto, 1974), pp 246–254; W.J. Eccles, *The Canadian Frontier, 1534–1760* (New York, 1960); A.S. Morton, *A History of the Canadian West to 1870–71*, second edition (Toronto, 1973).

Louisbourg and occupying Île Saint Jean. The success of the Americans appears to have surprised the French as well as the British, who had shown little interest in Shirley's plans.

Shirley quickly began to promote his next plan for an invasion of Canada. Again he solicited British assistance, and again the British were unenthusiastic, feeling that their energies had to be directed to more urgent matters at home where Bonnie Prince Charlie was assembling an army of Highland Scots to lay his claim to the British throne. The French were equally ill-prepared to support their colony on the St. Lawrence, so Governor Beauharnois decided that his best defence would be to launch a series of small raids along the New York frontier to preoccupy the Americans and prevent them from organizing a large-scale invasion. The New Yorkers responded by petitioning the Iroquois to join them in retaliation. For a time, the confederacy refused, insisting on its old policy of neutrality, but finally a number of warriors drawn primarily from among the Mohawk agreed to go to war. Native allies of the French soon found themselves pulled into the conflict as well.

The war in Europe dragged on for three years with neither side gaining any particular advantage. Finally in 1748, a treaty was signed at Aix-la-Chapelle to bring the war to an end. Louisbourg was returned to the French, but no real solutions to the problems of North America were negotiated, and no one seemed to expect the peace to last. In 1749, the British founded a new colony at Halifax, settled by discharged soldiers and naval men, and heavily funded to ensure a military stronghold that would reinforce the British claim to what they called Nova Scotia. The French retaliated by encouraging bands of native and French warriors to harass the new settlement, then constructed a fort named Beauséjour on the Isthmus of Chignecto to make clear their continued interest in Acadia.

The Seven Years' War

The continuing tensions were not confined to the maritime colonies. Conflicting claims among the French, Iroquois, and Anglo-Americans over the Ohio lands led to almost constant skirmishing in the West. The stakes escalated in 1754 when Governor Duquesne sent 800 troops into the Ohio Valley. They succeeded in destroying an American post under construction on the Allegheny River and replaced it with a French fort that they named Fort Duquesne. The Americans retaliated by sending a small force under the command of George Washington that attacked a party of French soldiers nearby, killing its leader and nine men. The French responded with a larger force of soldiers and Indian warriors who managed to send the Americans packing and re-established the French claim to the territory. Finally, the British became involved. They sent Major-General James Braddock with two regular regiments to North America with instructions to raise two new regiments in the colonies and to attack the French at four strategic points: Acadia, Lake Champlain, Fort Niagara, and Fort Duquesne.

Although war was not declared officially in Europe until 1756, the colonies were clearly drawing their parent countries into a major conflict. The colony of Canada was of little economic value to the French, but its strategic importance as a block to British colonial expansion warranted its protection, while the colony on Île Royale was important not only because of the economic value of the fishery but because the fishery had long been seen as a training ground for naval personnel. For their part, the British wanted to prevent the extension of French claims in the Ohio Valley as well as to protect their own fishery and trade interests in the North Atlantic.

A series of engagements on various fronts characterized the early phases of the war. Overall results were inconclusive. At sea, a British naval force engaged a French convoy taking soldiers to Quebec and Louisbourg, with minor losses to the French. General Braddock marched his troops against Fort Duquesne, where they were badly defeated by a much smaller French and native force. William Shirley, governor of Massachusetts, was given a military rank and put in command of a march against Fort Niagara. His troops made it only as far as Oswego on Lake Ontario, where they decided to remain for the winter since supplies were low and the ranks were seriously thinned by disease and desertion. William Johnson undertook to collect a large force of American frontiersmen and Iroquois allies from the Mohawk Valley; they marched to attack Fort St. Frederick on Lake Champlain. En route at Lake George, they met the French and Indian forces under the command of General Dieskau, but at the end of a bloody battle, neither side had won a clear victory.

Perhaps the most devastating series of events of this phase of the war occurred in Acadia. In the late spring of 1755, a combined force of British regulars and American militiamen succeeded in capturing Fort Beauséjour and found three hundred Acadians within its walls. Charles Lawrence, the British officer who was serving as governor of Nova Scotia, was more uneasy than ever about the loyalties of the Acadian settlers. He feared that if they learned of the Anglo-American problems in battles elsewhere, they would be inclined to rise up against the British. He decided to force the long-standing issue of the oath of allegiance and called a meeting of Acadian deputies in Halifax. When the Acadian representatives attempted to remain neutral in the affair and refused to swear the oath, Lawrence determined to expel the entire French population of Acadia. In October 1755, transport ships from Boston appeared at the major ports, people were rounded up, and the first of a series of expulsions began. The Acadians were shipped to other British colonies in North America or to Europe; some fled into the bush, while others made their way to Canada. A sizable majority of the population was deported between 1755 and 1762; exact numbers may never be known, although estimates have ranged as high as 90 percent. Eventually some of the Acadians managed to make their way homeward, but it was a horrific episode in Acadian history. The breakup of closely knit families and communities opened psychic wounds that remain unhealed in some circles even to this day.[6]

By 1756, it seemed that victory was within the grasp of the French and their native allies. Raids along the American frontier were highly destructive. Several thousand prisoners (men, women, and children) were taken, farm buildings and crops were destroyed, and an unknown number of people were killed. A more concerted campaign was undertaken in 1756 against Oswego and Fort George, which fell to a French and native force led by Louis-Joseph, the Marquis de Montcalm. The following year, the French-Indian allies won a similar victory at Fort William Henry on Lake George. Now in control of both Lake Ontario and almost the entire American frontier, it seemed as if the French and their allies were bound to triumph.

In 1758, however, the new British secretary of state, William Pitt, convinced his colleagues that much more money and effort had to be put into British military undertakings in both Europe and North America. Colonial militia were insufficient, he argued. And so several thousand

---

[6] On the deportation of the Acadians, see Naomi Griffiths (ed.), *The Acadian Deportation: Deliberate Perfidy or Cruel Necessity?* (Toronto, 1969). Political and diplomatic issues regarding Acadia are examined in J.B. Brebner, *New England's Outpost* (New York, 1927) and George Rawlyk, *Nova Scotia's Massachusetts* (Montreal, 1973). Also helpful are the maps in R. Cole Harris (ed.), *Historical Atlas of Canada*, Vol. 1 (Toronto, 1987).

British regular soldiers were shipped overseas, marking the largest commitment of resources for warfare in North America to that time. The overall strategy did not change much, however. Once again the British plan was to launch major assaults at four key points. Louisbourg was to be seized to clear the way for an invasion up the St. Lawrence to Quebec. Fort Frontenac on Lake Ontario was to be captured to prevent supplies from reaching French posts in the Ohio Valley. Fort Duquesne was to be attacked as the major French stronghold in the Ohio country. And finally, troops were to be dispatched to clear the French from the Lake Champlain frontier. After a lengthy siege, Louisbourg capitulated, although as some historians have commented, it was a somewhat pointless victory for the British since the French navy had already been defeated off European shores. Lieutenant-Colonel Bradstreet also won a victory for the British at Fort Frontenac. Elsewhere, however, the French continued to hold the upper hand. At Lake Champlain, over 15 000 British and American troops under Major-General James Abercromby suffered a devastating defeat at the hands of Montcalm's 3500 men. In the Ohio Valley, the British lost their offensive against Fort Duquesne, although the French position was undermined shortly afterward when natives of the area reached an agreement with colonial authorities in Pennsylvania, promising their alliance with the British in return for guarantees that the Americans would give up their interests in Indian lands west of the Allegheny Mountains. The French concluded that without the support of these Indians bands, they could not hold Fort Duquesne, and so they withdrew and destroyed the post.

In 1759, William Pitt decided to build on the successes of his earlier strategy and launch a major thrust against New France. It would consist of three elements: James Wolfe was to sail his troops up the St. Lawrence to take Quebec; another force would take Fort Niagara to permit troops to move down to Quebec from Lake Ontario; and Jeffrey Amherst was to lead a force up the Lake Champlain–Richelieu route. The Niagara campaign succeeded, giving the British control of the Ohio country and lakes Ontario and Erie. Amherst managed to move his army as far as Crown Point on the water route to Montreal where the men settled in to construct fortifications.

Wolfe reached Quebec, establishing his troops on the Île d'Orléans and directly opposite the city on the south shore, but found himself unable to take the fortress. Instead, the American Rangers who accompanied him contented themselves for the summer in terrorizing families throughout the district. Finally in September, Wolfe decided to attempt one last strategy and land his troops just above the town to force Montcalm and the French army to come out of the fortress to engage them. As a landing site, Wolfe chose the base of a steep cliff, anticipating that Montcalm would never guess that a landing could be made there. The tactic worked. Taken by surprise, Montcalm was able to muster less than half his troops and within minutes fell to defeat on a farmer's field known as the Plains of Abraham outside the town. A few days later the French gave up the fort at Quebec to the British.

The following spring, the Chevalier François-Gaston de Lévis led French soldiers back to recapture Quebec. Although he succeeded, his anticipated reinforcements failed to arrive and, learning that British ships were on their way, he decided to abandon Quebec and assist at Montreal, the anticipated site of the next British attack. However, the French position at Montreal was clearly hopeless. The three British armies converged on Montreal followed by the news that no French reinforcements would be arriving from Europe. Finally, on September 7, the French decided to capitulate. The British were victorious in New France.[7]

Brigadier-General James Murray was put in charge of the administration of the colony as a military governor until the war in Europe was over and the fate of New France could be decided by diplomats. It was not until February 10, 1763, that the Treaty of Paris determined the new outlines of European interests in North America. In that agreement, the European powers carved out their spheres of influence according to the new power relationships at home. France gave up its claim to New France and the lands east of the Mississippi River; the British agreed to grant them only the islands of St. Pierre and Miquelon and fishing rights off what was called the French shore of Newfoundland. The Caribbean Islands were divided between the French and the British, while Louisiana and Mexico were acknowledged as Spanish territory, although French administrators remained in Louisiana for a time. The Treaty of Paris was followed by the Royal Proclamation of 1763 whereby the British made clear the terms under which they intended to govern their new colony. A small adminis-

---

[7] On the military and political aspects of the Seven Years' War, see G.F.G. Stanley, *New France: the Last Phase, 1744–1760* (Toronto, 1968); I.K. Steele, *Guerrillas and Grenadiers: The Struggle for Canada, 1689-1760* (Toronto, 1969). Traditional military history can be found in C.P. Stacey, *Quebec 1759: The Siege and the Battle* (Toronto, 1959), while a nationalist interpretation can be found in Guy Frégault, *Canada: The War of the Conquest* (Toronto, 1969).

trative unit called the Province of Quebec was established along the St. Lawrence River between the Ottawa River and the Gaspé Peninsula. A line was drawn along the height of land running through the Allegheny Mountains; all lands between it and the Mississippi were declared to be Indian territory in which no non-native settlement would be permitted. Only by special arrangement through the Crown could any of these lands be alienated. The Proclamation of 1763 was thus, in part, a recognition of the important role played by native people who had allied themselves with the British cause during the war. They were clamouring for the removal of American settlers and speculators from their lands, and the British made it clear that they intended to respect those wishes. The proclamation was to become a crucial document in future struggles by natives to have their land claims recognized.

The French imperial order had been driven from the continent. In the wake of the Seven Years' War, a small population whose ancestry was French was left clinging to the shores of the St. Lawrence and the Atlantic coast, uncertain about their future under British rule. The Iroquois were generally pleased at the victory of their allies, although the loss of the French meant the old policy of playing one interest group against the other was no longer an option for the confederacy. The interior fur trade had almost collapsed during the war; now both native traders and their Canadian partners faced the dilemma of abandoning the trade or attempting to rebuild it through new supply sources in Europe. Members of Roman Catholic orders and congregations realized with concern that their faith was not recognized in Great Britain where they would not even have had the right to vote or hold public office. What would the future mean to them?

Conclusions

The history of New France and Newfoundland is neither an account of a glorious "heroic age" of explorers, traders, and missionaries nor is it an account of a "backward" and priest-ridden peasant population struggling to preserve itself in the New World. Both images have appeared in past histories, and both are misleading. Instead, the history of New France, in particular, is the story of people whose lives were very much bound up in the economics and politics of two worlds. The First Nations found themselves sharing lands with people whom they had invited to visit but who had come to stay. The French immigrants brought with them ideas and institutions from a homeland in transition between the ancien régime and modernity. They found themselves inextricably caught in the politics of the First Nations, upon whose lands they had settled, and also found themselves drawn to a number of aspects of indigenous culture: certain foods, clothing styles, transportation techniques, and habits of mind like pride, a love of public display, and a combined sense of individual autonomy and social responsibility. Unable and perhaps unwilling to reproduce in the New World their lives from the old, they evolved a society that represented something uniquely in between. It remained to be seen how that society would cope with the profound transition that took place in 1763.

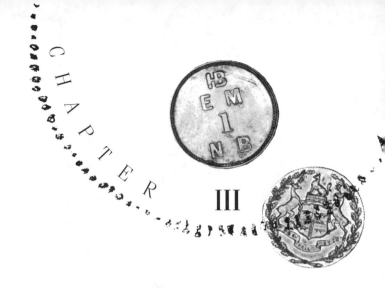

THE FUR TRADE

In mid-morning 6 July 1534, a French long-boat reconnoitering the coastline of a cove in the Baie de Chaleur came upon a flotilla of 40 or 50 Micmac canoes clearly intent on intercepting the Europeans. The Micmac landed and gestured enthusiastically for the French to join them, waving a number of furs on sticks to make their intentions clear. The French party was afraid because of their smaller numbers and rowed off in the opposite direction only to discover the Micmac in hot pursuit, dancing and calling out. The French fired two cannon shots and two "fire-lances" over the heads of their pursuers before they finally dispersed. The next day, the Micmac party reappeared where the French had anchored their ships, again holding up furs. This time the French felt that their position was more secure and they willingly bartered knives and other iron goods for the fur clothing that the Micmac offered. Next day, the Micmac returned again, now with their wives and families, to offer even more of their furs and clothing for trade.

The leader of the French expedition was Jacques Cartier, and although he was not particularly interested in the furs, he was so intrigued by this encounter with the people of the lands he claimed for France that he recorded the details at some length. He seemed a little surprised at the avid interest of the Micmac in French iron goods and was not entirely convinced that the furs that he had received were of particular value, but he admired the fine physique of the Micmac and their beautiful homeland.

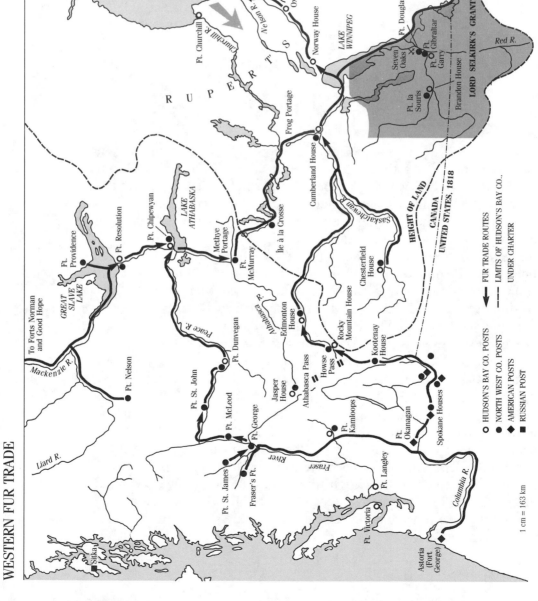

WESTERN FUR TRADE

HUDSON BAY

RUPERT'S LAND

HUDSON'S BAY CO. FROM ENGLAND

NORTH WEST CO. FROM MONTREAL

Ft. Severn

York Factory

Oxford House

Ft. Churchill

Churchill R.

Nelson R.

Norway House

LAKE WINNIPEG

Ft. William (After 1803)

Grand Portage (Before 1803)

Ft. Douglas

Seven Oaks

Ft. Gibraltar

Ft. Garry

Red R.

Brandon House

Ft. la Souris

LORD SELKIRK'S GRANT

Frog Portage

Cumberland House

Saskatchewan R.

HEIGHT OF LAND

CANADA
UNITED STATES, 1818

To Forts Norman
and Good Hope

Ft. Providence

GREAT SLAVE LAKE

Ft. Resolution

Ft. Chipewyan

LAKE ATHABASKA

Methye Portage

Île à la Crosse

Ft. McMurray

Athabasca R.

Chesterfield House

Mackenzie R.

Ft. Nelson

Peace R.

Ft. Dunvegan

Edmonton House

Rocky Mountain House

Kootenay House

Liard R.

Ft. St. John

Ft. McLeod

Jasper House

Athabasca Pass

Howse Pass

Ft. Kamloops

Ft. Okanagan

Spokane Houses

Ft. St. James

Fraser's Ft.

Ft. George

Fraser River

Ft. Langley

Ft. Victoria

Columbia R.

Sitka

Astoria (Fort George)

1 cm = 163 km

○ HUDSON'S BAY CO. POSTS
● NORTH WEST CO. POSTS
◆ AMERICAN POSTS
■ RUSSIAN POST

→ FUR TRADE ROUTES
--- LIMITS OF HUDSON'S BAY CO.
    UNDER CHARTER

Obviously the Micmac were already quite familiar with European visitors and keenly interested in obtaining metal tools. Although the first trade encounters on the Pacific coast occurred at a much later date, the patterns were similar. In the summer of 1774, a Spanish expedition led by Juan Pérez met the Haida offshore from Langara Island and found them anxious to exchange blankets, furs, and domestic utensils for the Spanish knives and beads. In these cases at least, it was the First Nations and not the Europeans who seemed most anxious to initiate an international trade.

Exchanges of fur during these early contacts between Europeans and native peoples should not really be considered a true fur trade, however. They were probably more important as part of ceremonies in which peace and friendship were pledged according to native traditions. A limited number of goods manufactured in Europe made their way into First Nations' communities through contact with fishers, through raids on fishing stations, and through scavenging from shipwrecks, and probably even fewer furs made their way across the ocean to Europe. So for almost a century, the offshore fisheries had far more economic significance to Europeans than trade in furs. Unfortunately, so little record (written or oral) exists of this period that we will probably never be able to recreate these contacts with any certainty. It was not until the late sixteenth century that the development of a fur trade in North America was encouraged, created by a demand for furs, which were now scarce in Europe.

Contrary to popular belief, the fur trade was not the first source of European goods for the First Nations since many inland people had access to European goods through their own trade networks prior to direct contact with European traders. Nevertheless, the fur trade did bring increasing numbers of natives into contact with both Europeans and their goods, beginning a long process of cultural change and political adjustment that would eventually span the continent. It is this process that will be considered in this chapter.

While the fur trade was not the initial drawing card for Europeans to what would become Canada, the patterns through which it developed came to have a profound impact on the native peoples, the territorial expansion of European interests, and the emergence of a unique society in the western interior. Thus, the fur trade cannot be considered solely as a business undertaking or an adjunct to imperialism, but must be understood for its social and political ramifications.

The Early Fur Trade

With increasing demand for furs in Europe at the beginning of the seventeenth century, a technique for producing felt from beaver pelts was developed in North America; the felt was made into the hats, which became a tremendously popular fashion item. For most of the first century of trade, it was almost exclusively the beaver pelt that Europeans sought.

The best furs for European purposes were made from the lovely, thick pelts of beavers that lived in northern areas. The regions in the immediate vicinity of the coast did not support particularly large numbers of such animals, so it was necessary to look further afield. North of the St. Lawrence in the lands of the Algonquin and Montagnais nations, the French found both a good supply and a people knowledgeable in the techniques of trapping beaver. The first step in the manufacturing of beaver felt was also undertaken by the natives. The animal was skinned, the inside of the pelt scraped clean and smooth, and several pelts were sewn together into a blanket or robe. These robes were worn with the fur next to the body for a season, and with time, the long guard hairs of the pelt worked loose. The skin itself also became smooth and soft. The fur was then ready for the remainder of the felting process, which was completed in Europe.

Another important aspect of early trade was the provisioning of European expeditions. Fishing crews and exploration parties knew little of the food resources in the "new" world and so relied on native people of the area to bring fish, meat, and agricultural foods for their sustenance.

In return for procuring food and furs and beginning the process of felt manufacture, First Nations trappers sought a number of specific goods from the Europeans and rejected items that did not suit them. Domestic utensils made of metal and particularly axes, knives, and agricultural implements were most desired. There was also a high demand for glass beads, which some commentators have interpreted as "trinkets and baubles" foisted on unsophisticated natives. More recent ethnographic study has suggested, however, that these beads were highly valued for their symbolic significance for use in religious ceremonies. There was initially

Opposite page:

Evolution of the beaver hat fashion: the engine that drove the fur trade for a time.

NATIONAL ARCHIVES OF CANADA/C17338

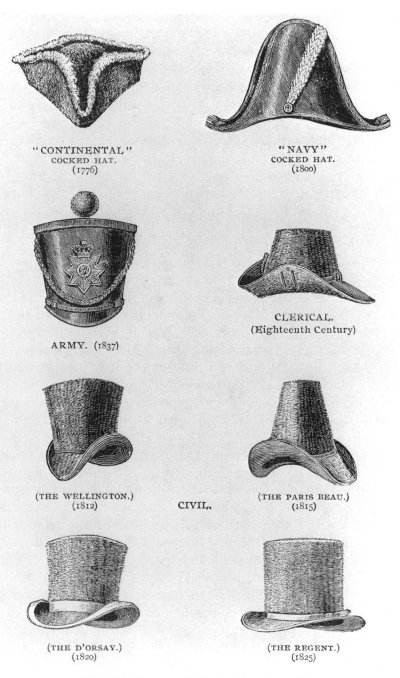

"CONTINENTAL"
COCKED HAT.
(1776)

"NAVY"
COCKED HAT.
(1800)

ARMY. (1837)

CLERICAL.
(Eighteenth Century)

(THE WELLINGTON.)
(1812)

CIVIL.

(THE PARIS BEAU.)
(1815)

(THE D'ORSAY.)
(1820)

(THE REGENT.)
(1825)

MODIFICATIONS OF THE BEAVER HAT.

little interest in cloth that was clearly unsuitable for clothing in a harsh climate or for bush life.

It was also the interests of native traders that determined the patterns and locations of early trade meetings. Tadoussac on the north shore of the St. Lawrence became an important site for the trade because it was here that large numbers of inland people met annually for a season of fishing amidst a round of political and social gatherings. The French found it convenient to meet with the traders at Tadoussac because so many of them gathered regularly at this one spot. Furs were brought here by the Montagnais and Algonquin along their regular northern travel routes. Thus, it was the native traders who did most of the travelling in the early days of the trade, while their European partners waited on the coast for their arrival.

During the French regime, the Canadian fur trade was a limited under-taking. Problems among early competitors led entrepreneurs like Champlain to demand a licensing system in order to limit the number of traders and control the trade. The king of France eventually agreed, and the trade was carried out through a series of monopolies, as described in Chapter One. Nevertheless, by 1663 the trade had not developed into a particularly lucrative or widespread undertaking for any of the participants. Demand remained limited in Europe, and problems of financing or staffing the business prevented much expansion on the European side. Limited demand for European goods and a preference to remain with more traditional economic activities limited participation on the First Nations' part.

Even with the direct involvement of the crown during the years of the Royal Colony, the fur trade did not expand particularly rapidly. In geographic terms, certainly, French traders began to move out into the Great Lakes, pursuing the trade that had been abandoned by the Huron following the breakup of their confederacy. However, with the decision makers unable to agree on a policy of a compact colony or extended imperial interests, internal disagreement hampered the development of the trade. Potential traders had to obtain official permission in the form of a licence, but initially only 25 of these licences were issued in the interests of preventing competition. Other regulations to control prices were also

Opposite page:

Popular trade goods from the Hudson's Bay Company (sketched by C. W. Jefferys).

NATIONAL ARCHIVES OF CANADA/C69578

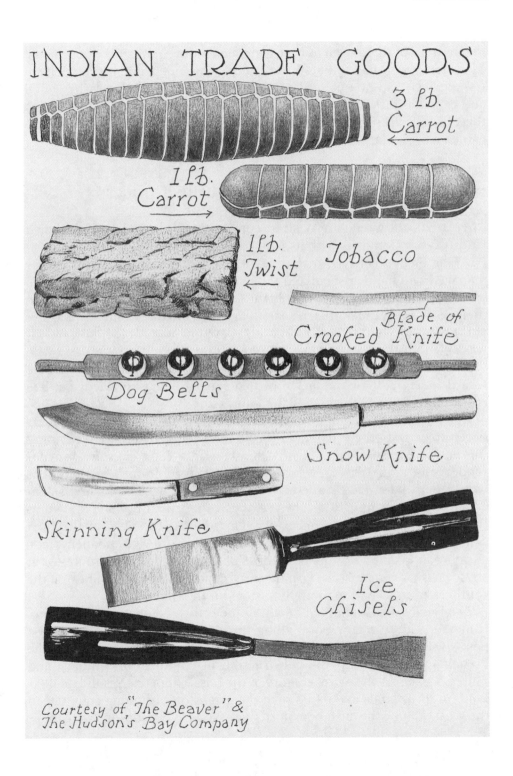

INDIAN TRADE GOODS

3 Lb. Carrot

1 Lb. Carrot

1 Lb. Twist Tobacco

Blade of Crooked Knife

Dog Bells

Snow Knife

Skinning Knife

Ice Chisels

Courtesy of "The Beaver" & The Hudson's Bay Company

attempted, but these seem to have generated more complaints than results. The French also had difficulty controlling the independent traders from Canada who had no qualms about taking their furs to the nearby Dutch and British if they could obtain a better price. Smuggling by men whom the officials referred to as deserters was commonplace; Fort Frontenac gained a particular reputation as a haven for these "illegal" activities.

Competition With British Traders

After 1670, the French also faced competition from the newly formed Hudson's Bay Company with its string of posts along the shores of Hudson Bay. The French believed they were in a superior position because their men were willing to travel inland extensively and live with the natives who were trapping furs for them, while the company men tended to remain in their posts along the northern coast. The Hudson's Bay Company was not entirely "asleep by the Bay" as one of its opponents charged, however. It was able to make use of the native population of the bay hinterland who did the inland travel and trading for it. Sometimes referred to as "Home Guard Indians," these families provided expertise and knowledge at less cost to the company than regular employees.

In response to the competition from the Hudson's Bay Company, traders began to move farther inland, following the Ottawa River to Lake Nipissing and a course along the French River into Lake Huron. A major rendezvous point developed at Michilimackinac from which flotillas would depart for Lake Superior or Lake Michigan. The businessmen-adventurers who undertook these extensive journeys became known as the *coureurs de bois*, and many of them adopted the lives of the First Nations with whom they lived and worked. More or less permanent trade sites began to emerge at the crossroads of key transportation routes or at strategic sites. Small-scale farming was conducted at a number of the southern posts as part of a supply system for the trade.

The French also attempted to cut off the British competition by seizing Hudson's Bay Company posts along the shores of the bay. When these posts were returned to the British by the Treaty of Utrecht (1713), the French responded with the construction of combination military and trade posts across the Ohio territory to the Mississippi to consolidate their hold on those lands and to assist in the extension of trading activities to the West. Among the most notable of these western expeditions were those

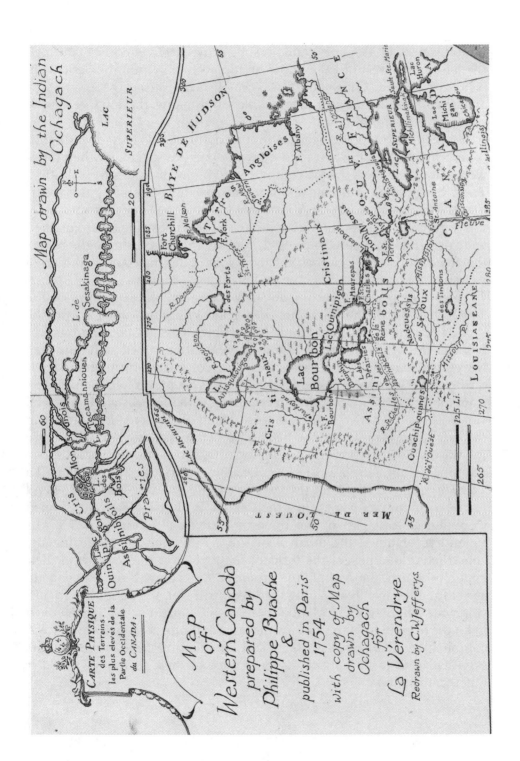

Map drawn by the Indian Ochagach

Carte Physique des Terreins les plus élevés de la Partie Occidentale du Canada :

Map of Western Canada prepared by Philippe Buache & published in Paris 1754 with copy of Map drawn by Ochagach for La Vérendrye

Redrawn by C.W.Jefferys.

Maps of the interior as seen by a native and a French cartographer.

undertaken by La Vérendrye and his sons between 1731 and 1743 through the lands northwest of Lake Superior and eventually into the Saskatchewan River system. A line of posts was established to attract the Assiniboine and Cree trade and discourage people from taking the long voyage to company posts in the North.

Another important change that occurred during this period was a shift from beaver harvesting to trapping a wider range of species for their fur as well as for their skins, which could be used in the manufacture of leather. There has been some debate about the reasons for this shift, but it seems that the European market was probably saturated with beaver and prices were dropping as a result. Traders looked to other possible furs to market, and demand gradually increased for alternatives. Although beaver remained the primary export, other furs like otter, raccoon, and marten were becoming important by the mid-eighteenth century.

These changes were accompanied by considerable disruption in the North and West. The lands between Lake Winnipeg and Lake of the Woods became the focus of competing Ojibwa, Cree, Dakota, and Assiniboine claims. Again and again, bands of each nation armed with European weapons descended upon bands that they considered intruders in their territories. There were also regular attempts to prevent French traders from moving farther west into direct contact with more distant bands who supplied furs to native intermediaries. Much of La Vérendrye's effort in this country was diplomatic as he and his partners attempted to convince the warring First Nations to give up their battles and devote their time to trapping for the purposes of trade. Unable to persuade the warriors, La Vérendrye agreed to permit the Cree to adopt his eldest son in 1734 and joined them in their war against the Dakota. With that alliance, he hoped to obtain at least part of the trade of their rich country. In 1737, La Vérendrye obtained the alliance of the Assiniboine by promising the construction of a post at the forks of the Red River in the heart of their lands. In return, the Assiniboine promised to meet with the Mandan, an agricultural people living along the Missouri River, to negotiate a friendship with the French. The Mandan contact with the French in 1738 proved to be the beginning of the end for the large and prosperous community. A combination of disease, warfare, and competition from white settlers eventually led to the virtual disappearance of their society in the later nineteenth century.

Impact on New France

In spite of the geographic extension of the trade that had occurred by 1760, there were no dramatic increases in the profits obtained. European demand was steady but not large, and the French continental trade system was expensive and slow. Competition among the French, Anglo-Americans in the South, and British in the North also limited returns. Furthermore, the fur trade was a peculiar economic activity in that it depended so heavily on supplies from Europe and developed almost no manufacturing or secondary investment in North America. The question of the impact of the fur trade on the economy and society of New France is one that has been discussed at considerable length by historians.

One of the first contributors to the debate was economic historian Harold Adams Innis. In his extensive study of the Canadian fur trade from its origins to the twentieth century, he argued that the development of the fur trade was the central determining factor in the economic and even social development of New France and later of Canada as a whole. Colonial policies and politics were primarily related to the demands of the fur trade, he suggested, and the economic problems of that trade contributed in no small way to the downfall of New France. Nevertheless, Innis argued, the geographic patterns of expansion that the fur trade produced laid out the pattern of the geography of modern Canada, and the economy based on the export of a "staple" resource was one in a series of economies based on staples like fish, timber, and wheat. The so-called "staples thesis" has had an important impact on the interpretation of Canadian economic development.

While Innis's interpretation of the central role of the fur trade has been very influential, not all historians have agreed with him. A better understanding of the role of the Iroquois in the fur trade has made it clear that the trade was just as much a north-south linkage as it was the east-west pattern that Innis chose to emphasize. Furthermore, the centrality of the trade in shaping the institutions of New France has been challenged in many different ways. The clerical historian Lionel Groulx emphasized instead the importance of agriculture in the history of New France, while E.E. Rich and John Galbraith preferred to interpret the fur trade as an imperial venture with little connection to the daily life of the people of the colonies. For W.J. Eccles, the military was a more important institution in shaping the lives and value systems of the people of New France. Louise Dechêne, in her study of seventeenth-century Montreal, concluded that the fur trade really had little impact on the development of that particular community. She noted, for example, that only a small group of men participated full time in the trade, while most others were only occasional participants. It may be difficult to settle the debate, since it is almost impossible to measure the actual rate of fur production or to trace the spin-off effects of fur trade money in the colony. The surviving records are limited and, of course, illicit trade can never be measured.[1]

Nevertheless, a romanticized vision of the early fur trade has been a remarkably persistent part of popular tradition in Canada. The colourful voyageur and independent coureur de bois have been depicted as a Canadian version of the frontiersman and the cowboy, with their lack of concern for authority, their machismo, and their pursuit of a life of freedom. Folk songs celebrate a life lived vigorously in the fresh northern air, free from the interference of women except, perhaps, for the adorable little sweetheart waiting patiently at home to hear of the exploits of her loved one.

The reality was somewhat different. Tethered to home through the necessity of a supply line for trade goods, the French traders were never completely independent. Many participated in the trade in order to earn money to invest in the family farm. Partnerships were often family affairs linking kinship and business as were most other economic activities of the time. Nor was it a life of ceaseless wandering along the inland waterways. More or less permanent posts emerged at key rendezvous points on and near the Great Lakes. The French traders learned the value of establishing family ties to cement economic relations with their native trade partners. First Nations' traditions linked personal and public activities through exchange of children or women, and the French soon learned to accommodate themselves to that aspect of native expectation, marrying important native women to help secure trade with their families and bands. By the end of the seventeenth century, there were probably several hundred

---

[1] For more on this interpretive debate, see H.A. Innis, *The Fur Trade in Canada*, (Toronto: 1970, revised edition); E.E. Rich, *History of the Hudson's Bay Company, 1670–1870*, 3 vols. (Toronto, 1960), *The Fur Trade and the Northwest to 1857* (Toronto, 1967); John Galbraith, *The Hudson's Bay Company as Imperial Factor, 1821-69* (Toronto, 1957); W.J. Eccles, "The Social, Economic and Political Significance of the Military Establishment in New France," *Canadian Historical Review* (March 1971); Louise Dechêne, *Habitants et marchands de Montreal au XVIIe siècle* (Montreal, 1974).

coureurs de bois living and working inland from the St. Lawrence. More or less permanent communities of mixed race began to develop throughout the fur trade hinterland, providing focal points as trade and provisioning centres.

While the early years of the fur trade may have been of limited economic significance to the French, the political aspects of that trade were of paramount importance. In the eighteenth century, the French recognized that their imperial interests in North America could not possibly be promoted without the involvement of the First Nations, either as active military allies or as impartial nonparticipants in the conflict with the Anglo-Americans. The fur trade was the major venue in which political agreements with the First Nations could be negotiated, with the French providing goods in return for military assistance and furs. Building on their successes in native diplomacy from the seventeenth century, the French proved remarkably successful with this strategy, obtaining the support of most of the eastern nations with the notable exception, of course, of the Iroquois Confederacy.

Thus, if one wishes to describe the impact of the fur trade on New France, it would probably be more helpful to look outside the St. Lawrence valley itself. In purely economic terms, profits from the early trade seem to have accrued primarily to merchants in Europe rather than to people in the colonies. Thus, it is possible to conclude that the trade had a limited impact on New France. But, in larger social and political terms, there can be no doubt that the trade was important to the position of France in America, in the creation of a new society, and in a not insignificant contribution to the mythology and folklore that helped to distinguish the people of New France from their old country roots.

The Age of Corporate Competition

With the fall of New France, the extensive network of trade partnerships and transportation routes that the French had developed seemed initially to fall by the wayside. At least, that was what the Hudson's Bay Company hoped, assuming that it would now have the field to itself under the guardianship of its royal charter. Instead, a new group of entrepreneurs rushed in to fill the vacuum. Even before the final political settlement, a number of young men from New York, including Alexander Henry, departed for the interior to make their fortunes. They hired Canadian voyageurs who knew the country and the trade and began to re-establish the network out of Montreal that had been disrupted by the Seven Years' War. There were setbacks. One of the first "adventurers" who left Michilimackinac for the northwest in 1765 was stopped by the people of Lac la Pluie, who did not want to see a trade opened with their neighbours. They raided the trader's canoes and forced him to stop. When he reappeared with a new trade outfit the following year, the Lac la Pluie people repeated their blockade. Finally, in 1767, the Montreal trader acquiesced and offered to leave most of his trade goods at Lac la Pluie for their benefit if they would permit him to take some of his goods farther west into the country around Lake Winnipeg. The natives agreed to permit him to pass and the success of his venture encouraged other young men from Montreal to come into the field.

The early adventurers were soon joined by British and Scottish entrepreneurs who made use of the skills, knowledge, and trade contacts of the old Canadian system to spread their interests remarkably quickly to the north and west of the Great Lakes. It was a time of ruthless competition, and dozens of small partnerships attempted to out-manoeuvre one another for furs. They established warehouses and offices in Montreal, exporting the fur harvest for annual auction in London and importing British merchandise via Montreal or Albany for carrying into the bush. Financial backers like James McGill and Isaac Todd made the entire system possible and grew wealthy in the process. Without the attempts of the French court to restrict trade competition and territorial expansion, the pursuit of furs probably provided more opportunities for more people in Canada after 1760 than it had for several decades.

The Hudson's Bay Company soon realized that it would have to respond, but its first moves were somewhat limited. In part, the explanation for the hesitation may lie in the fact that the London directors secretly still hoped that the Canadian traders were so poorly financed that it would be a simple matter of time before they would have to abandon the trade. The company's officers in the posts along the bay thought otherwise. Furthermore, they were very concerned about the loss of trade to groups of natives who were acting as intermediaries. When a group of Dogrib Indians visited the post at Churchill in 1766, it became clear to the company that much could be gained by direct trade with these inhabitants of the far northwest rather than permitting their furs to be channelled through the hands of the Chipewyan. Two years later, the officer in charge at Churchill travelled to London to convince the committee to finance an expedition into the lands of the "Far Indians." As an added incentive, he brought with him pieces of copper that the Chipewyan had brought to Churchill from these distant lands.

The promise of copper rather than an interest in countering the trade of the Canadians seemed to have motivated the London Committee of the Hudson's Bay Company at last. Samuel Hearne was commissioned to undertake the task. In 1769 he set out from Churchill with a group of natives who had promised to show him the way to the copper mines, but before a month was up, he was back at the post, the expedition a failure. Hearne made a second attempt in 1770 with a smaller party of Chipewyan and Cree guides; this attempt lasted six months, but after considerable hardship and the loss of his surveying instrument, he decided to return to base.

Limping back to Churchill, Hearne fell into company with an important Chipewyan trade chief named Matonabbee. Matonabbee rescued the starving party and guided them home, promising to assist Hearne should he decide to make a third attempt to cross the Barren Lands and find the source of the copper. Matonabbee clearly had his own motives for volunteering this assistance. He and his band were successful as intermediaries in the northern trade, and he recognized an opportunity to extend his influence through the northwest. And so in December 1771, Hearne set off from Churchill yet again, with a large party of Chipewyan under the leadership of Matonabbee. By the time they had crossed the Barren Lands, there were some two hundred people in the group.

This third expedition brought Hearne to the source of the copper: the mouth of the Coppermine River where it flows into the northern ocean. He was severely disappointed, however, to find that the great copper riches that had been described consisted only of a few surface deposits of native copper. It was also clear that the Coppermine River was not a suitable route for commercial purposes. Matonabbee was not similarly disappointed. His people had been skirmishing with the Inuit for some time in a conflict over territory and resources, and, at the Coppermine River, they discovered an Inuit camp. The Chipewyan descended upon the tents, killing everone they could find. The party then returned to Churchill where Hearne reported his findings. His journal and notes were forwarded to London as part of the argument for the establishment of an inland post to extend the trade of the company.

Andrew Graham, in charge at York Fort, was also strongly convinced that inland trade was now necessary and set about to prove his case to the company. In 1772, he sent his second-in-command, Matthew Cocking, along the rivers from York Fort to the Saskatchewan River country to gather information about the inland nations. Graham sent Cocking's journal to London as an argument in favour of the establishment of an inland post. Meanwhile, the London Committee appears to have been convinced already, and in 1773, instructions were sent out that a small post should be established at The Pas on the Saskatchewan River. Samuel Hearne was chosen to take charge of this important task.

In 1774, Hearne travelled inland and chose the site for the new post, which was christened Cumberland House. The site was advantageous because of its position on the main travel route and the potential access to all the other inland waterways. Hearne spent the winter at Cumberland House and conducted a successful trade there. It would prove to be an important post for the Hudson's Bay Company in years to come, and the Canadian traders recognized the challenge that the new company strategy posed to their trade. The response of the Montreal traders in the formation of the North West Company with its new trading strategies will be discussed in subsequent chapters. Suffice it to say that competition intensified throughout the 1790s and the first decades of the nineteenth century as British and Canadian businesses attempted to outmanoeuvre one another for advantage in the potentially lucrative trade. Eventually they decided that more profit could be had through cooperation than competition, and the rivals merged in 1821 under the name of the Hudson's Bay Company.[2]

The Pacific Trade

On the Pacific coast, a trade developed through somewhat different processes than the interior trade but with the same elements of commercial and political rivalry. Perhaps as early as the 1630s, Russian traders had made their way across Asia and established a trade for valuable sable pelts with the Arctic peoples of what we now call Siberia and Alaska. Russian

---

[2] There have been a number of histories of this period of the fur trade. Still useful is A.S. Morton, *A History of the Canadian West to 1870-71* (Toronto, 1939 and 1973). On the North West Company, see Robert Rumilly, *La Compagnie du Nord-Ouest*, 2 vols. (Montreal, 1980); Marjorie Wilkins Campbell, *The North West Company* (Toronto, 1957 and 1973). On the Hudson's Bay Company, see E.E. Rich, *The Fur Trade and the North West to 1857* (Toronto, 1967) and *The Hudson's Bay Company*, 3 vols. (Toronto, 1960).

claims to the lands and trade of the region were encouraged by the travels of Vitus Bering in 1728 and 1741. The Spanish became alarmed at these territorial claims and responded with a series of initiatives from Mexico, including the establishment of settlements in what is now California. In 1774, Juan Pérez was sent farther north still with intentions of claiming as much coastal land as possible for the Spanish. His exchange of goods with the Haida in Nootka Sound has already been noted. The British then joined in the competition. An expedition led by Captain James Cook, already famous for his exploits in the South Pacific, generated considerable excitement in Britain about the possibilities of profits in the North Pacific. The Spaniards were deeply concerned about British movement into the region, and war very nearly erupted in 1789–90. Finally, in 1795, the Spanish abandoned Nootka Sound entirely, leaving the northwest coastal trade to the Russians, British, and Americans.

The coastal natives quickly became astute traders. They demanded (and received) higher and higher returns in metal goods for their furs, and comparison shopped among the visiting ships to obtain the best goods for the best prices. Sea otter pelts formed the bulk of the early maritime trade, but these coastal peoples soon began to turn to inland trade partners for other types of land mammal pelts. Furs trapped by interior native bands thus found markets through the intermediaries of the coastal nations as old trade networks were put to new purposes and possibly expanded. As an adjunct to the trade, cultural influences from the nations of the northwest coast began to penetrate farther inland. Artistic techniques and designs, ceremonies, and even clan systems were all influenced by ideas that accompanied the exchange of goods.

The early decades of the coastal trade are often characterized as a "maritime" trade because the trade was conducted offshore, on board the foreign trading ships. The hope of establishing a land-based trade was not overlooked, however. Interestingly, it was the North West Company from Canada and not the Hudson's Bay Company that first gained a land base for British interests. Although Alexander Mackenzie reached the Pacific coast in 1793 after an arduous overland journey, the North West Company did not establish its first post until 1805 when Simon Fraser pressed across the mountains into the district that would soon be known as New Caledonia. Obviously, however, the wild mountain rivers were unsuitable as transportation networks and the North West Company continued to search for more useful routes. In 1811, David Thompson followed the Columbia River to its mouth only to discover a group of Americans hard at work

Sir Alexander Mackenzie — fur trader, adventurer, and businessman.

NATIONAL ARCHIVES OF CANADA/C69724

preparing for trade there. These men were representatives of the Pacific Fur Company, part of John Jacob Astor's network of trading concerns. The Nor'westers had been aware of Astor's plans for some time but had hoped to beat him to the coast. International commercial competition took on particular significance with the eruption of the War of 1812 back home. British command of the seas off the east coast of America prevented Astor's supplies from reaching his Columbia District post in 1814, and the traders finally agreed to abandon their post and sell it to the North West Company. After the war, the Americans reasserted their claim to the territory, initiating an international dispute over Oregon that would continue for 30 years. Yet again, trade and politics had become very much entangled.

First Nations and the Fur Trade

The men and women of the aboriginal groups who participated in the fur trade had business interests of their own, but their participation in the trade was also motivated by more complex considerations. It is necessary to recognize that cultural differences had an important role to play in dictating the development of the trade and the relationship between aboriginal traders and their partners from Canada and London. Native traders might seek prestige or increased leisure time from the trade rather than only profits. Furthermore, participation in the trade almost always precipitated changes in the lives of the native traders. However, the nature and extent of those changes has been the subject of considerable debate among historians and anthropologists. Because it is only recently that historians have paid any significant attention to the role of the First Nations in the fur trade, much work remains to be done.

First, it must be stressed that by participating in the fur trade and permitting Euro-Canadians to travel through their lands, the First Nations were in no way agreeing to foreign claims of territorial sovereignty. Nor did they consider themselves to be "subjects" of any foreign political power. Rather, they continued to see themselves as independent peoples who were merely allowing newcomers access for purposes of trade and military action. If the behaviour of a trader was contrary to their expectations, they wasted no time in making their dissatisfaction clear. Objections might take the form of a military raid on a post or a simple withdrawal of trade; in either case the Euro-Canadians would be forced to abandon their establishment. As they were vastly outnumbered and outgunned by the First

Nations, they could do no more than make symbolic claims to sovereignty. La Vérendrye, for example, attempted to claim one region in what is now South Dakota by secretly burying a plaque. When his action was discovered and challenged, he explained that he was merely commemorating his visit to the site. It was a lie that would eventually have grave consequences for the original inhabitants of the territory.

As the Europeans extended their trade westward, new groups were attracted to the prospects of participation in the exchange, but similar patterns of response have been observed throughout. Initially, people showed an interest in obtaining metal and manufactured goods such as knives, kettles, and cloth that were either an improvement on indigenous technologies or saved the trouble of a tedious manufacturing process. Nowhere did they encourage the trade as a purely economic exchange, however. Trading networks that had existed prior to the arrival of Europeans were interconnected with complex and delicate political agreements and kinship systems, so it is not surprising that the natives expected the European traders to conform to these arrangements. Hence, the Algonquin asked Champlain to assist them in their raids against the Iroquois, and the Huron agreed to permit Jesuits to live in their villages to cement the political alliance that was so necessary a part of the economic alliance. The French traders soon realized that personal and family ties were also important, so intermarriage between the Great Lakes people and the French traders became commonplace. Mixed populations sprang up following the extension of the fur trade across the country.

In a given region, many members of the first native group to meet with European traders frequently decided to establish themselves as traders rather than trappers. Sometimes the decision was a matter of necessity. If their homelands were depleted of fur-bearing animals and if they wanted European goods, they had to obtain furs elsewhere. At other times, the decision was a matter of choice if the bands saw an opportunity to obtain more prestige or more goods for less effort by acting as intermediaries. These intermediary groups would travel each year to more distant bands, obtain furs, proceed to the nearest trade post, and exchange furs for goods, then return to their inland trade partners, keeping some of the goods for themselves as payment for their efforts. Many intermediaries guarded their position jealously, using a variety of ingenious tactics to prevent the European traders from contacting the source of their fur supplies directly. Relations with both sets of trade partners were not always peaceful, but, for the most part, the system seemed to have been satisfactory for the native participants. The Europeans, however, were resentful of it, believing that they could maximize their profits if they traded directly with the people who actually trapped the animals. As the Europeans bypassed various groups in search of direct trade, open violence often resulted as the intermediaries attempted to maintain their control of the local trade.

Not all people chose to act as independent intermediaries. Opportunities for work existed in the vicinity of the fur trade posts, and many men and women chose to avail themselves of those opportunities on both short- and long-term bases. The Hudson's Bay Company posts were particularly dependent for survival on local native people who would hunt and fish for them. Because the company posts were maintained by a small staff who were unfamiliar with indigenous resources and methods of hunting, the men relied on supplies of fish, game, and wild fowl provided by people of the area in return for credit at the trade post. Women's skills at leather making and clothing construction were also in high demand. Initially, these products and services were provided by natives, but as intermarriage increased, the company found the Métis more interested in this type of employment. Some families became virtually permanent residents near the posts, combining their own hunting and gathering with work on behalf of the company. One of the most interesting examples of these native groups who chose to devote considerable time and energy to the trade developed in the late eighteenth century. Several groups of Iroquois from the Montreal area made their way into the far northwest, including the Athabasca district, where they established themselves as important trade partners and provisioners to both the Hudson's Bay Company and the North West Company. Their descendants remained in the northwest as distinct bands for several generations.

Other people expressed little interest in the fur trade and chose to continue their annual rounds of fishing, gathering, and hunting independently of the posts. Perhaps the most extreme example is the case of the Beothuk of Newfoundland who developed a strategy for complete avoidance of contact with Europeans despite sporadic attempts by British interests to establish a trade. In other regions, we know very little of those bands who chose to remain independent of the trade since most of the records of the period are those kept by fur traders who were primarily interested in the activities of the trading natives. Obviously not all people lived in areas well-supplied with the types of fur-bearing animals in demand for the trade. Others who lived in areas with marginal resource bases might trap for trade purposes in good years when game was plentiful and weather conditions conducive to hunting, but in other years, basic survival of their families took priority, and no attention was given to trapping. Certainly the fur company officers were constantly complaining that they could not persuade the natives to devote as much time and energy to trapping as the companies would have preferred. Traders accused them of being "lazy," but the truth was that the two sides of the trade partnership had somewhat different priorities. Profit might have been a shared motivation, but First Nations participants were also interested in maximizing personal prestige within the community and providing for increased leisure time. Work for the sake of work was an unacceptable ethic.

In yet another context, some people chose to participate fully and enthusiastically in trapping fur-bearing animals for purposes of trade. Indeed, in some districts, desirable species were overhunted to the point that viable animal populations were no longer sustainable and traders described the region as "cleaned out." Such behaviour raises perplexing questions for the historian, particularly since it is widely believed that most First Nations understood the necessity of conservation harvesting in both a material and a spiritual way. One attempt to explain the apparent conflict between behaviour and value systems was a thesis proposed by Calvin Martin based on his studies of Northeastern Woodland nations. Martin argued that these people blamed the animal spirits for the epidemics that were devastating their communities and so took advantage of the context of the fur trade to declare a "holy war of extermination" on the malevolent spirits. The theory received widespread attention, in part because of its intriguing attempt to recognize the important role of spiritual beliefs in native history. Subsequently, however, the work of other ethnohistorians has raised some serious questions about Martin's thesis. There is little evidence that any groups blamed disease on animal spirits. Most attributed disease to the activities of human beings. Either a shaman was deliberately inducing illness in an enemy or the individual affected had broken one of the many rules that maintained equilibrium in the world. Thus Martin's explanation for overhunting begins to come apart.

Nevertheless, the observation that religious values and beliefs had a role to play in the fur trade is an important one. The trade in beads and so-called "trinkets" and "baubles" was interpreted for a long time as evidence that wiley European traders were tricking naive natives into giving up valuable furs in exchange for worthless goods. An understanding of the religious and symbolic significance of these goods provides us with a very different picture of this trade. Studies of the "meaning" of colours, shapes, and particular articles among the Northeastern Woodland and northwestern Subarctic peoples have come to suggestively similar conclusions. Mirrors and white, black, and red beads were valued for their symbolism and had roles to play in ceremony and ritual, in much the same way that shells, copper, and crystalline rocks had played before the arrival of Europeans. They were not worthless items foisted on gullible natives, but precious entrés into the unseen world of mind and spirit.[3]

The political aspects of the fur trade operated on several levels. In terms of the immediate functioning of trade itself, elaborate ceremonials became part of the exchange. Before trade could begin in a region, a political alliance had to be negotiated. Subsequently, each time the parties met to trade, that alliance had to be reaffirmed through the exchange of gifts and a council meeting. Gifts such as tobacco, food, and brandy were offered to the visiting trade party and special clothing offered to a man designated as the trade chief. A great feast then followed, with dancing and music lasting into the night, sometimes even several days. Only then could the actual economic exchange take place. These practices were a traditional part of First Nations' politics; both the Canadians and the Hudson's Bay Company traders eventually recognized their importance and adopted them into the trade.

On the wider stage, the fur trade became integrated with trade patterns and political arrangements that had existed before the arrival of Europeans. Local and more extensive exchanges had probably always been a part of the continental economy. For example, the Huron provided agricultural products to the Algonquin in exchange for fish, meat, and animal products. Copper from lands near Lake Superior found its way far to the south and east, possibly as far as the eastern seaboard. People whose lands contained especially good-quality stone for spear points or arrowheads

---

[3] Calvin Martin, *Keepers of the Game. Indian-Animal Relationships in the Fur Trade* (California, 1978); Shepard Krech III, *Indians, Animals and the Fur Trade. A Critique of Keepers of the Game* (Athens, Georgia, 1981); Shepard Krech III, "The Early Fur Trade in the Northwestern Subarctic: The Kutchin and the Trade in Beads," in Bruce Trigger, Toby Morantz, and Louise Dechêne (eds.), *"Le Castor Fait Tout"* (Lake St. Louis, 1987) pp. 236–77; George Hamell, "Strawberries, Floating Islands and Rabbit Captains: Mythical Realities and European Contact in the North East During the Sixteenth and Seventeenth Centuries," *Journal of Canadian Studies*, vol. 21, no. 4 (1986): 72-94; George Hamell, "Trading in Metaphors: The Magic of Beads," in Charles F. Hayes (ed.), *Proceedings of the 1982 Glass Trade Bead Conference* (Rochester, N. Y., 1983), pp. 5–28.

would supply them to others in exchange for a variety of products. These exchanges were also part of a series of political alliance systems in which particular bands or nations negotiated agreements concerning territorial boundaries, rights of access to travel routes, and military cooperation against a common enemy. Economic agreements might be used to reinforce these arrangements, or perhaps political agreements would be used to support economic interests. Warfare was the frequent result of a breakdown of such agreements. If one nation infringed on the hunting territory of another or if a traditional travel route was cut off, the young men would set off to redress the grievance. Warfare could also result from personal feuds; the murder of a band member required revenge. With the constant possibility of war, a political system to maximize security was clearly a necessity. Alliances and confederacies such as that of the Six Nations and the Huron were the major component of First Nations' politics.

The fur trade system adapted itself to native political customs, and at the same time contributed a new factor to the tensions that already existed. It is difficult to know whether the series of wars that followed the introduction of the fur trade across the country was a direct result of the trade itself or simply an ongoing manifestation of older conflicts. Nevertheless, the fact remains that major changes in territorial arrangements accompanied the introduction of European weaponry and manufactured goods. The Cree, for example, appear to have inhabited primarily the lands between Hudson Bay and Lake Superior before their participation in the fur trade. With the establishment of Hudson's Bay Company posts on the northern fringes of their lands, they began to move farther and farther inland in search of furs or other nations from whom they could obtain furs. To the northwest, west, and southwest, they encountered Chipewyan, Assiniboine, and Dakota, generating widespread animosity and a reputation for being warlike. The French traders who moved into Cree land from their inland routes attempted to intervene in these battles and negotiate peace arrangements so that all parties would direct their energies to trade in the South. By the time La Vérendrye was reporting his activities west of Lake of the Woods, the Cree appear to have made their way onto the Prairies and across the parkland to the North. With time, these groups adapted to their new environment, so much so that anthropologists now speak of two distinct branches of the Cree: the Plains and the Woodland nations.

There has been considerable debate about the population movements of other groups. For example, some anthropologists have concluded that before the arrival of Europeans, the northern Ojibwa lived on the northern shores of lakes Huron and Superior and moved into the lands of the Canadian Shield during the early eighteenth century to take part in the fur trade and to avoid raiding bands of Iroquois. Others have argued that the Ojibwa have always occupied these northern lands and the earlier conclusions were the result of a confusion over band names. The Ojibwa themselves explain that they once lived on the Atlantic coast and moved gradually westward over an unknown length of time. There may never be sufficient surviving evidence to prove or disprove any of these statements conclusively.

The question of change is no less controversial when it comes to the social or cultural histories of the First Nations. What impact did participation in the fur trade have on people's daily lives or on their economic systems? Not long ago, most historians assumed that native societies were so anxious to obtain European goods that they leapt whole-heartedly into the trade, willingly abandoning their ancient way of life to trap full time and, in the process, losing their sophisticated knowledge of survival on the land and rapidly becoming dependent on European technology and even food for their livelihood. Thus the fur trade was interpreted as a massive intervention into native culture and significant social change and disruption were deemed to be the results. Marxist interpretations of the fur trade have taken such analysis one step further, arguing that the trade was a colonial institution imposed on the First Nations, forcing them into a new position as an "underclass" in perpetual debt to the Euro-Canadian companies and locking them into the capitalist economic system. Recently, a number of ethnohistorians have challenged these earlier conclusions, suggesting that they need to be modified somewhat. The debate has been a lively one, and, in the process, we are beginning to learn a great deal more about the native side of the fur trade story.

The first question is the extent of native participation in the fur trade. Because most of our knowledge of the business side of the trade comes from records kept by the trading companies and no census data exist for comparison, it is very difficult to estimate how many people out of the total population were involved. It is also difficult to know if the individuals who traded with the Euro-Canadians were trading simply on their own behalf, or whether they represented larger groups of people who trapped furs and obtained goods but never visited the posts themselves. Nevertheless, where there is surviving evidence, it seems to suggest that natives participated in the fur trade only very gradually, and in some areas participation did not occur until a relatively late date.

Within each nation, some bands clearly chose to participate to a greater or lesser extent than others. As has been noted already, some decided to take on the role of intermediary, devoting a substantial part of the year to travel for the purposes of trade. Other bands were dedicated to trapping for trade, travelling far beyond their home territories in search of good beaver lands. Other bands chose to remain on their traditional home territories and to incorporate occasional trapping for trade into their annual round of activities.

Until late in the nineteenth century throughout the North, few bands could possibly have become dependent on trading posts for their food supplies because the costs of transportation prevented the trading companies from importing much in the way of food. Indeed, the posts depended heavily on area food supplies for their own subsistence. It was not until the introduction of steam boats on the Saskatchewan and Athabasca–Mackenzie river systems toward the end of the nineteenth century that it became economically feasible to import significant quantities of food. Only at that time did items like flour and oatmeal begin to creep into native diets.

Certainly a variety of other changes were introduced through the fur trade. Territories of bands and nations shifted as they competed for advantages, while new political and economic alliances and animosities were created. Increasing numbers of imported goods for domestic use were adopted and European clothing gradually replaced indigenous costumes. Old specialty skills like basketmaking became increasingly rare. Outwardly, at least, people seemed to have given up many of the traditional ways.

Does a change in technology or material culture necessitate a change in world view or spirituality? Did the fur trade lead to important changes in the ways in which First Nations perceived the world and their place in it? These questions are even more difficult to answer than the questions about economic or political change. Some scholars have argued that the apparent need for European goods led native trappers to abandon their conservation ethic and overhunt animals for the sake of short-term gain. A number of anthropologists have argued that participation in the trade led to changes in how families were constituted or how marriages were arranged. Others have argued that old beliefs were remarkably persistent in the face of other changes and that First Nations were not, in fact, quick to give up the fundamental religious beliefs that structured their lives. Since it is so difficult to reconstruct the nonmaterial details of natives' lives before contact with Europeans, it is hard to compare their situation after extensive participation in the fur trade. It is even more difficult to evaluate intangibles like religious beliefs. Doubtless, debate will continue on these questions.[4]

Fur Trade Society

It would be misleading to consider the fur trade solely as an economic or even political activity. It was also the interaction of people, and given the nature of the trade, good relations on an individual and personal level were crucial. In the process of encouraging those personal relations, a unique society emerged in the North and the West. In some ways, the legacy of that society may have had more of an impact on the nation of Canada than the legacy of the fur trade as an economic system.

It is perhaps misleading to suggest that there was ever a single fur trade society. The experience of participants in the trade out of Montreal was different in significant ways from the experience of participants in the Hudson's Bay Company trade before the merger of 1821. The experiences of men and women were very different. The passage of time and changing circumstances also contributed to the development of different social experiences. Nevertheless, it is useful to consider some examples of the societies that developed through the process of fur trade history.

By the mid-eighteenth century, the focus of the French fur trade was the series of interior posts and settlements around the Great Lakes. Two of these, Detroit and Michilimackinac, served as major meeting places and depots. Both had year-round populations, but in the summer, visiting traders might double or even quadruple the winter population. At both

---

[4] There has recently been a great deal published on the role of the First Nations in the fur trade. Some examples include Charles Bishop, *The Northern Ojibwa and the Fur Trade* (Toronto, 1974); Daniel Francis and Toby Morantz, *Partners in Furs. A History of the Fur Trade in Eastern James Bay 1600–1870* (Montreal, 1983); Conrad Heidenreich and A. J. Ray, *The Early Fur Trades. A Study in Cultural Interaction* (Toronto, 1976); Shepard Krech III (ed.), *The Subarctic Fur Trade* (Vancouver, 1984), and *Indians, Animals and the Fur Trade* (Athens, Georgia, 1981); Calvin Martin, *Keepers of the Game* (Berkeley, 1978); A. J. Ray, *Indians in the Fur Trade* (Toronto, 1974); Abraham Rotstein, "Trade and Politics: An Institutional Approach", *Western Canadian Journal of Anthropology*, vol 3 (1972); Paul Thistle, *Indian European Trade Relations in the Lower Saskatchewan River Region to 1840* (Winnipeg, 1986); Bruce White, "'Give us a little milk': Social and Cultural Significance of Gift Giving in the Lake Superior Fur Trade," in Thomas Buckley (ed.), *Rendezvous* (St. Paul Minnesota, 1984).

sites, the imperial government had established a military garrison, and Jesuit missionaries were also an important part of the community. Outside the walled garrison at Detroit, small farms had grown up along both banks of the Detroit River, laid out in the strip pattern familiar along the St. Lawrence. Here, families raised corn and cattle to supply the community and the trade. Other garden products were grown in an area set aside for the military, the church, and the residents of the Detroit post. Four native settlements had become established nearby as well, inhabited by the three major nations in the vicinity: the Ottawa, the Potawatomi, and the Petun. With a population of about 2600, they far outnumbered the non-native population of about 500 farmers and 200 within the walls of the post.

Elsewhere throughout the Great Lakes region, dozens of small communities emerged during the eighteenth century with links to the fur trade economy. Initially, these centres were established near important native villages by the employees of Canadian trading companies and their native wives, but as time passed, the population base was composed primarily of their families who intermarried and raised more children who themselves participated in the trade. The communities also became physically distinct from the surrounding First Nations' villages. As historian Jacqueline Peterson has argued, during the French regime there were no significant class or status distinctions in these communities, and people depended for the most part on locally produced foods and domestic consumables rather than imported goods. Hence, in many ways, the outlook of the townspeople was directed to the surrounding native cultures and economy rather than to a distant Canadian or European metropolis. Clothing and tools were produced for home use or the fur trade and thus were manufactured to suit the tastes of native trade partners. Numerous coureurs de bois worked out of home bases in these villages without benefit of official licences, leaving little record for posterity but building important networks of family and community.

The Illinois country in particular developed into an important food supply centre for the trade since the rich soils in the valleys of the Mississippi, Illinois, and Missouri rivers provided excellent crops of corn and wheat. Many of the farmers who settled around the French posts were also active in the fur trade. It was an ethnically heterogeneous population with French, French Canadians, various First Nations, and Métis, as well as both black and native slaves.

In the country northwest of Lake Superior, sometimes known as the *petit nord*, community structure was somewhat different. Since agriculture was not really viable, local food supplies depended heavily on the vast fisheries where staggering numbers of fish like sturgeon were taken. Wild rice and maple syrup were also important dietary staples. Here, the French imperial presence was less obvious during the French regime, with only a few visits from Jesuit missionaries and no permanent garrisons. Some posts might be no more than a hastily erected shelter, while others were more significant with a small number of families settled year-round at or near the post. The traders would disperse from these centres to live with their native trade partners during the winter. Throughout the period of Hudson's Bay Company–North West Company competition, a number of major centres emerged in the petit nord at places like Grand Portage (and later, Fort William), Lac la Pluie, Osnaburgh House, and Oxford House.

Continuing into the northwest, trading posts large and small spread through the boreal forest. Those posts along the southern fringes of the forest served as pemmican-production centres at which Métis populations dominated. Some of the small posts might last for only a few seasons, while others became important centres with substantial buildings. The large posts were usually fortified, both against competing Euro-Canadian traders and against hostile natives, and had a variety of provisions including food and wood storage and a blacksmith shop.

The Hudson's Bay Company and the Montreal traders organized their corporate structures in very different ways before 1821, and historian Jennifer Brown has argued that these differences had an important impact on the ways in which the social organization of each fur trade community evolved. Of course, there were other factors that also contributed to differences. HBC personnel were relatively immobile compared with the Montreal traders, and HBC activities continued to be directed from Great Britain rather than from a colonial base throughout the period in question. As a result, it is helpful to consider the social aspects of each company separately.

As a number of independent and flexible partnerships before 1784 and a rather unstable corporate entity thereafter, the Montreal traders operated without much central direction or regulation. Individual personalities and situations could therefore be extremely influential in determining relations in a given district. Flexibility of response was another result that could be a considerable advantage to the Nor'westers. It could also be a problem. Without strict controls, some traders used whatever means available to obtain furs. Women were sometimes kidnapped and held for ransom to obtain a band's fur harvest, while intimidation, violence, and outright theft were not uncommon. The North West Company was also divided internally. By the late eighteenth and early nineteenth centuries, its labour force was composed overwhelmingly of French-Canadian men from the St. Lawrence colony, most of whom were apparently recruited from the parishes surrounding Montreal much as they had been during the fur trade of the French regime. Management, financial backing, and the senior wintering partners, however, had become dominated by English-speaking entrepreneurs. Most of these were actually Scots who had come directly from Scotland or via the United States. Like the voyageurs, management personnel were frequently related to one another so that family ties and nepotism formed an important part of the glue that held the organization together. Intermarriage between the new Scottish entrepreneurs and established French families helped to create a unique society in Montreal. For instance, Simon McTavish's brother-in-law, Charles Chaboillez, was also a chief partner in the North West Company. This tightly knit group of family and friends formed a close social circle as well as business partnership, enjoying a life of relative ease and material comfort. Even travel for business purposes could be a pleasure, as Simon McTavish wrote to a friend from New York in 1774: "For my part, I am now here, in the land of good cheer viz good Wine, good Oysters, & pretty Girls. . . ."[5]

The company not only adapted the techniques of the earlier French fur trade but also maintained much of the vocabulary. Men who signed on for specific periods of service in the interior as guides, interpreters, or canoeists were known as *engagés*. Canoeists were still called *voyageurs* and clerks were *commis*. The man in charge of a district was one of the company partners and was referred to as a *bourgeois*. The company encouraged enthusiasm for the work by enabling clerks to become shareholders in a system that had considerable success in motivating its members.

The Hudson's Bay Company, on the other hand, was organized quite differently in a system that clearly evolved from the British class system. There was a distinct hierarchy within the corporate structure that was reflected in all aspects of the lives of its members down to the spatial arrangement of living accommodations in the posts. The company was

---

[5] Simon McTavish to William Edgar, New York, 24 December 1774. In W.S. Wallace (ed.), *Documents Relating to the North West Company* (Toronto, 1934), p. 48.

directed from London through a central committee. Reporting to its members were the district governors and post factors who were referred to as "officers." Most of these men were born in England during the early years of the company, although later the London Committee found it advantageous to promote men with field experience who were usually of Scottish birth. Beneath the officers was a large body of labourers often referred to as "servants." These included a wide range of occupations like carpenters, blacksmiths, coopers, tailors, or ordinary labourers, each category with its own internal rank and wage scale. The company learned early in its history that men recruited from the Orkney Islands off Scotland's northwest coast were reliable employees accustomed to harsh climates and less than luxurious living conditions. Young, unmarried men signed on for a specific term, usually three or seven years depending on the position. In spite of the stratified organizational system, upward mobility was possible and indeed may have been a major incentive in drawing young men into the fur trade.

Within the Hudson's Bay Company posts, life was closely regulated and organized. The officer in charge obviously had a certain degree of auton-

The typical design of major Hudson's Bay Company establishments. Everything was intended to impress the visitor; the company even had its own flag.   NATIONAL ARCHIVES OF CANADA/C69703

omy, but the London Committee dictated the general parameters, often to the frustration of the officers who felt the committee members had no real understanding of the problem which they faced. Most of the trade activity occurred in the spring and fall; in between the men had to be kept occupied. Winters were particularly long and lonely. For those who could read, libraries were maintained at some of the major posts. Music, games, and dances were popular entertainments as they were at NWC posts. In the summer, the men tended small gardens to supplement their diets and were kept busy with an endless round of cutting wood, repairing tools, maintaining buildings, or keeping records. It was a much different life than that of the travelling voyageurs. One of the journal entries at Moose Fort in March 1785 summarizes the day's activities:

Wind N.E. Clear sharp weather four Men at the Doctors creek, and one to cook for them sawing timber for the *Beavers* repairs, shipwright and Mate employed at the large Boat, Armourer stocking hunting Guns, six Men cleaning the snow out of the Yard, three with the Cattle hauling home firewood, Cook and Cattle keeper as usual, two up the River fishing one away trapping, and one at hannah Bay hunting and one set off for there this day, A.M. a family of home guard Indians came in, brought a fine Trade of Martens.[6]

Any discussion of fur trade society must also attempt to come to terms with the nature of a third major variation: the Métis population. Today people tend to think of them as primarily part of the western Canadian mosaic, but racial intermarriage was a feature of colonization throughout the world, and eastern Canada was no exception. Nor was intermarriage solely a feature of the fur trade. Some connections between the Acadians and Micmac had developed in this way, for example, although perhaps not to the extent claimed by one mid-eighteenth century observer who suggested that most of the population of Acadia was a "mixed breed." French officials were ambivalent about such mixing, encouraging it through official policy in the early years of New France and discouraging it through social and moral pressure in later years. Clearly, however, the fur trade system encouraged intermarriage and contributed to the development of a significant mixed population that existed in some ways quite

---

[6] Moose Fort Journal entry for 28 March 1785. E.E. Rich (ed.), *Moose Fort Journals 1783–85*, (London, 1954), p. 106.

independently of the old French colonial society and that, in one region at least, came to define itself quite self-consciously as a "New Nation."

As has already been described, the villages of the Great Lakes region became an important meeting place for French and native participants in the trade. The children of the region grew to adulthood to find themselves in a uniquely advantageous position in the area's economy. Familiar with the languages and habits of both parent civilizations, they could act as brokers or go-betweens, providing goods, services, and information to both sides. It was here in the Great Lakes fur trade of the eighteenth century, according to Jacqueline Peterson, that the formation of a distinctive Métis population began. The British conquest of the French colonies in North America appears to have had relatively little impact on this development, particularly in the smaller and more isolated communities. In 1794, however, Jay's Treaty brought an end to the British presence in the areas south of the Great Lakes. American settlers began to work their way across the Appalachians soon afterward, and by the early nineteenth century the old fur trade economy had been seriously disrupted. It appears that significant numbers of the Great Lakes Métis people packed up and moved northwest. New villages were established along the Red and Assiniboine rivers, and the bison hunt became an important adjunct to their farming and trading. When the Hudson's Bay Company attempted to claim the area through Selkirk's settlement, violence erupted at Seven Oaks in 1816, an episode that later generations celebrated in song and folklore as a moment of glory in the formation of a "New Nation," the Métis of Red River.

Another element was added to the Métis population at Red River. Children of Scottish fur traders who had learned English rather than French and who were familiar with Protestant religious traditions instead of Roman Catholic ones also gravitated toward the settlement. Did a shared social role lead them to identify with the French Métis? Were religious and language differences obstacles to a sense of community? Or were the various economic niches occupied by the mixed population more important as dividing elements than were cultural aspects? as economic historian Irene Spry has argued. A lively debate among historians on these questions is still very much in progress. On one point, however, there seems to be general agreement. Rather than being marginalized because of their mixed racial heritage, for much of fur trade history, the Métis people of the northwest enjoyed a central role in the society, economics, and politics of a system that they helped to create. It was only when the fur trade ceased to be the main economic activity and racial attitudes hardened in the later nineteenth century that they were driven from prominence and marginalized.[7]

As has already been emphasized, because the fur trade involved the economic and political interaction of very different cultural groups, it could not possibly have occurred without the development of social arrangements that proved mutually satisfying to the participants. Primary among these was the recognition first by the Montreal traders and later by the Hudson's Bay Company that kinship ties were necessary among First Nations societies if the communities were to engage in economic partnerships. The North West Company learned of the importance of these alliances from the experiences of the French traders that preceded it, in no small way contributing to its domination of the interior trade by the beginning of the nineteenth century.

The clergy of New France were constantly complaining about what they saw as the "dissolute" and "lawless" behaviour of French traders in the interior, claiming these men were ransacking the countryside and debauching native women. These complaints contributed a lasting impression among Canadians that voyageurs and coureurs de bois were sexually promiscuous, taking advantage of more relaxed sexual attitudes among First Nations and enjoying a life of random pleasure seeking. While undoubtedly such cases could be found, by far the majority of the interior traders formed lasting marriages with native women. The Canadian traders were the first to recognize the importance of native women to their work. A trade relationship could be cemented through a marriage, with the woman's extended family bringing its furs to her husband. Essentially these marriages gave the traders political connections with their wives' families facilitating the economic relationships of the trade and giving them an advantage over their competitors. Native wives quickly learned French or English which enabled real communication instead of the gestures and broken trade jargon that characterized the earliest exchanges. Their translation abilities and knowledge of two cultures also gave them an important role to play as diplomats and negotiators, easing their

---

[7] The best recent work on the Métis is the collection of essays contained in Jacqueline Peterson and Jennifer Brown (eds.), *The New Peoples* (Winnipeg, 1985). Somewhat outdated by recent research but still of interest is Marcel Giraud, *Le Métis canadien* (Paris, 1945). Also, Richard Slobodin, *The Métis of the Mackenzie District* (Ottawa, 1966).

husbands' ability to accommodate themselves to native expectations in the elaborate process that accompanied the trade wherever it went. And of course these women provided companionship and stability in the lives of the Euro-Canadian traders, which encouraged the development of a unique fur trade society, initially in the region of the Great Lakes, and later in the West and Northwest.

Marriage arrangements were conducted *à la façon du pays* as the expression went. Historian Sylvia Van Kirk has described this marriage pattern as singular to the fur trade, a combination of the customs of the Europeans and First Nations. As far as the initial arrangements were concerned, the traditions of the First Nations involved were followed, usually a simple agreement in which the woman would move into the man's home. Sometimes the man would owe the woman's parents a period of service; sometimes gifts had to be offered as a "bride price." If either party tired of the arrangement, it was usually a relatively easy matter to break it off, but many fur trade marriages were life-long partnerships. One Canadian court, in an 1867 case, even recognized these marriages as legal in the European tradition, although they had not been solemnized by any Christian church or state. As racial attitudes hardened later in the century, however, a subsequent court decision deemed that such arrangements were not marriages in the British sense of the term. But mixed marriages were not confined to the lower ranks of the trading companies. Senior traders took care to arrange marriages with daughters of important chiefs whose families, in turn, also encouraged such matches, according them considerable prestige.

Both the Hudson's Bay Company and the Montreal traders recognized the importance of such marriage alliances to the trade, although somewhat different patterns emerged between the two groups. The London Committee of the Hudson's Bay Company remained ambivalent about the issue for many years, since it feared that families would become a costly burden on the limited supplies of its posts. Officially it prohibited marriages to native women. The men at the bay posts, however, did not always share the views of headquarters for both strategic and personal reasons, and many entered into marriage arrangements that were hidden from official eyes. In fact, several senior traders at the bay posts in the eighteenth century followed native tradition to the extent that they had more than one wife in spite of the heavy expense involved. North West Company men did not appear to favour polygamy, finding it too costly and awkward to support a large family in their more mobile lives. The HBC eventually relented somewhat and with the establishment of Selkirk's colony at Red River, encouraged retired fur traders to take their families to the settlement, where it was hoped that they would reinforce the company's claim to the lands, provide agricultural produce to supply the posts, and not become a burden on the company's stores.

The concept that women had a central place in the socio-economic arrangements of society was, in fact, shared by both First Nations and pre-industrial Europe. Specific duties might be clearly divided according to gender-defined categories, but both men and women were expected to participate in the support of the household and community. There was no concept that the "public" and "private" spheres were separate entities. Hence it is not surprising to learn that women played an important role in the fur trade beyond that already described. The trade was scarcely the male-dominated concern that most people believe it to have been. Women's skills provided a crucial support structure as well as an integral part of the trade itself.

Home guard women and wives of traders fed, clothed, and housed the post personnel. While men performed most of the big game hunting, daily diets were composed of fish, small game, berries, and vegetable foods, all of which women harvested. The women provided fresh provisions to the post in the summer and devoted considerable time to the preservation of foods for the long winters. Hundreds of fish were expertly filleted and dried on huge racks in the northern regions, while in the South, the women tended the crops and ground the corn. Families were fed first, then surpluses traded for the support of the rest of the post. Women tanned leather and manufactured the clothing necessary for life in the bush, particularly the moccasins, which wore out quickly but which were so much more serviceable than European footwear. At some posts, clothing, footwear, and snowshoes were provided solely for the use of the traders while at others, extras were made for the purposes of the native trade. Bands that had devoted their time to trapping sometimes were short of necessities like clothing and found it more convenient to obtain these at the trade post. Hence not all goods traded were of European manufacture.

Métis women on the plains had a particularly important contribution to make in the pemmican trade. The organized bison hunt expeditions of the early nineteenth century had grown to an enormous size, with parties of up to a thousand men, women, and children proceeding across the plains. Once the animals had been killed, the women moved in to butcher the carcasses and cut the meat into thin strips for drying on racks in the hot prairie sun or over a fire. Once the meat had reached the proper degree of dryness, the women pounded it into fine flakes that could then be mixed with melted grease in the proportion of 50 pounds (22 kg) of meat to 40 (18) of fat. Berries might be added. The pemmican was then packed into standard size 90-pound (41 kg) sacks, which the women had also made from the buffalo hides.

Some women traded small furs independently with the fur companies, but references to women as trade partners in the journals are few and far between. In the Columbia district, Chinook women of rank regularly brought their own furs in to trade, but elsewhere, we really have no way of knowing how many of the furs brought in by a male trade chief had been trapped by men and how many by women. We do know, however, that women were primarily responsible for preparing the furs. Unless the meat was carefully scraped from the hide and proper preservation methods followed, the hides would be unfit for shipment and would rot in transit. Women scraped, stretched, and softened the furs before they could be traded. It was also women who demanded manufactured domestic utensils for trade, which lightened the burden of homemaking. Thus women played a number of vital roles in the fur trade both as members of native communities and as wives of fur traders.

When the men retired from the service of the fur trade, they faced a very real problem. Should they return to their homes in Scotland or Quebec with their fur trade families, or should they remain in the country with their wives' people? Many of the Nor'Westers, in particular, chose the latter option, melting into native society and engaging in the occasional trade as "freemen," as they came to be called. After the establishment of the Selkirk settlement at Red River, Hudson's Bay Company traders had an option of living a more settled life without leaving the country entirely. Some men chose to pass their wives and families on to another trader who was remaining in the country; undoubtedly cases of abandonment occurred, as well.

With time, marriage customs and attitudes began to change. In the nineteenth century, Europeans developed a more limited view of the concept of race and racial differences, leading eventually to what is now sometimes referred to as "scientific racism": the belief that human beings could be categorized according to race and that a hierarchy of races existed, with the northern European at the top. At about the same time, white women began to arrive in the northwest. One of the first, Marie-Anne Lagimodière (Louis Riel's maternal grandmother), chose to accompany her trader husband and adopt the ways of bush living, which native women taught her. Others preferred to maintain their former ways in the new environment, however, and few of the arrivals at the newly formed Red River Settlement appear to have attracted the attention of the fur traders. After the merger of the two companies, and in keeping with changing attitudes, Governor George Simpson decided that it would be appropriate for senior officers at the larger posts to take wives suitable to their station, meaning white women from middle-class families in Great Britain. In 1829, he and his friend, Chief Factor John McTavish, took the lead while on leave overseas and brought back two women who met their standards of ideal womanhood: dutiful, pious, and genteel, the "lovely tender exotic" of their dreams. The fact that both men already had native wives in the Northwest whom they had not informed did not seem to concern them, although others were scandalized.

It was an important turning point in fur trade society nonetheless. Soon it was fashionable to acquire a white wife, and the increasing number of these women in the Northwest changed forever the attitudes to native women. These white women did not have any real role to play in the economy of the trade and, cut off from the comfort of family and friends, they suffered physically and emotionally. They set about to recreate a piece of their homeland in the new world, not only in the material sense, but also in the sense of establishing class and racial attitudes that set them apart from the old society. Nasty conflicts arose in places like Red River in which gossip and scandal mongering were the weapons, and white and Métis women were the primary combatants. Native women were increasingly denounced as "squaws," and by the mid-nineteenth century, social attitudes had won out over economic and political necessity. Except in the more remote areas, it was no longer considered desirable for a trader to take a native wife, and Métis women strove anxiously to imitate the conventions of their husbands' society. Miss Davis's school for young ladies was established at Red River in the 1850s; here, daughters of fur trade marriages could learn to play the piano and the harp, dance the British way, and dress and carry themselves like any respectable Victorian woman. Roman Catholic girls could learn the same graces at a school run by the Grey Nuns. Native ancestry was conveniently forgotten so that those who could might pass into white society and be accepted. It was a sad end to an interesting period of Canadian social history.[8]

---

[8] On fur trade social history, see Jennifer Brown, *Strangers in Blood: Fur Trade Company Families in Indian Country* (Vancouver, 1980); Sylvia Van Kirk, *'Many Tender Ties': Women in Fur Trade*

Conclusions

The fur trade was not the first economic engine that drove European interest in North American lands and resources, but it eventually became an important part of the history of certain regions of Canada. While the significance of the fur trade to the development of Quebec is a matter for some debate, there is no doubt that the trade was very important in the history of areas like the Great Lakes and the Northwest.

The fur trade became essentially a northern enterprise. It drew Europeans across the continent along the water routes that provided access to the most desirable fur-bearing lands. It brought northern First Nations into regular contact with the world of European commerce and technology. And, some would say, it ensured that the Northwest would become British territory rather than American.

Nevertheless, the process of territorial acquisition was more accidental than deliberate. Without the signing of treaties, the Europeans newcomers simply came to visit and decided to stay. Since the traders and the First Nations shared common interests in the pursuit of trade, there seemed little reason for the original inhabitants of the land to object except in local disputes over specific issues. Not until the newcomers demanded the land for purposes that conflicted with First Nations' interests did problems arise.

Canadians sometimes pride themselves in the belief that European expansion across the West was a relatively peaceful matter, but the fur trade period was never without conflict. Wars among the First Nations over access to resources and territorial expansion accompanied the trade and the acquisition of European weaponry. Conflicts between native traders and Euro-Canadians over the process and terms of the trade itself were also an important feature of the interaction. And perhaps most shameful of all were the violent encounters during the period of intense trade competition between the Hudson's Bay Company and the North West Company when alcohol, kidnapping, rape, and murder became tools of persuasion.

Society 1670-1870 (Winnipeg, 1980); Frits Pannekoek, "The Rev. James Evans and the Social Antagonisms of the Fur Trade Society, 1840-1846" in Richard Allen (ed.), *Religion and Society in the Prairie West* (Regina, 1974); Jennifer Brown, "Children of the Early Fur Trades," in Joy Parr (ed.), *Childhood and Family in Canadian History* (Toronto, 1982).

Trade relations could be mutually satisfactory for the participants as well. Through the political and social interaction that accompanied the trade, the foundations were laid for the formation of a unique society in the Northwest. The emergence of the Métis around the Great Lakes, at Red River, and in the Athabasca District was one element of that fur trade society. The experience of a shared history gave later generations of the Northwest a sense of identity distinct from that of the Canadians who would eventually acquire their territory. Whether that society would survive in the face of overwhelming pressures from later immigration and political schemes remains to be seen.

BRITISH NORTH
AMERICA, 1763–1791

The most apparent changes in British North America between 1763 and 1791 were political and constitutional. In 1763, at the time of the formal transfer of French territory to Great Britain by the Treaty of Paris, British North America north of the 13 American colonies consisted of one full-fledged British province (Nova Scotia), another substantial province (Quebec) still for all intents and purposes French, a rapidly growing fishing settlement in Newfoundland, and an ill-defined fur trade territory in the Hudson Bay drainage basin governed by the Hudson's Bay Company under Royal Charter. The British quickly added another vast western hinterland around and to the south of the Great Lakes inhabited by Indians and to be administered by British regulars, hived off from Quebec but not expected to acquire formal provincial status. By 1791, this ill-assorted collection of jurisdictions had become five full-fledged British provinces complete with legislative assemblies (Upper Canada, Lower Canada, Nova Scotia, New Brunswick, and Prince Edward Island), and two additional colonies (Cape Breton and Newfoundland) without representative government but ostensibly moving toward it. Moreover, with the independence of the 13 colonies to the South, these provinces and colonies had become the centre of Britain's North American Empire.

Such substantial political and constitutional change was on one level the product of larger forces over which Britain's northernmost territories had little control. Indeed, the governing British themselves seemed usually

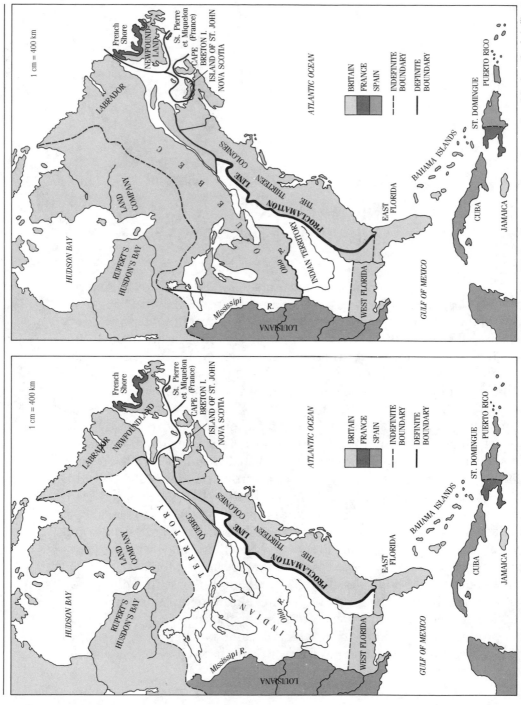

NORTH AMERICA, 1774

NORTH AMERICA, 1763

These two maps show the critical changes in British policy between the Royal Proclamation and the Quebec Act. The contraction and expansion of Quebec, the dwindling commitment of the British to First Nations' land, and attempts to contain the American colonists to lands east of the Appalachians are shown.

on the defensive, constantly reacting to new pressures from the obstreper-
ous Americans rather than developing any positive policy. But at the same
time, within the larger context of political turmoil and ultimate civil war,
the population of what would become Canada was constantly forced to
make choices that would contribute to the final outcome. Expelled
Acadians chose to return to their ancient territories at considerable
personal cost. French Canadians in Quebec passed up the opportunity to
become "liberated" from British tyranny by invading American armies in
1775–76, and Nova Scotians never provided sufficient encouragement to
the United States to produce a full-scale invasion. During and immediately
after the American war, thousands of residents and soldiers (white, black,
and red) chose to leave the United States and resettle in the remaining
British provinces, although some ultimately decided to return to their
homeland. And following a second Treaty of Paris in 1783, many Britons
(especially Scots Highlanders and Irish) determined to begin their lives
anew in British North America. Some of the choices of residence and
allegiance were voluntarily deliberate, others were unconscious, and still
others were forced upon those taking them. All decisions were, of course,
situational. They were taken in terms of the particular circumstances of
the time. To those circumstances we must now turn.

The Challenge of Expanded Empire

From the victory on the Plains of Abraham to the final conclusion of peace
with the French, the British public had been bombarded with literature
about French America and the relative merits of keeping it. The great
debate over the terms of peace was not conducted solely over France's
American Empire, of course. The Seven Years' War had been a truly
international conflict, and the chief issue in London was to balance British
territorial acquisitiveness against the widespread need for peace. Nevertheless, French America and especially Canada had figured prominently
both in the public discussions and in those conducted within Whitehall's
corridors of power. Most Britons held that French America was worth
retaining, partly for its economic potential but mainly in order to eliminate
the longstanding military threat it posed to the American colonies to the
South. An influential minority, however, insisted that the French menace

in North America was the principal protection for Britain against the independence of her seaboard colonies, which had been exhibiting signs of separatism for many years.[1]

While not everyone in the mother country could agree about the value of retaining Canada and other French American possessions, far greater consensus prevailed on policies to be pursued in the wake of that retention. The recent war had highlighted the extent to which the American colonists had slipped into assumptions of political and constitutional autonomy, operating beyond the control of Great Britain. The Americans would have to be returned to a "due subordination." The war had been very expensive, and fought largely—some would argue almost entirely—on behalf of those American colonists. The Americans were at least symbolically going to have to demonstrate a willingness to pay for the cost of its aftermath. What needed to be done administratively? The Indians who had supported the British during the war had been promised some security from settler encroachment on their lands. As for the new French subjects, they had an alien culture as well as a proscribed religion to add to a century-old tradition of military hostility to Britain and her colonies. All considerations pointed to the need for both a standing British army in North America and new American revenue measures to help support it as part of far-reaching reassertion of the power of Parliament over the colonies. The actions taken by Britain as a consequence of this thinking would, of course, lead almost inexorably to rebellion.

The Peace of Paris was formally signed in February 1763, although its terms had been general knowledge in the capitals of Europe since the preceding October. For the new province of Quebec, beyond final confirmation of the transfer of territory and subject populations from France to Britain, the peace treaty had little immediate impact. The British government continued to debate policy for North America through the spring of

---

[1] On the challenge of expanded empire, consult J. P. Greene, "The Seven Years' War and the American Revolution: the Causal Relationship Reconsidered," *Journal of Imperial and Commonwealth History*, VIII (1980), 85–105; J. M. Bumsted, "The Canada-Guadeloupe Debate and the Origins of the American Revolution," *Man and Nature/L'Homme et la Nature*, V (1986). For the text of the Treaty of Paris, see Adam Shortt and Arthur G. Doughty, eds., *Documents Relating to the Constitutional History of Canada 1759–1791* (Ottawa, 1907), 73–92. This work reprints most of the major documents discussed in this chapter and has been unjustly neglected by teachers of Canadian history in recent years.

1763, and until policy was agreed upon, Quebec would continue to be governed by the military regime headed by General James Murray, who would not receive a commission and instructions as civil governor until August 1764.

The British government produced its first attempt at overall policy in the wake of the Peace of Paris through the notorious Proclamation of 7 October 1763. Its "extensive and valuable acquisitions in America" were organized into four new governments (Quebec, East and West Florida, and Granada). Quebec was reduced in size to the agricultural settlements along the St. Lawrence; Newfoundland was given the fishing islands in the Gulf of St. Lawrence; Nova Scotia acquired Île St. Jean (now to be called the Island of Saint John) and Île Royale (now Cape Breton Island). Military men who had served in North America were entitled to apply for wilderness land grants "without fee or reward." No settlement was to take place in the region beyond the rivers flowing into the Atlantic Ocean. This territory—as far west as Rupert's Land (the Hudson's Bay Company's preserve) and as far south as the Floridas—was reserved for the Indians and was to be administered by the Crown, which would grant licences for trade under close supervision. Quebec and the other new provinces, almost as an afterthought, were guaranteed "the benefit of the laws... of England" immediately and promised elected assemblies as soon as possible.

The subsequent commission and instructions to the new governor of Quebec elaborated on the new arrangements for that province. The commission limited office-holding to those prepared to take the standard oaths against the papacy. The instructions created a governor's council and warned that without an assembly, "nothing be passed or done that shall in any ways tend to affect the life, limb or liberty of the subject, or to the imposing of any duties or taxes." Religious toleration was confirmed, although the Church of England should be established and the "said inhabitants...by degrees...induced to embrace the Protestant religion." The ecclesiastical jurisdiction of Rome was positively forbidden. Complex provisions for land granting were made in anticipation of a rush of settlers produced by a governor's proclamation publicizing the country's many advantages. The policy followed general guidelines of the time. Land was to be surveyed into 20 000 acre townships (8000 ha), with typical grants of 100 acres (40 ha) per head of the family and 50 (20 ha) for each dependant. Grantees would pay quitrents (small annual rentals in lieu of services) to the Crown of at least two shillings per acre. This system was ultimately followed more closely on the Island of Saint John than in Quebec itself.

Three related points must be made about this imperial policy. In the first place, little in it set Quebec apart from other provinces or regions. Indeed the absence of different treatment was its principal characteristic. The British had scarcely accepted French Canada as a "distinctive society" and planned to administer it within the overall rules of the existing Empire. Quebec would achieve full provincial status (including an elected assembly) as soon as its population had either acquired a large British base or had assimilated sufficiently to justify it. In the second place, the British government anticipated a substantial rush of American colonials to all its newly acquired territory, partly because the Americans were known to be land hungry and partly because they had been deliberately shut out of the interior of the continent. Finally, while the British were concerned to keep the Indians pacified, they had little notion of dealing with the Indian land claims in ways that the native peoples could accept or understand.

Since the British policy for all of the former French territory depended upon rapid settlement, it is important to appreciate both the encouragement given and the constraints upon such settlement. Great Britain was undergoing yet another major economic transformation, and it had no desire to people North America with its own citizenry, which would be required at home as a labour force. Equally, however, it felt financially strapped; there would be no subsidies for settlers such as had occurred in Nova Scotia between 1749 and 1763, when hundreds of thousands of pounds had been spent transporting and supplying new arrivals from Britain, continental Europe, and New England. Cheap land would have to be the principal inducement, and those already resident in America the chief recipients. The British acknowledged "Foreign Protestants" as acceptable settlers, but had no intention of assisting them in any way. Individual settlers from America could be attracted either as freeholders by inexpensive land grants or assisted by large landed proprietors who were usually required by the terms of their grants to provide settlers. Assisted settlers were typically expected to become tenants, reimbursing the landholder for his financial outlay with annual rentals.

Projections that seemed so promising on paper worked less well in practice. Few statesmen and politicians in London understood the realities of North American settlement. From the seventeenth to the early twentieth centuries, planned settlement seldom worked. American colonists did not flock to the newly acquired territories for a number of reasons. Settling wilderness land in a northern climate would at the best of times have proved attractive only with substantial financial inducement for the new pioneers. In the years after 1763, such financial assistance would come only from private entrepreneurs in exchange for limitations upon land ownership. American colonials, however, were not prepared to accept less than freehold tenure. The inability of the Quebec government to eliminate the seigneurial system further detracted from the attraction of that province for restless Americans, who were already suspicious of the climate, the prevalence of a foreign culture and religion, and the absence of familiar political institutions. Even without the colonial unrest that soon followed the Proclamation of 1763, Americans would not have been attracted north. In the meantime, the British government encouraged the granting of millions of acres of wilderness in Nova Scotia and the Island of Saint John to large, landed proprietors in anticipation of an influx of American settlers who never came. A trickle of new population recruited in the British Isles was arrested by the outbreak of the American Rebellion. Quebec was spared a wholesale land grab only by the complications of the seigneurial system in the territory under its control.

Quebec and the West, 1763–1774

Although the administrators of Quebec could not operate in total disregard of the mounting crisis to the South, the internal problems that they faced were in their own terms quite daunting. Some balance had to be struck between the needs of the dominant French-Canadian population and the demands of a small but vociferous British one, recently arrived since 1759 to take over much of the commercial activity of the province. Concessions to the Canadiens not only ran the risk of incensing the British minority in the colony (or the Americans beyond it), but of running afoul of British imperial policy or practice. Nevertheless, the overall dynamic in Quebec was a simple one, moving gradually from a province intended initially to become British to one recognized as already being French. The principal debates occurred over the nature of government, the laws and the legal system, and religion.[2]

---

[2] Most of the individuals discussed in this chapter have been sketched in volumes IV and V of the *Dictionary of Canadian Biography*, which represents some of the best recent scholarship on

For James Murray, who had to make the transition from military to civil governor in 1764, there was nothing but grief. Murray was sympathetic to the problems of the Canadiens, and very conscious of the problems he faced, writing, "It is by military force we are to govern this lately conquered Province in which there does not exist above 50 Protestant subjects exclusive of the troops and by my instructions of these 50 Protestants must be composed the Magistracy." As such comments suggested, Murray was in no hurry to establish an assembly, much less a judiciary, and he initially governed by a council made up entirely of Protestant newcomers. He and the council soon ran up against the thorny problems of adapting English and Anglo-British colonial practice to Quebec's conditions and were not assisted much by the appointed officials of the colony, who lacked either competence or imagination—or both. Everyone in the administration faced increasing hostility from a slowly enlarging body of anglophone merchants who wanted the terms of the Proclamation of 1763 fulfilled and were less than supportive of accommodations, such as permitting French-Canadian participation in the inferior civil courts.

The fundamental problem was that the Proclamation of 1763 was distinctly unfair, not only to the conquered population, but to Britain's Indian allies as well. Quebec's integration into the British Empire could not be predicated upon a simplistic imposition of new systems from without, particularly in view of the terms of surrender in 1760 and of transfer by France in 1763. The situation was a nightmare for a governor and a challenge to the best legal minds of the age. Canadians had in 1760 been guaranteed their property, which precluded any wholesale change in property law, the central cornerstone of any jurisdiction's civil law. They had only been guaranteed freedom of worship "so far as the laws of Great Britain permit," which was hardly much of a concession, since the Catholicism was legally proscribed. But to limit greatly the Roman Catholic

---

the period under consideration. Students are advised to consult it regularly. For Quebec in this period, see A. L. Burt, *The Old Province of Quebec*, 2 vols. (Toronto, repr. 1968); Hilda Neatby, *Quebec 1760–1791* (Toronto, 1963); Michel Brunet, *Les Canadiens Après la Conquête, 1759–1775: De la révolution canadienne à la révolution américaine* (Montreal, 1969). The debate over the meaning of the Conquest can be followed in Dale Miquelon, ed., *Society and Conquest: The Debate on the Bourgeoisie and Social Change in French Canada, 1700–1850* (Toronto, 1980). See also Fernand Ouellet, *Social and Economic History of Quebec, 1760–1850* (Toronto, 1980) and Allan Greer, *Peasant, Lord and Merchant: Rural Society in Three Quebec Parishes, 1749–1840* (Toronto, 1985). The Quebec Act is discussed in Hilda Neatby, ed., *The Quebec Act: Protest and Policy* (Scarborough, Ont. 1972).

Church would mock existing arrangements and to deny political rights to Catholics would disenfranchise virtually an entire population. Murray managed to pass the first religious hurdle successfully, encouraging Jean Olivier Briand to become consecrated in France to govern a hitherto bishopless church in Quebec. The willingness of the London authorities to turn a blind eye to their own laws, accommodating the religion of the Canadiens by allowing Rome to consecrate in France, says a good deal about the temper of the victors on both sides of the Atlantic. But Murray's legal ordinance of 1764, which introduced English law while not eliminating the Canadian codes, upset everyone by its confusion and eventually got the governor recalled.

Indian land claims ought to have provided an equal challenge to the best legal minds of the time, although it must be emphasized that the lawyers never took the native peoples very seriously at all. But if the Proclamation of 1763 confused Quebec administration, it really fell short for the Indians. The British understood that the Indians required a policy, but one that prohibited European settlement in the West was only half satisfactory. The Proclamation of 1763 tried to insulate the Indians from settlement, but made no attempt to guarantee them title to their lands, much less to provide them with some sort of political sovereignty over the territory that they claimed. The British never were able to regard the issue of Indian sovereignty as a real one, although Europe had plenty of examples of land arrangements in which both the ultimate authority of the Crown and the immediate autonomy of the territory were preserved. In truth, the real problem was that the British did not consider Indian concerns important issues and certainly did not regard them as a people entitled to as much attention as that given the *habitants* of Quebec.

The effect of the habitants of all the manoeuvring over high policy is difficult to assess. The Conquest has for over two centuries been viewed by historians as a turning point in Canadian historical development. By and large, historians writing from the British perspective have emphasized the difficulties of the administrative problems and the relative generosity of the conqueror. Those writing from the Canadien point of view have been gradually moving away from interpretations that concentrated on the sharp break with the French regime, although there remains the insistence that, for the "conquered," the new situation was traumatic and psychologically damaging. Evidence for psychological damage is not easy to provide in standard documentable form. However, the average Canadian did not articulate a reaction to either the transfer to Britain or the subsequent integration of Quebec into the British Empire. What we have, for the most part, are comments by elite observers, who usually saw what they wanted to see.

The Conquest brought peace and economic stability—perhaps even growth. Under the British, onerous military obligations were greatly reduced, and the new regime was not rapacious about taxation. Population grew and settlement expanded, probably increasing the enforcement of the hitherto dormant obligations of the seigneurial system. The bulk of the land remained in the hands of Canadian seigneurs, however, although perhaps 30 seigneuries passed into English ownership in the 10 years after 1760. The British support for the Roman Catholic Church was a mixed blessing. On the one hand, it provided access to the sacraments for a people undoubtedly Catholic in belief; on the other hand, it perpetuated the exertions of the tithe, one of New France's least popular institutions. The psychological impact of being ruled by foreigners under partially unfamiliar institutions is virtually impossible to measure or calculate. Canadian agriculture did begin to produce a regular surplus, particularly of wheat, reaching an export of nearly 200 000 bushels in 1771. Small landholders remained close to the margin of self-subsistence, however. The fur trade continued to expand, although its direction passed from French to British hands. For the several thousand habitants who worked in the fur trade, the difference between masters was probably not worth noting. The continuation of the fur trade without a pause also made regulation—at least without the substantial military presence in the West envisioned by the British in 1763 but never funded or instituted—quite impossible. In 1768 imperial regulation was abandoned, and the fur trade and Indian policy were returned to the several colonies. In some respects, this change was favourable to Quebec, since it implicitly enlarged the colony's sphere of trading. The fur trade elite in Montreal did provide a major base of opposition to Governor James Murray, who tended to view the traders as "Licentious Fanaticks" attempting to undermine the policies he was instructed to enforce.

James Murray quickly fell victim to the complications of British policy. He had done reasonably well under difficult circumstances in Quebec itself, but could not satisfy either the vociferous British merchant group in Montreal or the law officers of the Crown in London. The former protested Murray's "arbitrary" government, the latter his attempt to amalgamate the existing French judicial system with English common law. Like many a British colonial governor in British North America, Murray was viewed by the imperial authorities as having failed because he had not pleased everyone, and he was replaced in 1766 with Colonel Guy Carleton, who formally succeeded him as governor in 1768.

Carleton was an Anglo-Irishman who arrived in Quebec well-briefed on the problems faced by Murray and with far more military power than his predecessor had enjoyed. He had first to deal with a factious executive council composed chiefly of Murray supporters but soon brought it under control by dismissing his most critical opponents, Paul Irving and Adam Mabane. With the British merchants, he conciliated whenever possible short of accepting their program of allowing them an elected assembly. But Carleton had to keep one eye on the Americans, for Quebec would have to be defended in case of a rupture between the colonies and Britain. Few security measures would avail if the French population did not support the government, and Carleton searched desperately for both policies and local allies that would guarantee French-Canadian loyalty. He saw little possibility of substantial British immigration arguing that "barring a catastrophe shocking to think of this country must to the end of time be peopled by the Canadian race. . . ." Not surprisingly, he quickly found some potential local candidates for collaboration within the ranks of the seigneurial class of the colony.

Like most colonial administrators of people and systems different from their own experience, Guy Carleton elevated his own needs and assumptions into a policy. He did not wish to become dependent on the "English party" and managed to misinterpret completely the position of the seigneurs in the political structure of New France. In fairness to Carleton, the political functions of the seigneurial system were never clearly codified under the *ancien régime*, and the elimination of the intendant did alter the dynamic. In any event, the seigneurs resided mainly in the larger towns of the colony, and most had never enjoyed much local influence, particularly in terms of military leadership. But Carleton preferred to see them as English country gentlemen who could be co-opted into the political system. He also saw the value of the support of the Roman Catholic Church, both its hierarchy and its parish priests. His relationship with the church was on the whole a good one, quite different from that of the ancien régime since his government was quite outside it. Bishop Briand exercised power, particularly through the ultimate weapon of excommunication, which he would have had difficulty in wielding within the Gallican church-state relationship of Louis XV. He consolidated his authority to make himself the most powerful ecclesiastic French Canada had seen since the days of Bishop Laval. While Briand's control over his clerics was considerable, particularly after he had resolved the status of the parish church and cathedral chapter of Quebec in 1774, his positive authority with the habitants was never complete. Like most Canadian clergy, he constantly complained that the people went their own way in many matters related to religion and worship. Briand's church enjoyed a surprising amount of unofficial autonomy and governmental support under Carleton, who regularly allowed ecclesiastical disputes to be dealt with by the bishop, which would under the French regime have been matters for government intervention. In return, Briand insisted that the priests fully support the Carleton administration, and they generally complied.

As for the British merchants, Carleton did not entirely satisfy their demands. But he did attempt to offer them a *quid pro quo*. Although he did not institute the political and legal changes that the merchants had called for, he did acquiesce to their interests in the fur trade. All efforts at regulation of the fur trade from Quebec virtually ceased under Carleton. The traders were allowed to trade directly with the Indians north and west of the Great Lakes, and the ending of the annual licensing system freed them to head beyond the lakes, where journeys took far longer than one year. Even before Lord Hillsborough had officially abandoned the licensing system in 1768, the Hudson's Bay Company traders were complaining of a renewal of "French" trade on the Saskatchewan River, and by 1770 the "Peddlars from Quebec" could be found almost everywhere in the West.

Governor Carleton, content that he had established working relationships with the two most powerful elite groups carrying over from the French regime—and incorrectly assuming that these groups had more popular influence than was the case—went home to London in 1770 to regularize a "more effectual provision for the province of Quebec." The governor had made little effort to test seriously the murky waters of contemporary public opinion, although it was hard to know how this could have been done in the absence of general elections. Signed petitions for almost any action or policy could be generated and produced when needed at the appropriate time, and who could say how much "public opinion" was thus represented? The eventual result of Carleton's lobbying activities in Quebec and in London was the Quebec Act of 1774. This parliamentary legislation, as Hilda Neatby has trenchantly observed, was "based almost exclusively on the wishes of Canadians as interpreted by Guy Carleton."

Although the American colonists viewed the Quebec Act as one of the "Intolerable Acts"—it was passed by the British Parliament at the same time as a series of repressive measures resulting from the Boston Tea Party of 1773—it was less intended to deal with the American troubles than with the unsettled condition of Canada. The Americans saw sinister motives in four features of the legislation: the re-institution of feudalism, the recognition of the rights of the Roman Catholic Church, the withdrawal of the earlier promise for a legislative assembly, and the extension of the boundaries of Quebec into the Ohio Valley. Most of these offensive provisions had already been anticipated by earlier imperial decisions in which Guy Carleton had an important share. The home government had decided in 1771 to abandon thoughts of an assembly, and about the same time ordered the governor of Quebec to grant all lands "en fief et seigneurie," which quickly produced petitions for new seigneuries from both the French and British elites in the colony. The matter of extending Quebec boundaries had been inherent in the decision of 1768 to abandon the licensing of the fur trade, and thus the Indian reserve in the Ohio region. The council of Quebec had as early as 1769 argued that the western Indian lands be re-annexed to Canada. The power of the church had been restored unofficially by Carleton, with British approval because of earlier treaty provisions. The pacification of Quebec was indirectly connected with the American troubles, of course, since a discontented colony would be difficult to defend in case of a resumption of war. But the principles of that pacification were inherent in the internal affairs of the colony, however mistaken Carleton and the British may have been in accepting them as popular with the bulk of the population, and were not intended to provoke the Americans.

The Quebec Act was passed in 1774 fundamentally because British policy in the Proclamation of 1763 had proved unworkable. The French Canadians had not become assimilated, an English-speaking wave of new settlers had not come, and the army necessary to administer the western Indian policy had not materialized. As has already been suggested, the Quebec Act merely consolidated a series of imperial decisions already taken. Thus Quebec's boundaries, so sharply constricted by the Proclamation of 1763, were re-extended to their historical limits both east and west, giving the colony official control over the fur trade in the Great Lakes region to the Mississippi and over the fishery in Labrador. Roman Catholicism was legally recognized in two senses: the oath of allegiance was reframed so that Catholics in Quebec could take it and thus hold office; the clergy could now officially collect the tithe from its own adherents but not from Protestants. Instructions to the governor put the bishop and the clergy firmly under government control, but these provisions were in practice neglected during the emergency of the American Revolution. The promise of an assembly was positively revoked, and the size of the executive council nearly doubled. Governor and council were given legislative authority, but not the power to levy general taxation; a separate statute, the Quebec Revenue Act, provided a revenue through duties, licence fees, and the old feudal payments of the French regime. The Quebec Act provided the colony with English criminal law (although not habeas corpus) and the old French civil law, including the property provisions of the seigneurial system. As A. L. Burt pointed out more than half a century ago, for all its limitations, the Quebec Act "embodied a new sovereign principle of the British Empire: the liberty of non-English peoples to be themselves."

The Atlantic Region, 1763–1774

NOVA SCOTIA

Unlike Quebec, which received considerable attention from the imperial authorities between 1763 and 1775, Nova Scotia was virtually neglected and shoved to the peripheries of policy making. The colony had, of course, been centre stage between 1748 and 1763, when hundreds of thousands of pounds had been spent subsidizing the settlement of Halifax and then the Annapolis Valley after the Acadians had been forcibly removed. For many Britons, Nova Scotia became synonymous with government waste, and Edmund Burke could exclaim at one point in the House of Commons, "Good God! What sum the nursing of that ill-thriven, hard-visaged, and ill-favoured brat, has cost to this wittol nation." Imperial expenditures on both civilian and military business had turned Halifax into a boom town, and had attracted to the colony's political capital a large contingent of merchants, both English and American in origin, who flourished on government contracts and provision of drink for the soldiers and sailors stationed in and passing through the town. Nova Scotia had instituted in 1758 that symbol of "British Liberty" in America, a provincial assembly. North Americans never understood that from the imperial perspective, an assembly not only marked political but fiscal maturity. Within the Empire, only a colony with an assembly could tax itself. The Nova Scotia assembly knew how to spend the annual parliamentary grant from England, but was considerably less ingenious at figuring out ways to raise money when the subsidies dried up, as occurred in the early 1760s.[3]

Two major factors hampered a virtually bankrupt Nova Scotia as it attempted the transition from wartime prosperity to peacetime poverty. One was the political structure of the colony, in which Halifax existed in a world of its own with only a limited presence and power in the remainder of Nova Scotia. The capital had been created as a military centre of British power and, until 1760, had contained the bulk of the colony's non-Acadian population. The colony's official and merchant classes both resided in Halifax and had established cosy economic and personal interrelationships that had quickly translated into dominance in the legislative assembly when it was created. Even as settlement spread outside the capital, Halifax managed to maintain its dominance over both the government and the assembly. The incoming Planters, mainly New Englanders, had been promised political institutions with which they were familiar, but the central government systematically suppressed local town-meeting democracy in the New England settlements. The newcomers were not encouraged to participate in colonial government, and they often elected Halifax merchants to represent them in the assembly or else failed to send anyone. The Halifax oligarchy proved more interested in being able to acquire large amounts of undeveloped land for speculative purposes than in developing policies to give those lands any value. The lack of a back country counterweight to the power of Halifax both allowed the oligarchy to proceed unchecked in its rapacious land acquisition and prevented the government from obtaining cooperation from the outlying districts in any positive measures.

The second factor was the relative fragility of the Nova Scotia economy once it was cut loose from substantial public subsidies. Nova Scotia's prosperity had been artificially created before 1763, and its economic situation thereafter was fairly desperate. The province, very simply, was

---

[3] For Nova Scotia, the classic work remains John Bartlett Brebner, *The Neutral Yankees of Nova Scotia: A Marginal Colony during the Revolutionary Years* (1937, repr. Toronto, 1969). But see also Margaret Conrad, ed., *They Planted Well: New England Planters in Maritime Canada* (Fredericton, 1988); George Rawlyk, *Nova Scotia's Massachusetts: A Study of Massachusetts-Nova Scotia Relations, 1630–1784* (Montreal, 1973).

not sufficiently developed economically to pay its own way. The principal cash-producing commodity was fish, but much of Nova Scotia's fishery was in the hands of New Englanders, who took their catch in Nova Scotia waters and returned home with it. Fur was the second most important export, but the fur-producing hinterland was limited to begin with and bound to contract with settlement. First-rate agricultural land was in short supply, and markets were not readily available. In any event, the colony was not yet producing any agricultural surplus. Timber and lumber were promising commodities, but while they were sometimes marketed successfully before 1775, wood production was not an important industry. Rich mineral resources, included coal, were not systematically exploited. The picture in most economic areas is one of occasional successful forays by individual entrepreneurs, but no creation of an integrated commercial system. Many of the most successful harvesters of Nova Scotia resources were the New Englanders, who continued to utilize the colony as the furthest extremity of their own commerce. Lieutenant-governor Michael Francklin merely stated the obvious in 1766 when he reported to the Board of Trade that "we shall be a Province too much dependent on New England, and remain in a feeble, languid state."

Despite the prominence of the Halifax merchants, the colony lacked the rich commercial infrastructure that New England had spent over a century developing. It did not have autonomous trading connections with its best potential markets in Newfoundland and the Caribbean. The inability of Halifax to monitor activities in the outports and back country meant that most trade went unregulated and duties uncollected. Nova Scotia was unlikely to find salvation in any single staple commodity. Success would come, if ever it did, through the kinds of commercial carrying trades at which the New Englanders excelled: a bit of this and a bit of that traded here and there. A good deal of this trade did exist, but seldom in the hands of Nova Scotian traders. The colony needed to free itself from New England, although how such step could be achieved was hardly clear in 1774.

THE ISLAND OF SAINT JOHN

The early development of the Island of Saint John—it was not renamed Prince Edward Island until 1798—offers a splendid illustration of British settlement policy for the newly acquired French territory apart from Quebec, where 70 000 inhabitants made a special case. The British had forcibly removed 3500 Acadians from the island following the surrender of Louisbourg in 1758. Although a small contingent of Acadians and Micmacs still remained in residence, the British government regarded the island as virtually unpeopled and of great potential value because of its fertile land and commodious harbours. Nevertheless, the Proclamation of 1763 had done little about the island except annexing it (with Cape Breton) to Nova Scotia.[4]

Over the next few years the Island of Saint John became the subject of a considerable debate among the imperial authorities. The issue was how best to go about developing and settling this attractive piece of real estate. One faction was led by the Earl of Egmont, an important political figure, who led a syndicate of merchants and military officers applying to the Crown for a grant of the entire island. They offered to develop it at no expense to the public by reinstituting a feudal system (based on military obligation) that would ultimately provide thousands of soldiers for the British army in America, as well as place the island into the hands of "the Peers, great Commoners, eminent Merchants, and Other Gentlemen of Distinction" in Great Britain. Opposed to Egmont was the Board of Trade, which insisted that any special conditions of landholding in North America were "impolitick, inexpedient, and anti-commercial." Both sides agreed that a substantial quitrent payment to the Crown was not detrimental to settlement, however.

In the end, the Board of Trade won out. A feudal aristocracy would not be permitted on the Island of Saint John, although many of the provisions of the final scheme for settlement had been influenced by the Egmont proposals. The island was surveyed into 67 lots or townships of approximately 20 000 acres (8000 ha) each, and these townships were allocated by lottery in 1767 to "proprietors." The grantees were expected to move to the island to supervise the development of their holdings, were required to pay quitrents "proportional to the value of the lands," and were given ten years to settle one person per each 200 acres (80 ha) of grant. The settlers had to be either European Protestants or individuals resident in America for two years before receiving the land. The proprietor could either sell or lease land to the individual settler, who would have come to the island either on his own money or with the assistance of the proprietor.

---

[4] On Prince Edward Island, see J. M. Bumsted, *Land, Settlement and Politics in Eighteenth-Century Prince Edward Island* (Montreal and Kingston, 1987).

The concept of tying large land grants to proprietors with settlement at the proprietor's expense was a time-worn practice in both the French- and British-American empires, although it had never proved very successful. Most of the grantees added land on the Island of Saint John to their portfolios as speculative holdings and did not intend much immediate activity. Their hand was forced by the Nova Scotia government, however, which responded to news of the lottery by moving a complete colonial government to the island in 1768, hoping to recover its costs from the British authorities. Nova Scotia's lieutenant-governor Michael Francklin was recalled for his precipitate actions, and the island proprietors felt pressured to produce a plan for a separate government to keep the island out of the hands of the rapacious Nova Scotians. They argued that the cost of an autonomous civil government could be paid out of the revenues from the quitrents at no expense to Great Britain, and the Island of Saint John became a separate colony with its own government (although not yet with an assembly) in 1769.

The new administration of the Island of Saint John faced a number of great difficulties. One, of course, was that the island would have to become settled, a process really in the hands of the proprietors of the 1767 lottery. A few of these men became active in recruiting settlers, almost exclusively in the British Isles and chiefly in the Highlands of Scotland. The largest early settlement was composed of Roman Catholics from the Scottish western Highlands and Islands, hoping to escape religious disabilities while maintaining their traditional culture away from the modernizing trends in their homeland. By 1774 perhaps one thousand new settlers had been relocated on the island, not a bad record for private recruitment. The other problem was government revenue. The quitrents, if fully collected, would barely serve to pay the salaries of the colony's officers, and the British authorities—while providing some money for necessary buildings—made clear that Parliament would not make up salary arrearages. Although island quitrents were more thoroughly collected than had ever been the case in North America, many proprietors were holding their grants for speculative purposes and did not fully pay. The colony's officials became desperate for their salaries and, when informed that legislation to enforce quitrent collection would be legal only if adopted by a legislative assembly, immediately organized one. The number of eligible voters for the first assembly elections held in 1773 was tiny, both because of the small size of the population and the prevalence of Roman Catholics (who were not allowed to vote) among it. The first bill considered by the new assembly was one to enforce quitrent collection.

Thus in 1773 the Island of Saint John became the third full-fledged colony in what would become Canada and the second to have the full British constitutional apparatus of governor, executive council, and legislative assembly. By later Canadian standards, the land area of the island was miniscule, less than 2 million acres (810 000 ha) or 2184 square miles (5656 km²). But to compare the island with later Canadian provinces would be anachronistic. At the time it was organized as a colony, it was not regarded as either unusual or small. Several of the 13 colonies (particularly Rhode Island and Connecticut) were of the same approximate size, and the island was most commonly compared by contemporaries with Caribbean islands within the British Empire, many of which were substantially smaller in land area.

NEWFOUNDLAND

A substantially larger island than the Island of Saint John was Newfoundland, one of the earliest regions for British settlement in North America. Although Newfoundland had always been regarded by Great Britain as a place of enormous economic importance because of the fishery, it was very slow to acquire regular colonial status and was often regarded by London as outside normal colonial government. Certainly by 1763 British mercantilists were quick to emphasize that the accumulated monetary value to the nation of the Newfoundland fishery was as great as or exceeded that from Spain's American gold and silver mines, but the island was still by imperial standards irregularly administered. If the obstacle was not economic importance, neither was it an absence of inhabitants. After the initial settlement activity of the first half of the seventeenth century, most of Newfoundland's population for the next 50 years came from Europe to fish in the summer months. But gradually the proportion of year-round inhabitants (or "winterers," as they were called) had increased from 1200 in 1700 to 3500 in 1730 to 7300 by the 1750s. British authorities, however, sought to encourage the migratory fishery, which was held to be advantageous as a "nursery of seamen" for the navy, and equally sought to discourage settlement by withholding residential institutions of government.[5]

---

[5] For Newfoundland, consult C. Grant Head, *Eighteenth-Century Newfoundland: A Geographer's Perspective* (Toronto, 1976); Keith Matthews, *Lectures on the History of Newfoundland, 1500–1830* (St. John's, 1973).

The increased pressure of year-round population had gradually forced Britain to provide some of the trappings of administration, including winter magistrates appointed from the ranks of the principal local residents, a full-fledged governor in 1729, and courts to hear capital crimes in 1749. But otherwise, Newfoundland was ignored administratively, and land was occupied and transferred on the island without any formal civil system of law to govern or even record these transactions. Newfoundland's government was re-examined by the Board of Trade after 1763 as part of the overall evaluation of the new empire, and in 1765 that body recommended that it be given a proper administrative system such as prevailed elsewhere in British North America. The fall of the Grenville ministry because of the American Stamp Act Crisis ended liberal thinking in the corridors of power, and a subsequent report from the Board of Trade went back to emphasis on the migratory fishery.

The British support for migratory fishing went against the overall pattern of development of the fishery itself, although this pattern did not unfold smoothly and inevitably. By 1763 the inshore cod fishery, involving daily voyages from harbour to fishing ground by small boats, dominated the industry. Many of these small boats were named by year-round residents, who usually sold their catch to merchants from the West Country of England or from America. The "winterer" domination of the inshore fishery had constantly increased. After 1763, however, the migratory fishery received something of a new lease on life through the introduction of larger vessels that remained for long periods on the more distant Grand Banks. These "bankers" were encouraged by three factors. One was the beginning of shortages of cod close to shore (the problems of fish availability and the need for management of the resource that would bedevil the fishery to the present day had already emerged). No one could say whether the lack of fish was a result of overfishing or changes in the migratory patterns of the fish, but it was a serious problem. A second factor was positive encouragement of banking by the British authorities on the spot, particularly Governor Hugh Palliser. The third and most important factor was economic. The offshore fishery required a smaller number of fishermen proportionate to the catch involved and was regarded as far more profitable to the merchant, particularly since he was able to eliminate the resident middlemen. According to one contemporary calculation, in 1764, 238 British ships had brought 7000 men to Newfoundland, while by 1768, 389 carried over 12 000. At the same time, the totals of resident fishermen dropped from 10 000 to 7000 and the numbers who returned home for the winter more than doubled. The swift appearance of "banking" led both merchants and British authorities to believe that the day of the resident fisherman was past, and so it seemed before the onset of the American Rebellion.

The Coming of the American Rebellion

Neither the leading officials nor the population of the northernmost colonies were always well placed to predict accurately the course of events between the recalcitrant Americans and the British. Only Guy Carleton, who had returned to Quebec in the late summer of 1774 with the Quebec Act in his pocket, had any real notion of the emergency. What Carleton had learned in England about the possibility of open rebellion was reinforced within a day of his return, when the commander-in-chief of the British Army in America wrote from Boston for immediate reinforcements. Carleton responded with alacrity to the request, and filled his correspondence to London with reports of the favourable response of the French population to the Quebec Act. Within a few months, however, he was less certain of Quebec's response to increasing American pressure, including an invitation to the province to be represented at the next meeting of the Continental Congress scheduled for May 1775. The British merchants were unhappy, the Canadiens were not enthusiastic about militia service, and the colony was virtually denuded of troops.[6]

Carleton's problem was that he had deluded himself into thinking that his policies would make loyal subjects of French Canadians. In Nova Scotia, Governor Francis Legge's delusions were somewhat different. Arriving in the colony late in 1773, Legge soon found himself at odds with the cosy oligarchy of officials and merchants who had long controlled its government. In November 1774, he appointed a committee to audit the provincial books, which had been irregularly kept for years. Much of the money in default to the province was owed by its leading politicians, and Legge created a special jury to try two of them, ostentatiously sitting in the

---

[6] Marcel Trudel, *Louis XVI, Le Congres Américaine et le Canada, 1774–1783* (Quebec, 1949); Gustave Lanctot, *Les Canadiens Français et leurs Voisins du Sud* (Montreal, 1941), and his *Canada and the American Revolution* (Cambridge, Mass., 1967).

courthouse gallery throughout the subsequent trial. With the colonies to the South on the verge of rebellion, a leading Nova Scotia merchant was in jail, a martyr to "persecution," and Halifax muttered about "Stuart despotism." Francis Legge had failed to appreciate that political quiet in Nova Scotia depended upon an alliance between the governor and the local elite.

On the Island of Saint John, Governor Walter Patterson understood local politics far better than he did the deteriorating imperial situation. Patterson wanted to be in London lobbying for Crown approval of legislation enforcing quitrent collection and for parliamentary payment of salary arrearages, and in September 1774 he had requested a leave-of-absence on the grounds that he would be "of more service to the Island, by spending a little time among the Proprietors at Home, than I can possibly be of, in the same space, by remaining here." His request was granted in the spring of 1775 before the first shots of rebellion at Lexington and Concord in April, and he sailed from Charlottetown in early August in obvious ignorance of the severity of the situation. By the time of Patterson's departure, the shooting war had begun.

Given the volatile nature of the escalating crisis between the colonies and the British, it was hardly surprising that the final rupture was so swift. The Americans had been gearing for war since Parliament had responded so harshly to the Boston Tea Party with the "Intolerable Acts" of 1774. Delegates from the colonies had begun meeting at a Continental Congress in Philadelphia in September 1774 and had not managed to work out among themselves any satisfactory compromise scheme likely to meet with British acceptance. Most delegates accepted the logic of separation. When in April 1775 General Gage in Boston attempted to seize rebel arms stored outside the city, the Americans attacked the British troops, and the continent quickly found itself at war. Part of the swift American mobilization in the spring of 1775 included a number of actions that would affect the northernmost colonies not represented in the Continental Congress. These included an invasion of Quebec, the authorization of privateering vessels to harass British shipping on the Atlantic but especially in the more sheltered waters of the Gulf of St Lawrence, and the termination of trade with Newfoundland. Such actions symbolized three of the most crucial consequences of the war for the northern colonies: invasions and threats of invasion; privateering and guerilla conflict; and the interruption of commerce, including immigration from Europe.

The Warfare of the American Rebellion

INVASIONS: REAL, THREATENED, AND IMAGINED

Once the shooting had started, the Americans immediately thought about Canada. There were two major reasons for this reaction. One was that Canada, now in British hands, had for a century posed a northern military threat to the colonies. It might well do so again if not prevented by a pre-emptive strike. The other, not quite contradictory, was the belief in many rebel quarters that the Canadiens, suffering under the burden of British tyranny, were ripe for liberation from their oppressors. In early May 1775, a small force led by Ethan Allen captured the traditional gateway fortresses of Ticonderoga and Crown Point, the guardians of the Lake Champlain invasion route to Montreal. The Continental Congress approved plans for an invasion of Canada. Over the summer, American soldiers poured into the upper Lake Champlain region, encouraged by word that Quebec was not heavily defended and hopeful of Canadien assistance. The Americans breached the British defences of Montreal in early November, leading Governor Carleton to evacuate Montreal and remove to Quebec. Mean-while, another army led by Benedict Arnold marched overland from the coast of present-day Maine, losing half its numbers but arriving at Quebec almost simultaneously with Governor Carleton, and was soon joined by the Lake Champlain contingent led by General Richard Montgomery in an extended siege of the Quebec capital.[7]

Although the siege carried on through the winter of 1775–76, the Americans had lost their momentum in a desperate attack on the city on New Year's Eve. Montgomery was killed and Arnold wounded, while the garrison held. Short on supplies and money, faced with troops returning home, ravaged by disease, and unable to win the support of the Canadian population (although several hundred Canadiens did enlist in an American regiment recruited by Moses Hazen), the Americans finally withdrew when British reinforcements arrived in early May. Despite his new military

---

[7] Justin Smith's *Our Struggle for the Fourteenth Colony* (New York, 1907) says it all in the title. Later studies include G.F.G. Stanley, *Canada Invaded 1775–1776* (Toronto, 1973); Robert M. Hatch, *Thrust for Canada: The American Attempt on Quebec in 1775–1776* (Boston, 1979); Allan S. Everest, *Moses Hazen and the Canadian Refugees in the American Revolution* (Syracuse, 1976).

strength, Carleton failed to pursue the retreating Americans, allowing them to escape with their boats. He was replaced soon after as military commander by General John Burgoyne, who would lead the disastrous British invasion south in 1777 that resulted in the surrender of the British army at Saratoga and the entrance of France into the war. But after May 1776, Quebec was free of American troops and remained so for the remainder of the war. The Americans and their French allies projected several new campaigns into Canada, but none ever reached beyond the planning stage. Particularly in the relative absence of direct military threat to Quebec after 1776, Carleton's policy of alliance with the church and the seigneurs had some effect. Bishop Briand's threats of excommunication of habitants who helped the Americans probably had little impact during the actual invasion, but the church's staunch support for the British throughout the war had a cumulative importance.

While the American Congress (and its military advisers) enthusiastically embraced a Canadian invasion in 1775, proposals for similar action against Nova Scotia were rejected as too risky, chiefly because of British naval superiority, but also because there was insufficient evidence that an army would be greeted as liberators. Nevertheless, ambitious residents of the northern district of Massachusetts (now Maine) decided to act without government assistance. The small American force, led by Colonel Jonathan Eddy, focused on Fort Cumberland on the Chignecto Peninsula connecting modern Nova Scotia with New Brunswick, chiefly because it was expected that many residents would support the invaders. The resulting action in November 1776 was more a raid than an invasion, and it was both a disaster and a fiasco from the American perspective. Nova Scotians proved more loyal than anyone expected, and Eddy's motley "army" and a handful of Nova Scotia sympathizers escaped back into the United States after an unsuccessful siege of Fort Cumberland. Although the Americans would turn to guerilla raids along the St. John Valley for the remainder of the war, the province was never again actually threatened with invasion.

PRIVATEERS AND GUERILLAS

If full-scale invasion was not characteristic of the experience of most of the inhabitants of the northernmost colonies, privateering and guerilla activity kept the war constantly in everyone's minds. The Americans may have lacked a navy, but they had hundreds of small vessels in New England that could be and were granted permission by the authorities to operate as legalized pirates in coastal waters. The privateers captured British vessels at sea and treated both vessel and cargo as prizes of war. Small coasting vessels had difficulty defending themselves against other vessels often no larger but fitted out and manned entirely for aggressive purposes. The privateers often responded angrily when they could not find victims at sea and took out their frustrations on coastal communities, looting, pillaging, and occasionally taking prisoners. Few communities in the Atlantic region escaped unscathed, particularly in the early years of the war when the British naval force was inadequate to the task of coastal defence. All communities were forced to look to their own protection by organizing local militia companies, and the threat of the looting privateer forced many a native Yankee to choose a side. In the later years of the war, Nova Scotia coastal villages mounted their own privateers under the protection of the British navy, with considerable success.

Since most of the population of the northernmost colonies lived on the seacoast, along a navigable river, or relatively close to an ill-defined American border, the privateer and his land-based equivalent, the guerilla raider, were constant reminders of the omnipresence of war. Both the British and the Americans recruited and employed irregular troops for lightning raids across the borders. These troops were frequently accompanied by Indian parties, and the fighting that ensued was typically fierce and bloody. The St. John Valley in what would become New Brunswick was one constant battleground, and the Upper Mohawk Valley another. By its very nature, guerilla activity bore little relationship to larger strategic objectives and often involved essentially personal vendettas between former friends and neighbours.

THE INTERRUPTION OF COMMERCE

The American use of privateers turned the shipping lanes of the Atlantic region into a battleground that greatly disrupted commercial activity. Small coasting and fishing vessels were at constant risk, but even more exposed were larger merchant vessels of greater value to the privateer. The early years of the war were particularly difficult. No merchant wanted to venture into the unknown, and shortages of food and supplies were common occurrences, particularly in communities without access to agricultural surplus. Although every area had its shortages, no region suffered more from commercial interruption than Newfoundland.

For the Newfoundland fishery, the years of the war were in many ways disastrous. Banking vessels were at particular risk from privateers, and the catch of the offshore fishery dropped tenfold between 1775 and 1781. The inshore resident fishery fell off less precipitously, but the resident population was exposed to another problem by the onset of war. The American colonies had supplied the bulk of the foodstuffs—bread, flour, livestock—for the Newfoundland fishery in the years before the war, since fishermen had neither time nor the land to grow their own food supplies. American goods were cheaper than those imported from elsewhere, and by 1774 at least 170 American vessels entered the ports of Newfoundland, most carrying food and taking away fish for the West Indies. The American supplies quickly dried up with the onset of war, and by 1776 only three American vessels landed at Newfoundland ports. Privateers helped prevent supplies from elsewhere arriving. The years 1775 and 1776 in particular saw much starvation and malnutrition, although famine continued to be common in isolated outports throughout the war. Newfoundland was forced to turn to British sources and to its neighbouring colonies—especially the Island of Saint John and Quebec—for food, and the amount of land under cultivation on the island increased substantially between 1775 and 1781. Even when food was available, however, prices greatly increased. Since only St. John's was adequately protected against privateers, because of a naval presence that injected money into the local economy, many resident outporters moved there during the hostilities, where they increased the ranks of the restive unemployed.

Similar patterns could be observed elsewhere in the Atlantic region. Many isolated outports and settlements were abandoned and the population flocked to the larger communities, especially those like Halifax and Charlottetown where military expenditures provided the major economic activity. Among the ranks of the unemployed, military recruiters had a field day, and a number of residents of all the northernmost colonies ended up in British and provincial regiments. Both Halifax and Charlottetown flourished during the later years of the war, but they did so at the expense of the backcountry settlements, which also experienced the emigration of American settlers who had decided to return to the United States. Not only did war and commercial interruption depopulate many tenuous settlements only recently established in backcountry Nova Scotia and the Island of Saint John as well as much of outport Newfoundland, but they brought to a virtual halt any new infusions of immigration from Europe to all these colonies. Nova Scotia did make some population gains from refugee American loyalists, again mainly in Halifax, but during the wartime years total population actually declined in each of the three Atlantic colonies.

An inflationary increase in the price of food and the threat of food shortages were consequences of the war common to all the loyal colonies, including Quebec. Inflation and shortages were caused partly by disruption, partly by the increasing demands of a constantly expanding British military presence in the colonies. Soldiers and sailors had to be provisioned, and transatlantic logistics made it impossible to supply the British forces entirely from the mother country. Colonial governments attempted to deal with these problems by internal regulations, usually without much success. In Quebec, Governor Frederick Haldimand, who had replaced Carleton in 1778, actually suggested in 1779 that habitants be forced to sell grain at prices fixed by the government. Quebec routinely forbad the export of grain over the winter months, and the Island of Saint John on several occasions prohibited any export of foodstuffs from its jurisdiction.

Civil War and the Question of Loyalty

THE AMERICAN REBELLION AS A CIVIL WAR

Canadian historians have traditionally accepted the terminology of their American counterparts with regard to the war that disrupted Britain's North American Empire. The use of the label "the American Revolution" provides considerable difficulty from the standpoint of the Canadian experience, however, and has been deliberately avoided in this chapter. It suggests that revolution—a term that implies not only rebellion against existing political authority, but also profound alterations in social, economic, and cultural spheres—was the prevailing norm of the time. The northernmost colonies neither rebelled nor made a revolution, and one of the results is that Canadian historiography has spent a good deal of energy attempting to explain why not, often with implicit or explicit criticism of those in Quebec and the Atlantic colonies who did not respond favourably to the American call to action. If we assume that the American experience is the overriding one, Canadian inaction and failure are what require explanation.[8]

---

[8] See, for example, George Rawlyk, ed., *Revolution Rejected, 1775–1776* (Toronto, 1968), or W. B. Kerr, *The Maritime Provinces of British North America and the American Revolution* (Sackville, 1941).

Whatever the nature of the American response to Great Britain—and not all American historians are persuaded that it was truly "revolutionary"—it is clear that what transpired was a great imperial and North American civil war where sides had to be chosen and that resulted in the loss of Britain's North American Empire. From the Canadian vantage point, the label "The North American Civil War" rather than "The American Revolution" has considerable advantages. It suggests a deep internal division of opinion rather than a necessarily forward movement, for example. It also enables Canadian historians to ask slightly different questions and perhaps get slightly different answers. Instead of having to ask why Canadians failed to join the Americans, the question can be rephrased in terms of the choices Canadians did make. Americans typically reserve the phrase "Civil War" for their great internal upheaval of the mid-nineteenth century, but there is no reason why Canadians need be bound by such considerations. For the northernmost colonies, the issues were not those of revolution but choices of loyalties within an established imperial framework never seriously internally challenged or interrupted.

That the imperial rupture was a civil war is indisputable. It produced more refugees and exiles per capita than the French Revolution, the Russian Revolution of 1917, or the Cuban Revolution of 1957. Many of the leading political and military leaders on both sides were former friends and colleagues, often having shared experiences in earlier conflict with the French. Thus Guy Carleton himself sadly buried General Richard Montgomery, whom he regarded as, however infatuated with a spirit of rebellion, "a genteel man and an agreeable companion." Many of the American settlers and merchants who had come to the northern colonies after the military defeat of the French had relatives in the United States, as the inhabitants of Yarmouth, Nova Scotia, so poignantly observed in a petition to the provincial authorities late in 1775: "We were almost all of us born in New England, we have Fathers, Brothers & Sisters in that Country, [and we are] divided betwixt natural affection to our nearest relations, and good Faith and Friendship to our King and Country." The new settlers themselves often took different sides. Moses Hazen, who had come to Quebec after the Seven Years' War, eventually served in the American army and even attempted to enlist a Canadian regiment for its service. His brother William had settled in the lower St. John Valley in what is now New Brunswick and remained loyal throughout the conflict, ultimately becoming a member of the executive council of New Brunswick. In the American states themselves, the war against Britain divided families, and when Loyalist refugees came to the loyal colonies and enlisted in military service—as they often did—they ended up fighting against friends and kin.

THE QUESTION OF LOYALTY

No group of people suffered more from the demands that civil war made upon their loyalty than the Six Nations of the Iroquois Confederacy. Located as they were in upper New York, squarely in the middle of any invasion routes from north or south, the Indians inhabited some of the most coveted land on the continent. Famed warriors, the Iroquois were traditional allies of the British, and the Americans would have been content with their neutrality. From the Iroquois point of view, the most important issue was the continued maintenance of their lands and sovereignty from European encroachment. The confederacy was badly divided over whether its interests were best served by a treaty of neutrality which the Continental Congress agreed to in 1776, or by renewed support of the British, who promised to deal fairly with the Indians when the rebellion had been settled. Joseph Brant of the Mohawks led the loyalist contingent, joined by the Senecas and some of the Onondagas, into active military combat in 1777. The ancient Confederacy of the Six Nations was torn apart at the battle of Oriskany in the summer of 1777, in which Brant and his warriors participated, and would never be restored in the same form. With some of the Iroquois active participants in the warfare between loyalist guerillas operating out of Quebec and American forces, the Continental Congress authorized a major military expedition against the Iroquois in 1779. The American army marched through Indian country in a ruthless war of extermination fully supported by military leaders like George Washington, burning and destroying farms and houses as they went. Many of the soldiers were amazed at the prosperity of the Iroquois, who had long been horticulturalists and had adopted many European institutions, including Christianity.[9]

The destruction of Iroquois territory forced loyalist Indians north into Quebec, where they gathered around Fort Niagara. It also produced a spirit of revenge, and the loyal Indians were more prominent in British guerilla activity in 1780 and 1781. In the end, the British did not honour their promises and allowed Iroquois land in New York to be included in

---

[9] On the Indians, see Barbara Graymount, *The Iroquois in the American Revolution* (Syracuse, 1973).

the cessions of land to the United States at the peace treaty that concluded the American War. The Six Nations tribal council insisted in 1783 "that the Indians were a free People Subject to no Power upon Earth, that they were the faithful Allies of the King of England but not his Subjects—that he had no right Whatever to grant away to the States of America, their Rights or properties without a manifest breach of all justice and Equity," and Joseph Brant declared that the King had "sold the Indians to Congress." The British administrators in Quebec felt sufficiently guilty to offer in 1784 new land in the Grand Valley (near present-day Brantford, Ontario) to their Mohawk allies, having hastily obtained it by purchase from the local Mississaugas. Those Iroquois who remained in the United States were informed at Fort Stanwix in 1784 that they were "a subdued people" rather than a free nation, and while the pro-American Oneida and Tuscaroras were able to retain the lands they inhabited, they were required to sign away all other Iroquois claims. The Americans moved quickly after 1784 to acquire much of what remained of Iroquois land in New York.

Attempts to remain neutral did not work any better for other inhabitants of British North America than for the Iroquois Confederacy. Both sides in the civil war sought commitment, and the course of events sooner or later required it. But we do need to remember that unless one began the war as either an enthusiastic rebel or loyalist, noncommitment and neutrality were the natural response to the confusion of the situation. Thus there was nothing distinctive about the response of the inhabitants of Quebec and Nova Scotia in attempting to stand to one side. A large proportion of the population within the United States, including most eventual Loyalists, adopted a similar position. We must also keep in mind that as the war progressed, more and more people had to make a choice. The Canadiens faced that decision in the course of the American invasion of 1775–76, and while some joined the American army, most ended up supporting the British tacitly or openly. In Nova Scotia, similar early efforts at neutrality were replaced by support, however sullen in some cases, for the British authorities, who rejected declarations of neutrality as "being utterly Absurd and Inconsistent, with the duty of Subjects."

The situation in Nova Scotia was complicated by the emergence of a potential counterdevelopment to the American war, a movement of religious revivalism usually called "The Great Awakening." Begun by a young ex–New Englander named Henry Alline, who symbolically wrestled with the question of whether he had a call to public preaching during the confused early period of warfare in 1775 and 1776, the Awakening may well have helped resolve an identity crisis for many New England settlers.

To turn to religion for meaning and coherence in a time of personal confusion and bewilderment is, of course, as natural a human reaction as to seek "neutrality." The religious experience preached in Nova Scotia by Alline and others emphasized an individualistic pietism that could be separated from community affairs, desirable qualities in the divided and atomized state that characterized Nova Scotia in the early years of the war. Some historians have seen the religious revival helping to transform traditional American values into ones more appropriate to a Nova Scotia cut off from the United States. Nova Scotians, in this sense, retreated less to revivalism than employed it as a dynamic factor to remake their world. Certainly the end product was a home-grown religion that satisfied many in the Maritime region for decades to come.

The West in the Years of North American Civil War

Developments to the west of the Great Lakes help remind us that not everything that happens can be fit neatly in the chronological compartments of national or international significance. The fur trade had a dynamic of its own, often not seriously affected by external factors. The Montreal-based fur traders continued to expand their activities throughout the 1770s and 1780s, perhaps further energized by the arrival of a number of Americans (possibly loyalist in intention) who moved into the Hudson Bay drainage basin after 1775, such as Peter Pond. If the spread of the fur traders west of the Great Lakes had a life of its own, so too did events on the Pacific Slope. The Montreal-based fur traders and even the Hudson's Bay Company ones were inexorably moving west, each heading toward a route into the Pacific Ocean. The Hudson's Bay Company concentrated on searching for a northwest passage from the bay into the Pacific, sending Samuel Hearne on several journeys of exploration between 1769 and 1773. Hearne ended up demonstrating that the Coppermine River was not that passage. The Montreal traders were more concerned with virgin trading territory than exploration, but they too were on the verge of sensing that their westward penetration was bringing them within travelling distance of the "western ocean."[10]

---

[10] For the Pacific thrust, see G. Williams, *The British Search For the Northwest Passage in the Eighteenth Century* (Toronto, 1962); J. C. Beaglehole, *The Life of Captain James Cook* (London, 1974); Robin Fisher, *Contact and Conflict: Indian-European Relations in British Columbia, 1774–1890* (Vancouver, 1977).

Meanwhile, while interior fur traders pressed westward, Captain James Cook landed on Vancouver Island in 1778 as part of a major scientific expedition to search for the fabled northwest passage from the Pacific side of the continent. Like many of his contemporaries caught up in the American war, Cook had seen service in North America during the Seven Years' War and had made his reputation charting the coastline of Newfoundland. He made two circumnavigations of the globe in the early 1770s, lifting many of the rumours and myths that surrounded the South Pacific. In 1774, word of Samuel Hearne's journey to the Coppermine River reached London. Hearne had sighted the Arctic coast while demonstrating the absence of a strait connecting the bay and the Pacific. His findings and a recently published Russian map suggested that Alaska was an island, with a southern strait that might be approached from the Pacific. Cook was almost immediately dispatched to search for such a passage, departing England in July 1776 and arriving in North America by sailing east around the Cape of Good Hope and via New Zealand and the Sandwich Islands (Hawaii). He was ordered to begin his search at latitude 65°N, but was forced to put in for repairs in late March 1778 in Nootka Sound. Cook's ships spent nearly a month at Nootka and were impressed with the trading skills of the local Indians and with their furs, taken mainly from the sea otter.

Cook then sailed far enough north to round the Alaskan peninsula and discover a wall of impenetrable ice. Turning back, he headed toward the Sandwich Islands, where he was killed in early 1779. His ships headed back to England, and the official account of his voyage was published there in 1784. The outline of the shape of the northwest coast of America was now to become well known to Europeans, although the immediate importance of Cook's voyage was its publicity for the commercial possibilities of the region, particularly since the sea otter pelts collected at Nootka proved to be worth large sums on the Chinese market. A number of seaborne fur traders fitted out—in India, in China, in Europe, in New England—and rushed to make their fortunes by exploiting the trade that Cook had identified. Cook himself had seen little value in the region beyond the fur trade, but the new activity attracted European imperial interest, and Spain and Britain would very nearly go to war in 1790 over their competing interests (the "Nootka Crisis"). Britain sent Captain George Vancouver to complete Cook's surveys and deal with Spain in 1791. The result was cooperation between Vancouver and the Spanish officer Juan Bodega de Quadra. Since the Spanish had been independently charting the Northwest coast for a generation, this alliance greatly improved British knowledge of its waters. As for the Indians of the region, they were rapidly inundated by European traders who had little interest in anything other than making a quick killing in furs.

The Coming of the Loyalists

From the onset of hostilities between Britain and its American colonies, some Americans who opposed their countrymen had chosen or were forced to go into exile. Originally known as "Tories," the supporters of the Crown soon acquired the more attractive label of "Loyalists," and this one has stuck with them over the centuries. In the early years of conflict, most Americans who fled the United States for political reasons were members of the elite, often officeholders who had supported the British, but in any case sufficiently prominent to be singled out by the rebels for harassment and proscription. Most of these early exiles went to Britain, but there was a constant trickle into Halifax and Nova Scotia. Later in the war, as the British finally encouraged supporters to organize militarily and attempted to find popular backing within the American population, larger numbers of people were branded with the Loyalist mark. Perhaps as many as half a million Americans of European origin (20 percent of the European population) supported the British cause. The British had also encouraged both free and slave blacks to oppose the Americans and, as we have seen, forced the Indians along the frontiers to choose sides as well.[11]

The British lost the military struggle in 1781 when Lord Cornwallis surrendered at Yorktown. They turned to extricating themselves from a lost cause at minimal cost by negotiating a peace treaty with the United States. In the process, they sacrificed most of their commitments to their American supporters. While negotiations dragged on in Europe, Loyalist

---

[11] Some overview of the Loyalists is provided by J. M. Bumsted, *Understanding the Loyalists* (Sackville, 1986). See also L.F.S. Upton, ed., *The United Empire Loyalists: Men and Myths* (Toronto, 1967); E. C. Wright, *The Loyalists of New Brunswick* (Fredericton, 1955); David Bell, *Early Loyalist Saint John: The Origin of New Brunswick Politics 1783–1786* (Fredericton, 1983); Ann G. Condon, *The Envy of the American States: the Loyalist Dream for New Brunswick* (Fredericton, 1984); James Walker, *The Black Loyalists* (Halifax, 1976); Neil MacKinnon, *This Unfriendly Soil: The Loyalist Experience in Nova Scotia, 1783–91* (Montreal and Kingston, 1986); Larry Turner, *Voyage of a Different Kind: The Associated Loyalists of Kingston and Adolphustown* (Belleville, Ont., 1984).

refugees and soldiers were drawn to New York, the major centre of British authority and military power on the eastern seaboard, already the wartime home of thousands of pro-British. The Loyalists waited anxiously for word about the outcome of the peace negotiations and ultimate treatment for those who had supported the mother country. In the meantime, agents fanned out across Britain's remaining American empire, from Nova Scotia to Quebec to the Caribbean to Florida, investigating land and political conditions in the event of the worst.

By the autumn of 1782 it had become fairly clear that the Americans were not likely to forgive and forget—or that the British would hold firm to their friends—and Sir Guy Carleton (who had been transferred from Quebec to New York earlier in the war) began arranging for the movement of large bodies of Loyalists to Nova Scotia. There Governor John Parr had been warned to reserve as much land as possible for their arrival. Providing land for thousands of newcomers was no easy matter, since much of the land in Nova Scotia had been granted to absentee proprietors and would have to be legally returned to the Crown. The Island of Saint John, Cape Breton, and Newfoundland had no land readily available and were not destinations for the primary migrations of 1782 and 1783.

On 22 September 1782, Carleton sketched out a policy for Loyalist relocation, emphasizing that land grants were to be "considered as well founded Claims of Justice rather than of mere Favor," to be made without fees or quitrents. He expected that families would receive 600 acres (243 ha) of land and single men 300 acres (120 ha) and promised tools from New York stores. Carleton initially had overlooked those soldiers in the various provincial regiments recruited in America to fight the rebels, and this oversight was pointed out to him in a memorial from the regimental officers early in 1783. "The personal animosities that arose from civil dissension," the memorialists maintained, "have been so heightened by the Blood that has been shed in the Contest, that the Parties can never be reconciled." The regiments wanted land grants and assistance parallel to that extended to civilians, and their claims were accepted. At this point Carleton did not know the details of any compensation schemes that the British might work out for the Loyalists. He was concerned mainly with the process of resettlement itself.

Moving and compensating the Loyalists would be an expensive business, representing a major act of public support for colonization, probably the largest ever executed by the British government in its history. The ultimate cost of Loyalist resettlement figured in the millions of pounds and made the earlier expenditures on colonizing Nova Scotia appear puny. Not all of the the colonies in the remaining North American Empire benefited equally from British generosity. Newfoundland received no Loyalists, while Cape Breton and the Island of Saint John (the latter very indirectly) received about 1000 each. About 35 000 arrived in Nova Scotia, and about 10 000 sought refuge in the colony of Quebec. The British prewar policy of insisting that settlement must be self-financing was swept away, and under emergency conditions the loyal colonies of her empire received a publicly subsidized injection of those much-desired English-speaking American colonists. At the same time, it should be emphasized that large numbers of the incoming "Loyalists" were Indians and blacks, and even among those of European origin there was a rich ethnic mixture, especially of former Scots, Irish, and Germans.

The great migration of Loyalist refugees to Nova Scotia took place in 1783, with troop transport ships bringing thousands of newcomers to the region. There were two principal destinations in the spring of 1783: the mouth of the Saint John River and Port Roseway (renamed Shelburne) on the southwest shore of Nova Scotia. Two instant cities sprang up as the transports disgorged their passengers. Shelburne was surrounded by some of the most marginal agricultural land in the region, and its 10 000 people quickly dispersed. But Saint John had a rich agricultural hinterland up the Saint John River where hundreds of newcomers went, and it managed to survive as a centre, although not without growing pains. The city witnessed a fierce struggle between the old Tory elite, attempting to re-establish its authority in the new land, and an equally ambitious Loyalist middle class, mainly artisans and shopkeepers. With the aid of the colonial authorities, the old elite would emerge victorious.

The "spring fleets" brought civilian refugees, but they were joined later in the year by the Loyalist soldiers and their families, as well as by merchants attracted by the promise of good trading connections within the empire. Among the new arrivals were 3000 freed blacks. The disbanded soldiers scattered around the region, some being attracted to the Island of Saint John or Cape Breton. Battalions often stayed together under the leadership of former officers. Civilian refugees also became quickly dissatisfied with their locations (especially around Shelburne) and moved on to the Island of Saint John and Cape Breton, neither of which had really been part of Carleton's earlier plans.

Smaller contingents of Loyalists made their way into Quebec, some 2000 remaining in along the St. Lawrence (Sorel was a noted Loyalist centre) and 7500 journeying into the Mississauga country on the frontier. Concentrations gathered in what is now southeastern Ontario (Glengarry County), at Cataraqui (later Kingston), and in the Niagara peninsula. Many of the Niagara contingent had taken refuge around Fort Niagara in the last days of the guerilla fighting in New York, often those associated with units such as Butler's Rangers. Those at Cataraqui had served in one of three other provincial corps (the King's Royal Regiment, Jessup's Loyal Rangers, and Roger's King's Rangers) based in Quebec and active in the New York fighting. They were joined by several hundred Associated Loyalists who came north from New York City. By late summer of 1784, some 4400 Loyalists and, by 1786, 5800 resided west and southwest of the Ottawa River, mainly in the Bay of Quinte area. Another 1200 were at Niagara and a few hundred near Detroit. These settlers brought about 500 black slaves. In addition, some 1800 Iroquois from northern New York and 300 to 400 Indians from northwestern tribes sought refuge in Quebec.

By 1784, the combination of the American peace and the resettlement of thousands of Loyalists had completely altered British policy for the northernmost colonies. Instead of being marginal jurisdictions, they were now the remaining North American Empire. A first round of imperial reorganization took place in that year. Cape Breton was recognized as a separate colony (although without an assembly), and both it and the Island of Saint John were put under the authority of the governor of Nova Scotia. Continued controversy between Loyalist newcomers and the government of Nova Scotia resulted in the creation of New Brunswick as a separate colony, one that Loyalists could dominate and that could serve as a model of what could be produced by men and women of loyalty and intelligence. Guy Carleton's brother Thomas was appointed lieutenant-governor, and a number of prominent Loyalists leaders were given official positions in the administration. For Newfoundland, still not granted official colonial status, 1784 was nonetheless a critical year, since by agreement between the British government and the Vatican, James O'Donnell arrived as Prefect Apostolic, the first officially recognized Roman Catholic priest on the island.

In economic terms, the British were prepared in 1784 to allow the loyal colonies to replace the Americans in the old transatlantic commercial network. Such imperial preference without American competition would be but a fleeting opportunity that could not be seized. British North America was not sufficiently developed to fill the old American role, especially in the West Indies. Most of its new population was not yet established and consumed any agricultural surplus. Years of bad harvests, especially in Quebec, did not help. Throughout the 1780s, economic vitality came chiefly from the ripple effect of government expenditures on Loyalist resettlement. The British, moreover, quickly discovered that political independence did not make the Americans any less anxious to trade. Commercial connections between the United States and Great Britain were informally established, and the Americans resumed their traditional position as the mother country's most important trading partners.

The Loyalist resettlement created much political turmoil throughout the decade of the 1780s. The new conflicts took a variety of forms, although in general they involved the development of new political factions, often employing American colonial political experience and rhetoric and doing battle with existing oligarchies and with one another. On the Island of Saint John, for example, Governor Walter Patterson had finally resolved the question of quitrent arrearages in 1781 by government seizure of the lots of the delinquent proprietors. The lots were sold at auction, chiefly to Patterson and his officers, at bargain prices. The proprietors insisted that they had not been properly informed of the island actions and fought to get the seizures and sales overturned in London. When Loyalists began arriving on the island late in 1783, they were systematically located on the contested lots. In 1784 local opposition to Patterson produced the first organized political factions in what is now Canada, with each side in the assembly elections of that year running formal slates of candidates. A year later, Patterson had co-opted the Loyalists, who recognized that only by supporting him could they hope to retain their lands. The issues of the contested lots and the Loyalists became inextricably intertwined and were resolved only with great difficulty by Patterson's successor, Loyalist Edmund Fanning.

In Nova Scotia, the Loyalists finally developed that rural-based faction of opposition in the assembly that had been lacking before 1775, although it did not become as well organized as the opposition on the Island of Saint John. Not even New Brunswick, the province intended to be "The Envy of the American States," was free of trouble. The provincial government, located at Fredericton, had intervened in the Saint John struggle between the old Loyalist elite and the new urban middle class on the side of the elite. It managed to allow the elite to emerge triumphant in municipal elections but stirred up the emnity of many ordinary settlers who would find their spokesman in the person of James Glenie of Sunbury County in

1791. In all three colonies (and in Cape Breton as well), the main targets of the opposition were the well-entrenched elite oligarchies and the principal rhetoric was the standard "country party" line developed in England and imported into the American colonies before the American Rebellion. "Country" opposition feared centralization of power and sought to defend traditional liberties and rights against what was regarded as corrupt and self-serving oligarchies sheltering under the power of the colonial governor and his council.

The situation in Quebec was enormously difficult from the perspective of the incoming Loyalists. Although they had suffered much for their support of the Crown, indeed because they had suffered much, they were quite unable to come to terms with a government minus a representative assembly, that quintessential institution of "British Liberty." From the outset, the Loyalists had joined the English merchants of Montreal in demanding political reform. They not only insisted on an elected assembly and the institution of familiar English laws but also wanted local systems of government to replace a central administration located in Quebec. In 1786, Lord Dorchester (formerly Guy Carleton) was dispatched back to North America to deal with the emerging discontent as governor general of all British North America and governor of Quebec. He made concessions of local administration (chiefly judicial and under English law) to the western Loyalists in 1788 and 1789, but these were not sufficient to stem the complaints.

Loyalist demands and British policy came together in 1791 with the passage of the Constitutional Act of 1791. The British had long maintained that elected assemblies were an essential part of a proper colonial constitution. The absence of such an institution in Quebec was always regarded with some guilt by many British leaders, especially since after 1778 the British Parliament (attempting belatedly to satisfy earlier American criticisms) had agreed that Britain had no right to tax colonies without their consent, something that could be given only through local assemblies. The major question was not whether there would be an assembly for Quebec, but rather how many assemblies would be granted. Montreal merchants wanted a single assembly, while up-country Loyalists wanted two. In the end, the British decided on the partition of Quebec into Upper and Lower Canada, chiefly on the grounds that the up-country people needed to be separated from the dominant French-Canadian population on the St. Lawrence. Neither colony was to receive a particularly democratic government in 1791, however. Governors and appointed councils were given strong executive powers and control over colonial patronage. The 1791 legislation provided for the creation of Canadian peers with a hereditary right to attendance at the legislative councils, and Upper Canada was to have a strong established Anglican Church. The creation of elected assemblies in the Canadas was not intended, any more than in the Maritimes, to do more than allow the electorate or those they chose a minimal share in governments, which were still intended to be dominated by the central administration. How these new imperial arrangements would work out in practice had still to be determined.

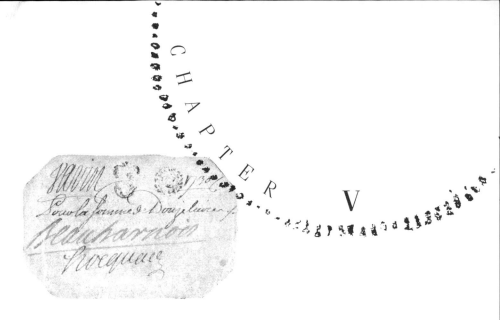

THE ORIGINS OF
COLONIAL SOCIETY AND
CULTURE

At the end of the eighteenth century, the colonies of British North America were populated by a heterogeneous collection of people with little in common culturally or historically. Many of them were recent arrivals still attempting to establish themselves. While the official mythology of Canada speaks of two "founding peoples"—the British and the French—such a modern conceptualization disguises more than it reveals from the historical standpoint. The notion of two founding peoples is one that has been with us since before the creation of the Dominion of Canada in 1867. It has most often been associated with a theory of compact or contract among the parties to Confederation, which has served as a principal constitutional interpretation of Canadian union. In the 1960s, as Quebec's francophone population became increasingly restive within Confederation, the federal government attempted to head off Quebec separatism by an official policy of bilingualism and biculturalism. A royal commission was created to provide intellectual respectability for the new federal initiative, and a number of Canadian scholars became associated with the commission, its findings, and its recommendations. The concept of biculturalism may have made enormously good sense politically, but it could only with great difficulty be derived from a reading of the historical development of Canada. A textbook in Canadian colonial history is not the place to second-guess Canada's official policies, but it is

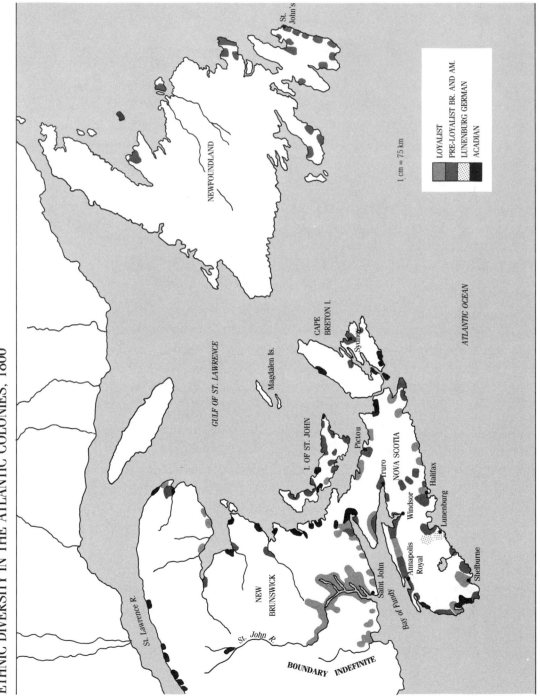

ETHNIC DIVERSITY IN THE ATLANTIC COLONIES, 1800

LEGEND:
LOYALIST
PRE-LOYALIST BR. AND AM.
LUNENBURG GERMAN
ACADIAN

1 cm = 75 km

NEWFOUNDLAND

St. John's

GULF OF ST. LAWRENCE

Magdalen Is.

CAPE BRETON I.

Sydney

ATLANTIC OCEAN

I. OF ST. JOHN

Pictou

St. Lawrence R.

NEW BRUNSWICK

St. John R.

Saint John

Bay of Fundy

BOUNDARY   INDEFINITE

Truro

NOVA SCOTIA

Windsor

Annapolis Royal

Halifax

Lunenburg

Shelburne

certainly the place to affirm loudly and clearly that the concept of two founding peoples—fundamental to bilingualism and biculturalism—was and is a grave distortion of the historical record.[1]

Neither the British nor the French were ever completely homogeneous peoples, and to emphasize these two groups as "founders" is to simplify Canadian historical development by selectively ignoring others: Indians, mixed bloods, and Afro-Americans. The simple fact of the matter is that the colonies of British North America were inhabited by a complex racial and cultural combination of peoples distinguished from one another by language, religion, lifestyles—and attitudes. This mixture had not congealed by the end of the eighteenth century, at least outside the boundaries of Quebec (or Lower Canada, as it was known after 1791). If the eighteenth-century record will not support any theory of two original peoples, what founding characteristics can be derived from it? At least three long-standing social tendencies had melded by the end of the eighteenth century. One of those tendencies was that Canadian society was profoundly racist. Another was that it was equally profoundly sexist. The final was that it was singularly diverse. It is, therefore, to racism, sexism, and diversity that we must now turn.

The Problem of Racism

In 1975, the American historian Francis Jennings wrote:

European explorers and invaders discovered an inhabited land. Had it been pristine wilderness then, it would possibly be so still today, for neither the technology nor the social organization of Europe in the sixteenth and seventeenth centuries had the capacity to maintain, of its own resources, outpost colonies thousands of miles from home. Incapable of conquering true wilderness, the Europeans were highly competent in the skill of conquering other people, and that is what they did. They did not settle a virgin land. They invaded and displaced a resident population. This is so simple a fact that it seems self-evident. All historians of the European colonies in America begin by describing the

---

[1] *Report of the Royal Commission on Bilingualism and Biculturalism*, 5 books (Ottawa, 1967), especially Book 1, *Official Languages*, and Book 5, *Other Ethnic Groups*.

natives' reception of the newcomers. Yet, paradoxically, most of the same historians also repeat identical mythical phrases purporting that the land-starved people of Europe had found magnificent opportunity to pioneer in a savage wilderness and to bring civilization to it.

As Jennings went on to point out, generations of Americans had suppressed facts and created a mythology to cover up treatment of native peoples. Some of the same suppression and mythologizing occurred in Canada, of course. They were clearly in evidence in the report of the Royal Commission on Bilingualism and Biculturalism, which systematically ignored the native peoples on the grounds that their situation was not part of the commission's political mandate. But a systematic schizophrenia about Canada's aboriginal population—they were there first but their presence somehow did not count—had characterized Canadian history for centuries. While French and English may have differed in the particulars of their response to the native peoples, in an ultimate sense they behaved identically, dispossessing those peoples of their land in the name of progress whenever there occurred a conflict between European settlement and native occupation/ownership. The First Nations may have received better treatment in what became Canada because more of the land was not required for settlement for a much longer period, but both French and English dispossessed whenever necessary. What was striking about the English, however, was their relative lack of ambiguity from the beginning about the inferiority of the "savage" state of the aboriginal. Until the nineteenth century, and probably then under English influence, the French alternated between notions of noble primitivism and barbarity in the connotations of the term "sauvage." Such an alternation characterized overall French perceptions of the native peoples. For the English, particularly settlers, the word "savage" unequivocally meant bestial and barbaric and translated informally into "the only good Indian is a dead Indian." English policy toward native peoples was from the beginning characterized by hostility and violence, which soon became the dominant feature of relations between the races in areas of English intrusion.[2]

Racism refers to unequal treatment of some peoples because they are regarded as not only different but as inferior. Racism can be enacted by

---

[2] For overviews of Canadian Indian policy (as opposed to the history of the native peoples), see E. Palmer Patterson, *The Canadian Indian: A History since 1500* (Toronto, 1972), and J. R. Miller, *Skyscrapers Hide the Heavens: A History of Indian-White Relations in Canada* (Toronto, 1989). There is no good general history of Canada's First Nations.

individuals in particular or by the institutions of society in general. The basis of racism is often but not always skin colour. In the case of the aboriginal peoples of Canada, their colour was probably less important than their social characteristics, which permitted the European intruder to see them as "savage barbarians," and their presence, which made it necessary for Europeans to displace them somehow, a process made more palatable by ethnocentric European assumptions of superiority. Social superiority was not only essential to conquest but also to settlement, for the newcomers came mainly from the bottom end of a hierarchically graded society and needed "inferior" populations to demonstrate their own advance in status. The entire vocabulary of European intrusion was based on ethnocentrism, particularly in English-speaking areas. North America was "settled" by Europeans, a concept that implies that aboriginal peoples had not already settled it. Indians were "converted" to Christianity while Europeans captured by them were "brutalized" into accepting native ways.

European policy toward native peoples in North America was not always based directly upon violence, but in the eighteenth century, it was seldom guided in the so-called "settlements" by assumptions of absolute equality between native and intruder. At least the facade of equality was maintained in the western fur-trading country, partly because the native inhabitants were economically essential, partly because the European intruder had not achieved a power supremacy in the region. Nor was violence always advocated by imperial authorities or central governments in settlement regions, where it was no longer perceived to be necessary. But those authorities and governments were prepared to make military alliances with Indians when these proved useful and to invoke complaints against policies of violence. Ironically, one of the principal charges against George III in the American Declaration of Independence was that he "has excited domestic insurrections among us, and has endeavoured to bring on the inhabitants of our frontiers, the merciless Indian Savages, whose known rule of warfare is an indistinguished destruction of all ages, sexes, and conditions."

Insofar as the imperial authorities had an Indian policy after 1763—and in particular circumstances they often had none except expediency—it was to isolate and separate native peoples from Europeans by negotiating the extinction of Indian territorial rights and removing Indians farther west or to unwanted land. Locating Micmacs in Nova Scotia on relatively small tracts of land was not in a policy sense much different from the Proclamation of 1763, which declared "that the several Nations or Tribes of Indians with whom We are connected, and who live under our Protection, should not be molested or disturbed in the Possession of such Parts of Our Dominions and Territories as...are reserved to them, or any of them, as their Hunting Grounds," adding any lands not "ceded to or purchased by Us as aforesaid, are reserved to the said Indians." The proclamation also suggested the principle that the government had a monopoly over land negotiations with the Indians. It insisted that "no private Person" could purchase land previously "reserved" to Indians. Such purchases could be made only at public meetings called "by the Governor or Commander in Chief of our Colony." The proclamation thus sought to prevent private land deals between speculators and unrepresentative Indians, but it also could be interpreted as indicating that from its perspective land was reserved to Indians only until the Europeans had need of it, at which point the state could renegotiate the arrangement. Whatever the proclamation meant to say in terms of Indian land—and it is subject to many different readings, including that of promising strong safeguards for native territory—it was not an agreement negotiated with the First Nations but a policy pronouncement issued unilaterally by one party.

The proclamation enunciated an imperial policy that would rapidly be swept away in the military needs of the American Rebellion, but that would be restored after the emergency, when the need for land by the British was greater and the need for military alliance with the Indian was greatly reduced. Not all inhabitants or all governments accepted such a policy. The British returned to purchasing land from Indians in the West for lump-sum payments before 1818 and for annual annuities after that time. In the eastern region of the Maritimes, existing Indian reserves were simply overrun by settlers without intervention by the Colonial authorities. In 1830 the British government shifted jurisdiction over Indians from the military to the civil authorities, explaining that the policy was now the "settled purpose of gradually reclaiming them from a state of barbarism, and of introducing amongst them the industrious and peaceful habits of civilized life." Isolation on reserves was now replaced by gradual assimilation into white society, by coercive bureaucratic means if necessary. Such shifts in policy, of course, merely continued rather than eliminated racism.

The Problem of Sexism

Like racism, sexism had its origins in the earliest development of humankind. It gradually developed into both a set of attitudes and, in the case of peoples who wrote down and codified their laws, legislative and judicial disabilities. Europe did not invent discrimination against women on the basis of their sex, for some native peoples had similar practices, although there was little uniformity of gender relations among the First Nations. When Europe transplanted itself to North America, it brought its attitudes and its laws along. What was striking about the European colonization experience in the relatively liberating North American environment of land availability and upward social mobility was not only that it was based on the illicit seizure of land from native peoples, but that it produced minimal movement toward a re-evaluation of traditional differences between men and women. Some scholars have even argued the similarity between the treatment of the First Nations and the treatment of women, beginning in the seventeenth century.[3]

While the process of colonization was not itself an inherently masculine business, historical writing about that process was long dominated by male assumptions and categories. If history concentrates on what are almost exclusively male preserves of the past—politics, government, war, public commerce—and the chronology that surrounds them, it will inevitably overlook women, whose preserves were not in the public arena but in the private one of home and family. As the bearers and rearers of children, as well as through their other labour, women were crucial to the European colonization process. Only in recent years, however, have historians begun asking questions about the nonpublic sphere and exploring the place of women in earlier societies in a serious way.

A combination of legal limitations and informal restrictions controlled the position of women in colonial society. European legal concepts distinguished between males and females, but particularly between males and females in marriage. Both French and English law regarded husbands as heads of the household and the dominant partner, although French law in the *Coutume de Paris* provided more protection to women, particularly in terms of property, than did the English common law. Under the *Coutume de Paris*, marriage property was held jointly although managed by the husband; to prevent abuse many couples signed written contracts spelling out property rights within the marriage. Under English common law, a married woman lost not only her property rights but most of her personal

---

[3] On women, see Alison Prentice et al., *Canadian Women: A History* (Toronto, 1988). On women and natives, see Karen Anderson, *Chain Her By One Foot: The Subjugation of Women in Seventeenth-Century New France* (Toronto, 1990).

rights, becoming a "femme couverte," under almost total control by her husband; far fewer such women signed formal marriage contracts. The liberation of women in Canada from the masculine patriarchy of the English common law would occur only gradually over much of the nineteenth century. French law as practised in New France probably allowed considerably more freedom to women, particularly unmarried ones, than would be the case after 1763.

The experience of women in the colonial societies of British North America was a distinctly mixed and complex one. On the one hand, the socio-economic-legal fluidity of the New World allowed women more opportunity for independent action than was the case in Europe. On the other hand, the value of women as childbearers and economic partners encouraged marriage, which distinctly constrained female freedom of action both legally and practically. Moreover, opportunities for female autonomy generally greatly increased as one moved up the social scale, where women were better educated and had more property of their own. Most of the overt movement for further autonomy would come from the upper- and middle-class women of Canadian society, and neither of these classes was well formed outside Quebec before the nineteenth century. Finally, in the political culture that developed in British North America after 1763, women were fairly rigorously excluded by both law and custom, with few exceptions allowed neither to vote nor to hold public office.

Historians of Canadian women have found increasing numbers of examples of autonomous women in operation in the colonial period, demonstrating that opportunity did exist and that the neglect of women by previous generations of historians was scarcely justified. But for the majority of women in the formative era, life was lived in the private world of household and family. It consisted of hard work in the home (and often in the fields or gardens as well), complicated by the dangers of childbearing in an age before the existence of germs was understood. The lives of such women are clearly recoverable through careful and extensive research, but they are not often connected to the larger events that constitute "history" for most Canadians.

We do know something about the experiences of Loyalist women in the American Rebellion, thanks chiefly to the process by which claims for compensation were presented to the British government after the war. Of the 3225 claims that were made, 468 (or 14.5 percent) came from refugee women. By definition these were women without spouses, since the husband would have filed the claim had he existed. Such women came from all sections of North American society. What was most striking about their claims was their general inability to offer any precision about their family's economic situation, reflecting the control over property and finances exercised by husbands. Women could be most precise about their own property brought into marriage, and generally had much descriptive knowledge about that on which they lived, but were often woefully ignorant about their family's larger economic contexts. Some women were left with management of estates and businesses while their husbands and brothers were away fighting, but by and large, women's place was in the home, and husbands did not share information on family finances with their wives.

Many women claimants who had lost husbands perceived themselves as "helpless"—the word was repeated continually in the written claims— although they had often behaved with great independence and bravery in surviving the turmoil. But they were now without a "Husband and Protector." One woman in Nova Scotia argued that she had missed the deadline for claim submission because of "being a lone Woman in her Husband's Absence and not having any person to Advise with." Almost all the claimants fully recognized both their own femininity and the limitations that entailed, and many argued that they would have done more had they been males. "Had she been a man," wrote one petitioner, "instead of a poor helpless woman—should not have failed of being in the British Service." A second striking feature about female Loyalist claimants was how much worse they fared than their male counterparts. Partly this was because they had imprecise information about their losses, but it was mostly because they were women being dealt with by men. The all-male Commission on Loyalist Claims apparently believed that women's expenses were less, and it failed to take into account either the fact that women had difficulty in performing public acts of loyalty (which could be particularly rewarded) or that they could often not easily obtain employment to provide for their own maintenance.

Legal and practical inequality between the sexes, as well as laws that at least in theory worked special hardship on women's lives, such as those governing infanticide and abortion, were well established in colonial British North America before the end of the eighteenth century. They would only become more entrenched in the first half of the nineteenth century, as new British (especially English) legal concepts were introduced, loopholes in the laws were tightened up, and a fresh concept of domesticity spread across the colonies. Thus, following British practice, all abortion was made criminal in the early years of the nineteenth century. An Upper Canadian law of 1837 protected fathers' rights to their daughters against "seduction" by other males, recognizing "the wound given to parental feelings, the disgrace and injury inflicted upon the family of the person seduced." Women were formally barred from political participation, first in Lower Canada, where propertied women had frequently voted after 1791, but then in other colonies. By 1851 women were specifically excluded from the franchise in both Canadas (1849), Nova Scotia (1851), and Prince Edward Island (1836), and by implication and practice from holding office in these provinces. Such actions were thoroughly consonant with the growth of the concept of domesticity, in which home and work were clearly separated and women became custodians of the home (nurturers of the family that resided in it). Women, especially unmarried ones, continued to exercise economic and social autonomy so long as they did not challenge the prevailing norms of society, but those norms and values were plainly male dominated. Formal feminine protest against British North America's sexist structures was isolated and uncoordinated until well into the nineteenth century.

The Problem of Cultural Diversity

BRITISH CULTURE

The official culture (that of government and business) everywhere in British North America after 1763 was English in language and proto-British in imperial institutions, but this fact informs us about very little.[4] The problem was not simply that the bulk of the population in Quebec was French Canadian. An equally profound difficulty revolved around the complexities of English as a language and the concept of "Britishness." Perhaps we can consider the problem of "Britishness" first.[5]

---

[4] On cultural concepts and definitions, consult A. L. Kroeber and Clyde Kluckhorn, *Culture: A Critical Review of Concepts and Definitions* (Cambridge, Mass., 1952) and J. M. Bumsted, "Toward an Understanding of Popular Culture," *Alberta*, 2, number 1 (1990), 1–15.

[5] For a general history based on the principles of analysis of this chapter, see Hugh Kearney, *The British Isles: A History of Four Nations* (Cambridge, 1989). On Wales, consult E. D. Evans, *A History of Wales 1660–1815* (Cardiff, 1976). On Scotland, see T. C. Smout, *A History of the*

The British Isles in the eighteenth century consisted of a number of historically distinct nations that had been more or less incorporated into a larger political entity. England was the largest and most dominant component, and it had for many centuries politically integrated Wales into its governing system. Wales had no separate and distinct body of law, politics, or church establishment. The same could not be said for Scotland and Ireland. Scotland had been a separate kingdom, ruled by the same monarch as England since the early seventeenth century but with its own Parliament, established church (the Church of Scotland), and legal system. In 1707 the Act of Union had consolidated the two Parliaments. But the union was not complete. Scotland retained its own legal system and its own established church. Moreover, even parlimentary consolidation was not total. Only a limited number of the peers of Scotland (18 out of 70-odd) were allowed seats in the House of Lords, and they were chosen by election from among the total body of Scottish peers.

As for Ireland, it was ruled essentially by the United Kingdom of Great Britain as an overseas colony until 1801, with Westminster appointing the officials of the Irish government and retaining a veto power over legislation of the Irish Parliament. For most of the eighteenth century, Catholics could neither vote for members of the Irish Parliament nor hold seats in it, and while Catholic emancipation in 1793 allowed Catholics the vote, they still could not sit in Parliament. Ireland, too, had its own church (the Church of Ireland) and its own legal system, although both were largely controlled from London. Only in 1801 was the Irish Parliament consolidated with the British one, the Act of Union producing the United Kingdom of Great Britain and Ireland. Until 1775, Ireland politically had more in common with the various American colonies, each of which had its own legislative assembly, church establishment, and legal system (based loosely on English common law but with many changes and modifications).

While the established churches of England (including Wales), Ireland,

---

Scottish People, 1560–1830 (New York, 1970). For Ireland, see Nicholas Canny, Kingdom and Colony: Ireland in the Atlantic World, 1560–1800 (Baltimore, 1988). Ulster's origins are considered in Philip S. Robinson, The Plantation of Ulster: British Settlement in an Irish Landscape, 1600–1670 (New York, 1984). For the American colonies, see J. P. Greene, Pursuits of Happiness: The Social Development of Early Modern British Colonies and the Formation of American Culture (Chapel Hill, N.C., 1988). On the English language, see Robert McCrum et al., The Story of English (New York, 1986).

and some of the American colonies were part of the Anglican community, there were many anomolies. Before American independence, the colonial Anglican Church had no bishops, and when the Americans finally acquired some, they were ordained by the Episcopal Church of Scotland, which was not the national church in that country. The established Church of Scotland was not Anglican but rather Presbyterian in organization (without bishops) and Calvinist in theology. The Scottish church was also the prevalent Protestant one in the northern counties of Ireland. Several American colonies, particularly in New England, also had state churches that operated without bishops and with a chiefly Calvinist theological orientation.

In the eighteenth century, none of the four "nations" of the British Isles were in any sense culturally—or even linguistically—homogeneous. All were collections of regions quite distinctive from one another and from which a "national" culture had not yet really emerged. The area around London perhaps came closest to producing the "typical" English person, but it represented less than a quarter of the total population of England and Wales. The West Country counties of Cornwall and Devon, which supplied much of the English population of Newfoundland, were quite different from northern counties like Yorkshire, which provided a substantial immigration to Nova Scotia in the early 1770s. Some of the traditional Cornish language (a Celtic tongue with affinities to Welsh, Erse, Gaelic, and the language of Britanny in France) still survived, and both Cornwall and Devon, as well as Yorkshire, spoke distinctive dialects of English that were virtually incomprehensible to anyone not familiar with them. If England was regionalized, Wales, Ireland, and Scotland were all even more significantly divided, along lines that were simultaneously historic, linguistic, religious, and geographical.

In Wales, the border and southern counties were considerably more assimilated with England than were the north and west coastal regions. In the latter, the Welsh language was still commonly spoken, and was even being rejuvenated as a modern language in the eighteenth century by Welsh nationalists. The "eisteddfod"—the famed musical and poetic competition of Wales—while having its roots in the distant past, became organized and institutionalized only during this period. Welsh speakers were less likely than English speakers in Wales to belong to the Church of England, many of them having become members of dissenting or nonconforming religious denominations that grew with the expansion of the language during the eighteenth century.

Scotland was divided into Lowlands and Highlands. The former spoke an independently developed dialect of English, complete with its own vocabulary and distinctive pronunciation. The Lowland middle and upper classes gradually anglicized their speech during the century—many, like James Boswell, took special elocution classes for the purpose—but the agricultural communities retained the "lallans" Scots dialects of their ancestors. Most Lowlanders were communicants of the Church of Scotland, although there were pockets of Anglicans and Catholics scattered throughout. North and west of the Highland fault, a society and culture quite different from southern Scotland prevailed. Although Highland Scotland was under considerable pressure throughout the eighteenth century to modernize, it was still, especially the farther north or west one went, dominated by clan organization and traditional livestock raising rather than extensive agriculture. The Gaelic language was commonly spoken and was particularly strong in pockets of Roman Catholicism in the western Highlands and Islands.

In Ireland, the situation was singularly complicated. The northern counties, notably Ulster, had been systematically resettled by the English conquerors in the sixteenth and seventeenth centuries. The new population had been recruited partly in England and Wales, but chiefly in the Lowlands of Scotland. These "Scotch-Irish," as they were often called, began moving to the American colonies in the eighteenth century. They were fiercely Protestant of a Presbyterian doctrine. The northern counties also contained a substantial Irish population, usually Roman Catholic in religion and far more traditionally oriented than the later settlers. In the south of Ireland, a small number of Anglo-Irish landlords (descendants of the Elizabethan conquerors) ran the country throughout the eighteenth century as the only politically recognized inhabitants. The bulk of the southern Irish population remained Roman Catholic in religion and traditionally peasant in outlook, farming on plots of land decreasing in size, since official policy was to transfer land into Anglo-Irish hands. There were at least three "Irish" populations, therefore: the small number of Anglo-Irish, a class that provided the bulk of the North American colonial officials of Irish origin; the Protestant Irish of the North, almost but not quite identical with the "Scotch-Irish"; and finally, the vast bulk of the Irish population, devotedly Roman Catholic and traditional in outlook, normally very poor and marginalized in Irish society. Centuries of repressive measures by the English had imposed English as the common language of Ireland, although Irish Gaelic was still spoken by half of the Irish population in 1800, and over one-third of five million Irish were bilingual. The extent of repression had not produced enthusiastic English folk in any political sense out of the Irish, however.

If the British Isles were regionalized, so, too, were the 13 American colonies that achieved independence. Contemporaries were astounded that the Americans had managed to cooperate to achieve a military standoff with the British that amounted to victory, since their earlier history had been one of local, provincial, and even regional squabbling over boundaries, military activities against the French and the Indians, and trade. Each colony cum state had its own political and institutional autonomy, and these seaboard colonies were commonly divided into three general regions, quite different in background and makeup: New England, the southern colonies, and the middle colonies.

New England was a region of small yeoman farms and substantial seaboard commerce. Its population was relatively homogeneous in background, having originated in the Puritan migrations to America of the first half of the seventeenth century and having had well over one hundred years to work out its own cultural adaptations in the New World and to achieve some measure of assimilative coherence. It was overwhelmingly English in origin and dissenting Puritan in religion. The southern colonies were economically characterized by market monocultures (chiefly tobacco) based upon the use of black slave labour. The first southerners were English, recruited chiefly from the urban areas, but large numbers of Scots and Scots-Irish had moved into the region, particularly in back-country Virginia and in North Carolina, during the eighteenth century. The Church of England held sway in this region, although there were large numbers of dissenters, often Presbyterian in persuasion. Between New England and the South were the middle colonies. Their ethnic origins were far more complex: Dutch in New York, Swedes in New Jersey and Delaware, Germans, Scotch-Irish, and English Quakers in Pennsylvania. The ethnic complications made it impossible to establish national churches or cultural homogeneity. The middle colonies were the "melting pot" of colonial America. While there were small pockets of Catholics and Jews in the colonies, they were in the eighteenth century overwhelmingly Protestant in religious adherence and English-speaking in terms of language. Nevertheless, there were strong regional accents and dialects. Americans could talk to one another more easily than could Britons, a fact that helped create cohesion during the American Rebellion, but there was no typical American. One of the effects of American independence was a considerable movement to create and codify a national American culture commensurate with the new political status—much the same thing would happen in Canada after Confederation—but not until the nineteenth century would that culture really take shape on a national level.

Given such realities, the dominant British fact was that there was really little quintessentially British (as opposed to English or Scottish or Irish or American colonial) to which conformity could be demanded on the part of the population of British North America before or immediately after the American Rebellion. The imperial economic and political rules and regulations ostensibly originated in the British Parliament, and those who enforced them and governed the various colonies (typically appointments by those who could not achieve much success at home) operated in an indisputably "British" world at the highest official level. But even the political rules and regulations were not really British, except in inspiration. Britain, of course, had no written constitution. Its political operations were based on long and gradual historical development, in which those involved often themselves did not understand exactly what was happening. During the eighteenth century, the monarch became a virtual figurehead, the prime minister emerged as the effective head of government, and the cabinet system (in which the executive was loosely responsible to the House of Commons) emerged. Contemporaries did not clearly comprehend these constitutional innovations, and part of the reason the Americans rebelled was because they were still stuck in the seventeenth century ideologically and conceptually. Perhaps even more to the point, the British parliamentary system did not transfer neatly to the North American situation and had to be inventively reconceptualized by imperial administrators. That rethinking had occurred essentially in the period before 1775.

Parliament in the eighteenth century was usually described as having three parts: the monarch, the House of Lords, and the House of Commons. Most political theorists of the time insisted that the inherent strength of the British system was in its balances among these three elements, labelled the monarchical, aristocratic, and democratic from the three "pure" forms of government identified by Aristotle. Balance of these elements had been sent askew by the constitutional developments of the eighteenth century, but the real problem for America was in finding equivalents for the three central factors of mixed government. Governors served in place of the monarch and houses of assembly in place of the House of Commons. But the House of Lords was based on a hereditary aristocracy that simply did not exist in the New World and could not be artificially recreated. Attempts to use governor's councils in lieu of the House of Lords simply did not work, and the role of the councils (the ancestors of the Canadian Senate) in North American government was always a difficult one to work out theoretically. But such equivalents, however well-intentioned, were not replications. The several colonies of British North America had no resident monarch and no resident aristocracy. It was scarcely surprising that the houses of assembly, which were able to rely more directly on British precedent and imitation of British models, came closer to British practice than the remainder of the constitutional arrangements. Even so, British imperial and constitutional practice before and after the American Rebellion was based far more on North American precedents than directly on British originals.

The legal situation was equally complicated. There was a body of English common law, much of which was only receiving codification in the second half of the eighteenth century in works such as those produced by the great jurist William Blackstone. There were also English judicial models of courts and practice, including a long-standing distinction between common and equity law, the latter practised in the chancery courts. This distinction was of considerable consequence with regard to property and the legal situation for women and children, since the common law was very male-oriented and equity law considerably less so. If common law was not the only body of law in England, it was also not British. Scotland's legal arrangements were considerably different, based far more on Roman law as filtered through French practice. A Scottish-trained jurist or lawyer, therefore, was far more familiar with the general principles of the Quebec legal system inherited from the French than with English common law. Many of the early "British" jurists in Quebec and elsewhere in what would become Canada had Scottish, rather than English, training and experience. Those who came from Ireland or the American colonies understood the common law, but their systems had modified common law substantially to suit local conditions.

Even leaving aside the complications of Quebec, the legal system that developed on a colony-by-colony basis in the northernmost colonies of British North America was neither wholly English or even British, but rather a hybrid. Acknowledgment was made to English common law as the guiding principle, but in reality what was practised depended a good deal on the legal training and experience of the early colonial legal officials, jurists, and lawyers. On the Island of Saint John, for example, the first chief justice was a Scot, and the colony in 1793 introduced a court of chancery to which decisions in the Supreme Court could be appealed. Chancery courts were equity courts not bound by the common law, and most Island property disputes were thus settled outside the common law, much as was the case in Quebec. In Nova Scotia, a civil divorce court was created in 1758, although England dealt with divorce either through ecclesiastical courts or directly in Parliament. The Nova Scotia divorce court owed much to New England legal practice, for the Puritans who founded New England had hated ecclesiastical courts and rolled most matters that were considered in them over into civil courts.

In terms of religion, there was a substantial chasm between theory and practice, even within the British Isles. Theoretically, everybody in Britain belonged to a "national church"—the Church of England, the Church of Ireland, the Church of Scotland. Only the first two, of course, were "Anglican." Even within the broadly based Protestantism of the Anglican communion, however, there had been many schisms. The Puritans had separated from the Church of England in the seventeenth century because it was not sufficiently Protestant and Calvinist; many had ended up in New England. Another major split occurred in the second half of the eighteenth century, when the evangelical Methodists founded by John Wesley went their own way. And then there were the Roman Catholics. Officially proscribed everywhere in the British Isles, Roman Catholicism experienced a rejuvenation during this period, particularly in the western Highlands of Scotland. Despite the best efforts of the English to suppress it, Catholicism held firm in Ireland. Indeed, the desire to avoid precedents that might lead to Catholic recognition in Ireland was a major reason for imperial reluctance to accept Catholicism fully in Canada. In any event, if the population of the British Isles was considered as a whole, Anglicanism was the faith of considerably less than a majority. Nor was it dominant in most of the American colonies before 1775.

Linguistically, the eighteenth century saw many gains for the so-called "King's English" in the British Isles. Codification of the language occurred in the form of dictionaries, the most notable of which was produced by Dr. Samuel Johnson. But much regional variation remained in terms of accents and vocabulary, occasionally in the form of distinct dialects such as Lowland Scots. The American colonials had their own form of English, much closer to seventeenth-century pronunciations and vocabulary (with many Indian words added) than to the English spoken by the English ruling classes in the eighteenth century. Celtic languages such as Welsh and Gaelic still retained vitality in parts of the British Isles, and both these languages even experienced reinvigoration in this period, thanks chiefly to their association with historical national aspirations. On the written level, English appeared relatively homogeneous by the middle of the eighteenth century. But as spoken, it came in many forms. Moreover, the Celtic tradition was an oral rather than a written one and influenced the speech patterns of many people who no longer spoke their ancient languages. Any Canadian who doubts the oral communications problems, even in English, should spend some time in places like rural Cumbria in the north of England, where heavily accented and dialected forms of English are still commonly spoken.

FRENCH CULTURE

Ironically enough, in any struggle of cultures within Quebec or within some larger geopolitical framework, French Canadians had enormous advantages. They had enjoyed over a century of development of their distinctive version of French culture and did not experience most of the divisive factors that characterized the culture of their British conquerors. French-Canadian culture was relatively uniform within a circumscribed geographical area. The people were members of the same Roman Catholic Church. That church may have not been a monolithic agent of social control, at least before 1837, but it never produced a major movement of doctrinal heresy or schism. French Canadians spoke the same language the same way, Parisian French having achieved virtually universal acceptance by the end of the seventeenth century. Foreign commentators in the eighteenth century were struck by the extent to which "the King's French" was spoken—and spoken well—in New France. The culture of New France had been oral rather than written; no printing press had been introduced during the old regime. As with Celtic culture in the British Isles, the absence of a written tradition may have disguised the extent of cultural vitality, especially to English-speaking conquerors who could not get inside the *mentalités* of the habitants. But in the standard fare of an oral culture—music, poetry, folk tales and legends—French Canada was extremely strong.[6]

Regional cultural variations, which certainly still prevailed in France— at least before the French Revolution—had been largely homogenized in

---

[6] On the French language in New France, see Philippe Barbaud, *Le Choc des Patois en Nouvelle-France, Essai sur l'histoire de la Francisation au Canada* (Sillery, 1984), and on Canadian French in general, Mark M. Orgin, *Speaking Canadian French*, rev. ed. (Toronto, 1971).

French Canada by nearly a century of development in which little immigration had occurred. Neither new cultural input nor the need for assimilation had taken place in New France since the 1670s. The French-speaking population of Quebec shared a common history sufficiently lengthy to provide them with a sense of communal identity hardly possible in the other colonies of northern British North America. The imperial authorities could not muster the power to suppress either the language or the religion of the French Canadians, and it is hard to know what form of "Britishness" might have replaced the traditional practices. Although deeply Roman Catholic in belief, Quebec was not yet dominated by its clergy in its early years under the British, and there was a clear distinction between popular belief and institutional structure. Outside the towns, there were not enough parish priests to provide a regular influence.

At the same time, we ought not to assume that the relative cultural homogeneity of the French in Quebec meant that all French-speakers in British North America were French Canadians. The Acadians of the Maritime region, for example, were not culturally identical with the inhabitants of Quebec. Acadians had come from a different group of French regions in the southwest and retained a distinctive spoken dialect that had not been influenced at all by Parisian French. Although it shared a confessional allegiance to Roman Catholicism with French Canada, Acadia's historical development had been considerably different. For Acadians, the dominant factors were the expulsions of the 1750s and their subsequent quiet re-establishment in the region as far away from British authority as possible. In addition to the Acadians, there was also a small but expanding francophone culture developing in the western fur-trading country. This culture was in large measure a product of intermarriage between French-speaking fur traders and local Indian populations. The linguistic result was a modified French with several fur-trade dialects that mixed French and Indian languages. Much of this developing western mixed-blood society was formally transferred to the United States when British negotiators gave up the Ohio Valley in the 1783 Treaty of Paris, but remnants of its remained in the trading territory of the Hudson's Bay Company and would surface at Red River in the nineteenth century.

THE FIRST NATIONS

By 1763, the population of native peoples in the settled and settling colonies, particularly in the regions of heaviest population concentration, had been marginalized. The First Nations had been decimated by epidemic disease and war, pushed outside the territory of settlement, and often placed on reserves by the colonial governments. Although the native peoples had been a critical cultural factor in the earlier years of European intrusion—the newcomers had arguably learned more from the native inhabitants of North America than the reverse—they were now no longer a dynamic cultural influence on the Europeans who had adopted what they needed of Indian knowledge and expertise. At the same time, if European settlement was able to marginalize native peoples, it was not able to assimilate the Indians to European culture. Despite centuries of effort by missionaries, especially the French Jesuits, only a handful of native people had ever fully assimilated European values.[7]

In the vast territory west of the St. Lawrence, as well as in the Subarctic and Arctic North, the First Nations were still in control of their own lives. Because of the relative slowness of European settlement in these regions, the continued importance of the fur trade, and the increasing liaisons between European fur traders and native women, the native peoples of British North America would continue to be an important autonomous cultural factor until well into the nineteenth century. Whatever the continued influence of Indians upon the development of transplanted European cultures and the extent of their control over their own destiny, the natives undoubtedly represented a series of separate and unassimilated cultures or subcultures extending across the western and northern parts of the continent. There was simply too much territory not suitable for agricultural settlement, which only Indian culture with its symbiotic relationship with the environment could appropriately utilize, to permit Europe to dominate culturally over the native inhabitants.

The Population of the 1760s

Population data are notoriously unreliable for British North America between 1763 and the mid-nineteenth century. We have far more detailed information during the French period, for the French—even in Acadia—

---

[7] Cornelius J. Jaenen, *Friend and Foe: Aspects of French-Amerindian Cultural Contact in the Sixteenth and Seventeenth Centuries* (New York, 1976); James T. Axtell, *The Invasion Within: The Contest of Cultures in Colonial North America* (New York, 1985).

took more careful and detailed censuses than did their British successors. The absolutism of the old regime both required information and undertook to obtain it. After 1763, careful census taking lapsed for many decades, and no attempt at national data collection was undertaken until the 1871 census following Confederation. Before 1871, what censuses existed were executed by the individual colonies without any overall coordination. Colonial governments became more concerned to obtain detailed information in the nineteenth century, however, and some census material—at least for individual colonies—is quite decent for years before Confederation. Such was not the case in the eighteenth century. Census data are spotty, sporadic, and often do not include very much information beyond simple head counts of the population. Even the head counts are limited in nature, since British administrators made little effort to collect information on native people or on populations outside the heavily settled districts. Generalizations from such data can only be extremely tentative but nevertheless can reveal some interesting patterns. We can perhaps begin by examining the population of British North America in the 1760s. We can then discuss the movements of people that altered at least some of the patterns by the 1790s.

NEWFOUNDLAND

The population of Newfoundland in the 1760s was an unusual one in a variety of ways. Unlike that of the typical settlement colony, it was divided into those who resided on the island only during the summer and those who lived there year-round. The proportion of wintering residents in the total population (as well as the total number of winterers) increased constantly in the eighteenth century, although there were cyclical variations in almost every region, usually associated with peacetime and wartime. Migratory activity decreased during war, and each eighteenth-century conflict had added to the growth of the year-round population, an effect that cumulated over the century. By the 1760s, wintering and summering residents were equally divided in a total population of about 20 000.[8]

---

[8] On Newfoundland, consult C. Grant Head, *Eighteenth Century Newfoundland: A Geographer's Perspective* (Toronto, 1976).

The division into year-round and summering residents to some extent overlapped with ethnic and religious divisions on the island. Almost half of the winterers had originated in the Roman Catholic south of Ireland, and Newfoundland had the largest total number and the most significant concentration of Irish Catholics anywhere in North America in the 1760s. The Irish were not equally distributed along the coastline, however, but tended to congregate together in certain districts. They also increasingly gathered in the town of St. John's. The Irish had begun moving to Newfoundland in large numbers in the 1740s, when a combination of increased Irish trade with the island and Irish conditions of food shortage and unemployment made it possible for them to board vessels for Newfoundland, usually as unskilled labourers. The migratory population of Newfoundland came chiefly from the traditional English fishing communities of Devon and Cornwall. While the Irish were almost exclusively Catholic, the English were almost exclusively Church of England, although Methodism had begun to make some inroads among the Protestant adherents. These ethnic-religious divisions of Newfoundland also were reflected in socio-economic terms. The merchant class was almost exclusively Protestant English, usually not year-round residents. The most important wintering class were the boat owners or masters, who controlled the small vessels that engaged in the inshore fishery. Masters were chiefly Protestant, while those who worked on the boats (the "servants") tended to be disproportionately Irish. Thus in Trinity Bay in 1764, there were 109 Protestant and 27 Roman Catholic masters, 74 and 22, respectively, were winterers, and 559 Protestant male servants and 756 Catholic male servants, 309 and 345, respectively, stayed the winter.

All colonial societies in their early stages of development tended to be skewed by gender and often by age as well, particularly if the economy was based, as was the case in Newfoundland, on exploitation of natural resources. Younger males naturally tended to dominate under such conditions. Newfoundland was no exception, although the relative absence of formal settlement activity—as opposed to decisions to remain made by those coming out as labourers for the fishery—significantly reduced the number of female arrivals and thus the proportion of females, even in the wintering population. At best, only 10 percent of the year-round population were women, and they tended to concentrate at St. John's and Conception Bay. The shortage of women reduced the number of younger children, and women of Irish origin were particularly absent. Thus in Trinity Bay in 1764, there were 91 Protestant "mistresses" (i.e., married women) 24 women servants, and 298 children, but only 8 Catholic mistresses, 4 women servants, and 21 children. Irish women were conspicuously lacking in St. John's, where one report in the early 1770s indicated a 16:1 male female ratio among the Irish population.

In addition to this population of European origin, there were a number of native peoples: Beothuk on the island of Newfoundland itself, Naskapi in the interior of Labrador, and Inuit (or "Esquimaux," as they were called in the eighteenth century) in the northern reaches of Labrador. None of these people was ever accurately counted in the eighteenth century. The Beothuk had long since retreated from the settled coast into the northern interior of the island. They were a hunting and fishing people; probably not more than 50 remained by 1763 and they soon became extinct. The Beothuk were continually harassed by the settlers and, like all Indian groups, suffered continually from epidemic disease imported by the Europeans. The Naskapi were more isolated, being contacted only by the occasional fur trader. They did not number more than 1000 in the Labrador area. Only a handful of Inuit moved in and out of Newfoundland's territory.

NOVA SCOTIA AND THE ISLAND OF ST. JOHN

The population of Nova Scotia had altered swiftly in numbers and composition during the period between 1749 and 1763. Nova Scotia at this time included the territory that would become New Brunswick, as well as Cape Breton and the Island of Saint John. Halifax had been settled, and nearly 7000 Acadians had been removed from the colony (and from French territories added to it in 1763) in the 1750s in two expulsions, the first in 1755 and the second in 1758 following the capture of Louisbourg. Not all Acadians in the region had been involved in the expulsions; many had retreated beyond the power of the British authorities to remove them, and others had subsequently returned. An official statement of the non-Acadian population in 1762 showed 8104 people representing 1692 families, with 14 340 acres (5800 ha) under cultivation and 63 000 additional acres (25 500 ha) in marshland. That estimate grew by 1763 to 1797 families with 19 980 acres (8085 ha) under cultivation and 73 300 (29 700 ha) in adjoining salt marshs. Neither official calculation included Acadians, although one subsequent estimate for the year 1764 indicated

2600 Acadians still in Nova Scotia, and another has suggested 10 000 still remained in the region. None of these early figures are very reliable, but a 1767 census, which included the Island of Saint John, does offer much more information.[9]

In 1767, Nova Scotia proper contained 11 072 people, with an additional 707 in Cape Breton, 1196 in the northern section (now New Brunswick), and 519 on the Island of Saint John. The gender figures were 6147 males and 4925 females for Nova Scotia, 414 males and 293 females for Cape Breton, 664 males and 531 females for the northern section, and 366 males and 151 females for the Island of Saint John. Broken down by distinctions between men and boys, women and girls (the cut-off point presumably at age 15, as it usually was in the eighteenth century), the data are shown in Table 1 below:

TABLE 1

Section	Men	Boys	Women	Girls
Nova Scotia	3282	2796	2400	2502
Cape Breton	270	141	128	161
North section (NB)	347	317	242	289
Island of St. John	266	100	72	79

As this breakdown indicates, both Nova Scotia proper and its northern section had been settled chiefly by families and came close to the normal breakdowns for recently settled agrarian colonies of numerical equality between sexes and between adults and children. Cape Breton and the Island of Saint John were chiefly extractive areas, where women and children (hence families) were in considerably shorter supply.

This 1767 census also offers a good deal of information on religion and national origin. That the census-takers found such information essential to record is in itself interesting, as are the results. In terms of religion, the data are shown in Table 2.

---

[9] Early census data have been reprinted in volume IV of *Census of Canada, 1870–1871* (Ottawa, 1876). For Nova Scotia in this period, consult John B. Brebner, *The Neutral Yankees of Nova Scotia: A Marginal Colony during the Revolutionary Years* (New York, 1937, reprinted Toronto, 1969), and Margaret Conrad, ed., *They Planted Well: New England Planters in Maritime Canada* (Fredericton, 1988). On Prince Edward Island, see J. M. Bumsted, *Land, Settlement, and Politics in Eighteenth-Century Prince Edward Island* (Montreal and Kingston, 1987). For the Acadians, see Jean Daigle, ed., *The Acadians of the Maritimes: Thematic Studies* (Moncton, 1982).

TABLE 2

Place	Protestants	Catholics
Nova Scotia	9 674	1 398
Cape Breton	287	420
North section (NB)	1 024	152
Island of St. John	243	276
Total	11 228	2 246

The census-takers broke the national origins into six categories: English, Irish, Scots, Americans (by which they meant American-born), Germans, and Acadians. Any Welsh would have been subsumed under English, but otherwise the "national" distinctions within the British Isles were maintained. Most of the Irish had arrived in the region aboard the first transports settling Halifax in 1749 and 1750. The Scots had not yet discovered the Maritime region as an immigration destination in 1767, although the beginnings of their influx would occur within a few years. The Americans were regarded as a separate people, most of them having come from New England. Germans had been brought to Nova Scotia as "Foreign Protestants" in the 1750s, and the Acadians were the survivors of the expulsions.

TABLE 3

Place	English	Irish	Scotch	Americans	Germans	Acadians
Nova Scotia	687	1831	143	5799	1862	650
Cape Breton	70	169	6	170	21	271
North section (NB)	25	53	17	874	60	147
Island of St. John	130	112	7	70	3	197
Totals	912	2165	173	6913	1936	1265

In addition, the returns showed 94 "Negroes" in Nova Scotia proper, seven in Cape Breton, two on the Island of Saint John, and one in the northern section of Nova Scotia. Over half of them were in Halifax County. Most of these blacks were household servants, and many of them were undoubtedly slaves. Only 28 "Indians" were reported, 20 of them in Cape Breton.

A few observations on this data are in order. In the first place, both Indians and Acadians were severely underreported in this census, partly because the census-takers did not regard them as important and partly because both groups tended to reside away from the main centres of population where it would take too much effort to enumerate them. There were perhaps around 1500 Micmacs and Malecites residing in the region in 1763. In the second place, it should be obvious that this population was extraordinarily mixed ethnically, religiously, and culturally. Less than 8 percent were of actual English origin, and despite the emphasis placed upon recruiting settlers in New England, only slightly more than half the population of the region was of American origin. The American settlers were located in three districts: the Annapolis Valley, the southwest coast of Nova Scotia, and the upper Chignecto Peninsula. The vast bulk of the Catholic population was either Irish or Acadian, and, assuming that all of the 1265 Acadians were tallied as Catholic, this means that 981 Catholics were left, most of whom could be credited to the Irish. Even so, more than half of the Irish total of 2165 would not be Catholic, indicating that many of them had come from the northern counties.

QUEBEC

The 1765 census of Quebec does not offer as rich a source of information as the 1767 Nova Scotia one.[10] It separates Montreal and Quebec from the remainder of the colony and provides no details for these two urban areas. Moreover, it fails to identity national origin (although the number of non–French Canadians probably did not much exceed a thousand, mainly residing in Montreal and Quebec) or religion, and even more regrettably, since most people counted could be presumed to be French-Canadian Catholics, it does not permit us to distinguish adults from children. Nevertheless, the data show (outside Montreal and Quebec) 10 660 families and a total population of 55 110, to which 14 700 were added for the cities. Those 55 110 broke down into 28 316 males and 26 794 females, of whom 21 431 were married. Most of the 17 394 males and 16,285 "Children & Unmarried" would have been under the age of 20. As in Nova Scotia, the census-takers did not attempt to report on native population, although one British estimate of 1763 placed the number of Algonquin, Ottawa, Potowatami, Sauteux, Cree, and other related tribes from the Ottawa Valley to Manitoba at 20 650, and the Hurons of Quebec

---

[10] For Quebec, see Fernand Ouellet, *Economic and Social History of Quebec 1760–1850* (Toronto, 1980).

at 1450. The number of Indians west of the farthest extent of the fur trade was beyond the knowledge of any European of the era. Far more than the Nova Scotia census, however, the Quebec one suggests a well-developed agricultural society of considerable cultural homogeneity. This pattern— of cultural togetherness in Quebec and great diversity and divisions outside it—would continue to characterize British North America throughout the eighteenth century.

In summary, the population of the northernmost colonies in the 1760s consisted of 20 000 Europeans in Newfoundland (half of them year-round residents), about 12 000 Europeans in Nova Scotia, and 70 000 Europeans in Quebec. If one excludes the Newfoundland summer population, the permanently resident European population was just over 90 000. In addition, there was an uncounted population of native peoples, relatively small in numbers in the settled colonies but extensive west of present-day Manitoba. At this period, the total number of native people in what is now Canada probably still substantially outnumbered the population of European origin.

Population Change to 1775

The Proclamation of 1763 was predicated on the assumption that large numbers of American colonials could be attracted to the northernmost colonies by the availability of land. As has already been discussed, British policy did not attract large numbers of Americans after 1763. Most of the New Englanders coming to Nova Scotia and merchants moving to Quebec had already arrived by that date, and few Americans were lured northward in an era without public subsidy. The bulk of the newcomers from 1763 to 1775 came from sources the British had not intended to tap. The Acadians, twice deported, gradually returned to the Maritime region, not always to their old lands. Immigrants from the British Isles began to arrive in substantial numbers, particularly from Highland Scotland, although there was a substantial movement from Yorkshire to Nova Scotia and a continual influx of Irish into Newfoundland. British immigration to North America was always arrested by war and was slow to resume after peace. But, after 1763, a major new wave of immigration swept over all the American colonies, which was ended only by the outbreak of the American Rebellion. Most of the post-1763 immigrants went to the 13 seaboard colonies to the South; and the northernmost colonies received some of the overflow but were not the preferred destinations for most of the new arrivals. Many of the immigrants from Britain to the northern colonies came as communities or at least together as passengers aboard transatlantic vessels. They tended to settle in isolated pockets, particularly in the Maritime region.[11]

The New England Planters ought to have been a far more dominant population in Nova Scotia than they became, especially in terms of their potential influence. The New Englanders were not sufficiently numerous and widespread to control culturally more than a few circumscribed regions of Nova Scotia, however. They had begun in time-honoured New England fashion, organizing themselves into communities to receive and distribute land. The Nova Scotia authorities had not allowed those communities to become fully autonomous towns, however, and cultural leadership in the form of clergy and schoolmasters was in short supply. Always isolated, the Planters were almost totally cut off from their roots by the American Rebellion. Afterward, they found themselves in conflict with an incoming Loyalist population with which they eventually merged. Without the political upheaval, the Planters would doubtless have gradually re-established more substantial cultural ties with New England than was possible under the circumstances. Without the Loyalists, the Planters would probably have lost their American roots more quickly.

The Acadians almost by definition became an isolated and defensive population. Although the authorities had given up on formal persecution, they still insisted on an oath of allegiance, and memories of previous British treatment remained strong. On the other hand, the Acadians could no longer take France seriously as a protector. When they returned to the Maritime region, the Acadians did not resettle their previous lands but tended instead to choose isolated and less attractive regions in western Nova Scotia, Cape Breton, the Island of Saint John, and the northeast coast of the northern section of Nova Scotia. The wisdom of choosing places not in demand by other settlers was shown after 1783, when many of the Acadians who had settled in the upper Saint John River Valley were removed again by the arrival of Loyalists. Although they had previously been an agricultural people, many of the returned Acadians found a new livelihood in fishing. As Catholics they remained politically disenfran-

---

[11] For the period 1763–1775, see Gordon Stewart and George Rawlyk, *A People Highly Favoured of God: The Nova Scotia Yankees and the American Revolution* (Toronto, 1972).

chised in Nova Scotia until 1784, in New Brunswick until 1810, and in Prince Edward Island until 1830. Even when granted the vote, they did not immediately exercise it. Even more so than the Planters, the Acadians lacked cultural leadership. The church in Quebec, which according to Rome continued to have authority in the Maritime region, found it difficult to supply them with clergy, and most of the early priests were Irish and Scottish in origin. Nevertheless, the Acadians had their distinctive language, isolated locations, and a strong defensive sense of survival nurtured by their history. They would quietly expand in numbers, particularly in what became New Brunswick, for nearly a century, before becoming a visible and articulate people.

After 1763 some emigrants from the British Isles did end up in the northernmost colonies. Immigration began in the late 1760s and swelled in 1770, fuelled by unfavourable economic conditions in Britain (economic depression and another round of agricultural rationalization), and assisted by the acquisition of large tracts of unsettled land by former soldiers and speculators in the territories recently acquired from France. Most of the emigrating Britons went to the more established colonies in the South; they represented a less Americanized population at the time of the outbreak of rebellion; many re-migrated northward as Loyalists. But there was a continued outpouring of Irish into Newfoundland, nearly doubling the resident population on that island to 15 000 by 1775. And a major movement from Scotland, especially from the Highland region, often including Gaelic-speaking Roman Catholics, was building as well.

The Maritime region became the principal northern destination of the Highland Scots. The Island of St. John, where a number of parties including over 200 Roman Catholics were brought by proprietors between 1770 and 1775, was particularly attractive. A few parties also went to Quebec, to territory that later became part of Upper Canada. The Highlanders of this period came mainly from the more isolated western region and adjacent islands, where Gaelic was still the common language and where Roman Catholicism survived and even flourished semiclandestinely. They tended to emigrate in extended family groupings and to set sail together on chartered vessels for isolated destinations that allowed them to replicate their Old World communities. Lowlanders were more attracted to Nova Scotia, and a beachhead of settlement was established on the coast of Northumberland Strait around what became Pictou in 1774. A number of Yorkshiremen were included in the 2000 English arrivals in the province in the early 1770s. Most settled in the Cumberland region on the

Chignecto Peninsula, where they came into political and cultural conflict with the Yankees. This process of transatlantic migration was not favoured by the authorities in Whitehall, many of whom were landlords not anxious to lose tenants, and steps were undertaken to limit both land granting in America and recruiting in the British Isles on the eve of the rebellion. But immigration was gaining momentum to the northernmost colonies when the American war effectively ended it for the duration of hostilities.

The Coming of the Loyalists, 1775–1785

Imperial acceptance of the cultural and institutional values of the French-Canadian majority in Quebec came simultaneously with the disruption of the British Empire in North America, which would produce a major migration northward of English-speaking settlers. Loyalists began moving into Quebec and Nova Scotia from the beginning of open warfare between the colonies and Britain. Many of the migrating refugees to Quebec avoided the St. Lawrence, preferring more isolated territory in the Niagara Peninsula and northwest of Lake Champlain. Although no overall settlement policy for Loyalist exiles was produced until after the war had ended, the governments in Quebec and Nova Scotia did their best to accommodate the new arrivals. They found, particularly in Nova Scotia, where exiles mixed freely with earlier Planter settlers, that the newcomers did not get on very well with the resident population. Much jockeying occurred for place and preferment in an already constricted environment, and the incoming Loyalists were persuaded that the existing population had not shown sufficient commitment to the Crown.[12]

The Loyalists present complex problems for the historian. In theory their cultural and demographic impact ought to have been even more substantial than it was. The older Canadian view that the Loyalists represented the "cream" of American society, "the choicest stock the colonies could boast," is no longer tenable. It has been replaced by one that sees the Loyalists as a representative cross-section of the American population at the time of the rebellion, including large numbers of blacks and native Indians. Arriving at an operational definition of a Loyalist has

---

[12] For a general historiographical introduction to the Canadian Loyalists, see Bumsted, *Understanding the Loyalists* (Sackville, 1986) and footnote 11 on the Loyalists in Chapter 4.

always been difficult, and the larger problems of assessing the cultural impact of the newcomers are even more complex. But recent scholarship suggests some of the factors that limited a long-term Loyalist influence.

One factor was the number of soldiers among the Loyalist arrivals. Contemporaries in the northern provinces clearly distinguished between Loyalist refugees (the civilian exiles) and those soldiers disbanded from the various units fighting in the British army. The two groups were in some cases mixed aboard vessels evacuating the colonies. Soldiers were dealt with by the same officials under similar programs and were often recipients of land grants and subsidies from the colony in which they were demobilized. Since, at the close of the war, a substantial proportion of the British army was based in the northernmost provinces, many soldiers were able to take advantage of the government largesse without actually moving very far. No exact figures are available, but probably close to half of the total usually regarded as "Loyalist" settlers were actually disbanded soldiers.

The British army was a polyglot mixture of Loyalists, German mercenaries, British regulars (usually Highland Scots and Irish), and even men recruited in the northernmost colonies themselves; Newfoundland supplied men for several regiments, for example. Loyalist units (or "provincials," as they were often called) were initially recruited within a specific region or colony but had their ranks supplemented from wherever replacements were available. Army units were therefore not necessarily coherent or homogeneous even when originally comprised of Americans loyal to the Crown, and many soldiers were not American colonials at all, thus lacking the political commitment usually associated with Loyalists. Anglican clergyman Jacob Bailey, for example, characterized his new neighbours in the Annapolis Valley as "a collection of all nations, kindreds, complexions and tongues assembled from every quarter of the globe and till lately equally strangers to me and each other."

Soldiers, especially the professionals, tended to be single males. Many took land locations and provisions upon demobilization, subsequently exchanging them for ready cash or drink, and moved on. Provincial regiments often acquired land together under their officers, thus forecasting some sort of coherent community, but few such communities emerged. Most historical discussion of Loyalists focuses on their immediate arrival and initial location rather than upon their subsequent dispersion. High rates of transiency were common everywhere to North American settlement, and the Loyalists were no exception to the rule.

Few Loyalists stayed where they received their initial land locations.

Surveying and obtaining formal title was a very slow process, for the colonies were not equipped to deal with an influx of people on the scale involved. On the Island of Saint John, Loyalists became pawns in an internal land grab, and very few ever received titles. Shelburne, Nova Scotia, a town of over 10 000 people at its height in the mid-1780s, was virtually a ghost town within ten years. In Adolphustown, Upper Canada, one-quarter of households turned over every two years. On the Island of St. John, less than 25 percent of Loyalist land grantees were still on the island for the nominal census of 1798, almost none of them on their original locations. In Wallace, Nova Scotia, 40 percent of grantees never took up their lands and another 36 percent were gone within two years. Nearly half of the black Loyalists in Nova Scotia departed the colony for Sierra Leone in 1792. No detailed study of forward linkages has been done with most of this highly mobile population, and so we do not know whether it remained within British North America or—as contemporaries claimed—returned to the United States when the dust settled and subsidies ended.

Whether civilian refugee or disbanded soldier, Loyalists typically lacked the homogeneity and cohesiveness to exert a power and influence commensurate with their numbers, despite their ostensible American origins. They came from all parts of the American colonies, from all walks of life, from a variety of ethnic and religious groups. Although a majority were farmers, the agricultural situations with which they had previously dealt were quite disparate. They had chosen loyalty for a variety of reasons. Loyalism was particularly attractive to ethnic and religious minorities who found the tolerance of the British Empire preferable to the aggressive national ethos of the new republic. More recent immigrants to the colonies, particularly among the Scots, were overrepresented among the Loyalist population. But rank-and-file Loyalists were at best united mainly in the common experience of adherence to the Crown, in distaste for the American republic, and often in fervent dislike of the Loyalist elite. Religious differences were symptomatic of the lack of cohesion. Many of the Loyalists were at least technically adherents of Anglicanism. But they came from a religious tradition strong in the American south that emphasized low-church practices more akin to Protestantism than Anglo-Catholicism, including church organization without bishops. The British authorities provided British North America with bishops (Charles Inglis in Nova Scotia in 1787, Jacob Mountain in Quebec in 1793), but neither was able to draw into his flocks the numbers necessary to give credence to Anglicanism as an established colonial church. Roman Catholicism remained the unofficial national church in Lower Canada, and Protestant sectarianism flourished in the English-speaking colonies.

The Loyalist elite, drawn from the ranks of colonial officials, merchants, professionals, and clergy, had considerably more cohesiveness, representing as they did a single social class in the American colonies. But most members of the colonial Loyalist elite did not settle in British North America, and they were able to dominate the governments of only New Brunswick and to a lesser extent Upper Canada. Even so, there was considerable class-related controversy between the elite and other Loyalist groups almost everywhere. Blacks and native peoples had their own reasons for becoming Loyalists and their own agendas in the new land.

In theory, the coming of the Loyalists ought to have imported and reinforced American cultural values, particularly at the vernacular level. Unfortunately, however, we do not know whether the Loyalist arrivals were predominantly "Good Americans," "Un-Americans," or "Non-Americans." The newcomers helped reinforce American patterns in some respects, such as speech patterns and domestic architecture. But the colony that was most obviously American, Upper Canada, was not necessarily so because of the Loyalists. American westward movement into British North America after 1783 was an ongoing process until the eve of the War of 1812, and the "late Loyalists" have always posed a problem for Canadian historians.

While the Loyalist resettlement has probably been given more credit than it deserves for reshaping development in British North American after the American Rebellion, it did help produce three new provinces (New Brunswick in 1784, Cape Breton from 1784 to 1820, and Upper Canada in 1791) that would officially have British cultures, as well as reinforce the Anglo American component of two others (Nova Scotia and Prince Edward Island). Moreover, a number of Loyalists made their way into the western fur trade. Newfoundland was itself not much affected by Loyalism, although many of its former residents may have settled elsewhere as disbanded soldiers. As for Quebec (or Lower Canada as it became known after 1791), its official British culture still remained weakly superimposed upon a French-Canadian one, which after the Constitution Act had a political outlet. The church and the seigneurs continued to be more important under British rule than under French, and a professional class emerged to provide political leadership for the habitant.

In what became Upper Canada and New Brunswick, the Loyalist infusion produced complex conflicts. English or British elements jostled with varieties of "Loyal Whiggery" (American democratic ideas minus the rebellious elements). In these "Loyalist provinces," the official imperial culture amalgamated with Loyalist ideals but displayed little consonance with vernacular American, which tended to be far more concerned with practical political and economic matters than with ideology. Official Loyalism exhibited a hostility to the United States not shared at the grass roots level. It also allied with British elements in a commitment to well-defined social hierarchies, including notions of a North American aristocracy, political deference to one's "superiors," and the importance of an established Anglicanism. Finally, official Loyalism combined its support of an established Church of England with a paternalistic policy of tolerance for ethnic, religious, and racial minorities at variance with the post-1775 American thrust to civil conformity and national identity.

After the Loyalists

Another movement of immigration from the British Isles was released after the coming of peace in 1783. Again slow in gaining momentum, and viewed with some hostility by colonial officials already overburdened with Loyalist resettlement, this wave was of short duration, for the coming of the French Revolution in 1789 soon led to a resumption of Anglo-French wars in 1793. British immigration to the United States was not ended by American independence, although some potential newcomers were uneasy about the new republic and chose the remaining loyal colonies instead. The Irish resumed their passage to Newfoundland, and the Highland Scots theirs to those northern districts previously established by their compatriots before the American war; few Highlanders went to the United States at this time. The principal destinations were Nova Scotia, the Island of St. John, and the Glengarry district of eastern Upper Canada. To all these settlements both Highland Catholics and Protestants, as well as Gaelic-speakers and non-Gaelic speakers, congregated. Gaelic-speaking Catholics were more likely to immigrate and settle together as a community, however, and by 1815 Gaelic (Irish and Scottish varieties) would become the third most commonly spoken European language in British North America.[13]

Few French-speaking immigrants came to British North America after

---

[13] On the post-revolutionary period, see Graeme Wynn, "A Region of Scattered Settlements and Bounded Possibilities: Northeastern America 1775–1800," *Canadian Geographer*, 31 (1987), 319–38; Jane Errington, *The Lion, the Eagle, and Upper Canada: A Developing Colonial Ideology*

the American Rebellion, although the handful of French priests driven from France by the anti-clericalism of the French Revolution who made their way to the British colonies had an influence far in excess of their numbers. The newcomers became the only Catholic clergy in many places, and as men of learning assumed important roles as teachers and educators. They provided an infusion of traditional European values into Canadian Catholicism. While the French received few immigrants, both in Quebec and in Acadia the population grew rapidly through natural increase.

French Canadians continued to seek employment in the fur trade, which required increasing numbers of servants as competition intensified between the Montreal-based traders and those of the Hudson's Bay Company. Indeed, French Canadians were the dominant cultural group in the trade, although usually confined to the lower ranks of employment with little chance for advancement into positions of authority. In 1804, for example, the North West Company had 113 English-speaking and 718 French-speaking traders, with 625 of the latter serving in the lowest ranks of voyageurs and other such trades. Larger numbers of European males meant larger numbers of relationships with native women. By the end of the eighteenth century, a number of changes had taken place regarding those relationships. They had become more regularized, taking on aspects of marriage "according to the custom of the country," despite the absence of clergy to solemnize marriage vows. Moreover, there were now greater numbers of mixed blood women, the daughters of earlier liaisons. Traders often preferred them to native women as marriage partners. The trading companies were coming to appreciate that these relationships not only were unpreventable but both useful and necessary to assure loyal and satisfied employees. Since by far the majority of Europeans in the West was of French-Canadian background, it was not surprising that many children born there were likely to be French-speaking and Roman Catholic, as were their fathers. At the end of the eighteenth century, a separately recognized mixed blood society had not yet emerged. The norm was that most children took their mother's rather than their father's culture. But already observable was a tendency for the children to retain some of their fathers' identities, if only in a supplementary sense.

All these developments confirmed the tendency of the Protestant population of British North America to diverge from the officially supported Church of England and for there to be a substantial Roman Catholic

(Kingston and Montreal, 1987); John Garner, *The Franchise and Politics in British North America, 1755–1867* (Toronto, 1969).

element. The official Anglican Church in early British North America was outnumbered not only by Protestant dissenters, therefore, but more importantly by Roman Catholics. Indeed, Catholics were in the overwhelming majority in Lower Canada, a majority in Rupertsland (still without priests), close to a majority in Newfoundland, and the largest single denomination in Cape Breton and Prince Edward Island by the end of the century. In the 1780s, the imperial authorities gave up attempting to enforce proscriptions against Catholics in British North America, although full acceptance was slower to come. By the end of the eighteenth century, Catholics were enfranchised only in the Canadas (by the Constitutional Act of 1791) and in Nova Scotia by a 1789 legislative enactment. New Brunswick withdrew political privileges from Catholics after its initial elections and did not restore them until 1810. Prince Edward Island did not allow Catholics to vote until 1830. Newfoundland, Cape Breton, and Rupertsland had no popularly elected political bodies, in the former two partly because of the prevalence of Catholics. More to the point, until 1830 the Canadas alone allowed Catholics to sit in the legislative bodies for which they could vote. Catholic restrictions encouraged British North Americans of that denomination outside Canada to think of themselves as outsiders, and encouraged their communities to operate as autonomous cultural units.

The Population of the 1790s

In the mid-1760s, permanent residents of European extraction in British North America stood at about 90 000. By the 1790s it had more than doubled to something over 225 000. Newfoundland's total population had recovered to its 1760 level, but now had 15 000 winterers. There were 161 000 people in Lower Canada, 15 000 in Upper Canada, 20 000 in New Brunswick, 30 000 in Nova Scotia, 4000 on the Island of St. John, and perhaps 1000 year-round inhabitants in the West. Most of these figures are estimates, since only Quebec (in 1790) and Prince Edward Island (in 1798) produced careful census data. Only the PEI census, which was done on a name-by-name basis, is sufficiently detailed to permit ethnic analysis.[14]

---

[14] Andrew Hill Clark, *Three Centuries and the Island: A Historical Geography of Settlement and Agriculture in Prince Edward Island, Canada* (Toronto, 1959), 57–60.

The 1790 Quebec census, which does not include districts that would become Upper Canada and provides no details for Montreal and Quebec, is particularly interesting in its breakdown by age and marital status of the rural districts.

TABLE 4

Males		
Married	19 375	
Unmarried		
under 8	17 883	
under 16	13 151	
16 to 60	11 886	
over 60	3 718	
		66 013
Females		
Married	20 569	
Unmarried		
under 8	17 288	
under 16	12 001	
16 to 60	10 315	
over 60	3 125	
		63 298
Total		129 311

What this census clearly reveals is a society that has achieved a stable balance between males and females, but one that has an extremely high birth rate, resulting in substantial numbers of children under 16. On the other end of the scale, the numbers over 60 are small, reflecting the fact that average life expectancies, even for those who had survived childhood, were still well under that age. Quebec society was extraordinarily tilted toward the young, a characteristic of all British North America throughout the nineteenth century. This population continued, of course, to be almost exclusively French-speaking in language and Roman Catholic in religion.

Some notion of the ethnic and cultural diversity in other colonies can be gained from the Prince Edward Island material. The 1798 nominal census there permitted geographer Andrew Hill Clark to assign ethnic origins on the basis of surnames. The result showed 669 Acadians, 1814 Highland Scots, 310 Lowland Scots, and 1579 others, chiefly of initial English extraction. There were several hundred Irish and a handful of Germans, most of whom had anglicized surnames. Perhaps half of the "others" had come from the American colonies, many as Loyalists. Highland Scots and

Acadians particularly clustered together in a few contiguous settlements. The 1798 census also permits distinctions according to age (see Table 5).

TABLE 5

Males		
over 60	104	
16-60	1014	
under 16	1217	
		2335
Females		
over 60	78	
16-60	867	
under 16	1092	
		2037
Total		4372

Comparisons of this material with the Quebec census is instructive. Quebec's population in terms of sex breaks down into 51 percent male and 49 percent female, while that of PEI distributes 53.4 percent male and 46.8 percent female. In terms of the percentage of those over 60, the figure in Quebec was 6 percent, while in PEI it was 4.2 percent. In Quebec, those younger than 16 represented 46.7 percent of the total population, and roughly 20 000 married couples had 66 000 children. On PEI, the proportion of children below 16 in the total population was even higher than Quebec, at 52.8 percent. A census on the island taken only seven years later in 1805 shows that the population over 60 had dropped to 3.7 percent of the total, while the proportion of children under 16 held constant at 52.3 percent. While high birth rates among French Canadians are part of Canadian legend, it is worth emphasizing that similar or even higher rates were characteristic of the other colonies in the late eighteenth and early nineteenth centuries. Upper Canada's birth rate would persistently exceed that of Lower Canada throughout the nineteenth century. Given the continued absence of French-speaking immigration to British North America, however, the fact that the non-French population grew from natural increase at a rate equal to French Canada's *and* from immigration meant that despite "the revenge of the cradle," French-Canadian population would persistently decline as a proportion of the whole.

Crude birth rates in excess of 50 per thousand (today the figure is around or under 20 per thousand) were to some extent balanced by high crude death rates of over 25 per thousand (ours today runs around 7 per thousand). Infant mortality ran especially high. People aged more quickly and died earlier; as late as 1830, average life expectancy for males was 40.2 years and for females 42.4 years (figures today are well over 70 years). Countless observers noted, in particular, the premature aging of women, hardly surprising given the expectations that they would give birth to substantial numbers of children. Lowered birth rates are associated either with severe limitations on access to land for a rural population or with extensive urbanization. Obviously neither condition prevailed in British North America at the end of the eighteenth century. The population was well over 80 percent rural, with higher percentages outside Quebec than within it. Most of this rural population were farmers and fisherfolk. While landholding systems meant that not all farmers owned their own land, the family farm continued to be both the reality and the ideal. The basis of such farming was the exploitation of the labour of the family. Large families secured success under these circumstances, although they would rapidly exceed existing family holdings and produce a dynamic for the expansion of new agricultural settlement that would have prevailed even had substantial new immigration not occurred.

Conclusion

Many Canadians have always assumed that from at least 1763 onward there were in Canada two historic cultures: the French and the British. That assumption was elevated to the level of national policy in the 1960s. But the important points about British North America from 1763 to 1800 are far more complex than a simple model of biculturalism would allow. In addition to an official imperial British culture and an unofficial well-established French one, a variety of other cultures flourished and had not yet amalgamated. The authorities were quite unable to foster any real cultural hegemony out of the disparate parts.[15]

The extent of cultural complexity in British North America in the 1790s can hardly be overemphasized. Only the French in Lower Canada had a reasonably mature and stable culture, dominating most of a province

---

[15] See H. Brook Taylor, *Promoters, Patriots, and Partisans: Historiography in Nineteenth-Century English Canada* (Toronto, 1989).

governed by men with an alternative set of cultural values and assumptions. But the French culture of Canada was not the only French one present. In the Maritime region, the Acadians were redeveloping and re-entrenching their own particular version of North Americanized culture. In the West, the Métis offered yet another French variant, in which European origins were subordinated to Indian ones. Moreover, the extent of miscegenation in western British North America reflects the relative importance of the Indian population. Large portions of the territory on the continent claimed by Great Britain had few European inhabitants beyond the male fur traders. As for the British, their official imperial culture dominated among the ruling elites in provincial capitals and commercial centres. Even in colonies where the French did not predominate, outside the major towns American culture, mixtures of American and regional British culture, isolated regional British culture (such as Irish or Highland Scots), and occasionally even other European cultures flourished, constantly adapting to their new situation.

Except for the loose framework of the British Empire, operated through individual colonies of considerable autonomy, there was no coordinating agency to encourage conformity. Unlike the United States, which was equally complex culturally, there was no powerful fusion force of a national revolution in British North America and no development of a corresponding national political and sociocultural ideology. The provinces that would become Canada would move toward nationhood and dominion status gradually, and while the process was hardly free from ideology, those that developed were difficult to translate into cultural symbols and icons. Without a national perspective, the importance of a culture such as that of French Canada remained geographically limited. The governments in the eastern provinces had no need to take French Canada into account in formulating their policies.

In short, British North America as of the beginning of the nineteenth century was a collection of relatively autonomous and culturally heterogeneous provinces with weak colonial administrations incapable of melding their cultural components into a coherent whole or of assuring equality, even had that been recognized as a priority. What had congealed in the eighteenth century were racist and sexist attitudes and practices that further fragmented an already diverse society.

BRITISH NORTH
AMERICA, 1791-1841

Introduction

At the close of the eighteenth century, British North America consisted of seven political units: Newfoundland, Prince Edward Island, Cape Breton, Nova Scotia, New Brunswick, Lower Canada, Upper Canada and a vast western domain under the nominal control of the Hudson's Bay Company. Tied in various ways to Great Britain, the seven had much in common. None enjoyed political independence. Via a system of Crown-appointed governors and governor-appointed local executives, and, in Upper and Lower Canada, legislative councillors, the imperial centre exercised great control over most significant political matters. All depended to some degree for their economic prosperity on financial and commercial links with Great Britain. All but the western region experienced substantial population growth. Finally, and most importantly, the seven political units that made up British North America in 1791 were part of a pre-industrial world.

This last feature is most significant because of the tendency to look with nostalgia on eras that seem to predate the stresses and strains and competitive pressures of modern times. Many historians portray a society in British North America that is more simple, orderly, and stable than today's complex, individualistic, and disorderly society. Too often we look at the past through rose-coloured glasses. Sometimes museums encourage

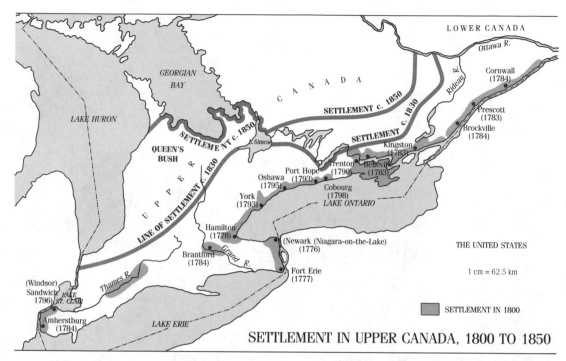

SETTLEMENT IN UPPER CANADA, 1800 TO 1850

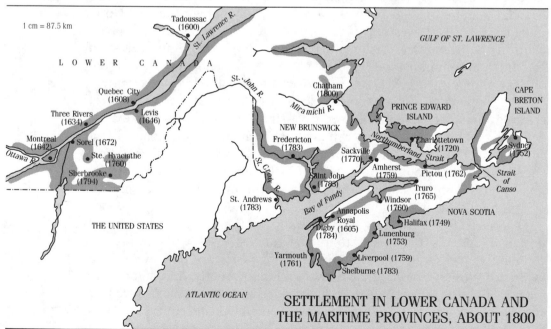

**SETTLEMENT IN LOWER CANADA AND
THE MARITIME PROVINCES, ABOUT 1800**

this: examples are the pioneer villages, such as the one at Morrisburg, Ontario, or King's Landing Historical Settlement at Prince William, New Brunswick, or the Canadian Museum of Civilization at Hull, Quebec. Such exhibits do not include violence, poverty, and harsh living conditions as central themes.

Some scholars take this depiction one step further and argue that the roots of Canada's national "character" were planted in the 1791–1841 period. Far from seeing this period as a contrast to present-day Canada, they argue that the reality of a "Peaceable Kingdom" emerged then and has endured since. For these writers, the contrast between the pre-1841 period and the present is not to be found in Canada; rather the contrast is with Canada's powerful neighbour, the United States. Canada is, apparently, less boisterous, less aggressive, less individualistic, less crime ridden, more stable and tolerant because our peculiar society crystallized at a particular moment in time. In much of our historical writing, the pre-1841 era has become a touchstone—a basic element in the definition of Canada. For some, the era becomes a kind of refuge, and nostalgia highlights the contrasts with the present. For others, the era contains the beginnings of Canada's distinctive character and our independence on the North American continent.

Another perspective on this period is possible, one based upon the proposition that pre-industrial people experienced pain, inequality, failure, and fear of the unknown future to at least the extent we do today. And the era prior to 1840 was clearly a pre-industrial one. Or put more precisely, we are presented with British North Americans "making it" within the bounds of a pre-industrial economic, political, and social system, a system gradually becoming part of a more industrially oriented world. The nature of life in a pre-industrial context bounded by an increasingly industrial world forms the focus of these chapters.

Five overlapping themes or tensions recur in the following discussion. The first is depopulation vs. population: natives had to be dispossessed of land and property before white Europeans could set down roots. While the process began well before 1791, its pace and impact accelerated in the following century. The second theme is stability and rootedness vs. mobility and rootlessness: some people came, some stayed, some moved within and some left. What did stability or mobility mean to an early nineteenth-century British North American? The third theme focuses on poverty vs. wealth: a common assumption is that rural pre-industrial Canada was relatively equalitarian, that wealth had yet to be funnelled into the hands of the few. A closer look suggests that social and economic gradations were common. A fourth and related theme is power vs. dependency: power was manifest in political, economic, and social life. To "make it" in pre-industrial British North America one had to please the proper people. Birthplace, ethnicity, gender, colour, and class counted and conditioned one's expectations, behaviours, and rewards. The fifth theme is isolation vs. links to the outside world: this tension existed at many levels. At first glance, rural people might seem to have lived isolated, self-sufficient lives, with few links to the world beyond their farm or village. In fact, this was rarely the case. Credit, food, social and trade needs bound rural farmers, Atlantic fishers, and interior lumbermen to each other, to rural- and urban-based merchants and, increasingly, to a wider, non-rural, industrializing world. Many tried to use political, economic, and social means to benefit from these links between British North America and points beyond.

While the above themes form the foundation of the following discussion, organization is on regional lines in order to better reflect the differences as well as similarities existing among the various colonies that made up British North America in this era. By introducing BNA society in regional terms, different rates of development become apparent and the importance of regional differences becomes clear. A regional focus also puts time in perspective. In a political, socio-economic sense, 1841 had meaning for Upper and Lower Canada because they were politically reunited at that time. It has little significance for the Maritime/Atlantic region and still less for the West. Thus, to guard against a tendency in the historical literature to "fit" all of British North America within a common chronology (this tendency has its counterpart in fitting all of women's and children's history into a period based upon the experiences of adult males), discussion about each region will focus on the above themes. Chronological end points will, to some extent, vary both within and across regions.

Upper Canada: The Planting of White Society

INTRODUCTION

Upper Canada, a colony three and one-half times the size of the British Isles (413 000 square miles), grew in population (white) from 6000 in

1784 to about 60 000 in 1811, a rate of increase equal to that of adjoining New York State. Because of relatively cheap lands, lower taxes, and reputedly quiescent native peoples, westward-bound Americans viewed Upper Canada as a favourable destination. Following the War of 1812, Upper Canada's white population grew from about 75 000 in 1815 to about 450 000 in 1842. Between 1815 and 1826, some 37 000 emigrants arrived and 100 000 more followed in the next nine years. Most of the postwar emigrants came from the British Isles where land enclosures and a decline in industrial growth after the Napoleonic Wars caused much unemployment and hardship. As European population increased, native population declined from roughly 14 000 in 1770 to about 9000 in 1830.

While 90 percent of people lived in rural areas, urban centres did develop. In 1811 only one community, Kingston, boasted 1000 people. By 1841, 20 communities had over 1000, 4 exceeded 3000, and Toronto (York) reached 14 250. Despite their small size, Upper Canada's communities were centres for commerce, transportation, communication, and political and judicial power.

Historians are engaged in a debate concerning the nature of Upper Canada's economy and the links between that economy and social and political change in this period. Some historians argue that the staple model or staple approach best explains the nature of Upper Canada's economic, social, and political development. A staple is a raw material or natural product that is exported. The staple model asserts that a country's economic, social, and political characteristics are to a great extent dependent on the production, processing, and sale of usually one dominant staple product. Some historians believe that the export of wheat and timber fuelled Upper Canada's growth. Protected by Corn Laws, which gave colonial wheat cheaper entry than foreign wheat to the British wheat market when British production was down, and by timber tariff preferences, Upper Canada became a dependent supplier of raw resources to an industrializing mother country who, in turn, supplied her colony with the required manufactured items. The linkage between this staple model and political change is direct. The periodic closure of the British market to wheat and to a lesser extent lumber products had, it is argued, a devastating effect on the colonial economy. Because of excessive dependence on these exports, the economy went through a number of crises or booms and busts. Political upheaval, as witnessed by the rebellion of 1837, was caused, staple theorists argue, by the fragility of Upper Canada's economy and its subservient economic relationship to Great Britain.

A second perspective, one that is adopted here, cautions against portraying Upper Canada as caught in the classic staple trap—excessive and narrow dependence on the export of one or two natural products. This alternative interpretation argues that economic diversification did occur in rural and urban regions. The colony did not depend simply on staple production. Those in the colony who worked for diversification also pushed for corresponding institutional change. Those in the colony who opposed them had their own vision of progress. Political unrest and institutional change must, this second interpretation emphasizes, be understood within the context of an evolving society and a modernizing economy. Staples were important but far from determining factors in structuring economic, social, and political behaviour in Upper Canada.[1]

Making It in the Bush: Society and Economy in Rural Upper Canada

DISPOSSESSING NATIVES

Clearing the land was the foremost preoccupation of white settlers, and natives were the first to be cleared. The Proclamation of 1763 recognized native rights to certain lands. It also made the British Crown the sole authority for extinguishing those claims. Natives could possess their land, but they could only sell it to the Crown. Between 1783 and 1806, in part to satisfy Loyalist demands, the Crown acquired most of southern Ontario from some 1000 Mississauga. Early land agreements exhibited several common characteristics. Land was often defined in vague terms. A blank deed was all that "testified" to the nature of one transaction. Arriving on the scene in 1792, Lieutenant-Governor John Graves Simcoe reported this sloppy documentation and was warned "not to press that matter" since it "throw(s) us entirely on the good faith of the Indians for just so much land

---

[1] A number of articles by Douglas McCalla nicely explore these themes: D. McCalla, "The Loyalist Economy of Upper Canada, 1784–1806," *Histoire sociale/Social History*, 16 (1983), 279–304 and "Rural Credit and Rural Development in Upper Canada, 1790–1850," in Roger Hall et al., eds., *Patterns of the Past: Interpreting Ontario's History* (Toronto, 1988), 37–54 are two of them. Consult their footnotes for further references. A readable and insightful overview of the economy is provided in K. Norrie and D. Owram, *A History of the Canadian Economy* (Toronto, 1991).

as they are willing to allow. . . ." A corollary to a subsequent agreement seems to have papered over the blank deed problem. In other cases, including one involving what is now Canada's capital, the legal title remains under dispute. The natives also ceded immense amounts of land in return for very little. The Mississauga, for example, exchanged 3 000 000 acres (1 214 000 ha) of land running along the Niagara Peninsula and inland in 1784 for under £1200 of gifts.

The costs of rewarding the loyal in Upper Canada were heavy and those costs were borne by the Mississauga and eastern Iroquois rather than by the British. How did this happen? A number of explanations have been suggested: the slow and unthreatening rate of white influx; the increasing lack of unity among the Mississauga; greater dependence on and demand for European goods; the conduct of negotiations by agents from the military/Indian department, who were men experienced in relating to natives, and in whom natives had trust. While none of these factors can be discounted, the best answer may be that initially the natives did not believe that they were, irrevocably, giving away their land. Even in English,

As depicted by W. H. Bartlett in 1840, the native village of St. Regis on the St. Lawrence near Cornwall was dominated by European structures: the church in the background and the wooden buildings throughout.   NATIONAL ARCHIVES OF CANADA/C2335

the surviving documents are confusing. Imagine the quality of the translations. In the case of the Niagara Peninsula surrender, the interpreters did "an atrocious job." Even more importantly, the concept of ownership as understood by the whites was very likely not that understood by the natives. The Mississauga "owned" land in a communal sense: no particular individual or group could lay exclusive claim to it. In return for presents, the Mississauga were willing to allow the whites a share in the use of the land, but the idea of exclusivity, as understood by the whites, only gradually, with the advance of white settlement, became understood by the Mississauga.

Following the War of 1812, imperial policy toward natives underwent substantial change. No longer considered subsidized warriors, natives received fewer annual presents. Desperate for money and supplies, they ceded some 10 million acres (4 million ha) to the Crown between 1815 and 1836. The decline in presents coupled with deteriorating hunting made alternative sources of income necessary. The British government, by instituting yearly payment rather than lump sum grants, seemed to guarantee a prosperous and protected future. Because of disease and alcohol, the native population declined at least until the mid-1850s. By contrast, white population grew substantially. Finally, a change in leadership resulting from the death of the elderly probably further undermined resistance.

The most dramatic land grab occurred in the mid-1830s. The newly arrived lieutenant-governor, Sir Francis Bond Head, coveted one and a half million acres (600 000 ha) of land in the Saugeen region, and in return offered 6000 natives perpetual rights to nearly barren islands north of Georgian Bay. Joseph Sawyer, a Credit River chief, exclaimed:

...if we go to Manitoulin, we could not live, soon we should be extinct as a people; we could raise no potatoes, corn, pork or beef; nothing would grow by putting the seed in the smooth rock....We have been bred among the white people, and our children could not live without bread, and other things, to which they are now accustomed.

Pressure from Methodist and other British religious leaders caused the Colonial Office to veto Bond Head's plans and to institute policies designed to assimilate rather than segregate Upper Canada's native peoples. The Crown kept the Saugeen land, however, and the most vocal opponents of the sale, the Credit Valley Mississauga, led by the fully ordained Methodist missionary, Kahkewaquonaby (Peter Jones), lost their hold on wealthy land at the junction of the Credit River and Lake Ontario in 1847.[2]

RURAL ECONOMY

White settlers found uprooting trees more difficult, expensive, and time consuming than displacing natives. Stumps were the physical signposts of frontier living: one traveller coined the phrase "Stumpology or the science of stumps" and advised that the first Canadian encyclopedia should contain an entry under that title. For five to ten years, settlers operated a farm in the making. Survival depended on the astute marshalling of the energy resources of one's immediate family. Yet early settler families tended, like the farms they owned, to be families in the making. Pregnant wives had to tend to young children as well as to demanding domestic household business—cooking, cleaning, washing, gardening, doctoring. While children entered the world of work at a much earlier age than they do today—as early as their eighth year—they could perform only tasks such as planting root crops and burning debris, not chopping, clearing, and piling. One could hire a chopper, but choppers charged handsomely and often performed poorly. Detailed written contracts covering chopping and piling testify to both the learned skills required and to the calculating nature of the frontier dweller. While chopping usually fell to the male household head, the family's resources were simply insufficient for logging and piling. Farming bees emerged, not from some spirit of bonhomie and brotherhood bred from a presumed egalitarian frontier, but from necessity. Labour was offered in return for copious food and drink (one yoke of oxen equalled one gallon of whiskey) and for the promise of labour in return. At the outset, the environment necessitated interaction and precluded self-sufficiency.

The insufficiency of the nuclear family as a self-sufficient farm enterprise is further illustrated by the composition of rural households. Existing evidence suggests an average household consisted of between six and

---

[2] A general overview of treaty agreements is provided in R. Surtees, *Indian Land Surrender in Ontario, 1763–1867* (Ottawa, 1984); L. F. S. Upton, "The Origins of Canadian Indian Policy, [*JCS*], 1973; a path breaking biography of an important Mississauga leader is Donald B. Smith, *Sacred Feathers: The Reverend Peter Jones (Kahkewaquonaby) and the Mississauga Indians* (Toronto, 1987). Leo A. Johnson provides a good analysis of one land surrender in "The Mississauga–Lake Ontario Land Surrender of 1805," *Ontario History* [*OH*], LXXXIII (1990), 233–53.

seven persons, at least one of whom tended to be a male working-hand. In the bush, males consistently outnumbered females because of the demands of the workplace. Simple nuclear families were disadvantaged and could rarely survive alone. They had to augment their labour force by natural increase (a long-term strategy), transient labour, short-term boarding of older children from neighbouring established families and, when necessary, by farmers' bees.

Merchant capitalism permeated the Upper Canadian bush. This is true despite the fact that, typical of most "frontier" economies, Upper Canada lacked cash. Goods were exchanged for goods. Farmers' and merchants' account books make it clear, however, that each item had a monetary value. A dollar's worth of wheat was exchanged for a dollar's worth of

This lithograph illustrates the land-clearing process in rural Upper Canada. Perhaps the only discordant element in the picture is the association of the wife and children with the home (cabin). In fact, women and children also worked in the fields.
NATIONAL ARCHIVES OF CANADA/C44633

sugar. Many, if not most, farmers went into debt before any land was cleared in order to purchase initial supplies, seeds, and implements. Their crops were planted not simply to feed their families but also to satisfy creditors.

What crops would creditors find suitable? Most historians have argued that wheat filled the bill. But does this emphasis on the importance of one staple reflect reality? One farmer's diary covering the period 1819–22 mentioned 39 different crops on his farm. While this variety was exceptional, few farmers simply planted wheat. Most participated in a dynamic local (as opposed to export-directed) economy and sold crops and goods other than wheat: firewood, hides, hay, pork, ashes, teaming services. While wheat was the dominant crop, its cultivation in 1803 required only 50 percent of the land under tillage, and the production of the export portion required only 20 percent of the land under cultivation. Fluctuations in the export of wheat did occur between 1794 and 1812, but these fluctuations did not deter immigrants. With the exception of the rebellion year, 1837–38, a similar pattern of economic development occurred from the mid-1820s until well into the 1840s. Yearly increases in population, cultivated land, grist and saw mills, houses, stores, pleasure carriages, horses, oxen, and cows took place. Dips in British wheat demand and/or poor wheat crops in Upper Canada did not seem to affect dramatically this steady growth picture. This is, of course, inconsistent with what the staple model would predict (boom and bust), and suggests the rural economy was more diversified than many have believed. In fact, wheat was far from the only export cash crop: the value of timber and wood exports from the St. Lawrence–Great Lakes area equalled in value wheat and flour exports during the 1815–1840 period. And, like wheat, exports of timber products predated British tariff protection. As well, demand for wood was strong in Upper Canada's internal economy—in most years more saw than grist mills were in operation. If, in any year, an export demand for a particular product fell, other possibilities existed for economic sustenance.

LAND POLICY AND RURAL SOCIETY

From the beginning, land appropriation in Upper Canada seems to have proceeded at a swift and unequal rate. The following cases illustrate the general pattern. Situated in the heart of eastern Upper Canada, Montague Township in Lanark County had had nearly half of its 112 square miles (290 km^2) appropriated by absentee landowners by 1810. These speculators sat on the land and began to sell it only after 1830. A similar pattern occurred in the Home District, the site of the colony's capital, York. By 1800, well before many settlers had arrived, between one-half and two-thirds of land in that district's central townships had been alienated, primarily by absentee speculators. The same pattern appeared in western Upper Canada. Of the 211 000 acres (85 400 ha) patented in the Western District by 1815, speculators owned 43 percent, including much of the best land. Despite tax increases on wild land following 1818, speculation continued throughout the colony. Even the executive government profited when in 1825 it sold 2 500 000 acres (1 012 000 ha) of Crown land to a private corporation, the Canada Company, for £295 000 payable over 16 years. In 1826 the executive also instituted the sale by auction of the remaining Crown lands. The prospect of starting a farm did not become easier as time passed.

This pattern of land ownership suggests that, even in an environment characterized by abundant vacant land, hierarchical social division based on land ownership could and did emerge. Speculation in choice lands by absentee owners forced poor settlers to look for cheaper land in townships more distant from roads, waterways, and emerging ports. Those relatively few settlers with money who could afford to purchase better-located land often found themselves bounded by vacant lands (including Crown and clergy reserves set aside by the Constitutional Act of 1791), thus intensifying their difficulties in terms of travel, labour pools, and general marketing.

Who were the speculators? A case study of the Western District up to 1825 is illustrative. In that area, the Baby and Askin families, long-time fur traders, well connected to both the Montreal merchants and the military/Indian departments, owned just over one-quarter of all patented land. Eight of the top 15 speculators (owners of 400 plus acres or 162 ha) in the Western District were merchants, most often active in the fur trade, and four were militia officers. Many of the top 15 were connected by marriage and were either themselves or had relatives in important political positions. The activities of John Askin are revealing. He used his marriage to a native woman to obtain native land at cheap cost. He also used his political contacts, in particular the colonial surveyor-general, D. W. Smyth, whom he had helped become elected, to protect his property. "[F]or God's sake," a financially pressured Askin urged Smyth in 1799, "get me thro this difficulty, ways and means are better known to you than me. It badly suits my present circumstances to lose 14 lots." As a group, the Western District speculators had patented 63 percent of all potential lands by 1825. Speculators routinely evaded taxes: less than one-half of their holdings were taxed, whereas 75 percent of nonspeculative holdings paid taxes. As John Clarke, a close student of this period has written, this tax evasion "must have had a dire effect upon the economic, social, and educational development of the area." Government land policy and speculative activity spawned conditions reminiscent of those that many settlers had hoped to have left behind in the Old World.

A closer look underlines the hierarchical structure of rural society in this period. A wheat farm of at least 100 cleared acres (40.5 ha) generated approximately $1500 per year. This equalled salaries paid to the highest government officials, although most such officials had access to additional income. Only 2 to 5 percent of Upper Canada's farmers held over 100 acres (40.5 ha), of cleared land. About 20 percent held between 50 and 100 acres (20.2 and 40.5 ha), and 50 percent held under 30 cultivated acres (12 ha). The average farm size in one eastern township in 1840 was 120 acres (48.5 ha), but only 10 percent of the landowners in that township had over half their land cleared and some 45 percent had less than a quarter cleared. These figures clearly point to a stratified rural structure. The few were in a position to live comfortably; the many were obviously struggling and, very likely, working part time elsewhere. At one level, the figures suggest at least the hope of being able to progress up the ladder. If the average holding was 120 acres (48.5 ha), then was it not only a matter of time before one's farm would be cleared and a high income realized? Perhaps, but the time and energy involved was formidable. During initial settlement when the focus was almost totally on land clearing, roughly 4 to 5 acres (1.6 to 2 ha) could be cleared in a year. Later, however, the increasing demands of operating a producing farm reduced clearing to less than 1.5 acres (0.6 ha) per year. The poor could ascend the social ladder, but only, to the elite's delight, slowly. That, after all, was the essence of social stability: the poor had prospects and therefore would be less likely to rebel; they could, however, only realize those prospects in a deliberate and measured way. The cost of land may not have precluded land purchase by a majority of emigrants, but it may have limited the amount of land emigrants could purchase and/or limited what they could spend on hiring help to clear land. It thus retarded rates of clearage and general economic advancement.[3]

---

[3] John Clarke, "Geographical Aspects of Land Speculation in Essex County to 1825: The Strategy of Particular Individuals," in K. G. Pryke, et al., eds., *The Western District* (1983), 69–112, gives many other references. Peter Russell, "Forest into Farmland: Upper Canadian Clearing Rates, 1822–1839," *Agricultural History*, 57 (1983), 326–39.

At another level, policies implemented to foster agrarian development led to a more radical transformation. Between 1821 and 1838, the colonial government amassed a debt in excess of £1 000 000 for the construction of canals, roads, and general public works. The Welland Canal, improvements on the St. Lawrence, and the Rideau Canal were all commenced in this period. The prime object, as William Hamilton Merritt, the main mover behind the Welland Canal put it, "was connecting the great chain of Lakes bordering on the Province with the Oceans." Upper Canadian and even American wheat could then be sent through British North America to Great Britain. The competition provided by the newly constructed Erie Canal in the United States could, Merritt, other Upper Canadians, and Montreal merchants hoped, be met and surpassed. In this, they were brought up short by Lower Canada's refusal to spend accordingly on their sections of the St. Lawrence.

Even in the 1870s, as this picture of canal construction near Montreal indicates, pick, shovel, and horse dominated the workplace. Working conditions had changed little from the 1830s.

NATIONAL ARCHIVES OF CANADA/C61471

Nevertheless, the extent of debt did necessitate more sophisticated financial instruments, institutions, and arrangements than had existed before. The Bank of Upper Canada, the colony's first chartered bank, opened for business in 1821, in part to serve the resident merchants and in part to serve the fiscal needs of the state. During the 1830s, six new banks commenced operations, and banking capital increased by over five times.

Canal construction signalled the beginnings of an economic transition from agrarian to industrial capitalism. Between 1826 and 1832, some 9000 men laboured on the Rideau and Welland canals each year. Large gangs worked side by side, controlled by a contractor/manager answerable to the ultimate owner of the enterprise, the state. This separation of labour from ownership constituted a dramatic step toward industrial capitalism and signified the increased complexity of the local economy. The men received extremely low wages, faced notoriously poor working conditions, and were cast aside upon the project's completion. Strikes did occur. Violence and rioting erupted. But, due in part to military assistance in containing the unrest, construction continued.

The government's program of economic development wrought changes of a sort few had anticipated. Crop diversification, land clearage, exports of wheat and flour, as well as lumber and wood products, and a buoyant internal economy all contributed to the outward success of elite policy. Yet canal construction engendered new economic and social relations in the workplace; financial needs demanded the creation of new and sophisticated institutions and new and binding ties to the mother country. Immigration brought needed capital to the colony; but it also brought tens of thousands of destitute labourers, impoverished widows, children, and old people. Rising costs of land coupled with at best stable and very likely declining wage rates made it increasingly difficult for new emigrants to become what both they and the elite desired—farmers. Instead many became paupers or, at best, labourers.

In Pursuit of Power: Politics and Politicians in Upper Canada

ELITE EMERGENCE TO 1815

The Constitutional Act of 1791 created the political structure within which Upper Canada would evolve. That Constitution reflected the values of a powerful land-based group of British "gentlemanly capitalists" who believed that a proper governmental system had to include elements of the monarchy, the aristocracy, and the democracy or common people. Upper Canada received a lieutenant-governor who, acting as the Crown's representative, could withhold or reserve royal assent to any legislation. He also appointed both the executive council, whose appointees sat at his pleasure and offered him advice, and members of the legislative council, the "upper" section of the bicameral legislature, whose members would hold their seats for life. The assembly, the "lower" section of the bicameral legislature, was elected for no longer than four years by male British subjects 21 years and older, who satisfied minimal property qualifications. This was a complex structure, one which over time and with special focus on the powers of the two councils, would generate a great deal of debate and dissatisfaction in Upper Canada.

British policy makers provided that one-seventh of the land of each township be set aside for the maintenance "of a Protestant clergy" and later that another one-seventh be reserved for the Crown. While many then and later assumed that "Protestant clergy" meant the established Church of England, the Anglican Church, the wording was unclear on this point. Certainly, many British policy makers hoped the Anglican Church would become the colony's "state" church. In light of the fact that Anglicans were a small minority in Upper Canada in 1791, this intent could only rankle many Loyalists. And, of course, over and above the problem of special treatment favouring one church, the system of clergy and Crown reserves meant that less land was available for individual settlers.

The political elite that emerged reflected an uneasy balance between commerce and administration, British ideals and North American practice, and regional loyalties and bureaucratic placelessness. Initially, British bureaucrats dominated the capital, York. By 1803 roughly 100 major appointments had been made; then York's families began to provide for their own. Sixty percent of the major appointments made between 1803 and 1812 went to members of already established families. This strong proprietary attitude toward office holding—the sense that one could aspire to owning an office and bequeathing it—contrasts markedly with the rules governing civil service operations today. The York group controlled land, judicial, and civil functions, which would in one way or another touch every resident.

Variations on this theme took place outside York. The "Baron," Colonel Thomas Talbot, a large landowner in the St. Thomas–London area, exercised his paternalist power in the classic fashion of the eighteenth-century British gentry. Having acquired much of his land in return for the promise of settling British emigrants, Talbot looked on all the region's settlers as his "children." Uninterested in commerce and disdainful of York's bureaucrats (as they were of him), Talbot ruled his fiefdom with a dextrous system of handouts—liquor, land, local preferment, and the threatened sting of autocratic power. Settlers' names were pencilled in on Talbot's surveys: they could be erased at the slightest hint of unbecoming conduct. Rarely sullying his own hands in political affairs, Talbot used a number of local placeseekers as his political and business agents. When necessary, he manipulated electoral returns, as in 1812, by bribing voters with land grants and by situating the polling booth 60 miles (96 km) from the opponent's home!

Those who emerged to positions of power in other areas outside York tended to be less in the mould of the British squires and more in the mould of the ambitious merchant. The Upper Canadian merchant, Robert Hamilton, consciously constructed a network of family alliances centred at Niagara. So too did Richard Cartwright at Kingston and, as we have seen, the Askins and Babys in the Western District. When Lieutenant-Governor Simcoe attempted to consolidate regional affairs more firmly in York's hands, he found it necessary to appoint merchants to newly created local positions simply because there were too few qualified alternatives. Merchants and bureaucrats had to learn to co-exist.

For all their differences, merchants like Robert Hamilton from Niagara and British-appointed government leaders such as Lieutenant-Governor Simcoe were united in their pursuit of conspicuous consumption. Hamilton owned what was reputedly Upper Canada's finest home. Simcoe could sup there at ease. Social life in tiny York was an incestuous round of balls and suppers. If Simcoe's wife could complain of the "want of servants," others, like the aspiring William Jarvis, kept his two and one-half storey log home with the aid of six black slaves. This peacocklike display of wealth and power had the effect of social closure. Intermarriage, liberal land grants, proper education, and displays of wealth helped both to solidify the emerging elite and, at the same time, to separate it from the mass of Upper Canada's settlers.

"Launching" children was a major preoccupation of this emerging elite. Even non-merchant and non-bureaucratic members of the middle/upper class, like the Reverend John Stuart, a Loyalist and the first rector of St. George's Anglican Church in Kingston, spent considerable time and money in providing his eight children "proper and respectable places in society." While the children of bush farmers entered farm employ at age eight, children of the middle and upper classes on the make went to private schools like the Reverend John Strachan's at Cornwall, to academies in New York State, to article with suitably accredited Upper Canadian lawyers, or to clerk in their father's governmental office.

That is, of course, if the children were male. Females had different roles to play. They did not require substantial education. For the aspiring middle and upper classes, the concept of separate spheres—women in the house to rear families, handle social affairs, and generally assist their ambitious husbands to succeed in the outside world—permeated family organization. Yet for upwardly mobile families, the social roles played by women were often crucial. In a small and hierarchically structured society, who you dined, danced, and dallied with mattered. As Ann Powell, wife of the chief justice, wrote in 1806 on the eve of a ball in honour of the Queen: "Their rank will be settled and I fear some who claim precedence, will find themselves of less importance than they expect." Upper-class women were far from retiring belles closeted in protected homes. In social affairs, affairs so central to political success, they were on the front lines.

Even before 1812, tensions existed within elite households. Servants tended to be unruly, independent, and hard to retain. After the early 1790s, no new slaves could be imported and, besides, slaves were too expensive to retain. How could York's elite maintain face without the assistance of dependable underlings? Even more worrisome was the presumed breakdown of "the well-regulated" family. In 1804, six prominent parishioners in tiny York kept "Mistresses," the local Anglican pastor lamented. Newspapers regularly carried notices like the following:

Whereas Sibyel, my wife has eloped from my bed and board, without just cause; All persons are forbid harboring or trusting her on my account, as I will pay no debt of her contracting after this date.

For women to leave their families in this male-dominated society—as an 1802 newspaper explained, women were, after all, created to be a "help meet" for man—suggests both the degree of abuse that existed within some families and the amount of independence that some women exhibited. Not that desperation always underlay independent action. Newspaper advertisements document the growing presence of single women in many business pursuits, including merchants, innkeepers, and artisans.

Despite the anger of many men, some courageous women had begun to challenge social norms concerning proper female behaviour as early as the beginning of the nineteenth century.

Between 1800 and 1812, the Reverend John Strachan kept an especially close eye on the changing fortunes of the Upper Canadian family. By 1811 he despaired of the "self-interested," "wicked," "deceitful," "debauched," "drunken," "liars," who seemed to make up so much of the young generation. He detected a decline in respect for elders and more importantly for the values elders held dear. He linked the alleged disaffections to family breakdown and to a republican spirit loose throughout the colony. Affection had to be tempered by the inculcation of respect for family, community, and Crown. "To regulate a family and keep children in proper subordination is much more difficult than is commonly supposed," he warned his listeners in 1812. He might well have said the same concerning the proper regulation of a society.

In fact, many Upper Canadians had begun to oppose elite activities. Methodists, probably the colony's largest religious group, not only resented official preferences given to Anglicans in matters of land, but also seethed at restrictions on their right to conduct marriages. Rural settlers resented the placement of schools, financed in part by their taxes, in hard-to-reach urban areas. Country as opposed to court (York) leaders competed for patronage and other spoils. By 1812 a broadly reform-oriented group of 11 of the assembly's 23 members voted for legislative control of money bills, lower salaries for bureaucrats, lower land assessment rates, and easier access to land. In the language used by the Reverend John Strachan, Upper Canadians on the eve of the War of 1812 seemed to lack all sense of "proper subordination."[4]

The War of 1812, fought by England and her colonies against the United States, dealt a solid blow to the emerging Upper Canadian reform movement. That fact is one of the most important significances of this overly

---

[4] A standard, if somewhat dated, treatment of politics and society in this period is G. Craig, *Upper Canada: The Formative Years* (Toronto, 1966). For a more recent treatment from a different focus consult S. J. R. Noel, *Patrons, Clients, Brokers: Ontario Society and Politics, 1791–1896* (Toronto, 1990). For insights into early reform activity, see the biographies of William Weekes and Joseph Willcocks by G. H. Patterson and E. H. Jones, respectively, in *Dictionary of Canadian Biography* [*DCB*] Vol. 5 (Toronto, 1983). For the role played by upper-class women see K. M. J. McKenna, "The Role of Women in the Establishment of Social Status in Early Upper Canada," *OH*, LXXXIII (1990), 179–206. A good survey of Canadian women's history is A. Prentice et al., eds., *Canadian Women: A History* (Toronto, 1988).

glorified war. Confrontation seemed unlikely following 1794 when Britain had ceded its western forts to the United States. Yet the situation changed rapidly after 1803. Britain and France renewed their European conflict. With her superior navy, Britain began to interfere with neutral shipping, and, in June 1807, attacked and boarded an American frigate, the *Chesapeake*. The United States reacted in a predictably belligerent way, shattering the calm that had enveloped the Upper Canadian frontier. War Hawks, congressional members who represented western and westward-bound settlers, argued that the easiest way to damage Great Britain was by annexing British North America, especially that part of it known as Upper Canada. It would not be difficult. Most who lived there, they believed, were Americans secretly awaiting deliverance from despotic (i.e., monarchic) British rule.

Clearly one group who lived there did not fit that description. Many western native peoples were at this time coming under the influence of a millenarian religion preached by the prophet Tenskwatawa. Animated by other-worldly visions, the prophet followed in the tradition of the native revival movement of the 1750s and 1760s over which Pontiac had assumed leadership. Tenskwatawa's brother, the Shawnee chief Tecumseh, increasingly embittered by the resolute nature of American expansion—natives had ceded over 30 million acres (12 million ha) to American whites between 1803 and 1805—gradually transformed this religious movement into a fighting force for the defence of native lands. This force existed independently of British aid or encouragement. In fact, native leaders, remembering the double-crosses of 1783 and 1794 (where the British, by leaving the western forts, reneged on their promise to protect the natives against American expansion), were very wary of new British promises. These suspicions were shared by the Six Nation Iroquois in Upper Canada who in 1808 complained "of the great distress they are in for bread" and stated that they intended "to sit quiet in case of any quarrel between the King's America." The Mississauga centred at York, although much weakened by liquor, hunger, and disease (their population in this area had dropped from over 500 in 1787 to about 320 in 1801) and much abused by the molestation of British soldiers and settlers, were equally wary of British overtures. Nevertheless, following 1807, the British Indian department covertly attempted to supply and encourage the western natives to stand ready for a joint British/native offensive against United States.

Such encouragement could hardly be secret. Sporadic fighting between American settlers and western natives revealed the use of British guns.

British incitement and support further heated an already incendiary situation. Despite belated British attempts to keep native allies on a short leash, by the fall of 1811 the native frontier was a virtual war zone. Harassed on the seas, frustrated on the frontier, and enticed by what appeared to be "easy pickings" in Upper Canada, the United States declared war against Great Britain in June 1812.

Fear of American invasion intensified the administration's reaction to government critics and their Upper Canadian followers. The assembly refused to pass measures the executive deemed necessary to ready Upper Canada for war. General Isaac Brock correctly worried more about "the disposition of the people" than the enemy. Upper Canadian militia were as raggedly trained and reluctant to fight as their American counterparts. Early victories spearheaded by Brock leading British regulars and native allies at Detroit and Queenston Heights (where he lost his life) eased local dissent. A massive American campaign levelled York in April 1813, but the Americans quit the area after a week of pilfering. The York raid led to criticisms of the British garrison's failure to defend the capital. Governor General Sir George Prevost replied by appointing government agents to report on dissension and disloyal activity. Many reform leaders, fearing the strengthening of appointed government agencies at the expense of the elected assembly, quit Upper Canada, some to fight alongside the Americans.

Americans achieved success in the Lake Erie region in September and October 1813, but, worried about a native counterattack, failed to hold their gains. The Erie battles, however, shattered the confederation that the native leader Tecumseh had assembled to fight with the British. Abandoned by the British, Tecumseh and 500 followers fought on against 3000 Americans at Morristown on the Thames River. Tecumseh was killed and the confederation rent apart. Peace talks between the Americans and 3000 natives commenced in July 1814, months before war's end. For the native peoples, the War of 1812 marked the decisive finale to a longstanding, if often uneasy and rarely satisfactory, alliance with a European nation operating out of Montreal. Since the Conquest of 1760, that alliance had been marked by three major British betrayals: 1783, 1794, and now 1813. There would not be a fourth. The natives, not the British, ended that alliance.

Americans did not learn from their Lake Erie successes. In 1814, instead of massing for an assault against Kingston—the seat of British naval construction on Lake Ontario and the crucial commercial linchpin between that lake and the St. Lawrence—they undertook yet another advance through the Niagara region. In July, after the war's fiercest fighting, they were turned back at Lundy's Lane.

On 24 December 1814 the Treaty of Ghent provided for commissions to examine the most contentious issues in Anglo-American relations—Great Lakes naval armaments, fishing off the Maritime shores, navigation rights and boundary disputes—and required a return of all conquests. The Rush-Bagot Agreement of 1817 provided for naval disarmament on the Great Lakes. The convention of 1818 set the boundary west of Lake of the Woods at the 49th Parallel up to the Rocky Mountains and dealt with the Atlantic fisheries. While this did not mean an undefended border in Upper Canada (forts, canals, and roadways continued to be constructed with military purposes in mind) or an end to hostile feelings, it did ease considerably the tensions that existed before and during the war.

Of all the British North American colonies, the war hit Upper Canada the hardest. Yet not all Upper Canadian regions were equally affected. The Niagara area suffered much battle damage and even greater economic problems because of its disruption as a shipping centre for an already declining fur trade. York's merchants, in contrast, profited from a growing trade in wheat and foodstuffs. York's bureaucratic elite began to equate dissent with treason; political opposition with Americanization. They also came to believe that those on the spot could best implement British policy: after all, they affirmed, look how the British regulars failed to protect York. As the seat of political and bureaucratic power, York benefited from the growth of a centralized civil-military presence in Upper Canada. This power touched many Upper Canadians whether through militia service, the sale of agricultural products to the military, or through a heightened awareness of the need to defend against a common threat.

As the centre of shipbuilding, a major military port, and an essential shipping point, Kingston enjoyed a buoyant economy uninterrupted by the physical devastation of battle. Kingstonians were close in spirit to the Federalist Tory party in the United States. During the war, goods, news, individuals, and ideas continued to cross the border. Yet that war swept away the Federalists as an ongoing force in American society. Kingston's elite determined that the same would not happen in Upper Canada. Although the process had been different at York, the end was the same. The war stiffened the elite's resolve to create, on the British North American frontier, a Tory fortress impervious to extreme democratic influence.

CONSERVATIVES, REFORMERS, AND REBELS

Coming on the heels of the American and French revolutions and the Irish rebellion of 1798, the War of 1812 hardened conservative attitudes in Upper Canada. Some historians have argued that this period represented the birth of Canada's conservative tradition: a concern for order and stability; the measured recognition of group rights; a distrust of things American; and a fervent loyalty to the ideals of the British monarchy. This is an important interpretation, although it underemphasizes the impact that economic and social change had on political behaviour in the post-1815 period. By 1841 the seeds of modern political parties and modern governmental behaviour were planted in Upper Canada. While these seeds received sustenance from eighteenth-century British Tory traditions and from the hothouse effect created by the War of 1812, their ultimate flowering depended on nourishment derived from a gradual transition in local economic and social practice.

Between 1818 and 1828, a Tory elite, the so-called Family Compact, was firmly in control of the executive and legislative councils. In close collaboration with the lieutenant-governor and in command of the judicial system, the Family Compact alienated many Upper Canadians who, by the end of the 1820s, began to coalesce as "His Majesty's faithful opposition." One complex issue known as the Alien Question excited much opposition. Americans born in the United States after 1783 were denied the right to own land and to vote in Upper Canada. Given the large number of Americans in Upper Canada, this was no trivial matter. While the Tory-controlled courts—the executive council represented the highest court of appeal in the colony—and the Tory legislators backed off on the denial of land rights, since many Tories were themselves speculators who had sold Americans land, they equivocated and stalled on the matter of political right. One American, Marshall Spring Bidwell, was even stripped of his seat in the assembly in 1822. Increasingly frustrated, the Tory's opponents ignored the lieutenant-governor and petitioned directly to England for justice. Much to the Tories' shock, in 1827, redress was granted and those who were American born were guaranteed equal political rights.

Other incidents kindled growing dissent. In 1818, a fiery Scots reformer, Robert Gourlay, had the temerity to conduct a survey of Upper Canadians, encouraging critical statements of government and politicians. He responded to Tory attempts to stifle the questionnaire by calling John Strachan, a leading Anglican clergyman and member of both the executive and legislative councils, a "monstrous little fool of a parson" and by chairing a public convention to discuss public problems. Arguing that such conventions smacked of French revolutionary happenings, the Tories banned them. Gourlay was jailed for eight months and banished for disturbing the colony's "tranquillity." Many of his supporters were dismissed from public posts.

This water colour by F. H. Consitt of the 1828 electoral campaign in Perth, Upper Canada, suggests the excitement and violence that accompanied such events. There was no secret ballot, and voters were regularly "influenced" by whiskey, money and force.

In the midst of this rising disaffection, John Strachan, responding to the increased immigration of British Anglicans, began to promote what he considered to be the proper prerogatives of the state's church. He became head of the General Board of Education through which he could control school textbook selections. He lobbied for an Anglican-controlled colonial university. When Strachan presented the Colonial Office with a biased perspective on the colony's religious affairs, the reform press organized a counterattack, sending a petition with 8000 signatures decrying a "clerico-political aristocracy" to England in 1827.

These and other "outrages" led to the election in 1824 and again in 1828 of the first clearly reform-dominated assemblies. Reform-minded politicians began to organize at grass roots constituency levels. Yet reformers themselves possessed no common party platform. Nor did they possess a very committed electoral following. Given the reality of the stable, hierarchically structured rural society, it is a wonder that political passions escalated to the extent that they did. For many reform leaders and most reform voting farmers, the arrival of a new lieutenant-governor, Sir John Colborne, represented sufficient reform. He held prominent elite members at arm's length; distributed patronage to non–Family Compact members, even broadening the legislative and executive councils; and supported a number of economic and development measures proposed by the assembly between 1828 and 1830. The rural population seemed to believe that Upper Canada was indeed a poor man's country: they were willing to defer to acceptable moral leadership, probably in the expectation that someday they, too, could make it up the social and economic ladder. Colborne successfully pacified discontent: the Tories swept the 1830 election.

At a micro or personal level, the political career of John Willson aptly symbolizes the connection between political outrage and rural economic structures in the late 1820s. Before 1812, he stood with the reform opposition and, during the war, voted against the suspension of habeas corpus. Throughout the 1820s, known as "Honest John," he cultivated the rural electorate around the head of Lake Ontario (modern Hamilton) by promoting universal education, attacking civil court inequities, defending women's right to own property (they were, he believed, equal workers on the land), opposing the clergy reserves, and supporting general economic development. He argued that if more farmers were in Parliament expenses would decline and the economy would grow. He called himself a "plain farmer" ready "to reap the advantages of the country." He also saw himself as an independent conservative, ready to support the Compact party, if they deserved it, i.e., if they stood for moral government and economic development. In 1828 he was happy that the people "had at last been roused to save their liberties." He was equally happy to accept Colborne's resolution of those "complaints."[5]

Many historians characterize Upper Canadian politics as "marked by tranquillity, even somnolence rather than by violence and strife." For them the Rebellion of 1837 becomes "uncharacteristic," if not anomalous. Yet even in the 1820s, Tories were quick to smash the printing press of a reform editor, William Lyon Mackenzie; to tar and feather and threaten the dismemberment of a hapless reform clerk in the Gore District; and to jail yet other Reform editors, but never Tory editors, if they wrote too critically of the governing elite. If violence simmered in the 1820s, it escalated in the 1830s. Before 1850 some 400 riots took place throughout British North America. At least 51 of them occurred in Upper Canada between 1824 and 1840, 44 of which erupted in the 1830s. Rising criminal activities seemed to parallel the increase in violence.

As one Tory politician put it, "Everything seems tending toward revolution...." The 1825 Decembrist uprising in Russia, revolutions in central and western Europe, the chartist movement and electoral reform in England, and the threat of Jacksonian democracy in the United States intensified anxiety. To contain disaffection (both imagined and real), Upper Canada's elite began to abandon voluntary, localized, community structures and looked for support instead to the state and state-supported institutions. The 1830s marked the beginnings of the rise of the modern institutional state and, in its shadow, the emergence to power of a new ruling class.

Hospitals were constructed to, as one doctor put it, "repress [the] vices" of the sick. Along with houses of healing, state-supported "houses of industry" were set up to contain, cure, and reform their inmates so that on release they would fit well into a changing social and economic milieu. Legislation was passed to construct a "Lunatic Hospital." Anxious debate took place over education, setting the stage for the institutionalization of schools in the 1840s. In 1835, the largest public building in Upper Canada, the Kingston Penitentiary, opened for business. It became a monument

---

[5] A popular treatment of the War of 1812 is Pierre Berton, *The Invasion of Canada 1812–13* (Toronto, 1980) *Flames Across the Border, 1813–14* (Toronto, 1981); H. C. W. Goltz, "Tecumseh," *DCB*, V, 795–800 and C. P. Stacey, "Sir Isaac Brock," *DCB*, V, 109–115 are both useful.

and symbol for the cleansing of disease, destitution, and disorder from the social body. Its architecture embodied the moral values of the elite. Its massive and imposing exterior cowed and impressed. The penitentiary became society's showcase. It became what society should be, but was not.

To strengthen their political position, the Tories reached out to two groups of new immigrants. The first was the Protestant Irish, some of whom brought with them a fierce antagonism toward Catholics and, since they had been living as a loyalist minority in Ireland, a sensitive antenna to the cry of beleaguered loyalism. Some organized into Orange lodges, a protective Protestant society that provided them social cohesion and collective strength. Between 1830 and 1834, riots against reformers occurred in Hamilton, Toronto, and the districts of London, Newcastle, and Johnstown. Orangemen, in alliance with local Tory leaders, substituted physical force for the rule of law. A second group, the Upper Canadian Methodists, no longer primarily American in origin, and led by Egerton Ryerson, erstwhile critic and foe of Strachan, moved closer to the Tory fold. Traditional practices like rural camp meetings and public emotional demonstrations declined and were replaced by urban churches led by educated and professionally trained preachers: Methodism came more and more to opt for the rational principles along which Anglicanism was structured. The possibility of sharing in clergy reserves money plus the right to solemnize marriages, finally granted in 1831, eased tensions.

A short-lived reform assembly of 1834 was swept from power in a violence-filled election in 1836. Sir Francis Bond Head, the lieutenant-governor and self-appointed leader of the Tory troops in that election, dismissed from office all those who had had the temerity to oppose him. Defeated, many moderate reformers, in despair, quit politics, a fact that left reform leadership open to those of a more radical bent, like William Lyon Mackenzie. Taking his cue from Lower Canada, on 25 December 1837 Mackenzie led around 1000 ill-armed followers down Yonge Street to Toronto in an attempt to overthrow the colonial regime. The attempt failed abysmally, as did a second uprising in western Upper Canada led by Dr. Charles Duncombe. The rebels, pursued by Loyalist militia, fled to the United States where some staged throughout 1838 a series of border incursions that kept the colony in a state of tension.

Rebel motives are not easy to categorize. We know that in western Upper Canada, rebels tended to be more often of American or Scottish rather than English heritage, to be Presbyterian or Baptist rather than Anglican, and to be similar in socio-economic background to those of their neighbours who did not rebel. Whatever political grievances the rebels had were intensified by a severe financial crisis that beset the colony in late 1837. Triggered by a recession in Great Britain and the United States, the crisis was compounded by Bond Head's pig-headed refusal to allow the colony's banks to adopt a policy that would have lessened debt foreclosures and ameliorated the ensuing credit crunch. But Bond Head equated "speculation" (i.e., debt) with Americans and both with disloyalty. Tight credit would, Bond Head believed, "tend most materially to assist in crushing the enemy of Civilization—democracy."

At both the local community level and at the provincial level, a new breed of political leader began to emerge in the 1830s. These leaders were from a business, mercantile, or professional rather than farming background. While common to both political groups, this trend was most pronounced among the Tories. This suggests that, for some, the Rebellion of 1837 represented an attempt to preserve an agrarian lifestyle by unseating an increasingly non-agrarian-based political and economic elite.[6] The extent to which that attempt failed, and the degree to which this emerging elite consolidated its power in the post-Rebellion era, can best be examined following a discussion of developments in the second colony created by the Constitutional Act of 1791 and the only other colony to revolt in 1837, Lower Canada.

Lower Canada: The Transition, 1791–1838

INTRODUCTION

Bold interpretations have been offered about the "reality" of life in Lower Canada. The interpretation most often found in textbooks combines

---

[6] In addition to Craig and Noel cited in footnote 4, see David Mills, *The Idea of Loyalty in Upper Canada, 1784–1850* (Montreal, 1988); Paul Romney, *Mr. Attorney: The Attorney General for Ontario in Court, Cabinet and Legislature, 1791–1899* (Toronto, 1986), 1–201. This is a much more wide-ranging and provocative study than the title suggests. J. K. Johnson, *Becoming Prominent: Regional Leadership in Upper Canada, 1791–1841* (Kingston, 1989) is a mine of information. R. L. Fraser's biography of John Willson in *DCB*, 8 (Toronto, 1985), 945–46 is useful. Colin Read, *The Rising in Western Upper Canada, 1837–8* (Toronto, 1982) and C. Read and R. J. Stagg, *The Rebellion of 1837 in Upper Canada* (Toronto, 1985), cover the rebellion. For institutional development see T. Brown, "The Origins of the Asylum in Upper Canada, 1830–39," *Canadian Bulletin of Medical History*, 1 (1984), 37–58.

elements of the staple theory with a notion of a colonial or conquered mentality that allegedly beset Lower Canadians following the Conquest of 1760. This traditional view argues that Lower Canadian farmers failed abysmally in their dogged attempt to supply the staple, wheat, to Great Britain. After enjoying some success in the 1790s, their fortunes declined dramatically after 1803. A number of factors are offered as reasons for this decline: soil exhaustion, improper farming techniques, overcrowding, growing competition from other North American centres, and by the 1830s, a series of insect infestations, all of which laid the hardy habitant low. In their increasing desperation, Lower Canadian farmers listened to a reactionary feudal-minded rural elite of lawyers and other professional sons of seigneurs and a few successful habitant farmers who, in an attempt to find security for themselves, blamed a growing anglo elite for the poverty of the countryside and preached a reactionary nationalist message, all of which culminated in the Rebellion of 1837–38. This vision juxtaposed an ostrichlike, head in the sand habitant with a dynamic, aggressive, but frustrated anglo business elite.

A new interpretation emerged on the eve of Quebec's Quiet Revolution in the 1960s. After Québécois began to take charge of their economy and political bureaucracy in the 1960s, historians sought for the past roots of such aggressive behaviour and suggested that those roots extended back at least to the early nineteenth century. These scholars argued that a spirit of entrepreneurship, not a docile, defeated sense of resignation, permeated the countryside. Modernization did not bypass, but rather transformed, the habitant. French-Canadian farm families, in their own way as market driven as the urban-based anglo merchant elite, actively participated in a broad restructuring of traditional lifestyles. In the course of so doing, they ran up against that anglo elite and contested its political, social, and economic position. That challenge lay at the base of the 1837–38 rebellions.

These are extreme interpretations. It is possible to find a more moderate position, one that will be offered here. It accepts the reality of agrarian hardship especially evident in the 1830s. It acknowledges that this distress fuelled revolutionary behaviour. At the same time, this moderate perspective argues that the countryside was not a homogeneous society. All were not poor. Nor were all farmers. Modernization of rural practices occurred even as traditional rural behaviour persisted. Rebel leadership in the country reflected an emerging economic and social group. Not all rural dwellers were ostriches; nor were all entrepreneurs. In urban centres, too, poverty and distress existed. This combination of rural dissatisfaction and urban unease challenged the urban-based anglo elite in the Rebellion of 1837–38.[7]

POPULATION, LAND, AND THE RURAL ECONOMY

Population—growth, distribution and demographic characteristics—and amount of cleared and uncleared land are two key components in all interpretations of Lower Canadian life. As Table 1 indicates, Lower Canada's population doubled about every 25 years. Most of the francophone increase was due to a birth rate of 50 per 1000 and a death rate of 25 per 1000. High when compared to European rates, this birth rate approximated that experienced by other New World settlements in this era. Before 1815, most of the anglophone growth was the result of immigration into the Eastern Townships from New England. Between 1815 and 1844, about 400 000 immigrants from the British Isles entered the port of Quebec. Some 40 000 stayed in Lower Canada, the rest moved on to the United States or Upper Canada. While many English settled in the larger urban centres—by the 1830s, over one-half of Montreal's population was English-speaking and by 1851, 40 percent of Quebec City's—a full two-thirds of the anglophone population lived in rural areas in 1844. Anglophones did dominate the urban mercantile elite, but not all anglophones were wealthy and well connected. By the early 1830s, two out of every five of Montreal's day labourers were English.

---

[7] The traditional view can be followed in Fernand Ouellet, *Economic and Social History of Quebec, 1760–1850* (Carleton University Press) (first published 1966) translated 1980, and *Lower Canada, 1791–1840* (Toronto, 1980); for a shorter version that follows most of Ouellet's arguments see Susan Mann Trofimenkoff, *The Dream of Nation: A Social and Intellectual History of Quebec* (Toronto, 1983). For a recent and forceful statement of the modernizing view, see G. Paquet and J.-P. Wallot, *Lower Canada at the Turn of the Century: Restructuring and Modernization*, CHA Historical Booklet #45 (Ottawa, 1988). This booklet provides access to some of the central literature in this debate. Serge Courville's writings come closest to a moderate perspective. See "Villages and Agriculture in the Seigneuries of Lower Canada: Conditions of a Comprehensive Study of Rural Quebec in the First Half of the Nineteenth Century," in *Canadian Papers in Rural History*, 5 (1986), 121–49 and with N. Séguin, *Rural Life in Nineteenth Century Quebec*, CHA Historical Booklet #47 (Ottawa, 1989). A useful overview of social and economic development is provided by Brian Young and J. A. Dickinson, *A Short History of Quebec: A Socio-Economic Perspective* (Toronto, 1988). For the early period Allan Greer, *Peasant, Lord and Merchant* (Toronto, 1985), should be consulted.

TABLE 1

LOWER CANADA: POPULATION GROWTH AND DISTRIBUTION

	Total	Percentage French	Percentage English	Urban	Rural
1791	165 000	94	6	6	94
1815	335 000	88	12	11	89
1831	512 000	82	18	11	89
1844	691 200	75	25(est.)	12(est.)	88
1851	890 000	75	25	13	87

The potential for conflict along ethnic lines in urban centres existed at all class levels.

Economic activity in rural Lower Canada encompassed more than farming. Ten to 12 percent of people in the seigneurial territory of the St. Lawrence lowlands lived in hamlets or villages and were not farmers. The number of villages grew from 51 in 1815 to 210 in 1831 to over 250 in 1851. These villages were often more than distribution centres; they also became centres of diverse industrial activity. Especially in the Montreal region, these commercial/industrial centres were well linked by roads to rural farmers who found there a local market for their produce as well as a source of needed material items. Clearly, the habitant farmer could and did produce far more than wheat. By the 1830s, increased diversity in crop production—barley, peas, corn, potatoes, tobacco, hemp—reflected the variety of markets available to the habitant farmer: overseas, continental, urban/regional, and local village. The communication links suggest that these villages provided a place to which rural dwellers could go for work— nearly 40 percent of workers in the countryside surrounding the village of St. Eustache in 1831 were day labourers who did not declare farming as their main occupation. In rural Lower Canada, and especially in the Montreal region, a process of industrialization and urbanization was well advanced by the 1830s. The diversified structure of this rural economy resembled similar development in some European countries and in New England where full-scale industrialization was preceded by decentralized industrial growth.

In the context of traditional writing on Lower Canada, the assertion of economic diversity and vitality in the seigneurial lowlands is startling. Some 80 percent of Lower Canadians lived on the approximately 195 seigneuries in the Montreal, Trois Rivières, and Quebec regions. The seigneurial system with its hidden charges and onerous dues payable by habitants to the seigneur has rarely been portrayed as an institution or structure capable of facilitating economic modernization. Generally, seig-

The assertion by the artist (circa 1805) that Canadians made their own clothes is somewhat misleading. Rural families regularly used imported British cloth, and urban dwellers rarely wore local homespun clothes. In fact, between 1792 and 1835 British commodities, cloth, linen, cups and saucers, and tastes — tea instead of coffee — became ever more pervasive throughout urban and rural Lower Canada. In part, this trend reflected the control exercised by British merchants over Lower Canada's wholesale import and export trade. NATIONAL ARCHIVES OF CANADA/C14835

neurs and the seigneurial system are held to be remnants of the precapitalist feudal era. But in this period of transition, old bottles were made to hold
new wine. As early as 1791, two-thirds of the seigneuries were owned in
whole or in part by French-Canadian and English-Canadian bourgeoisie.
This percentage increased dramatically with the decline of the fur trade as
a major preoccupation of Montreal merchants in the early years of the
nineteenth century. This new breed of seigneur facilitated economic
diversification even while exploiting rural dwellers using all the feudal
powers and privileges at his command. These seigneurs and resident
merchants, in fact, experienced the greatest income gains in the Lower
Canadian countryside. Modernization and exploitation were not incompatible. Perhaps the pace of economic development would have been
greater had the seigneurial system been abolished before 1854. But that is
different than claiming, as do many adherents of the traditional interpretation, that the system stifled all such development.

Just how poor were the habitants? Analysis of a wide range of personal
inventories left after death suggests that income differentiation and a more
hierarchically structured rural society emerged between 1791 and 1838 in
the Lower Canadian seigneuries. The very poor and the very rich grew
more quickly than other groups. Rural society became less homogeneous
and more class structured. Significant differentiation in the distribution of
wealth in the countryside is also suggested by the fact that over one-
quarter of farm families in the Montreal area owned less than eight acres
(3.2 ha) of cultivated land, seven or eight acres (2.8 to 3.2 ha) being close
to the minimum necessary for subsistence living.

It is important to suggest the probable causes of this process of social
and economic differentiation in the countryside. Many proponents of the
traditionalist argument state that smaller land holdings were a primary
cause of poverty and that these small holdings stemmed from the ancien
régime legal requirement to divide all assets equally among family heirs.
Yet in practice this legal requirement was often avoided. As well, in certain
old parishes with little available new land, family strategies lessened the
problem of land scarcity. For example, a high proportion of marriages in
old rural parishes involved an older woman with land and a younger man
without. Some parents entered into a contract with one of their sons who,
in return for providing his parents with ample food, clothing, shelter, and
money for the rest of their lives and on occasion also providing money to
his brother and sisters, received the family farm as his own. Moreover,
while detailed studies of land holdings over time are few, those that have

been done show little change in average size—one arpent (five-sixths of an acre or 0.33 ha)—and in the distribution of land owned; the number of small and large farms seemed to remain stable.

Seigneurial greed is a second major factor often mentioned as a cause of rural poverty. Seigneurial rents increased some 36 percent between 1790 and 1831. Regional studies correctly point to the harshness of these payments and to the misery they helped cause. At the same time, it should be noted that many seigneurs found it difficult to collect their dues. Habitants were adept at evasion. A third commonly mentioned cause of rural distress is the declining export market for wheat. Clearly the production and export of wheat did decline in this period. Was this decline symptomatic of rural distress? Some historians argue that the habitant diversified his crops in reaction to emerging local markets resulting from the growth of towns and villages and the expansion of larger urban centres. For these scholars, declining wheat exports are not synonymous with rural poverty; rather, they indicate modernization of agricultural practice and suggest that reliance on the production of a single staple, wheat, does not represent the more complex reality of rural life in the St. Lawrence Valley.

Although historians continue to debate these issues, the following conclusions seem warranted. Habitants were never simply pawns of forces beyond their control. Within the context of their environments, they reacted and adapted as well as they could to the pressures of changing social and economic structures. Because of overpopulation, the length of time a family had farmed, seigneurial greed, and crop failures caused by poor climatic conditions, disease, and bug infestations, many rural dwellers did experience grinding poverty. Yet others survived and even prospered during this period of economic and social transition in the countryside. Whether the general trend was in the direction of increased poverty or increased wealth must at this point in the debate remain, as one historian has noted, "an open question."

There is, however, no question as to the fate of one group of rural people. In what is now northern Quebec, where, until the 1840s, the Hudson's Bay Company restricted settlement, natives continued to hunt, fish, and trade for a living. In the St. Lawrence lowlands, by contrast, most natives (there are few reliable population statistics) lived a marginalized existence on one of several long-established Catholic missions. Those in the northwest seigneuries, the Lac des Deux Montagnes area, numbered just under 1000 in 1800 and were very active in the fur trade. With the decline of the fur trade, those natives moved into lumbering as forest workers and timber rafters, supplementing that activity by small garden farming. About 2000 mission natives lived in the rural regions surrounding Montreal in 1831. Over 80 percent farmed for a living, specializing in the production of corn and potatoes. But their farms were only about one-tenth the size of those of their white neighbours, and of 641 industries listed in the 1831 census, only one, a flour mill, was located on native land. Like their Mohawk brothers in the northern seigneuries, natives on the fertile Montreal plains looked to lumbering and, when possible, the fur trade to scratch out a meagre living as part of an increasingly marginalized existence. Like the landless habitant, the natives adjusted as best they could to an economy in transition.

URBAN ECONOMY AND SOCIETY

A simple staple thesis fails to explain the emergence of economic diversity and social change in the countryside. So, too, the staple thesis fails to account for the nature of urban development in this period. Montreal grew even as its traditional staple export, fur, rapidly declined and even as its new staple export, wheat, failed to take the former's place. The third staple export to affect Lower Canada in this period, lumber, was concentrated in Quebec City and the Ottawa Valley. Yet Montreal's growth outpaced Quebec City's in this and later periods. The consumption of lumber for building and firewood in Montreal and Quebec City alone in the 1820s probably equalled in value the amount of wood exported. One has to look beyond the staple interpretation in order to understand urban economic and social conditions in this period.

Even as Montreal merchants pushed for canals to link Upper Canadian and western American wheat producers and Quebec merchants profited from the export of wood, structural changes of a nonmercantile sort were taking place. Craft industries, small manufacturing, construction, saw milling, and ship building emerged. Between 30 and 40 percent of urban household heads were craftsworkers in this period. Nor were all workers male. Women comprised about one-quarter of the urban workforce in the 1820s and were engaged in such crafts as the needle and leather trades. They were also domestics, teachers, nurses, innkeepers, and prostitutes. The vitality of urban craft work, perhaps more than the linkage to export markets provided by staple products, set the context for economic change in urban Lower Canada.

A version of the traditional interpretation of Lower Canadian history argues "that French and Indians exhibited some child-like qualities that encouraged their organization into paternalistic labour systems. . . ." Yet a closer look at urban working conditions suggests that a father/child relationship between employee and employer was, if it had ever existed, fast disappearing. Rather, working conditions resembled those of a full-fledged industrial capitalist system. From the beginning of the nineteenth century and increasingly thereafter, workers were paid regularly in cash, room and board was rare, hours of work were long and closely supervised, no protection was given for unemployment in slack seasons, and no compensation was given for sickness or injury (in fact, in some cases absentees were fined two days' salary for each day absent). Apprenticed employees often quit, thus violating their contract. In 1802 the government enacted repressive legislation aimed at controlling apprentice behaviour. The authorities jailed strikers in 1815. When strike activity was decriminalized in the mid-1820s, a series of unions were formed and a number of strikes took place over the issues of shorter hours, better working conditions, and higher pay. Although large mechanized industrial factories only emerged at mid-century, the system of impersonal labour relations that were often linked to their emergence existed in Lower Canada's major urban centres a quarter of a century earlier.[8]

Like the Lower Canadian habitant farmer, the urban worker was hardly childlike, passive, and easily exploited. Despite evidence of a growing collective consciousness among urban workers, material conditions seem to have improved only marginally in this period. One historian who studied the working-class suburb of St. Roche in Quebec City between 1820 and 1850 concluded that, as in the countryside, merchants benefited the most in this period of transition. The wealth of unskilled labourers, already at a bare-bones level, remained unchanged. While some of the middle group, the skilled artisans, increased their economic well-being, more descended to the level of the general proletariat.

If class relations became increasingly tense in urban centres in this period of transition, so, too, did ethnic conflict. At times it is difficult to distinguish between the two. French and English craftsworkers competed for jobs, with the English appropriating more and more of the available

---

[8] B. Palmer, *Working Class Experience: The Rise and Reconstitution of Canadian Labour, 1800–1980* (Toronto, 1983) provides an overview. A more focused treatment is David Thiery Ruddel, "La main d'oeuvre en milieu urbain au Bas-Canada: conditions et relations de travail," *Revue d'histoire de l'amérique français*, 41 (1988) and J. Burgess, "The Growth of a Craft Labour Force: Montreal Leather Artisans, 1815–31," *Historical Papers* (1988), 48–62.

work in many industries in both Quebec and Montreal. A majority of merchants, general businesspeople, and doctors were anglophones. Only in the area of law were francophones better represented. Seventy-five percent of government salaries, 80 percent of government pensions, and 99 percent of government contracts went to anglophones. In the urban crucible of Lower Canada, conflict fueled by ethnic and economic grievances smouldered.

POLITICS IN AN ERA OF SOCIAL AND ECONOMIC UPHEAVAL

One's interpretation of political conflict in this period depends directly on how one characterizes social and economic development. Were the contending factions divided along the lines of a backward-looking francophone professional group versus an aggressive anglophone mercantile class? Or was the split more along the lines of a contending francophone petty bourgeois class with links of an economic and social sort to the rural habitant, pitted against an anglophone mercantile elite with connections to colonial and imperial power centres? The first scenario assumes that the economic and social transition bypassed the French. The second scenario assumes that all Lower Canadians were affected by changing economic and social conditions and reacted actively to those structural pressures. Despite the forcefulness with which the above propositions are put forward by their respective advocates, one is at times hard pressed to discern such stark contrasts in the available evidence. In fact, one might be surprised if such clear-cut divisions really did exist during a period of social and economic transition. New lines of cleavage emerged even as old lines of conflict persisted. As in Upper Canada, so, too, in Lower Canada, political struggle reflected the stresses engendered by a process of uneven economic and social change.

The Constitutional Act of 1791 institutionalized socio-political conflict in Lower Canada. That act granted the vote to most rural property holders and renters and to many urban artisans. Even women property holders could vote until the assembly rescinded that right in 1834. Anglophones, and especially merchants, were, of course, incensed by the separation of Upper from Lower Canada and were even more discomfited by the liberal franchise stipulations. While freehold tenure, as opposed to the seigneurial system, applied to all unceded public lands (mainly in the Eastern Townships), it was not clear whether English or French civil law was to apply in those areas. Also the continuance of French civil law meant that all merchants had to abide by, to them, often strange and restrictive French commercial law. Nor was it clear what rights the Roman Catholic Church held. The granting of clergy reserves to the Protestant Church in the zones of freehold tenure and the lack of explicit legal recognition of the Catholic Church left that institution's leadership in a state of unease. This unease was compounded by the confiscation of Jesuit land by the state in the early nineteenth century and by a sharply declining ratio of priests to population: 1:750 in 1780, 1:1400 in 1810, and 1:1800 in 1830. Throughout this period a weakened Catholic Church sought allies.

In the 1780s, English and French merchants and a smattering of French professionals—lawyers, doctors and surveyors—had petitioned for an elected assembly. Following 1791, the French "petty bourgeois" group no longer required anglo merchant support and began to concentrate instead on controlling the new, popularly elected assembly. The anglo merchants responded by gravitating toward the governor who appointed members to the executive and legislative councils. Conflict was muted in the 1790s, in part from the fact that the anglo merchants managed to control about 50 percent of the assembly's seats in that decade. The buoyant period of wheat exports in the 1790s and early years of the 1800s added new members to the French-Canadian middle class. Sons of prosperous rural families began to be educated as lawyers and doctors. Rising local merchants began to seek ways to consolidate their positions. Between 1801 and 1805, members of the rising middle class coupled with habitant farmers and local tradespeople for the first time occupied more assembly seats than did the English merchants. The assembly had begun to reflect the changing nature of Lower Canada's social and economic structure.

At the same time, political power became increasingly divided along ethnic lines: English in the appointed councils and French in the elected assembly. In fact, the political platforms of the various socio-economic groups were honed on the scythe of rising ethnic animosity. The urban-based English merchants found in Governor Robert Milne (1799–1805) a kindred spirit who attempted to gerrymander electoral boundaries on their behalf, and, more importantly, stocked his councils with their representatives. English bureaucrats, merchants, and some French seigneurs began to dominate the councils even as the French middle and agrarian classes took control of the assembly. The Constitutional Act institutionalized ethnic division. A new English newspaper, the *Quebec Mercury* (1804), called for policies to "unfrenchify" the colony, to which a new French paper, *Le Canadien* (1806), responded with anti-English critiques. French assembly members looked to British constitutional arguments to defend assembly prerogatives and to argue for greater control of executive appointees, even to the extent of demanding elected councils or at least councils that reflected the assembly's composition. Under the leadership of Pierre Bedard, editor of *Le Canadien*, the Parti canadien challenged the anglo alliance or Chateau Clique, demanding assembly control of the civil list (money allotted to pay bureaucratic salaries) and control of government patronage. When the Parti canadien attempted to expel from the assembly two members of the English party in 1809, the new governor, James Craig (1807–1811), dissolved the assembly and, in 1810, seized *Le Canadien*'s press, jailing Bedard along with 20 of his co-workers on trumped-up charges of "treasonous practices."

Underlying this ethnic-political conflict lay a less clear-cut divergence on economic issues. Certainly the Parti canadien resented English speculators' control of some 2 000 000 acres (809 000 ha) of Eastern Township lands, thus making rural expansion into that area difficult, if not prohibitive. Certainly, too, the English merchants were involved primarily in an export trade in fur, wheat, and, after 1807, lumber and tended to dominate the larger urban centres, while francophone merchants prospered from a developing local and regionally based rural and small urban economy. This difference in specialization and size accentuated the ethnic cleavage. Yet there were points of common interest. As we have already noted, as early as 1791 French and English bourgeois were equally active in purchasing seigneuries. There is evidence that both groups diversified the economies in their respective seigneuries. Both groups favoured the establishment of banks. Studies of assembly activities in the 1790s and 1830s have shown a wide range of consensus on matters relating to economic development. And, again, as we have noted, the assembly and councils were united in their determination to pass legislation that would "discipline" an emerging industrial workforce and thus strengthen the power and economic well-being of emerging industrial employers.

There may be a discernible difference over the issue of local economic development. The larger export-oriented merchants consistently opposed the taxation of imports to pay for local developments like jails, roads, and canals and proposed, instead, a tax on land. This was politically stupid. The Parti canadien adroitly used this cry for a land tax to rally the habitant to their camp and solidify opposition to the English party.

Out of this complexity two main points emerge. The first is that ethnic differences, intensified by the Constitutional Act and by a patronage system that systematically favoured one group at the expense of the other, made agreement between the contending economic and social groups virtually impossible. The second point to note is that both economic and social groups reflected the pressures of a changing rural and urban economy. Both camps exhibited gradations in economic policy and, if the extremes in each camp would never see eye to eye on how best to channel change, moderates would. As events transpired, however, and resulting directly from intransigence fostered by the situation outlined above, it would take a rebellion before those moderates could command events.

TOWARD REBELLION

The War of 1812 temporarily stilled internal dissension in Lower Canada. All major social groups rallied to keep the Americans out. Battles at Lacolle in 1812 and Chateauguay in 1813 were enough to dissuade Americans, especially those from the adjacent New England regions who were never keen on war, from further significant military activity in Lower Canada. The Catholic Church made the most of the war by proclaiming loudly and publicly its allegiance to the English Crown. The bishop was rewarded by an annual salary from the governor in 1813, by a place on the legislative council in 1817, and, the *pièce de résistance*, by official and legal recognition as Bishop of Quebec in 1818.

After the war, and the short-lived economic boom that it occasioned, assembly-councillor-governor conflict intensified. The Parti canadien, soon renamed the Parti patriote, brought forward a new charismatic leader, Louis Joseph Papineau, son of a seigneur and a lawyer-seigneur in his own right. As Speaker of the House, Papineau pocketed a large government salary and pushed for greater assembly control of civil salaries and government patronage. While happy to exact harsh levies from the habitants living on his seigneury in the Ottawa Valley and to allow English merchants to do the same, Papineau, through his charisma, focused habitant grievances against the English and reflected the fury of the francophone professional class who had been systematically denied government preferment. He also headed a party that demanded economic development at the local and regional level. By 1827 his party held over 90 percent of the assembly's seats.

The Parti patriote also took steps to enhance further its control of rural minds. In the late 1820s and early 1830s, the assembly passed several laws that gave it greater control over primary schooling. Although partly repealed by the councils in the mid-1830s, this legislation was a direct challenge to the Patriotes' major competitor in the countryside, the church. The challenge would not be forgotten.

Despite Patriote pressure, the governors and their councils remained entrenched. In 1822 under Governor General Lord Dalhousie (1820–28), the English party attempted for a second time (the first was in 1812 under Craig) to effect secretly the union of Upper and Lower Canada, raise electoral qualifications, and abolish French as an official language. When the attempt became public, 50 000 French Canadians signed petitions opposing the bill. Despite some conciliatory moves by an increasingly worried Colonial Office in London, dissent seeped out of the assembly and onto the streets. Riots and death occurred in 1832 at an election in Montreal. Strikes escalated. British immigrants brought cholera (10 000 Lower Canadians died in 1834 and 1836) and intensified ethnic pressure.

Emboldened by civil unrest, the assembly, in 1834, passed the Ninety-Two Resolutions advocating American republican institutions, the freeing of Eastern Township lands from the monopolistic control of the recently established British American Land Company, and the governor's impeachment along with other incendiary items. Papineau's re-election in 1834 was marked by bitter street fighting in Montreal. The Patriotes swept the elections and some 80 000 signatures accompanied the resolutions to London. English and French coalesced into armed factions: Doric Clubs, Legions, and Rifle Corps for the British and the Fils de la Liberté, echoing French revolutionary organizations of the 1790s, for the French. An attempt at conciliation by newly appointed Governor Lord Gosford failed. Early in 1837, Lord John Russell, the colonial secretary, issued the Ten Resolutions, which flatly denied all of the Parti patriote's demands and threatened to impose union with Upper Canada if dissent persisted.

Early in November 1837, the Fils de la Liberté and the Doric Club battled on the streets of Montreal. Gosford issued warrants for the arrest of Papineau and other Patriote leaders. Full-scale war took place in rural villages to the south and north of Montreal. Despite an initial Patriote success at St. Denis, the marshalling of 2000 British regulars soon put down the uprising. At St. Eustache, on December 14, 58 Patriotes died fighting a larger and better-armed force of British regulars. By mid-December, Patriote leaders had fled, Papineau among them, to the United States. Throughout 1838, rebels attempted to rekindle an insurrection and in February, November, and December of that year they mounted unsuccessful incursions. The rebellion suffered from a vacillating leadership

The artist, Katherine Jane Ellice, a member of a wealthy anglophone family, sketched this picture of rebels as she viewed events from a window in her home at Beauharnois, Lower Canada, in 1838.   NATIONAL ARCHIVES OF CANADA/C13392

exercised by Papineau, by somewhat conflicting economic and social goals—Papineau, for example, wished to preserve the seigneurial system, others to abolish it—by clerical resistance, and by a failure to coordinate and centralize the limited military resources at the rebel's hands.

Who rebelled and why? Despite leadership problems, organizational difficulties, and the reality of superior British forces, some 9000 Lower Canadians actively supported the revolts of 1837 and 1838. When viewed from the perspective of Lower Canada's total population of about 500 000 French Canadians, this is not a large number. Yet all rebellions succeed or fail through the actions of a minority. When it is also realized that rebel support came mostly from the Montreal region—the lumber regions of Quebec and, especially, the Ottawa Valley were relatively quiet—the concentration of such a mass of dissidents in one area could have had powerful results. The traditional interpretation as to why the Montreal plains spawned the greatest dissent points to the alleged agricultural crisis and rural poverty that beset that area more than any other in Lower Canada. At best this is only a partial explanation. It fails to take into account the differential nature of wealth in the Montreal countryside and the extensive diversification of economic endeavour concentrated in that area. In fact, rebel participation reflected the reality of this complex social and economic environment. Certainly disadvantaged habitants and artisans were ready to strike out against perceived oppressors. So, too, however, were merchants and local professional notables, men and women who were relatively well off but who felt disadvantaged vis à vis wealthier and often anglophone urban dwellers. "Urban villages" were the centres of rural revolt. Local merchants and local professionals led the regional uprisings. Emerging industrialists in the countryside fought to preserve their place against an encroaching urban dominance emanating from Montreal. The rebellion's roots sprung from traditional and emerging economic and social structures.[9] Its results favoured one group of the new social and economic order, that situated in the expanding central urban areas of Lower Canada.

---

[9] On Papineau, see F. Ouellet, *L. J. Papineau: A Divided Soul*, CHA Historical Booklet, #11 (1968) and R. C. Harris, "Of Poverty and Helplessness in Petite-Nation," *CHR*, 52 (1971), 23–50; Allan Greer, "From Folklore to Revolution: Charivaris and the Lower Canadian Rebellion of 1837," *Social History*, 15 (1990), 25–43 explores some of the popular roots of discontent.

Colonial Development on the Atlantic, 1791–1842

Many historians are reluctant to write of an Atlantic region, a concept susceptible to "a watery definition if ever there was one." Good reasons can be found for separating Newfoundland out from the maritime settlements of Nova Scotia (which Cape Breton joined in 1820), New Brunswick, and Prince Edward Island. Yet despite important differences, each colony did function within a staple economy, operate as a dependent colonial political system, and evolve an increasingly stratified and elitist-dominated social structure. Greater than was the case with the Canadas, staple ties to the mother country shaped and structured development in the Atlantic region.

POPULATION GROWTH AND DIVERSITY

In 1800 some 85 000 people lived in the Atlantic area. Less than 4 percent were descendants of the original native inhabitants. Forty percent had arrived as part of the Loyalist influx. The rest were earlier settlers from New England in Nova Scotia, English and southern Irish in Newfoundland, Acadian in northwest New Brunswick, and Scots in Nova Scotia and Prince Edward Island. By 1840, over half a million people lived in the Atlantic region. Waves of Irish and, in slightly lesser numbers, of Scots swept over the area. By 1815, a solid majority of Newfoundland's 40 000 people were Irish. Just as the Irish outnumbered Newfoundland's English population, so, too, they quickly outnumbered Loyalist New Brunswickers. Between 1815 and 1838 some 13 000 Irish came to Nova Scotia, but even more Scots, about 25 000 Protestants and Catholics from the Highlands and Lowlands arrived. By 1851 the Scots were Nova Scotia's largest ethnic group and comprised a significant proportion of Prince Edward Island's population. While 1200 black Loyalists left Nova Scotia in the early 1790s seeking a less racially bigoted part of the world in which to live, some 1700 freed black slaves reached New Brunswick and Nova Scotia after the War of 1812. By 1851 there were 5000 blacks in the latter colony.

This population mix gave the Atlantic region an extremely diverse cultural heritage. Many immigrants spoke little or no English. Gaelic, Welsh, and Irish were their mother tongues, and even English arrivals had trouble understanding one another if they were from areas of England marked by isolated enclaves of settlement. The Highland Scots were especially tenacious in preserving their language and culture throughout the nineteenth century. So, too, were the Acadians in New Brunswick and Prince Edward Island. If the Highland Scots congregated in culturally homogeneous settlements, often in Cape Breton, the Irish seemed to settle everywhere and were most noticeable in the major cities of the Atlantic region, a region where more people lived in urban centres with 1000 or more people than was the case in either Upper or Lower Canada.

The region's original inhabitants were less visible. The Beothuk of Newfoundland, a migratory hunting and fishing people of Algonquian stock, were increasingly denied access to essential coastal fishing areas by

A view of Halifax Harbour about 1820 painted by John P. Drake.

NATIONAL GALLERY OF CANADA, OTTAWA, CANADA

TABLE 2

ATLANTIC CANADA: POPULATION, 1800

Colony	Population	% Rural	% Urban
Nova Scotia	40 000	75	25
Cape Breton	2 500	100	
New Brunwick	25 000	90	10
Prince Edward Island	3 000	100	
Newfoundland	14 000	88	12

TABLE 3

ATLANTIC CANADA: POPULATION, 1841

Colony	Population	% Rural	% Urban
Nova Scotia	226 000	89	11
New Brunswick	156 000	77	23
Prince Edward Island	47 000	92	8
Newfoundland	86 000	71	29

English and Irish. They struggled unsuccessfully to live off meagre resources in interior areas. The last Beothuk, Shawnadithit, died in captivity in 1829. The Micmac and Malecite peoples of New Brunswick, Nova Scotia, and, to a lesser extent, Prince Edward Island, had, for 150 years, fought first the French and then the English to keep their land. This courageous and often overlooked struggle resulted in the granting of occupation licences to the Micmac and Malecite peoples for lands on which they could live, but only at the pleasure of British authorities. It was a tenuous and fragile existence best exemplified by one early settler's boast: "I do not mean to have an Indian Town at my Elbow." Between 1783 and 1810, New Brunswick natives received licences to one-half of one percent of the province's land area (100 000 acres or 40 500 ha). By 1838, primarily because of the steady encroachment of white squatters, they controlled only 60 000 acres (24 000 ha). The story was much the same in Nova Scotia. Gift giving and treaties such as occurred in Upper Canada never took place in the Atlantic region in the nineteenth century. The British argued that the French had already extinguished native land claims and the threat of American invasion was never sustained enough to warrant "purchasing" native support. Few government officials concerned themselves with native issues. Nova Scotia Micmacs struggled to maintain a traditional migratory lifestyle and in the process became increasingly impoverished and embittered.[10]

The Micmac conical wigwams, made of overlapped sheets of birch bark, commonly housed a single extended family. For two years prior to his first marriage, a male suitor would live with the family of his bride-to-be and work for his future father-in-law, thus proving his worth. During that period, sexual relations between the suitor and future bride were, officially at least, forbidden.

NATIONAL ARCHIVES OF CANADA/C36647

[10] A general but somewhat dated survey is W. S. MacNutt, *The Atlantic Provinces: The Emergence of a Colonial Society* (Toronto, 1965). L. S. F. Upton, *Micmacs and Colonists: Indian-White Relations in the Maritimes, 1713–1867* (Vancouver, 1979) is the best overview of this subject. On the Beothuk, see R. T. Pastore and G. M. Storey, "Shawnadithet," *DCB*, 6 (Toronto, 1987), 706–9.

"FRAGMENTS OF THE FEAST": STAPLE PRODUCTION AND THE RURAL ECONOMY

Fish from Newfoundland and the St. Lawrence Gulf, wood from New Brunswick, and coal from Cape Breton headed the list of Atlantic region exports. Fish, wood, and coal economies had many similar characteristics: dependence on exterior markets; a high degree of external ownership; minimal effect in stimulating complementary regional economic growth; and, harsh exploitation of local labourers. These staple economies did not, however, exist in a local vacuum. Family farming underlaid staple enterprise. Most Maritimers and many Newfoundlanders farmed; in fact, during this period, most heads of households listed farming as their principal occupation. This did not mean that they did not also fish or work as a lumberer or a coal miner. Although most had come to the Maritimes in pursuit of cheap land, few could enjoy the luxury of one occupation. Farming both facilitated and ameliorated the pressures exerted by staple production on colonial life.

THE FISHERY

In 1790 the migratory fishery dominated Newfoundland. Almost continuous international conflict between 1793 and 1815, however, led to the end of yearly migration to the banks and to the establishment of a more locally based economic activity. By 1820 most major fish merchants resided in St. John's, although many of them took extended seasonal and longer "holidays" in Britain and, indeed, ultimately retired to the mother country. Nevertheless, the shift in location was more than symbolic. Expansion of local activity from St. John's to the northern coast of the island opened up the seal hunt in late winter and early spring and thus proved supplemental to the summer dried salt cod fishery. Local control of the salt and seal fisheries stimulated boat building. As early as 1804, 149 ships involved in sealing had all been built in Newfoundland. Enterprising St. John's shippers worked through agents in major Irish ports to encourage the immigration of Irish workers.

Yet the shift in locus of control did not alter certain basic structural characteristics of the fishery. Large British firms continued to dominate. The fishery remained dependent on the vagaries of external market demand, the pressures of international competition, and the availability of the natural resource. Unlike the sale of wheat from the Canadas and wood from New Brunswick, both of which were primarily consumed in Great

Britain, Newfoundland's products were mainly sold in southern Europe and Brazil, areas over which England could exercise only intermittent influence. From 1815 to 1836, a period when population increased from about 40 000 to 75 000, the per capita export of Newfoundland saltfish declined form 23.4 to 9.8 hundredweight per person. Increased Scandinavian competition and protectionist policies in importing countries accounted for the difficult market conditions, conditions which, in the words of one scholar, led to "hardship, starvation, bankruptcy, and depression in Newfoundland."

After 1830, merchants took increasing advantage of the weakening position of outport families. "You will not," one merchant informed his outport agent, "purchase any fish unless the payment be made in goods." The truck system, the payment for produce by high-priced goods, diminished real wages and led to the exploitation by merchants of isolated local

The view of St. John's was taken from Signal Hill in 1831. NATIONAL ARCHIVES OF CANADA/C3371

labour forces. Since labourers could not accumulate savings, local economic diversification was curtailed and local demand for consumer goods limited. In the Gaspé region of the Gulf of St. Lawrence, wood, potatoes, and cabbage were at times sold to merchant-creditors to reduce debt. Even on the rugged rocky coastlines, family gardens and household production helped stave off starvation and, ironically, in so doing, facilitated the continuance of exploitation.

Only large-scale merchants could afford to diversify their economic activity, yet few did. Many merchants of St. John's, in fact, schemed against the development of local agriculture, preferring to profit from the importation and resale of food from the United States, Nova Scotia, and Prince Edward Island. Boat building occurred, but much of the material involved, other than wood, was imported from Great Britain. The international context within which the Atlantic colonial fishery operated precluded the guarantee of a stable living wage to local workers. The exploitation of these workers and their families by merchants was, however, the result of human decisions motivated by a conservative vision of colonial development and callous greed.

LUMBER

The closing of the Baltic, England's main source of timber, by Napoleon in 1807 stimulated a major economic boom in the Maritimes. The export of wood, lumber, and ships soon dominated New Brunswick's economy and that of parts of Nova Scotia and Prince Edward Island. Although the Baltic opened after 1815, England, determined to control supplies, maintained a strong imperial preference for colonial wood until the early 1840s. New Brunswick's exports of ton timber increased from 5000 tons in 1805 to 417 000 tons in 1825, levelling off to 200 000 tons annually until the 1840s. Shipyard output in New Brunswick increased 13 times between 1806 and 1811 and continued growing thereafter. Wooden ships accounted for 80 percent of the value of Prince Edward Island's exports in 1825. Nova Scotia may have earned £90 000 annually via the export of ships.

Both industries owed much of their existence to the protection of preferential duties and to the Navigation Acts that excluded foreign shipping from most British colonial trade. Both industries suffered severe boom and bust swings dictated by demand in the British market, and both depended to a great extent on capital, materials, and labour imported from Great Britain.

The decades of the 1830s and 1840s were a time of transformation in the timber sector. In both New Brunswick and Nova Scotia, exports of ton timber took second place to the sale of boards, planks, and deals produced by saw mills. The centralization of control into the hands of several large British-based timber firms accompanied the diversification into saw milling. The granting of timber licences for five years enabled large well-capitalized merchant houses to dominate the trade. Owners and workers became more distinct. By the mid-1840s, some saw mills employed 80 workers, the first, along with shipbuilders, industrial proletariat to emerge in nineteenth-century New Brunswick. The extent of social and class division is clearly, albeit unintentionally, caught by the Chatham *Gleaner's* account of a "substantial repast" put on by the lumber baron Samuel Cunard in 1836. The day following the party, the paper reported, "the poor people were requested to attend at the mill where the fragments of the feast were distributed among them."

A lumber mill at Stanley, New Brunswick, in 1835.   NATIONAL ARCHIVES OF CANADA/C3552

As with the fishery, the profits generated by the wood industry normally ended up in England. With the exception of boat building and the construction of saw mills, the industry's owners invested little in the colony. Nor did resident merchants in Halifax and Saint John. These urban centres grew rapidly, and many merchants made substantial sums from the lumber and shipbuilding trades, but few invested in any major manufacturing sectors. Most urban economic leaders were content to live and prosper within a commercial economy producing for protected imperial markets.

COAL

Granted monopoly rights to Cape Breton coal by the British government in 1827, the General Mining Association, by the late 1830s, employed 1500 workers, paid $5000 a month in wages, and had investments worth $250 000 in Nova Scotia. Their Cape Breton coal operations represented one of the largest concentrations of industrial workers and industrial investment in any of England's North American colonies. Yet the General Mining Association's business fitted well within the staple-focused, mercantile-managed colonial economy. Capital, technology, skilled workers, and experienced managers were imported from Scotland and England. General labourers from Newfoundland and Cape Breton performed unskilled tasks. By 1835, according to one miner, "the greater part of the men on the concern was in debt" to the company, in part, because of a modified truck system that forced miners to purchase high-priced goods at the company's stores. Labour disputes and running battles with coal poachers who supplied coal to "the greater part of" Sydney challenged the monopoly. But few strikes were successful: the labourers, divided on ethnic grounds and isolated from other job opportunities, had little option but to accept company wages and company work conditions. Coal took Nova Scotia to the brink of industrialization in this era: but it was industrialization of a truncated sort; the owners allowed limited linkages and diversification to occur and all activity took place in socially stratified, export-oriented coastal zones.

AGRICULTURAL SETTLEMENT

Measured by export figures, the Atlantic region was undistinguished in agriculture. Both Nova Scotia and New Brunswick imported food from the United States to feed their inhabitants throughout this period. Measured by household activity, however, agriculture was the region's most important economic endeavour.

While environmental constraints, especially the pressure of increased immigration on limited good land, set bounds to the possibilities for success in the rural Maritimes, socio-economic decisions played an equally important role in structuring rural life. Behaviour in the area of land acquisition went far in defining and creating rural poverty and wealth. Community studies indicate that the first settlers quickly monopolized the best land and made it very difficult for later arrivals to acquire sufficient land at a reasonable price. In some communities, the first settlers practised social and economic closure by intermarrying and by withholding local credit from newcomers. Very early in the century extreme poverty coexisted with at least modest affluence in many rural areas. In 1791 about one-half of the total workforce in one Nova Scotian rural county were wage labourers. By the second quarter of the nineteenth century, two-thirds of Prince Edward Island's population were tenants or squatters, and, by 1837, one-half the population of Cape Breton Island, some 20 000 people, were also squatters. After 1827, Nova Scotia and New Brunswick began to sell rather than give away land, a policy that led to a five-fold increase in fees in Nova Scotia and that "severely restricted" the chances of immigrants acquiring property in New Brunswick. The emergence of the rural poor resulted as much from social decisions as from environmental restraints.

Farming and lumbering were interdependent enterprises in this era. Large family farms could profit from the sale of provisions. The owners of smaller farms on poorer land required winter lumber work at low wages just to survive. Logging may have reduced out-migration, but it did not reduce poverty; rather, lumber barons profited from the existence of a rural proletariat of marginal farmers who accepted low-wage lumber work in order to live close to kin and friends.[11]

---

[11] S. Ryan, *Fish Out of Water: The Newfoundland Salt Fish Trade, 1814–1914* (St. John's, 1986) is a good introduction to a major component of Newfoundland's economy. S. J. Hornsby, "Staple Trades, Subsistence Agriculture and 19th Century Cape Breton Island," *Annuals of the Association of American Geographers*, 79 (1989), 411–34 is a clearly written analysis. G. Wynn, *Timber Colony* (Toronto, 1981) is essential for understanding New Brunswick. Eric Sager with G. Panting, *Maritime Capital* (Kingston, 1990) is an exhaustive treatment of shipping and the Maritimes. On agriculture see R. MacKinnon and G. Wynn, "Nova Scotia Agriculture in the 'Golden Age': A New Look," in D. Kay, ed., *Geographical Perspectives on the Maritime Provinces* (Halifax, 1988), 47–60 and R. Bitterman, "The Hierarchy of the Soil: Land and Labour in a 19th Century Cape Breton Community," *Acadiensis*, 18 (1988), 33–55. The journal, *Acadiensis*, which specializes in Maritime history, should be consulted for all topics covered in this section.

STAPLES AND THE FAMILY

If well-attired ladies in "pink and lilac high-heeled shoes" were common in Saint John, most women suffered a more frugal and penurious existence. Women performed two main functions: production of goods in the home and reproduction of the next generation. Individual experiences in the performance of these roles varied according to ethnicity, age, class, and colour. Acadian women, for example, tended to marry earlier and have larger families than did women of Scottish origin. Women and their children who managed farm households on Cape Breton's rocky backland soil endured both poverty and loneliness as they waited wondering if their husbands, off seeking supplementary wage work in the fishery, coal mines or lumbering camps, would return healthy or return at all. Black and native women, who suffered from racism as well as sexism, struggled to survive via the sale of Micmac quiltwork and, in the case of some black women in Halifax, by the sale of homemade baskets and brooms.

Children also participated in the production of household goods. "[N]othing of any consequence has happened to day," Louisa Collins, an 18-year-old daughter of a rural Nova Scotian family, confided to her diary in September 1815, after having spent the day making butter, ironing, spinning, and sewing. She did admit to not feeling "very well and... retire[d] early." Sons worked in the fields at an early age and tended to the smaller garden plots near the house. In these contexts, formal schooling took second place to the maintenance of household sufficiency.

Until the 1840s and 1850s, propertied women could vote in most Atlantic colonies. The legal proscription of their political rights in succeeding decades followed current British notions concerning the proper sphere for women's activity. Women should remain in the house and raise and nurture children. Work and home were to be separate gender-distinct domains. Father would be the family provider, mother would be the family moulder, the spiritual and moral backbone of the family unit.

The behaviour of prominent Atlantic-region politicians underlines the reality that women lacked power and protection in the political sphere. Joseph Howe, Nova Scotia's leading reform politician, lecturing in 1836 on the "Moral Influence of Women," sharply criticized "the more reckless and daring apostles" of women's rights. For him, women clearly belonged in the home, where his wife, Susan Ann, described by Howe as "no great reasoner," raised, with little help, his ten children. Small wonder that it was

Howe's 1851 reform government that took the franchise from Nova Scotia's propertied women.

Other politicians went even further. "To protect his son's reputation," Newfoundland's fiery reform activist, Dr. William Carson, "entered the home of a female patient and, without authorization...conducted a painful, searching examination of the most intimate kind." New Brunswick's leading reform politician, the wealthy merchant and land-owner, Charles Simonds, "pawed," an acquaintance reported, his married housekeeper "three or four different times, and went on, till she would stand it no longer." In 1843 Simonds was convicted by a jury of five counts of rape and one of common assault, charges later reduced by the Supreme Court to two of assault with carnal intent and one of common assault. The reform careers of both men seemed little affected by these incidents and, in fact, the St. John's press ignored the Simonds' case. For men, privilege and power could provide timely and silent acquiescence.[12]

POLITICS AND SOCIETY

Canada's historians have characterized Atlantic politics as quiescent, conservative, undemocratic, and patronage ridden. The really interesting and exciting events and conflicts occurred in central not Atlantic Canada. This central Canadian focus has, however, obscured the degree to which political development in the Atlantic colonies parallelled that in central Canada. As in the Canadas, political conflict escalated in the 1820s and 1830s. Family Compacts, an uneasy alliance of aristocrats and improve-ment-minded merchants, dominated Atlantic as well as central Canadian political affairs. In the three Maritime provinces, as in the Canadas, political battles over control of colonial finances, general development policies, and religious/educational matters were waged between appointed councils and elected assemblies. Finally, in the Atlantic, as in the Canadian colonies, appointed lieutenant-governors struggled with varying skill and success to maintain political order, non-party government, and British hegemony. Yet these similarities were tempered by local geographic,

---

[12] M. Conrad, et al., eds., *No Place Like Home: Diaries and Letters of Nova Scotia Women, 1771–1938* (Halifax, 1988). For a general appraisal of writing on women in Atlantic Canada, see Gail G. Campbell, "Canadian Women's History: A View from Atlantic Canada," *Acadiensis*, XX (1990), 184–98.

ethnic, and economic differences. The political cultures of Atlantic Canada can only be understood via a close analysis of those local conditions that structured the pace of political change, the intensity of political conflict, and the social distribution of political power.[13]

A PERIOD OF CALM, 1791–1820

If political criticism was understated in the years before 1820, the seeds of future dissension were nonetheless planted. In Newfoundland, no assembly existed, and a year-long resident lieutenant-governor was not appointed until 1818. Newfoundland residents had limited institutional means available for the political expression of social and economic discontent. Yet problems did exist. In 1800 the right to own property had not been established. Roads, hospitals, newspapers, schools, and churches were almost nonexistent. St. John's became increasingly stratified along the lines of poor Irish Roman Catholics and moderately wealthy to rich Anglican English, Presbyterian Scottish, and Protestant Irish merchants. The reformer, William Carson, did protest the lack of an assembly but to no avail.

In Prince Edward Island, "the one party seems to contend for a Democratical Institution, the other for an Aristocratical one...," the lieutenant-governor warned in 1804. By 1812 a precursor to a political party did control the local assembly. Called the Loyal Electors, the group was far from "Democratical": led by lawyer and land agent D. B. Palmer, the organization did not advocate land reform or the granting of civil and political rights to Roman Catholics, who had none. Rather it attempted, unsuccessfully, to supplant an already-entrenched elite with self-avowed "persons of unimpeached characters." The "Aristocratical" party took the

---

[13] A good introduction to the literature dealing with these themes is P. Buckner, "Limited Identities and Canadian Historical Scholarship: An Atlantic Provinces Perspective," *Journal of Canadian Studies*, 23 (1988), 177–98. The *Dictionary of Canadian Biography*, volumes 5–8 should be consulted for excellent studies of major (and minor) Maritime political figures. Each biography is accompanied with an excellent bibliography. Access is provided via a geographical/thematic index. P. Buckner, *The Transition to Responsible Government: British Policy in British North America* (Westpoint, 1985) is a detailed analysis. J. M. Beck, *Joseph Howe*, Vols. 1 and 2 (Montreal, 1982 and 1983) is the standard treatment. P. McCann, "Culture State Formation and the Invention of Tradition: Newfoundland, 1832–55," *Journal of Canadian Studies*, 23 (1988) and Linda Little, "Collective Action in Outpost Newfoundland: A Case Study from the 1830s," *Labour/Le Travail*, 26 (1990), 7–36, are useful introductions to politics and society in Newfoundland.

Loyal Electors seriously. Arriving in 1813, a new lieutenant-governor, Charles Douglas Smith, advised by members of the "old party," quickly muzzled the opposition by suspending the assembly and not allowing it to meet until 1818.

Political conflict in early New Brunswick also provided a precedent for public dissent and opposition. In the mid-1790s, a loose and fluctuating alignment of religious dissenters, merchants, early landowners, and various combinations of regional leaders argued for increased assembly rights vis à vis the appointed council. While this conflict often resembled little more than bickering between the "ins" and "outs," reformers did take public stands on judicial and educational issues that had meaning and importance to more than simply themselves. Moreover, James Simonds, a rich merchant and leading proponent of assembly rights, bequeathed his opposition mentality to his sons, Charles and Richard, both of whom were to lead reform-oriented groups in the 1820s and 1830s.

In Nova Scotia, a mixed bag of assembly advocates emerged and challenged a council dominated by merchant leaders from Halifax. Regional suspicion of Halifax motivated most assembly advocates. Political disputes in Nova Scotia, while at times leading to rough tactics at the polls and even to the threat of duals between rival candidates, seemed the most self-serving and lacking in concern for constitutional principle and populist needs. Later reformers would find little in the colony's immediate past from which to take support and sustenance.

The War of 1812 brought prosperity to the Atlantic region. Newfoundland residents benefited from greater local control over the fisheries. Nova Scotia merchants became or financed privateers who captured American ships and cargoes. Some profited from increased access to the West Indies trade occasioned by the denial of American entry. Others took advantage of a large smuggling trade between the Maritime and the New England states. Since military demands were few, public displays of British patriotism were ubiquitous. Elite attitudes, values, and the British connection were solidified. Reform and dissension were further quieted and subdued.

THE EMERGENCE OF CONFLICT, 1820–42

The quarter century following the war's end witnessed a deepening of political participation throughout the Atlantic region. During this period of increasing social and economic stratification, political players began to search for institutions that would facilitate elite dominance while permitting structured rural participation in the political process. Nor was this a zero sum game. If elite dominance was not irreparably undermined, neither was populist pressure completely co-opted.

Newfoundland outport residents were especially hard hit by the economic downturn following 1815. In 1820, two bankrupt Catholic fisherman, James Handrigan and Philip Butler, received 14 and 12 lashes, respectively, for resisting attempts to confiscate their property for unpaid debts. In fact, their wives had seemed the most militant: one threatened "to blow" a constable's "brains out" and the other had to be forcibly removed from her home. The state's cruel action sparked a reform response in St. John's where 180 mainly Irish merchants signed a petition for redress. Reformers argued for an elected assembly as a panacea for social and economic ills. Even English Protestant merchants could agree on the need for representative institutions; gradually the plight of outport families like the Handrigans and Butlers receded from the main reform agenda. Intransigent lieutenant-governors and a Colonial Office fearful that under a representative system the St. John's elite would not be able to control the outports, let alone St. John's, delayed the granting of an assembly until 1832.

Institutions accompanying the new constitution in 1832 favoured the Church of England in matters of religion and schooling despite the fact that half the population was Irish and mainly Catholic. The new Roman Catholic bishop, Michael Fleming, Irish-born and follower of the Irish nationalist Daniel O'Connell, would have none of it. He strengthened the local clergy by adding 21 young Irish-born and trained priests to Newfoundland in the 1830s. His open support of political candidates led to harsh public criticism from the Protestant press, to Catholic mob intimidation of a Protestant newspaper editor, and to the calling out of the militia by the lieutenant-governor to maintain peace.

Troops visited outports as well. Riots occurred in the early years of the decade in Conception Bay and a particularly large and successful protest against the truck system by sealers caused much attention from St. John's Protestant merchants. Indeed, throughout that decade, at least 30 different instances of protest ranging from the intimidation of merchants by an aggrieved customer to organized electoral violence took place at Conception Bay. Working-class rule opposed the order of merchants and magistrates. Local witnesses of violent acts were cowed into silence by such written threats as the following:

Mrs. Jackman
If you allows your Son to swear against Kiley mark
the consequence ye Protestant Buggarr
depend on it it shall be a damned sore swear for him
for his life. . .the young scoundrell
and you as bad as him to allow it he will not escape much longer

One historian has concluded that by "the late 1830s and early 1840s something very like a class struggle was being waged in Newfoundland." The hapless lieutenant-governor, Henry Prescot, reported in 1841 that it was "war to the knife" between the Liberal Catholic assembly and Tory Protestant council. Yet reform unity was fragile and St. John's reformers had only limited contact with and understanding of outport sentiment and grievance. The Protestant mercantile elite mounted a strong counterattack: representative government was a mistake, they now admitted; the Catholic-Irish threatened to subvert British institutions; social chaos seemed imminent. The Colonial Office responded by suspending the constitution in 1841 and enacting the Newfoundland Act the following year. This legislation went far to mollify Protestant fears: a more restricted franchise and an assembly composed of elected and appointed members were the two keynotes. It remained to be seen whether the new constitution would contain sectarian and class violence.

In the early 1820s, Prince Edward Island's lieutenant-governor, C. D. Smith, began to enforce the annual collection of an imperial land tax known as the quitrent. The tax hurt small resident landowners and many tenants whose leases required them to pay all taxes. Warned by the executive that they would lose their land and thus their livelihood, some tenants travelled up to 70 miles (112 km) to the capital with produce to pay the quitrent. Many owners were dispossessed, and much of their land ended up in the hands of C. D. Smith's officials. With the colony on "the verge of an open rebellion in 1823," the Colonial Office recalled Smith.

In Prince Edward Island, three political factions emerged to contend for power following the mid-1820s: an old, declining, but still powerful aristocratic, landed elite; an emerging middle-class faction, commercially and industrially oriented proponents of progress; and, a rural-based populist group, advocates of rural equality and "people's rights." These political and social divisions clearly echoed similar developments in the Canadas and Newfoundland.

The attitude of the middle class and the rural groups to the judicial process known as escheat sharply indicates their differences. Under escheat, lands not appropriately developed by proprietors could be restored to the crown. George Dalrymple, a merchant and leader of the middle-class group, sought a limited escheat levied against those who, by doing nothing, blocked "general prosperity." This plan bypassed most tenants since it affected absentee owned and unsettled land. William Cooper, who in the early 1830s formed the Escheat Party, wanted to end all proprietorial-based control and give ownership to those who worked the land.

Cooper's radical egalitarian vision excited much support in the colony in the 1830s, in part because, in 1829, Catholics, who represented the poorer half of the Island's population, had finally been given the right to vote. In 1831, Cooper entered the assembly after a hotly contested by-election in which he defeated, among others, Thomas Irwin, a candidate running on a platform of justice for natives, the original landowners entirely ignored by the Escheat party, and other parties. In 1838 Cooper's party controlled 75 percent of the assembly's seats, and many rural tenants met quitrent collectors with force. In the face of widespread dissent, Lieutenant-Governor Sir Charles Augustus Fitz Roy, no friend of escheat, but sympathetic toward the plight of tenants, acted with moderation. Aided by the Colonial Office, which refused to meet Cooper in 1839, he managed to diffuse the escheat movement and to limit violence to out-breaks against local landowners rather than to a general uprising against the government itself. Blocked by the appointed council and the Colonial Office, the Escheat Party passed no laws helpful to tenants between 1839 and 1842. They were defeated in the ensuing election and the party disintegrated thereafter, but its existence forced social and political matters touching the lives of the majority of the colony's residents to centre stage. Future political parties could continue to ignore them only at their peril.

In New Brunswick, political conflict remained at the level of a struggle between two elites over power. Geography played a role: discrete communities with localized interests led to factionalism—not to party groupings. One of the most restricted franchise acts in British North America probably inhibited populist expression. Individual assembly members were assured of re-election if they could extract money from the public purse for local development. Since the assembly controlled all appropriation for roads and bridges and the committee that allocated these expenditures consisted of representatives of each of the colony's ridings, most constituencies received their due.

The appointment of Thomas Baillie as commissioner of Crown Lands in 1824 interrupted this period of stability. Ambitious and headstrong, Baillie, via a rigorous system of land tax collection and a new program for Crown land sales, challenged both the assembly, which had no control over land revenue, and leading timber operators, who, accustomed to the cheap existing leasehold system, correctly feared that the sale of land would benefit a few large and monopolistically oriented lumber barons. Those timber operators who failed to purchase or were denied access to choice timber lots gained control of the assembly in the early 1830s and agitated for legislative control over both Crown land revenues and Thomas Baillie, who seemed to be personally profiting from the new regulations. Lieutenant-Governor Sir Archibald Campbell compounded problems by promoting the Anglican Church and its control of higher education in the face of a predominantly Presbyterian populace as well as by defending Baillie's excessive expenditures and high-handed activities.

Entrepreneurially minded politicians like Charles Simonds, in many ways similar in outlook to Prince Edward Island's George Dalrymple, led the assembly's attack throughout the 1830s. After much bitter conflict, the Colonial Office replaced Campbell as lieutenant-governor with Sir John Harvey, in May 1837. Harvey's instructions were clear: avoid at all costs any deepening of dissent like that which was occurring in the Canada's. In return for a guaranteed annual civil list, the assembly acquired control of Crown land revenues in 1837. Members of the assembly not favoured by Campbell and Baillie were appointed to the executive council. Harmony ensued while the assembly busily spent £133 000 more than it collected between 1837 and 1842. Simonds viewed such expenditure with increasing unease. How to harness and centralize economic development became for Simonds, as it did for middle-class, "progressively" minded reformers in other British North American colonies, the next challenge on the political agenda.

In Nova Scotia, as in New Brunswick, geography facilitated the development of scattered, isolated communities, a separateness reinforced by distinct ethnic and religious settlements. The Nova Scotia assembly acted in a manner similar to that of New Brunswick's: local interests took precedence over matters of a more general concern. In the 1820s, the assembly did demonstrate some unity on issues of religion and education, reflecting the Presbyterian and dissenting outlook of most of their constituents. The continual blockage by the council of assembly support for the Presbyterian Pictou Academy gradually led to a wider battle over assembly prerogatives in money matters. But, the assembly, not the executive, controlled most colonial revenue and the Church of England was not a large and wealthy enough target to merit much sustained attention.

A severe economic downturn in the mid-1830s, the arrival of Lieutenant-Governor Sir Colin Campbell, a man determined to uphold direct British hegemony, and the entry on to the reform stage of the mercurial Joseph Howe ended a long quiet period. A moderate newspaper editor, Howe, when publicly prosecuted for criminal libel in 1835, successfully and spectacularly defended his case. He, then, sought election to the assembly in 1836, where he assumed leadership of the reform-minded faction. Especially opposed to the Halifax elite's control of the council, this reform group, further strengthened after the 1837 election, demanded an elected council or at least a major change in personnel. In response, Campbell split the old council into executive and legislative councils and staffed both with Anglican and no Reform leaders. This obstinance, made all the more extreme when compared to the moderate accommodation occurring in neighbouring New Brunswick, provoked reform activity, although reformers were quick to disassociate themselves from any suggestion of rebellious activity such as was occurring in the Canadas. Instead, Howe and other reformers petitioned for Campbell's recall and personally lobbied the Colonial Office in London. Yet 3000 Nova Scotians counter-petitioned in Campbell's support, and he persisted in office until October 1840. In the election of that year, Howe and the reformers received a majority, but Howe failed in his bid to be speaker, suggesting that sectional and regional realities continued to be dominant over any sense of party discipline.

Commerce and Conflict in Western Canada, 1790–1846

WESTERN PEOPLES

We do not know the number of native peoples in the West in 1790. One accepted estimate for the prairie region is 40 000. Nor do we know the number of fur-bearing animals that inhabited the West. We do know that both declined precipitously over the 50-year period considered here. Epidemics of whooping cough and measles from 1818 to 1820 and smallpox from 1837 to 1838 decimated the Assinboine and Cree and affected West Coast natives, although less traumatically. Fur-bearing species like the West Coast sea otter and, in parts of the Prairies, the beaver, were seriously depleted before 1810. The white population grew slowly. Far more spectacular was the emergence of a bi-racial people,

This painting of a Saulteaux native in 1828 by Peter Rindisbacher, probably near the modern border between Manitoba and Ontario, almost seems to suggest that the Saulteaux had a premonition of things to come.   NATIONAL ARCHIVES OF CANADA/C1935

composed of Métis, the offspring of French fur traders and native women, and country-born, offspring of English and Scottish traders and native women. Some 6000 (3000 French-speaking and 3000 English-speaking) people of dual native-white ancestry lived at Red River by 1845. Countless others congregated at inland and West Coast posts. Typical of the coastal posts was Fort Vancouver where, in 1846, one visitor reported, "The men, with their Indian wives, live in log hunts near the margin of the river, forming a little village—quite a Babel of languages, as the inhabitants are a mixture of English, French, Iroquois, Sandwich Islanders, Crees and Chinooks." Fur-trade posts were far from being isolated British ghettos.

On the Prairies, Algonquian-speaking tribes, like the Cree and Ojibwa to the East, Siouian speakers like the Assiniboine to the South and Athapaskan speakers like the Chipewyan in the North were at different times and in different ways affected by the fur trade. With but few exceptions for all the people, the period before 1821 was a time of relative prosperity and independence, conditions well on the way to being reversed by the early 1840s.

In British Columbia the diversity of native peoples defies easy description. Divided by language, dialect, ethnicity, and social and political behaviour, there were at least 24 separate native nations and within some of those there existed different linguistic groupings. Relative to the Prairie natives, British Columbia's natives were still independent and powerful in the 1840s.[14]

THE COMPETITION FOR FUR, 1790–1821

Hudson's Bay Company dominance of the fur trade did not come easily, nor would any reasonable observer have predicted it in 1790. By that date, it seemed that the St. Lawrence trade had been firmly grasped by one firm, The North West Company. Yet the Hudson's Bay Company persisted. Following 1811, new personnel assumed control. A profit-sharing incentive system similar to that of the Nor'Westers was introduced. Covert plans were laid to expand into the Athabasca region. Most importantly, at the insistence of one of the new directors, the Scottish peer and philanthropist, Lord Selkirk, a scheme to establish an agricultural colony at Red

---

[14] Overviews can be found in R. Fisher, *Contact and Conflict: Indian-European Relations in British Columbia, 1774–1890*. (Vancouver, 1977); G. Friesen, *The Canadian Prairies: A History* (Toronto, 1984); and J. R. Miller, *Skyscrapers Hide the Heavens: A History of Indian-White Relations in Canada* (Toronto, 1989).

River, astride the Nor'Westers transport system, was set in motion. If Selkirk saw the colony as a way to provide a decent life for hard-pressed Scottish agriculturists, the Hudson's Bay Company believed the colony could be the source of cheap labour and cheap food and help satisfy one of the original conditions in its charter, that of western colonization.

Between 1812 and 1814, some 200 settlers struggled to set up a farming community. They came from Scotland and Ireland and suffered great hardship during their arduous trips to Red River. But on arrival their troubles had just begun. Miles Macdonell, Selkirk's vain and ineffectual agent, antagonized the already extremely suspicious North West Company by, among other incidents, issuing the so-called pemmican proclamation in January 1814. By forbidding the export of any foodstuff from the colony, Macdonell both threatened the Nor'Westers' business, since pemmican was the main food traders carried inland, and challenged the rights of the large Métis settlement who supplied the Nor'Westers with that food. Encouraged by the North West Company—although it is a moot point as to how much encouragement was necessary—the Métis initiated a series of harassing raids on the settlement, destroying crops and houses. These raids culminated in the Battle of Seven Oaks, where a Métis contingent under Cuthbert Grant engaged the new governor, Robert Semple, killing him and 20 of his men. While the battle itself was unplanned, the prospect of violent confrontation was very much a part of Métis plans and an almost inevitable result of the challenge posed to the North West Company by Selkirk's settlement. It was the last major battle at Red River. Selkirk, along with some 90 Swiss and German mercenaries, reached the colony in 1817 after having captured and pillaged the North West Company's headquarters at Fort William and apprehended some North West traders on charges varying from murder to sabotage.

Even as Selkirk travelled to Red River, the Hudson's Bay Company mounted a sustained competitive assault against the Nor'Westers in the Athabasca territory. Both sides hired "bully-boys" to intimidate the local natives and rival traders. The Nor'Westers adopted an official policy not to assist "Hudson's Bay servants. . .in case of starvation." One Nor'Wester expressed "exultation" when "no less than 15 men, 1 clerk with a women and child died of starvation going up Peace River." Both companies attempted to acquire furs destined for and prepaid by their rivals. Both companies suffered large financial loss during the waging of what was in reality a private war for control of the North West fur trade.

Financial and competitive pressure plus the threat of Colonial Office intervention pushed the companies to the bargaining table. In 1821 the two companies merged: the Hudson's Bay Company retained its name, but of the 53 trading partners, the North West Company supplied 32. More significantly, the merger meant the end of Montreal's century-long link to the fur trade. Provisions, goods, and furs now flowed only through the bay: "The fur trade," as one old Nor'Wester, exclaimed, "is forever lost to Canada." In terms of trade, so it was. Yet, as had the North West Company before it, the Hudson's Bay Company continued to hire stalwart and poor peasants from "voyageur parishes" in rural Lower Canada. Crumbs continued available for those Lower Canadians too poor to say no.

NATIVES AND THE FUR TRADE, 1821–1840

Most West Coast native peoples continued, as they had before 1821, to profit from the fur trade. Cultural change and in some cases enrichment took place; but it was change over which white fur traders exerted no control. Some tribes, indeed, unwilling to alter traditional lifestyles, simply refused to trade with Europeans. Others, like the Tsimshian chief, Tegiac, and the Carrier chief, Kwah, established close and mutually profitably relations with chief factors at coastal forts. Kwah, at his death in 1840 probably the most influential chief in New Caledonia, did not see himself as in any way subservient to fur traders. As he once asserted, "Do I not manage my affairs as well as you do yours. . .I never want for anything; and my family is always well clothed."

Competition from fur traders did permit some prairie natives the luxury of playing off rival fur traders as they had prior to the 1821 merger. The natives near Norway House, a Hudson's Bay post just north of Lake Winnipeg, seem to have profited from a combination of trading with fur traders from Red River, working for the local Hudson's Bay men, and pursuing traditional hunting and food-gathering activities. Yet, further in the interior en route to York Factory, at Oxford House, the local Cree became increasingly dependent on the Hudson's Bay Company for work and provisions. Free traders seemed not to have penetrated that far inland; the natives were paid lower wages compared to other areas; and they were increasingly tied by debt to the company's traders.

Those Cree and Assiniboine west of Red River experienced increased competition from skilled Red River Métis in the hunting of buffalo and the supplying of food to fur traders. They, as had been the case before 1821, were also subjected to greater competitive pressures from inland natives who had easier access to the southern horse trade as well as access to interior posts. Concerning natives who lived close to the more isolated northern and interior posts, one is tempted to compare their situation to those around Oxford House. Yet detailed evidence for such a conclusion is not yet available. One should be wary of writing as if one reaction or situation could typify the condition and behaviour of all natives. As we saw in the pre-1821 era, so, too, in the post-merger period, native peoples acted in a variety of ways resulting from a combination of different tribal traditions and specific local conditions.

SETTLING IN THE WEST

"Some of the most worthless of God's creatures, in one of the most miserable countries on the face of the earth": such was Governor Andrew Bulger's opinion of Red River in 1823. Beset by crop failures, fear of attacks by the Sioux, internal disorder, and Hudson's Bay restrictions on trading rights, Red River settlers worked hard to maintain a bare subsistence living. They were a polyglot lot: Scottish settlers, German and Swiss soldiers, French-Canadian farmers, and French- and English-speaking bi-racial inhabitants battled themselves, natives, the company, and the elements during Red River's early years. By the 1830s, schools, churches, and

White fish from the Red River was a major part of the diet of settlers in that region, as this painting by Peter Rindisbacher in 1827 makes clear. NATIONAL ARCHIVES OF CANADA/C1932

several years of successful crops brought order to a community fast becoming dominated by English and French peoples of mixed North American native and European descent.

In 1836 the Hudson's Bay Company took formal control of the colony: the company virtually appointed the governing council; the local chief factor was the colony's governor; the court system reflected company influence; and, settlers depended on the fur trade company as a market for their produce. Red River seemed a company town *par excellence*.

Yet appearances were deceiving: early Red River should be remembered for two reasons that have little to do with Hudson's Bay Company dominance. Within the Company's shadow, a potentially bi-cultural people struggled to emerge to prominence. English-speaking people of mixed race had great difficulty in articulating a distinctive sense of self. The reasons for this are complex and not completely understood. Some historians argue that they followed the leadership of their more aggressive French-speaking Métis neighbours. Others maintain that they too closely aped the minds and manners of the English Hudson's Bay Company elite.

A profile of the French-speaking Métis can be more sharply drawn. Having gained a strong sense of self-worth and national consciousness at the Battle of Seven Oaks, the Métis were especially prominent. Although no bi-racial person sat on the political or judicial councils in the early 1830s, the settlement, nevertheless, relied more on the Métis than on the Hudson's Bay Company for its existence. The Métis provided settlers with food from the buffalo hunt when crops failed; protected the settlement from Sioux attacks; manned the transportation system on which the fur traders depended; engaged in subsistence farming; and, increasingly, traded freely in fur, resisting the Hudson's Bay Company's attempts to control them. In the process, they affirmed and reaffirmed their own implicit claims to territorial suzerainty.

In a second and equally pointed way, Red River symbolized change. Its existence warned of the supplanting of a mobile fur trade frontier with one characterized by settled agrarian communities. The Hudson's Bay Company as a commercial fur-trading empire had always resisted such a scenario and would adjust to it only ponderously in the years ahead. For the Métis people, too, even as they challenged the Hudson's Bay Company and staked emotional and economic claims to Red River territory, the Red River settlement constituted a profound threat, albeit a threat in embryo. It was for what it presaged, as much as for what it was, that early Red River should be remembered.

THE BUSINESS CULTURES OF PRE-CONFEDERATION CANADA

Contact between North American natives and European interlopers took place on many levels, but few were as important or as constant as trade. This was especially the case in that part of North America that became known as Canada. Trade facilitated interaction between natives and whites for a much longer period than in regions further south. Any discussion of business practices in pre-Confederation Canada, then, must first focus on its first traders, the natives of North America. Most who have examined the role of natives in trade have adopted one of two perspectives. The first perspective holds that native trade cannot be understood in market-oriented terms. Natives did not trade to make a profit; rather, trade was an adjunct to diplomacy. Those who fought together traded together. Trade followed a diplomatic/military alliance and could not take place without such a formal liaison. Supply and demand did not set price or determine bargaining: the need for allies and the relative military and political strength or prestige of the trading groups set the level of exchange.

A second interpretation, which focuses on a somewhat later period, accepts that traditional native trade operated according to nonmarket considerations. Over time, however, these considerations became secondary to the imperatives of a capitalist market-based trade. Alliances no

265

TRADE AND ECONOMY OF MID-19TH CENTURY BRITISH NORTH AMERICA

MAJOR IMPORT/EXPORT ROUTES
AMERICAN CANALS USED
AMERICAN RAILWAYS USED
OLDER TRADE ROUTES NOT USED AT
TIME OF CONFEDERATION

* EXPORTS
* IMPORTS

ATLANTIC OCEAN

1 cm = 212 km

This map offers a glimpse of primary exports and imports and should make comprehensible the nature of colonial trade. Note that the American canals emphasize the dependence on American routes, particularly for Upper Canada.

* MANUFACTURED GOODS *
* FISH *
* FOODSTUFFS *
* TIMBER GOODS *
* MASTS, TIMBER, SHIPS *
* MANUFACTURED GOODS *
* MANUFACTURED SHIPS *
* FOODSTUFFS *
* FISH *
St. John's

* FURS (UNTIL 1821) *

* WHEAT *

Halifax

* FISH, LUMBER *

* MOLASSES, RUM *

* FOODSTUFFS *

Saint John

* FOODSTUFFS *

Rivière-du-Loup

* TIMBER AND FOODSTUFFS FROM 1853 *

Portland

* TIMBER *

* FOODSTUFFS *

Boston

Quebec

* TIMBER *

* TIMBER AND FOODSTUFFS *

Montreal

* TIMBER AND TIMBER *

* FURS AND TIMBER *

Rupert House

* FURS *

Moose Factory

Fort Albany

HUDSON BAY

Kingston

New York

Ottawa

* TIMBER AND FOODSTUFFS *

Buffalo

York

* TIMBER *

* FOODSTUFFS *

Detroit

* FURS TO BRITAIN *

York Factory

Fort Severn

* FURS *

* FURS UNTIL 1821 *

* LUMBER *

Fort William

Chicago

Fort Churchill

* FURS *

* FURS *

* FURS *

St. Paul

Fort Garry

* FURS, WHEAT
MANUFACTURED
GOODS *

TRADE AND ECONOMY OF MID-19TH CENTURY BRITISH NORTH AMERICA

longer played an important role in setting trading terms although traditional protocols, procedures, and ceremonies remained. Native trade was in a process of transition from traditional nonmarket behaviours to more modern market-governed activity.

This market versus nonmarket polarization presents a somewhat idealized and abstract picture of traditional native trade. In fact, a closer examination of how and why North America's first traders conducted their business suggests that traditional practices were in some respects congruent with market behaviours, although they had emerged from a noncapitalist-oriented culture. Few of the First Nations you read about in Chapter 1 lived in isolated "palaeolithic poverty"; rather, most native bands interacted with other groups at the levels of war, marriage, and trade. Recognition of the fact that exchange and interaction were integral aspects of native life before the arrival of Europeans makes it easier to understand the ease with which natives and Europeans cooperated and traded during the early contact years.[1]

Pre-Contact Exchange in North America

Archaeologists have determined that before 1000 B.C. natives around Lake Superior chipped and polished local copper into tools that were traded as far east as modern Labrador and as far west as modern Saskatchewan. For the most part, this early trade occurred in a step-wise process: one band would exchange goods with a neighbouring and often genetically linked band, and, in this way, the copper implements would travel along pre-contact trade networks. All participants in the trading process, however,

---

[1] See Bruce Trigger, *Natives and Newcomers: Canada's "Heroic Age" Reconsidered* (Kingston/Montreal, 1985), 183–94, for a short review of this debate. For work that focuses on trade in the pre-contact and early contact periods, see C. A. Bishop, "The Indian Inhabitants of Northern Ontario at the Time of Contact: Socio-Territorial Considerations," in M. G. Hanna and B. Koozman, eds., *Approaches to Algonquian Archaeology* (Calgary, 1982); W. A. Fox and R. F. Williamson, "Free Trade in Prehistory: A Lesson from the Past," *Ontario Archaeological Society Newsletter*, 89, 4 (1989), 9–11; R. C. Cole, ed., *Historical Atlas*, Plate 14; and M. W. Spence, et al., "Hunter-Gatherer Social Group Identification: A Case Study from Middle Woodland Southern Ontario" in S. P. De Atley and F. J. Findlow, eds., *Exploring the Limits: Frontiers and Boundaries in Prehistory* (Great Britain, 1984).

were not equal. Rather, each trading network contained centres of activity where powerful social and economic groups tended to dominate the exchange process. One such centre emerged along the north shore of Lake Erie between 1000 and 500 B.C. Meadowood blades made from local sources of flint were exchanged as far as Ohio and northern New York. By 500 B.C., however, stiff competition from Ohio natives who had begun to manufacture and trade a similar product led to the demise of the Meadowood industry, making it the first documented casualty of free trade!

A second example underlines the complexity of trading networks in the pre-contact era. Large burial mounds—one measuring 53 metres long by 7.5 metres wide by 1.8 metres high—mark the landscape around Rice Lake in southeastern Ontario. These date from A.D. 500 and provide evidence of habitation by the same bands for generations. While primarily hunting and gathering peoples, the Rice Lake natives also participated in an exchange system centring on the so-called Hopewellian culture of southern Ohio. Silver from what is now Cobalt, Ontario, 350 kilometres north of Rice Lake, was reworked by elite craftspeople at Rice Lake and distributed by them throughout the Hopewellian exchange system. That this was an elite-controlled manufacturing and trading system is suggested by the fact that only a small minority of individuals had silver items buried with them. At the same time, Rice Lake natives also received goods from what is now the eastern United States and traded throughout their local region. Rice Lake was both the northern node of the southern-centred Hopewellian system and a participant in several other exchange systems as well.

While it is very likely the case that step-wise trade continued to characterize the exchange process, the connection between Ohio and Rice Lake was nonetheless direct. Both centres declined at the same time (A.D. 300). While the exact causes of the decline remain unknown, it is clear that hunter-gatherers were far from isolated groups unto themselves. Complex trade interaction linked cultures and economies and, indeed, as was the case with the Rice Lake craftspeople, led to the emergence of specialization and status groupings within native bands.

Such "trade chains and middlemen systems," according to one ethnohistorian, "extended throughout most of the eastern Subarctic" and existed on the British Columbia coast in the pre-contact era. Trade sparked the emergence of status and hierarchical relations within the participating societies. Just as the Huron, in the Georgian Bay area, had by the eve of contact developed a trade system based on descent—i.e., the family that initiated a trade route could bequeath control of that route—so too did a similar practice emerge among some Upper Great Lakes Algonquin–Ojibwa groups. Ojibwa and Huron families and individuals closely controlled these trading rights, and, based on these prerogatives, an extensive alliance system had evolved by the time of contact. An even more pronounced ranking system based on the hereditary control of desired trade goods and central exchange routes had evolved in pre-contact times among natives such as the Tsimshian on the Pacific coast.

The argument concerning the existence of social differentiation based on control of trade—the emergence of status and elites within pre-contact native societies—is somewhat controversial. After all, it is commonly held that traditional native cultures were based on egalitarian notions, otherworldly spiritual beliefs, and nonacquisitive habits. The nonmaterial notion of wealth is often, and justifiably, pointed to as a major difference

This painting by Robert Hood in 1819 depicts Inuit meeting incoming Hudson's Bay Company ships in the Hudson Strait. Presumably such enterprising Inuit had first crack at incoming trade goods.   NATIONAL ARCHIVES OF CANADA/C40364

between native and European societies. Native practices of gift giving during trade, burial, and other ceremonies seems to underline the importance of the nonmaterial ethic. While the commencement of this behaviour is obscure, public redistribution of spiritual and functional goods was established before contact. Redistributing or sharing rather than hoarding or stockpiling goods enhanced one's status in native society. Some native societies displayed social rank through conspicuous giving rather than through conspicuous consumption. Gift giving and the holding of burial feasts demonstrated a family's generosity and worth even as they publicly proclaimed the bequeathment of trading privileges. Gift giving during trade helped cement relationships between trading groups and affirmed the rights and privileges of the various groups involved. While such behaviour is at one level clearly antithetical to the capitalist imperative of acquisition and personal reinvestment, it is nonetheless similar in the sense that wealth display was firmly embedded in native notions of social status. Once, for example, one's goods were distributed, it was imperative to acquire more goods for future public disbursement in order to maintain social standing. This imperative facilitated exchange in pre-contact native societies and provided a point of affinity for initial relations with Europeans following contact.

The Hudson's Bay Company and Native Traders

Native trade in the post-contact period is dealt with in detail in an earlier chapter. One aspect of the Hudson's Bay Company–native trade, however, deserves a closer look in this chapter on early business practice. Hudson's Bay Company traders and natives conducted their business according to a set of rules that became known as the "Standard of Trade." The concept of the "made beaver"—one prime beaver pelt—equalling a fixed amount of European trade goods became the currency of North America's fur trade for two centuries. For example, one gallon of English brandy equalled four made beaver, one pound of Brazilian tobacco equalled one made beaver, and one gun equalled 14 made beaver. Fixed price and bartered trade have been seen as accommodations to native nonmarket traditions. Yet such a view oversimplifies the actual operation of trade in the New World and the reality of current European trading practices in the Old World.

The Standard of Trade permitted much scope for bargaining at the trading posts. What, for example, constituted a prime beaver pelt? Moreover, Hudson's Bay traders gave light weights and short measures of various products, such as gunpowder, tobacco, and diluted brandy. As their demand "give us good measure" suggests, natives were only too well aware of this possibility. Gift exchanges also provided a further means to augment gain. Bargaining had limits, however. Native demand for goods was itself relatively constant, governed by limited carrying capacities and by an ethic that abhorred hoarding and encouraged public distribution of goods. Thus, for the Hudson's Bay Company to offer more goods per "made beaver" meant that natives needed fewer made beaver to satisfy their demand for European goods. In this context, the company would receive fewer not more pelts. Therefore traders rarely exceeded the prices set by the official Standard of Trade and were quite concerned to reduce gift giving whenever possible. Bargaining occurred but was limited by the contrasting ethics of the two cultures: one predisposed toward no growth and the public distribution of goods; the other, toward growth and accumulation.

The establishment of a maximum price, which is what the official Standard of Trade became, and the use of barter as the money of exchange reflected what one writer has termed "the structural weaknesses in the European economy" in the seventeenth and eighteenth centuries. Given that it took about two years to communicate market information from Europe to the Hudson's Bay Company and then to the natives (assuming they even cared), the difficulties of operating a market-driven long distance trading system in a period of primitive communications become apparent. The implementation of a constant trading standard or a stable price structure provided some clarity and reduced uncertainty in a pre-industrial economy. Barter exchange characterized many trading transactions in both the Old and New World in an era marked by severe shortages of metallic currencies and the difficulties of transporting such specie over long distances. One well-used bookkeeping manual even had a separate chapter for barter transactions. Old World practice and New World tradition were both well served by that means of exchange.[2]

---

[2] Consult A. J. Ray and D. Freeman, *"Give Us Good Measure": An Economic Analysis of Relations Between the Indians of HBC Before 1763* (Toronto, 1978) and E. Mancke, *A Company of Businessmen: The HBC and Long-Distance Trade, 1670-1730* (Winnipeg, 1988) for further discussion of these themes.

This discussion of Canada's first traders suggests that, even during the first century of the Hudson's Bay Company's trade, persistence of traditional practice rather than transition to the imperatives of a more-modern market economy characterized native behaviour. Prepared by their own traditions and motivated by their own culturally determined reasons, natives were traders in search of a good deal. It is why they desired such a deal and what they did with the fruits of their trade that set them apart from European traders. The discussion also points to the problems of assuming that European economic behaviours were mirror images of our own. As we shall see in more detail in the following section, such was not always the case.

Old Regime Business in the New World, 1620–1763

Merchants straddled the Atlantic providing the essential connection between New and Old France. Merchants built, financed, and outfitted the ships that sent people, mail, and goods between the two regions. New France was never self-sufficient: it depended on merchants for all kinds of goods, brandy, grain, hardware, and household items. In war and in peace, merchants were the umbilical cord that linked colony and mother country. Given the intimacy of the connection, any exploration of old regime business in the New World must start at home in Old France.

As were native traders, European merchants were part of the communities within which they lived. The problem is to place them within the appropriate community. Were merchants simply middle-class men on the make, the bourgeois of whom we hear so much today? Can they be fully understood in terms of class, their relationship to economic activity? Is national affiliation important? In other words, did the manner of doing business differ if the merchant were English or Dutch or French? How important were religious affiliations, ports of residence, family ties? A substantial historical debate surrounds many of these questions.[3]

---

[3] Introductions to these issues can be found in Roberta Hamilton, *Feudal Society and Colonization: The Historiography of New France* (Gananoque, 1988); Dale Miquelon, *Dugard of Rouen: French Trade to Canada and the West Indies, 1729–1770* (Montreal and London, 1978); and especially J. F. Bosher, *The Canada Merchants, 1713–63* (London, 1987).

NATIONAL STATES AND ECONOMIC STRUCTURES

One of the most important of these debates focuses on the way the economic structures of England and France influenced business behaviour. Some argue that the agricultural revolution that took place in seventeenth-century England led over time to the creation of a wage labour–consumer class. As agricultural fields were enclosed and peasants forced off the land, urban areas based in part on wage labour developed. An aristocratic marketplace was being superseded by a mass marketplace and traders, merchants, and manufacturers were on hand "to serve and create its needs." While this process only slowly gained momentum, it is nonetheless true that after the mid-seventeenth century it was increasingly possible to invest in the production of goods for a British mass market. This was not the case in France. It took the French Revolution of the 1790s to begin the creation of a comparable mass marketplace. Up to that point, merchants traded primarily in luxury goods for an aristocratic clientele. Because peasants were still tied to the land by feudal bonds, they could only rarely produce more than they consumed or paid in various dues to others. A mass consumer market could not evolve under the old regime in France. In this context, merchants saw little economic reason to invest in manufacturing or producing mass commodities. Rather, they looked to business to provide them with enough wealth to acquire lands, government offices—which were bought from the Crown and all subsequent returns went into the owner's pocket—and, above all, noble status.

This interpretation has much explanatory power. It provides a plausible explanation for the relatively greater mass exodus of English (who were pushed off the land) as compared to French (who remained relatively tied to the land) to the New World in this era. The notion of an evolving mass market does help one understand the greater diversity of economic activity in England and its colonies as compared to France and its colonies. The separation of government finance from strong private control in England as compared to France, with its decentralized system for the collection, spending, and managing of government funds, certainly permitted greater financial stability and at least the possibility of a coordinated state-financial policy to emerge in England.

Two cautions are appropriate at this point, however. The temptation to overdraw these contrasts must be avoided. England could not and did not transform itself from a feudal subsistence society to one of mass consumer and diversified production overnight. The process of change, while real and important, was gradual and evolved over the course of a century, at least. Vestiges of the past co-existed with economic and social change. Old attitudes, including those related to investments in land and the quest for aristocratic status, never completely died. Throughout this and later periods, merchants and their heirs often sought the trappings of the country gentleman. And, in fact, the form of economic behaviour that emerged in Britain in these years has been called "gentlemanly capitalism."

The second caution is, in a way, the reverse image of the first. Change did take place within old regime France. Dale Miquelon, in his study of one important merchant firm involved in the Canada trade, Robert Dugard of the Port of Rouen, has concluded that Dugard's mode of organization, method of financing, and rate of return appear very similar to comparable English enterprises. Moreover, if in 1701 a national business council in France could complain that "the profession of trader is vilified and despised by officers and gentlemen," it, nonetheless, remained true that officers and gentlemen dabbled, at times quite deeply, in many commercial affairs. It also remained the case that one sure way to ascend to gentleman status was via a successful mercantile career.

RELIGION, FAMILY, AND PORT OF TRADE

It is within the overlapping circles of family, religion, and port of residence that most old regime mercantile behaviour occurred, and it is within the extensive circumference of religion that wider European and more narrowly French economic activity converged.

Merchants engaged in the Canada trade congregated in the ports of southwestern France, especially Bordeaux and La Rochelle, where they lived cheek by jowl in compressed areas close to the water. Ports and their satellites competed with each other for government preferment in matters of tax and custom duties. Within each port, merchants built up personal contacts from which ties of credit and debt emerged. Allegiance to and pride of place were undoubtedly important influences on merchant activity. Yet individual ships engaged in the Canada trade were often owned by merchants from several competing ports. Moreover, Canada merchants tended to be recent arrivals and were not among the wealthiest or established elite of those ports. Port of origin does not adequately account for the activity of the Canada merchants.

Family ties provide a better key to the nature of mercantile activity. In fact, trade between Old and New France was a family affair. Agents and partners of Canada merchants living in Quebec had more often than not followed a relative there and/or were related to the owners of the parent company in France. Marriages were business propositions: in one businessman's journal, he mentioned his marriage of that day and then entered into a long enumeration of the capital, business assets, and contacts that the union had made possible. For many merchants, wives brought more than money and contacts; they also brought their own talents and were accordingly often active members of the mercantile affair. Other partners, agents in satellite and colonial ports, debtors, and creditors were, it seems whenever possible, linked by family. In an age of uncertain communication and in the business of long-distance trade, it was essential to know and trust those with whom one did business.

Religion overlapped and reinforced family links. Few married outside their own religious circle. Catholics, Protestants, and Jews would trade with one another but only rarely did partnerships involve those of different religions. Children inherited and ultimately bequeathed religious affiliation, but religion was more than a private affair. In this, the era of the Counter Reformation, the French state was an active ally of an aggressive, proselytizing Roman Catholic Church. The religious foundations of New France reflected this link. The revocation of the Edict of Nantes in 1685 represented the culmination of this "relationship": all Protestants or Huguenots were outlawed from France, and in the next decade some 180 000 left. One had to be a Catholic in order to advance in economic, social, and political circles in France in this era. Accordingly, many Huguenots who remained became New Converts and many New Converts were active in the Canada trade.

Most New Converts, in fact, remained Huguenots at heart. They tended to marry other New Converts. And what is of crucial significance for our discussion of the nature of trade, New Convert merchants in France, including those involved in the Canada trade, tended to have close links of a family, financial, and mercantile sort with what has been called a "Protestant International," an expanding and powerful group of financiers, merchants, and capitalists headquartered in the Netherlands, England, and extending even to Quebec. New Converts could not anticipate opportunities similar to those of Catholic merchants for upward mobility in France. They thus naturally cultivated different client and support groups, and these were to be found in the international rather than national context. While French Catholic merchants remained firmly embedded in old regime France, French New Convert merchants were becoming part of a different milieu, a context structured by social and economic developments in Britain and Holland, changes that had yet to affect France itself.

Commerce in the Colony

IMPORT-EXPORT MERCHANTS AT QUEBEC CITY

Few of those representatives of Canada merchants who went to Quebec looked on the colony as their future home. Living in the narrow streets of Quebec's Lower Town, these agents viewed the colony as a stepping-stone to future preferment in France. Often of humble, artisan origin themselves, their role as agents, generally acquired via family links, was a first move in that direction. Within the colony, however, these agents had power and influence. In the course of handling the affairs of the metropolitan merchants, they determined when and to whom to extend credit; set prices; assessed local market needs; evaluated and priced fur for export; prepared cargoes for shipment to French colonies in the Caribbean and, after 1715, to Louisbourg; liaised with Montreal merchants through whom they became connected to a hinterland beyond their direct reach; and even, on occasion, built ships to be used in the Atlantic trade.

While much money could be made from the export of fur, that trade only accounted for some 11 percent of gross domestic colonial production between 1695 and 1739. Agricultural output accounted for over 75 percent, and the rest was generated by miscellaneous nonagricultural activity. It is no surprise, therefore, that the profits of most Canada merchants depended on good harvests. When harvests were poor, import consumption dropped and profits declined. The uncertain harvests of the 1740s and 1750s, coupled with and in part caused by war, fatally weakened the import-export merchants. Like Old France, New France was an agricultural community and, to be successful, merchants had to adjust to that reality.

FUR MERCHANTS AT MONTREAL

The Quebec agents of relatively wealthy mercantile ventures in France were important men of business in the colony, but they were not the only merchants there, nor, as in France, were merchants the only ones who engaged in commercial affairs. In Montreal, the fur trade occupied most commercial minds. But it would seem to have filled the pockets of few merchants. By 1725 less than a dozen Montreal merchants had capital assets equalling 50 000 livres. Only about one-third of the profits from the trade in beaver remained in the colony. In the 20 years up to the Conquest, Montreal merchants had little wealth, married within their social and economic group, i.e., experienced horizontal not upward social and economic mobility, and generally invested only in their immediate commercial affairs. By the late 1720s, the fur trade was closely regulated by France: the state restricted the number of traders in the interior and, the Compagnie des Indies, a chartered company, held a monopoly over beaver sales. In this protected and restricted environment, the established local merchants in Montreal maintained a moderate level of prosperity.

Others in the Montreal region also received moderate, but nonetheless significant, returns from the fur trade. Between 1730 and 1745, 6493 engagés were hired by fur merchants to transport goods into the interior and carry furs back to Montreal. The engagés were paid a total of 1 513 347 livres or an average of 233 livres each. This was not a large salary in an era where the average nonrural worker earned close to 400 livres a year. Small wonder that 62 percent of them called themselves "habitants" or "habitant-voyageurs": for them the fur trade was supplemental to other occupational pursuits.

Yet some at least of those other occupational pursuits were themselves tied to the fur trade. Anywhere from 20 to 50 percent of the goods sent into the interior were grown, milled, or manufactured in the colony. Local craftspeople, farmers, and millers in the Montreal region all benefited from the roughly 60 000 livres spent on local goods in 1727 and from the over 110 000 livres spent each year in the early 1740s. In fact, in the early 1740s, money spent by the fur trade on goods and salaries in the Montreal region equalled about one-half of all money spent by the Crown in the colony and amounted to one-tenth of the value of the colony's exports for those years. Historians have tended to evaluate the trade's worth in terms of mercantile profits. Evidence currently available suggests that few resident merchants got very rich from that trade. For many others in the Montreal region, however, the trade was at least a supplement to other occupations, and for some, a valuable addition to their primary business.

Those in Montreal, at the midpoint of the trading process, would seem to have benefited in important, but moderate, ways from the fur business. What can one say concerning participants at the extreme ends of the trading cycle: the natives in the interior and the merchants in France? The Compagnie des Indies, which, following 1717, enjoyed a monopoly on the beaver trade, made an annual profit of 200 000 livres between 1727 and 1743. This represented a 26 percent return on invested capital, about twice what the average transatlantic firm received. Since the price charged by the Compagnie to French and European buyers was not above the going international rates, it follows that the price Montreal merchants received for beaver was low. To some extent the colonial merchants would offset this by smuggling fur to Albany, New York, from where they were shipped to London. When the Compagnie offered very low rates compared to Albany's, London imports from New York rose, suggesting an increase in smuggling. Yet even at its peak, London's imports from New York represented only 20 percent of Quebec's exports to France. Smuggling never really compensated the Montreal merchants for their low returns from the Compagnie des Indies.

Could Montreal merchants offset these low prices in their trade with the natives in the interior? The simple answer is yes. How is less simple. From the early 1700s, the French state had viewed the fur trade less as a money-making venture than a means of keeping native allies in the interior and thus protecting the French colony from English expansion. In the early years of the century, the state was willing to subsidize the trade for imperial reasons. By 1720, old supplies of fur in Paris had rotted and an increased consumer demand made such imperial subsidies unnecessary. Nevertheless, the state remained very sensitive on the issue of native allies and continued to see the fur trade as the best way to maintain friendly links. In this context, Montreal merchants combatted the low prices offered by the Compagnie des Indies by petitioning the Ministry of the Marine and warning that such prices would be scoffed at by the natives who would desert to British traders at Oswego, Albany, and Hudson Bay. The French Empire, they warned, would be put at risk. The strategy was effective: especially in the war years following 1745, Compagnie prices were raised, if only a little, and presumably colonial merchants benefited.

Were the merchants' petitions anything other than a clever ruse? Did natives systematically seek out the best prices available? Clearly, some did and when price differentials, i.e., when French traders offered a considerably smaller amount of goods than did British traders for fur, then more natives would move to the better offer. On balance, however, it would seem that the source of that better offer had to be close by. When British and French posts were relatively close, natives took regular advantage of the competition. But few posts were very close in the era before the Conquest. The Hudson's Bay Company did not leave the bay until the 1770s, and few New York merchants went into the interior. Moreover, the French state allowed only a restricted number of licensed French traders into the interior in any one year. As a result, the possibility of playing off one French merchant against another was limited. Most natives who continued to trade with the French in the years before the Conquest, in effect, subsidized the Compagnie des Indies' large profits and the colonial merchants' moderate prosperity. They tolerated a relatively low return in order to avoid the alternative of long-distance travel to the posts of merchants who offered more.[4]

BOURGEOIS GENTILHOMMES

If you don't have enough wits to make some money where you are, you should be beaten since everyone knows what civil servants do and those who do not have a profitable trade are treated as idiots. You don't pay enough attention to these matters. It is all very well to do one's duty, but you should try to look after your own affairs as well.

Such was a mother-in-law's advice to her son-in-law, a colonial office holder in New France. It was an appropriate admonition. Governors, intendants, and military officers used their positions to pad their pockets through commercial speculation. Governor Frontenac went to the colony to acquire money to repay outstanding debts. He speculated in merchant shipping as well as the fur trade. Officers at interior posts, in return for protecting local monopolies, took a cut of the returns and often traded directly themselves. The revelations of trade speculation involving the intendant François Bigot (1748–59), while dramatic, were probably not untypical. Like the agents of the Canada merchants, Bigot and other colonial officials came to the colony to make their fortunes and move up in French society. Similar practice dominated all other local regions in France. Bigot profited from privately held fur monopolies and from partnership in mercantile ventures that received contracts from him to supply the state at inflated prices. He lived a sumptuous life. His penchant for aping the royal court at Versailles at a time when New France was under a virtual state of siege and grinding poverty was the lot of most citizens typified the attitudes of his class. It is hard to know just how much

---

[4] J. E. Igartua, "The Merchants of Montreal at the Conquest: Socio-Economic Profile," *HS/SH*, 8, 1975, 275–93; and Louise Dechêne, *Habitants et marchands au Montréal au XVII siècle* (Paris, 1974) are standard works. Thomas Wein, "Selling Beaver Skins in North America and Europe, 1720–1760: The Uses of Fur Trade Imperialism," *Journal of the Canadian Historical Association*, 1 (1990): 293-318 and G. Allaire, "Fournitures et engagements 1715–60: l'impart economique du commerce des fourrures dans la region de Montréal," unpublished paper, CHA (Windsor, 1988) are very useful.

money he grossed through private deals made possible by his public position. Consistent with social dictates of the era, these gains were shipped to France so that, upon retirement, he could "live like a country gentleman on a country property in an agreeable French province surrounded by family, friends and servants." He ended up in the Bastille, and, on December 10, 1763, was banished from France for life. The French state prosecuted Bigot and others because it required scapegoats upon whom to pin the debacle of defeat. That, too, was part of the rules of the game; one of the risks speculators in office knowingly undertook on the road to ennoblement. Commercial activity in New France was tied by kin, religion, finance, custom, and motive to business in the old regime. The one cannot be understood in isolation from the other.

COD AND THE LOUISBOURG MERCHANTS

New France was not the most important North American commercial colony under French control. Île Royal (Cape Breton Island), founded in

The Newfoundland dry cod fishery.   NATIONAL ARCHIVES OF CANADA/C70648

1713, was by the 1720s exporting cod worth three times the value of New France's beaver exports. The colony traded with France, New France, Acadia, New England, and the Caribbean. The merchant class that emerged to handle that trade differed in several ways from that in New and Old France.

Louisbourg became the centre of commercial activity. In contrast to New France, the merchants who controlled trade had generally been born in the colony or had prior experience in the cod trade in Newfoundland. Few major French metropolitan firms had agents at Louisbourg. Local merchants gradually took over the fish trade, directly controlling about 50 percent of the catch by the 1750s and successfully limiting wages of fishers throughout the period. On average, they would seem to have been much wealthier than the fur trade merchants of Montreal. They also would seem to have enjoyed greater social prestige than their confrères in New France. They held many administrative posts including a significant percentage of the seats on the Superior Council. In part, their prominence can be attributed to the fact that there were relatively few competitors: a seigneurial elite comparable to New France did not exist in Île Royal, although the military officials were closely involved in the cod trade and, in some cases, general mercantile affairs.

The absence of institutional restraints—outside control and competing elites—on commercial activity at Louisbourg probably, as one historian has argued, "promoted the dissemination of commercial values" as well as the local riches and upward mobility of merchants. Certainly Louisbourg's merchants were able to react more quickly during the war years of the 1740s and 1750s in redirecting trade flows and revamping the local fishing industry than were the merchants in New France who were more closely tied to metropolitan centres in the old country. The Louisbourg example does exist as a contrast to New France. When freed from the fetters of economic bondage to French mercantile companies and the old regime state, colonials could profit from local commercial activity.

Two caveats should be mentioned here. The first is simply that Louisbourg merchants enjoyed the pomp and splendour of courtly affairs and were quite prone to displaying conspicuously their gains from selling cod. The second point is perhaps more fundamental and relates to exactly what is meant by "entrepreneurial enterprise [which] could thrive within the legal and political structures of New France" at Louisbourg. Certainly local control of and local profit taking from the growing triangular trade between the Caribbean, New England, and the colony were higher in

Louisbourg than in New France. Most definitions of entrepreneurship, however, go beyond that of simple profit taking. They focus on the transformation of existing economic structures. Is there any evidence that Louisbourg merchants operated at that level of enterprise? Certainly they bent the rules of mercantilism by including New England as a major trading partner. But did they transform the economy by developing enterprise outside of trade and commercial exchange? We do know that Louisbourg merchants spent significant sums on conspicuous consumption. But they did absolutely nothing to develop agriculture, mining, or logging on Île Royale. They preferred to import from New France and New England. Although over time they became boat owners, few of their boats were built in the colony. The frustrated local financial commissary complained in 1743 that

I make every effort to enlist the inhabitants in building, but I am unable to succeed because of the benefits they see in purchasing English ships, these purchases procuring for them the disposal of their rum and molasses, so if that harms construction, it on the other hand is good for the sale of the cargoes coming from the islands [the West Indies].

In the sense of transforming the economy, then, Louisbourg's merchants were not entrepreneurially minded at all. Like many merchants elsewhere, they did little to reorient a social and economic structure from which they were making sufficient profits. In the end, their impact on the colony's development was negligible. As one scholar has concluded, "With the fall of Louisbourg, France disappeared from the scene and left so scanty a legacy from nearly half a century of occupation as to make clear that Cape Breton Island was largely underdeveloped in the 1713–58 period."

ACADIANS AND MASSACHUSETTS

Acadian commercial activity in the late seventeenth and early eighteenth centuries underlines one point suggested by the Louisbourg experience: local colonials could engage in economic activity independent from the control of France. The Acadians farmed the rich lowlands around the Bay of Fundy. They were successful in this endeavour because they ingeniously constructed a series of dykes that allowed excess fresh water to flow out to the bay but prevented salt water from inundating their land. The French officially forbade trade between Acadia and the English at Massachusetts. Acadian entrepreneurs ignored those restrictions: furs obtained from natives and surplus farm products were sent to Massachusetts in return for

West Indian products (sugar and rum) and manufactured goods (knives and dishes). This trade occurred in an unsettled context of intermittent war between the French and English. Despite such conditions, Acadian entrepreneurs travelled to Boston to trade and even, at times, sought recourse for grievances in Massachusetts law courts.

When Acadia was ceded to England by the Treaty of Utrecht in 1713, enterprising Acadians engaged in illicit trade with the French at Louisbourg, sending 16 ships with agricultural produce in 1740 alone. Not until the dispersals of the mid-eighteenth century took place did the Acadians cease to engage in profitable and independent commercial and agricultural activity.

CONQUEST AND COMMERCE

The nature of the impact that the Conquest of New France had has been called "the most fundamental issue in the historiography of Canada in the eighteenth century." Did the overthrow of the French lead to the decapitation of an allegedly dynamic colonial bourgeois class and to the subsequent retardation of economic development in what became Quebec? When the umbilical cord between New and Old France was severed, did the colonial economy and its leading men of business wither away in the face of dynamic, aggressive, and unfair competition from British commerce? A series of assumptions that underlie these questions must be examined before any answer can be provided.

Was New France's economy buoyant in the years prior to the Conquest? Judgments are very mixed on this issue, but a recent study by Morris Altman, an economic historian, has argued that per capita economic growth in New France parallelled economic development in the British American colonies to the South between 1695 and 1739. Far from being stagnant, Altman concludes that "Canada was economically dynamic and prosperous, even when compared to British North America." If one accepts Altman's appraisal (and his evidence is the most comprehensive yet assembled), then, how can one explain such growth? As noted earlier, the fur trade contributed only a minor role. Of slightly more importance was nonagricultural activity—artisans like carpenters, masons, shoemakers, joiners, tailors and their families made up about one-quarter of New France's population in this era. But the crucial and most consistently dynamic production occurred in the agricultural sector, accounting as it did for some 75 percent of gross domestic output.

Against this backdrop, the role played by merchants seems somewhat insignificant indeed. Perhaps too much of the debate on the Conquest has focused on a relatively minor sector of that colony's economy, those involved in its purely commercial affairs. With the exception of some import-export merchants at Quebec, few commercial men invested outside of their immediate businesses. Few Montreal merchants, as we have seen, accumulated much wealth to invest anywhere. When one traces the fate of Montreal's fur trade merchants after the Conquest when they were faced with a new market (Great Britain), stiff competition from better-financed British merchants, and discrimination from British state appointees, one discovers that the traditional scale of their operations, never very large, remained constant. In this sense, they were not so much decapitated as bypassed. Clearly, the change in the business context made life difficult for them. But viewed from a wider perspective, one has to question their importance to New France's economy before the Conquest.

But what of the fate of Quebec's import-export merchants? Two points can be made here. The first relates to a change that occurred before the Conquest. By the 1730s and certainly during the war-torn years of the 1740s and 1750s, the French state had begun to look to the contacts and skills of the New Convert, Huguenot merchants in order to facilitate the transport of men, arms, and material to the New World. Many Catholic families involved in the Canada trade began to move from trade to the greater security of land in the hopes of acquiring noble status. Few Huguenot merchants had that option. The Canada trade was becoming a cosmopolitan Protestant-controlled domain well before the Conquest: the Conquest was simply a further step in that direction.

The second point is that the Conquest and its aftermath did exact a terrible toll from those mainly Huguenot merchants who had remained in the Canada trade. Disruptions occasioned by the Seven Years' War sank many merchants. When, following the Conquest, the French state refused to honour its debts, many others fell into bankruptcy and quit, not only Canada, but commerce too. Yet a number of Huguenot merchants elected to stay and were joined by other Huguenots who had earlier fled from France. Some colonial merchant families, like that of Pierre Guy who had dealt with Huguenot merchants in the Canada trade in France, salvaged what they could of their assets and then went to London to, as Pierre wrote, "make acquaintances here, which is very easy to do." Significantly, Guy's first London link was with a Huguenot import-export merchant, Daniel Vialars. While Guy would complain bitterly in subsequent years about unfair discrimination from the British and would become quite active in pushing for the granting of an elected assembly, his business did prosper, and the essential first link that facilitated that prosperity was provided by Huguenot connections. Even before the Conquest cut the cord between New and Old France, a second lifeline was being laid down, one that drew the Canada trade out of France and into a wider Protestant-dominated Atlantic community. While the existence of these links hardly put Quebec merchants on a position of equality with their new English-raised and -speaking competitors, they did provide a known haven in a changing and hostile world.[5]

A Mother Country on the Move?: Colonial Enterprise in a British Mode

The Conquest substantially restructured commercial patterns. The influx of some 200 British merchants ushered in a period of greater competition in the fur trade and in other colonial commercial sectors. As we have seen, many Canadian merchants did not fare well in this altered milieu. Did these changes, therefore, represent the beginning of a new economic order? Did the Conquest transform colonial entrepreneurial activities and in that sense accomplish what French colonial entrepreneurs had failed to do? A traditional response to these queries has been yes: coinciding with the British Industrial Revolution (1750–1850), the Conquest gave to North America a new, dynamic mother country, a social, political, and economic system permeated with bourgeois notions of freedom, thrift, industry, and a competitive spirit. More recent scholars have suggested that this depiction is grossly overdrawn. In the first place, they argue, the Industrial Revolution is itself a misnomer. Even in Great Britain change occurred gradually and unevenly across various economic sectors. In

---

[5] The best study of Bigot is J. F. Bosher and J. C. Dubé, "François Bigot," *DCB*, 4, 59–70. For Louisbourg, see Christopher Moore, "The Other Louisbourg: Trade and Merchant Enterprise in Île Royale, 1713–58," *HS/SH*, 12 (1979); and A. H. Clark, "New England's Role in the Underdevelopment of Cape Breton Island During the French Regime, 1713–58," *Canadian Geographer*, 9, 1 (1965). For the general economic picture, see Morris Altman, "Economic Growth in Canada, 1695–1739: Estimates and Analysis," *William and Mary Quarterly*, XLV, 1988.

some areas, very little had changed by 1851. Gradual rather than revolutionary economic transformation had its counterpart in social relations. Men of business remained second-class social citizens in England throughout much of this period. At best, a form of gentlemanly capitalism set the contours of social, political, and economic change. Landed or *rentier* capitalists who engaged at arm's length in commercial agriculture constituted the nation's social and economic elite.

This recent interpretation emphasizes continuity of social status amidst gradual economic transformation. Existing social structures were able to accommodate and shape capitalist development rather than be reshaped by such economic change. This is an important (although far from unchallenged) perspective. It forces us, as students, to be cautious about attributing great consequences to presumed watershed events like conquests and revolutions. This is not to imply that nothing ever changes: rather dramatic events rarely sweep all before them. What the Conquest transformed in terms of North America's economy had more to do with ethnicity and direction of trade than with business practice and structure.[6]

Commercial Communities in British North America

Much has been made of the role played by Scottish businesspeople in British North America. They have been described as a "self-conscious new capitalist order of confident entrepreneurs." Reflecting Scotland's rise as a commercial power in the late eighteenth century, many middle-class Scottish entrepreneurs emigrated to British North America. They forged commercial links with Scottish ports, like Glasgow, that would last throughout the nineteenth century. They monopolized the upper levels of the fur trade. They played an active role in the early nineteenth-century

---

[6] A general overview of research works on the Industrial Revolution is provided by Julian Hoppit, "Understanding the Industrial Revolution," *Historical Journal*, 30, 1 (1987), 211–24. For insights into business practice and the lives of businessmen in the various British North American colonies the relevant biographies should be consulted in the *Dictionary of Canadian Biography*. The geographical/thematic index can be used to identify appropriate people. Other helpful studies are P. Goldring, "Governor Simpson's Officers: Elite Recruitment in a British Overseas Enterprise, 1834–1870," *Prairie Forum* (1985) and Bruce Wilson, *The Enterprises of Robert Hamilton: a Study of Wealth and Influence in Early Upper Canada, 1776–1812* (Carleton, 1983).

Newfoundland trade. The Scottish-born dominated early business in New Brunswick: the major business area of Saint John was known as "Scotch Row"; the local St. Andrews Society resembled a chamber of commerce; and a prominent Scots entrepreneur, John Black, built up a trading network of only Scottish firms in North America, the West Indies, England, Scotland, and even the Mediterranean. One frustrated Upper Canadian critic complained about the "scotch pedlars," a "Shopkeeper Aristocracy" which, in the early nineteenth century,

had insinuated themselves into favour with [the Scots-born lieutenant governor] General Hunter...there is a chain of them linked from Halifax to Quebec, Montreal, Kingston, York, Niagara and so on to Detroit. . . .

This standard picture of a Scottish "mafia" controlling the upper levels of British North America's commercial affairs is in danger of becoming a caricature, where one important element of reality is blown up to represent the whole. In the first place, Scottish businesspeople did not constitute the only significant commercial ethnic enclave operating in the New World. Patrick Morris, for example, the Irish-born merchant reformer in Newfoundland, succeeded in a Protestant British mercantile world via "an ethnically focused" trade that included a dozen merchant businesspeople in St. John's alone. Six of these Irish Catholic businesspeople were elected to the assembly in 1842 and five sat on the appointed council. Ethnic bonds underlay Morris's political and mercantile affairs.

A second point about which more care is needed is the timing of Scottish commercial prominence. Existing evidence suggests that the power of the Scottish group peaked in the early nineteenth century: certainly prominent Scottish entrepreneurs remained active throughout the century, but during the pre-Confederation era, other commercial groups challenged or surpassed the Scottish cliques in most of British North America. Take the celebrated case of Scots dominance in the fur trade, for example. While the Scottish-born controlled the very highest levels of the Hudson's Bay Company throughout the pre-Confederation era, the extent of that prominence declined after about 1850. Sixty-three percent of the chief traders appointed between 1834 and 1849 were born in Scotland. Only 31 percent of the 70 chief traders appointed between 1850 and 1869 could claim Scottish birth.

A similar changing of the guard would seem to have taken place even earlier in Nova Scotia. Many of the Scottish merchants who had arrived in the 1780s had died or were past their prime by 1820. Significantly, four of the five most prominent directors of the colony's first bank, the Halifax Banking Company, formed in 1825, were born in Nova Scotia and the fifth was a Roman Catholic born in Ireland. Reflecting the increasing ratio of native to foreign born, an indigenous family capitalism began to dominate the Nova Scotian business scene in the 1820s. A similar trend was evident in New Brunswick: by 1850 one-half of the merchants in Saint John were native born. In Upper Canada, too, Scottish shopkeepers, while still prominent, began to share pride of place with others. The changing composition of the directorship of that colony's first and most pre-eminent bank, the Bank of Upper Canada, reflects this evolution. In 1825 the Scottish-born occupied 33 percent of the seats, in 1835, 25 percent, in 1845, 11 percent, and in 1855 only 8 percent. Clearly the power of the Scots in commercial affairs must be situated within a chronological frame.

Ethnic ties were obviously important to British North American traders. Ethnic groups preferred to trust members of their own enclave. The cultivation of ethnic links was one way of assuring trust in the conduct of long-distance trade during an era of primitive communications. Yet few traders could afford to be as single-minded as John Black of Nova Scotia. To succeed, most Scottish traders had to deal, on a regular and close basis, with members of other ethnic groups. The links formed to ensure trust and confidence in these cases transcended and broke down the simple enclave behaviour often described in current historical literature.

A closer look at an oft-pointed-to example of Scottish commercial control, that of the forwarding and fur trade between Montreal, Kingston, Niagara, and Detroit in the late eighteenth and early nineteenth centuries, suggests the importance of other, as well as, ethnic bonds. Many of the prominent families involved in this important commercial network were Scots: James McGill of Montreal and Robert Hamilton of Niagara are two examples. Yet rarely is much made of the fact that other active members of these overlapping partnerships were not Scottish. Isaac Todd at Montreal and John Askin of Detroit were Irish and Richard Cartwright of Kingston was a New York–born Loyalist whose father hailed from England and mother from Holland. Marriage was one way of solidifying commercial bonds between different ethnic groups. As one worldly wise Upper Canadian put it: "Love. . .matches may fill the belly of women, but not of men." The amount of "metal" women "carried" was far more important than their beauty. Not surprisingly, then, in 1785 Hamilton married his daughter to John Askin, thereby solidifying a long-lasting commercial alliance. For his part, James McGill, one year after establishing permanent residence in

Montreal, enhanced his local commercial position by marrying into a well-connected French Roman Catholic family.

In the absence of ethnic ties and family links, more intangible but nonetheless crucially important common qualities underlaid successful commercial operations. At this level, such concerns as general breeding, education, and politics became important. In Saint John, New Brunswick, the merchant elite were drawn from old patrician Loyalist families. The long-lasting Upper Canadian partnership of Hamilton and Cartwright commenced in 1780 in the business of the southwest fur trade and military provisioning at Niagara and succeeded where at least three-quarters of their competitors failed. Both merchants were well educated and had the breeding, respectability, and proper social bearing to gain the respect and attention of military personnel on whom they came to depend for much of their business. Military personnel deemed some other potential competitors, too "deficient in education and liberal sentiments" to warrant commercial or bureaucratic patronage.

In British North America, commercial bonds were forged in community crucibles similar to those that existed in New France. While religion would seem to have been less a touchstone for commercial contact (except perhaps in Newfoundland), family, birth place, and social standing remained important strands in the commercial webs woven by merchants after the Conquest, as they had been before. Such criteria were valued by merchants as one way of lessening risk and decreasing the unknowns that pervaded commercial life in the colonies. Contacts and confidence continued to rest on such personal qualities throughout the nineteenth century. The pre-eminent form of commercial organization, the family partnership, embodied these values. Yet pressures generated by a modernizing economic world encouraged some entrepreneurs to experiment with new modes of business organization in an attempt to capitalize on emerging economic opportunities.

Beyond the Family Partnership: Business Organization in British North America

Through much of the pre-Confederation era, even the largest mercantile partnerships tended to do a general business (as a guard against sudden fluctuations in the price of any particular commodity) rather than a specialized trade. They tended to be managed by family members situated in Scottish or English ports and colonial entrepôts. Only rarely were managerial decisions delegated below the partnership level. Inbred control, however, often led to disaster rather than success. A series of major bankruptcies of family-linked mercantile and fur-trading firms in Montreal in the mid-1820s encouraged many to search for better organizational structures within which to conduct business. One organizational solution was the limited liability stock company. Shares could then be purchased by many investors who would be liable only for the amount of their investment. Unfortunately for would-be colonial entrepreneurs, English promoters had been down that road a century earlier, and the result had been a series of burst bubbles and financial disasters.

Despite an increased use of the corporate form in the 1830s and 1840s, the imperial government continued to look askance at such organizations and, even in the case of colonial banks chartered in the 1830s, the mother country required that each shareholder be liable for double the amount of his or her personal investment. Gentlemanly capitalists professed disdain at attempts to hide personal wealth behind the shields of corporate anonymity and limited liability. Not until 1850 in the Canadas was a general law passed permitting ordinary mercantile, commercial businesses to incorporate under the protection of limited liability. Yet even this law preceded the passage of a similar one in England by five years and in Nova Scotia by over twelve years.

The real impetus for change in traditional modes of business organization lay outside the local mercantile context. Some historians have pointed to the Hudson's Bay Company and similar large internationally active trading companies as the precursors to modern multinational enterprises. Having received its charter before a series of spectacular corporate failures in the early eighteenth century caused the British state to shy away from such organizations. The Hudson's Bay Company, it is argued, resembled modern international firms in two ways. It set up a managerial hierarchy of salaried administrators who were given responsibility to manage matters concerning production, distribution, and pricing. It incurred the costs of instituting this hierarchical structure because of the very large number of economic transactions that the company routinely undertook. In the Hudson's Bay Company's case, these transactions, the transfer of goods and services, numbered in the tens of thousands and took place between natives and local traders, traders and ship captains, ship captains and company principals in London, company principals and British and

European buyers. Because of the volume of these exchanges—similar in volume to many late nineteenth-century enterprises—it made economic sense for one firm to take control of the total field of activity. By managing the purchase of trade goods in London and their sale in North America and the purchase of furs in North America and their sale in London, the firm could generate and control systematically gathered information on supplies, prices, market tastes, and preferences.

It is true that the Hudson's Bay Company did come close to what economists call the modern vertically integrated enterprise. However, that trading company did not produce the goods that it traded: it remained dependent on market forces for the purchase of trade goods in London, and it remained dependent on native hunters and traders for fur in North America. In both cases, however, the company attempted to stabilize prices by entering into contracts with London suppliers in advance of delivery and using the Standard of Trade mechanism as well as instituting a policy of conservation and fur management following 1820.

The second way in which the Hudson's Bay Company anticipated the operations of modern multinational enterprises concerns the system set up for overseeing its managers. The Hudson's Bay Company banned private trading, experimented with incentive contracts, required extremely detailed reports of activity, and even exacted oaths, which included swearing commitment to the company's goals. All these mechanisms for controlling managers far from head office are part of modern practice. In at least one aspect relating to the administrative sector, the Hudson's Bay Company would seem, however, to have been very much a part of its premodern, mercantile environment. After 1820, the Hudson's Bay Company, like the North West Company before it, began to rely on a system of kin-based appointments, a form of recruitment common to other large trading companies and to the British government itself. This was simply, as one senior company director explained, "mercantile usage and...the usage of public and private services."

A second group of historians have argued that the real precursor to modern enterprise did not emerge until changes in transport and communication technology made possible the ability to oversee a far-flung managerial hierarchy and facilitated a great enough volume of transactions to make the costs of such administration bearable. Certainly the advent of the transcontinental telegraph in the 1840s and the transatlantic cable in the 1860s facilitated rapid and routine transmission of commercial information and made the traditional, tightly controlled partnership less necessary. The routine acquisition of commercial information meant that one did not have to rely as much on a partner in another port: hired agents could do the job just as well. Moreover, the very companies set up to create and manage new transport and communication systems often required the hiring of large labour forces, the close supervision of routine schedules, the efficient processing of a large volume of transactions completed at a speed impossible to contemplate in the pre-railroad and steam era, and the careful management of the complexities of maintaining and depreciating fixed physical assets. For most historians, it is such corporate structures as those that emerged to manage railroads that contained the seeds of modern corporate enterprise. Railroads began to manufacture much of their capital needs, thus exhibiting, to an even greater extent than the large multinational trading companies, evidence of vertical integration.

These pictures dramatically depict the contrast between the beginnings of the railroad era in the 1830s when men cleared a roadbed for the Canadas' first railroad, the Champlain and St. Lawrence, and the large industrial shops of the Great Western Railway at Hamilton, some thirty years later.   NATIONAL ARCHIVES OF CANADA/C40332

A brief look at the troubled transition from mercantile to modern management in the sphere of railroads in Upper Canada will help make clear the complexities involved in this process of change. Most local railroad directors had little experience in managing railroads. Many were merchants who viewed railroads as an adjunct to or extension of their main occupational concerns. Improved transportation was of obvious benefit to the merchant. Despite potential monetary returns, wholesale import-export merchants, like Peter Buchanan and Robert Harris from Hamilton, bitterly complained of the time railroads took from their main interests. "To a man of business," Buchanan affirmed, "railway matters are a great curse." Yet merchants did acquire managerial responsibility and attempted to exercise much managerial control in the early years of Canadian railroad development. Drawing on skills acquired from the running of their own businesses, merchant directors were adept at cultivating local financial contacts. These links, bolstered by the government's guarantee, opened significant banking capital for short-term use by railways. Most merchant directors were foreign-born and generally involved

STRATFORD-PERTH ARCHIVES

in import-export functions rather than simply "local traffic." International contacts attracted British and in some cases American capital for local railroad development.

Having raised money, the merchant was reluctant to relinquish control over it. Generally, merchant directors received the proxies of the foreign investors and were trusted by these investors to handle local problems and administration with, in the beginning, only general guidelines provided. They had first to supervise the activities of American and British contractors and engineers. The former had nominal power and ultimate managerial responsibility; the latter possessed real power and no commensurate responsibility. "The Directors are Ninnies...," the exasperated chief engineer of the Bytown and Prescott Railway declared, "and I plainly foresee that I will have to teach them everything." For many Upper Canadian railways, such education was all but ruinous. American contractors, for example, wasted little time in taking advantage of the inexperienced Northern and Great Western railway merchant directors. The letting of construction contracts is a case in point. In Great Britain, contracts contained final estimates of a road's cost. In the United States contracts contained only the costs of materials: the amount of material to be used was determined as work progressed. In the Northern and Great Western's cases, the contracts not only contained no final costs but also left unstated the quantities and the unit price of the required materials. Taking full advantage of this open-ended agreement, the contractors in both cases secured the appointment of friendly American engineers whose job it was to estimate on a monthly basis the value of the completed work. On the Northern and the Great Western, this led to poorly constructed roads at costs far in excess of normal contracts.

And so the pattern went. Whether the contracting company and the engineers were, as in the case of the Grand Trunk, British in origin, or, as in the case of most other railways in Upper Canada, American, construction tended to be low in quality, cost overruns immense, and ultimate accountability on the part of those who did the construction evasive. The prevalence of this predatory behaviour deserves explanation. In the first place, the main personnel and the networks on which the contractors and engineers relied were not local to Upper Canada. The prime objective of many of the chief British and American contractors was simply to construct the road and leave the country. Given this attitude and given the ignorance of Upper Canadian railroad directors, the behaviour of the contractors probably differed in degree if not in kind from their activities in their native lands. This is probably true if only because they could not have negotiated the same type of contract in England or the United States.

Why then were Upper Canadians so woefully unable to control the imported contractor-engineers? Put simply, the problems of managing large-scale business enterprises had rarely been confronted in the Upper Canadian economy. Significant canal construction had taken place, but before the 1840s this had been largely completed by British and American engineers, few of whom stayed in the colony. When the Canadian government took control of the Welland Canal in 1841, it let out numerous small contracts. Thus few large contractors emerged within the country. In the United States, the military provided a source of managerial personnel; in Upper Canada, professional military personnel were themselves generally imported from Great Britain. Finally, many Upper Canadians participated in this predatory behaviour. Politicians of the status of Allan Napier MacNab, John A. Macdonald, Alexander Tilloch Galt, and Luther Holton all profited in varying degrees from inside information during construction of the Great Western and/or Grand Trunk railways.

The inability of colonial businesspeople to oversee railroad construction and operation, most of which was being financed by foreign capital, elicited quick response from those foreign investors. British shareholders set up their own boards of directors which, by the early 1860s, had increasingly firm control over most major Upper Canadian railroads. These British directors also sent over to the colony relatively well-trained professional managers (answerable to them) for the conduct of corporate affairs. In turn, these salaried managers usually hired subordinate administrative personnel from British railroads on which they themselves had previously worked. On the eve of political nationhood, the managerial structure of Canada's most modern corporate enterprise remained in the embrace of mother England.

At the end of the pre-Confederation era, the family firm still dominated local business organizations. While railroads, large internationally based trading companies and, perhaps, several large manufacturers in the steel and iron sector were taking on the characteristics of modern, vertically integrated corporations, these changes found few imitators in the wider business community. Indeed, one large, Toronto-based furniture manufacturer failed in an attempt to set up a branch plant 72 km away to supply his firm with materials and in that sense to integrate production and distribution. He could not implement a managerial structure that would provide him with reliable information and ensure adequate supervision of his extended operations. Throughout the attempt, he relied on family for personnel appointments. Accustomed to the more closely focused world of an earlier phase of manufacturing, he proved unable to adjust to an emerging world of integrated diversification and centrally controlled but physically dispersed branch-plant operations. In terms of business organization, the pre-Confederation era marked a period of troubled transition from mercantile to modern.[7]

This discussion of organizational change in pre-Confederation business leads to a final speculation. It may be that the tri-patterned evolution outlined here—the persistence of family mercantile and manufacturing firms; vertical integration as exhibited by large multinational trading companies; and the managerial and production structures of railroad corporations went far to condition the emergence of later forms of Canadian enterprise. Some of the largest merchant firms like Eaton's and Simpsons, for example, were, and in the case of Eaton's continue to be, prime examples of family-run enterprises. In fact, the extent of family control of Canada's largest corporations is oft remarked upon in the twentieth century. Yet Canada has also been, at various times, quite active as the headquarters of multinational undertakings. Many of these enterprises have emerged from the transportation sector, and indeed even in the pre-Confederation era, some railroads owned branch railroads in the United States. In two other sectors, echoes from the past can also be clearly heard in the present: the first concerns matters of credit and finance; the second relates to business-state interactions. It is to these matters that we now turn.

Credit in the Colonies

While colonial banks did not exist in British North America before 1817, part-time bankers did. Merchants engaged in what outwardly resembled a barter economy. In reality, all goods traded had precise monetary values.

---

[7] On these issues see A. W. Currie, "The First Dominion Companies Act," *CJEPS*, 28, 3 (1962); A. M. Carlos and S. Nicholas, "'Giants of an Earlier Capitalism': The Chartered Trading Companies as Modern Multinationals," *Business History Review*, 62 (1988), 398–419; A. D. Chandler, Jr., *The Visible Hand: The Managerial Revolution in American Business* (Cambridge, 1977); P. Baskerville, "Professional vs. Proprietor: Power Distribution in the Railroad World of Upper Canada/Ontario, 1850–81," *Historical Papers* (1979); and Ian Radforth, "Confronting Distance: Managing Jacques and Hays' New Lowell Operations, 1853–73," in P. Baskerville, ed., *Canadian Papers in Business History* (Victoria, 1989), 75–100.

Quality coinage or specie did not circulate long in British North America. Such specie was often worth more elsewhere, and there was never enough to supplant barter-based exchange at the best of times. Not surprisingly, pressure arose for institutions that could issue money—bank notes—and thus help simplify commercial transactions.

In addition to goods, merchants received and issued as cash promises to pay at a future date. Related to these promissory notes was the bill of exchange, a promise to pay foreign suppliers, generally British, in their own currency. As the economy grew, the buying and selling of promissory notes and bills of exchange required detailed attention. Few could know the personal worth of those whose signatures were on the notes or bills. A centralized agency became increasingly necessary. A medium of exchange in which the mercantile community could have confidence, a currency backed by real gold or silver and not just the presumed worth of a not well-known individual, was needed.

It has been argued that the control of credit and the barter system gave merchants great power over their local communities. For this power to be exercised, however, certain conditions had to be in place: the merchant had to enjoy a monopoly situation; the local community had to be isolated; local residents had to be poor and tied to the production of one staple; that is, there had to be little possibility of local economic diversification. These conditions held true in certain areas of the Atlantic region in the pre-Confederation era. Such conditions were less prevalent in the Canadas. Even in Lower Canada, merchant competition in rural areas, both from resident and itinerant traders, was stiff. Such was also the case throughout much of Upper Canada. In 1846, at least 160 Upper Canadian communities had two or more local stores. Competition made it difficult for merchants to extort high prices. Local farmers proved quite willing to travel to where the best prices were offered. Moreover, while merchants were often the wealthiest individuals in local communities, this was not always the case. Farming communities were not economically homogeneous, and in certain cases farmers, not merchants, headed the local economic elite and were able to set, not simply accept, prices for local produce. Merchants also, of course, depended on continued production by local farmers in order for their own credit needs—money advanced by merchants in Toronto, Montreal and England—to be met. Local merchants, like local farmers, were tied to an international line of credit. For the system to work, stability and continuity of supply and demand were the *sine qua non*.

It is this last point that brings us back to banks. All involved in the colonial economy wished to buy cheap and sell dear. Few were consistently able to do so. Most required credit, often continual credit in order to remain productive. Merchants pushed for banks as one means for providing more stability to the financial side of commercial affairs.

Just as merchants desired to operate in a monopoly situation, so too did the colonies' first banks. Six chartered banks were in operation by 1825: the Bank of New Brunswick, the Bank of Upper Canada, The Halifax Banking Company, the Quebec Bank, the Bank of Canada, and the Bank of Montreal. The political connections and commercial prominence of the bank directors protected initial monopoly positions. Five of the eight Halifax Banking Company incorporators sat on Nova Scotia's legislative council. Nine of the first 15 Bank of Upper Canada directors held high political appointments. In the late 1820s, seven or eight "great" merchants and office holders owned over 50 percent of the Bank of New Brunswick's shares. By the 1830s, however, competition had emerged in New Brunswick and in Nova Scotia. And during that decade Upper and Lower Canada each chartered five new banks.

Yet it is in the manner of operation as much as in the number operating that British North America's early banks left themselves open to charges of exclusive and monopolistic practice. Many historians have in fact suggested that pre-Confederation banking behaviour delayed and weakened the development of Canada's industrial sector. Echoing reformers like William Lyon Mackenzie and Joseph Howe, they point to the fact that banks loaned money primarily to merchants engaged in the exchange of actual goods; that banks could not legally lend on the direct security of factories, machines, or land; that they favoured short-term rather than long-term loans; that a small, politically well-connected merchant elite ran them; and that banks tied up too much of their capital in conservative loans to local governments. The rules of the game made diversified development, the transition from a mercantile to an industrial economy, difficult indeed.

This interpretation has much force. While the Canadian banking system was the most advanced and independent in all of Britain's colonies in this period, it nonetheless remained true that it was a *colonial* banking structure. Banks did have particular roles to play within the colonial-imperial relationship. Primary among those tasks was underwriting the export of natural products to England and the import of finished products from the mother country. The constant resistance by the colonial office to permitting colonial banks to invest in fixed capital enterprises reflected the primary economic goal of that empire. Yet certain qualifications are necessary. Mercantile principles also underlay the banking structures of England and the United States. Both those nations experienced significant industrialization. In fact, industrialists did not always require long-term loans. Short-term advances for working capital often sufficed and these advances could be acquired by having one or more reputable community businesspeople endorse their promise to pay the bank—to act as personal security for the loans advanced. In this way, for example, the Bank of Upper Canada provided money for canal construction in the 1830s: the personal wealth of the canal company directors, not the physical assets of the canal itself, represented the security for such advances.

If banks had, in fact, done what they were supposed to do, the standard critiques would still have force. A closer look at actual banking practice suggests that many banks extended their operations well beyond the rules of the game. Prominent merchants did receive priority. But in attending to merchants' needs, banks, such as the Bank of Upper Canada, regularly extended initial 90-day loans to periods up to 15 months, thus rendering suspect the notion of short-term. Nor did the Bank of Upper Canada tie up excessive capital in government loans. Rather, that bank (and others)

In the pre-Confederation era, banks printed their own money. This bill captures both the traditional and the emerging economy of the 1850s.

NATIONAL CURRENCY COLLECTION, BANK OF CANADA. PHOTOGRAPHER JAMES ZAGON. BY PERMISSION.

willingly acted as agents for the sale of government debentures. In so doing, the banks operated as typical merchants: instead of acting as intermediaries on the sale of goods, they acted as agents for the sale of financial securities. This practice, according to the Bank of Upper Canada's general manager, brought "much foreign capital into the country."

Because banks tended to lend to well-connected and well-known commercial men, that is, to lend on reputation, they often found themselves, somewhat inadvertently, financing something other than strictly mercantile activity. Lending to friends and relations of bank directors—surely a policy consistent with traditional mercantile behaviour—did lead some banks to underwrite economic diversification. This trend is especially clear in the transportation sector. As more and more merchants became involved in building and operating steamships and railroads, so too did the banks with which those merchants had personal connections become involved in the financing of those operations. Within this closed system, economic change, supported but not initiated by bank capital, could and did take place.

The financing of railroads, the largest capital projects undertaken in the pre-Confederation era and the projects that symbolized the transition from a mercantile to an industrial economy, provides a good case study of the role played by colonial banks and imperial financiers in Canadian colonial economic development. In particular, such a study suggests that the recipients of loans granted by financial intermediaries rather than the intermediaries themselves may have reaped the greatest rewards.

There were several reasons why banks became increasingly involved in financing railroad affairs. As the goals of empire changed in the 1840s from direct to indirect economic control, the role of colonial banks also shifted. London investor-bankers looked for local institutions capable of supporting their colonial investment programs. The local government assumed an important role in this context. So, too, did that government's bank, the Bank of Upper Canada. Imperial investors wanted that bank to tide over or prop up large capital-intensive projects during periods of drought in the London financial market. London investment houses knew that most capital for colonial railroad development would come from England. What they had not counted on or were unable to control was the extent of capital desired and the swiftness with which huge amounts became necessary. Those decisions were made by local political leaders and local capitalists, often indistinguishable from each other, who consistently ignored advice from London bankers to proceed slowly and cautiously. These local politicians and capitalists who sat in the Canadian cabinet, on the various railroad directorates, most notably that of the colony's largest railroad, the Grand Trunk, and on the boards of local banks, like the Bank of Upper Canada, desired railroads immediately in order to tap the grain trade of Upper Canada and the American Midwest. The construction of the St. Lawrence Canal in the 1840s had failed in that purpose. For a number of reasons, primarily relating to the degree of American competition, the Grand Trunk also failed in this respect.

A severe economic and financial downturn in 1857 pushed an overextended Bank of Upper Canada to the wall. It could no longer assist imperial investors and the local state. London investment bankers, Thomas Baring and George Carr Glyn, had staked the reputation of their firms to the success of the Canadian ventures. They had also committed a substantial amount of their personal fortunes to the Grand Trunk's future (in Baring's case this personal investment reached £600 000). They could not pull out and continue to enjoy their reputations as first-class financial houses in the city of London. As a result, both the London bankers and the Bank of Upper Canada, which closed its doors in 1866, took a drastic loss on Canadian railroads. For colonial capitalists, now heading a bankrupt colonial state, a larger political union offered some hope of financial (to say nothing of political) stability. The financial entanglement precipitated by colonial capitalists provided Canada yet another reason to confederate. Many wreckages were strewn along the road to political nationhood and economic modernity.

A slightly broader perspective is useful. Thirty-six chartered banks commenced operation between 1820 and 1860 in the four colonies that formed Canada in 1867. By 1870, 21 had failed or, because of weakness, been taken over by other banks. This high rate of instability is generally explained by referring to the cyclical and seasonal swings associated with a trading economy. Yet the timing of failure suggests a different interpretation. Coinciding with a period of dramatic economic transformation, nine of the thirteen Upper Canadian failures occurred after 1850. Upper Canada, ahead of other British North American colonies, was industrializing in these years. Lower Canada/Quebec, for example, only equalled Upper Canada/Ontario's rate of industrial growth during the 1870s. Significantly, Quebec suffered more bank failures in the 1870s than in any other decade before 1900. Also, for the first time, failures exceeded new starts. Similarly, three of the four New Brunswick failures took place in the 1860s, a time of economic change in the shipping industry. Banks would seem not to have failed because of instability in the pre-industrial economy. Financial institutions suffered at the point of economic transition. As we have noted, for merchants and some manufacturers, adjusting to new, emerging economic realities was difficult. Many bankers failed to change traditional habits quickly enough to master the needs of a new economic regime.

We would be wrong to leave our discussion at this point. Many traditional institutions did fail during this period of economic transition. People, however, created and invested in those businesses. Most who invested in banks had little or no access to privileged information. Upper Canadian bank presidents regularly denied the public and, on occasion, even the government access to their internal affairs. When the Bank of Upper Canada began its slide into oblivion, its published statements covered up the reality of its troubled financial state. The government's system of bank inspections did not prove any more helpful to the unsuspecting shareholders and depositors.

Some knew the real state of affairs. The Bank of Upper Canada's collapse did not surprise John Rose, soon to be minister of finance in the new Dominion. He did not think that anything "disastrous. . .beyond loss to the shareholders" would occur. And what of the shareholders? "Is there any probability of the poor shareholders getting anything. . .?" Lydia Payne wrote the bank's trustees in September 1866,

The failure is of serious consequence to me, as I depended on my stock invested in it, for support in my old Age—. . .I wrote to Mr. Cassels [the bank's manager] before the Bank suspended payment to dispose of my shares, but I was not favored with an answer—. . .I hope you will kindly pardon the questions I have asked—Pray do what you think is best for me.

Lydia owned 215 shares. The trustees did nothing for her. Neither did the government, headed by Sir John A. Macdonald, who was himself personally indebted to the bank for some $17 000—a debt the trustees, headed by Clarke Gamble, the bank's long-time lawyer, wiped out unpaid in the early 1870s.[8]

---

[8] P. Baskerville, *The Bank of Upper Canada*; D. McCalla, "Rural Credit and Rural Development in Upper Canada, 1790–1850," in Roger Hall et al., eds., *Patterns of the Past: Interpreting Ontario's History* (Toronto, 1988); Allan Greer, *Peasant, Lord and Merchant* (Toronto, 1985), Chapter 6; and D. C. M. Platt and J. Adelman, "London Merchant Bankers in the First Phase of Heavy Borrowing: the Grand Trunk Railway of Canada," *Journal of Imperial and Commonwealth History*, 18, 2 (1990), 208–27.

Business and the State

THE IMPERIAL CONTEXT

Country gentlemen...were undoubtedly the best and most respectable objects of the confidence of the people...they had the greatest stake in the country after all and were the most deeply interested in its welfare.

The British Parliament applauded these comments made by a British Lord in the 1770s. Property owners dominated the British Parliament; cities were barely represented. It was the era of "rotten" and "pocket" boroughs where one large landowner could control his client-constituency. Only gradually did merchants and industrialists acquire noticeable political power in England. By 1825, however, another British Lord could complain:

Trade, manufacturers, and money, are everything. The landed proprietors are mere ciphers, they are of no consequence, either with Ministers or with Opposition.

While this was an exaggeration, it did point to real change: by 1830 lawyers, merchants, traders and bankers represented about one-quarter of all members of the House of Commons. Moreover, middle-class entrepreneurs were quite active in the affairs of the local state. Lords and gentry adapted to these political changes and they, too, became active at local administrative levels. Gentlemanly capitalists and middle-class men on the make merged in municipal forums as well as in the House of Commons. Legislation gradually reflected middle-class bourgeois dictates: free trade, a tax policy that did not favour landed interests, maintenance of public order, and the cultivation of a free labour market were the most prominent. Finally the Victorian state, itself, became more professional and bureaucratic as "the methods of the counting house and factory [were applied] to matters of law and government."

Similar changes took place in British North America during the pre-Confederation era. In part reflecting local economic and social realities and in part influenced by British and American examples, colonial states became more active and businesspeople became more dominant in political affairs. By 1867, politics embodied bourgeois values.

Business and the Colonial State: 1770–1850

The 200 or so merchants who flocked to Quebec after 1763 are often depicted as being at loggerheads with British governors, the British army, French seigneurs, and Roman Catholic prelates. Soon known as "factious traders," they pressed for two major changes: the granting of a Parliament and the institution of British civil law. It may be, however, that historians have overemphasized the importance of these divisions. British merchants were prepared to go only so far in arguing for change. Before and after the Quebec Act, they petitioned for English civil law, trial by jury, and habeas corpus. They tended to be more circumspect regarding political change. In common with the other elites, they did not want habitants to achieve political power. As well, they understood that commercial men in London, their potential supporters, opposed an assembly for the same reason. Moreover, colonial merchants were reluctant to antagonize a governor upon whom they depended for favours in the fur trade, the army provisioning trade and, in the late 1770s and early 1780s, mercantile credit. Patronage of this sort bound them to established authority.

Some, like the crusty Scot, George Allsopp, would stand up to governors and be dismissed from the legislative council for his temerity. Most curried favour and patronage where and when they could. The result was that as a group Quebec merchants did little to influence political and judicial change in the late eighteenth century. The Constitutional Act of 1791 did grant an elected assembly, but by splitting the colony into two, Upper and Lower Canada, it left the Montreal and Quebec merchants isolated with little alternative than to move closer to the governor and seigneurial factions. The Constitution of 1791 assured the existence of the Chateau Clique. Francophone and some anglophone merchants, however, did make their presence felt in the elected assembly. Between 1791 and 1838 they never held less than one-third of the seats. As has been previously mentioned, the commercial policies of francophone and anglophone merchants did differ on several matters, but perhaps the more important point to note is that by 1840, Lower Canadian businesspeople were accustomed to involvement in all levels of the political process. This perspective helps explain the rise to power of lawyer-businessman-politicians like George Etienne Cartier and Hector Langevin in the Union era. These Fathers of Confederation did not emerge from a social and economic vacuum. They built on a strong tradition of direct participation by businesspeople in politics. In this sense their success represented the honing of already well-developed skills.

Merchants faced less resistance in the area that became Upper Canada. In 1788, the governor divided the old Mississauga land into four districts, each district receiving Courts of Quarter Sessions and Common Pleas and a local land board, all to be administered under the rules of English law. Merchants and retired military personnel contended for control of the legal/administrative system. It soon became evident to some local observers that Loyalist officers were barely "sustain[ing] an appearance of consequence and the shadow of former power." Merchants played the leading role in adopting to local economic realities. Rarely learned in the complexities of British common law procedure, the merchants opted instead for informality, simplicity, and economy. These attitudes reflected mercantile ideas in New York and, to an extent, in England, too. In addition to administering the courts, the merchants were the courts' heaviest users. They tended to be the initiators of suits, at the other end of which were often retired Loyalist officers struggling to maintain payments. Merchants also tended to centralize court activities at Niagara, Kingston, and Detroit, thus making it impossible for rural settlers to enjoy equal ease of access. The general result was the strengthening and solidifying of merchant endeavours throughout the old Mississauga territory.

After 1791 Governor Simcoe challenged mercantile power in Upper Canada. He found support from the agrarian-dominated assembly. As a first step, he restructured and centralized the legal system under the Court of the King's Bench at York. He also introduced a centrally controlled system of local government. To Courts of Quarter Sessions he appointed justices of the peace whose duties included some judicial responsibilities as well as extensive administrative and patronage functions. At this point, Simcoe came squarely up against the reality of merchant power. There were just too few people of sufficient worth, talent, and energy to fill the regional positions available. Merchants were willing: in the absence of others they had to be enlisted. Thus the structure Simcoe had hoped would provide the foundation for consolidating a patronage/client network exclusive of and competing with merchants had, ironically, to recognize commercial power as prime criteria for place and prestige in early Upper Canada. At the outset, businesspeople achieved significant administrative/political power at the level of the local state.

In fact, in Upper Canada and probably in the Maritimes, too, the local state provided an important forum where, as in England, "a self-confident middle class built its characteristic institutions and culture." In Upper Canada, the old system under the justices of the peace could not cope with increasing crime, riots, disease, fire, pollution, demand for roads, and effective market regulation. As a result, eight Upper Canadian communities incorporated in the 1830s and five more followed before 1847. A rising middle class lobbied for incorporation and moved quickly to control the new system. Lawyers and merchants held about two-thirds of the seats on the elected common councils and boards of police in the 1830s. Between 1840 and 1860, 80 percent of elected municipal officials came from the business sector. A prohibitively high property qualification precluded the majority of town residents from standing for election. A similar high property qualification kept the right to vote from many town dwellers. The municipal state became a closed preserve for the bourgeois class.

Not surprisingly local laws reflected the goals of that class. Laws concerning market regulation, for example, banned itinerant salespeople and centralized mercantile transactions, thus consolidating the municipality's hold on the regional economy. Municipal councils in Upper Canada and in Saint John, New Brunswick, raised money for infrastructural development. Municipalities also moved to enforce social and moral control: chivaris, traditional expressions of popular justice that took place when citizens felt offended by the actions of a fellow resident, were banned; the transient poor were closely controlled; moral and civil order offences dominated the calendars of local courts. The local state was, in many ways, the crucible within which bourgeois values were tested and then extended to a wider political and social arena.

The bourgeois middle class also moved to increased prominence at the provincial political level in this period. While Upper Canada's population remained overwhelming agrarian, the socio-economic composition of the elected house of assembly changed fairly dramatically in the 1830s. Before 1820, 64 percent of the members of the house of assembly (MHAs) had been farmers at some stage in their career. Only 34 percent of MHAs elected between 1830 and 1841 had farmed, and, of those, over one-half engaged in some other business pursuit. Those who only engaged in some business pursuit outnumbered those who only farmed by a two to one margin in the 1830s. Clearly, MHAs reflected an emerging urban-oriented, business-minded, capitalistic society. They also, in Upper Canada, at least, were concentrated in the emerging Conservative Party: in the 1830s, 51 percent of the elected Conservatives and only 26 percent of the elected Reformers were businesspeople or lawyers.

The business orientation of the emerging Conservative Party was, to a degree, reflected in the activities of the patrician-dominated legislative and executive councils, the second component of the colonial state. Promoters like William Hamilton Merritt who wished to develop large capital-intensive projects such as the Welland Canal focused their efforts on currying favour from that political elite, the so-called Family Compact. Cut from the gentlemanly capitalist mould, these lawyers, merchants, and assorted landholders, typified by John Beverly Robinson, felt it their duty to develop the agrarian potential of their adopted home. Conservative to the core in a social and political context, they were willing to extend state powers and commit state money for infrastructural development. By so doing, they provided the foundation for similar state activity in the era of railroads.

Business and the Colonial State: The Canadas, 1850–64

Many historians caution against a tendency to assume an exact identity of interests between the state and the general business sector. Clearly, at the level of personnel there was a profound overlap. Yet divisions of interest existed within the business community: not all sectors of that community could capture the state and employ it for their own interests. Moreover, politicians had to satisfy a clientele of which the business community was only one, albeit an increasingly dominant, part. It may indeed be that the Canadian state came over time to exercise the role of broker, balancing the competing interests of labour, business, and general populist concerns within the contours of a general market economy. The fact is, however, that in the pre-Confederation era the business sector had few real rivals to contest its political influence. Even more importantly, neither the business class nor the colonial state was in a position to maintain and balance established relationships. Rather, they were grappling with change of a dramatic sort.

Only by recognizing that both government and business were undergoing fundamental structural change can one appreciate the nature of state-business interaction in the Canadas after 1850. Both the state and large businesses like railroads were beginning to professionalize and systematize their operations, to "apply the methods of the counting house and factory" to their respective spheres. Managerial change and the implementation of a more bureaucratic procedure proceeded in a symbiotic, inter-connected, and parallel manner in the public and private spheres. Thus, in 1854, the government appointed an auditor general to oversee and reform the state's extremely decentralized financial system. Such reform was, of course, delicate since past and current speculation by politicians had to be protected. Nevertheless, while halting and imperfect, the process did lead to the passage of a bill in 1864 that marked a substantial advance over the informal, decentralized, and paternalistic system within which public works and public financing had operated in the early 1850s.

Politicians who interacted with foreign lenders realized that unless they modernized their local procedures, capital would be difficult to acquire. Yet it made little sense for government to transform its managerial system when the colony's largest business organizations continued to operate in an inefficient manner. This point was driven home in the mid-1850s by a series of railroad accidents and by the virtual bankruptcy of the colony's three largest railroads. The state responded by upgrading existing and passing new legislation designed to restrict worker autonomy, strengthen the punitive power of managers, and enhance punishments available to the judiciary. Acting to shield the Canadian public from undue careless-ness, to preserve social stability in the polity over which it ruled, to safeguard its own large capital investments, to encourage foreign invest-ment, and to protect its own political future, the Canadian government in the 1850s and 1860s pressured railroad corporations to implement reform. It created a small bureaucratic structure staffed by experts to oversee and inspect existing managerial structures. This process assisted efforts under-taken by British investors to modernize colonial railroad operations. In the course of these actions, the state helped move the Canadas from a predominantly commercial economic, social, and political environment to an increasingly industrial capitalist milieu. And, in the course of these actions, the state favoured the needs of the rising bourgeois class and subordinated and restricted the freedoms of the growing class of wage labourers.[9] The birth of the bourgeois state predated and provided the context for Confederation.

---

[9] For insights into the nature of state-business relations in the various colonies see: A. Greer and I. Radforth, eds., *Colonial Leviathan: State Formation in Mid-Nineteenth Century Canada* (Toronto, 1991); David Milobar, "Conservative Ideology, Metropolitan Government, and the Reform of Quebec, 1782–1791," *The International History Review*, 12, 1 (1990), 45–64; W. Wylie, "Instruments of Commerce and Authority: The Civil Courts in Upper Canada, 1789–1812," in D. Flaherty, ed., *Essays in the History of Canadian Law*, 2 (Toronto 1983); J. K. Johnson, *Becoming Prominent: Regional Leadership in Upper Canada, 1791–1841* (Kingston/Montreal, 1989); R. Langhout, "Developing Nova Scotia: Railway and Public Accounts, 1848–67, *Acadiensis*, 14 (1985), and B. Young and J. Dickinson, *A Short History of Quebec* (Toronto, 1988).

CHAPTER VIII

BRITISH NORTH AMERICA, 1841–1864

Introduction

Historians often emphasize change and development and seek to "uncover" the seeds for the present in the past. This temptation is especially strong when discussing the quarter century before the formal creation of the Canadian nation in 1867. Yet not all people who lived in that era sought change. And for many who did, their ideas and hopes never took hold. By focusing solely on the theme of modernization, the aspirations of many British North American are lost to view for ever. Certainly significant change did take place in this period. In many ways, such change marked the making of a modern Canada. Yet protest accompanied change. Different visions of the future contended for supremacy.

Economic imbalances along regional lines did come clearly to the fore in this period. Yet despite economic restructuring, especially in central Canada, most colonists east of Red River and west of Newfoundland continued to farm for a living. Few got very rich and many, especially in the Maritimes, had to work at several occupations in order to support a family. The persistence of farming as the basis for economic activity is often taken to mean that little "progress" in the economic sphere took place. Such a perspective is condescending toward rural life and fails to appreciate the degree to which development could and, again especially in central Canada, did occur in the farming sector. It is wrong to see

BRITISH NORTH AMERICAN RAILWAYS ON THE EVE OF CONFEDERATION

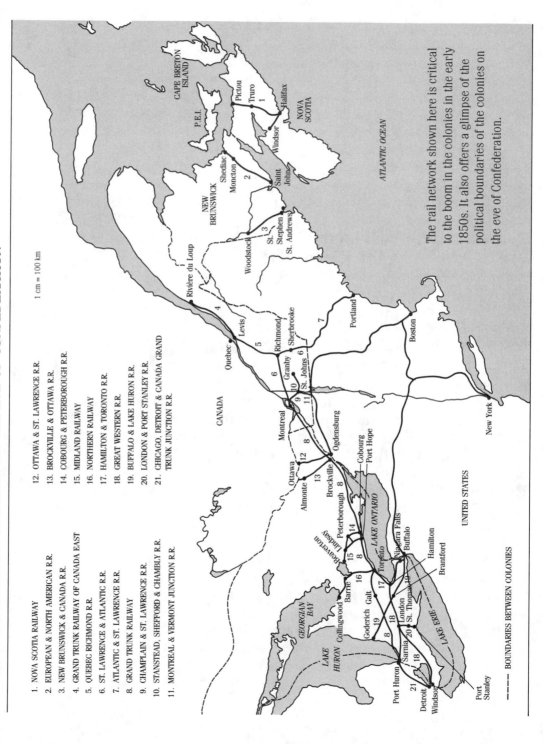

1 cm = 100 km

1. NOVA SCOTIA RAILWAY
2. EUROPEAN & NORTH AMERICAN R.R.
3. NEW BRUNSWICK & CANADA R.R.
4. GRAND TRUNK RAILWAY OF CANADA EAST
5. QUEBEC RICHMOND R.R.
6. ST. LAWRENCE & ATLANTIC R.R.
7. ATLANTIC & ST. LAWRENCE R.R.
8. GRAND TRUNK RAILWAY
9. CHAMPLAIN & ST. LAWRENCE R.R.
10. STANSTEAD, SHEFFORD & CHAMBLY R.R.
11. MONTREAL & VERMONT JUNCTION R.R.

12. OTTAWA & ST. LAWRENCE R.R.
13. BROCKVILLE & OTTAWA R.R.
14. COBOURG & PETERBOROUGH R.R.
15. MIDLAND RAILWAY
16. NORTHERN RAILWAY
17. HAMILTON & TORONTO R.R.
18. GREAT WESTERN R.R.
19. BUFFALO & LAKE HURON R.R.
20. LONDON & PORT STANLEY R.R.
21. CHICAGO, DETROIT & CANADA GRAND
    TRUNK JUNCTION R.R.

------ BOUNDARIES BETWEEN COLONIES

The rail network shown here is critical to the boom in the colonies in the early 1850s. It also offers a glimpse of the political boundaries of the colonies on the eve of Confederation.

industrialization and farming as polar opposites: the one indicating progress; the other stasis. In fact the two went hand in hand. Industrial activity emerged first in areas where farming was most profitable.

The achievement of responsible government did facilitate the emergence to political and social power of a growing middle class composed of commercially minded and some industrially oriented businesspeople. From that new elite, the Fathers of Confederation did step to the fore. Throughout the period, from Newfoundland to the West Coast, middle-class people on the make did strive to create institutions that would instill uniformity, obedience, and dependable work habits in those whom they aspired to rule and lead. Yet such activity rarely completely achieved the desired end. Opposed by often informal but recurring working-class or plebeian resistance, fractured by persistent ethnic and religious strife, resisted by prairie and West Coast natives and Métis, and confronted by American goldminers west of the Rockies, bourgeois leaders lived their lives on contested terrain.

Life on the Eve of Economic Transition: Economy and Society in Mid-Nineteenth-Century Canada

DISMANTLING THE MERCANTILE SYSTEM

Protective duties on lumber and wheat and restrictions on foreign-owned vessels trading in Britain and British colonial ports were swept away in the 1840s. A severe Irish famine in the mid-1840s provided the spur for the repeal of the Corn Laws in 1846. Colonial wheat no longer enjoyed a preference over foreign wheat in the British market. The immediate need for cheap food reinforced the more general argument current in Britain for free trade. The free trade agreement had two assumptions: one, cheaper trade meant less cost for life's necessities, and therefore capitalists could lower the wages required to keep workers at a subsistence level; and, two, England was economically superior to other nations and could nicely prosper in a free-trade system. Accordingly, timber duties were lowered throughout the 1840s, and in 1849 the Navigation Acts, which had provided protection for British boats, were repealed.

In Lower Canada, these repeals led to a brief Annexation Movement led by frustrated Montreal merchants who feared their lucrative transshipment roles would be undercut. Those who suffered, like the Bank of Montreal, some Montreal merchants, and several Upper Canadian millers and shippers, based too much of their financial and economic activities on attracting the wheat of the American Midwest down the St. Lawrence to British markets. The Corn Laws had facilitated this by allowing all American wheat milled in the Canadas to be treated as Canadian wheat.

The Annexation Movement found little echo in Upper Canada. While Canadian wheat exports to Great Britain via the St. Lawrence dropped by some 40 percent between 1847 and 1848, total wheat exports from Canada to Britain actually rose between 1846 and 1849. The explanation for this is simple. Instead of shipping their products via the more costly and time-consuming St. Lawrence–Britain route, Upper Canadian farmers and merchants increasingly shipped by the Erie Canal–New York–Britain route. They were encouraged in this by American legislation called the Drawback Acts of 1845–46, which allowed transshipment of produce in bond through the United States free of all duties. In addition, local American prices were, throughout the 1840s and 1850s, high enough to allow Upper Canadians to sell in that market despite American tariff charges.

Montreal merchants hoped that the completion of the St. Lawrence canal system in 1849 would re-attract American produce. Shipments to Britain via the New York route, however, continued to be cheaper. In one respect, the completion of the St. Lawrence canal did benefit the Upper Canadian wheat and flour trade and Montreal's merchants. Since Lower Canadian wheat growers did not provide sufficient food for their local market, Upper Canada had a nearby market to supply. As well, demand for wheat and flour in the Maritimes was increasingly filled by Upper Canada following an intercolonial trade agreement in 1849. In fact, by 1851 British North American colonies purchased about 50 percent of all of Upper Canada's wheat exports. By the end of the 1840s, Upper Canada had, in many ways, become British North America's breadbasket. Secure in both their economic linkage to the United States and to British North America, Upper Canadians could piously promote, through the newly founded British North American League, an alternative to annexation, continuance of ties to the mother country.

In Upper Canada, after 1850, land under cultivation rather than land under settlement became the main index of agricultural growth. In this sense, the years immediately following mid-century marked the transition to an era of intensive as opposed to extensive rural development. In this changing context, wheat exports remained an important part of Upper Canada's economy, doubling in volume and tripling in value between 1850 and 1856. A Reciprocity Treaty with the United States in 1854, which allowed free trade in minerals, fish, forest products, and agriculture, and the Crimean War in Europe in 1855–56 created major markets for this crop. Yet, despite these impressive statistics, king wheat did not represent the real action in Upper Canada's rural areas following 1850. Even in 1851, over 40 percent of the provinces' cultivated land produced something other than wheat. Diversification intensified throughout the next two decades, with the growth of dairy, livestock, and mixed farming. While total area devoted to wheat declined only slightly between 1851 and 1871, area used by other crops increased dramatically. By 1871 wheat acreage represented less than a quarter of all cropland. This emphasis on mixed farming did not represent a sharp break from the past. Even before 1850, farmers produced and sold products other than wheat. Mixed farming did not commence after 1850; rather, in response to changing market forces, it intensified.

Similar, if less dramatic developments occurred in rural Lower Canada. Diversification rather than reliance on one crop marked most agricultural areas. Due mainly to poor soils and a shorter growing season, overall output, however, did not match that of Upper Canada. Following the Reciprocity Treaty, Lower Canada exported butter, cheese, wool, cattle, horses, and sawn lumber to American markets.

The dismantling of Britain's protective system, then, did not severely undermine the economies of Upper and Lower Canada. The Annexation Crisis was short lived. Internal trade within and between Upper and Lower Canada continued buoyant. The Reciprocity Treaty with the United States in 1854 did increase an already growing north-south trade in natural products. But its cancellation by the United States in 1866 did not weaken the Canadas economically. Moreover, the economy of both regions encompassed more than the production and sale of natural products.

URBAN AND INDUSTRIAL GROWTH, 1841–71

Between 1841 and 1871, urban population increased at a remarkably similar rate in Lower and Upper Canada: from 12 percent to about 22 percent in each section. The distribution of urban population represented just as remarkable a contrast. In 1871 Upper Canada boasted 96 communities with over 1000 people, a fivefold growth. Lower Canada had less than

25 communities with over 1000 people, but this represented a threefold growth since 1831. Two cities, Montreal and Quebec, contained over three-quarters of Lower Canada's urban people in 1871, while the two largest cities in Upper Canada, Toronto and Hamilton, contained under one-quarter of that province's urban population.

Railroad construction reinforced this pattern of urban growth. Stimulated by a series of government measures promising financial guarantees, by the establishment of a Municipal Loan fund, and by a receptive British capital market, railroad construction boomed in the 1850s. Upper Canadian workers built 1400 miles (2250 km) of track, about two-thirds of all track laid in that decade. By 1853 Montreal was connected by three lines to Boston and New York. Upper Canadian railroads also emerged from the existing urban system, which by 1850 stretched along Lake Ontario's

This peaceful picture by W. H. Bartlett of the steamboat *Cobourg* outside Cobourg, Upper Canada, in the early 1840s belies the competitive nature of urban competition in that era. Despite having been built in Cobourg and named after that centre, the *Cobourg* was, in fact, owned by a syndicate of Toronto businesspeople. On its maiden run, the *Cobourg* did not even stop at the town of Cobourg!   NATIONAL ARCHIVES OF CANADA/C11865

north shore into the Grand River Valley and on to London in central southwestern Ontario. The Northern railroad running north from Toronto to Barrie and Collingwood (1855) strengthened Toronto's hold on its hinterland and facilitated increased exports of wood and flour across Lake Ontario.

The two major lines constructed in this period, the Great Western and the Grand Trunk, were intended mainly to link American routes on the eastern seaboard and New York State with lines running through Michigan and the Midwest to Chicago. While local feeder lines were built throughout the 1850s, their construction did little to alter the north-south trade orientation. Such construction did facilitate the growth of small urban communities in Upper Canada, whereas in Lower Canada fewer north-south feeder lines penetrated the regions north of the St. Lawrence, and fewer small urban sites developed. For most lake communities, the construction of a railroad into their hinterlands represented the last hope they had of narrowing the gap between themselves and Toronto and Hamilton. Thus Port Dover and Port Stanley along Lake Erie, and Brockville, Prescott, Port Hope, Cobourg and, of course, Toronto and Hamilton along Lake Ontario, sponsored, promoted and constructed railroads. By the end of the decade, however, Toronto, Hamilton, and Montreal had consolidated positions already enjoyed in 1850. In Upper Canada, the key factor distinguishing urban centres was less the role of exporter and more that of importer. In this context, Toronto benefited not simply from north-south trade but also, especially following the construction of the Grand Trunk, distribution of goods imported from Montreal. By 1870 the urban pattern of contemporary southern Ontario was in place.

Industrial development reflected the pattern of urban growth in both provinces. In 1850 small, crafts-based manufactories, often saw or grist mills, were the rule. Exceptions in Lower Canada included shipyards and large sawmills at Quebec City, iron mines and forges at Trois Rivières, and a series of large water-powered industries along the Lachine Canal in the Montreal region. In the following two decades, Montreal took advantage of water power, abundant cheap labour, and a strong local capital market and emerged as the dominant industrial centre in the Canadas, capable of competing effectively in the Upper Canadian as well as Lower Canadian marketplace. Outside of Montreal, Quebec City, Sherbrooke, and Hull, little significant manufacturing occurred in Lower Canada by 1871. Railroad and canal construction had led to consolidation of industrial production in a few major centres.

Industrial production was much more dispersed in Upper Canada, although here, too, the trend was toward centralization. The Reciprocity Treaty helped open up the American market for sawn lumber. A relatively buoyant agricultural economy in Upper Canada created a greater demand for manufactured items. Cash income per Upper Canadian farm averaged three to four times that of Lower Canadian farms. This spending power had an impact throughout the economy. Because Upper Canadian farmers could better afford to buy their own clothes, farm production of woollen textiles declined much more quickly in Ontario than in other British North American colonies. The agricultural sector began to mechanize more quickly in Upper Canada than elsewhere. By 1870 Ontario's farmers owned seven times as many reapers and mowers as their Quebec counterparts. Local purchasing power stimulated centralized factory production.

Railway construction also facilitated industrial growth and the beginnings of industrial concentration. Railways provided relatively cheap and efficient transportation, which permitted manufacturers to extend their markets. As a result, local artisans increasingly had to compete against larger and centralized producers. Railways also created a demand for manufactured items. Rails, locomotives, and all manner of hardware items began to be produced in Upper Canada to help meet this demand. By 1870 domestic production of machinery, furniture, agricultural implements, and boots and shoes exceeded 90 percent of local demand, while production of paper, woollens, and foundry products met 80 percent or better of local needs. Perhaps most significantly, railways themselves became effective producers of many of the above items. The largest of these railroads, the Grand Trunk and the Great Western, ranked not only among the largest industrial plants in Canada before 1870 but also led in terms of managerial and technological expertise. They were the first large, integrated corporations to operate in the Canadas.

While Montreal profited from strong Upper Canadian demand, so too did many Upper Canadian manufacturers. Reflecting Upper Canada's stronger and more widely dispersed agricultural sector, and despite the consolidating impact of railroad construction, rural areas accounted for 62 percent of industrial establishments and 42 percent of the industrial labour force in 1870. Yet the trend was to concentration. Larger industries congregated in Toronto and Hamilton: 70 percent of workers employed in establishments with over 50 employees worked in these two cities in 1870.

Industrialization did not follow a simple linear path from a small hand-driven artisan craftshop to a large power-driven factory. In 1870 all industrial sectors contained a mix of craftshops, power-driven factories, and manually operated manufactories. Woollen, cotton, and knitting mills and wood processing and paper mills had a high proportion of operations in large, power-driven, factorylike settings. Most other sectors, like cotton, chemicals, printing, furniture, and tobacco, contained a mix of large and small hand-driven manufactories, artisan craftshops, and some power-driven factories. The change from a pre-industrial to a modern industrial

Bothwell, Upper Canada, boasted one of the earliest oil wells in the Canadas. This picture is from the early 1870s, although the well pre-existed Confederation.

structure did not occur at one time or in the same fashion whether one examines different industrial sectors or simply looks within a single sector. The paths to the future were diverse, and if by 1870, central Canada's industrial structure forecast that future, it also exhibited many links to the past. Parts of that region were truly at the point of economic transition. Yet the final point to note is that most workers were still employed in the agricultural sector. Industrial workers doubled in Upper Canada between 1850 and 1870, but they still represented only 14 percent of the working population. Despite significant economic change, the reality is that both provinces remained predominantly rural in orientation throughout the pre-Confederation period.[1]

A Society in Motion

UPPER CANADA

As it had for almost every decade since 1791, Upper Canada's population doubled in the 1840s, reaching 952 000 in 1850. Population growth and net immigration slowed thereafter, and by 1870 Ontario had 1 926 922 people. The Irish potato famine of the mid-1840s contributed the greatest single influx of migrants in this period: between 1846 and 1851, 200 000 British subjects, two-thirds from Ireland, migrated to Upper Canada, perhaps 40 000 moving on to the United States.

The idea of the Irish as urban dwellers and unskilled industrial labourers is an American cliché. About three-quarters of all Upper Canadian Irish

---

[1] A general survey of the economy can be found in K. Norrie and D. Owram, *A History of the Canadian Economy* (Toronto, 1991). B. Young and J. A. Dickinson, *A Short History of Quebec: A Socio-Economic Perspective* (Toronto, 1988) provides a good treatment of Lower Canada. Some more specialized studies include P. Craven and T. Traves, "Canadian Railways as Manufacturers, 1850–1880," *Historical Papers* (1983); D. McCalla, *The Upper Canada Trade: A Study of the Buchanans' Business, 1834–72* (Toronto, 1979); J. McCallum, *Unequal Beginnings: Agriculture and Economic Development in Quebec and Ontario until 1870* (Toronto, 1980); O. J. McDiarmid, *Commercial Policy in the Canadian Economy* (Cambridge, Mass., 1946); D. McCalla and P. George, "Measurement, Myth and Reality: Reflections on the Economic History of 19th Century Ontario," *Journal of Canadian Studies*, 21 (1986); M. McInnis, "Marketable Surpluses in Ontario Farming (1860)," *Social Science History*, 8 (1984); G. A. Stelter, "Urban Planning and Development in Upper Canada," in W. Borak, ed., *Urbanization in the Americas* (1980). J. McCallum, *Unequal Beginnings*, and S. Courville, "Une Monde rurale en mutation: le Bas-Canada dans la première moitie du 19th siècle," *HS/SH*, 20 (1987) are useful for Lower Canada statistics.

lived and worked in rural regions. How can one explain this? How were often destitute and at times disease-weakened migrants able to settle in rural Upper Canada at a time of rising costs for farmland and diminishing arable land? In the first place, most Irish migrants were already experienced, small tenant farmers. They came equipped with technological knowledge, if not always material wealth. Many also came equipped with artisan skills that allowed them to work and accumulate capital to commence farming. Finally, the notion of the outcast migrant is belied by numerous examples of protection by previously settled friends and kin. Migration and settlement, not just for the Irish, was a stepwise process, involving many links and many stops before a final destination was reached. The trek to, from, and within rural areas in Upper Canada continued unabated in this period.

Historians have often characterized transients as people in flight: rootless, dispossessed and doomed to a life of struggling subsistence. Doubtless many were, but the very prevalence of transiency in rural areas suggests the possibility of a different explanation. Rather than assume that all people who moved were in flight, passively reacting to larger economic and social forces, one could postulate that many of those who moved did so with concrete goals. Some evidence suggests that transients were active shapers as much as passive reactors to the world around them. Consider the process underlying the settlement of part of Upper Canada's last best west: the bushland of Euphrasia Township in Grey County in the late 1840s. In 1851, 70 percent of Euphrasia's 97 heads of households had lived elsewhere in Upper Canada. Most had spent at least three years at their last place of residence. Moves were dictated by capital needs and, as importantly, by the stage of family composition. No one moved to Euphrasia without at least two dependants; most households only moved to Euphrasia when they had children of working age (eight years or older). Not only were most heads of household still living in Euphrasia in 1861, but a majority of their adult sons had also established farms in the same township. Family values and family structure interacted with larger social and economic forces to condition the migratory process.

As the 1850s wore on, it became more difficult to duplicate the Euphrasia Township pattern within Upper Canada's boundaries. The necessary land simply was not available. In this context, a number of strategies were employed in an ongoing effort to maintain family linkages. In the rich agricultural region of Peel County, population pressure on the land escalated sharply in the 1850s and 1860s. Inheritance practice began to recognize the necessity of some migration by no longer dividing existing land equally among all sons. At the same time, the primary heir had to underwrite the costs of migration for those forced to leave. Family responsibilities therefore remained intense. In an attempt to balance family size with existing land resources, people married and began their families later.

People often worked in industry as a first step to owning a farm. Almost 40 percent of labourers in southern Upper Canada listed in the 1861 census and who could be traced to the census of 1871 had become farmers. Before 1870, the lumber industry in the Ottawa-Prescott area allowed single men to postpone marriage and establish some capital to set up a farming household. These same men could supplement farming on the relatively unproductive Prescott terrain with seasonal shanty and sawmill work. Industrialization in rural areas did not supplant, but, for a time, co-existed with agrarian pursuits.

Farmers did not enjoy identical living standards. The foreign-born and relatively young were overrepresented amongst tenants. One estimate of stratification within the farming community of Peel County in 1861 puts 39 percent of farmers at the bottom level, those not having "moved beyond the primitive amenities of a pioneer society." Recent immigrants, Irish Catholics and Protestants bulked large in this category of least-improved families. One in every six farm households in Upper Canada did not produce enough food to feed its own family, and only one in six were "substantially commercial." Just as before, farming was not a quick way to become rich. An untold number never made it up the ladder at all, having abandoned their plot or been evicted by creditors, "picked," as one complained, "as bare as a bird's ass."[2]

---

[2] For migration patterns and discussions of how various ethnic-groups adjusted to life in the Canadas see D. Akenson, "Ontario: Whatever Happened to the Irish?" *Canadian Papers in Rural History*, III (1983); C. J. Houston and W. J. Smyth, *Irish Emigration and Canadian Settlement: Pattern Links and Letters* (Toronto, 1990); B. S. Elliott, *Irish Migrants in the Canadas: A New Approach* (Montreal and Kingston, 1988); David Gagan, "Land, Population and Social Change: The Critical Years in Rural Canada West," *CHR*, 59 (1978); D. Gagan, *Hopeful Travellers: Family, Land and Social Change in Mid-Victorian Peel County, Canada West* (Toronto, 1981). D. A. Norris, "Migration, Pioneer Settlement and the Life Course: The First Families of an Ontario Township," *Canadian Papers in Rural History*, 4 (1989). Chad Gaffield, *Language, Schooling and Cultural Conflict: The Origins of the French Language Conflict in Ontario* (Montreal, 1987); A. Gordon Darroch and M. Ornstein, "Ethnicity and Class, Transitions Over a Decade: Ontario 1861-71," *Historical Papers* (1984).

LOWER CANADA

By 1871, Lower Canada's population had increased to 1 200 000, 1.7 times its size in 1844. This represented a considerably slower growth rate than Upper Canada's whose population quadrupled in the same period. English, as a percentage of Quebec's population, peaked in 1851 (25 percent), declining to 20 percent in 1871. Relatively few immigrants stayed in Lower Canada. Moreover, between 1840 and 1880 about 340 000 mainly French-speaking people left the province. Lower Canadian agriculture, even when combined with lumber and mine work, could not sustain the expanding rural population.

As in Upper Canada, families moved with a purpose. Some moved to Lower Canadian urban centres. Others moved as part of church-sponsored colonization societies within Quebec, but most left to seek work in New England. Before 1850, those families who left Quebec tended to have fewer children, a male household head who was at least as likely to be as skilled as an unskilled worker, and a wife who tended to stay in the home rather than acquire wage labour outside the household. This family configuration fitted well with the needs of the still pre-industrial economy of northern New England. Factories and mills had yet to dominate. Artisan skills were still prized. Opportunities for the employment of women and children were limited. Lower Canadian families adopted strategies appropriate to the economic environment.

After the mid- to late 1850s, when textile mills and other large manufactories became increasingly common in the New England states, Lower Canadian families on the move had more children. The family consisted most often of an unskilled labourer as household head and a wife who accepted wage work outside the home. Factories could employ children and women as well as men. More children meant a healthy family economy. Once again, strategy underlay family movement. Clearly, linkages did exist between families in Lower Canada and French families in the New England region, and information and aid resulted from those links.

URBAN WORK

Early industrialization imposed harsh conditions on the maintenance of the family unit. Some families brought parts of their farm with them to urban centres and, as in Montreal, raised pigs, cows, and maintained a productive family garden. Many more began to work outside the home. By

1871 women represented 26 percent of the employees in Toronto's five largest industrial sectors, and children accounted for 10 percent. Thirty-three percent of Montreal's labour force were women and one-quarter of all boys between the ages of 11 and 14 worked outside the home in Montreal. Such work took place under the supervision and control of nonfamily overseers. In this context, exploitation of female and child labour became commonplace. A federal commission of investigation into working conditions in mills and factories in Ontario reported in 1882 on the extensive employment of women and children in poorly ventilated attics, wet basements, and overcrowded rooms with little or no sanitation facilities. Women and children, some under ten years of age, often worked 60 hours a week for meagre wages.

This picture of row housing in the Beaver Hall Hill area of Montreal was taken in 1852.
NATIONAL ARCHIVES OF CANADA/C47354

In Montreal skilled and unskilled workers found it more difficult to own homes as the period progressed. In large cities, residential segregation reflected class distinctions. By 1871, in Toronto, for example, skilled workers, who had lived side by side with middle-class entrepreneurs and factory owners in the 1850s, comprised a large percentage in Toronto's oldest working-class slum, Cabbagetown, on the banks of the Don River. Family formation patterns further separated classes. Upper income earners in Hamilton lowered their family size, as did certain members of the successful farming class, possibly to ensure that their children would inherit a stake sufficient to guarantee their future success. By contrast, skilled workers and labourers, especially recent immigrants, increased their number of children. As in rural areas, families nearer the bottom of the socio-economic ladder depended on the number of people working rather than on the income of one wage earner. Length of residence also varied according to class level: those who moved most often formed what has been called "a reserve army of the underemployed." Those who persisted tended to dominate civic politics, own land, enjoy a high income, and shape cities to suit their own interests. In Toronto, for example, services like paving, sidewalks, sewers, piped water and gas were only granted to those who could, on a street by street basis, afford to pay. Over time, this requirement accentuated residential differences, filtering out those who could not afford the attendant taxes.

Similar work place and residential and family experience helped create a sense of working-class consciousness, one forged also on the canals and railroads of the 1840s and 1850s. At least 61 strikes occurred in Lower Canada between 1843 and 1879. Forty strikes led by skilled workers protesting the introduction of machinery and demanding higher wages took place in Upper Canada in 1853 and 1854. On railroads, strikes were, as one Great Western railroad engineer reminisced, as regular as the "croaking of the frogs." In both Canadas, unions were formed by moulders, tailors, joiners, machine workers, printers, firefighters, and others. Class distinctions, not easily perceived in the 1830s, became clearer with the emergence of industrial capitalism.[3]

---

[3] R. Rudin, *The Forgotten Quebecers: A History of English-Speaking Quebec, 1759–1980* (Quebec, 1985) is a provocative treatment. B. Beattie, "Opportunity Across the Border: The Burlington Area Economy and the French Canadian Worker in 1850," *Vermont History*, 55 (1987) is useful. B. D. Palmer, *Working Class Experience: The Rise and Reconstitution of Canadian Labour* (Toronto, 1983) is a good introduction. B. Bradbury, "Pigs, Cows and Boarders: Non-Wage Forms of Survival Among Montreal Families," *Labour/Le Travail*, 14 (1984) and C. Gaffield and G. Bouchard, "Literacy, Schooling and Family Reproduction in Rural Ontario and Quebec," *Historical Studies in Education*, 1/2 (1989), 201-18, highlight special themes.

INSTITUTIONAL CULTURE

In this period, state-operated institutions like schools, asylums, and prisons were often created by the elite to modify, manage, and manipulate other people. Almost without exception, however, those other people, whether living in urban or rural areas, went far in reconstructing those institutions to suit their own individual and class ends. This formative period of institutional growth, therefore, must be understood as a dialectical process: agency, or freedom to act, existed at both ends of the class spectrum.

The rise of state-supported schools provides an excellent example of institutional growth. In Lower Canada, church and state acted together to establish an elementary school system that grew from 800 schools to 4000 in this period. Literacy rates increased. Close to 200 000 students attended elementary school in 1867. A corresponding growth occurred in religious communities, especially in the enrolment of nuns, who were the main source of teachers. The state's hope was that the growing Catholic Church, willing investor in state-sponsored enterprises like railroads, would prove able to instil the bourgeois values of obedience and steady work habits into the rural classes and thus fit them for factory and industrial work.

The Catholic Church became more conservative in its allegiance to the pope, more aggressive in asserting its primacy over the state, and more energetic in instituting devotional societies at the popular level. These policies were known as Ultramontanism, and they had a profound impact on the Canadian people.

Quite understandably historians have viewed these activities within the larger context of Protestant fears of "papal aggression." To many Protestants in the Canadas and, indeed, in the Maritimes, the fear of Catholic expansion was fanned by the increase of Catholic migrants and the re-establishment of Catholic political and religious rights in many European countries. Religious tension did play a powerful role in political and cultural matters, as will be described in Chapter 11. Yet there is a danger in overemphasizing Catholic-Protestant hatreds. A common commitment to capitalist development, to growth along bourgeois-guided lines, overlay sectarian strife. Through educational reform and social teaching in both Canadas, the Catholic Church performed a modernizing role in conjunction with the goals of the rising political and economic elite. Ignace Bourget, the Bishop of Montreal, for example, advocated a modern curriculum with less Latin and more emphasis on trade and farming. The Church also took the lead in the 1840s in the Lower Canadian temperance crusade, which was managed in other colonies by middle-class business-peoples. Temperance, priests like the charismatic lecturer Father Charles Chiniquy argued, marked the only hope for the salvation of French-Canadian nationality. Only sober, prudent, thrifty and industrious habitants could compete effectively against a rising sea of anglo immigrants. Chiniquy made the link between temperance and industrialism explicit:

We ought not to bring from Europe what we can get at home...we manufacture nothing. . . . We suffer from a want of nationality, a want of union, a want of energy.

Temperance would help cure these problems. Through educational reform and general moral teachings, the Catholic Church attempted to act as a bridge linking a pre-industrial and industrializing society.

How successful was the church in this regard? The number of priests per population and general church attendance, like school attendance, certainly increased over this period in Lower Canada. The consumption of alcohol dropped precipitously at the height of the temperance crusade in the late 1840s. Yet it climbed again throughout the 1850s. Labour unrest also increased in this period. Moreover, while much more research needs to be undertaken, there is good evidence that rural families used schools to suit their own ends. They sent boys to school when farm work routine permitted. Girls attended school more consistently and for a more extended period of time, since they were not as required for heavy farm labour. Rural families saw schools as useful for acquiring religious training and limited literacy. Measured against farm needs, schooling had little value. Small wonder that, in 1849, violent uprisings against compulsory schooling and school taxes occurred in many Lower Canadian rural areas.

In Upper Canada, in the mid-1840s, a state-administered, tax-supported system was set up to transmit "useful knowledge" through regulated reading, standardized texts, and the professionalization of teaching to working-class children. "The rich with grammar schools and more can take care of themselves," the system's founder, Egerton Ryerson, affirmed.

Success was limited. Local school boards, because of entrenched custom and financial restraints, adopted the state's slate for proper school texts only slowly, if at all. The teacher's religion and ethnic background plus, in some areas, the language of instruction at the local school house dictated whether a rural family would send children to school. State-run lending libraries could not compete with the sale of banned books by itinerant Yankee booksellers. The state's attempt to discipline the reader even led to the formation of "underground" lending services within some public schools. One student-run venture featured "Sylvanus Cobb with his love and murder, stories of highwaymen from Dick Turpin to Paul Clifford, lives of opera girls *et hoc genus omne* and the worst of Reynold's filthy and exciting publications." Compared to the spotless condition of books in the state-supported library, the student selections were, according to school investigators, "tattered and torn," dirty and coverless, evidently extensively loaned and carefully studied. Schools may, indeed, have been successful in teaching people to read. The irony is that the state could not control what was being read. Rather than quieting the possibility of social unrest, subversion, and independent thinking, the emerging educational system may have provided alternative avenues to those ends.

Moreover, the educational system of the 1840s rested on an increasingly fragile assumption that middle and upper classes could afford to underwrite two educational structures: public and private. Economic pressures dictated otherwise. As a result, state aid to private schools increased and, more significantly, better teachers, more subjects, separate female classes, and modern school houses came to characterize the upper grades of the public system. Since most working-class urban families, like most farm families, required the labour of their children in order to survive, children of more prosperous families dominated the upper grades. In response to economic pressure, middle and upper classes transformed a school system initially set up for other people's children into one suitable for their own offspring.

Asylums and prisons also failed to conform to their founders' hopes. When "cure" rates failed to reach expectations, money for asylums dwindled, and they became places of incarceration. The failure of the penitentiary to act as a beacon of reform led to the transformation of local judicial and policing routines from a voluntary to a professional and bureaucratic system. In Lower Canada, this process had commenced immediately following the Rebellion. A criminal class existed and could not be rehabilitated: but it could and had to be controlled.

Land purchases from natives continued in Upper Canada, but in both provinces concerted efforts were made to break the communal and dependent aspects of native life. In order for native people to become free and independent actors in a market economy, a series of government committees recommended that communal ownership of reserve land be discouraged. The government passed an Enfranchisement Law that gave voting rights to all natives who opted for individual ownership of land, who could read and write English or French, and who could pass a skill-testing exam (naming the world's continents). There was a Catch-22 to this process of enfranchisement, however. Natives who opted for the vote lost their status as Indians under Canadian law. To vote, one had to ape white, middle-class values. By 1860, three years after the passage of this act, only one native had elected to do so.

The changing nature of religious institutions, as indicated by membership, message, and architecture, sheds further light on the materialistic ethos so prevalent in the Canadas in the middle years of the nineteenth century. Between 1841 and 1871, membership in Upper Canadian Protestant churches, like that of Lower Canada's Catholic Church, increased dramatically. Even as they worshipped material progress, Upper Canadians swelled the ranks of the established churches where they listened to an increasingly other-worldly message symbolized by the dramatic change in church architecture in this period.

By 1880 Gothic church buildings loomed over Ontario's secular cities, towns, and rural villages, where, as the *Canada Farmer* observed in 1865, "straightforward square houses" predominated. In the Family Compact era, Anglican churches were constructed to reflect that church's dominance within secular society. Seating arrangements, for example, reflected social differentiation: the wealthy and privileged purchased special pews with tables and other accoutrements. In this sense, churches reflected and emphasized society's hierarchical social structure. By 1850, that structure had been transformed. A new Upper Canadian elite, one adverse to close state-church relations, now sat atop secular society. In this changed context the church sought to separate itself from the new social mores; Gothic architecture with its spires and calculated ornamentation provided the perfect form for proclaiming this intent. The growing use of the Gothic style in the construction of public schools symbolically linked church and schools and reinforced the moral message taught by both. For many, the rush for wealth carried with it a profound sense of unease. The acquisition of church membership represented, in part, a recognition that the schools, prisons, asylums, poor houses, and reserves were not working: street peoples, criminals, natives, the insane, the poor, and the rural farmer seemed incalcitrant, incapable of being assimilated. The failure to resolve these perceived problems underlined the fragility of capitalist culture in the years following mid-century: within secular society, industrial capitalist values did not yet reign supreme. An other-worldly church offered relief, if not assistance.[4]

Political Restructuring: Patronage, Parties, and Politics, 1838–64

INTRODUCTION

Union politics can be approached from at least three perspectives. The traditional, often called Whiggish, interpretation focuses on the coming of responsible government in 1848 and sees that event as a step to democratic and independent nationhood. A second, not incompatible, interpretation emphasizes duality within the Union. Far from creating a unitary state, the Act of Union in 1841 facilitated the emergence of a federal or dualistic governing structure. English and French, Catholic and Protestant experimented with a political structure within which they could co-exist. In this sense the Union era is a period of gestation from which confederation issued in 1867. The third perspective cuts across the first two. Both responsible government and the emergence of duality are seen as major events, but their significance is given a different slant. Responsible government, in this view, while facilitating independence from the mother country, also fostered greater centralized political control within the colony. Tighter executive decision making and closer control of party development followed the granting of responsible government. The watch words of the political leaders who acquired power at this time were not democracy and independence: they were economic development, efficiency, and collaboration both between French and English and between the Canadas and Great Britain. During the Union period, an upwardly

---

[4] On education see: Alison Prentice, *The School Promoters* (Toronto, 1977); N. McDonald and A. Charton, eds., *Egerton Ryerson and His Times* (Toronto, 1978) and Bruce Curtis, *Building the Educational State: Canada West, 1834–71* (London, 1988). On the general issue of the role of the state see A. Greer and I. Radforth, eds., *Colonial Leviathan: State Formation in Mid-Nineteenth Century Canada* (Toronto, 1991). W. Westfall, *Two Worlds: The Protestant Culture of 19th Century Ontario* (Montreal, 1989) and J. W. Grant, *A Profusion of Spires: Religion in 19th Century Ontario* (Toronto, 1988) are useful studies. Susan Mann Trofimenkoff, *The Dream of Nations: A Social and Intellectual History of Quebec* (Toronto, 1983) can be consulted on issues of education and religion in Lower Canada.

mobile French and English socio-economic elite took political power. While the emergence of this new elite cannot be seen as a simple movement toward greater democracy, its policies and actions did facilitate French-English collaboration and the attainment of Confederation. It is to these matters, matters of crucial importance in terms of understanding the foundations of the Canadian nation, that we now turn.[5]

SETTING THE STAGE: THE REBELLION'S AFTERMATH, 1838–41

Disciplining the rebellious took different forms in Upper and in Lower Canada. Of 81 rebels tried before Upper Canadian juries, 48 were acquitted and two were executed. In Lower Canada, thousands were arrested, property was systematically destroyed, and many habitants in the countryside around Montreal were terrorized. Martial law was declared and the constitution was suspended. Denied the rights of a jury trial and, instead, tried before a court martial, 99 of 108 rebels were condemned to death, of whom 12 were publicly hanged and 58 banished to New South Wales. The rest of those arrested were eventually released without charge.

In Lower Canada an appointed Special Council ruled between 1838 and 1841. The autocratic council initiated a series of important changes in areas of landholding, law, welfare, local government, and education. By beginning to do away with seigneurial tenure (on the island of Montreal), to construct state-run asylums, to fund a school system under church control, to found a rural police force heavily concentrated in the Montreal hinterland, and to extend central control into the country via a revamping of local government, the council set the stage for the emergence to power

---

[5] A general treatment which emphasizes politics is J. M. S. Careless, *The Union and the Canadas: The Growth of Canadian Institutions, 1841–57* (Toronto, 1967). Other, somewhat more specialized treatments include: Jacques Monet, *The Last Cannon Shot: A Study of French Canadian Nationalism, 1837–50* (Toronto, 1969); W. G. Ormsby, *The Emergence of the Federal Concept in Canada, 1839–45* (Toronto, 1969); P. A. Buckner, *The Transition to Responsible Government* (West Point, 1985); G. T. Stewart, *The Origins of Canadian Politics: A Comparative Approach* (Vancouver, 1986); S. J. R. Noel, *Patrons, Clients, Brokers: Ontario Society and Politics, 1791–1896* (Toronto, 1990); and P. Romney, *Mr. Attorney: The Attorney General for Ontario in Court, Cabinet and Legislature, 1791–1899* (Toronto, 1986). Biographical studies of leading politicians in this period are available in various volumes of *Dictionary of Canadian Biography*, e.g., Francis Hincks, Louis La Fontaine, John A. Macdonald, Robert Baldwin, Allan MacNab and A. W. Morin. J. M. S. Careless, ed., *The Pre-Confederation Premiers: Ontario Government Leaders, 1841–67* (Toronto, 1980) is also useful.

of a new Lower Canadian elite. Those Lower Canadian commercially oriented bourgeoisie who saw the seigneurial system and pre-industrial French law as impediments to economic and social development were, even as the council enacted its draconian legislation, looking for ways to accommodate to and manipulate the new order.

The most dramatic legislation passed by the Special Council sanctioned the reuniting of Upper and Lower Canada in February 1841. The notion of union emerged in part from the report of John Lampton, the Earl of Durham. A British emissary empowered to resolve the Canada problem, Durham disembarked at Quebec in June 1838 in full ceremonial dress astride a white horse and accompanied by an orchestra. The Durham Report received mixed reception from contemporaries in 1839 and from historians since. For Durham, the Lower Canadian conflict was racial in origin, and the solution was to assimilate the French. Union with Upper Canada would, he believed, "elevate" the French from a "hopeless inferiority." No French Canadian could accept Durham's racial slurs. But some could and did accept the rest of his program.

His proposal that the assembly should initiate public policy and appoint "the persons by whom that policy was to be administered" seemed to many Lower and Upper Canadian reformers to be responsible government, a system that required that the executive be chosen from and reflect the political composition of the elected assembly. The executive council would become the equivalent of our modern cabinet. Many moderate Upper Canadian reformers led by Robert Baldwin had been arguing for just such a system throughout the troubled 1830s. By establishing a direct linkage between the assembly and the executive, Durham proposed a system within which disagreements could be resolved rather than exacerbated. A structure that made the executive's existence at least partly dependent on the assembly's composition and policy desires forced executive members to conciliate rather than ignore assembly wishes, should they desire to maintain their conciliar position. Durham did not conceive that this would weaken the executive's role. By linking the executive council to the assembly, he put forward a structure that would deepen the former's power and give to the council the credibility necessary to administer an increasingly complex economic and social state.

On two related issues, however, Durham remained firmly wedded to the principles that underlay the Constitutional Act of 1791. Despite the fact that the Crown in England no longer played a central role in selecting British ministers, Durham continued to allocate a great deal of that power to the lieutenant-governor. In fact, the governor was the lynch pin of his system and would, if governing properly, receive the support of all reasonable assembly members. He believed this to be possible because he felt that political parties would never develop in the colonies. Executive councillors would act as individuals, not as party representatives.

It is difficult to assess the impact of Durham's Report in British ruling circles. Durham was somewhat of a radical reformer who may have been given the Canadian position simply to get him away from the centre of British politics. His decision to banish some rebels to Bermuda, taken without consulting imperial authorities, led to his premature resignation in November 1838. He arrived back in England in a combative and belligerent mood. And besides personal issues, his report represented simply one in a long line of investigative commissions stretching over the last decade. Finally, as had been the case throughout the 1830s, British politics were, themselves, extremely unstable. The balance between the Whig and Tory parties was close throughout this era. In a period of eleven years, eight different men had headed the Colonial Office. Under these circumstances, sustained policy making was difficult. Yet the rebellions did focus Colonial Office minds. Matters could drift no longer. While British political leaders ignored some of Durham's specific points, they followed closely the report's major thrust, that of more closely linking the executive and the assembly components of colonial government.

In fact, Durham's myopia concerning the governor's powers and party development was shared by many in the Colonial Office. Following Durham, a succession of governors were sent over to rule according to the principle of harmony, with the governor in the conductor's seat. Neither Durham, nor the Colonial Office, however, constructed the ultimate rules of the game. Within the Canadas, Durham's sketch formed the basis for a more comprehensive blueprint, a game plan devised by an emerging set of moderate, business-oriented, conservative and reform politicians from Upper and Lower Canada.

REDEFINING RESPONSIBILITY, 1841–51

Charles Poulett Thomson, Durham's successor as governor general, saw to it that Upper Canada's Tory-dominated assembly voted for the union proposal. The promise of a 1.5 million pound sterling loan from Great Britain was in itself enough. The terms of union were simply icing on an already very rich cake: each section—officially Canada East and Canada West, but in practice always Upper and Lower Canada—received 42 assembly seats, notwithstanding that Lower Canada had 200 000 more people; debt was merged, despite the fact that Upper Canada's debt was 13 times the size of Lower Canada's; the capital was at Kingston, Upper Canada, a bastion of Anglo-Saxon loyalism; English was the only official language. To commemorate his success, Thomson demanded the title "Lord St. Lawrence"; this was a little too grandiose for the Colonial Office and he settled for Lord Sydenham.

In the context of the themes of responsible government, duality, and centralization of power, Sydenham, like Durham, was very much a transitional figure. His idea of responsible government meant governing through an executive council picked by himself to reflect the assembly's composition. That council could, he believed, only advise the governor general; it could not dictate to the Crown's colonial representative. Already in close correspondence, politicians like Robert Baldwin and Francis Hincks from Upper Canada and Louis La Fontaine from Lower Canada had different ideas. They believed that executive councillors should be the central actors in political administration. The gulf between the governor and the reform group was no less significant over the issue of duality. Sydenham clearly hoped that the union would be a crucible wherein the French could be effectively subdued and assimilated. Yet to achieve greater reform party strength, Baldwin and Hincks were ready to stand by La Fontaine in the latter's attempt to bend the union toward the goal of *la survivance*, the retention and enrichment of French culture in Lower Canada.

All major political actors in the 1840s emphasized the need for a strong central executive. In part, this attitude reflected the continued influence of the old Constitutional Act of 1791 with its emphasis on executive power. But even more importantly, the unanimity on the issue of strong central authority derived from a general perception that the Constitutional Act had failed to achieve this end: it had rather resulted in the rebellions of 1837. The rebellions, many concluded, arose from the executives' inability to govern properly. The separation of executive administration from the assembly precluded effective control by the country's elected representatives. Executive control needed to be more deeply embedded in the colony's political structure. Disputes arose concerning which component of the executive branch should have primary authority: the council or the governor. Those who advocated responsible government believed that conciliar control of patronage was essential. Those who supported rule by "harmony" gave the power of patronage to the governor.

The union's first general election sharpened and clarified lines of contention and consensus. Louis La Fontaine, a Patriote supporter, argued for developing interior resources, abolishing seigneurial tenure, and constructing canals, all consistent with pre-1837 anglo-merchant economic programs. Although he lost the election, his program found ready sympathy among Upper Canadian reformers, who found him a safe Upper Canadian seat, thus cementing, at the leadership level, an accommodation or alliance between "progressive"-minded politicians from the union's two sections. Using all means at his command, Sydenham, for his part, attempted to create a following in his own image: he selected his own candidates, cajoled votes via bribery, gerrymandered electoral boundaries, handpicked electoral officers, located polls close to his area of strength, and employed violence to keep opposition voters away. He swept Upper Canada, ensured the election of some English Lower Canadians, and even enticed Baldwin to sit on the executive council.

Yet this was harmony via sleight of hand. Discordant notes were soon heard. When Sydenham would not add La Fontaine or any other French Canadian to the executive council, Baldwin resigned. Sydenham, exasperated, commented privately, "Was there ever such an ass!" Yet to govern effectively, even Sydenham had to recognize that the union's two sections possessed separate languages, religions, civil codes, judicial systems, and forms of land tenure. To deal with these differences, he set up the beginnings of a dual administration and appointed two law officers, two commissioners of Crown lands, and two provincial secretaries. Far from moving toward a unitary governmental system, Sydenham set the foundations for the emergence of a federal or dual governing structure.

Following Sydenham's sudden death in 1841, the Canadas were sent three governors in the space of four years. The first of these, Sir Charles Bagot, and the second, Sir Charles Metcalfe, were both able men who were determined to follow the Durham/Sydenham view of the governor as active administrator. Neither enjoyed Sydenham's success. In September 1842, Bagot invited five reformers to join the executive council, two of whom, La Fontaine and Augustin-Norbert Morin, were francophones from Lower Canada. This trend toward duality was further entrenched when Bagot appointed two deputy superintendents of education in order to reflect the different religious composition of Upper and Lower Canada, allowed French law to remain in place in the lower colony, and appointed the francophone, Étienne Parent, as clerk of the executive council. Despite the stacked deck in favour of Upper over Lower Canada and English over French at the union's commencement, the reality of the French fact became quickly and increasingly reflected at the centre of power.

The Colonial Office viewed these trends with alarm. Metcalfe arrived in April 1843 with instructions to hold the fort against further change. Quickly recognizing that assimilation was not feasible, he repealed restrictions on the use of French language, approved Montreal as the new seat of government, and even advocated a general amnesty for most rebels. On the more contentious issue of executive control, Metcalfe dug in his heels. So, too, did La Fontaine and Baldwin. In May 1843, La Fontaine demanded

Sir Charles Metcalfe opening Parliament in Montreal, 1846.
NATIONAL ARCHIVES OF CANADA/C315

that the executive council be accorded the right to distribute all patronage in the country. And Baldwin assured an office seeker that same year that "I have always been in the strictest sense of the word *a party man*; therefore patronage will be dispensed in a manner calculated to strengthen and support that party."

For Metcalfe to accede to this demand would entail two revolutionary changes. First, executive power would be transferred from the governor to the council. As we have seen, this was inconsistent with the Durham/Sydenham line of reasoning and, indeed, with the beliefs of many colonial politicians, including the old Tories. Secondly, it would lead to, as Baldwin obviously believed, the *de facto* recognition of party government. Up to 1843, governors could maintain the reasonable fiction that council members were picked for their individual following in the assembly and in the country generally. Members of such an executive had two loyalties, one to the Crown and one to the region from which they were selected and in which they lived and/or invested capital. Baldwin and La Fontaine proposed a third allegiance: to party, an allegiance that would subsume the other two.

This impasse could not be bridged. Reformers had long since tired of trusting governors. Metcalfe believed party government would sever the bonds of empire: "I have avowed my adherence to Responsible Government views to the fullest extent which it can be avowed in a colony and it must be either Blindness or Disaffection that can desire to get further." An election ensued. The venting of long pent-up emotions led to bitter recriminations and to the spectacle of the determined Metcalfe, disfigured and dying from a cancerous growth on his cheek, leading a motley array of Conservative-minded Reformers, moderate Conservatives, and old Family Compact Tories under the banner of loyalty to the Crown. The emerging Reform Party was badly beaten in Upper Canada (30–12), but their French-Canadian allies, under La Fontaine, the champion of *la survivance*, swept the lower province (29–13). The Hincks-Baldwin determination to ally with La Fontaine again paid dividends. Weakened by disease, Metcalfe gave to his moderate Conservative appointees, William Henry Draper from Upper Canada and D. B. Viger from Lower Canada, virtual autonomy in making appointments, a freedom increased under the brief reign of his successor Earl Cathcart. But even patronage could not bond old Tories and moderate men on the move. Draper returned to the bench in 1847. The Reformers, having tightened party organization while in opposition, swept to power in both sections of the province.

The La Fontaine–Baldwin government in 1847 was the first true party government to exercise power in the Canadas. It marked the first of a long line of bifurcated ministries representing at the highest political level the reality of duality. The transferral of power was, in the context of the Canadas' turbulent and violent political past, suitably symbolized by the passage of the Rebellion Losses Bill in 1849. This bill promised to compensate those French Canadians who had suffered property damage in the rebellion. Coming on the heels of the repeal of the Navigation Acts and the seeming abandonment by Britain of loyal colonists, it aroused the frustrated fury of old Family Compact Tories and anglo merchants in Montreal. When Lord Elgin, the governor general, signed the legislation over Tory cries, some, like Samuel P. Jarvis, an elder Toronto Tory, prayed "they would...string him up as a caution to other traitor governors." Others did more than wish. They burned the Parliament Buildings in Montreal. They pelted Elgin with rotten eggs and tomatoes. But even Tory vigilance could not turn the clock back. By 1850 the seeds of Canada's modern political system had been well sown.

Bishop John Strachan might lament declining morality and charge that "the ministry, as they call it, whether Conservative or Reform seems to have no other object than to get good places." But an exasperated rising moderate conservative, John A. Macdonald, caught Strachan's real meaning when he complained in 1847 that Family Compact Tories "cannot abide promotion or employment of anyone beyond their pale." Implicit in both these comments is the recognition that social change accompanied political transformation. A new elite had grasped the reigns of power.

Bourgeois Politics in the 1850s

On cultural and political matters, Baldwin and his co-leader, La Fontaine, attempted to end years of acrimonious debate. They entrenched the equal status of French by having the throne speech read in both French and English. They sponsored the Rebellion Losses Bill and granted all rebels of 1837 amnesty. They attempted to pacify Catholic-Protestant conflict by permitting Catholic public schools where a sufficient number of residents wanted it. By passing a secular public schools act and by creating a secular university—the University of Toronto—they hoped to end forever Anglican hopes of state-church status. Through the Municipal Corporations Act, they made more local offices elected. In the end, they were overly optimistic.

In Lower Canada, a small group called the Rouges, concerned about increasingly close ties between the government party and the Catholic Church, argued for the complete separation of church and state and a secular education system. They even supported the brief movement for annexation to the United States led by disgruntled Montreal merchants as a protest against the repeal of the corn laws, abandonment of timber preferences, withdrawal of the Navigation Acts, and passage of the Rebellion Losses Bill.

A group of Upper Canadian radical reformers, Protestant-voluntarist to the core, known as the Clear Grits, demanded the immediate end to the Clergy Reserves, balked at allowing any religious teaching in public schools, opposed all concessions to French language instruction, demanded cheaper and more representative government, and, when they discovered in 1851 that Upper Canadians outnumbered Lower Canadians, pushed for representation by population in place of equal representation by section.

While Baldwin showed energy on cultural and political matters, he temporized on developmental issues. He opposed Francis Hincks's legislation, which enabled municipalities to borrow money for developmental purposes. He disagreed with Hincks concerning the propriety of railroads running lotteries for raising money. He threatened to resign when Hincks decided to extend state backing of railroad construction from the guarantee of one-half the debt of railways over 120 km in length and to substitute provincially backed debentures for those of railroad companies. He attempted to stop the passage of a general Companies Incorporation Act for manufacturing, mining, and chemical industries, but Upper Canadian representatives outvoted him 22 to 6. Clearly, Baldwin felt uncomfortable with state involvement in expansive developmental issues. And equally clearly, a growing number of his past and potential supporters felt differently. In 1851 Baldwin resigned, followed soon thereafter by La Fontaine.

Gentry born and legally trained, Baldwin remained closer to the politics and politicians of the pre-1840s than those of the emerging 1850s. So, too, did La Fontaine, who, to indicate noble aspirations, if not reality, had had the "f" in Fontaine capitalized. In this sense, their resignation from politics and the assumption of reform leadership by the sharp-witted banker, Francis Hincks, and his lawyer co-leader, Augustus-Norbert Morin, neatly symbolize the transition from gentry to bourgeois rule. Yet there was also continuity amidst change. The economic policies through which Hincks hoped to structure the Canadas' economic future drew from past tactics and worked within traditional frameworks. Public works programs financed by British capital would provide jobs for Britain's "redundant population." Land sales by the Canadian government to British immigrants would help underwrite any necessary government aid to railroads. The program built upon Upper Canada's and to a degree Lower Canada's experiences as far back as canal construction in the 1820s.

These economic policies helped conciliate business-Conservative interests: Allan MacNab, for example, a lawyer, Anglican, and sometime Family Compact supporter from Hamilton, readily admitted that "all my politics are railroads." Others, from the so-called radical reform stream, demanded different policies. Hincks and Morin promised to secularize the clergy reserves, abolish seigneurial tenure, extend the franchise, increase representation (for both sections equally), and institute an elective legislative council. While they carried through on some of these—representation increased from 42 to 65, and the franchise was somewhat broadened—Hincks's attempt to merge two fundamentally antagonistic groups ran aground over the issue of business-government interaction. His propensity to speculate in railroads and land transactions and to profit from his own government policies left him vulnerable to charges of corruption. Rising reformer and owner of the influential Toronto *Globe*, George Brown skilfully exploited Hincks's vulnerability. Hincks's defence that he had "the same right to accept compensation for services rendered to private individuals or Corporations that the Attorney General has to receive fees for his advice, or for services rendered by him to similar parties," in other words to exploit his office as a normal businessperson/lawyer might do, found widespread support in the assembly at large but met with little sympathy from Brown and his followers. The fact that Hincks also supported Catholic schools, created a denominational collegial system at the University of Toronto, and with Morin delayed abolishing seigneurial tenure and the clergy reserves for fear of losing French Roman Catholic support further alienated him from the Clear Grits, Brown's supporters, and the small Rouge Party.

The resulting split in the Upper Canadian section of the old Baldwin–La Fontaine party led to a watershed in Canadian political history. The election of 1854 saw a realignment of political groups. French-Canadian nationalists led by Morin and George-Etienne Cartier joined with an Upper Canadian Conservative group composed of some old Tories like MacNab and young moderate Conservative leaders like the lawyer and businessman John A. Macdonald. This alliance of moderate Conservatives

from Upper Canada and moderate Reformers from Lower Canada supplanted the old grouping of Upper Canadian Reformers with their Lower
Canadian counterparts and remained the norm in central Canadian politics from 1854 until 1896. It represented the triumph of common economic goals over religious and ethnic differences.

In Lower Canada, the new government acted quickly and abolished
both the clergy reserves and the seigneurial system: clerics and seigneurs
were, however, amply compensated, and the new elected legislative council, because of high property qualifications, remained in the hands of the
rich. As had the Reform Party, the new Conservative group continued to
work closely with an increasingly powerful Catholic Church. These
initiatives were logically followed by a revamping of the pre-industrial law
codes that had underlaid the seigneurial way of life. In 1859, Cartier, a
former Patriote accused of treason during the rebellion, appointed a
commission to codify Quebec's civil code. On that commission, he put
Charles Dewey Day, a judge, who in 1839 had sentenced Lower Canadian
rebels to death. That Day and Cartier could easily unite to uproot one of
the most basic and fundamental of French Canada's institutions—its legal
system—acutely underlines the extent of political and social change
during the union.

In two ways the political reshaping of 1854 fractured the union and
facilitated Canadian Confederation. By continuing the economic policies
of Hincks, Macdonald and his Lower Canadian allies, Cartier and Alexander Tilloch Galt, a politician, land speculator, and businessman from the
Eastern Townships, brought the union to the brink of financial collapse.
By 1857 railroads and municipalities began to default on government
guaranteed loan repayments. A wider tax base and the acquisition of richer
resources to finance and underwrite continued economic expansion
appeared to be the only feasible answer. In 1858 Galt, especially, pushed
for a wider union of all British North American colonies. The British
Colonial Office considered the idea to be premature and shelved it, but not
long enough to gather dust. The union's tangled finances prevented that
from occurring.

The reshaping of politics that took place in 1854 resulted in more than
the emergence of a bourgeois party and the union's near financial collapse.
It also led to the virtual collapse of the union's political structure. This
occurred because a majority of Upper Canadians refused to accept cultural
differences and rejected a party based on the primacy of business. They
rallied instead around George Brown and the *Globe's* incendiary if not

racist and bigoted leadership. Brown and his followers hoped to relegate Catholics and French to a subordinate position. Arguing that too much of Upper Canada's cultural legislation, like that relating to schools, had been created by Lower Canadian votes and capitalizing on Upper Canada's larger population, Brown centred his platform on the principle of representation by population. Not surprisingly, this simple but powerful appeal found little support in the lower province. Brown also correctly sensed a growing restlessness in rural areas as good farmland became less easily available. He began to proclaim the benefits of westward expansion, adroitly tapping the latent imperialism within Upper Canadians. Finally, at a large and masterfully controlled Reform Convention in 1858, Brown and his followers advocated the introduction of a federal political system that might include representation by population at one level and, at another, some form of sectional equality. All this was not well spelled out. But it did point to some form of federation and in that sense anticipated the future while pandering to racist and imperialist pressures in the present.

In election after election following 1858, Reformers dominated the Upper Canadian polls and the moderate reformers/Conservatives (the Bleu Party as it came to be called) dominated in Lower Canada. The smaller Upper Canadian Conservative Party under John A. Macdonald allied with the Bleus from Lower Canada led by Cartier, while the Brownite Reformers sought an uneasy alliance with Reform Rouge Lower Canadians. This produced a situation of equality amongst antagonists, or what historians have termed political deadlock. A moderate Reform coalition led by John Sandfield Macdonald from Upper Canada and Louis-Victor Sicotte (1862–64) from Lower Canada attempted to break this political log-jam by the application of a double majority system. This system held that any law primarily affecting one section required both a majority vote in that section as well as an overall majority in order for it to become law. Such a system was unwieldly and, besides, J. S. Macdonald declared as law a school bill that granted privileges to Upper Canadian Catholics despite a majority of Upper Canadian votes opposing it. Upper Canadians saw this as a negation of the system they thought had emerged in the 1840s, a system John A. Macdonald, somewhat cynically, described as

a Federal Union; that in matters affecting Upper Canada solely, members from that section claimed and generally exercised the right of exclusive legislation, while members from Lower Canada legislated in matters affecting only their own section.

The crossing, both before and during John Sandfield's tenure of these boundaries, constituted a major reason for the union's destruction. By 1864 political deadlock and near bankruptcy had created an environment conducive to further substantive political restructuring.

Economy and Society in the Maritimes: A "Golden Age" or a "Dark Vale of Sorrow"?

INTRODUCTION

The 20 years prior to Confederation are commonly seen as the golden age of nineteenth century economic and social development in the Maritime region (excluding Newfoundland). Pre-industrial rhythms dictated by dependence on wood, wind, and water underlay and conditioned economic growth. When wood markets became increasingly unstable, when iron steamers began to compete with wooden sailing vessels, and when ocean freight rates dramatically fell, the Maritime economy floundered. Relative to the Canadas, there seemed little movement toward a modern industrializing economy.

This interpretation is open to two critiques. Those who view the 20 years before Confederation as a "golden age" generally point to macro economic indexes, to average or mean rates of growth and development, and rarely focus on how material resources were actually distributed among the people who lived there. An investigation of the social distribution of resources tarnishes the nostalgic notion of a "golden age." The second critique focuses on the most common reasons given for the decline of prosperity: the technological triumph of iron and steam over wood and sail. In the context of this impersonal new technology, Maritimers were somehow disadvantaged, unable to compete, and fell victims to forces beyond their control. This argument, however, makes humans mere pawns of impersonal technological imperatives. This notion oversimplifies a much more complex set of causes that are rooted not in technological dictates but in local human agency, in decisions taken by nineteenth century Maritimers.

THE AGE OF SAIL

Colonial shipping and shipbuilding grew within the protective confines of the old mercantilist system. It also survived that system's dismantlement in the 1840s. Following 1850, some shipyards grew in size; ship owning became concentrated in Saint John, Yarmouth, Windsor, and Halifax; shipbuilders and owners became increasingly separated; and technology began to replace skilled labour. In the 1860s and 1870s, British North America's sailing fleet ranked in the top five of the merchant marines in the world, and about 75 percent of that fleet was located in the Maritimes. The Reciprocity Treaty, the Crimean War, and the Civil War all opened up new shipping opportunities for maritime capitalists. The advent of the telegraph allowed maritime shippers to keep abreast of world shipping needs and far-flung markets as readily as their major competitors. A swiftly rising rate of world trade and a decline in the size of the American merchant marine further contributed to growth in the shipping sector. Mercantile investment in shipping and shipbuilding emerged from a sensible appraisal of economic opportunities. Profits remained high well into the 1870s.

The sailing sector had an impressive impact on the Maritime economy. Shipping ranked next to timber as the most important component of New Brunswick's economy. The sale of ships put Prince Edward Island's exports ahead of imports throughout this period. And, as a Pictou County paper noted in 1854, shipbuilding had a noticeable ripple effect within local economies:

...besides giving employment to several hundred men—carpenters, riggers, blacksmiths, etc., also gives much work to a large number of persons from the country who supply ship yards with timber, or the merchants with top timber for exportation, thus causing the circulation of large amounts of capital.

One historian has estimated that up to 12 percent of all wages to labourers in the 1860s came from shipbuilding. Twelve percent of sawmill output in Nova Scotia and New Brunswick went to shipbuilding in 1871. Clearly the shipping sector had substantial links to other areas of the Maritime economy. Yet in one sense shipping had less contact with Maritime commerce than it had had at the height of the mercantile period. After 1850 ship owners became more and more a part of world trade and less and less interested in the shipment of local products. In the postmercantilist context, ships were no longer simply "the oceanic extension of the [local] merchant's warehouse"; rather, voyages increasingly began and ended outside of British North America.

Like coal mining, shipbuilding brought Maritimers to the edge of industrialization; it did not carry them over that threshold. It remained an enterprise anchored in a commercial/mercantile era. It is important to understand in what way this was the case because the pattern of economic development in the pre-Confederation era set the stage for much subsequent economic endeavour in the Maritimes. In the first place, shipbuilding in the Maritimes did not lead to a decline in the pursuit of subsistence-based agriculture or primary staple-based economic activity. On the contrary, shipbuilding co-existed with and fed off the persistence of such traditional pursuits. Farmers, fishers, and woodworkers could and did obtain seasonal employment in shipyards, work that supplemented but did not transform traditional economic activity. Other links that would have had a transforming impact on the local economy were possible, but merchants ignored them. Merchant shipbuilders, for example, continued to import most of the high-value metal materials required for construction. Had all metal inputs for New Brunswick ships been manufactured in that province, the value of output from the local metal sector would have increased by close to 25 percent in 1871. Expansion of this heavy industry would itself have had significant ripple effects throughout the economy, effects that the staple industries and independently run family farms could not possibly generate. Instead of encouraging the breakdown of precapitalist, low productivity economic enterprise, merchant-owned shipbuilding and mining perpetuated and profited from its continuance.

In 1850 the level of industrialization in Nova Scotia and New Brunswick was roughly comparable to, if not greater than, that of Upper Canada. By 1870 per capita industrial output was 60 percent higher in Ontario than in the two Maritime provinces. Upper Canada had significantly higher investments in machine shops, railways, and iron foundries. Maritime investment bulked relatively greater in wooden ships. Dispersed, small family, subsistence-level farming and fishing, coupled with supplementary mine, shipyard, and wood work failed to generate excess capital for local industrial diversification. Those who did profit, the merchants, chose to invest in a particular way in wooden shipbuilding. This decision led to the continuance of a pre-industrial local economy, even as that type of economy was being transformed in other parts of British North America.

Staples and Society During the Golden Era

Economic trends originating in the 1830s and 1840s continued in Newfoundland. The fishery became increasingly consolidated in the hands of relatively few, generally Protestant, St. John's merchants. Merchants, traders, and professionals made up only 2 percent of the working population in 1857; almost all the rest were employed in the fishery, a proportion that remained constant for the rest of the century. By 1865 there had been a severe decline in old, British-owned outport firms. St. John's merchants worked through independent, small outport merchants who dealt directly with the fishers and their families. The export of fish measured on a per capita basis continued, as one historian has noted, to fluctuate "around a declining trend." Agriculture remained little developed. Perhaps the brightest sector of the economy in these years was the seal fishery: the exploitation of the seal herd even encouraged some merchants to invest in steam ships in order to better navigate through the northern ice flows. Thus of all the Atlantic region colonies, Newfoundland, the one with the least diversification of staple industry and often characterized as the least successful economy, was the first to venture into the modern era of steam and iron vessels.

Prince Edward Island was the only colony to export more foodstuffs than it imported. But problems with land ownership, tenants' rights, and costs of shipments undermined agricultural prosperity at the household level. Shipbuilding and wood work supplemented farm labour throughout the period. Farming in Nova Scotia and New Brunswick failed to generate enough food to feed the region; both colonies imported substantial amounts of wheat and flour. Income distribution remained highly inequitable throughout the farming sector. In some regions of Nova Scotia, one-half of the farm families did not produce enough food to feed their household. Sixty-two percent of all farms in six New Brunswick districts in 1861 were worth less than $500; 12 percent were worth over $2000. Social and economic stratification marked rural Nova Scotia and New Brunswick during the "golden age."

A brief look at the contrasting fates of two rural households in Nova Scotia in the 1850s provides further insight into social conditions in the countryside. John Murray's hundred acre (40 ha) "New Rhynie" farm in Pictou county valued at $3500 in 1851 produced a wide array of products for sale to local markets. Butter, beef, pork, lamb, fowl, potatoes, flour, and oatmeal were sold in 1853 and netted $112 for the year after all farm expenses were paid. The sale of this diversified produce was similar to the practice of many Upper Canadian farmers during this period. The 60-year-old Murray, a member of the local agricultural society and an elder in the local church, was among the elite of rural Pictou County: his wife, Jane, 39 years old, employed a servant in 1851 to help with household chores and the raising of four children under the age of eight. At least two other children attended school. While John left the farm over a hundred times on various buying and selling trips in 1853, Jane's place was clearly at home—she left, so far as we know, only three times in that year.

Also of Pictou County, Ariel Brown, a cordwainer, produced boots and shoes for the local population and farmed six acres (2.5 ha) of cleared land, valued at $200. He, his wife, and family of seven children under 12 years of age were among the poorest of households in their local district. During 13 days in February 1853, his wife and five children died of dysentery. While exceptional, such tragedies were not unknown: dysentery struck the poor and young regularly in this era. Nor was medical help usually available. Even Halifax lacked a full-fledged hospital. After a period of intense grief, Brown remarried but, beset by competition from New England shoe factories, he, his new wife, and two children hit the road. By 1861 he was in Portland, Maine, having moved at least three times and worked at at least five different jobs, twice as his own employer. In fact, he represented the vanguard of Maritimers who would leave the region in search of employment in New England mills or lumber camps. Natural growth accounted for the region's 15 percent population increase in the 1860s. During that decade, 13 000 more people left than arrived, a number that grew dramatically thereafter. Struggling to find decent employment for himself and his son, Brown, like many other Maritimers, took solace in religion "to us a guide and a light to pass through/this Dark vale of Sorrow."

New Brunswick's lumber industry, while recovering from dire predictions of ruin following the end of British protection, never re-achieved the strength of the 1820s. The Reciprocity Treaty and Civil War did provide a strong new market in the United States but costs of production increased in this period and overall profitability declined. Nor did Nova Scotia fare well, despite reciprocity. Her overall exports declined in this period and the fishery, which continued to dominate that colony's economy, provided only a poor and uncertain income for individual families. Relatively few Maritimers flourished during the Golden Era; an estimate of wealth distribution in Nova Scotia in 1871 suggests that 10 percent of the families owned 81 percent of the wealth.

RAILWAYS AND URBANIZATION

Politicians like Joseph Howe were strong proponents of railway construction through much of this period. With other Maritimers, he pushed
unsuccessfully for an intercolonial railway stretching from Halifax to
Quebec City, a railway they hoped would establish that port as British
North America's main entrepôt. Financing from Britain and the Canadian
government was not forthcoming, and maritime promoters had to settle
for shorter internal lines. Even to construct these lines, however, Nova
Scotia and New Brunswick had to contribute significant financing and, in
the case of Nova Scotia, to take ownership of one small line. State
involvement in railroad affairs marked the beginning of a more interven-
tionist-minded government, a government willing to engage in developmental activities. It also helped to create a vested interest fixed to railroad
expansion and the development of locally controlled coal and iron enterprises. Thus in 1858, pushed by Nova Scotia's conservative government,
the Colonial Office rescinded the General Mining Association's monopoly
over local coal mining. By the eve of Confederation, a locally based
economic elite interested in railroad growth, industrial development, and
increased ties to the continental interior, rather than to the oceanic
frontier, had emerged in Nova Scotia and New Brunswick.

Three Atlantic cities exceeded 25 000 people in 1861: St. John's, Halifax,
and Saint John, the latter by far the largest with 38 800 residents. Fire,
rebuilding, and the search for fiscal autonomy occupied the various city
councils. Parts of St. John's burned several times; fire also created havoc in
Saint John in the 1840s. Municipal services—police, fire fighters, water—
were improved, albeit slowly, in most major municipalities. The provincial
state in almost all cases only reluctantly granted fiscal power to municipal
councils and equally reluctantly provided money for infrastructural and
local institutional development.

Major urban centres in Upper and Lower Canada had by 1855 well-
established systems of regional communication via roads, urban newspapers, and telegraphic communication. A similar integration of regional
information had not occurred in Atlantic Canada. Relative to the Canadian
cities, Atlantic Canada's urban places remained aloof from the rural
countryside and smaller towns and villages. Shipping dominated the
economy of most urban centres, and nonlocal market information dominated their newspapers.

The converse, however, was not true. Rural dwellers, beset by hardship,
increasingly looked to urban places as beacons of opportunity. Thousands

of Cape Bretoners, beset by a series of potato crop failures in the late 1840s, sought employment and relief in maritime as well as Lower Canadian and New England urban centres. Halifax carpenters resented the competition constantly offered by rural job seekers. Ariel Brown's first stop was Moncton, New Brunswick, a small urban place of 2600 people in 1851 that because of the shipbuilding boom, seemed to offer economic opportunities. Brown was not alone in his quest for security: almost a quarter of Moncton's households contained two or more families in 1851, and most of those were young, recent immigrants who sought work in the shipbuilding or general industrial sector. A business failure made Brown trek elsewhere. The downturn in shipbuilding in the late 1860s forced many other recent arrivals to do likewise. Like the Canadas, the Atlantic region was marked by individuals and families in motion. In this sense, the barriers between rural and urban were minimal.

The sudden arrival of Irish famine migrants in the mid-1840s sparked Orange (Protestant) and Catholic Irish conflict. Orange lodges grew dramatically in that decade in New Brunswick. In fact, sectarian violence in Saint John was a major catalyst for the creation of a professional police force. Urban justice tended to favour white Protestants over other ethnic groups; Catholic Irish rioters were generally more severely dealt with than were their Protestant antagonists.

Since most major urban centres were situated on the sea, itinerant sailors formed a significant portion of society. Local residents regarded sailors as low-life vagabonds who frequented rough waterfront districts in search of liquor and women. Reality was somewhat different. Maritime cities, in fact, dealt harshly with visiting sailors; they were much slower than other national ports to provide special medical facilities for injured and sick sailors. Local ordinances made it difficult for sailors to find accommodation away from waterfront boarding houses, which often doubled as sites of gambling and prostitution. Residential centralization also made it easier for boarding home owners to help organize crimping activities—the kidnapping and impressment of sailors. Sailors had few support systems when in maritime ports in this era.

Sailors and soldiers regularly stationed at the garrison in Halifax often entered into temporary family liaisons with local women. Along with their offspring, these women faced a difficult and uncertain future once the sailor or soldier left. In part because of this social situation, Halifax had many prostitutes who, over time, developed their own communities in seedy waterfront areas. As the historian Judith Fingard noted, "Prostitutes lived together, worked together, drank together, went to court and jail together." Bawdy houses, jail houses, and courts formed their institutional context, prostitution their only way to survive. Mary Young declared in 1862: "I know no other means of getting a livelihood without sleeping with men."[6]

INSTITUTIONAL CULTURE

Religion played an important role in the lives of people on the Atlantic coast. The conflict in Saint John between Protestants and Catholics occurred in a less violent form in Halifax, where, after the Irish famine immigration, 40 percent was Catholic and throughout Newfoundland, where the population was about equally divided between English Protestant and Irish Catholic. Halifax boasted 25 churches in the 1860s. Catholics and Protestants formed separate urban missionary efforts to uplift prostitutes and others who lived in "the very worst and most destitute localities of the city." The fact that most people in those districts were themselves Catholics led many to link the underclass and Catholicism in unfavourable ways. Sectarian bias permeated the city.

Religion was no less important in the countryside. We have seen how Ariel Brown's deep Protestant faith comforted him during his tragic life. Yet, as in the city, various churches sent different and often conflicting messages. If one Calvinist Presbyterian minister could justify Cape Breton's potato famine as God's punishment for "unthriftiness and offensive indolence," and a Catholic priest could defend proprietor's rights against those of Prince Edward Island tenants, other evangelical preachers were more sympathetic to the poor and critical of the elite. Social class

---

[6] For shipping, see E. Sager with G. Panting, *Maritime Capital: The Shipping Industry in Maritime Canada, 1820–1914* (Kingston, 1990). For agriculture, see footnote 11, Chapter 6. For mobility in the Maritimes, see G. Wynn, ed., "This Dark Vale of Sorrow," *Nova Scotia Historical Review* (1986), 55–62 and P.A. Thornton, "The Problem of Out-Migration from Atlantic Canada, 1871–1921," *Acadiensis* 15 (1985). For the Nova Scotia economy in the early 1850s, see J. Gwyn, "'A Little Province Like This': The Economy of Nova Scotia under Stress, 1812–53," *Canadian Papers in Rural History* 6 (1988), 192–225. For an introduction to railway policy, see R. Langhout, "Developing Nova Scotia: Railways and Public Accounts, 1848–1867," *Acadiensis* 14 (1985). Urban life and politics are treated in T. W. Acheson, *Saint John: The Making of a Colonial Urban Community* (Toronto, 1985) and J. Fingard, *The Dark Side of Life in Victorian Halifax* (Nova Scotia, 1989).

divisions in the countryside may have been supported by different religious denominations. While the impact of religion was profound, in complex ways it was constrained and influenced by matters of ethnicity (especially Irish) and class.

As in the Canadas, schooling was seen, by those who superintended it, as "a necessity, as preventative. . .of crime [and] as underlying the sources of productive industry and consequently the prosperity of the country." With these objectives in mind, formal schooling did spread throughout the Atlantic region. The bitter religious conflict that swept the Atlantic colonies in this period complicated the enactment of public schooling. Compounding Catholic-Protestant enmity was the reality that in Newfoundland especially and in the other colonies to a lesser extent, a substantial middle class did not exist from which to draw tax revenue for the support of a public school system. In Newfoundland, grants-in-aid drawn from fluctuating custom duties had to suffice. Despite religious conflict and financial difficulties, Prince Edward Island may have been the first colony in the British Empire to introduce "a complete system of free education" in 1852, followed in the Maritimes by Nova Scotia in 1864 and New Brunswick in 1871. Most colleges or institutions of higher education remained under the control of various churches. The immediate result of Prince Edward Island's initiative strongly suggests that the rural people desired affordable education; by 1854 the number of enrolled students had doubled, and their attendance in proportion to population was one-third higher than that of New Brunswick and Nova Scotia.

The extent and duration of school attendance in the rural Maritimes was probably not high given the economic problems of maintaining rural households. It may be that some rural families used the school system as a means for bettering their daughters, many of whom became teachers in this period. The nature of the household economy in Newfoundland, however, militated against even this degree of participation. Girls helped their mothers at home and in the curing of fish. Boys went with their fathers in the fishing boats. Few of either sex attended school after the age of eleven or twelve. Yet even in Newfoundland, if more slowly than on the mainland, women became teachers, encouraged as one inspector explained in the 1850s, because they required "a smaller salary for their maintenance than males." Newfoundland women contributed to the colony's central staple enterprise. By accepting a lower wage than men, they helped raise the educational level of that colony, although measured in terms of literacy, Newfoundland's population lagged far behind that of other nineteenth-century British North American colonies.[7]

As in the Canadas, asylums, hospitals, work houses and penitentiaries all were built in this period and enjoyed the same failure to meet elite expectations. It would take more than institutions to effectively change the oppressive lives of the struggling majority of Atlantic residents during the "golden age."

POLITICS AND SOCIETY

In a general sense, political developments in the Atlantic region in the later pre-Confederation period parallelled events in the Canadas: parties developed; a stronger executive emerged; government's role expanded in social and especially economic sectors; sectarian strife and class conflict underlay political division. As before the mid-1840s, these general trends evolved in different ways in each colony, emerging, as they did, from different social and economic contexts.

Nova Scotia's political development at times set the stage for Canadian events and at times followed central Canadian precedents. In the 1840s a Reform Party, managed by Joseph Howe, and a Conservative Party, led by J. W. Johnston, emerged as fairly cohesive opposing forces. When Sir John Harvey arrived as lieutenant-governor in 1846 determined to effect a nonparty coalition, he and the Colonial Office that supported him were out of touch with the times. From the Colonial Office's viewpoint, responsible government managed by an executive council of ministers was possible for the larger province of Canada but was inappropriate for smaller colonies like Nova Scotia and other Atlantic region jurisdictions. Political events in Nova Scotia forced Harvey and the Colonial Office to change their minds and accept, after a victorious Reform victory in 1847, the first "administration based on party in British North America." By 1849, the reformers had transformed the executive council into a cabinet of ministers and had doled out substantial amounts of patronage at the expense of conservative supporters. The assembly did retain some control over money bills, so centralization of power occurred more slowly in Nova

---

[7] P. McCann, "Class, Gender and Religion in Newfoundland Education, 1836–1901," *Historical Studies in Education*, 1/2 (1989) and I. R. Robertson, "Reform, Literacy and the Lease: The Prince Edward Island Free Education Act of 1852," *Acadiensis* 20 (1990), 52–71, are good introductions to aspects of educational policy in this period.

Scotia than in the Canadas. Nevertheless, the reality of responsible government and party management in Nova Scotia meant that the Colonial Office could delay but not prevent rising pressure for similar systems in the other Atlantic colonies.

The Reform governments of the 1850s (the opposition held power only briefly in the latter part of the decade) were conservative in their social policy and active in economic measures. Railroads received strong support, and by 1864 per capita indebtedness had increased by more than tenfold. As in the Canadas, a development-minded administration had mortgaged the colony's future. The reformers were much more cost conscious in the area of education. Not until a conservative administration under Charles Tupper achieved power in 1864 did Nova Scotia exhibit a similar activist policy in education by creating a publicly financed school system.

As the historian Phil Buckner has suggested, Joseph Howe, the preeminent reformer in Nova Scotia in this period, closely resembled George Brown of Upper Canada. Both men were editors of major newspapers situated in the most dominant and expanding urban centre in their provinces. Both reflected the attitudes of the expansive urban, commercial/industrial elite of their cities. Both opposed universal male franchise. Both exhibited strong anti-Catholic attitudes. In Brown's case, this prevented him from heading a Canadian administration for longer than two days. In Howe's case, it led to the overthrow of the Reformers in 1857 after he had publicly villified Catholics and advocated the formation of a Protestant party to safeguard society from the "Papists." In all of this, Howe and Brown and the Reformers who followed them exhibited many of the beliefs of mid-Victorian British liberalism. Responsible government co-existed comfortably with such elitist, sectarian and anti-democratic views. Nor were such attitudes limited to the Canadas and Nova Scotia.

Political developments in New Brunswick demonstrate how responsible government was at the same time a movement toward democracy and a measure for the centralization of power. Even though New Brunswick's executive council had been drawn from the assembly in the late 1830s and early 1840s, responsible government, as we understand the term today, was still not in place. Those who sat in the executive council were not beholden to a majority party in the assembly and were not bound to act as a cohesive group. Nor did all holding ministerial positions sit on the council. In this context, the lieutenant-governor could continue to pick policy options from among those put forward by individual councillors and, in effect, act as a prime minister. Assembly members rested content with this strong degree of imperial representation in New Brunswick's political affairs because financial control rested in their hands. Responsible government would curtail their powers of financial appropriation. Assemblymen argued that if the executive obtained the right to initiate money bills and to impose a strict party system of government, then their individual democratic rights would be infringed.

This system persisted until the mid-1850s because political parties developed slowly in New Brunswick. The financial power enjoyed by individual assemblymen gave them much scope for the exercise of the art of brokerage. Judicious and timely expenditures at the constituency level forestalled the emergence of volatile religious, ethnic or economic grievances until the mid-1850s. Both leaders of the Anglican and Roman Catholic churches were, in comparison to those in many other colonies, moderate-minded, consensus-oriented men who counselled compromise in matters of ethnic and denominational rivalry. Economic discontent, because of the abolition of timber preferences, did arise in the late 1840s, but the major policy disagreement concerned tariff implementation, and that issue cut across rather than solidified party groupings.

By the early 1850s, a small faction of middle-class, commercially oriented politicians did argue for responsible government and the executive's right to initiate money bills. Such issues failed to excite the electorate's imagination. Temperance agitation did. Sixteen new members entered the assembly in 1854, and most followed reformers like Charles Fisher in favour of responsible government, Samuel Tilley, in favour of temperance, and William Ritchie, in favour of railroad promotion. The old Family Compact, Loyalist families were quickly outvoted and, for the first time, the executive council became the preserve of one party.

Like the bourgeois-oriented party that emerged in the Canadas, the Fisher-Tilly Reformers believed in an activist government: they extended the franchise, but only a little; weakened the legislative council; consolidated financial control in the executive's hands; provided financial support for railroad construction; and passed a Prohibition Act. The latter proved impossible to enforce and caused their resignation and the election of the old Conservatives virtually on a one-plank platform of repeal of prohibition. After acting on that plank, the Conservatives lost control of the assembly, and in 1857 the Reformers were re-elected and retained power for the next eight years.

Temperance is generally seen as the issue that solidified party groupings in New Brunswick. For the first time, the electorate could choose between two clearcut platforms. Most made their choice on the basis of the moral teachings of their religion. Anglicans and Presbyterians voted for the Conservative, anti-temperance slate; Methodists and Baptists voted Reform; Catholics, traditionally pro-reform, had great difficulty on the temperance issue and, where possible, voted a nonparty ticket. Yet the transition to party voting was gradual: most of those who voted for or against temperance in 1856 and 1857 voted, as one close student of this period has written, "for men who were, in fact, very like themselves," men whom they had supported in the past when they had run as individuals and for whom they would vote in the future when they ran as party members. In this sense, the temperance issue helped create a more sophisticated political electorate.

One final point deserves comment concerning temperance and politics in New Brunswick. That issue provides a dramatic example of the active role that women could play in politics in the mid-nineteenth century. Although unable to vote, women could and did petition government on a wide range of issues. They were particularly active on moral matters like temperance, and their pressure was instrumental in pushing the Reformers to pass the Prohibition Bill. Although prohibition ultimately failed, the point remains that New Brunswick women had crossed the threshold of the household and entered the political arena.

The 20 years following the imposition of the Newfoundland Act in 1842 were pivotal ones in Newfoundland's political history. Responsible government was attained in 1855; clerical involvement in politics and sectarian violence peaked in 1861; the beginnings of a local political culture, one that in some ways bridged religious, ethnic, and class divisions, emerged.

Lieutenant-Governor Frederic Harvey, self-proclaimed "Peace Maker," used the substantial power available to him under the imposed constitution of 1842 to calm dissent and began to encourage the growth of a political perspective or culture that would include within it loyalty to the Crown as well as attachment to the colony. He supported the newly founded Native's Society, composed of middle-class Newfoundlanders who saw the island as their home and the monarch as their leader; temperance organizations, which preached total abstinence in drink and moderation in all other pursuits; and literary societies and mechanics institutes designed to ameliorate intemperate and radical attitudes. He also sponsored many public displays of loyalty to the Queen of England attended by all classes, religions, and ethnic groups. A useful comparison here is to Upper Canada, which attempted through its educational system to construct a political culture amenable to bourgeois goals of economic progress. Given Newfoundland's weak educational system, Harvey sought the same result through different agencies.

He made progress in marrying public commitment to the British Empire with loyalty to a developing Newfoundland. Sectarian strife and political dissent, however, remained strong despite the passage of the Education Act of 1843, which created state-funded Catholic and Protestant schools and the implementation of state-funded poor relief the same year. By 1847 it had become clear that the Newfoundland Act could not bind the colony's many factions into a stable whole and the assembly and conciliar system re-emerged.

The Liberal Catholics held about 60 percent of the seats in the first two assemblies and made reciprocity and responsible government their key planks. By 1855 they had achieved both, yet their hold on power was none the less precarious. Relations with their premier vote getter, the outspoken Roman Catholic bishop, John Mullock, deteriorated throughout the 1850s. Mullock had dared to characterize the pre-responsible government situation as "irresponsible driveling despotism...depending for support on bigotry and bribery." He became disenchanted with the Reformers, in part because they were slow in implementing what he considered to be needed reforms and in part because, through government-administered poor relief funds, they seemed to be acquiring independent control at the constituency level, often at the expense of the Catholic Church. Even as the Reform Party struggled with internal divisions, the Tory Party worked to conciliate a growing Methodist group that had in the past voted Reform. Reform Catholic fears mounted when the 1857 census revealed that Protestants outnumbered Catholics 64 000 to 55 000. Events came to a head at a riotous election in 1861, which was followed by a four-hour siege of the assembly, the calling out of troops, the shooting deaths of several people, the stoning of the Anglican bishop, and the destruction of property owned by the Conservative Party's leader.

When the dust settled, even Bishop Mullock realized that moderation was required. The victorious Conservative leader, Hugh Hoyles, agreed and began to distribute patronage according to the numerical strength of the various religious denominations and invited Liberal Catholics to take office in his government. These actions helped to diffuse the violent sectarian nature of Newfoundland politics. It became increasingly difficult to identify Reformers as Catholics and Conservatives as Protestants. Both parties sought and required a broader spectrum of support in subsequent years.

The study of Prince Edward Island's politics in the volatile pre-Confederation period underlines the complex intertwining of class and religion as codeterminants of political behaviour in British North America in the mid-nineteenth century. Following the collapse of the Escheat Party in 1842, the colony's entrepreneurially minded, middle-class politicians, those who desired a stable and vibrant local economy in which to sell their products, searched for more moderate ways to reform the land question. By the late 1840s, a reform group led by George Coles, a local merchant and manufacturer, had focused on responsible government as the best means of achieving reform unity and, perhaps, of allowing the beleaguered tenants some power in the political arena. A reluctant Colonial Office granted responsible government in 1851 but remained determined to protect the rights of absentee land owners.

The passage of the Free Education Act, the widening of the franchise (1855), and the implementation of the Land Purchase Act (1853) did promise significant benefit for rural dwellers. Three other measures designed to ease the grip absentee landowners had on the colony were overturned by the Colonial Office. And the only purchase made under the Land Purchase Act ended in scandal when local agents of the absentee proprietor skimmed £10 000 off the sale. Other landowners refused to sell. The Reform policy of gradualism, compensation, and resale to tenants had accomplished little; squatters and tenants comprised 60 percent of all land occupiers in 1861.

Following the granting of responsible government, a Conservative group led by Edward Palmer, the son of the leader of the Loyal electors in 1812, slowly realized that attempts to reinstate the old political system were unlikely to achieve either local or colonial government support. At the same time, they, like the Colonial Office, remained determined to uphold the status quo in the land arena. They seized on some inadvertent, but incendiary, comments made by a Roman Catholic bishop in 1856 concerning the reading of the Bible in the publicly funded school system to divert attention from land problems. Thanks to Coles's failure at several crucial points to handle effectively the so-called Bible question, Palmer was able to cynically manipulate religious beliefs and fears strongly held by Prince Edward Island's electorate.

Of Palmer's cynicism in this regard there can be little doubt. Equally, there can be no doubt that Protestant-Catholic enmity was deeply rooted in the colony's countryside, of whom 55 percent were Protestants and 45 percent Catholic, the majority of the latter Irish, Acadian, and Scots

Highlanders. In 1859 Palmer's party took power, and no Catholic sat with them. He passed a measure that sanctioned Bible reading but permitted opting out. Sectarian controversy, however, was quieted only temporarily. Not until 1876 would church roles in the public education system be finally resolved.

Palmer's party had little constructive to offer in terms of resolving the land issue. He referred the matter to a Land Commission, which advocated the old Reform policy, but once again the Colonial Office, despite a trip by Palmer to England to defend the commission's resolutions, refused to sanction the policy. The Confederation debates seemed to provide a further pretext for doing nothing. In 1864 a frustrated group of more radically inclined and populist-minded land reformers organized the Tenants League and began to advocate civil disobedience. Neither the Reformers, who desired a stable market place, nor the Conservatives could support such initiatives. It was an all-too-common juxtaposition: matters of religion and nationalism were used by a political elite to blunt and forestall more radical economic and social reform.[8]

Monopoly's Demise: Transforming the Fur Frontier, 1840–64

INTRODUCTION

Measured by population statistics, the Métis were clearly the most vital and expansive of the prairie people in the middle years of the nineteenth

---

[8] A modern synthesis of Atlantic Canada's political history in this period is required. For an overview covering part of the period from the British perspective, see P. Buckner, *The Transition to Responsible Government*. Once again *The Dictionary of Canadian Biography* must be consulted for information on leading politicians from all the Atlantic colonies. Volumes 8, 9, 10, and 12 are especially valuable. Other work on Nova Scotia includes: J. M. Beck, *Joseph House*, Vol. 2 (Montreal, 1983); on New Brunswick, Gail G. Campbell, "'Smashers' and 'Rummies': Voters and the Rise of Parties in Charlotte County, New Brunswick, 1846–1857," *Historical Papers* (1986), 86–116; "Disfranchised but not Quiescent: Women Petitioners in New Brunswick in the Mid-19th Century," *Acadiensis*, Spring, 1989, 24–54, and "The Most Restrictive Franchise in British North America? A Case Study," *CHR*, LXXI, 2 (1990), 159–89; Newfoundland: P. McCann, "Culture, State Formation and the Invention of Tradition: Newfoundland, 1832–55," *JCS*, 23, 1 & 2 (1988), 86–103; G. E. Gunn, *The Political History of Newfoundland* (Toronto, 1966); and on Prince Edward Island, Ian Ross Robertson, ed., *The Prince Edward Island Commission* (Fredericton, 1988) and "The Bible Question in Prince Edward Island from 1856–1860," in P. Buckner and D. Frank, ed., *The Acadiensis Reader*, 1 (Fredericton, 1985), 261–83.

century. At Red River they increased from 6000 in 1845 to 9800 in 1871; 58 percent were French speaking and 42 percent English speaking. Native people declined to between 25 000 and 35 000, while the white population remained little changed, numbering under 2000 in the early 1870s.

More dramatic population swings occurred west of the Rockies. The native population probably exceeded that of the Prairies in 1870. The white population swelled from a relative handful in the mid-1850s to over 30 000 in 1858 because of a gold rush on the Fraser River, dropping off to 10 500 in 1871. A Hudson's Bay Company sponsored settlement struck roots at Victoria on Vancouver Island, which by the mid-1850s represented the largest concentration of non-natives west of Red River and surpassed in size white settlements in neighbouring Washington Territory.

These population trends call into question two commonly held assumptions: one, that white settlement expanded in a linear east-west fashion; and two, that so-called "progressive" economic development proceeded in a similar lock-step manner. Even on the Prairies, population growth and economic development did not proceed in that way. The area north and west of Lake Winnipeg developed separately from and parallel with the area between that lake and Lake Superior. West of the Rockies, white settlement fluctuated in response to local economic circumstances, a process quite distinct from that of the Prairies. By 1870, British Columbia's white population was about four times greater than that east of the Rockies and west of Lake Superior. In this period, the Hudson's Bay Company probably promoted a wider range of economic enterprises on the coast than on the Prairies. Indeed, the company's transformation from a purely fur-trade-based enterprise to one willing to diversify into land development, retailing, and resource ventures, a move given corporate sanction in 1871, owed more to experimentation on the coast than to developments further east. Finally, and related to the differential rates of population growth and economic development, the life experience of native peoples varied not simply between the coastal and prairie regions, but also within each region.

Challenge at the Core: "Le Commerce est libre"

From the Hudson's Bay Company's perspective, there were too many people in Red River by the mid-1840s. The company could not profitably employ them all. Frosts, floods, droughts, mice, blackbirds, pigeons, and locusts meant that full-time farming could feed few households. Between 1812 and 1870, there were over 30 reports of serious crop failures. Unemployed, able-bodied men presented potential competition to the company's control of the fur trade. Even before the 1830s, George Simpson, the Hudson's Bay Company's manager, had granted several merchants licences to trade in furs in the expectation that they would sell them to his

This photograph of Wegwan, a Métis who lived near Red River, was taken in 1858.
NATIONAL ARCHIVES OF CANADA/C16447

company and not to Americans. In 1841 he encouraged 23 families to push west to the Columbia River in a futile attempt to reduce Red River's population. When in 1844 Norman Kittson, an American fur trader, established a post at Pembina, 112.5 km south of Red River and entered into a vigorous trade with Red River merchants James Sinclair and Andrew McDermott, Simpson tightened his grasp. He denied independent merchants the use of Hudson's Bay Company's boats; read their mail; terminated their trading licences; and successfully solicited troops from the imperial government, ostensibly to protect Red River from American expansion during the Oregon Crisis, but really to police the settlement. Unfortunately for Simpson, the troops stayed only a little over a year, leaving in 1848. Moreover, his restrictive measures stirred up widespread opposition. Two Métis, James Sinclair and Alexander Isbister, presented a petition signed by 1000 Red River residents to the Colonial Office in 1847 decrying the company's high-handed measures.

When the Colonial Office ignored them, pressure mounted within the settlement. Protests against restricted trade expanded to include demands for more adequate bi-racial representation on the governing council, for subsidized Catholic schooling, and for fairer judicial appointments—the highest judicial officer in Assiniboia, Adam Thom, was a racist who had confided to Simpson his belief that the French possessed 1/100 of the intelligence and abilities of the Anglo-Saxon and the Métis even less. The landmark test of the Hudson's Bay Company's ability to control rising dissent at Red River took place in 1849. Pierre-Guillaume Sayer and three others were arrested for illegal trading in furs and brought before the district's highest court. Armed and angry Métis, led by Louis Riel senior, massed outside. The jury found Sayer, who was defended by Sinclair, guilty but recommended mercy on the improbable grounds that the accused had misunderstood the law. The court accepted the pretext and, by freeing Sayer, freed as well Red River's commerce from Hudson's Bay Company control.

Even as they chanted "le commerce est libre," the jubilant Métis began to push for more concessions. In 1850, French-speaking magistrates were appointed. Adam Thom was demoted. In 1851, an annual grant to Catholic schools commenced. Métis representation on the 15-person governing council increased, although they never numbered more than five at any one time, and of the 14 who sat on the council between 1850 and 1870 only four were free of Hudson's Bay ties and three of those were clerics. Radicals received no representation.

While political rights were granted grudgingly, if at all, commercial freedom seemed unrestrained. By 1855 some 400 Métis transporters followed "the cart line" between Red River and St Paul. In 1856, Kittson, now married to a Métis, set up a general store in St. Boniface and, along with other merchants, shipped £120 000 worth of fur to St. Paul the following year. By 1858 four American rail lines reached the Red River's banks, and 62 steamboats had made 1000 trips from St. Paul to Red River.

Prairie Natives in the "Free Trade" Era, 1840–1870

It is common to view the period following 1840 as one of increasing erosion of native independence, culture, and self-reliance. Most historians see the 1840s and 1850s as benchmarks signalling the end of nondirected cultural change and the beginning of a long period of declining economic opportunity and directed cultural change. An impressive amount of evidence is available to support this view. Missionary activity escalated in these decades: Wesleyan Methodists, Anglicans, and Roman Catholics vied with each other in seeking Hudson's Bay Company support to proselytize natives. One historian has described this competition as the "Race to the Northern Sea." In many areas, too, natives, like the Riding Mountain Ojibwa, became dependent on the Hudson's Bay Company. They traded fur for food and became, in the process, virtually company employees tied by the truck system to the large mercantile firm. Other plains natives suffered both economic and military incursions at the hands of the Métis. In organized fashion and aided by the large carrying capacity of their red river carts, the Métis became one of the premier prairie hunting peoples, supplanting natives as major suppliers of food to the fur trade. After a dramatic military victory over the Sioux in 1851 at the Battle of Grant Coteau, Métis military might had also to be respected. American hunters and settlers to the South provided further grave threats to native autonomy. Moreover, Plains natives, struggling for control over ever-diminishing space and declining food resources, engaged in major battles among themselves, culminating in the Cree-Blackfoot wars of the late 1860s. Thus a Cree leader, Chief Sweet Grass, could petition for relief in 1871: "We are poor and want help—we want you to pity us...our country is no longer able to support us."

These enormous pressures on prairie natives can not and must not be dismissed. Yet what requires closer attention is the variety of native responses, the surprising persistence of traditional behaviours, and the adaptability of native cultures in the face of the ever-encroaching missionary and agricultural and industrial frontiers. Two general points can be made here. The first is that native culture should not be viewed as a static whole. Cultures demonstrate vitality by adapting to change. Native cultures had been adapting to change for centuries before the arrival of Europeans. While pressure for dramatic change may have been greater in the mid-nineteenth century, the idea of change and adaptation was not new. Secondly, the various pressures exerted on the native peoples were not all of a piece. Missionaries and Hudson's Bay traders were often at odds. For the most part, Hudson's Bay people looked askance at missionaries and suffered their presence in order to protect their trading monopoly from further criticism in England. In fact, after the revocation of the company's monopoly in 1859, Simpson virtually withdrew support for missionary activity.

Native adaptation and uneasy fur trade–missionary relations set the context for proselytizing on the Prairies. Fur traders resisted missionary attempts to set up agricultural settlements, especially when native trappers employed by the company were involved. Despite these road blocks and despite differences of approach between the various denominations—the Methodist initiative fluctuated dramatically in these years; other Protestant faiths remained "palisade bound"; the Catholics moved most widely over the Prairies—native peoples were attracted by missionary activity. Yet few became the farmers desired by missionaries. And what is more indicative of the resiliency and adaptability of native cultures is that many took from Christian doctrine that which seemed to fit best within their traditional lifestyle. Abishabis, a Cree religious leader, spread just such a synthesized message until his murder in 1843. His memory and message lived on. An anthropologist interviewing Moose Factory natives 90 years later discovered that they attributed the introduction of Christianity to Abishabis and had no recollection of white missionary activity!

A similar resilience and ability to adapt to change is apparent in the economic sphere. By the late 1850s, the Hudson's Bay Company had come to depend primarily on natives to run their transport system. Mutinies and strikes were commonplace. As one frustrated trader complained, "Tis a perfect plague having every year a lot of men giving notice of retirement, and a ceremony of talk and palaver with them annually, knowing that they have it in their power to distress you. . . ." The natives at Norway House successfully integrated Hudson's Bay Company work with traditional subsistence routines. Historians have yet to recognize fully the strengths of native resistance and the creativity of native adaptation in this period. Until they do, white understanding of native resistance today will be incomplete, perhaps tragically so.

Coastal Concerns, 1845–1858

American challenges to Hudson's Bay Company sovereignty were not unique to Red River. As early as the 1830s, Governor Simpson had dealt with what he termed "worthless and lawless characters of every description from the United States," in the Columbia River district. In 1843, three years before the resolution of the Oregon Crisis, Simpson had "prepared for the worst" and commenced construction of a new coastal headquarters, Fort Victoria, on the southwestern tip of Vancouver Island. As chief factor, James Douglas began to consolidate the company's operation. The British government sought a more permanent resolution of the coastal situation by setting up a Crown colony on the island in the hopes of blocking American northern expansion. The Hudson's Bay Company agreed to oversee this colonization project and was given a five-year grant to island lands: 90 percent of the sales revenues went to the colony's upkeep and 10 percent into the company's pockets. The company also agreed to relinquish its trading monopoly on the island. Because of the upset price of £1 per acre, the stipulation that at least 20 acres (8 ha) of Vancouver Island land had to be bought at one time, and a comparison with land south of the border that was virtually free, historians claim the company blocked settlement and opposed diversified economic growth in order to protect its fur trade operations. According to this sleepy hamlet version of island development, Victoria and other island communities, to the extent that they grew at all, consisted simply of retired and often cantankerous fur traders. Recent research has qualified this view, however. In fact, the Colonial Office, not the Hudson's Bay Company, set the policy concerning land sales. The Colonial Office believed that land should be priced just out of reach of the average settler in order to ensure the existence of a colonial landless proletariat ready to develop other people's properties. Such a policy would lead to the suitably restricted and stratified society desired by British policymakers.

Simpson and Douglas did not object to social stratification, but they did object to the impracticality of the Colonial Office's scheme. In practice they mitigated the official program by adopting a three-tiered sales policy that allowed small city lots to be purchased for £10, larger suburban lots for £25, and 20-acre (8 ha) country lots for £100. They instituted an instalment purchase plan, granted 20-acre (8 ha) allotments to retiring Hudson's Bay Company traders and permitted liberal allowances for rock and swamp when charging for country lots. By 1857, 180 settlers had purchased some 17 000 (6880 ha) acres of land on southern Vancouver Island. By the same date, probably over 900 people of European origin resided on the island.

Just as the company adopted a relatively flexible policy concerning land sales, so, too, it embarked upon a fairly wide-ranging commercial program of resource development. Sensitive to the winds of change that were sweeping the area and doubtless influenced by concurrent pressures in the Red River region, Simpson realized that the company had to broaden its operations and concentrate less on fur and more on agriculture, lumbering, salmon fishing, whaling, and mining. In the 1850s, the company engaged in all these activities and permitted its employees to set up private concerns as well. While most of the 180 people who purchased land on southern Vancouver Island had been affiliated with the Hudson's Bay Company, the diversity of their occupations suggests that the company was much more than a simple fur-trading concern. Individual careers also spanned many occupations: J. W. Mckay, a Hudson's Bay employee, noted in 1872 that he had "been Sailor, Farmer, Coal Miner, packer, Salesman, Surveyor, explorer, Fur Trader and Accountant in Your Service." Moreover the company and private individuals traded with the Sandwich Islands, San Francisco, Alaska, mainland British Columbia, and Great Britain. This diversified commercial program predated by some 20 years the company's 1871 decision to adopt a wide-ranging commercial strategy for the rest of its operations.

As in Red River, the company exhibited little such flexibility in political and social matters. Although Vancouver Island received the first elected assembly west of the Canadas in 1856, the franchise requirements were extremely high (higher than Douglas desired). Thus a small elite of Hudson's Bay personnel enjoyed, as they did at Red River, political power over a wider and more ethnically and occupationally diverse nonvoting populace.

Monopoly's Demise: Red River, 1857–1864

Despite Douglas's best efforts, the extent of West Coast settlement and commercial development satisfied few, and the extent of the company's political control angered many. This dissatisfaction dovetailed with rising discontent concerning the company's management of Red River affairs. In a broader context the fur company's ancient monopoly seemed out of step with Britain's official free trade policy. In 1857, the British Parliament struck a committee of investigation. It resulted in the transfer of Vancouver Island to the Crown and the loss of the company's trading monopoly on the Prairies and in mainland British Columbia.

For many interested observers, however, more was at stake than the fate of the Hudson's Bay Company's monopoly. Minnesotans claimed it was their manifest destiny to appropriate Red River for the United States. Even as Minnesota merchants moved north, land-hungry farmers from Upper Canada began to trek west. Excited by expansionist-minded Upper Canadian politicians and newspaper editors like George Brown, by the optimistic reading of the reports of two scientific surveying expeditions in the late 1850s—the Palliser and Hinds/Dawson expeditions—and frustrated by the lack of available good arable land in Upper Canada, many looked to the west as a new frontier. Aggressive Toronto businesspeople joined with Métis Red River entrepreneurs to form the North-West Transportation Navigation and Railway Company in 1858. It obtained a charter to ship mail and goods from Toronto directly to Red River. That settlement and its hinterland had fast become central to several "manifest destinies": that of the resident bi-racial peoples; of Minnesota expansionists; and of central Canadians on the make.

Some of the central Canadians did their best to poison the political and cultural climate at Red River in the early 1860s. Several arrivals from Upper Canada, Dr. John Schultz, William Caldwell, and William Buckingham prominent among them, started a newspaper, the *Nor'Wester*, a name intentionally selected to excite memories of central Canada's direct links to the West and direct competition with the Hudson's Bay Company. The paper attacked company control and disparaged Métis intelligence. Rifts within the settlement ran deep in the 1860s. A prominent Anglican missionary, popular among the English-natives, was convicted of attempting (five times) to induce an abortion on his 16-year-old servant girl who was carrying his child. When jailed, English-native vigilantes freed him. The Hudson's Bay Company looked on, impotently.

By 1864 Red River and its hinterland, lacking a government, had attracted many suitors for the position. Only Sioux violence on Minnesota's northern frontier and the Civil War stymied expansion from the South. Part of the Upper Canadian drive to confederate stemmed from the realization that this breathing space was only temporary. By 1864, the Colonial Office began to apply increased pressure on the Hudson's Bay Company and the Province of Canada to come to an agreement on the transferral of political power in the West. The bi-racial people of Red River, able and willing to govern themselves, were on the eve of oblivion. The West was about to be claimed by forces that had never been a central part of its past: citizens of an agricultural and industrial world were flexing their muscles. If Red River had been but a nascent threat in the 1820s to the Métis and native peoples of the West, that threat had become full grown by 1864.

Monopoly's Demise: Governing Gold Diggers, 1858–1866

The discovery of gold on the Fraser River in 1857 and the influx of 30 000 gold seekers the following year accelerated trends already visible on the coast. Late in 1858, Douglas formally quit as chief factor of the company's Vancouver Island operations and became the Crown's representative for the island and the mainland. During the gold rush, the Hudson's Bay Company acted as a general retailer and wholesaler of goods to miners. It also took advantage of its continuing control of Victoria lands (as per the 1858 transfer agreement), and by 1862 had netted over $300 000 in profit from their sale. This marked the company's debut as a retailer of urban land in British North America. Its success undoubtedly whet the appetite of a syndicate of entrepreneurs and land speculators called the International Financial Society, which purchased the Hudson's Bay Company from its old fur trade masters in 1863. Once again events on the coast precipitated change at centres of eastern power.

As the Crown's representative west of the Rockies, Douglas faced an awesome task: that of governing a potentially unruly mass of young, single, male miners in pursuit of a quick fortune. To benefit Victoria's merchants, maintain high prices for local land, and exert some control over the influx of fortune seekers, he made Victoria and Nanaimo the only free trade ports on the coast and, for a time, required all miners to obtain a licence at Victoria. The Colonial Office supplemented these measures by instituting a system of Gold Commissioners who travelled to mainland mining camps collecting fees and hearing minor civil suits; setting up a circuit court system under the dynamic and forceful control of Matthew B. Begbie; and sending a force of Royal Engineers to help construct roads and upgrade communication systems.

How successful were these measures in controlling a potentially unruly population? "It is clear," Begbie affirmed in 1861, "that the inhabitants almost universally respect and obey the laws," especially when compared to other gold-mining regions. Most historians have echoed Begbie's assertions. Yet recent work by an historian, Tina Loo, forces a reconsideration. Her calculation of a homicide rate parallels that found in other gold camps in San Francisco, Australia, and New Zealand and far exceeds that of mid-nineteenth century England. Moreover, violence of a lesser order seemed equally prevalent: armed skirmishes and battles among natives trading at Victoria; clashes between Vancouver Island settlers and resident natives over grazing rights; robbery in the interior mining camps; or, drinking,

This anonymous drawing of early Yale neatly captures the rough and tumble nature of British Columbia goldrush towns.   NATIONAL ARCHIVES OF CANADA/C2824

brawling and organized prostitution rings in Victoria, a town one contemporary described as "a Rising Sodom on Vancouver's Island."

Loo has also documented extensive use of the courts for civil matters, especially concerning the collection of commercial debts. Against a backdrop of a society without community bonds—few women, families, friends, or permanent settlements—courts and violence became dual forums for the resolution of disputes. Given the "bondlessness" of the society, more informal, less adversarial means for dispute reconciliation did not exist. At base, most of British Columbia's mining population and especially the merchants, saloon keepers, and even barbers that served that community sought some stability and protection while they pursued profit. For most, dispute resolution by courts was preferable to resolution by violence. But both mechanisms were well used, and both emerged from and reflected the characteristics of British Columbia's society of young rootless gold seekers and the prostitutes, saloon keepers, and merchants who serviced them. A common desire for profit and a web of credit and debt were the ties that bound that "flotsam and jetsam" into a social whole.

The social costs of providing infrastructural supports—roads, courts and communication systems—soon proved more onerous than the local government and the Colonial Office were prepared to bear. Nor were all disputes during the Gold Rush era concerned with social and economic order. Pressured by an emerging reform-minded group loosely led by two newspaper editors, Amour de Cosmos at Victoria and John Robson at New Westminster on the mainland, the Colonial Office realized political change was required. The first attempt at solving the political and financial problems, that of joining Vancouver Island and the mainland in 1866 and in the process abolishing the island's assembly, hardly satisfied the political reformers, nor did it resolve the financial difficulties. In that context, expansion-minded central Canadians would find fertile grounds for negotiations in 1871.

Crown Colonies and Coastal Natives, 1849–1864

Before 1849 the major change in native-white relations on the coast had been the gradual shift after 1821 from a sea-based to a land-based fur trade. With the granting of Crown colony status to Vancouver Island in 1849, a new stage in relations commenced. Conferral of colonial status required that rights to land be transferred from native to colonial control. This process had two phases: that overseen by the so-called fur trade governor, James Douglas, 1851–1864, and that following Douglas's departure when administrators more oriented to settlement and agriculture took control.

James Douglas exhibited much sympathy and considerable acumen in his native dealings. Whenever possible he counselled moderation and the punishment of individuals, not tribes, for alleged misconduct. At the same time, he believed that the Crown could not hope to control coastal natives without frequent recourse to intimidation provided by the Royal Navy. Both aspects of his policy proved, however, ineffective. Natives never understood justice by trial. And besides that, a frustrated Attorney General Thomas Wood wrote in 1864: "It is mere theory to suppose that English law prevails...[coastal natives] are to all intents and purposes Independent tribes...." Very likely English gun boats were more symbols of assurance for Europeans than they were effective measures for native pacification.

In terms of his dealings with natives, Douglas is best remembered for having negotiated 14 treaties on Vancouver Island and several more on the mainland. One-time grants of store materials facilitated white settlement in choice island regions. As in Upper Canada some 60 years earlier, it is not known with certainty just what natives thought had been transacted. That Europeans believed they had acquired total control is clear. In the British Columbia context, however, Douglas, whose wife was a Métis, must be seen as a relatively positive factor for native peoples: he did attempt to provide via treaties some, albeit meagre, living space for them and he did deal sympathetically with judicial matters. In this sense, he represented a transitional figure bridging the end of the fur trade era and the beginning of the settlement period. After 1864, native lands were appropriated without treaties of any sort. There is a profound irony here: in the context of present-day native land claims in British Columbia, the fact that most land was appropriated without recourse to treaties gives to native people their strongest and most effective bargaining and legal power.

Just as on the Prairies, missionaries on the coast worked hard to convert natives to Christianity. Prominent among them was the famous Anglican missionary William Duncan who constructed a model village, Metlakatla, that in limited ways attempted to blend native/white behaviour. In reality, like the missions set up by Methodists and Catholics, its primary goal was assimilation. And like the efforts of his contemporaries on the coast and on the Prairies, these efforts met with, at best, fragile success. The sophisticated native cultures west of the Rockies, like that of the Kwakiutl, withstood white proselytizers more often than not.

Despite frequent conflict during the brief but intense gold-rush era—natives wished to pan for gold on land they considered their own and profit directly from its sale—British Columbia's native peoples, in contrast to those on the Prairies, had not yet had to make serious compromises in traditional ways of life. The era of compromise and adaptation commenced in earnest after Douglas departed.[9]

---

[9] The following provide useful introductions to the West in this period: G. Friesen, *The Canadian Prairies*; A. Gluek, *Minnesta and the Manifest Destiny of the Canadian Northwest* (Toronto, 1965); D. Owram, *The Promise of Eden* (Toronto, 1980); J. W. Grant, *Moon of Wintertime* (Toronto, 1984); A. J. Ray, *Indians in the Fur Trade* (Toronto, 1974); J. R. Miller, *Skyscrapers Hide the Heavens: A History of Indian-White Relations in Canada* (Toronto, 1990). On British Columbia see the somewhat dated but still the only good survey, Margaret Ormsby, *A History of British Columbia* (Toronto, 1958). Some useful essays covering this period can be found in W.P. Ward and R.A. J. McDonald, eds., *British Columbia: Historical Readings* (Vancouver, 1981). The standard treatment of native-white relations in British Columbia is R. Fisher, *Contact and Conflict*.

THE PRE-CONFEDERATION ROOTS OF CANADIAN REGIONALISM

In Canada, regionalism is a concept that arouses strong emotions. For some Canadians, regional diversity is a matter for celebration. It represents the distinctive texture of a country that exists and flourishes despite its vast internal variations. By others, regionalism is bemoaned as a dreary fact of life, especially of political life. Federal policies have to be tailored according to how they will play in "the regions." Contracts must be awarded so that regional sensibilities are not offended. Mediocrity and patronage politics, so it might be argued, crowd out flair and even rationality in federal policy making, and regionalism is largely to blame. Conversely, those who believe that the historical development of the Canadian economy has resulted in unhealthy domination by central Canada would also take a jaundiced view of regionalism, but for different reasons. Eastern and western regions, they argue, have been reduced to peripheral status and—short of basic economic and constitutional reform—the only recourse is to the necessary evil of federally supported regional-development programs. Too often, though, the real nature of Canadian regionalism is lost in a welter of stereotypes and canards. Some of these are self-inflicted, as in the case of tourist promotions that portray Atlantic Canada as a series of rugged, lighthouse-strewn coastlines, Ontario as Toronto writ large, or British Columbia as a land fit only for

THE MARITIMES AS AN ECONOMIC REGION, 1800

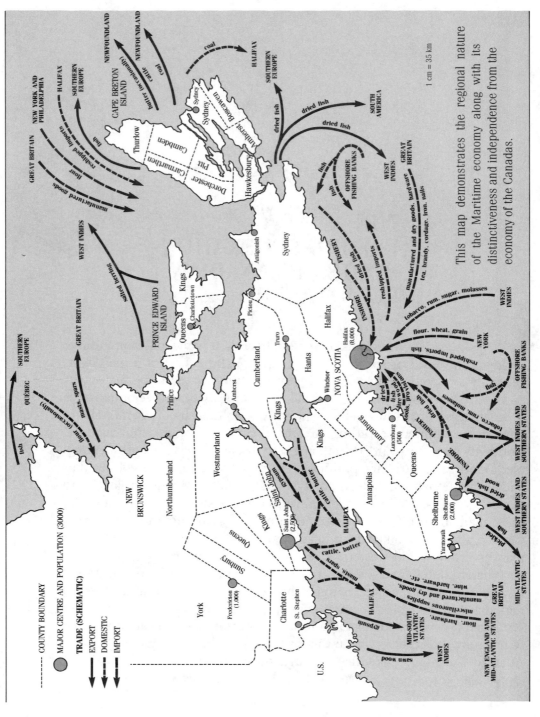

This map demonstrates the regional nature of the Maritime economy along with its distinctiveness and independence from the economy of the Canadas.

1 cm = 35 km

FROM R. COLE HARRIS, ED. *HISTORICAL ATLAS OF CANADA I: FROM THE BEGINNING TO 1800.* REPRINTED BY PERMISSION OF UNIVERSITY OF TORONTO PRESS.

mountaineers. Other stereotypes are hurled bitterly from one part of the country at another—at what might be seen as the urbanely cynical political culture of Quebec, or at the combination of chronically indebted farmers and prickly oil producers that some might take to represent the Prairies. What all of this demonstrates is a prevailing confusion about the significance of regional diversity for Canada. There are different kinds of regionalism—cultural and linguistic, economic, societal, and political. They generate different responses from Canadians. What they have in common, though, is that they have deep historical roots. Regionalism in Canada, as it has evolved since Confederation, needs to be understood in the context of its earlier development.

Even on 1 July 1867, Canada was a country of regions. Its four founding provinces had been brought into Confederation for different reasons and with varying amounts of reluctance and dissension. By the same date in 1873, when the joining of Prince Edward Island was proclaimed to a silent crowd of three persons in Charlottetown, the complexity had become even greater. Seven provinces and a vast northwestern territory were now included. The approximately 86 000 km^2 of the original dominion had been extended to almost 8 million. Although Newfoundland had opted decisively in 1869 to stay out, it was plausible to speak of a land stretching from ocean to ocean. The question was what to do to make sense of it all. Or, as the Toronto-based weekly *The Nation* put it in 1875, "Will our statesmanship [ten or fifteen years hence] still consist of a perpetual effort to hold together by 'better terms' and bribery under various forms and names, a motley army of political contingents, drawn from districts which care little for each other, from self-seeking interests, from warring religions; or will this wretched and degrading necessity have been in some measure superseded by the ascendancy of a higher bond of unison?" Four years later, the newly elected Conservative government of John A. Macdonald began to implement its answer to the question. The National Policy, based on the stimulation of Canadian manufacturing industry by a protective tariff and on railway linkages among the provinces, was intended to weld the country into an economic unit. Initially, it had some success. By the early decades of the twentieth century, however, shifts in the balance of population and the consolidation of capital in major urban centres had ensured for central Canada a dominant economic role. The policy was now "national" only if Ontario and Quebec were accepted as being the permanent heartland of a nation that also had peripheral regions. It was also the early twentieth century that saw the effective establishment of a professionalized discipline of history in Canada and of Canadian history as an identifiable field. An earlier milestone had been the appointment of George M. Wrong, a prolific scholar on the history of Canada, at the University of Toronto in 1894. But after the turn of the century, further important developments followed: the establishment of history professorships at other universities, including the appointment of Lionel-Adolphe Groulx at the Université de Montréal (then still part of Université Laval) in 1915; the launching of the *Canadian Historical Review* as a full-fledged historical journal in 1920; the inauguration of the Canadian Historical Association in 1922. Published works on Canadian history now appeared in increasing numbers. Not surprisingly, the most influential of them reflected Canada's ongoing search for its identity as a nation of almost baffling complexity, but one in which the ascendancy of the central provinces might be the key to historical as well as political understanding.

These studies explained important elements of Canadian history in terms that could be simply understood. Not that the historians themselves thought simplistically. But they did reduce Canada's development to the operation of certain well-defined processes. For Groulx, the central reality of the history of Quebec was the cultural threat posed to the survival of francophone, Roman Catholic civilization by the intrusion of Anglo-Saxon materialist values. This process, he argued, had begun with the Conquest of Canada and had been intensified by nineteenth-century industrialization. For Groulx's younger anglophone contemporary, Donald Creighton, of the University of Toronto, the commercialization of the St. Lawrence valley was also crucially significant, but in a different way. Influenced by the earlier work of Harold Innis on the fur trade, Creighton set out in 1937 his influential "Laurentian thesis" in a book entitled *The Commercial Empire of the St. Lawrence*. The building of Canada, he argued, had been accomplished on the basis of the trading activities of the merchants of the St. Lawrence. Through them, the economic influence of central Canada had been felt from the Atlantic Ocean to the West. It was legitimate, therefore, to look at the country from a centralized perspective. Groulx and Creighton were very different historians, ideologically as well as in their methods, but they did have certain characteristics in common. Both believed absolutely in the primacy of historical events taking place in central Canada—for Groulx in Quebec and for Creighton in Quebec and Ontario. Neither had any great interest in other parts of Canada except insofar as they represented cultural or economic hinterlands. The Acadians, for example, or the Red River colonists, were appraised not for their own intrinsic importance but for whatever significance they might have in terms of the supposedly more important processes taking place elsewhere. The influence of these perceptions stretched forward well into the 1960s. Not only was Groulx active as the editor of the *Revue d'Histoire de l'Amérique Française* until his death in 1967 and Creighton a vigorous and increasingly polemical author throughout that decade, but also their younger colleagues and former students frequently wrote from similarly centralist perspectives. There were dissenters and they often addressed themselves to the politics of centralism as well as to purely historical questions. University of Manitoba historian William L. Morton boldly declared in a 1945 critique of the Laurentian thesis that "until...the concentration of wealth and population by national policy in Central Canada ceases, Confederation must remain an instrument of injustice." Eleven years later, W. Stewart MacNutt of the University of New Brunswick similarly suggested in the *Atlantic Advocate* that events since 1867 had reduced Atlantic Canadians to the status of "a minority that has experienced economic rather than military conquest."

By the late 1960s, scholars such as Morton and MacNutt were no longer isolated voices. The celebrated adoption by many Canadian historians of the concept of "limited identities"—groups defined by class, ethnicity, gender, or region—as the essence of Canada's overall identity meant that researchers could fan out over a broad terrain of social history. It was a liberating experience. To study the concepts of Maritime or Prairie regional identity, for example, could no longer be dismissed as a trivial, antiquated activity. Rather, fields such as these were significant both in themselves and as contributions to the understanding of Canadian history in all its new-found complexity. The same could be said for examinations of the experience of native people, of immigrant communities, of women, of the working class. In Quebec and increasingly in Ontario, meanwhile, these trends were accompanied by another. Regionalism *within* those provinces was being explored by historians influenced, in Quebec, by the pioneering social studies of scholars such as Fernand Ouellet and Louise Dechêne and, in Ontario, by the shift of interest that was symbolized by the establishment in 1971 of the provincially funded *Ontario Historical Studies Series*. "Does 'Ontario' exist?" was the half-serious question pondered by the senior Queen's University historian Arthur Lower in the pages of *Ontario History* in 1968, and his conclusion was that the province was really a collection of regions that each had "a character of [its] own." Since the late 1960s, the use of regionalism as a tool of analysis in Canadian history has continued to expand. The trend has been especially marked in studies of the post-Confederation era, in which Atlantic and western scholars have led the way in exploring the marginalization of their regions. But the impact has also been felt in pre-Confederation scholarship in a variety of innovative works in cultural, economic, social, and political history. To be sure, the concept of a "region" raises tricky questions of method and definition. A useful definition is offered by the historical geographer L. D. McCann: "A region...is a homogeneous segment of the earth's surface with physical and human characteristics distinct from those of neighboring areas. As such, a region is sufficiently unified for its people...to possess a sense of identity distinct from those of other regions."[1] Even this statement leaves questions to be answered. How can the term "region" have any consistent meaning when it could be taken to signify a province (such as British Columbia), an area within a province (such as the Beauce region of Quebec), a group of provinces (such as the Maritimes), or an area stretching outside of the boundaries eventually established for Canada (such as the Abenaki lands covering large areas of modern Maine and New Brunswick)? How does Quebec fit into a regional framework when it is, in one sense, a region of Canada and, in another sense, a national society in itself? The study of Canadian regionalism is no less complex than Canadian social history itself. Yet faithfulness to the true character of the Canadian experience demands that regionalism be explored as a historical theme. And the place to start is with its earliest origins.

Foundations of Canadian Regionalism

Human societies are profoundly influenced by both their physical and human environments. This is a simple truth that, until recently, was often

---

[1] L. D. McCann, ed., *Heartland and Hinterland: A Geography of Canada* (Scarborough, Ontario: Prentice-Hall, 1982), p. vii. Other works relevant to the questions discussed in this section include: Carl Berger, *The Writing of Canadian History: Aspects of English-Canadian Historical Writing Since 1900*, 2nd ed. (Toronto: University of Toronto Press, 1986); Ramsay Cook, "Canadian Centennial Cerebrations," *International Journal*, 22 (1967), pp. 659–63; W. L. Morton, *The Critical Years: The Union of British North America, 1857–1873* (Toronto: McClelland and Stewart, 1964); and Frank H. Underhill, *The Image of Confederation* (Toronto: Canadian Broadcasting Corporation, 1964).

overlooked by historians. Many studies of North American colonial settlement assumed that European settlers would begin by faithfully reproducing in the New World the kind of societies they had left behind and would simply conquer nature and indigenous peoples insofar as it was necessary to do so. A celebrated 1964 study, *The Founding of New Societies*, edited and partly written by Louis Hartz, argued that colonial societies in the Americas, South Africa, and Australia should be understood almost entirely in terms of the European societies and ideologies they sprang from. They were "fragments of the larger whole of Europe." While it was true that contact with aboriginal peoples might have an influence on the character of colonial ideology, by being able in some respects to "twist it out of shape," this did not obscure for Hartz the prime importance of the European parent society. Physical environment found no significant place in the scheme. Since Hartz wrote, historians' perceptions have changed radically. One influence has been the sharpening general awareness of the centrality of ecological questions. Another has been a greater openness to interdisciplinary study, which has allowed historians to benefit from the insights of human and physical geographers. Finally, sophisticated studies of native cultures have elucidated the extent to which environmental influences affected both native and non-native peoples and have suggested new ways of examining the interactions between peoples and the land that occurred at the time of contact between colonizers and native societies. Thus, to understand the origins of Canadian regionalism in the era of colonial societies, we have to look first at the configurations of physical environment and of aboriginal cultures. Both show enormous spatial variations, and these in turn affected the nature of the contact experience. But there were also variations in time. Processes such as first contact, integration of colonies into European commercial networks, and the later development of industrial capitalism occurred at different times in different places. The result of these complex patterns in space and time laid the foundations for Canadian regionalism.

That Canada is a country of vast diversity in its natural environment is a reality that needs no laboured efforts at proof. Ranging from the ancient rock of the Canadian Shield, of which the oldest is more than 2.5 billion years, to the much younger continental shelves on the east, west, and northern coasts, Canadian geology has produced many different terrains. Soil types, rock formations, and vegetation are all testaments to this variety. But geology is only one factor in determining environment. Climate is another, and, during the thousands of years of human occupation of the territory that is now Canada, major climatic changes have taken place. As recently as 11 500 years ago—the era when the first clear archeological evidence is found of a human presence—much of what is now Canada was covered by sheets of ice. There were also extensive areas of tundra in the northwest and near the coasts, and only limited areas of scrubby woodland close to the present border with the United States. There followed a period of warming and forestation as the ice receded. Also changing was the coastline, as melted ice caused the oceans to rise. It was only some 5000 years ago, for example, that Prince Edward Island was separated from the mainland by the flooding of the coastal plain that became the Northumberland Strait. By the year 1500, when native-European contact was beginning, a recent study in the *Historical Atlas of Canada* identified a dozen ecological "provinces." Defined by climate, soil, and vegetation, the provinces went from the cordilleran boreal forest of the northwest to the cool, temperate mixed vegetation areas of the southeast and from the tundra of the Arctic northeast to the humid and temperate Pacific coast of the southwest. The potential for human occupation was obviously affected by these enormous variations. The availability of food resources, whether harvested on land or at sea, directly affected the density of population that the land could support. Accordingly, smaller native populations lived in the North as compared with, say, the West Coast, with its more easily available supply of fish and sea mammals as well as land animals. Ecological variations would also affect the patterns of European settlement, though in ways that reflected the greater importance to the newcomers of the extraction of commercially valuable resources.

Aboriginal societies immediately prior to European contact were numerous and distinctive. There are several ways in which these cultures have been classified by anthropologists and other scholars. One scheme would be to classify purely by ecological region: Arctic, Subarctic, Northeast, Great Plains, Plateau (that is, between the Rockies and the coastal mountains of the West), and West Coast. A related alternative is to group native cultures according to subsistence patterns: the fishing economy of the West Coast, the large prairie and northern areas where hunting predominated, the small but populous agricultural territory of the Iroquoian peoples adjoining the eastern Great Lakes, and the hunting-gathering-fishing areas of the East Coast and the subarctic. A third possibility is to differentiate according to language, identifying at least 12 native language families. The Algonquian, Athabaskan, and Inuktituk (Inuit) groups were by far the most widespread in terms of territory, although the Iroquoians and the West Coast peoples—the Salish, the

Wakashan, the Tlingit, the Tsimshian, and the Haidan—were more densely populated on their smaller territories. The Beothuk, Siouan, and Kootenaian peoples were the remaining groups. All of these schemes of classification have some value in conveying the diversity of aboriginal cultures. Yet in themselves they are not satisfying, because they are too abstract to convey the breadth of human experience on which native societies were nourished. Political cultures were based on well-established leadership structures that depended on varying combinations of heredity, consent, and personal qualities of individual leaders. Religious belief was fundamental to all native societies, and it was expressed not only in rituals such as those accompanying healing or the hunt but also in a host of artistic forms ranging from rock etchings to ivory sculptures and from oratory to dance. Many native societies, as well as pursuing their domestic economy, lived by trade. At the time of European contact, there were widespread trade networks in commodities such as copper, obsidian (volcanic) glass, silica, marine shells, and no doubt in other, more perishable, commodities that are less clear from the archeological record. For trading and diplomatic purposes, command of more than one language was commonplace in some native communities. The self-confidence of the Micmac he met caused a French missionary to observe in 1611 that "they think they are better, more valiant and more ingenious than the French; and what is difficult to believe, richer than we are." The same observation would have held true for the many other native peoples who made contact with non-natives in the centuries to come.

It was also true, of course, that interaction was ultimately destructive for native people. Epidemic disease, cultural change based on the adoption of non-native material goods, and economic adaptations to the presence of an alien commercial system took their toll. But interaction was a two-way process. In regard to disease, the early European visitors to the East Coast and the St. Lawrence valley gave much more than they got. Exchange of material culture, however, was more reciprocal. The technology of transportation—canoes, toboggans, snowshoes—was one in which native practices were widely adopted by non-natives. In economic life, too, native and non-native frequently became interdependent. While the fur trade obviously depended ultimately upon European demand and had adverse ecological consequences for native people, it was also shaped by the willingness or unwillingness of native groups to participate. Since contact led to this mutual influence—even though in each case it would degenerate into consequences that were damaging for native cultures—the meeting of diverse native societies with Europeans who varied by nationality, social class, and purposes in North America inevitably produced a wide spectrum of results. Herein lay one of the prime determinants of post-aboriginal regionalism. The patterns of early interactions in what is now eastern Canada had important results for both native and colonial populations.

English and Beothuk in Newfoundland had limited direct contact. Although some trading took place initially, it came to an end after violent clashes between the two peoples in 1612–13. From that time, the essential Beothuk strategy was one of withdrawal from English-occupied areas. The Beothuk refusal to adopt the use of firearms allowed the English to pursue unopposed an aggressive harvesting of coastal resources that had primarily supported the native population. For the Beothuk themselves, withdrawal was an effective way of avoiding violent confrontation for the time being but also meant an increasing and destructive reliance on the slim natural resources of the interior of Newfoundland. By contrast, French and Micmac in Acadia forged a lasting bond of economic partnership as early as 1605, leading to religious and military alliances and eventually to kinship ties. The relationship was influential on both peoples. The Micmac gained, though at a high, long-term price, secure access to trade. They also prolonged the presence of a colonial population that presented neither a territorial nor a military threat and thus protected their own remarkable resilience as a native people in an increasingly European-influenced part of North America. The Acadians, in turn, gained economically and militarily through this interdependent relationship. In the St. Lawrence valley and in forays to the Great Lakes, French colonizers were quickly plunged into dealing with pre-existing native trading networks and with conflicts between native peoples. The early efforts of leaders such as Samuel de Champlain and of religious missionaries were distinguished only by a profound lack of understanding of the complexities involved. The future development of the colony of Canada would be shaped not only by the alliances made with some native peoples but also by the long-standing alienation of others, notably the Iroquois. Thus, in the early seventeenth century, three contrasting patterns emerged. No valid generalizations can be made regarding native-European contact in this era, unless regional differences are taken into account.

If these contacts differed from region to region in the same period, then there were also regional differences that were created through time. Interaction between native and non-native people, though varying widely in specific results, was characterized by certain essential processes. One of these was the process of early contact, with its potential for initial cultural change and the spreading of disease. A second, usually following hard upon the first, was the effort of non-native people to cull for profit the natural resources of the territory involved. Thus, the resources became commodities in an ultimately European-dominated mercantile network. The third process, which might begin long after the first two (more than a hundred years after, in Newfoundland and Acadia) or might take place at virtually the same time, was actual colonization by non-natives. The combined results of the three processes invariably included ecological as well as social and cultural change. The fur trade, for example, could lead quickly to the depletion of beaver stocks, and, by more gradual steps, the same could happen to timber and fish. Colonization, with its introduction of European agricultural methods, also had serious ecological implications. The initial conversion of native hunting lands for crop growing or the raising of livestock was soon compounded by the search for new lands to accommodate a growing colonial population or to compensate for soil exhaustion and overgrazing. Even where colonial land use did not encroach largely on lands used by native people, as in Acadia, land-use techniques could have ecologically destructive side-effects. Acadian dyking of coastal marshes and the building of river sawmills and gristmills, for example, altered fish habitats and inadvertently disrupted Micmac fishing. The long-term effects of overusing resources and altering land-use techniques were formidable. As William Cronon remarked in an influential 1983 study of the ecological history of colonial New England, "Economic and ecological imperialisms reinforced each other."[2] But these processes

---

[2] William Cronon, *Changes in the Land: Indians, Colonists, and the Ecology of New England* (New York: Hill and Wang, 1983), p. 162. Other important and stimulating works in the areas covered by this section are: R. Cole Harris and Geoffrey J. Matthews, *Historical Atlas of Canada: From the Beginning to 1800*, volume I (Toronto: University of Toronto Press, 1987); Louis Hartz, *The Founding of New Societies: Studies in the History of the United States, Latin America, South Africa, Canada, and Australia* (New York: Harcourt Brace, and World, 1964); R. T. Naylor, *Canada in the European Age, 1453–1919* (Vancouver: New Star Books, 1987); Bruce G. Trigger, *Natives and Newcomers: Canada's "Heroic Age" Reconsidered* (Kingston and Montreal: McGill-Queen's University Press, 1985). In the writing of the section, especial use has been made of Plate 4 (by J. H. McAndrews et al.), Plate 14 (by J. V. Wright and Roy L. Carlson), Plate 17 (by J. H. McAndrews and G. C. Manville), Plate 18 (by Conrad E. Heidenreich and J. V. Wright), and Plate 69 (by Conrad E. Heidenreich and Robert M. Galois) in Harris and Matthews, *Historical Atlas of Canada*, volume I.

occurred at different times in different parts of North America. In historical studies of the United States, the notion of a continually westward-moving frontier remains defensible even though much debated since first put forward a century ago. The Canadian experience does not lend itself to such neat packaging. The existence of the St. Lawrence River as a great inland waterway meant that European-native contact could occur almost as early along its length as on the East Coast. French explorations to the Great Lakes and further west quickly extended interactions far ahead of any colonizing frontier. Nevertheless, these processes still varied according to time.

By the early nineteenth century, there remained a large stretch of territory that could be described realistically as outside the scope of non-native contact, but it was in the extreme north: much of Baffin Island, the other Arctic islands, adjoining parts of the mainland, and land west toward the Alaskan border. There were other large areas where contact was infrequent or where traditional economies could still coexist with a limited commitment to the fur trade: in Labrador and today's northernmost parts of Quebec; in what is now the western half of the Northwest Territories; in much of Alberta and noncoastal British Columbia. In the remaining areas—the coast of British Columbia, a large area directly west of Lake Winnipeg and everything directly east of it, including the southerly half of the coastline of Hudson Bay and all the coast of James Bay, native economies and ways of life had already suffered from depletion of animal stocks. Across today's Ontario and Quebec, food shortages had become frequent, except where Iroquoian communities continued their successful agricultural production. In the East, including the extreme southeast of Quebec and today's Atlantic provinces, 300 years of contact and 200 years of colonization had extracted their price. Native economies had been largely destroyed, and native people, while still resilient in their cultural values, had become small and virtually powerless minorities. Thus, in the configuration of native peoples, there was still a vast diversity. Now, however, it was based not only on aboriginal characteristics and on the varied particular circumstances of the contact experience, but also on differences arising from the timing of non-native intrusion. The resulting variations in regional experience were readily apparent to those who travelled widely in British North America. They were made especially plain to Thomas Douglas, fifth earl of Selkirk, who as a Scottish aristocrat and colonial promoter enjoyed success in settling a Highland community in 1803 on lands he had bought in Prince Edward Island. When he turned his attention to the Red River in 1811, he quickly found out not only that he had unwarily become involved in the ongoing conflict between the two great fur-trading companies but also that Métis hunters could put up stiff resistance to the founding of an agricultural settlement. When the Red River colony finally did attain a significant population, after Selkirk's death in 1820, it had a multicultural character that arose from the predominance of Métis families. Regional distinctions in British North America at this time continued to depend heavily on the state of relations between native and non-native peoples, and on the ecological consequences of those relationships.

"In Nova Scotia and New Brunswick," wrote Selkirk in a pamphlet published about 1814, "the Indian tribes are almost extinct; and nothing remains of them, but some scattered families, among whom there is no opportunity for any extensive improvement. In the north and west," he continued, "numerous tribes are to be found, some of which are in all circumstances highly favorable to their progress in civilization." The statement was ethnocentric, and also exaggerated the decline of native population—severe as it was—in the Maritime colonies. Nevertheless, Selkirk's comments and the experiences on which they were based did convey an important truth: that there was already a fundamental regionalism in British North America based on the interaction of native people, non-native people, and the physical environment. The meeting of native and European changed the nature of both kinds of society as they existed in North America. It also changed landscapes and environmental balances. And it did so in ways that varied according to place and time. There were, of course, other processes that entered into the making of regions. Military conflicts, the continuation and increase of immigration from Europe, and the rise of industrial capitalism were among the most important. But the foundations of regionalism in colonial society were laid down through the early processes of intercultural and ecological adaptation.

Components of Regionalism

As New France and then British North America increased in non-native population and as the major military and socio-economic processes of change affected all those who lived there, the varieties of regional experience became increasingly complex. For the historian, this presents some serious problems. In defining Canadian regionalism, it is not helpful to see only a mass of different historical experiences. The historian's task is to interpret the past, not just to describe it, and any attempt to make regionalism meaningful requires a clear and consistent way of differentiating regions. To be sure, there are some complexities that cannot and should not be avoided. One is that regional experiences vary in time. The regional distinctions that might be valid for New France in 1700 are not necessarily defensible for British North America in 1800 or for Canada in 1867. A second consideration is that there can be no one criterion for identifying regions because there were different kinds of regionalism. To put it another way, any proper analysis must take full account of the components of regionalism. There is no point in looking only for areas in which people speak the same language. Although that may be one important component of regional identity, it is unlikely to be the only one. Similarly, it is not enough to look only for areas with a single dominant industry or trade, or where relationships between social classes follow an established pattern or that are governed by the same political institutions. Significant as these factors may be, they cannot be considered alone. Regional analysis requires that all the components should be accounted for and that an effort be made to deal with perceptions of regionalism. Did the people in a particular area at a particular time feel themselves to be bound by common ties? Were such affinities recognized by other people in neighbouring areas? Although the historian might on some occasions argue that a region existed independently of these kinds of perception, a conscious sense of identity is normally part of any regional experience. It too, though, rests upon identifiable component influences.

The first of these can be described as cultural regionalism. The concept of culture is a complex one in itself. One study found that it had been defined in more than 300 ways in the English language alone. In the present context, it refers to the ethnic, religious, and linguistic characteristics of the peoples occupying a given area. In all of these respects, pre-Confederation Canada was diverse. As the first Canadian census in 1871 would later show, there were substantial populations of native people, of French, English, Irish, Scottish groups, and of those of other European or African origin. Languages varied accordingly, and religious attachments included many Christian denominations as well as native beliefs. But the patterns were regional and local. There were many rural areas where a person could live a long life with only infrequent encounters with others of different ethnicity or religious affiliation: whether in the Irish communities of the "Cape Shore" on Newfoundland's Avalon peninsula, on the seigneuries of the St. Lawrence valley, or on northern native lands not yet directly reached by the fur trade. To be sure, it was a rare individual whose life was entirely untouched by persons of different cultural background. Continuing interaction between native and non-native peoples, immigration, and the presence of military garrisons and European-based commercial networks saw to that. Again, though, the patterns of contact were distinctive by region. The coexistence of Orkneymen and Cree was just as peculiar to the northern areas controlled by the Hudson's Bay Company in the eighteenth and early nineteenth centuries as was that between Acadians and the agents of lowland Scottish and Jersey merchants to the shores of the Gulf of St. Lawrence at the same time. The cultural results in each case were expressed in informal bilingualism, in religious accommodations, and in adaptations of material cultures in such forms as tools and housing styles. On a wider scale, similar observations could be made of entire provinces. The domination in Newfoundland of Irish and English language and culture groups was one example, as was the cultural modification of Loyalist Upper Canada by successive waves of Irish, English, and Scottish immigrants. Cultural regionalism does not imply that regions had a uniform cultural character. The concept does signify, however, that the pre-Confederation period did not witness the invasion of an anarchic mass of culture. Distinct patterns emerged. They can be identified geographically. And, collectively, they form one important component of the more general phenomenon of regionalism.

A second component is economic regionalism. It is clear enough that, as colonial societies, New France and British North America were economically integrated with European parent countries that they served by producing natural resource commodities. For reasons that had to do both with natural environment and with access to transportation routes, the particular products varied geographically. Fish from the North Atlantic and the Gulf of St. Lawrence were both plentiful and easy to transport by sea to European markets. Beaver furs from the northwest were of good quality, and, following the trapping out of beaver in eastern areas in the seventeenth century, were more readily available than elsewhere. By following river and overland routes to Montreal and to Hudson Bay, they could be made ready in large quantities for transatlantic shipping. Timber, in the early nineteenth century, became another lucrative export commodity, drastically changing the economies of such areas as New Brunswick and the Ottawa Valley. Yet the predominance of staple trades was never as simple or complete as it might seem at first glance. In Newfoundland, for example, the fishing economy operated until well into the eighteenth century in a way that ensured that most of those who were present during the summer season were short-term residents only and that even those who "overwintered" were not necessarily permanent inhabitants. This contrasted with the purely resident fisheries of Acadians in the Bay of Fundy and the Gulf of St. Lawrence. Nor did staple trades rule entire economies as strongly as they dominated export statistics. Agriculture was practised in all of the colonies for subsistence and for supply of local markets and, as well, as provided export commodities such as wheat. Military expenditures were essential to some local economies—especially in urban areas such as Quebec and Halifax, and in rural areas through demand for food supplies for garrisons. The nineteenth century brought further economic complications to British North America. The introduction of railways, beginning in Lower Canada and Nova Scotia in the 1830s, was a prelude to a mid-century surge in industrialization and urbanization, while the Reciprocity Treaty began in 1854 to bring about a temporary realignment of export markets to the United States. As with cultural patterns, economic regionalism did not necessarily follow neat lines of demarcation. But neither were the combinations of fishing, fur trading, timber cutting, military and governmental influence, agriculture, and industrialization randomly distributed. Anybody in the 1850s who stood in Halifax with Province House and the Citadel on one side and the export wharves on the other, or who watched the clustering of industrial growth along the railway lines skirting Lake Ontario, or who travelled between Fort Victoria and the interior trading forts of what was to become British Columbia would gain at least a partial sense of the regional economies that had emerged by that time.

The third component is societal regionalism. Closely related both to cultural and economic elements of regional experience, societal questions relate to social class and gender. Class and gender relations are fundamental to any human society, and in Canada they too have varied regionally. To pursue the example of the 1850s: as that decade opened, Prince Edward Island, rural Canada East, and the city of Toronto with its 30 000 inhabitants were all societies in which there was obvious class conflict. In Prince Edward Island, the efforts of tenants—together with political allies in the colonial assembly—to reform or abolish the proprietary system of landholding were frequently accompanied by crowd action directed at frustrating rent collection or reinstating evicted tenants. The land question in Canada East, here involving the struggle over seigneurialism, raised some similar issues. In Canada East, however, commercialization of land was more clearly the issue than in the predominantly agricultural proprietary lands of the island. As well as tenants, potential industrial promoters objected to seigneurial control of land and to the extensive legal rights of seigneurs in such matters as milling and pasturage of animals. This opposition of a new commercial class to the traditional structure of landholding contributed to the formal abolition of the seigneurial system in 1854. In Toronto, the beginnings of industrialization were already leading to class conflict centred in growing workshops and factories. Workers' responses were finding expression in the foundation of trade unions such as the Toronto Typographical Association, which had a continuous existence from 1844. To be sure, class conflict cannot be understood entirely, or even predominantly, as regional phenomenon. Processes such as the commercialization of land and the development of industrial capitalism transcended regional and national boundaries. But important regional diversities existed. The same can be said of gender relations. Although certain general principles hold true regardless of region, such as the integral importance of the labour of both genders in family economies, there were distinct patterns that can be geographically identified. Eighteenth-century Newfoundland, for example, had an abnormally male-dominated population. Even by the early 1770s, the proportion of women among the year-round residents was as low as 10 percent; 25 percent were children and 65 percent were adult males. The disparities were even more marked in the summer, with the arrival of large numbers of males for the seasonal fishery.[3] Those women who did live in

---

[3] C. Grant Head, *Eighteenth Century Newfoundland: A Geographer's Perspective* (Toronto: McClelland and Stewart, 1976), p. 145. The themes briefly summarized in this section can be explored further in a wealth of more specialized studies. Among them are J. M. Bumsted, *Land, Settlement, and Politics on Eighteenth-Century Prince Edward Island* (Kingston and Montreal: McGill-Queen's University Press, 1987); Allan Greer, *Peasant, Lord, and Merchant: Rural Society in Three Quebec Parishes, 1740–1840* (Toronto: University of Toronto Press, 1985); Gregory S. Kealey, *Toronto Workers Respond to Industrial Capitalism, 1867–1892* (Toronto: University of Toronto Press, 1980); John J. Mannion, *Irish Settlements in Eastern Canada: A Study of Cultural Transfer and Adaptation* (Toronto: University of Toronto Press, 1974); A. I. Silver, *The French-Canadian Idea of Confederation, 1864–1900* (Toronto: University of Toronto Press, 1982); Sylvia Van Kirk, *"Many Tender Ties": Women in Fur-Trade Society in Western Canada, 1670–1870* (Winnipeg: Watson and Dwyer, 1980); Graeme Wynn, *Timber Colony: A Historical Geography of Early Nineteenth-Century New Brunswick* (Toronto: University of Toronto Press, 1981). A collection that presents stimulating approaches to the interaction of regionalism with other social phenomena, although primarily focusing on the post-Confederation period, is Gregory S. Kealey, ed., *Class, Gender and Region: Essays in Canadian Historical Sociology* (St. John's: Committee on Canadian Labour History, 1988).

Newfoundland at this time had an increasingly important economic role, as their labour in processing fish on shore steadily replaced that of imported male workers, but it would be well into the nineteenth century before Newfoundland's population attained a more equal gender distribution. A distinct pattern of a different kind is apparent in the northwest, where gender relations had a crucial cultural and economic significance arising from women's mediation between native and non-native participants in the fur trade. Thus, societal characteristics formed an important component of regionalism.

So did political structures. Some critics of the use of regional analysis in Canadian history argue that the concept of regionalism is an unnecessary complication of the simple principle that Canada is a country of provinces. The regions are the provinces, and vice versa. The proponents of regionalism reject this argument, contending not only that cultural, economic, and societal criteria cannot be ignored in identifying regions but also that regions do not necessarily conform to political boundaries. Some regions may consist of clusters of provinces, others of areas within provinces. Nevertheless, there can be no question that political divisions have an important influence on regionalism and deserve to be considered along with other components of it. The effort to create political entities, and to define them according to established boundaries, was fundamental to the existence of European colonies in North America. With a breathtaking disregard for existing native societies and their possession of land, seventeenth-century European charters made vast claims of territory. Acadia, in 1603, was defined by France as stretching from the latitude of present-day New Jersey to Cape Breton Island. Even more extravagantly, in 1627, the Company of New France was awarded all the lands from Florida to the Arctic Circle as "the country of New France, known as Canada." Easy as it is, in retrospect, to ridicule these pretensions, they deserve serious historical consideration on at least two grounds. First, because the notion that European nations had a right to make such allocations of land, even if they could not always defend them against all competitors, has proved to be extraordinarily tenacious in Canadian ideology and jurisprudence. It is the essential reason why native peoples have to attempt in legal battles to prove their ownership of claimed lands rather than—as would be better justified by the historical record—the burden of proof resting on the non-natives. Second, these European claims point to the general reality that in colonial societies political divisions were provisional by their very nature. Just as the boundaries in the early charters were often proved unrealistic, so other colonial entities came and went. Some designations, such as Rupert's Land, for the territory granted to the Hudson's Bay Company in 1670, endured but meant little. Others were extinguished by conquest: Acadia, Île Royale, the colony of Canada. Some, such as the province of Quebec (1763–91) or the province of Nova Scotia (1763–84), survived in altered or restricted forms. Others did not: the province of Cape Breton (1784–1820), the province of Canada (1841–67), the province of Vancouver Island (1849–66). There was nothing absolute about the political boundaries set down in the pre-Confederation era, no matter how loftily they were proclaimed. Yet they could have an influence on regional formation. Although the French colony of Acadia ceased to exist in 1713, the descendants of its inhabitants continued to use the name. The provinces of Cape Breton, New Brunswick, and Upper Canada, when founded in the late eighteenth century, were self-consciously seen by Loyalist residents as expressions of their peculiar identity and as monuments to their political struggles. That other inhabitants looked bitterly at the Loyalists' pretensions was only another indication of the symbolic and practical significance that such political structures could have. Political divisions, tentative as they were, represent a significant component of regionalism.

The question of regional senses of identity leads on to a final element in the nature of regionalism: perception, and the existence of "regions of the mind." The existence of a region, like the existence of a nation, depends, at least in part, on a consciousness of it as such. When a contributed editorial declared in the Halifax Methodist newspaper, the *Provincial Wesleyan*, in 1861 that "Eastern British America is our home," it referred to the Maritimes and Newfoundland. A French-language newspaper published in New York described in 1865 the "Franco-Canadian nationality, which today has a very real existence on the banks of the St. Lawrence." In 1869, assembled Métis representatives declared in the context of the transfer of Rupert's Land from the Hudson's Bay Company to Canada that "being established, living and working on these lands, which they have assisted the Company in opening, the people of the Red River having thus acquired incontestable rights in this country, the representatives of the Métis population of the Red River emphatically proclaim these rights." Leaving aside the question of the relationship between nation and region— depending upon the context, Quebec can justifiably be regarded as either, while native peoples and Acadians also have proper claims to distinctive nationality—all of these statements asserted strong senses of common identity tied to geographical areas. None of them coincided exactly with political boundaries, although all were influenced by political realities of the 1860s. By that decade, with colonial populations established for some 250 years, diverse senses of regional identity had emerged. They drew upon shared historical experience and collective memory. They were shaped by the different components of regionalism. These regional identities were not only based upon the fundamental diversities of physical environment and native society but had also evolved through French and British regimes. Both New France and British North America were characterized by profound regional distinctions that in turn contributed to the conscious regionalism that pervaded the Confederation era.

Regionalism in the French Regime

At its height, at the turn of the eighteenth century, the French empire in North America covered extensive territories and extended its economic influence far beyond its areas of colonial settlement. Yet the diversity of the French experience was long overlooked by historians who concentrated their analysis on the colony of Canada. Before 1713, New France (this term is used to encompass the entire French empire) included colonial settlements in Newfoundland, Acadia, Canada, and Louisiana. French claims had also been advanced to the Hudson Bay territories, and the Mississippi and Ohio valleys. Trading networks in the Great Lakes region and further west were strengthened by missionary and military outposts, as well as by the settlement at Detroit. After 1713, under the terms of the Treaty of Utrecht, Newfoundland and Acadia were given up to Great Britain, as was Hudson Bay, but were replaced by the new colony of Île Royale, incorporating Cape Breton Island and Île Saint-Jean, later Prince Edward Island. New France remained, until the era of its final conquest by the British in 1758–60, a vast empire. It was also an empire of profound regional variation. As in other European empires in the Americas, the French colonies resolved themselves during the seventeenth centuries into different cultural and socio-economic forms. While colonial administrators in France and in Quebec had firm ideas of what constituted a successful colony, their mercantilist assumptions frequently led them into judgments that did no justice to the diverse ways in which colonial societies could develop. When, for example, Jacques de Meulles visited

Acadia in 1685 as intendant of New France, his dismissal of the colony as "si peu de chose [such a small thing]" was understandable in the context of its small population and lack of economic links with other parts of the French empire. Those very characteristics, however, had led to the development of a society different from any that would be found in the St. Lawrence valley and in its own terms a successful one. The challenge to historians, given the extent to which research in this period depends on the records of government officials, is to move beyond such perceptions to evaluate the regional structures underlying the French colonial presence.

Culturally, the regional variations began with colonial immigration. Immigration from France to North America was always small in scale compared to that of the English, and among the French, the majority of immigrants arrived on what was initially a temporary basis, often as short-term contract workers or as soldiers. More than two-thirds of those who came to Canada during the French regime did eventually return to France.[4] They came from specific areas: from Paris and its vicinity, from northern and western coastal provinces such as Normandy, Brittany, and Poitou. Given the cultural diversity of France at this time, even these areas were enough to ensure variation in such matters as language and legal custom. Religious diversity was less evident, as the French government's ban on immigration of Protestants and Jews discouraged those people even though it was never strictly enforced. Canada experienced the full range of this immigration, while the experience of Acadia and French Newfoundland was different. French Newfoundland, centred on the port of Plaisance, had a tiny resident population by comparison with either Acadia or Canada. All but a few of the original immigrants came from the

---

[4] See Peter N. Moogk, "Reluctant Exiles: Emigrants from France in Canada before 1760," *William and Mary Quarterly*, 3rd series, 46 (1989), pp. 463–505. Further reading on the themes of this section can be found in the following books and articles: Jean Daigle, ed., *The Acadians of the Maritimes: Thematic Studies* (Moncton: Centre d'études acadiennes, 1982); W. J. Eccles, *Essays on New France* (Toronto: Oxford University Press, 1987); W. J. Eccles, *France in America* (New York: Harper and Row, 1972); N. E. S. Griffiths, *The Acadians: Creation of a People* (Toronto: McGraw-Hill Ryerson, 1973); Dale Miquelon, *New France, 1701–1744: "A Supplement to Europe"* (Toronto: McClelland and Stewart, 1987); Christopher Moore, "The Other Louisbourg: Trade and Merchant Enterprise in Ile Royale, 1713–58," *Histoire sociale/Social History*, 12, No. 23 (May 1979), pp. 79–96; Marcel Trudel *The Beginnings of New France, 1524–1663* (Toronto: McClelland and Stewart, 1973); Alan F. Williams, *Father Baudoin's War: D'Iberville's Campaigns in Acadia and Newfoundland, 1696, 1697* (St. John's: Memorial University of Newfoundland, 1987).

western coastal areas of France, particularly from the port of La Rochelle, with a significant minority of Basques. The thread that bound together the residents was their origin in, and their continuing trade connections with, the seaports in which the French Atlantic fishery was based. Thus, there was an initial cultural homogeneity that did not exist in Canada. The same was true in Acadia, though for different reasons. The majority of the group who settled in Acadia in the 1630s and 1640s and formed the core of the Acadian population came from a single specific area in Poitou: from the personal lands of the colonial promoter Charles de Menou d'Aulnay Charnisay. They came in families, and there is no evidence of any significant migration of these settlers back to France. To be sure, the Acadian population assimilated many others whose origins were elsewhere in France—and some who were English or Portuguese—and whose reasons for coming to North America were, in terms of overall French migration, more conventional. These included soldiers, artisans, and fishers, who decided to remain in Acadia when their engagements expired. But the existence of a cohesive group of families centred on d'Aulnay's settlement at Port Royal gave the Acadian population a firm basis of cultural coherence that was not evident in Canada. Over time, the Acadian cultural experience diverged further. To an extent unparallelled in either Newfoundland or in Canada, the Acadian cultural milieu extended not only to native people but also to colonists of other nationalities. Close Acadian ties to the Micmac can be compared to the relationships established by Canadian traders with allied native peoples, but there were important differences. The Acadian experience was one of affinity with all of the native peoples of the area, including Abenaki and Maliseet-Passamaquoddy, rather than differentiation between some peoples who were allied and some who were not. By 1700 it was expressed in kinship ties that extended to formal intermarriage. The Acadian relationship with New England traders was another significant influence. Not only did it affect material culture, since most of the colony's manufactured goods were imported from or through New England, but it also encouraged travel between English and French communities, and linguistic adaptations. Just as there were New England merchants long before the conquest of Acadia in 1710 who maintained houses and warehouses in Port Royal, so there were Acadian merchants and seamen who had just as close a familiarity with Boston and Salem as had their Canadian counterparts with La Rochelle or Bordeaux. By cultural origin and by later cultural milieu, the French communities in North America had distinct, though related, experiences.

The same was true in terms of economy. All of the French colonies drew economic strength from export trades in natural resources, domestic food production through agriculture and fishing, and cash inflows from France directed toward military and administrative expenses. There were important differences, however, in the relative importance of each. Canada and pre-conquest Acadia shared a substantial reliance on agriculture and the fur trade, but military expenditures in Canada were vastly greater than in Acadia. When the first substantial French infusion of military spending reached Canada in the mid-1660s, Acadia was under temporary English occupation and was ignored. The disparity thus created was never made up. "War," one of the most prominent historians of the colony of Canada, W. J. Eccles, has commented, "and the threat of war, was one of the great staples of the Canadian economy." Strategic considerations also dictated French support for the western fur trade after 1713, by which time its purely economic value to the parent country had become questionable. For Canadiens, the benefits of the fur trade were beyond doubt, but the maintenance of its military framework by France was the prerequisite for its continuation. On the East Coast by this time, the principal French economic centre was at Louisbourg. The colony of Île Royale, of which Louisbourg was the headquarters and principal town, shared with Canada its partial economic reliance on military expenditure. As a centre for naval protection of the French fisheries and a strategic location near the entry to the Gulf of St. Lawrence, Louisbourg had a military importance that was evident in the scale of its fortifications and the size of its garrison. Yet this was also the French trading colony *par excellence*. It continued key economic characteristics of both French Newfoundland and Acadia, the

Louisbourg Harbour, 1731. Fortress in the background.
NATIONAL ARCHIVES OF CANADA/C23082

two colonies that had been its predecessors: the prime export of salt cod, as at Placentia, and the Acadian practice of trading regularly with New England. Île Royale also traded extensively with Canada and the French West Indies, and the value of its cod exports (in most years for which records are available) far exceeded that of Canadian exports of fur. Île Royale's overall trade figures were at a comparable level to those of Canada, though its population was much smaller. The island colony, in fact, had to live by trade. It had little agriculture, and cod was its only salable product. All of its other supplies had to be imported. In the 1750s, some attempts were made by Governor Jean-Louis de Raymond to expand cultivation of the land and develop timber production, but the results were soon overtaken by the conquest of 1758. The economic consequences of the Conquest of Canada in 1759–60 were also profound, bringing to an end the existing mercantile structure of the fur trade, though not the involvement of Canadian voyageurs. Prior to the conquest era, Canada and Île Royale had widely divergent economies. Though existing in the same European empire, with the same mercantilist beliefs, their products and the degree of their reliance on external trade differed. Both in the seventeenth century and in the changed circumstances between 1713 and 1760, therefore, New France accommodated a clear economic regionalism.

It was equally evident that economic diversity implied societal distinctions. Again, there were common elements. The importance of metropolitan French expenditures to colonies such as Canada and Île Royale was reflected in the degree of control exercised by administrative and military officers. Land ownership structures were crucial to agricultural areas. And in all the colonies external trade implied the existence of a merchant middle class and a preindustrial working class employed in the production of resource commodities and as seafarers. Gender relations, throughout New France, were based on a legal framework that confirmed the authority of husbands and fathers. Women were denied entry to professions or official positions, although entry into the religious orders provided an alternative for some, and middle-class widows frequently took over the property and business interests of deceased husbands. For most women, domestic labour or work on farms and fish wharves formed their economic contributions to the family. Within all of these societal characteristics, there were significant regional variations. In eighteenth-century Île Royale, the class structure was relatively straightforward. Members of a military, administrative, and merchant governing class presided over soldiers, artisans, and members of fishing crews who were frequently temporary, male residents. By contrast with the more complex society in Canada, where the seigneurial system and the presence of the clergy at all social levels brought about an additional series of social relationships and where the larger population ensured more gradation of military and administrative officers and merchants, Île Royale was dominated by Louisbourg and by its military and trading preoccupations. The more profound societal divergences within New France, however, involved Acadia and the fur-trading territories of the West. The distinctive class and gender characteristics of fur-trade society and their implications for French-native relations are clear from the thriving historical literature in the field. The Acadian case has been less thoroughly explored. The effective throwing off of seigneurialism by the Acadians of Port Royal in the 1650s—taking advantage of a temporary English occupation that weakened the seigneurial bonds—had profound consequences. While Acadia did not cease to be a society differentiated by class, the structure was one that evolved from the ruins of a tentative seigneurialism rather than one in which seigneurial relations regulated a peasant class. Nor, in the absence of any large military presence in the colony—even at the time of the conquest in 1710, the entire strength of the Port Royal garrison was not more than 300—and with the clergy only infrequent visitors to most communities were other outside influences evident. Social class was a product of relations within the communities, and the Acadian merchants who traded with Massachusetts by the late seventeenth century did so on the basis of capital accumulation that was small in scale and recently generated. Their commerce was also squarely North American–based and depended little on links with France.

Acadian distinctiveness also had implications in the political regionalism of New France. Although the governor, intendant, and bishop, based in Quebec, had extensive theoretical powers over the entire French empire in North America, historians have often been misled by taking those powers too seriously. Not only were they mitigated in Canada itself by the economic influence of merchants and seigneurs and in some years by popular crowd actions to protest against food shortage or government-enforced labour, but also the authority of senior officials weakened once it moved beyond Canada's boundaries. The frequency of proclamations against young Canadians travelling west for the fur trade or against Acadian merchants trading illegally with New England showed the ineffectiveness of such curbs. In preconquest Acadia, governors came and went frequently and faced a fundamental problem that was rooted in the political culture of the colony. If they attempted to govern in accordance with mercantilist principles (as they were frequently instructed to do in directives from Versailles and Quebec) by discouraging trade with New England, they would be resisted or ignored by communities that were fully accustomed to making their collective will known through local meetings. If governors gave way to community pressure, as almost all eventually did in permitting the New England trade to continue, they risked dismissal on the ground that they had failed to carry out orders. The wars that preceded the conquest of 1710 raised the prestige of royal governors somewhat because of their military role. Nevertheless, it was not for nothing that Governor Frontenac of New France complained in 1678 of the "parliamentary tendencies" of the Acadians and that a later governor of Acadia repeatedly referred to the inhabitants he met soon after his arrival in 1701 as "republicans." The political culture of the Acadians was also an important element in their long-term response to British rule after 1710. Their experience in acting independently of imperial administrators was put to good use in establishing—especially in communities outside the garrison town of Annapolis Royal—an effective separation between population and British authorities, except for mediation when necessary of elected deputies sent to Annapolis. It was also true that this distant relationship ultimately produced a dangerous insulation of Acadian communities from British political and strategic preoccupations and contributed to the rapid passing of events beyond Acadian control in 1755. Yet, as evidence of the regional diversity in the political culture of New France, the Acadian experience is crucial. Politically, the colony of Quebec and later the colony of Île Royale operated more nearly as they were intended to. Senior royal officials, though their power was by no means absolute, firmly held the initiative. Administrative, military, and judicial systems were highly developed. Elsewhere, it was not necessarily so.

New France was always thinly populated by comparison with other European empires in North America. A generous estimate of the number of French in North America in 1701, when New France was at its greatest territorial extent, would be 25 000, just one-tenth of the English population in the much smaller area along the eastern seaboard. The very complexity of the French empire, with its widely separated colonial settlements and its dependence on influencing large western areas to which France made no claim of possession, invited simplistic attempts to rationalize its nature. Given also that Canada was the most populous of the colonies, that in the late seventeenth century it bore some resemblance to Jean-Baptiste Colbert's mercantilist ideal of the compact colony, and that in the eighteenth its fur trade was increasingly seen as having strategic value for France, it was not surprising that the view from Quebec would predominate in official accounts. Historians have often reproduced this model, seeing Canada as the essence of French North America and the other areas as appendages. Canada was, of course, the nominal seat of government, and its economic influence was widespread.

Nevertheless, New France was more than this view of it allows. It was a vast empire, encompassing human societies that, like the British colonies or even, though the population scale was vastly greater again, those of Spain, were remarkably diverse. New France, as much as the others, was an empire of regions and of consciously distinctive senses of identity. That this was true of the Acadians, for example, became especially clear following their conquest, as they confronted hard choices as to whether to stay under British rule or move to Île Royale. Presented with an oath of allegiance by the British in early 1718, the inhabitants of the communities of Minas asked for more time on the ground that they must "assemble the whole Colony in order to decide," and in any case rejected the current form of the oath for reasons that included the statement that "when our ancestors were under English Rule, such oaths were never exacted from them." Acadian political culture, and the collective historical memory that was essential to it, were clear in the statement. The regionalism of the French regime, as well as being significant in its own right, reveals important elements of the overall regionalism of the pre-Confederation era. First, it was a demonstration of the variations in colonial society that could proceed from interactions with the physical environment and with native people. French settlement was not just French settlement. It implied a range of human and environmental influences that differed from place to place. Secondly, the regional identities generated by New France left continuing legacies. Although the society that characterized Île Royale was effectively destroyed in 1758, those of the Acadians, the Canadiens, and of the voyageurs during their western sojourns were not. They survived the British conquests, although they changed in important respects, to influence later regional patterns. In British North America, however, a lengthy process of evolution would take place before the regionalism of the Confederation era emerged.

Regional Evolution in British North America

Regionalism is not a static concept. The century that followed the final conquest of New France by Great Britain was a time of significant evolution in the regional character of British North America. An apparent consolidation of regional identities was followed by a steady process of division and subdivision that resulted in the creation of new regions and subregions. The consolidation was political, while the pressures leading to division were cultural and socio-economic. They stemmed from war, immigration, and international economic relationships. The American Revolution, of course, radically changed the scale of British North America. The British territories were still large after the revolution, but the division of the Great Lakes severely diminished the province of Quebec, and the Thirteen Colonies took with them the great majority of the population. The rump of British North America in 1783, in fact, bore a striking geographical resemblance to New France. It covered much of the same territory, and British settlers were still outnumbered by both French and native inhabitants, though their numbers were soon to be augmented by Loyalist and Celtic immigrants. While the adherence to Britain of the colonies acquired in 1763 was not entirely coincidental, it was unpredictable in 1775. Many revolutionary leaders had confidently expected Quebec and Nova Scotia to join the cause. Now that they had not, the reduced British North America began to develop along regional lines that resembled those of New France, although with a greater complexity that came from large-scale immigration and from military and economic developments. Both the provinces of Nova Scotia and Quebec were broken up—politically and culturally—while Newfoundland and the West underwent important societal transitions.

Newfoundland, in 1783, was not part of British North America in any practical sense. The official British view that Newfoundland represented a fishery rather than a settlement was increasingly inadequate, and yet the island was still demonstrably not a colony along the lines of those on the mainland. Its government structures were loosely defined, and, societally, the proportion of women and children remained low after the turn of the nineteenth century, although winter proportions of 13 percent women, 33 percent children, and 54 percent adult males in the early years of the new century did show an evening trend. It continued as immigration further raised the permanent population, reaching over 124 000 by 1857. By that time, Newfoundland had formal judicial structures and an elected assembly that had operated since 1855 on the principle of responsible government. Economically, it was still largely separate from the mainland of British North America—its major trade links with Great Britain, southern Europe, and other parts of the Americas made its minor connections with Nova Scotia appear tiny by comparison—but there was no longer any question of its being generically different in a political sense. The colony could be considered as a region of British North America in a way that it could not have been 50 years earlier, even though there was no indication that it wished to establish any closer direct ties with the mainland.

Newfoundland was also a regional society now in a second sense. The older, settled areas of the eastern Avalon peninsula—the southern shore and Conception Bay—were the first to attain a more even gender distribution and a high proportion of permanent residents, while the more recently settled outlying areas continued to be dominated by adult males. St. John's was the major exception to this pattern: although now an established urban centre, it received large numbers of single, male immigrants on their way to other destinations in Newfoundland or on the mainland. Newfoundland, by 1860, therefore, was not only a colonial society in a full sense but also had its own regional complexity.[5]

The same was true of the area, which corresponded to all of the later Maritime provinces, that from 1763 to 1769 had composed Nova Scotia. The expulsion of the Acadians had drastically reduced the non-native population, while the Micmac and other native peoples struggled to recover from the military setback that the defeat of their French ally had represented. It was true that immigration had already begun the process of repopulation as New England Planters and Scotch-Irish settlers founded new communities close to the ruins of the old Acadian villages. They would soon be joined by Celtic immigrants, returning Acadians, and then Loyalists. For the moment, however, the enlarged province of Nova Scotia plausibly had an opportunity to remake itself in a form suitable for membership in Great Britain's extensive North American empire. The first

---

[5] For the statistics and other characteristics cited on Newfoundland, see Head, *Eighteenth-Century Newfoundland*, pp. 82—232; Shannon Ryan, "Fishery to Colony: A Newfoundland Watershed, 1793–1815," *Acadiensis*, 12 (Spring 1983), pp. 34–52; and W. Gordon Handcock and Michael Staveley, chapters 1 and 2 of, *The Peopling of Newfoundland: Essays in Historical Geography* edited by John J. Mannion (St. John's: Institute of Social and Economic Research, 1977).

retrenchment of Nova Scotian territory in 1769, when autonomy was granted by the British government to the Island of St. John, did not essentially change Nova Scotia's configuration. However, the arrival of the Loyalists brought a new surge of political regionalism and the splitting off of Cape Breton and New Brunswick in 1784. The province of Cape Breton, with its relatively small population—some 6000 by 1815—of Micmacs, Acadians, Loyalists, and Scots, was reintegrated with Nova Scotia in 1820. Among the three more lasting Maritime colonies, political culture shared significant similarities: a restricted franchise, personal patronage, and the increasing power of merchant elites as trade developed in the early nineteenth century were common to all. Nevertheless, there were also differences. The Island of St. John—Prince Edward Island from 1798— was unique in the extent to which the land question, greatly embittered by the settlement of many Loyalists on land disputed by rival would-be owners, became a central and continuing political question. New Brunswick's founding Loyalist elite, meanwhile, loudly proclaimed the distinctive virtues that would govern that province's political life. "Yes—by God!," proclaimed one of the Loyalist leaders, Edward Winslow, "We will be the envy of the American states." The vision of New Brunswick as a prosperous and ordered society was never fully realized, and the intolerance of opposition that characterized the idealism of the Loyalist elite soon led to bitter political conflicts. But of the conscious distinctness of New Brunswick there was no doubt. In Nova Scotia, Loyalist refugees ultimately reinforced existing political patterns, notably the persistent tensions between the governmental influence of the Halifax merchant elite and the interests of the smaller towns and rural areas of the province. In each province, political issues developed differently, despite the more general characteristics of political culture that existed in common.

Cultural and economic regionalisms, however, did not respect political boundaries. By the early nineteenth century, the Maritime colonies could be divided into three economic regions. All were defined by their coastlines or by their access to the coast through river transportation. Only one of the economic regions lay within a single political jurisdiction: the Atlantic coastline of Nova Scotia from Cape North to Yarmouth. Depending predominantly on fisheries, though with extensive subsistence agriculture and increasing coal production and export from Cape Breton and with commercial, government, and military activity in Halifax, this coastline exported to the West Indies, Great Britain, and—notably in the era of reciprocity—to the United States. It was a region of ports, ranging from the smallest fishing communities to the commercial centres of Sydney, Guysborough, Halifax, Liverpool, and Yarmouth. Between it and the second economic region, the Bay of Fundy, there was no sharp dividing line. The Bay of Fundy too relied on export trades, and, as on the Atlantic coast, its shipping and ship-building activities grew steadily in the early and middle decades of the nineteenth century. Nevertheless, distinctions can be made. In the Fundy region, fisheries were less important than on the Atlantic coast, and timber and agriculture more so. As had already been evident before the Acadian deportation, the most productive agricultural areas of the Maritimes surrounded the Bay of Fundy: the Annapolis Valley and the environs of Cobequid Bay; the isthmus of Chignecto and neighbouring areas to east and west; and the St. John and Kennebecasis valleys of New Brunswick. Products from these areas were extensively traded around and across the bay and found their way to virtually all of the significant urban centres of Nova Scotia and New Brunswick. But the Fundy export economy was dominated by timber, notably from the St. John River system. Economic links to the British Isles were strong, although weakened as the nineteenth century progressed and Britain increasingly abandoned imperial tariffs for free trade. The Reciprocity Treaty of 1854, which provided for free trade in natural products between the United States and British North America, brought a southward shift in orientation. The third economic region was also an area of enormous cultural diversity. On the maritime coastlines of the Gulf of St. Lawrence, including Prince Edward Island, four languages were commonly spoken: Micmac, Acadian French, Gaelic, and English. Linguistic diversity implied variation in ethnicity—notably arising from Acadian resettlement in western Cape Breton, western Prince Edward Island, and the north shore of New Brunswick, as well as Scottish and Irish immigration—and in religion. Although Roman Catholicism predominated, it was deeply divided on ethnic lines. The gulf economy combined characteristics of the other two regions with distinct ones of its own. Like that of the Atlantic coast, the economy of the gulf depended heavily upon fisheries. But timber and agriculture were also important in certain areas: timber in the Miramichi and Restigouche districts of New Brunswick, agriculture in Prince Edward Island. From the island, agricultural products were exported to Great Britain and, again increasingly after 1854, to the United States. Also distinctive to the gulf region was the existence of economic affinities with Lower Canada. The links were evident at the level of merchant investment: major fish and lumbering merchants frequently had interests on both sides of the gulf and upriver. The cultural complexity of the gulf region and its participation in an interprovincial economy set it apart from either of the other two.

Both politically and in cultural and economic terms, therefore, the greater Nova Scotia of 1763 was soon subdivided. As the Confederation era approached, the economic complexity become even greater with the development of railways and the associated potential for industrialization. Meanwhile, the greater Quebec of 1774 was affected by similar forces, although the resulting patterns were different. The boundary provisions of the Quebec Act were short-lived, as the recognition of the United States by Britain involved the loss to Quebec, of the Ohio country, and half of the Great Lakes region. More boundary adjustments were soon to follow in the Constitutional Act of 1791. While the parallels between New Brunswick and Upper Canada should not be overdrawn—as there were significant differences in size of non-native population, proportions of native and non-native peoples, and physical geography—the foundation of both provinces was brought about by the dissatisfaction of Loyalist refugees with an existing government that they considered distant and alien. In the case of Upper Canada, there was an additional cultural and societal

Montreal, 1863.   NATIONAL ARCHIVES OF CANADA/C46677

dimension. Upper Canadian Loyalist leaders had no intention of being politically associated with the much more numerous Catholic and francophone population of the St. Lawrence valley and also rejected the socio-legal framework of seigneurialism. Although the Constitutional Act provided identical administrative structures for Upper and Lower Canada, the political cultures of the two colonies were divergent from the beginning, and the division of 1791 can be understood, in part, as the formal recognition of an already-existing political regionalism in the old province of Quebec. Yet here as in Nova Scotia, political regionalism was soon complicated by economic change and the development of distinct regions within both Upper and Lower Canada.

In Lower Canada, the starting point for economic regionalism was the seigneurial agriculture of the rural areas of the province. And the province was overwhelmingly rural, with fields closely adjoining even the largest urban centres. The nineteenth century witnessed rapid changes. The growth of merchant capitalism intensified the commercial exploitation of land, as did the development of the export trade in timber and other commodities. Railway development, from the 1840s onward, combined with steam shipping on the St. Lawrence to create the conditions for industrialization in urban areas. This industrializing process was most evident in Montreal. Culturally diverse, with an anglophone majority for a number of years at mid-century and with its harbour reconstructed, the province's largest city emerged effectively as a region by itself, with a hinterland that was already spreading beyond the boundaries of Lower Canada/Canada East. At the opposite pole were the rural areas of the St. Lawrence lowlands. Although affected by commercialization of land, by climatic and other environmental problems between 1815 and 1840, and by outmigration to urban centres as population grew and available land became scarce, these areas had been settled on the basis of seigneurialism and clearly bore its marks in arrangements of land lots long after 1854. The other distinct regions of pre-Confederation Lower Canada were formed or reformed in response to mid-nineteenth century economic and cultural change. The Eastern Townships had remained effectively as Abenaki territory until the Conquest of Canada, and had been settled by Loyalists and other immigrants from United States in the 1780s. The 93 townships themselves, based on freehold land tenure rather than seigneurialism, had been created by the British government in 1791. From 1840 onward, however, francophone immigration remade the region, so that by Confederation anglophones were in a minority in most townships. This immigration was partly a simple result of the overflowing population of the seigneurial areas, but in part was deliberately encouraged by the clergy in the form of colonization. Colonization efforts in the Appalachian highlands of the Eastern Townships did not, however, accomplish their professed goal of establishing prosperous agricultural settlements. Instead, settlers found themselves making a precarious living from a combination of subsistence agriculture on poor soil and wage labour in the woods, cutting timber for expanding lumber companies. In the Saguenay–Lac Saint-Jean region, and the Saint-Maurice valley, both located on the other side of the St. Lawrence valley from the Townships, a similar pattern emerged to an extent that prompted one historian, Normand Séguin, to argue that colonization was essentially a device for providing the lumber barons with the labour they needed.[6] Whatever the motivations involved, colonization should be understood as part of the series of socio-economic changes that informed the development of Lower Canadian regionalism in the nineteenth century.

Similar processes were at work in Upper Canada. There too agriculture and timber were the chief bases of the early nineteenth-century economy, although railway development brought a noticeable increase in urban manufacturing in the decades immediately preceding Confederation. Upper Canadian regionalism did not follow neat geographical patterns because one of the most important distinctions was between the urban centres that fringed the northern shore of Lake Ontario—Kingston, Belleville, Cobourg, Port Hope, Whitby, Toronto, Hamilton—and the rural areas that adjoined them. By the 1840s, Toronto was clearly emerging as the centre of an industrial region that encompassed Hamilton and was steadily outpacing the growth of the other lake ports. High rates of immigration, continuing capital accumulation from exports of wheat and timber, and the elaboration of a transport network composed of railways, steam transportation on Lake Ontario, and an increasing number of roads leading north from the lake: all of these contributed to urbanization. But there were also other recognizable regional experiences in Upper Canada.

---

[6] See Normand Séguin, *La conquête du sol au 19e siècle* (Sillery: Boreal Express, 1977). Other useful treatments of this question can be found in Paul-André Linteau, René Durocher, and Jean-Claude Robert, *Quebec: A History, 1867–1929,* translated by Robert Chodos (Toronto: James Lorimer, 1983), and J. I. Little, *Nationalism, Capitalism, and Colonization in Nineteenth-Century Quebec: The Upper St. Francis District* (Kingston, Montreal, London: McGill-Queen's University Press, 1989).

One region comprised the Ottawa valley and the eastern counties between the Ottawa and St. Lawrence rivers. Separated from the rest of Upper Canada by the southwestern tip of the Canadian Shield, this area was culturally diverse, including Loyalist and other immigrants from the United States and Glengarry Scots, and combined agriculture with the commercial development associated with the Ottawa valley timber trade. Economically, and as an area of crucial river transportation routes, it was as much part of Lower as Upper Canada. The experience of western Upper Canada was again distinct. The territory *par excellence* of the land companies and settlement promoters—major examples included the Huron Tract of the Canada Company and the townships on the north shore of Lake Erie that were settled by Thomas Talbot—this region experienced rapid immigration and agricultural development in the first half of the nineteenth century. Urban development took place in a number of centres, but notably in London, which emerged as a transportation centre and, following the involvement of western townships in the Rebellion of 1837, as a military centre also. Finally, the districts on Georgian Bay, south of Lake Nipissing, constituted a lumbering area. Although non-native settlement was slight before Confederation, except from the 1840s at the southern end of Georgian Bay in places such as Collingwood, Barry, and Penetanguishene, which had already functioned as a naval and military centre, the region did represent the furthest northward penetration of Upper Canadian resource exploitation. Thus, while all of Upper Canada and after 1841 Canada West was affected by large-scale immigration and by the influence of export trades, chiefly in wheat and timber, the balances varied by region.

West and north of the province of Canada's ill-defined borders, the effects of the non-native presence were widespread but were not associated with large-scale settlement. Diverse in native societies and profoundly influenced by the fur trade, except in certain extreme northern areas, the North and West in the first half of the nineteenth-century contained only three areas where colonial settlement existed in any sense recognizable to non-native North Americans: on Hudson Bay, at York Factory; on the Red River; and on the Pacific coast. All three were areas of continuing contact between native and non-native peoples, and York Factory always retained the character of a trading centre. It was an unusual one, however, in the relatively high number of Hudson's Bay Company employees who made up its permanent complement at any time—the total ranged between approximately 35 and 65 in the early and mid-nineteenth century—and

Red River Colony scene, 1823.   NATIONAL ARCHIVES OF CANADA/C8155

one resident, Letitia Hargrave, declared in 1849 that it was "by far the most respectable place in the Territory."[7] The company employees were overwhelmingly Scottish, and the length of their service at York Factory varied from those who served out only one contract to those who considered the northwest as their lifelong home and a place to raise their families. Conventional accompaniments of colonial life such as church and school

[7] Quoted in Michael Payne, *The Most Respectable Place in the Territory: Everyday Life in Hudson's Bay Company Service at York Factory, 1788 to 1870* (Ottawa: National Parks Service, Environment Canada, 1989), p. 27. For further reading on the areas to the West and North of Lower Canada, see G. M. Craig, *Upper Canada: The Formative Years, 1784–1841* (Toronto: McClelland and Stewart, 1963); Robin Fisher, *Contact and Conflict: Indian-European Relations in British Columbia, 1774–1890* (Vancouver: University of British Columbia Press, 1977); Gerald Friesen, *The Canadian Prairies: A History* (Toronto: University of Toronto Press, 1984); David Gagan, *Hopeful Travellers: Families, Land, and Social Change in Mid-Victorian Peel County, Canada West* (Toronto: University of Toronto Press, 1981); Michael B. Katz, *The People of Hamilton, Canada West: Family and Class in a Mid-Nineteenth Century Canadian City* (Cambridge, Mass.: Harvard University Press, 1976); Margaret A. Ormsby, *British Columbia: A History* (Toronto: Macmillan, 1958).

were not always available: schooling depended on the intermittent availability of teachers, and the first church was completed in 1858. Nevertheless, with its extensive permanent buildings and its summer vegetable gardens and livestock rearing, York Factory reproduced important elements of a colonial settlement, albeit one in which the native presence was pervasive and in which native and mixed-blood participation in the fur trade was the sole economic support. The Red River, while also based on the coexistence of native and non-native people, was differently patterned. The foundations of agricultural settlement were laid by the Selkirk colonists after their arrival in 1812, but after the troubled period of conflict with the North West Company and of environmental disasters culminating in the flood of 1826, population growth depended largely on retired employees of the Hudson's Bay Company with their native and mixed-blood families, and on French-speaking Métis. A multicultural society resulted, although its geographical situation inhibited economic development. Métis buffalo-hunting prospered as long as the stock lasted, but there was little market for agricultural products: the Hudson's Bay Company's

York Factory, 1878.   NATIONAL ARCHIVES OF CANADA/PA123668

demand was small, while distance prevented effective marketing in the populated areas further east. Only with the beginning of substantial westward movement out of the province of Canada in the 1860s was a new commercial structure created, though this immigration also threatened the distinctive cultural character of the Red River.

Until the late 1850s, the Pacific coast outposts of Britain's North American empire also retained the imprint of the fur trade. To be sure, the British trade on the West Coast had had a troubled history from its beginnings in the early nineteenth century. There was no short or easy route by which furs could be brought to market. Russian competition had not materialized on any significant scale, but an active rivalry with United States fur-trading interests had given place by the early 1840s to the even more serious threat of population movement from the South. In the 1844 presidential election in the United States, Democratic candidate James Polk was victorious on a platform that included the slogan "Fifty-four forty or fight." Some American interest groups wanted the U.S. northwestern

Victoria, 1858.   NATIONAL ARCHIVES OF CANADA/C741

boundary to adjoin Russian Alaska at the latitude of 54° 40 north. By that time, Britain's Fort Victoria had been established, partly for defence purposes but also as an alternative to the existing Hudson's Bay Company West Coast headquarters at the mouth of the Columbia River. When Polk's dramatic threat gave way to serious negotiation, and agreement was reached in 1846 to extend the British North America boundary to the coast on the latitude of 49° and then to the south of Vancouver Island, Victoria accordingly took on its new status. In 1849, Vancouver Island was granted to the Hudson's Bay Company by the British government as a colony, requiring that settlement be established within five years. As previous experience at the Red River showed, the fur trade and agricultural colonization were not naturally complementary, and it was questionable whether the company could be expected to take its colonial mandate seriously. Together with the hazards of the voyage from Britain by way of Cape Horn, the company's lack of support for Vancouver Island, despite the efforts of the colony's second governor, James Douglas after 1851, kept its British population to a total of about a thousand on the eve of the Fraser Valley Gold Rush of 1858. At that time, British presence on the mainland was slight and was centred at the small Fort Langley in the Fraser valley. The gold rush, though small by comparison with its California predecessor of 1849 and even with the Caribou Gold Rush that drew prospectors further into the interior of British Columbia in the early 1860s, altered decisively the population characteristics of the British Pacific coast. Rapid non-native population growth in the Fraser valley, even though much of it was temporary, led to the proclamation of the new mainland colony of British Columbia. By the time it was united with Vancouver Island in 1866, the combined non-native population had reached some 12 000, while acculturation and violent conflicts had resulted in widespread native displacement from the areas of immigrant settlement. For the first time in British North America west of the province of Canada, a region had emerged where the full effects of non-native colonization were being felt. Only at Red River had similar immigration already been initiated.

Regionalism and the Era of Confederation

During the century that had passed between the Conquest of Canada and the 1860s, the regional structure of British North America had become increasingly complex. The colonies of Nova Scotia and Quebec, formed from territories ceded to Great Britain by France, had experienced not only political division but also cultural and economic subdivision. Newfoundland had attained colonial status but was also economically subdivided into regions. The regional character of the North and West was still largely derived from the variation of native cultures and from the interactions associated with the fur trade, but, in certain areas, non-native settlement was influential by the 1860s. The complexity was such that Britain's sprawling empire in North America apparently defied any attempt at logical management. It was, it seemed, a mass of conflicting regions and subregions, only loosely grouped together in political units that over the years had shown an alarmingly high rate of attrition.

Yet by the 1860s new questions were being posed that demanded the revival of a simpler and stronger regionalism. In part, the origins of this process were cultural. Writers and painters increasingly portrayed British North America in terms that underlined the distinctness of regional landscapes and ways of life. The existing pattern of popular and folk cultures, expressed in native and Celtic languages as well as in French and English, and in folk art that ranged from religious images to ships' figureheads, was as complex as British North American society itself. More formal was the work of the writers and artists who, from the late eighteenth century onwards, increasingly found a middle-class clientele in the major urban centres. Portrait painters and itinerant musicians depended directly on this growing demand for their work. Writers of exploration and travel literature had long enjoyed a European as well as a British North American audience, while the topographical painting of military officers reflected contemporary British notions of the picturesque in landscapes. Closer to the real cultural values of British North Americans—or at least of those qualified by literacy and social class—were the many local publishing houses that grew up in the Atlantic colonies and the Canadas in the early nineteenth century and later on the Red River and on Vancouver Island. Newspapers and literary magazines led on to book publishing. Fiction writing, poetry, historical narrations, satire, and political commentary proliferated.

Out of this ferment came articulations of identity within British North America that became especially clear in the writing of history. In Newfoundland, the nationalistic imagery of a hardy population labouring under the oppression of West Country fish merchants and the British government had already had its genesis in John Reeves's *History of the*

Government of the Island of Newfoundland, published in London in 1793, and was passionately affirmed in pamphlets by the reformers William Carson and Patrick Morris during the campaign leading to representative government in 1832. The "intellectual awakening" of Nova Scotia produced, among other prominent writers and works, the historical studies of T.C. Haliburton who combined pride in Nova Scotia's past with faith in its future by tying the province's identity to the ideal of the independent farmer. Most notable was his 1829 *Historical and Statistical Account of Nova Scotia*. Haliburton had counterparts in the other Maritime provinces in authors such as Peter Fisher, historian of New Brunswick, and John MacGregor in Price Edward Island.

Historical writing in Upper Canada/Canada West, meanwhile, had to take account of sectional conflict and the Rebellion of 1837. It did so, as reflected in the widely read *History of Canada* by John McMullen and published in 1855, by celebrating the reforming achievements of responsible government and the steady economic progress that the author believed had followed the upheavals of the 1830s. In Canada East, François-Xavier Garneau published his three-volume *Histoire du Canada* between 1845 and 1848, portraying the struggle of the Canadiens for survival: a military struggle in the days of New France, and then a cultural and political struggle within British North America. Garneau's work gave a stimulus both to the production of historical novels evoking the glory and the tragedy of the French-Canadian experience and to the sophisticated literary and historical periodicals—primarily *Les Soirées canadiennes* and *Le Foyer canadien* that appeared during the 1860s. The paintings of Cornelius Krieghoff, meanwhile, embodied in vivid colours and sly, satirical humour the rural life of the St. Lawrence valley. It must be noted, however, that his work was more eagerly received by English-speaking patrons in the Canadas than by members of the francophone middle class who objected to his portrayals of bucolic habitants as representative of French Canada. His contemporary Paul Kane, who began his career as a portrait painter in Upper Canada, painted landscapes and scenes of native life he encountered during lengthy travels in the West and North in the 1840s. Out of all this, the regional variety of British North America was clear, but it was a variety in which broad patterns of conscious identity—limited as the perspectives were by the social class, ethnicity, and gender of the producers—were being articulated and portrayed for Newfoundland, the Maritime colonies, the Canadas, and the West and North.

These patterns were also reflected in the more general history of the

1860s. That this was a decade of crisis for British North America is clear enough from many historical accounts. What is not so evident is that there were different crises for different regions. In Newfoundland and the Maritimes, the crisis was primarily economic, though it had clear political implications. In Newfoundland, declining productivity in the fishery was becoming evident as population growth outpaced increases in production. There was also the more general question of how Newfoundland should adapt itself to meet changes in technology, to steam and steel, and to what extent the colony should attempt to emulate mainland industrialization. The Maritimes also had questions to face. Not that the economy of any one of the provinces lacked strength, as the health of sea-borne trade attested. Nevertheless, there was room for serious debate on strategies for the future, especially in the context of the transition that was already taking place from older technologies to steam traction and industrial production based on steel rather than on wood. Should the maritime economy be held steady on its existing course, with modern technologies used chiefly to strengthen existing trade connections? Should the provinces move aggressively to develop land links with the United States, particularly through the building of a railway from Saint John to Boston and thus seek continuing trade as well as industrial development? Or, should the Maritimes opt for a continental economy in association with the rest of British North America involving a railway link with Canada and new inland trading relationships? This was the argument that favoured Confederation, and it prevailed in the face of widespread scepticism. The Confederation question in the Maritimes was debated in the context of fundamental economic questions that had no simple or reliable answers. They were, moreover, regional questions in the sense that they were common to all three provinces. Prince Edward Island, to be sure, was more remote until the early 1870s from railway construction and industrialization, but it too had to face the hard realities of shifting trade patterns. Thus, for the Maritime provinces, Confederation was considered because it offered one possible resolution of uncertainties over the economic future. Of course there was more to it than financial considerations. Feelings of loyalty to Great Britain and the need for military defence were among the other issues involved, but the intercolonial railway and the prospects for east-west continental trade were crucial matters.

The province of Canada faced a very different crisis. It was both long-standing and acute, and it was essentially cultural and political. By what political arrangements could the largely francophone Canada East be reconciled lastingly with the overwhelmingly anglophone Canada West? The separation of Upper and Lower Canada in 1791 had been, among other things, an effort to create stability by separating the different political cultures of Canadians and Upper Canadian Loyalists. But it did not resolve the class and cultural conflicts within Lower Canada, as Lord Durham's famous comment of 1839 illustrated: "I found two nations warring in the bosom of a single state." Durham's preferred solution of uniting the two Canadas, however, did not have the desired result of bringing about the acculturation of the francophone population into a British society. Rather, the war between the two nations was transferred to a larger political arena and was embodied first in conflicts over the lesser representation of Canada East in the provincial Parliament and then in the lengthy debates over representation by population after Canada West had attained a majority of the population. The centrality of the problem, compounded by the equally acute financial crisis of the time, was evident in the political paralysis that gripped the province of Canada in the early 1860s. Again, the possible solutions were not clear-cut. The status quo was untenable. At the other extreme, complete division into renewed provinces of Upper and Lower Canada might solve the immediate political impasse but it carried a risk of economic instability in view of the economic and transportation links that existed within the Province of Canada. Like the economic dilemma of the Maritimes, this conundrum was a genuinely regional issue. That is not to say that relationships between language groups were unimportant elsewhere, but only in Canada had they attained constitutionally significant dimensions. For both Canada and the Maritimes, Confederation could be seen as a plausible avenue toward solution of a regional crisis. But they were not the same crises.

The North and West also faced an uncertain future in the 1860s. To suggest that there was a single crisis for all of that immense territory would run the risk of being simplistic. Nevertheless, there were certain matters that had a wide significance. First among them was the untenability of the situation whereby the Hudson's Bay Company had operated, as defined in 1858 by one friendly observer, as "the custodians of the whole of that vast territory for the British Empire."[8] Advocates of western colonial settlement

---

[8] Edward Ermatinger, quoted in Doug Owram, *Promise of Eden: The Canadian Expansionist Movement and the Idea of the West, 1856–1900* (Toronto: University of Toronto Press, 1980), p. 207. For other reading on questions relating to the regionalism of the mid-nineteenth century,

saw the company, and the fur trade itself, as an obstacle to progress. Experience on the Red River and on Vancouver Island had indicated that, at best, it was an ineffective mediator in the intercultural tensions that non-native settlement inevitably brought. A second, and related, consideration was the momentum that western settlement had attained by the 1860s. Again, British Columbia provided an example, and migration from Canada West to the Red River was another. Canada West, as the 1860s opened, was hardly overcrowded, in that large areas of uncultivated land still existed. Readily available land of good quality, however, was increasingly hard to find, and the western peninsula was virtually closed as an area of further settlement. Expansion thus became an attractive possibility. It was stimulated by scientific findings that suggested new uses for the western territories. Meteorologists such as Henry Youle Hind of Trinity College, Toronto, argued that the prairie northwest, contrary to previous assumptions, was not only habitable by settled populations but would prove fertile enough for agricultural development.

Geologists such as Sir William Logan, provincial geologist in the province of Canada from 1842 and first director of the Geological Survey of Canada, identified both the lack of commercially valuable mineral resources in the existing settled areas of the province and their availability on the Canadian Shield. The surrender of Rupert's Land to the dominion by the Hudson's Bay Company in 1869 was obviously in the interests of Canadian expansion and a solution to the northwestern dilemmas of the 1860s by the simple expedient of invasion by colonial settlement.

In reality, matters were not quite so straightforward, as the Red River Resistance showed in late 1869 and early 1870. The negotiations conducted by Louis Riel's provisional government with Ottawa produced some recognition of Métis rights in the new province of Manitoba, although no lasting security. More successful were the representatives of

---

see James Hiller and Peter Neary, eds. *Newfoundland in the Nineteenth and Twentieth Centuries: Essays in Interpretation* (Toronto: University of Toronto Press, 1980); Morton, *The Critical Years*; Patrick O'Flaherty, *The Rock Observed: Studies in the Literature of Newfoundland* (Toronto: University of Toronto Press, 1979); George L. Parker, *The Beginnings of the Book Trade in Canada* (Toronto: University of Toronto Press, 1985); Dennis Reid, *A Concise History of Canadian Painting* (2nd ed.; Toronto: Oxford University Press, 1988); John G. Reid, *Six Crucial Decades: Times of Change in the History of the Maritimes* (Halifax: Nimbus, 1987); M. Brook Taylor, *Promoters, Patriots, and Partisans: Historiography in Nineteenth-Century English Canada* (Toronto: University of Toronto Press, 1989); Suzanne Zeller, *Inventing Canada: Early Victorian Science and the Idea of a Transcontinental Nation* (Toronto: University of Toronto Press, 1987).

the 12 000 non-native residents of British Columbia who obtained terms from Ottawa that included assumption of the new province's public debt and the promise of a transcontinental railway. Yet even in this case, tensions soon developed, notably over the federal government's lengthy delays in fulfilling its railway obligation. The westward extension of the Dominion of Canada between 1869 and 1871 was a significant advancement of the regional interests of Ontario and—if the language provisions of the Manitoba Act were to be believed—of Quebec. It also offered some scope for negotiation by those who lived in the Northwest, aimed at protecting their own interests. Not only was this true of the Métis of Manitoba and the settlers of British Columbia but also of the native leaders who negotiated the first group of seven numbered treaties between 1871 and 1877. Where native and federal interests came into serious conflict, events proved that the dominion could wield sufficient military power to have its way. Such would be the lesson of the defeat of the North-West Rebellion in 1885. Non-native grievances, however, could not so easily be suppressed and proved to be politically more tenacious. Thus, in the formative years of the creation of the Canadian West, as in the initial forging of Confederation in the mid-1860s, there were different regional agendas. Their legacy would continue to be seen in recurring instances of western alienation in federal affairs.

Regionalism and the Nature of Canadian History

Whether Canadians like it or not, regionalism is essential to the nature of Canada. Whether Canadian historians like it or not, regionalism is inherent in Canada's past. Historically, Canadian regionalism has been complex. There have been different regional patterns at different times, and they have arisen from different combinations of cultural, economic, societal and political regionalism. The Confederation era saw an apparent simplification of regional interests, as immediately pressing questions confronted the Atlantic colonies, the province of Canada, and the Northwest. Confederation could be portrayed as an important part of the solution to all of these questions. But whether it would operate that way in practice would be revealed only gradually in the post-Confederation development of the country. As a response to the regional agendas of the 1860s and early 1870s, the union of British North America brought with it a tendency toward interregional tension. This was partly because of the differences in the regional agendas themselves. A Maritimer who believed that the real purpose of Confederation was to enable the various provinces to pool their economic fortunes in a way that was profitable and equitable for all did not necessarily see eye to eye with an Ontarian or Quebecer who saw it primarily as a device to reconcile language groups. Neither would have had much in common with the westerner who regarded Confederation as a framework within which inevitable societal changes in the West could be accommodated through negotiation. The very urgency that the crises of the 1860s produced made it temporarily possible for these implied conflicts to be ignored. In the political proceedings of the Confederation era, there were strong elements not only of conviviality and visionary enthusiasm but also of willing suspension of disbelief in the compatibility of the motives and interests represented at the bargaining tables. This artificial conviviality could not last forever, and signs of disillusionment soon began to emerge. When the Halifax *Morning Chronicle* endorsed repeal of the British North America Act on May 18, 1886, by declaring on behalf of Nova Scotians that "we thrived before we endured the exactions of the Canucks, we shall thrive when we are once again free from these exactions," it expressed feelings of betrayal corresponding to those that would later accompany proposals for secession in Quebec and the West. If Ontario was exempt from such feelings, it was because it alone experienced the satisfactions from Confederation for which others had hoped in vain: its linguistic and cultural character was maintained, and, at the same time, its economy grew both absolutely and relatively to other parts of Canada.

But there was even more than that to the regional tensions that Canada would experience. Although the crises of the 1860s forced political leaders to think in terms of broadly defined regions, the environmentally and historically generated diversity of British North American societies never lay far beneath the surface. Each of the regions was subdivided along cultural, economic, and societal lines. Each contained a variety of strongly held senses of identity that proceeded from shared historical memory and would not easily, if at all, be replaced by the notion of Canadianism. This was most conspicuously true of those whose nationality was consciously distinct from and prior to the creation of the Dominion of Canada—native peoples, Acadians, Canadiens, Métis—but it held good also for Maritime anti-Confederates who believed in the continuing dynamism of the British Empire, or for Vancouver Islanders whose distance from central and eastern Canada would be only partly offset even by the arrival of the first transcontinental passenger train on the other side of the Strait of Georgia in 1886. Thus, to the conflicting expectations of the larger regions were added those of a host of competing subregions and limited identities. It is no accident, given this complexity, that for Canada the process of constitutional reform has invariably proved to be agonizing, just as efforts to produce a common sense of economic or cultural purpose have frequently dissolved in the face of regional contradictions. However, the conclusion to be drawn is not that regional distinctions are a national liability and should be abolished or ignored but rather that they must be understood and worked with. Regional divisions were built in to Canada when it was created, and they have continued to be fundamental to the nature of the country. Historians—and others who seek to understand Canada as a nation and as society—need to recognize this reality, as they have increasingly done in recent decades. The centralist perspective that was understandable enough in early twentieth-century scholars who lived and wrote in the era of increasing central Canadian ascendancy is no longer excusable in their successors of the 1990s. Regional diversity can be celebrated, deplored, or simply observed, as the individual scholar wishes. Of its central importance, however, and of the rightful place of regional analysis in Canadian historical methodology, none should be in doubt.

THE CONFEDERATION QUESTION, 1864–1867

The making of Confederation has been among the most celebrated and least understood processes in Canadian history. Although generations of historians have interpreted and reinterpreted the events that led to the proclamation of the Dominion of Canada on July 1, 1867, the historical character of the country has continued frequently to be defined by Canadians according to myths and symbols rather than precise analysis. Not that there is anything inherently offensive in myths and symbols. All countries have them, and Canada is never likely to shed them entirely. However, the particular mythologies that have grown up around the question of Confederation—even, perhaps especially, those that have been intended to celebrate and glorify the achievement of 1867—have seriously oversimplified both the events themselves and the nature of Canada. The resulting confusion has underlaid much of the recurring intellectual agony that some Canadians have experienced in trying to define the elusive national identity. It has also bedevilled the tortuous processes of continuing constitutional reform. Some myths of Confederation are simply foolish, even though they may have been mouthed at times by some of the most august personages in the land. An example is the notion that there were two founding peoples, French and English. Convincingly rebutted by native leaders as insulting to the First Nations, this assertion might also be taken as slighting the large Celtic populations of all the original provinces of the dominion. More subtle and

CANADA AT CONFEDERATION

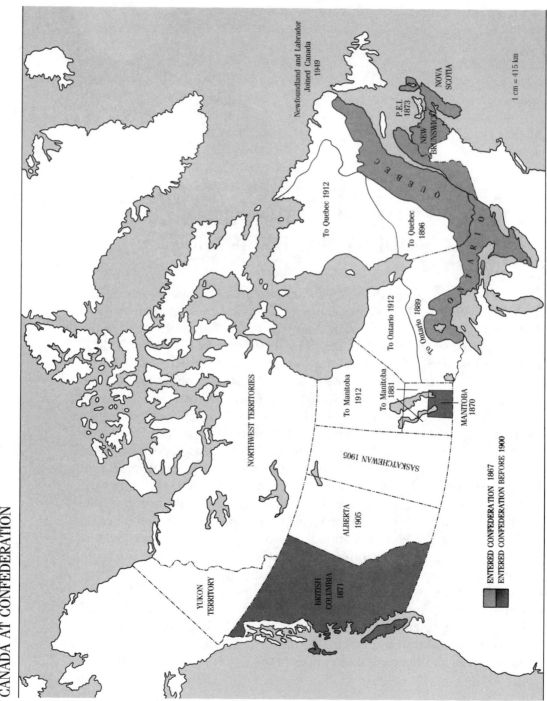

Newfoundland and Labrador
Joined Canada
1949

1 cm = 415 km

P.E.I.
1873

NOVA
SCOTIA

NEW
BRUNSWICK

Q U E B E C

To Quebec 1912

To Quebec
1896

O N T A R I O

To Ontario 1912

To Ontario 1889

NORTHWEST TERRITORIES

To Manitoba
1912

To Manitoba 1881

MANITOBA
1870

SASKATCHEWAN 1905

ALBERTA
1905

BRITISH
COLUMBIA
1871

YUKON
TERRITORY

ENTERED CONFEDERATION 1867
ENTERED CONFEDERATION BEFORE 1900

not at all foolish is the contention that the Confederation agreement implied a compact by which two language groups, French and English, would coexist. It would take a falsely legalistic interpretation of the British North America Act and a refusal to acknowledge much of the rhetoric of pro-Confederates in the province of Canada to argue that there was no such understanding. And yet to assume that the reconciliation of language groups was the prime and fundamental principle of Confederation would be to simplify the character of a union formed by colonies that had, as the

The Fathers of Confederation. Photographs taken at the Quebec Conference and brought together to mark the fiftieth anniversary of Confederation.   NATIONAL ARCHIVES OF CANADA/C2780

Montreal pro-Confederate and future Canadian finance minister John Rose observed in 1865, "many separate and distinct interests and local differences." Even so apparently safe a belief as the notion that Confederation represented the founding of a new nation requires qualification. There were strong hopes in 1867 that it would do so. "We are laying the foundation of a great State," declared the British colonial secretary during the parliamentary passage of the British North America Act. But the act itself was explicit in its denial to Canada of any sovereign powers in its foreign relations and envisaged that the union of 1867 was only a stage on the way to "the eventual Admission...of other Parts of British North America." In other areas that were as much political as constitutional, such as federal-provincial relations, there were long evolutionary processes to come. Confederation, important as it was, must be seen as a stage in the ongoing association of provinces that were diverse before they united and were not homogenized when the union took place.

Part of the responsibility for the existing confusion over the nature of Confederation must be borne by historians. Despite the volume of historical writing on the Confederation question and the high quality of some of it, the role of historians as the public's guardians against facile assumptions about the past has not been satisfactorily fulfilled in this case. During the early and middle decades of the twentieth century, separate schools of interpretation emerged in the French and English languages, and there was little contact or debate between the two. Historians writing in English tended to celebrate Confederation. "Consciously," wrote Donald Creighton in 1944, "with a glad sense of release from the past, and an excited confidence in the future, the 'fathers of Confederation' turned their backs on the pettiness and inferiority of provincialism and dependence." Confederation, agreed A. R. M. Lower in 1946, was "a wise and far-seeing" effort toward "building out of scattered and parochial colonies a great continental nation."[1] These verdicts of the 1940s were contained in

---

[1] Donald Creighton, *Dominion of the North: A History of Canada* (Toronto: Macmillan, 1944), p. 304; Arthur R. M. Lower, *Colony to Nation: A History of Canada* (Toronto: Longmans, Green, and Co., 1946), p. 334. Other works referred to in this section include: R. G. Trotter, *Canadian Federation, its Origins and Achievement: A Study in Nation Building* (Toronto: Dent, 1924); William Menzies Whitelaw, *The Maritimes and Canada Before Confederation* (Toronto: Oxford, 1934); Donald Creighton, *John A. Macdonald: The Young Politician* (Toronto: Macmillan, 1952); Creighton, *John A. Macdonald: The Old Chieftain* (Toronto: Macmillan, 1955); Creighton, *The Road to Confederation: The Emergence of Canada, 1863–1867* (Toronto: Macmillan, 1964); P. B. Waite, *The Life and Times of Confederation, 1864–1867: Politics, Newspapers, and the Union of*

general histories of Canada and drew upon the works of the two authors and other historians in earlier years, such as Reginald Trotter's 1924 work, *Canadian Federation: Its Origins and Achievement* and W. M. Whitelaw's less congratulatory but generally compatible 1934 study, *The Maritimes and Canada Before Confederation*. Some dissenting voices were raised in the late 1940s and 1950s, but their complaints were more of the way Canada had come to be dominated by its central provinces than aimed at tarnishing the lustre of the 1867 achievement. Significantly, the outstanding work in the English-Canadian historiography of the 1950s, to judge from its influence on a generation of historians, was Creighton's massive and laudatory biography of John A. Macdonald. Within this tradition, there was little scope for a detached, critical scrutiny of the Confederation process.

Although the early 1960s brought forward some sophisticated works that continue deservedly to be read—P. B. Waite's *The Life and Time of Confederation* and W. L. Morton's *The Critical Years*, as well as Creighton's *The Road to Confederation*—they presented no fundamental challenge to the overwhelmingly celebrationist historiography that had gone before. The problem was not that it was necessarily wrong to raise a case favourable to Confederation but rather that the arguments of the anti-Confederates of the 1860s were ignored or undervalued. Thus, the quality of the political and intellectual exchanges of that era was underestimated, and much of the real drama of the events could easily be lost.

Writings in the French language tended to be more sceptical. The Abbé Lionel-Adolphe Groulx, the leading Quebec historian of the first half of

British North America (Toronto: University of Toronto Press, 1962); W. L. Morton, *The Critical Years: The Union of British North America, 1857–1873* (Toronto: McClelland and Stewart, 1964); Lionel Groulx, *La Confédération canadienne, ses origines* (Montréal: Le Devoir, 1918); Jean-Charles Bonenfant, *The French Canadians and the Birth of Confederation* (Ottawa: Canadian Historical Association, 1966); D. A. Muise, "The Federal Election of 1867 in Nova Scotia: An Economic Interpretation," *Collections of the Nova Scotia Historical Society*, 36(1968), pp. 327–51; William M. Baker, *Timothy Warren Anglin, 1822–96: Irish Catholic Canadian* (Toronto: University of Toronto Press, 1977); Kenneth G. Pryke, *Nova Scotia and Confederation, 1864–1871* (Toronto: University of Toronto Press, 1979); J. Murray Beck, *Joseph Howe: The Briton Becomes a Canadian, 1848–1873* (Kingston and Montreal: McGill-Queen's University Press, 1983); David Weale and Harry Baglole, *The Island and Confederation: The End of an Era* (Summerside: Williams and Crue, 1973); Phillip Buckner, "The Maritimes and Confederation: A Reassessment," *Canadian Historical Review*, 71 (1990), pp. 1–30; Stanley B. Ryerson, *Unequal Union: Confederation and the Roots of Conflict in the Canadas, 1815–1873* (Toronto: Progress Books, 1968). For a valuable collection of recent perspectives, see Ged Martin, ed., *The Causes of Canadian Confederation* (Fredericton: Acadiensis Press, 1990).

the twentieth century, wrote in 1918 on *La Confédération canadienne, ses origines*. For Groulx, Confederation had served a legitimate purpose in fending off the imperialisms of both Great Britain and the United States, but it had failed to provide an adequate framework for the cultural health of French Canada. Groulx's verdict did not go unchallenged by other Quebec historians at the time or later, but it did set the agenda for debate centring on the significance of Confederation for the relationship between French and English language groups, the question of whether there was an implied pact between language groups, the extent to which the British North America Act had provided for a federal system decentralized enough to allow such a pact to be fulfilled, and the related matter of whether French-language minorities outside Quebec were important in themselves or whether only Quebec was the heartland of francophonie in Canada.

By the early 1960s, Quebec historians such as Jean-Charles Bonenfant had concluded that the notion of the pact was a myth and that the reality was one of a centralized union. Accordingly, Quebec nationalists of the era drew the further conclusions that only through secession, or at least a fundamental reappraisal of the Constitution, could Quebec protect itself and that French-language minorities elsewhere must fend for themselves. The evolving French-language historiography, therefore, had little in common with the pro-Confederation thrust of the English-language writers, and yet its critique was focused squarely on linguistic and cultural duality and how far the arrangements of 1867 could accommodate the needs of French Canada or, in the terms increasingly characteristic of the writing of the 1960s, those of Quebec. Then came the profound historiographical changes of the late 1960s, which affected all historical writing in Canada regardless of language. Old-style political history was displaced from its leading position as social and economic studies explored the experience of those who had been ignored or slighted before: women, the working class, native, African, and Asian groups, as well as other non-English and non-French immigrants. Region, ethnicity, gender, and social class became the preferred tools of analysis. While political history did not disappear, historians in general had other concerns than to expend more energy on what seemed to be the tired question of the Confederation process. It was true that the regional approach yielded important studies by authors such as D. A. Muise, William Baker, J. Murray Beck, Kenneth G. Pryke, Harry Baglole and David Weale, and Phillip Buckner that revised existing interpretations of the role of the Maritime provinces and invited reappraisal of the basis for both pro- and anti-Confederate activity. But a general reassessment, synthesizing old and new scholarship, was slow to emerge.

A modern view of the history of the making of Confederation must examine certain essential questions. What were the arguments for and against Confederation and how did they vary between provinces? What were the problems that Confederation was intended to address, and why did the pro-Confederates think that it could resolve them? What were the dynamics of the process, according to class, gender, ethnicity, and region? Confederation was the project of a few well-heeled and well-connected males whose ethnic origins were exclusively Anglo-Celtic or French and who as politicians had regional interests to advance. What did their actions mean for the great majority of British North Americans who might share one or two of these characteristics but certainly not all? Some of these questions were broached by Stanley Ryerson in his *Unequal Union*, published in 1968, but the upsurge of specialized scholarship since then has provided the scope for more comprehensive answers than were open to Ryerson. The historiography of Confederation, while including works by many of Canada's finest historians of the past hundred years, has been a curiously limited one: limited, that is, by the tendencies of writers to celebrate Confederation, to interpret it only in relation to cultural and linguistic dualism, or to bypass it in favour of newer areas of study. Only by shifting attention back to the Confederation debates and interpreting them in the light of modern scholarship can historians of the 1990s frame new answers to questions that bear on the fundamental character of Canada.

The Geopolitics of 1864

In 1864, British North America was in a state of crisis. The complexity of the crisis—or rather of the crises, for there were at least four of them— defied any attempt at a simple solution. Nevertheless, in the minds of some, a union of the British North American colonies was the nearest approach to a feasible remedy. Three of the concurrent crises were internal to British North America and were centred in particular geographical areas. But the fourth stemmed from external pressures, and it was this one that gave much of the plausibility to the notion of union. It concerned the place of the British American colonies in the troubled international arena of the 1860s. The American Civil War was still a bitter and destructive conflict as 1864 opened, though the war of attrition that had prevailed in 1863 made it unlikely that the South could hope any longer for a military victory. Public opinion in British North America was predominantly pro-southern, especially as the northern cause was widely perceived as aiming solely at preserving the union rather than abolishing slavery. There were significant exceptions to this pattern. George Brown, leading reform politician in Canada West and editor of the *Globe* newspaper, was an abolitionist of long standing and used the *Globe* to counteract the pro-southern thrust of other journals. Some 35 000 British North Americans enlisted in the northern army, including many black fugitives who had crossed the border to escape from slavery. One fugitive, the antislavery activist and Methodist preacher Josiah Henson, stood trial for recruiting activities in Canada West—an offence when undertaken for a foreign army—though he was eventually acquitted. Nevertheless, sympathy for the South was conspicuous and was intensified by the *Trent* affair in late 1861. The British steamship *Trent* was stopped by a northern naval vessel off the Bahamas, and two southern agents were arrested on their way to Europe. Charges and counter-charges between Britain and the Union government led to fears of a northern invasion of British North America and the hasty dispatch of 14 000 British troops to meet the threat. The invasion never came, but tensions lingered. The actions of some Nova Scotians some two years later in attempting to free the arrested southern hijackers of the New York–Portland passenger steamer *Chesapeake*, eventually captured by an American navy vessel and towed into Halifax harbour following the initial seizure on 7 December 1863, provided yet another well-publicized incident. Southern agents and sympathizers continued to be active in towns along the border and in Montreal.

In this climate, relations with the United States could hardly flourish. Already, there were signs that the Reciprocity Treaty might be in political trouble in the United States as northern opinion demanded some form of reprisal. Military tension, although much reduced from the level it had attained in the wake of the *Trent* affair, still existed, and a future invasion of British North America was not inconceivable. At the same time, British attitudes were also causing concern. The long process of British movement away from preferential economic treatment of its colonies and toward free trade had been under way for generations, but the damage wrought by the major British retrenchments of imperial preference in the 1840s was still a fresh memory. Now, in 1864, Great Britain was increasingly questioning its defence commitments in North America. In late 1863, a European international crisis had arisen when Prussia and Denmark confronted each other over the ownership of the territories of Schleswig and Holstein. Great Britain gave public support to Denmark but lacked the military resources to intervene in February 1864 when the matter led to war. British embarrassment at this conspicuous display of weakness was compounded when its ally went down to defeat within six months, and it was easy to assign part of the blame to the presence of many thousands of troops in British North American garrisons. Now more than ever, Britain wanted a way out. For all the British American colonies, the potential economic and military hostility of the United States combined with the slackening economic and military commitment of Great Britain to pose serious questions concerning the best route to survival.

The economic threat was especially crucial to the Atlantic colonies. Newfoundland's situation was exceptional in that its geographical position isolated it from any serious military threat from the United States and in that its economy, although in a poor state in the mid-1860s because of declining catches of cod and seal, depended more on exports to southern Europe, Brazil, and the West Indies than to either Great Britain or the United States. The three Maritime colonies, however, had difficult choices to make. The crisis that confronted them in the 1860s was not characterized by any lack of immediate prosperity. The continuing expansion of the already-large fleet of merchant sailing vessels operating from the Maritimes gave clear evidence of a flourishing trading economy. In an era of rising freight rates—partly caused by the disruption of United States shipbuilding during the Civil War—there were opportunities for entry into new international carrying trades, and competition from steam could be offset by the construction of larger and better-constructed sailing ships. Nevertheless, changes would eventually have to come, as Maritime merchants and politicians were well aware. For a region whose leaders took pride in being on the cutting edge of enterprise in the world's most expansionist economic association, the British Empire, there was no inclination to rest on past achievements. For all the existing prosperity of the trading and shipbuilding ports, adaptations would be demanded both by technological change and by shifting international trade patterns.

Therein lay the crisis, for there was deep disagreement as to which direction should be taken. One possibility was to retain the essential character of the existing economy but make the transition to steam-driven, steel-hulled vessels as necessity dictated. The fleet, therefore, would continue to be, as it always had been, modern and efficient. Coal would be a growing export commodity, and steam technology would increase production of more traditional staple trade goods such as timber. As a version of the region's future, this view had its merits, but it also raised difficult questions. What was the guarantee that trade patterns would remain stable, especially in view of the unreliability of Great Britain? What if freight rates stopped rising and went sharply downward? A possible answer was economic diversification gained through links to the United States. As well as maintaining existing overseas and coastal trends, a railway connection with New England might promote new exchanges and encourage industrial growth in the Maritimes. Again, though, there was uncertainty, arising in this case from the tensions caused by the Civil War and the implied threat even to the Reciprocity Treaty. A third strategy would also involve diversification and a railway: the construction of an intercolonial railway to the province of Canada, to open up new markets for Maritime products, and stimulate the export of Canadian goods through Maritime ports. This possibility, as well as defence considerations, had influenced Maritime interest in negotiations with Canada in 1862, which had seemed—until Canada reneged a few months later—to have produced a workable financial agreement. However, questions could be raised as to whether a close association with Canada would be beneficial for colonies that previously had had a coastal rather than a continental orientation. And how close would the association have to be? If it implied a basic shift away from the traditional seaborne economy, it could be seen as a reckless gamble. In 1864, there still seemed to be time to consider all of these options, but of the difficulty of the choices involved and the unpredictability of the results there could be no doubt.

The crisis in the province of Canada was more conspicuous and more obviously urgent. Politically unstable and plagued by public debt, the province was close to collapse. The depth of its problems became evident during the first half of 1864 in unsuccessful attempts to maintain a stable government. Since the spring of 1862, two successive reformist ministries had been headed by John Sandfield Macdonald, the first led jointly with Louis-Victor Sicotte and the second with Antoine-Aimé Dorion. The Sandfield Macdonald governments had attempted necessary financial reforms, but in doing so had alienated both the British colonial office and entrenched British financial interests, which feared for their railway investments in Canada. Macdonald might have survived these problems had it not been for the depth of sectionalism in the province. The

Macdonald-Sicotte ministry had attempted to govern on the basis of the "double majority"—the principle that any measure passed by the legisla-

George Brown, 1818-1880.   NATIONAL ARCHIVES OF CANADA/C8359

tive assembly would have to be approved by a majority of the members in Canada East and in Canada West, so that no legislation could be imposed by the will of only one of the two sections. The attempts had collapsed, however, in the face of religious tensions aroused by a private member's

John A. Macdonald, 1815-1891.   NATIONAL ARCHIVES OF CANADA/C21597

bill that provided for greater privileges for separate Roman Catholic schools in Canada West. The Scott Act, named for its author, Richard W. Scott, passed on the basis of a majority from Canada East. The resulting uproar from Protestants in Canada West greatly embittered the sectional tension that already existed and contributed to the fall of Sandfield Macdonald's first ministry. Reorganized in partnership with Dorion, the government emerged from an election in the spring of 1863 with a small overall majority, but without a majority in Canada East. The notion of the double majority was now fatally weakened, and the government itself fell in March 1864. It was replaced for less than three months by a Liberal-Conservative government headed by Etienne-Paschal Taché and John A. Macdonald. Their defeat on 14 June, on a motion of no confidence, underlined how desperate the province's predicament was.

Most political leaders could now agree that some form of constitutional change was needed in order to resolve the deadlock that proceeded from the tensions between Canada East and Canada West and, ultimately, between French and English language groups. To achieve the needed reform, however, would require more unity than the Canadian Parliament had yet been able to muster. There was a way out in June 1864, though it was a difficult one. On the same day as the Taché-Macdonald ministry was defeated, an all-party committee on constitutional reform, chaired by George Brown, clearly the leading reform politician since the collapse of the Sandfield Macdonald ministry, presented its report. It favoured "a Federative system, applied either to *Canada* alone, or the whole British North American provinces." The committee had not been unanimous. Two of its fifteen members favoured new attempts to refurbish the principle of the double majority, while John A. Macdonald favoured a more centralized legislative union of British North America rather than a federation. But Brown quickly indicated that he would support a new ministry dedicated to the search for constitutional change, and on 22 June the "Great Coalition" was inaugurated. Nominally headed by Taché, the coalition was dominated by John A. Macdonald, Brown, and George-Etienne Cartier. Involving as it did the coming together of old political enemies, its formation was a desperate move. The new ministry could not be expected to outlive the crisis that had created it, but, in the meantime, it enjoyed wide parliamentary support in its efforts to break through the constitutional impasse. Brown would have preferred to explore first the possibility of a federation including only Canada East and Canada West, but Macdonald insisted on beginning with the notion of a British North American

George-Etienne Cartier, 1814-1873. NATIONAL ARCHIVES OF CANADA/C6166

union. Failure in both was inconceivable, as it would leave Canada in an ungovernable state, but the immediate question was whether other parts of British America could be persuaded to join in resolving the Canadian crisis.

There was a further internal crisis in the British North America of 1864, one that would have to affect the plans of the Canadian coalition to include annexation of the Northwest in their proposed union. Although characterized by a vast geographical area and profound human diversity, the entire territory represented by the Northwest and the Pacific coast was in an era of great transition. The population in 1864 was still overwhelmingly composed of native people, although the impact of the fur trade and the influence of the Métis gave evidence of the way in which the non-native presence had had at least an indirect effect on virtually every area south of the Arctic Circle and on some to the north of it. On the Red River, on Vancouver Island, and, since the late 1850s, in the Fraser valley, non-native colonization was growing. Scientific surveys indicated that mineral resources as well as hitherto-unsuspected agricultural possibilities might beckon. And if prospective immigrants from Britain or from Canada West did not come forward in sufficient numbers, there were many south of the United States border who could fill what was, from a non-native perspective, a vacuum. The likelihood of increasing non-native settlement raised political as well as cultural and environmental questions. Since 1670, the Hudson's Bay Company had exercised a loose form of jurisdiction over Rupert's Land, and since 1834 and 1849, respectively, its officers had governed on the Red River and on Vancouver Island. Whether a fur-trading company was an effective body to provide government to growing centres of population, however, was doubtful, and the doubts were not lessened in 1863 when control of the Hudson's Bay Company passed to a syndicate of investors known as the International Financial Society. More interested in real estate profits than in governing, the new owners soon began negotiations with the British government aimed at removing overall company control of the West in return for ownership of certain potentially profitable lands. It was clear in 1864 that the entire north and west of British America was about to undergo political and demographic changes, but what the results would be was still an open question.

Thus, for diverse reasons, British North America entered on the mid-1860s in a state of instability. The individual crises that were at hand varied widely in their causation and their degree of urgency, but in every part of British North America, the status quo was becoming untenable. The attitudes of Great Britain and the United States only added to the danger-ous uncertainties of the time. It was unlikely that any simple solution could be found for all of the problems that existed, but the Canadian proposal for a British North American union was a start toward working on some of them. Much depended, of course, on how the initial proposal would translate into practical initiatives. It was against this geopolitical backdrop that the "Fathers of Confederation" began the deliberations that took them to Charlottetown and Quebec.

The Charlottetown and Quebec Conferences

The conferences of 1864, in Charlottetown in September and Quebec City in October, were crucial to the series of developments by which Confeder-ation eventually came about almost three years later. At the conferences, the pro-Confederates gained the initiative. Although hard-pressed at times, especially in New Brunswick, they succeeded in retaining it. Although their anti-Confederate opponents marshalled serious arguments and enjoyed substantial public support, the momentum generated in Charlottetown and Quebec was formidable. The two conferences were totally different events, and yet together they constituted a single process. The Charlottetown meeting was not concerned primarily with detailed planning for the proposed union of the colonies. Although some specifics were discussed, the real significance of the occasion lay in the success of the Canadian participants in shifting attention away from Maritime union—the ostensible subject of the conference—and toward British North American union, and in the social ties that developed among all the delegates. These were essential preconditions for the bargaining that took place in Quebec, from which emerged the 72 Quebec Resolutions that formed the first explicit effort to shape the union. Even the Quebec conference did not make Confederation inevitable. But by the end of October 1864, there was a detailed blueprint and an organized network of powerful support for an idea that four months earlier had only been a vaguely defined part of the program of a shaky coalition government in the province of Canada.

The idea of Maritime union had gained a momentum of its own in early 1863, following the collapse of the railway scheme agreed between Can-ada, Nova Scotia, and New Brunswick in the previous year. For Maritime advocates of the railway, with its economic and defence implications, this decision was not only a setback but also an indication of the unreliability of the Canadians. Calls for Maritime union followed. If Canada could not be trusted, the Maritimes must fall back on their own united resources. The British colonial secretary, the Duke of Newcastle, agreed. Newcastle had welcomed the 1862 railway agreement as a step toward British North American union; now, he supported Maritime union in the hope that it would eventually lead in the same direction. The lieutenants-governor of the Maritime colonies took their lead from London and also became advocates of Maritime union. Arthur Hamilton Gordon, lieutenant-governor of New Brunswick, was an especially strong supporter. The problem was, however, that anger at the Canadians was an emotion that soon died down. As it did so, it was replaced by a renewed awareness of the loss of political power by each of the provincial elites that would result from a legislative union of the Maritimes and by questioning whether the scheme would contribute to resolving the economic questions of the time. The three provincial legislatures passed general resolutions in the spring of 1864, indicating their willingness to discuss the matter at an interprovincial meeting, but nobody was in any hurry to fix a date or appoint delegates. Then, in July, the new lieutenant-governor of Nova Scotia, Sir Richard Graves MacDonnell, received a surprising letter from his Canadian counterpart, Viscount Monck. The province of Canada, Monck wrote, was interested in the forthcoming conference and would like to send a group of observers. Hurriedly, MacDonnell set the wheels in motion. The conference was called for Charlottetown—the lack of firm support for Maritime union in Prince Edward Island meant that only by meeting there was the presence of Island delegates likely to be ensured—on 1 September. The designation of the delegates was still slow, but by the time the Canadian observers steamed into Charlottetown harbour on board the *Queen Victoria*, all was ready. The presence of a circus in town, the first in 21 years, offset any popular excitement that the conference might have generated. But at least the discussions could now proceed.

The first session was a short one, on the afternoon of the first day. The Maritime delegates met by themselves, decided to set aside the question of Maritime union until the Canadians had been heard, and then the meeting adjourned for the day after the Canadian observers had been formally admitted. It was not surprising that the Canadians should have succeeded so quickly in gaining the attention of the conference. Their intervention had, in effect, prompted its calling. For Maritime union, there was only lukewarm support, while the idea of a wider Confederation had been extensively discussed in Maritime newspaper columns during the summer, after the hopes of the new Canadian government had become known, and had aroused widespread interest if little outright support. The Charlottetown delegates were at least willing to hear what the Canadians had to say. And they had a great deal to say. Meetings were held from 10:00 a.m. to 3:00 p.m. on the succeeding days. Cartier and Macdonald led off the speeches, both laying out a general case for Confederation. They did not emphasize the details of the proposed union, although later speeches by Brown and by Canadian finance minister Alexander Tilloch Galt did so. Brown dealt with the possible workings of federation, an area where the Canadian arguments were strong: in a federation, the individual provinces would not lose their identities and their legislatures as they would in a legislative union of the Maritimes. Galt had the unenviable task of explaining how the finances of the new united British North America could be so arranged that the Maritime provinces would not end up paying for the vast debts of the province of Canada. He was apparently successful in arguing that it could be done, although the issue would continue to arise frequently in the public debates of 1865 and 1866. By 6 September, the Canadians rested their case. The next morning the Maritimers met to decide that Maritime union was a lost cause and that the Canadian proposal should be pursued to see if acceptable terms could be worked out. With that, the conference adjourned for brief sessions in Halifax and Saint John. Little real business was transacted in either place, but by the time the last session closed, the decision had been made to call a further conference in Quebec in October. The Charlottetown conference had decided virtually nothing with any certainty, but it had thrust the question of union to the head of each colony's political agenda. Even Newfoundland would become involved. Although not represented at Charlottetown— uninvited until the last moment, Newfoundland was unable to send delegates—its premier had expressed interest in the discussions. Macdonald, Cartier, Brown, and the others had good reason to be pleased with their sojourn in the lower provinces.

There was, however, a further important element of the meetings in Charlottetown. Each day, the afternoon adjournment of the conference was followed by a social function. A dinner at Government House on the first evening was followed by another the next day hosted by W.H. Pope, Prince Edward Island's provincial secretary. On 3 September, the Canadians entertained on the *Queen Victoria*. The fourth, a Sunday, was a more sober day, but on the fifth it was the turn of Island opposition leader George Coles to entertain. The Charlottetown portion of the festivities— for more were to come in Halifax and Saint John—closed with an elaborate dinner-dance that, according to one Island journalist, represented "the gilded scene of fashion's vices, and the reeking slough of debauchery."[2] This was an exaggeration, but there was no doubt that social occasions rather than formal deliberations took up most of the delegates' time. That this should be so was not an indication that the conference was a mere excuse for carousal but rather that it was a ritualistic occasion of which an important product, one assiduously cultivated by the convinced pro-Confederates, was the creation of a sense of communal solidarity among the participants. In this process, women were as important as men. Although denied any formal access to the workings of politics, some middle-class women could nevertheless exert influence in areas where the public and private spheres overlapped. When George Brown reported to his wife, Anne Nelson Brown, on the "number of handsome daughters, well educated, well informed, and sharp as needles" who had assisted George Coles on September 5, he recognized the importance of this role. The mingling of delegates with wives and daughters also had a further significance. Underlying the political discussions were the sensibilities of a group of males who closely resembled one another in terms of social class and who, whatever the differences between reformer and conservative, interpreted their task as one of safeguarding public and private values that could be threatened by political instability, economic decline, or even military invasion by the unruly democracy to the South.

The female presence at social occasions created an association between public issues and the private ideal of the middle-class family. It thus contributed to the forging of an idealism based on class and gender that would help to sustain the pro-Confederates even in the face of strong political attacks by their opponents. The advocates of Confederation often, in fact, compared British North America to a family. "If one member

---

[2] John Ross, in *Ross's Weekly*, September 15, 1864, quoted in Waite, *The Life and Times of Confederation*, p. 79. For other treatments of the Charlottetown and Quebec conferences, see Francis W. P. Bolger, *Prince Edward Island and Confederation, 1863–1873* (Charlottetown: St. Dunstan's University Press, 1964), and Morton, *The Critical Years*. The important question of women's participation in the Confederation process was discussed in CBC's *Ideas* series on September 6, 1989: see Moira Dann, *Mothers of Confederation* (Montreal: CBC Transcripts, 1989).

in a family insists upon having all his own way," remarked Taché in introducing the resolution approving Confederation to the Canadian Parliament in 1865, "there will be trouble, and so through all possible relations of humanity." Taché referred specifically to the relations between French and English, but his remark revealed an important and often overlooked element of the discourse of Confederation.

The ambience of the Charlottetown conference was carried over to Quebec. Many of the 33 delegates who assembled there on October 10 brought family members with them, and the journals of such participants as Mercy Ann Coles, one of the daughters of George Coles, and Frances Monck, sister-in-law of the governor general of Canada, attest to the frequent mingling of business and socializing. These women were not always impressed by what went on. Mercy Ann Coles, for example, found John A. Macdonald "an old Humbug," and both she and Monck remarked

Governor General Lord Monk and family, 1866.   NATIONAL ARCHIVES OF CANADA/C21006

on the drunken behaviour of some of the leading delegates as the evenings wore on. On one occasion Coles was congratulated by the premier of Prince Edward Island, John Hamilton Gray, for her restraint in pretending not to notice when her dinner partner, the Canadian minister of agriculture, D'Arcy McGee, "got so intoxicated he was obliged to leave the table." The pro-Confederate rhetoric at such occasions could be intoxicating, too. But at this conference, more than in Charlottetown, the formal sessions did get down to negotiation on specific issues. Canada was represented by its entire 12-member cabinet, which met daily before and after the five-hour sessions of the conference. The seven-strong delegations of New Brunswick and Prince Edward Island were enlarged from those that had attended in Charlottetown. Nova Scotia sent five and Newfoundland became formally involved for the first time by sending two representatives. The Canadians, aware of their success in Charlottetown but also of its inevitable hollowness if detailed terms could not now be agreed upon, came well prepared to each session. The conference was chaired by Taché and was addressed first by John A. Macdonald. On his resolution, the principle of British North America union was unanimously endorsed at the end of the first day. This was a reaffirmation of the agreement reached in Charlottetown, but did not add to it. It was left to George Brown the next day to broach the first of the issues that were likely to prove divisive. "The system of government," Brown moved, "should be federal with local governments in each province and provision for admission of the North West Territories, Newfoundland, British Columbia, and Vancouver Island." Now the real battles could begin.

One question that arose immediately concerned the relationship between the central and the "local" governments. Just what did "local" mean? Did it mean what Brown, as the ensuing debate revealed, intended it to mean: that is, essentially municipal units, which would involve elected local legislatures but would be unmistakably subordinate to the central government? If so, then the use of the word "federation" would hardly mask the similarity of the scheme to a full-scale legislative union, where all effective power would lie in the central Parliament and in the cabinet ministers who enjoyed its confidence. For John A. Macdonald and for the British colonial office, who shared the belief that only a legislative union would be fully workable, this was an attractive prospect. It also had its merits for Canada West, which, with its large and growing population, could expect to wield enormous power through such a constitutional arrangement.

It was viewed quite differently by francophones from Canada East, who could see themselves greatly outnumbered by anglophones in the central Parliament and deprived of a strong Quebec legislature to act as a counter-balance. Similarly, the Maritime provinces could envisage themselves overwhelmed by the superior numbers of the Canadians. The crux of the debate came when the New Brunswick delegate Charles Fisher proposed "that the General and Local Governments shall be formed on the model of the British Constitution as far as possible." Although then reworded to remove the word "local," this motion was passed and effectively safe-guarded the continuation of responsible government in the provinces. The federation, therefore, would be a federation in a real sense. Nevertheless, the conference was not finished with this question. In the late stages, individual delegates from New Brunswick and Prince Edward Island protested against the principle, defended by Macdonald and others, that the federal government and not the provinces should control all powers not specifically attributed to either. On this issue, the centralist view prevailed. It was embodied both in the power of the federal Parliament to legislate in "all matters of a general character, not specially and exclusively reserved for the local Governments and Legislatures," and in the power of the governor general to "disallow" provincial legislation within two years of its passage. Nevertheless, the question of provincial rights would frequently be raised during the Confederation debates that followed, and, even after Confederation had become a reality, the relationship of federal and provincial powers would become a continual irritant in the politics of the Dominion of Canada.

A second vexing constitutional question was the matter of the composi-tion of the federal legislature. The make-up of the assembly—or House of Commons, as it would ultimately be designated—caused surprisingly little contention, with the one important exception that it was settled without the agreement of Prince Edward Island. The understanding reached in Charlottetown had been that the house would conform to the principle of representation by population. Accordingly, Brown proposed that the initial representation should be 89 members for Canada West, 65 for Canada East, 15 for New Brunswick, 5 for Prince Edward Island, 19 for Nova Scotia, and 7 for Newfoundland. All of the delegations concurred, except that a divided Island contingent finally agreed to ask for one additional member. They found no support from the other provinces, and this rebuff led to a perceptible cooling in attitude of the Island delegates toward the entire Confederation scheme. More contentious for the other delegations was the matter of representation in the upper house and the status of the Atlantic provinces. The initial proposal introduced by Macdonald was that the division should be sectional: that is, that of 72 members, 24 should be appointed from Canada West; 24 from Canada East; and 24 from the Atlantic provinces. The response was swift, and a counter-proposal from Leonard Tilley of New Brunswick would have increased the Atlantic representation to 32, of which 12 would go to Nova Scotia, 10 to New Brunswick, 6 to Newfoundland, and 4 to Prince Edward Island. While this might have seemed—and did seem to the Canadians— to be a matter of quibbling over numbers, the principle involved was fundamental. The Atlantic provinces would be grossly outnumbered in the House of Commons and were prepared to accept this. But, for them, there must be a safeguard in the composition of the upper house. Prince Edward Island delegate A. A. MacDonald went so far as to argue that, on the model of the Senate of the United States, "each Province should have equal representation in the Federal upper house," but found no support outside of his own delegation. Ultimately, a compromise prevailed. With only

Commemorative photograph of delegates at Quebec Conference, 1864.
NATIONAL ARCHIVES OF CANADA/C6350

Prince Edward Island dissenting, the conference endorsed the principle of equal numbers for Canada East, Canada West, and the Maritimes, but allowed that Newfoundland would have its own additional representation, as would other northern and western provinces if and when they were admitted. The issue was settled for the present, but it still had much potential for explosive debate when the issue of Confederation was taken back to the Maritime provinces.

The Quebec conference also reached conclusions on other substantial matters. The question of public debt was resolved, despite some uneasiness among the Maritime delegates, by a complex scheme for providing credits to those provinces that had lower debts than did Canada. The construction of the intercolonial railway was reaffirmed and also the importance of "the communications with the North-Western Territory, and the improvements required for the development of the Trade of the Great West with the Seaboard." With regard to language, specific discussion at the conference was sparse, though the issue clearly underlaid the debates over a number of other questions and was addressed in the final resolutions. Resolution 46 declared that both English and French languages could be used "in the General Parliament..., and in the Local Legislature of Lower Canada, and also in the Federal Courts and in the Courts of Lower Canada." The implication was that English would be used elsewhere. The special legal status of Lower Canada, or Quebec, was recognized in its omission from resolutions calling for the standardization of laws and court procedures among the other provinces. Another language-related clause safeguarded the existing rights of both Protestant and Catholic denominational schools in the province of Canada. The conference formally indicated that defence, hitherto the responsibility of Great Britain, would be taken over by the new central government. But the conduct of foreign affairs was conspicuously absent from the resolutions, as it was assumed that British power in this area would continue.

The deliberations in Quebec finally came to an end with a lengthy session on 26 October and an adjournment the next day. The resolutions passed numbered 69, and three more were added when the conference then reconvened briefly in Montreal. Among them was the significant requirement that "the Sanction of the Imperial and Local Parliaments shall be sought for the Union of the Provinces, on the principles adopted by the Conference." This resolution was, of course, no surprise. It was clear enough that the delegates alone could not commit their provinces to the union. Nevertheless, it was a statement that set the conference in perspective, and provided a balance for the emotional rhetoric in which many delegates indulged at a banquet hosted by the mayor of Montreal on 29 October. "A united nation, we shall become a great country," declared the leader of the Nova Scotia opposition, A. G. Archibald, "and the time is not far distant when a colossal power, growing up on the continent, shall stand with one foot on the Pacific and the other on the Atlantic." The truth was, however, that the union first had to be approved more widely than among the 33 delegates. The Charlottetown and Quebec conferences had taken on a momentum of their own. Helped along by the family atmosphere created by the female presence in Charlottetown and continued in Quebec and also by the rituals of late-night male drinking, the delegates had achieved a degree of personal solidarity that allowed even the Prince Edward Island delegates to join in the rousing chorus of idealism and self-congratulation that closed the proceedings, even though they had gained few concessions on the issues most important to them. One Island delegate, Edward Whelan, did admit that the process of swaying public opinion in favour of Confederation might be "tedious, difficult, and protracted." In most of the provinces, Whelan's prognosis was correct.[3]

The Confederation Debates in the Province of Canada

On 3 February 1865, Sir Etienne-Paschal Taché, 69 years old and with only a few months to live, rose in the legislative council of the province of Canada to move adoption of the Quebec Resolutions. "If we desired to remain British and monarchial," he declared according to the parliamentary record, "and if we desired to pass to our children these advantages, this measure...was a necessity." The alternative was absorption, whether

---

[3] Edward Whelan, *The Union of the British Provinces* (Gardenvale, Quebec, and Toronto: Garden City Press, 1927), p. 121. Other published contemporary accounts of the Quebec conference can be found in G. P. Browne, ed., *Documents on the Confederation of British North America: A Compilation based on Sir Joseph Pope's Confederation Documents Supplemented by Other Official Material* (Toronto: McClelland and Stewart, 1969); "Diary of Mercy Ann Coles," *Atlantic Advocate*, Vol. 56, No. 3 (November 1965), pp. 40–44; W. L. Morton, ed., *Monck Letters and Journals, 1863–1868: Canada from Government House at Confederation* (Toronto: McClelland and Stewart, 1970); P. B. Waite, "Edward Whelan Reports from the Quebec Conference," *Canadian Historical Review*, 42 (1961), pp. 23–45.

by violent conquest or gradual assimilation, by the United States. In the legislative assembly three days later, John A. Macdonald similarly evoked the threat from the South, and contrasted it with "the happy opportunity now offered of founding a great nation under the fostering care of Great Britain, and our Sovereign Lady, Queen Victoria." With this phrase, at the end of a lengthy speech, Macdonald sat down to loud cheers. In the province of Canada, the Confederation proposal began with the significant advantage that the political status quo had become untenable and that there was a potential enemy nearby that could be cited as an additional reason for proceeding quickly. The parliamentary opposition to the measure was fragmented. Among the representatives from Canada West, it encompassed both Conservatives and Reformers, but the numbers were small. Some disaffected Conservatives believed that federalism was an inherently unstable system of government and that—even worse, and despite the pro-British pronouncements of Taché and Macdonald—it smacked of republicanism. Macdonald was well placed to answer such criticisms because his own preference for a strong central government was generally known, and he was not averse to giving private assurances to conservative critics. "If the Confederation goes on," he wrote to one in late 1864, "you, if spared the ordinary age of man, will see both Local Parliaments and Governments absorbed in the General Power." Not all of the dissidents could be convinced, but there was no question of any general revolt. Nor, with Brown on the government benches, would the anti-Confederates from Canada West on the reform side pose any great threat. The central figure among them was John Sandfield Macdonald, the former premier who had tried and failed to govern by means of the "double majority." Distrustful of federalism, Sandfield Macdonald nevertheless had little to suggest as an alternative to Confederation, other than the continuation of efforts to make the province of Canada work. The impracticability of any such effort was all too obvious to most of those who had lived through the early 1860s.

More generally, the Quebec resolutions were manifestly advantageous for Canada West. Not only would Confederation break the political deadlock of the province of Canada, but it would also put Canada West in a strong political and economic position. Assured of more than 40 percent of the seats in the new House of Commons and more than 30 percent in the legislative council, Canada West would be the most powerful province by far. Furthermore, access to what A. T. Galt described at the Quebec conference as "the great resources" of the Maritime provinces would provide a further stimulus to economic growth. "We were trying to encourage manufacturing in Canada," Galt had continued. "A supply of coal was a most important element of success in this respect; and we had before us the fact that Nova Scotia possessed that element." It was hardly surprising that anti-Confederate feelings should be rare and scattered, for Canada West had good reason to be pleased with the work of the conferences. And the more Macdonald succeeded in his efforts to make the union more centralized than genuinely federal, the stronger Canada West would be. Conversely, the potential strength of Canada West in the proposed union was one reason why opposition in Canada East was much more formidable. Even pro-Confederates there were aware of the problem, as the Prince Edward Island delegate Edward Whelan recorded at the end of the Quebec conference. "Should the Union be consummated," wrote Whelan on 27 October 1864, possibly on the basis of a conversation with Taché earlier in the day, "Lower Canada will, most especially, be the firm and fast friend of the Maritime Provinces. The desire of her public men is, apparently, to secure the aid of the Eastern Provinces for the purpose of curbing the grasping ambition of Upper...Canada." Whelan then went on to make a further important observation. "The predominant feeling of the French members of the Canadian Ministry...is that of devoted and chivalrous loyalty to the British Crown. They appear to detest Democracy in any and every shape...." What Whelan was essentially confirming, though he did not analyse it for himself, was that the francophone cabinet ministers represented only a narrow portion of the political spectrum in Canada East. All of the provincial delegations to the Quebec conference had been bipartisan, and all but that of the province of Canada had included opposition as well as government politicians. Canada, of course, had been represented by the cabinet of the Great Coalition, which was bipartisan by its very nature. The Reformers in the coalition, however, were drawn exclusively from Canada West, while the Rouges of Canada East were not included. Consequently, at Quebec, only four of the 33 delegates were francophones, and all of them were Bleus. In Canada East, it was logical to expect that the Rouges would be the centre of organized opposition to the Confederation proposal.

The campaign was quickly begun by the leader of the Rouges, Antoine-Aimé Dorion. Formerly the partner of George Brown and later of John Sandfield Macdonald in two previous governments of the province of Canada, Dorion had refused to join the Great Coalition because of his suspicions of the proposal to unite British North America. On 7 November

1864, within days of the end of the Quebec conference, he issued a manifesto that signalled his opposition. At the time, no official announcement had been made of the content of the Quebec Resolutions, and this was seized upon by the anti-Confederates as an indication that what they

Antoine-Aimé Dorion, 1818-1891.   NATIONAL ARCHIVES OF CANADA/PA25382

contained was unfavourable to Canada East. While George Brown spoke openly in Toronto about the conclusions reached by the conference, Cartier and the other francophone delegates would say only that confidentiality had to be maintained. Dorion's manifesto, addressed to his constituents in the county of Hochelaga and then widely publicized in the press, set out his central argument: the proposed constitution was "quite simply, a disguised legislative union." As such, far from securing more autonomy for Canada East, it would ultimately threaten all that made French Canada distinct. Dorion had other objections, too, and was especially sceptical of any economic benefit for the province of Canada from union with the Atlantic provinces. He returned to that theme in February 1865 in the parliamentary debate on the Quebec Resolutions. Dismissing the intercolonial railway as a project being pursued by railway interests for their own corrupt purposes, Dorion scored significantly at the expense of prominent government figures such as Cartier and John A. Macdonald, who were known to have close relationships with the British merchant banks, Baring Brothers and Glyn Mills, which had financed previous railway development in the province of Canada. The proposed intercolonial railway, he argued, should be seen as a thinly disguised effort to provide an extension for the Grand Trunk, and thus to bail out that financially troubled railway and its British backers. Then Dorion again took issue with centralization, which the Quebec Resolutions would impose. The federal power to disallow acts passed by the provincial legislatures, he argued, would locate control firmly in Ottawa. Worse still, this power could easily be used arbitrarily if the central government disallowed a law for partisan reasons—for instance, that the provincial government was in the hands of an opposing party—even though it was supported by the majority in the province. All of these problems, Dorion maintained, would bear especially heavily on Canada East. "The French element," he predicted, "will be completely overwhelmed by the majority of British representatives." Quoting a speech made in Toronto by Galt, who had asserted that the delegates to the Quebec conference would have preferred legislative union to a federal one if they had thought it politically feasible, Dorion foresaw the day when an attempt would be made to push federalism aside. "The people of Lower Canada," he warned, "will not change their religious institutions, their laws and their language, for any consideration whatever. . . . Not even by the power of the sword can such changes be accomplished."

Dorion's warning was blunt. It called forth responses from the pro-Confederates of Canada East that rejected his interpretation of the Quebec

Resolutions. Among francophones, the issue was debated in terms that almost exclusively concerned the nationality, the culture, and the institutions of French Canada. That centralization, if it came about, would pose a lethal threat was not contested. The crux of the argument was whether the proposed constitution would produce this centralization, and Bleus such as George-Etienne Cartier and Hector Langevin maintained flatly that it would not. On the contrary, for them, the Confederation scheme would be the firm guarantee for the distinctness and autonomy of the province of Quebec that had been missing from the constitution of the province of Canada. Pro-Confederate speeches and newspaper editorials in journals such as Cartier's consistent supporter, *La Minerve*, resounded with the words "separation" and "independence." Confederation would mean, at last, the separation of the two Canadas. It would mean the setting up of an independent province and legislature in Canada East. Not that independence would extend as far as absolute sovereignty. But in all the matters that mattered to the maintenance of the nationality of the Canadiens, the new constitution would carry firm safeguards. Education, the pro-Confederates pointed out, was specifically put under provincial jurisdiction, and Canada East had been conspicuously exempted from the clause prescribing unification of civil and property laws among the other provinces. The Bleus frequently referred to Confederation as an "alliance," a pact formed between autonomous nations in which the province of Quebec would embody French Canada. In all of this, Cartier and the Bleus succeeded in portraying themselves as the voices of calmness and rationality. "All the moderate men," declared Cartier in the parliamentary debate, were "favourable to Federation." Thus, by implication, the anti-Confederates were hotheads and extremists. Having skilfully staked out this middle ground, Cartier and his supporters were not easy to dislodge.[4]

Predictably, the measure approving the Quebec Resolutions was passed in the Parliament of the province of Canada without difficulty. The vote of

[4] Useful works that include analysis of the Confederation debates in Canada East, and have been used in the preparation of this section, include Jean-Paul Bernard, *Les Rouges: libéralisme, nationalisme et anticléricalisme au milieu du XIXe siècle* (Montréal: les Presses de l'Université du Québec, 1971); A. I. Silver, *The French-Canadian Idea of Confederation, 1864–1900* (Toronto: University of Toronto Press, 1982); Brian Young, *George-Etienne Cartier: Montreal Bourgeois* (Kingston and Montreal: McGill-Queen's University Press, 1981); and Walter Ullmann, "The Quebec Bishops and Confederation," *Canadian Historical Review*, 44 (1963), pp. 213–34. A convenient anthology of major contributions to the parliamentary debates is P. B. Waite, ed., *The Confederation Debates in the Province of Canada, 1865* (Toronto: McClelland and Stewart, 1963).

91 to 33 incorporated a "double majority" of members from both Canada East and Canada West, and even the francophone members were 27 to 21 in favour. To be sure, there were still some parliamentary arguments to come. In 1866, during a summer made tense by the brief invasion of the province of Canada by the Fenians, Irish nationalists based in the United States who decided to attack British North America as part of their strategy to combat the British presence in Ireland, and associated rumours of war with the United States came a new effort by Dorion and Sandfield Macdonald. In June, they proposed to the Parliament that Confederation should not be carried into effect before an election was held to establish the wishes of the voters. They were defeated 79 to 19. In August, a flurry of controversy arose over government legislation intended to guarantee the maintenance of English-speaking Protestant schools in the future province of Quebec. Threatened with a divisive debate, the government withdrew its bill to the disgust of Quebec anglophones such as Galt, who immediately resigned from the cabinet. The education question would have to be left to the upcoming constitutional conference in London, which would finally produce the British North America Act. Before the conference started, though, came a last-ditch effort by the Rouges. A petition signed by 20 anti-Confederate parliamentarians was addressed to the British colonial secretary, now Lord Carnarvon. Going over the history of the steps taken toward Confederation since 1858, the petitioners portrayed each phase as the result of the selfish and partisan manoeuvres of the pro-Confederates and as an affront to the real wishes of the people of Canada East. It was inconceivable, though, that the British government would heed such a representation when its own policy was in favour of the union, and Carnarvon was accordingly unimpressed. The delegates would depart for London as planned. There, francophone Canada East would be represented by Cartier and Langevin, while Dorion and the other anti-Confederates were left to contemplate the proceedings from afar.

Thus, the anti-Confederate cause in Canada East, despite the eloquence of Dorion, had been a failure in parliamentary terms. Behind this, however, lay an even more important failure: the failure to mount an effective extraparliamentary campaign. Hopelessly outnumbered in Parliament by the Conservatives and Canada West Reformers who supported the coalition government, the Rouges had to show, if they were to be successful, that popular opposition to Confederation was so great in Canada East that the scheme would be unworkable even if implemented. That they did not do so was owing in part to their own divisions and apparent inconsistencies. As a former government leader, and at other times in opposition,

Dorion had been closely involved with earlier efforts to resolve the constitutional impasse in the province of Canada. In the Confederation debates, he had to expend valuable time and energy in denying allegations that, while in office, he had favoured principles that he now opposed. While Dorion might explain truthfully that the Confederation between Canada East and Canada West that he had once advocated had been more limited geographically and less centralized than the current proposal, the issue was one that could easily be exploited by opponents who sought to challenge his credibility. Furthermore, the Rouges never attained complete unity in their approach to the Confederation question. Some were reluctant to appeal to Canadien nationalism, regarding it as an essentially conservative force that was antithetical to their own liberalism. Some even speculated publicly on the possibility that union with the United States might hold the best future for Canada East, whether or not it was preceded by the union of British North America. All of this militated against any widespread mobilization of public opinion by the Rouges, and it also widened the distance between them and the one group that—however unlikely the alliance would have seemed—might have assisted toward this goal. That group was the Catholic hierarchy and clergy. An effective case could be made that the new united British North America would be a hostile environment for Catholics, dominated as it might well be by the Protestant elites of the predominantly anglophone provinces. Certainly, there were indications that the powerful Bishop of Montreal, Ignace Bourget, thought along these lines. For other members of the hierarchy, though, any opposition to Confederation meant flirting with the offensive liberalism and anticlericalism of the Rouges and even raised the spectre of annexation by the United States. The result was a curious collective silence, which the Bleus exploited by claiming that it signified approval. "The opinion of the clergy was for Confederation," declared Cartier, according to the records of the parliamentary debate in 1865, and he went on to assert that this included "those who were high in authority, as well as those who occupied more humble positions." This statement brought an indignant, though private, denial from one of Bourget's officials. But, in general, the bishops of Canada East only took a clear position on Confederation after it had become a *fait accompli* in the spring of 1867. Then they pronounced themselves in favour of it. Their previous silence had worked in favour of the Bleus, and the lack of endorsement of Bourget's reservations by his colleagues was an important factor in disabling the development of any powerful popular opposition.

Thus, the Confederation debates in the province of Canada resulted in approval of the Quebec Resolutions without serious difficulty. There was never any real parliamentary threat to the Great Coalition's proposal, and even in Canada East the extraparliamentary opposition was muted. Nevertheless, in Canada East, much more so than in Canada West, there were substantive issues that had to be addressed by the pro-Confederates. Whenever challenged over the likely consequences of Confederation for French Canada, they emphasized the autonomy that would be enjoyed by the future province of Quebec. It would have, they argued, all the powers it needed in order to ensure the preservation of the language, culture, and religion that were fundamental to it. Thus, Confederation itself would be, in effect, the guarantor of these characteristics because the federal system would be the basis of Quebec's new independence from Ontario. That rhetoric, which differed markedly from the way in which Confederation was being presented in Canada West by Galt, John A. Macdonald, and others, was significant for its promotion of the belief that Confederation was indeed a pact between French-speaking and English-speaking nations. Whatever may have been the collective intentions of the framers of the Confederation proposal—or whether or not there was any single set of collective intentions among them—and whatever the British North America Act might eventually say, Confederation was clearly presented in Canada East as an affirmation of the distinctness of Quebec. To be sure, this left significant questions unanswered. What was to be the status of French- or English-language minorities in the various provinces? What misunderstandings would later arise from the emergence of competing definitions of the purposes of Confederation? One immediate result of the debates in the province of Canada, however, was the entrenchment in francophone Canada East by the Bleu campaign of the notion that the fundamental virtue of the Confederation proposal was that it would relieve the tensions that had crippled the province of Canada by extending a new, autonomous status to the province of Quebec.

The Confederation Debates in the Atlantic Provinces

The Confederation proposal was debated in the Atlantic provinces with a much more realistic chance of defeat than in the province of Canada. For a time in 1865 and early 1866, it seemed that the electoral eclipse of Leonard

Tilley's pro-Confederate government in New Brunswick would be the final blow. In the end, two of the four Atlantic provinces were corralled, New Brunswick and Nova Scotia, but even in those the pro-Confederates had not dared to introduce the Quebec Resolutions into their legislatures for detailed discussion. In none of the four provinces did the opponents lack for serious arguments against the union. In all of them, the opposition forces had credible political leaders and substantial support both inside and outside of the legislatures. To be sure, those in favour of Confederation also had their arguments, and they had the valuable support of the British government, exercised through the lieutenants-governor. In the island provinces, however, even this was not enough to shore up the weakness of the pro-Confederate cause.

In Prince Edward Island, opposition quickly became overwhelming. The Island delegates to the Quebec conference had been frustrated by the meagre parliamentary representation offered to their province and by the failure of George Coles to persuade the conference to pass a resolution promising that the new federal government would resolve the land question by buying out the absentee proprietors. "At the Quebec conference," Coles later declared to the provincial assembly, "I said that if the grant for the purchase of the lands of this Colony was not conceded, they might as well strike Prince Edward Island out of the constitution altogether." Although some of the Island delegates returned as pro-Confederates, Coles and two of his colleagues became powerful opponents. They lost no time in taking their case to public meetings throughout the Island, and nowhere did they have difficulty in gaining support. By the end of December 1864, even the pro-Confederate W. H. Pope was declaring publicly that "the great majority of the people appear to be wholly averse to Confederation." The debates in the legislature in March and April 1865 served only to confirm the widespread hostility to the proposal, although they did provide for a thorough airing of the arguments on either side. The pro-Confederates, while clearly outnumbered, doggedly maintained that a negative vote would mean eventual assimilation by the United States.

The opponents attacked on a variety of fronts. All of them condemned the specific political provisions of the Quebec Resolutions and the conference's silence on the land question. Also cited by many of the speakers were the characteristic Atlantic arguments against the entire principle of union. Why should Prince Edward Island tie itself to the politically unstable and debt-ridden province of Canada? The results would be disastrously high levels of taxation for the benefit of railways and other projects hundreds or thousands of kilometres away and disruption of the Island's prosperous seaborne trade if the new federal government raised tariff barriers against imported goods. Trade with the province of Canada, the anti-Confederates continued, was not worth considering as an alternative. Canada did not need the Island's agricultural products, while protected Canadian manufactured goods would quickly swamp the Island market and ensure—though the anti-Confederates did not put it in these words—the establishment of an exploitive, colonial relationship. Prince Edward Island, in short, was better off as it was. These arguments easily carried the debates, and in the following year, 1866, the assembly responded to renewed pressure from the British government by passing a resolution, proposed by the premier, J. C. Pope, that expressed disbelief that the union "could ever be accomplished upon terms that would prove advantageous to the interests and well-being of the people of the Island." That was the finishing stroke. Although political realignments and financial problems would eventually bring Prince Edward Island into Confederation in 1873, there was now no possibility that it would agree to be a founding member.

Newfoundland took longer to decide, but the result was the same, except that in this case the refusal was not reversed for 80 years. The two Newfoundland delegates to Quebec had participated fully in the pro-Confederation euphoria with which the conference had closed. The future of the proposed union, Ambrose Shea had declared at a Montreal banquet, "was impossible for the wildest imagination to over-estimate." Nevertheless, this leading Newfoundland Liberal was also careful to bracket his statement with the observation that he and his Conservative colleague Frederic Carter were at the conference "simply expressing their own opinions on the subject." The Newfoundland delegation was small, and, even though it was bipartisan, it could make no pretence that its recommendations would necessarily be accepted at home. It was true that the premier, Hugh Hoyles, was sympathetic to Confederation and had been personally responsible for arranging for Newfoundland to be represented in Quebec. But Hoyles was in poor health. Before resigning in 1865, to be succeeded by Carter in a government that included Shea and some other pro-Confederation Liberals, Hoyles gave a firm commitment that no decision would be taken on Confederation before the voters had expressed their opinion in a general election. The election held later in 1865 was not the one, as the new government prudently held off on the Confederation question, and it did not emerge as a campaign issue. In parliamentary terms, the situation was now finely balanced, with the assembly divided but potentially favourable, while the merchant-dominated legislative council was firmly opposed. Here as in Prince Edward Island, though, economic issues and extraparliamentary opinions were crucial. The Roman Catholic clergy, including the Bishop of St. John's, gave forceful expression to a widespread Catholic belief that Newfoundland in Confederation would be vulnerable to the domination of the aggressively Protestant Canada West and that, more generally, it might well end up as a downtrodden appendage to the mainland. The telling comparison was often made by Newfoundland Irish Catholics with the status of Ireland in the United Kingdom since the union of 1801.

Meanwhile, the merchants of St. John's expressed their class interests but also scored significant debating points by demonstrating that Newfoundland's existing economic links with mainland British North America were marginal compared to those with Europe, the United States, the Caribbean, and Brazil. Their arguments paralleled those of the Prince Edward Island anti-Confederates in anticipating economic and financial chaos as the result of any association with the protectionist and profligate Canadians. The pro-Confederates were reduced to pointing out that the fishing economy was already in trouble and that Confederation might lead to new but unspecified options. For a time in the late 1860s—the pro-Confederation government was in no hurry to face the electorate even after Confederation was inaugurated on the mainland in 1867—it seemed as if the assembly might be persuaded, and a draft plan of union was approved by it in 1869. The promised general election, however, settled the matter later that year. The pro-Confederates' decisive defeat ensured that Newfoundland would continue on its autonomous path.

The debates in Nova Scotia and New Brunswick were different, and for good reason. First of all, the external pressures on those two provinces were greater than on either Newfoundland or Prince Edward Island. Desirable as it might be to the advocates of Confederation in Britain and Canada that the island provinces should be members, it was not essential. But a British North American union consisting only of Canada and New Brunswick would be too limited to be worthwhile, and one comprising only Canada and Nova Scotia would be geographically unworkable. Both of the mainland Maritime provinces, therefore, were indispensable to the proposal, and both had the power to make or break it. Second, there was a larger underlying body of support for the principle of union in Nova Scotia and New Brunswick than in the other two Atlantic provinces. Part of this

was prompted by economic concerns. The intercolonial railway offered
direct prospects of economic development, and there were powerful
merchant interests that had a long-standing interest in promoting the
growth of manufacturing industries. Arguably, Confederation might provide a sound basis for development and thus enable the provincial
economies to make the successful transition that new steam and steel
technologies demanded. There were also noneconomic reasons: the recognition that the current relationship with Britain was becoming untenable
and that, especially in New Brunswick, proximity to the United States

Joseph Howe, 1804-1873.   NATIONAL ARCHIVES OF CANADA/PA25486

suggested that new arrangements for defence were needed. Certain important questions remained, however. How much of this sympathy for the principle of Confederation would translate into firm political support for the scheme embodied in the Quebec Resolutions? Even if much of it did so, would it be enough to offset the arguments of those who believed, for similar reasons to those of the anti-Confederates in Newfoundland and Prince Edward Island, that any association with the province of Canada could only be politically and economically destructive and that other avenues toward economic development and military security must be pursued? In both Nova Scotia and New Brunswick, the outcome of the Confederation debates was unpredictable. There were strong arguments to be made both for and against, and the stakes were high. The long-term health and prosperity of the provinces were at issue, and the proponents of both sides of the argument were sure that the course of action advocated by their opponents would lead to economic and political decline.

On 28 July 1866, just over three months after he had seen the Nova Scotia assembly vote in general terms in favour of a union that would "effectually ensure just provision for the rights and interests of Nova Scotia," Charles Tupper wrote anxiously to Lord Carnarvon. The opposition to Confederation, he informed Carnarvon, was "active and formidable": so much so that "there can be no doubt that an appeal to the people would result in the reversal of the resolution of the Legislature in favour of the Union and the defeat of the measure for many years." Tupper had known from the start that an election on the issue would be dangerous for the pro-Confederation cause. But as long as he could hold on to a majority in the existing assembly, there was no need to call the election until 1867. The politics of Confederation in Nova Scotia, therefore, were simple enough in principle. The goal was to induce the assembly to give enough of an endorsement to allow Confederation to proceed and then to hold on in the hope that the union would be enacted by the time of the next election. In practice, matters were more complex. Opposition in Nova Scotia was slow to gather force. By the end of 1864, with the legislature not yet in session, most of the Halifax newspapers had committed themselves to the support of Confederation, and there was little visible dissent. One by one, however, the newspapers outside Halifax came out against the scheme and were soon almost unanimous. Likewise, the influential Halifax *Chronicle* changed its stand to one of opposition in early 1865. All of this indicated a groundswell of public opinion. The individual who was potentially the most powerful anti-Confederate, Joseph Howe, kept silent

Sir Charles Tupper, 1821-1915. COURTESY OF THE PUBLIC ARCHIVES OF NOVA SCOTIA

for the moment. As fisheries commissioner under the Reciprocity Treaty, he was a British-employed civil servant and could not participate openly. But in January 1865, he published the first in a series of anonymous letters to the *Chronicle* in which he referred to the union proposal as "the Botheration Scheme." The letters took issue both with the Quebec Resolutions—the provincial legislatures in the new union, Howe argued, would have no more status than Halifax city council—and with the principle of uniting prosperous Nova Scotia, with its low tariff and manageable public debt, with the discredited province of Canada. On both grounds, Howe appealed to Nova Scotian patriotism and to the benefits of direct membership of the politically and economically dynamic British Empire rather than being tied to a ramshackle continental union.

Then came a lull, when the pro-Confederates were defeated in the New Brunswick general election of early 1865, and it seemed that the scheme was dead. A year later, though, with the anti-Confederation government in political trouble in New Brunswick and the Fenians gathering on the Maine border, Tupper persuaded the Nova Scotia assembly to accept the principle of union. This was the signal for an open, all-out assault by Howe. Inside the legislature, Howe's ally, William Annand, carried on the fight but was outnumbered. In public rallies and on an extended visit to London to attempt to influence the British government, Howe personally led the attack. It failed. In strictly political terms, it did so because Tupper did not need to call an election. When the provincial election was eventually held in September 1867, it was overwhelmingly won by anti-Confederates committed to repeal of the British North America Act. By then it was too late. In the face of a hostile majority of public opinion, Confederation had been pushed through. Yet there was more to it than just that. Economic issues had increasingly dominated the debate, and a division had emerged between the areas of the province most likely to benefit from the intercolonial railway and those committed to existing trades. The pro-Confederates consistently stressed the industrial prosperity that a continental market would bring, and they were seconded by visiting Canadian speakers—Cartier and Galt were two prominent examples—who proclaimed the compatibility of Canadian and Maritime economic interests and the prosperity that the railway would bring. Most Nova Scotians were unconvinced, but in the provincial and federal elections of 1867 a substantial minority, some 38 percent in the federal vote, did support Confederation for economic or other reasons. The truth was that serious arguments could be marshalled on either side. Nova Scotia's entry to Confederation was carried out in conscious defiance of the will of the electorate, but it did represent one answer (and in places such as Tupper's personal stronghold of Cumberland County, which stood to benefit from the railway, a highly attractive one) to the question of what should be Nova Scotia's future strategy.

Samuel Leonard Tilley, 1818-1896.   NATIONAL ARCHIVES OF CANADA/C14587

Similar economic issues were important in New Brunswick, though questions of defence and ethnic divisions also played a role. Leonard Tilley and the other New Brunswick delegates to the Quebec conference returned home to face some harsh realities. One was that the Quebec Resolutions were controversial in New Brunswick from the start. One of Tilley's former cabinet colleagues, Albert Smith, published an open letter to his constituents in Westmorland County in November 1864 declaring that rebellion would be the only option if the Quebec scheme was carried out. In the same month, the influential Saint John *Morning Freeman* argued that for New Brunswick the proposal would amount to the loss of responsible government. These arguments were not necessarily against union on better terms, but their vehemence put Tilley on the defensive. Convinced that the existing legislature, which only had a few months left in its mandate, would not approve the Quebec Resolutions, the premier called a winter election. From the beginning, it was a disaster for the pro-Confederates. With Albert Smith emerging as the leader of the opposing forces, the opposition guns began to rake not only the Quebec Resolutions but also the intercolonial railway proposal and all the economic implications of the union. To an extent, this was misleading. Dislike of the centralized constitution envisaged at Quebec was stronger among the anti-Confederates than outright dismissal of the possibility of union on more acceptable terms. But in an election campaign, all the weapons had to be used. Tilley was ridiculed because he could not specify which route the intercolonial would take. Through the St. John valley? Along the north shore? Nobody knew, least of all the premier. Smith and the anti-Confederates, moreover, advocated the alternative of western extension: a railway from Saint John to Portland, Maine, and on to other points in the United States.

Rather than gamble on the unlikely prospect of trade with Canada, they argued, the existing seaborne trade with the United States should be solidified with a railway connection. With the Reciprocity Treaty facilitating this linkage and with the transatlantic timber trade continuing, New Brunswick would have better economic guarantees than Confederation could ever provide. So thought the electorate, for Smith took office after the election with a solid majority in the assembly. Especially strong was the anti-Confederation vote among Acadian and Irish Catholics—despite the vocal support for the scheme of the Archbishop of Halifax, which helped to carry certain key ridings. But the victory was not owed to those groups alone. Every one of the delegates to the Quebec conference who contested a seat was defeated. It was, seemingly, a decisive rejection of the scheme that, in Smith's striking phrase, had originated in "the oily brains of the Canadians."

The New Brunswick election was hailed by the Rouges in Canada East and the anti-Confederates in Nova Scotia as signifying the end of the Confederation proposal. Of course, it was not. Smith's government was soon in trouble. It contained an odd mixture of people who had opposed

Albert J. Smith, 1822-1883.   NATIONAL ARCHIVES OF CANADA/PA25257

Confederation for different reasons and who now found it difficult to work together. Damaging allegations of corruption also arose. The major blow, however, came soon after the election, when the United States announced that it was giving the required one year's notice of cancellation of the Reciprocity Treaty. By the spring of 1866 the treaty would be dead, and with it would go the very foundation of Smith's economic program. Now the lieutenant-governor could go to work. Arthur Hamilton Gordon was personally more committed to Maritime union than to the Quebec scheme, but he had orders from London. He also despised Smith and manoeuvred him into resigning in April 1866. Another election followed, and this time the Fenians were assembled at Eastport, Maine. Heavily armed, they presented a threat that was necessarily taken seriously. On April 21, early in the election campaign, they actually crossed the border briefly. The pro-Confederates—now nominally led by Peter Mitchell, although Tilley retained much influence—seized the opportunity to whip up anti-Irish, anti-Catholic feeling, and this joined with understandable fear of invasion to produce a wave of emotional support for the notion of union with other British colonies in North America. The pro-Confederates also profited from the blow dealt to western extension by the cancellation of reciprocity. Now, the intercolonial looked more attractive than it had in 1865. Not least, the pro-Confederation campaign was well financed. Tilley had asked John A. Macdonald for a subsidy of "some $40,000 or $50,000 to do the work in all our counties," and in a secret transaction in Portland, Maine, the cash was passed over. How significantly it may have influenced the election results was impossible to say. But the results themselves were clear. Only the Acadian vote had remained consistent since 1865, and the representatives of the three anti-Confederation counties were contemptuously labelled in the assembly as "the French brigade." They were far outnumbered by the pro-Confederates, and a short legislative session in June and July saw the resolutions committing New Brunswick to Confederation safely carried.

In the Atlantic provinces, therefore, the Confederation debates were vigorous. They could hardly be otherwise, for the stakes were high. Not only the constitutional provisions of the Quebec Resolutions were at stake but also the economic strategy with which the future would be faced. The decisions of Prince Edward Island and Newfoundland were clear. Nova Scotia and New Brunswick, which were essential to the entire Confederation proposal, experienced more tortuous processes. It was natural that they should, for there was more scope for argument as to the costs and benefits of Confederation for those provinces than for the other two. In

Nova Scotia, approval was gained because there was no obligation for Tupper to fight an election he would almost certainly have lost. In New Brunswick, it took a series of unusual events, including a cancelled treaty and a threatened military invasion, to prompt the electorate to revise its previous rejection of the scheme. Beneath all of this, however, lay a genuine and deep-seated division of opinion. At any given time in Nova Scotia and New Brunswick there was a significant minority—sometimes more than a minority—that was willing to be convinced of the merits of union. The pro-Confederates appealed strongly to this body of opinion by downplaying the centralizing tendencies of the Quebec Resolutions and emphasizing the compatibility of economic interest between Canada and the Maritimes. Thus was stimulated the belief that Confederation was a pact by which the mutual economic advantage of those two regions would be sought in the future. Whatever may have been the collective intentions of the framers of the Confederation proposal, and whatever the British North America Act might eventually say, Confederation was clearly perceived in the Maritime provinces as being based on a commitment to an equitable economic relationship among the partners. There was no mention as yet of matters such as railway rate making, which would later come to symbolize the health or the sickliness of the relationship, but the pro-Confederate rhetoric left no doubt as to what Maritimers ought to be able to expect in Confederation.[5]

The Underlying Issues

As the Confederation question was debated, there were some issues that were openly and frequently discussed. That Confederation was being

---

[5] A selection of works worth consulting on the Confederation debates in the Atlantic provinces would include the following: Baker, *Timothy Warren Anglin*; Beck, *Joseph Howe: The Briton Becomes a Canadian*; Bolger, *Prince Edward Island and Confederation*; James Hiller, "Confederation Defeated: The Newfoundland Election of 1869," in *Newfoundland in the Nineteenth and Twentieth Centuries: Essays in Interpretation*, James Hiller and Peter Neary, eds. (Toronto: University of Toronto Press, 1980), pp. 67–94; W. S. MacNutt, *New Brunswick: A History, 1784–1867* (Toronto: Macmillan, 1963); D.A. Muise, "The Federal Election of 1867 in Nova Scotia: An Economic Interpretation;" Pryke, *Nova Scotia and Confederation*; Léon Thériault, "Acadia, 1763–1978: An Historical Synthesis," in *The Acadians of the Maritimes: Thematic Studies*, Jean Daigle, ed. (Moncton: Centre d'études acadiennes, 1982), pp. 47–86; and Waite, *The Life and Times of Confederation*. Also valuable are the biographies of the protagonists as found in the *Dictionary of Canadian Biography*.

touted by its advocates as a means of resolving the political deadlock in the province of Canada and as an avenue toward the preservation of Maritime economic prosperity were points that could hardly be missed by anyone paying attention to the political rhetoric of the time. Also conspicuous were issues relating the defence in the context of the troubled relationship between British America and the United States. And the intention of Great Britain to move away from direct administration of its North American colonies was never far below the surface of the discussions. There were other important matters, however, that were not so visible. One was the question of western expansion. To be sure, the West was not ignored in the Confederation process. The Quebec Resolutions envisaged the eventual membership of the North-West Territory, British Columbia, and Vancouver Island, and this provision was carried forward into the British North America Act. Also contained in the Quebec Resolutions was a declaration that "communications with the North-Western Territory, and the improvements required for the development of the Trade of the Great West with the Seaboard" were matters that would be taken up by the new united colonies as soon as finances permitted. Behind this lay growing scientific awareness of the resources of the West, and the related expansionist movement in Canada West. Mineral resources on the Canadian Shield had been identified by geologists over a 20-year period, while the investigations of John Palliser and Henry Youle Hind in 1857 and 1858 had raised the likelihood that even the Prairies—hitherto dismissed as unproductive—could support agricultural settlement. Scientific developments also influenced the Confederation debates in more abstract ways. Scientific notions of progress, increasingly embodied in the concept of evolution, gave rise to the confidence that a united British America could stretch from one coast to the other, could comprehend a variety of landscapes and cultures, and could not only survive but even produce in time a new British American nationality. This kind of idealism was not always evident in the debates that were so often necessarily concerned with the grubbier realities of political compromise. Nevertheless, it existed. It gave rise to a sense of mission in the way the new Dominion of Canada would approach the Northwest, and it contributed to a more general sense of grandeur and generosity of vision that at times informed pro-Confederation rhetoric. "We hail this birthday of a new nationality," proclaimed the Toronto *Globe* on 1 July 1867: "A united British America...takes its place among the nations of the world."

However, there was one major problem that affected any and all of the grander expressions of the Dominion's character and destiny, and it represented in itself one of the underlying themes of Confederation. It lay in the extreme narrowness of the social basis on which the scheme was founded. The "fathers of Confederation" were, by definition, male. They were men of property, and by ethnic origin they were Anglo-Celtic and French. It was no accident that they should have these characteristics, for they were the products of a political system that could only produce leaders of this stamp. Although voting rights were more widespread in British North America than, say, in Great Britain at the same time, there were significant restrictions. The most conspicuous was the exclusion of women. Only in Lower Canada, where women who fulfilled the property requirements had regularly gone to the polls, had women had a significant history of voting. Elsewhere, despite some isolated exceptions, it seems that convention—as in Britain—had been a sufficient restraint. Starting in the 1830s, however, women had been specifically disenfranchised in each of the colonies. The trend had begun in Lower Canada in 1834. Although the legislation there had been disallowed on a technicality by the British government, women were disenfranchised throughout the united Province of Canada in 1849. By that time, Prince Edward Island and New Brunswick had passed similar legislation, and Nova Scotia followed in 1851. Property qualifications imposed a further constraint, although it varied between provinces. Prince Edward Island, for example, had an electorate that included virtually every adult male. The province of Canada, by contrast, had on its voting registers in 1861 only 13.15 percent of the population of Canada East and 13.9 percent of the population of Canada West. Even allowing for the number of women, children, and other disenfranchised persons in the general population, and for the vagaries of the registers, this was a long way from full male suffrage. Also excluded from the vote, in practice if not by law, were native people. By the mid-1860s, only British Columbia specifically disenfranchised potential native voters—Nova Scotia had done so between 1854 and 1863 when it experimented with a universal male, non-native franchise, but dropped the ban when it reintroduced the property qualification in 1863—but it is clear that almost all were excluded by property requirements. Thus, the political foundations on which Confederation rested were characterized by the exclusion from political participation of all women, virtually all native people, and depending on the province, significant numbers of working-class people, including many members of black and other ethnic minorities who lacked property.

The ability of merchant and professional elites to manipulate the system was strengthened even further by the pervasiveness of patronage as an instrument of political manoeuvring. Although more deep-seated in the province of Canada, with its bitter interparty divisions than elsewhere in British North America, provincial government patronage and the prospect of federal patronage were undoubtedly wielded effectively during the crucial Confederation debates in Nova Scotia and New Brunswick. Also important was the access to British investment that the state could provide. As a group, the "Fathers of Confederation" were disproportionately populated by men who had direct connections with major British merchant banking houses, especially with Baring Brothers and Glyn Mills. As heads of, or senior ministers in, governments that had expanded their interventionist economic role by their promotion of railways, many of the "Fathers" were longtime practitioners of the arts of attracting investment and awarding lucrative contracts. Nor had they been above personally profiting from the inside information they gained from their connections. As successful participants in the financial workings of the British Empire, they effectively combined economic and political power. These arrangements, not surprisingly, would continue long after Confederation: not until 1893 would Baring and Glyn be supplanted by the Bank of Montreal as Canada's fiscal agents in London.

Furthermore, it would be a mistake to think of Confederation as representing any sort of a new beginning with regard to extension of political participation. The British North America Act was quite explicit on the point: as to voting rights, "all Laws in force in the several provinces at the Union" would continue in force and would be used for federal as well as provincial elections. Also continued were the property laws that in each province embodied women's subordination. Even in an area such as relationships with native people, which was defined clearly in the British North America Act as a federal responsibility, the policy that was enunciated in the Indian Act of 1868 essentially established only a new administrative framework for the existing provincial policies and continued the assimilationist goals and pragmatism in method that had characterized them all. The truth was that, by its initiators, Confederation was not seen as bringing about societal changes. It *was* intended to resolve problems that were political, economic, and strategic. Inevitably, as the anticipated westward expansion took place, it would have to deal with the extensive societal and environmental changes that were taking place in the West. But the fundamental intention to preserve rather than alter existing social patterns was clear in the support for Confederation that came from Conservatives and in the Conservative rhetoric that so often accompanied the proposal, especially in the province of Canada. The promonarchical statements of leaders such as Taché and John A. Macdonald were consciously aimed at contrasting British and British American practice with the anarchically democratic institutions of the United States.

It was true, of course, that Confederation was not solely the project of political Conservatives, though it drew a great deal of its support from them. Even by reform politicians, however, outright democracy was often suspected and rejected. The Rouges in Canada East, their political philosophy influenced by French revolutionary ideals, did advocate universal male suffrage, but their position was not shared even by the reform leaders in Canada West. "The Constitution which makes the vox populi the 'all in all' [in] political or governmental power," commented the Reformist St. Catharine's *Evening Journal* in February 1865, "has an inherent weakness which must result in its own death." The same objections were made by prominent Reform leaders in the Maritime provinces. Throughout the uniting provinces, the central ground of English-speaking reformism was occupied by those whose main concern was to make the governing class more directly responsible to an existing propertied electorate rather than to open the doors to radically wider participation. The trend during the three decades prior to Confederation had been to define and even restrict the franchise rather than to expand it. Democrats, for George-Etienne Cartier when he addressed the legislature of the province of Canada in February 1865, were to be classified along with socialists and those who favoured annexation by the United States: all were "extreme men." Confederation was not a measure of social reform or of political levelling. Rather, it was intended to protect against infection by the democratic tendencies of the United States and to preserve the hierarchical principles of British America.

But how far would British Americans from outside of the political elite allow this intention to be fulfilled? That question would not be answered in 1867, or for years thereafter, but it was there to be posed. In the creative achievements of Confederation, certain upper-middle-class women had been important participants. Their influence had been expressed in their roles at the Charlottetown and Quebec conferences and in the advice they might offer—as notably in the case of Anne Nelson, wife of George Brown—to politically active male members of their families. Nevertheless, the mid-nineteenth century was a time of reduction in the direct political participation of women, as the male-propagated doctrine of "separate spheres" emphasized women's domestic role and led, among other results, to the specific denial of women's suffrage. The response of women would gather its full force only later in the century, but already in the 1860s there were signs of what was to come. Women could and did influence the political process by sending individual and collective petitions to legislatures. Middle-class women were pressing for fuller access to education, and within five years of Confederation, Mount Allison University in New Brunswick would become the first in Canada to open its degree programs to women. Already, in 1867, Emily Stowe had become the country's first practising female physician, although she still faced a stern battle to obtain a formal licence. These were early indications of the effort of such women to invert the doctrine of separate spheres by asserting that the nurturing qualities of women could justify opening the range of professional possibilities in fields that would eventually include teaching, nursing, and social work. At the same time, the establishment by church women of missionary and temperance societies was a forerunner of the later politicization of feminism and the campaign for women's suffrage. Working-class women faced different circumstances, with mid-century industrialization in the province of Canada bringing about large-scale migration to urban areas. The federal census of 1871, reflecting changes occurring during the 1860s, showed that 42 percent of the industrial labour force in Montreal consisted of women and children and 34 percent in Toronto. Although hindered in many cases by male domination of trade unions, female workers in future years would play an important role in organizing themselves to make demands on employers and the state. Despite the exclusion of women from formal participation in the Confederation process, they would not for long allow the Canadian state to maintain this status quo unchallenged.

The same was true of the industrial working class more generally. During the 1850s, a series of conspicuous strikes—notably involving railway construction workers in a variety of Canadian and Atlantic locations and a wave of strikes among skilled workers in Canadian urban centres in 1853 and 1854—had drawn attention to the increasing organization of the working class. The most common form of organization was the local union, representing skilled workers such as printers or carpenters. However, unskilled labourers were also organized in some areas, as in shipbuilding in major ports. The 1860s saw the continuation of working-class activism, and continuing industrialization led to further strikes and broadening of the base of the workers' response either through unions with international affiliations or though adaptation of union organization to increasingly large factories. Quickly, working-class organization gained a political dimension. In Great Britain from the late 1850s and the United States in the 1860s, demands for a shorter working day were frequently adopted by strikers, and in Britain the effective foundation of the Trades Union Congress in 1868 led to the beginning of concerted political action in this area and support for legislation to give clear legality to trade union activity. A similar struggle began in the Dominion of Canada in the early 1870s. The Nine-Hour Movement resulted not only in strikes such as the bitter dispute of 1872 between Toronto printers and employers such as George Brown's *Globe* newspaper but also in the establishment of a shaky political alliance between unions and the federal Conservatives. The Macdonald government's Trades Union Act of April 1872 was a direct response to the Toronto printers' strike and established that unions were not to be categorized as illegal conspiracies. The working-class movement that gathered strength so rapidly after Confederation was not solely a movement of the politically disenfranchised. Depending upon the province they lived in and the value of the property they owned or rented, many trade unionists—especially in craft unions—were also voters. However, without substantial private means they were denied any realistic chance of access to political office, and the effectiveness of their efforts to advance class interests depended upon extraparliamentary pressure. Thus, again, movements that were already developing at the time of Confederation were soon to exert an effective influence upon state institutions in whose foundation they had been largely denied an active role.

Native people and other visible ethnic minorities in the province of Canada and the Atlantic provinces had, in general, been excluded from the political process as individuals as well as collectively. For many communities, survival in the face of adverse social and economic conditions was a necessary preoccupation and excluded for the moment any direct effort to reverse their political disempowerment. For native people specifically, the adjustment to reservations was ongoing, and the removal to Ottawa of jurisdiction over government policies regarding native peoples represented a further loss of access to the political and bureaucratic decision makers. Not that native people were overawed. In 1863, Nova Scotian Micmacs raised what seemed to a non-native observer to be "many unreasonable objections" to subdivision of reserve lands.[6] Independence of thought remained and could be expressed at times in independence of action, but, for the moment, native people in the provinces that would initially unite in Confederation had limited practical scope for autonomy. Rather different was the situation of those in the West. Although much diversity of circumstances existed in the vast territories to the West of the province of Canada and although native peoples in British Columbia had already felt the effects of non-native colonization, any westward extension of the united British North America would inevitably involve negotiations and possible conflict with well-established native populations. The Métis of the Red River were especially well equipped to defend their territory politically and, if necessary, militarily.

Further west, Ojibwa, Cree, Assiniboine, Blackfoot, Piegan, and other powerful native peoples were similarly placed. Although acculturation and environmental change had reduced their manoeuvring room, native people had the advantage of being able to point to the successes—at least in the short-term—of native armed resistance to the western expansion of the United States. Once again, the confrontation between western native people and the Canadian state was necessarily a phenomenon of the post-Confederation era. It had to be preceded by the agreement with the Hudson's Bay Company that would transfer to Canada the assumed non-native power of jurisdiction over the vast northwest lands. Then, if non-native settlement was to expand, the process of interaction would begin. It

---

[6] Quoted in L. F. S. Upton, *Micmacs and Colonists: Indian-White Relations in the Maritimes, 1713–1867* (Vancouver: University of British Columbia Press, 1979). Other works dealing with the issues examined in this section include P. A. Baskerville, "The Pet Bank, the Local State, and the Imperial Centre, 1850–1864," *Journal of Canadian Studies*, 20 (1985–86), No. 3, pp. 22–46; Carl Berger, *The Sense of Power: Studies in the History of Canadian Imperialism, 1867–1914* (Toronto: University of Toronto Press, 1970); Gail G. Campbell, "Disfranchised but not Quiescent: Women Petitioners in New Brunswick in the Mid-19th Century," *Acadiensis*, 18 (Spring 1989), pp. 22–46; Micheline Dumont et al., *Quebec Women: A History* (Toronto: Women's Press, 1987); John Garner, *The Franchise and Politics in British North America, 1755–1867* (Toronto: University of Toronto Press, 1969); Doug Owram, *Promise of Eden: The Canadian Expansionist Movement and the Idea of the West, 1856–1900* (Toronto: University of Toronto Press, 1980); Bryan D. Palmer, *Working-Class Experience: The Rise and Reconstitution of Canadian Labour, 1800–1980* (Toronto: Butterworth, 1983); Alison Prentice et al., *Canadian Women: A History* (Toronto: Harcourt Brace Jovanovich, 1988); Gordon T. Stewart, *The Origins of Canadian Politics: A Comparative Approach* (Vancouver: University of British Columbia Press, 1986); and Suzanne Zeller, *Inventing Canada: Early Victorian Science and the Idea of a Transcontinental Nation* (Toronto: University of Toronto Press, 1987).

was inconceivable that it would be one from which the new Confederation would emerge without being significantly changed.

Underlying the question of Confederation, therefore, were important issues that were not part of the common currency of the Charlottetown and Quebec conferences or of the political debates that followed them. In the charmed circle of the "Fathers of Confederation," ladies were compared to "charming flowers...in their blooming beauty all around us." Working people, such as the Newfoundland fishermen who might serve with the Royal Navy in time of war, were to be valued for their "willing hands and stout arms." Disavowed alike were "bigotry of classes" and "bigotry of race," but the concept of race to which Thomas D'Arcy McGee referred—as was normal in the nineteenth century—was applied to French and English rather than to non-European groups. Native people, for example, seemed to impinge minimally on the consciousness of the conference delegates except insofar as native affairs represented an area of jurisdiction to be attributed to the proposed federal government. None of this was surprising, but it did impart to the proceedings a provisional quality that was none the less real for the fact that it was not fully evident in 1864 or for some years thereafter. Those who framed the Confederation scheme did so from a narrow social base. The state they created would soon have to contend with the organized demands of those who were held to be bound by decisions to which they had not had the opportunity to contribute. This, along with the more overt tensions between regional interests and between levels of government, ensured that the passage of Confederation in 1867 would be the beginning of a complex process of adjustment rather than a crowning achievement.

The Nature of the Union

Even as the delegates from the various provinces set off for the final constitutional conference in London, there were some remaining doubts. In late June 1866 the New Brunswick premier, Peter Mitchell, arrived in Rivière-du-Loup with his delegation for the transatlantic passage. In Halifax, Tupper and the Nova Scotians awaited a Cunard steamer in Halifax. Unexpectedly, telegrams reached both premiers from the province of Canada, informing them that the Canadian delegates could not leave until November. Mitchell was inclined to blame the entire delay on "Sir John A. Macdonald's condition and habits at the time," but whatever delays Macdonald's intemperance may have caused were compounded by the real crisis brought about in Canada by the Fenian threat. In any case, Mitchell and Tupper decided to leave on schedule. Tupper needed quick progress so as to ensure the safe enactment of Confederation before he had to face the voters. Even Mitchell believed that "if we went back it would be an end to Confederation." Once in London, the Maritime delegates were left to do very little during the late summer and early fall. Only after the arrival of the Canadians did the conference convene on December 4. There was not much scope for change to the Quebec Resolutions now that they had been specifically approved by the Parliament of the province of Canada. To reopen them would be to invite divisive debate, and none of the 16 delegates wanted that. The conference did resolve some difficult matters. A clause protecting separate school systems for religious minorities as far as they already existed by law—that is, in Quebec and Ontario— was unanimously adopted. And after some wrangling, agreement was reached for adjustments to the allocation of seats in the Senate, now that Prince Edward Island would not be a member: Nova Scotia and New Brunswick were allocated two extra seats each, which Prince Edward Island would take over if it were to join in the future. Thus, the regional balance agreed in Quebec was maintained. These questions settled, the conference turned to the tedious but necessary business of drafting final resolutions to form the basis of the legislation that the British cabinet would take to Parliament. By Christmas Eve, the task was complete. On Christmas Day, Macdonald wrote to the colonial secretary to let Carnarvon know that the resolutions would soon be on their way. On behalf of the delegates, he asked that no publicity should be allowed at this stage to prevent "premature discussion and imperfect information of the subject."

Macdonald and the delegates had specific reasons for this request. Howe and Annand, from Nova Scotia, were in London and actively lobbying against the union. Also present, and dissatisfied, was the Archbishop of Halifax, Thomas Louis Connolly, who wanted protection for separate schools in Nova Scotia and New Brunswick as well as in Ontario and Quebec. With these critics to be faced and the scrutiny of the resolutions by the British cabinet still to come, the proponents of union wanted matters kept as low-key as possible. They did not, of course, have much to worry about in practice. The British government was fully prepared to make changes to the details of the scheme, even to important details. On the insistence of the British cabinet, for example, provision was made for the creation of additional senators in case of a deadlock between the Senate and the House of Commons. But, in general, the union proposal was safe enough. Carnarvon dutifully considered the objections of Howe, Annand, and Connolly before rejecting them. Great Britain was not about to lose this opportunity to secure its goals in British North America. Many of the matters that were resolved in early 1867 were symbolic, though they were not unimportant. The two provinces into which the old province of Canada would be divided were named Quebec and Ontario. A British

Opening of the first Parliament of the Dominion of Canada, November 1867, as portrayed in *Harper's Weekly*. NATIONAL ARCHIVES OF CANADA/C11508

suggestion that Ontario be named "Toronto" was rejected as unnecessarily confusing. More complex was the decision on the formal title of the new united British North America. On the adoption of the name "Canada" there was no controversy, although Maritime anti-Confederates would point to this choice as an indication of where the real power in the negotiations had been located. The delegates would have liked the full title to be "Kingdom of Canada," and it was this that appeared in a draft of the British North America Act in early February 1867. The British cabinet, however, thought the term pretentious, and there were also fears that the republican United States would find it offensive. The eventual term "Dominion of Canada" still had a monarchical ring and had a precedent in the "Dominion of New England" that had existed briefly in the late seventeenth century. It had the disadvantage of lacking any proper French translation, but that detail was of little concern to Carnarvon as he rose in the House of Lords on 19 February to give his main speech in favour of the British North America bill. There was some support in both Houses for the objections from Nova Scotia, but by the end of March the bill had become an act with the signature of Queen Victoria.

1 July 1867 saw the inauguration of the new Dominion. Ceremonies were held in towns and cities from the Atlantic coast to the shores of Lake Huron and Lake Erie. Bands played and guns fired salutes, although in some Nova Scotian centres there were dissidents—perhaps readers of that day's *Morning Chronicle* editorial proclaiming the death of "the free and enlightened Province of Nova Scotia"—who insisted on hanging black crepe among the brightly coloured flags. In mid-September came the first federal election as well as the much-delayed provincial vote in Nova Scotia. Federally, in three of the four provinces, Macdonald's Conservatives won comfortably. In Nova Scotia, the anti-Confederates swept overwhelmingly into the provincial assembly and the federal Parliament. Of the 19 federal members elected, Tupper was the lone pro-Confederate, and even he won only narrowly in his old stronghold of Cumberland. Joseph Howe won personal election in Hants County and assumed leadership of the ultimately unsuccessful repeal campaign. The numbers of those elected were somewhat misleading, however, as the 38 percent pro-Confederate vote showed the strength of the minority view, especially in areas that stood to benefit from the intercolonial railway. What the Nova Scotian voting of 1867 really showed was how tortuous the Confederation process had been, how narrow had been the pro-Confederates' margin of overall political victory, and how strenuous a process of adaptation was to

come. Those who advocated Confederation had raised many expectations, and yet they had been unable to win the overwhelming support of British North Americans. In a sense, the political system did not allow them to do so: women, the working class, and disempowered ethnic minorities continued to have no choice but to put their demands on the new Canadian state from outside of the parliamentary process. Even within the confines of the male, propertied electorate, substantial opposition to Confederation had been recorded everywhere except in Canada West. The union of British North America seemed to offer convenient solutions to certain political and economic problems. It was an idea that could arouse significant support everywhere—solid support in Canada West—and one that could even inspire flights of idealism in some of its proponents. But its passage had been difficult at every stage. Now, in 1867, the task of making it workable had already begun.

PRE-CONFEDERATION CANADA AS A EUROPEAN SOCIETY

Thus far, this book has focused on trying to explain how Canada became and indeed always was a unique society. That is important, and it is accurate, but it is only half a truth. It is also true that Canada was and still is very similar to a large number of other societies and nations. Specifically, the dominant culture in Canada was and still remains European, and if we take as our vantage point the mid-nineteenth century, everything in that dominant culture either was imported from elsewhere or was a development closely parallelled by developments in other countries.

Is that not a contradiction? No. Consider an analogy. In elementary school you were probably taught that no two snowflakes are alike. That is an accurate fact, but it is only half a truth. Snow is only one of the forms that H_2O can take. So, although each snowflake is unique, nevertheless all snowflakes share a common fundamental character. They hold that character in sharp contrast to H_2O molecules that form ice, water, or steam. Therefore, to obtain a reasonable understanding of the physics of a snowflake, one must at the same time recognize both its uniqueness among snowflakes and that it belongs to a family that shares certain basic properties.

We have to make a similar recognition in the study of history, especially Canadian history. It is easy to become so fascinated with the tiny and

ORIGIN OF IMMIGRANTS TO NEW FRANCE, 1608-1759

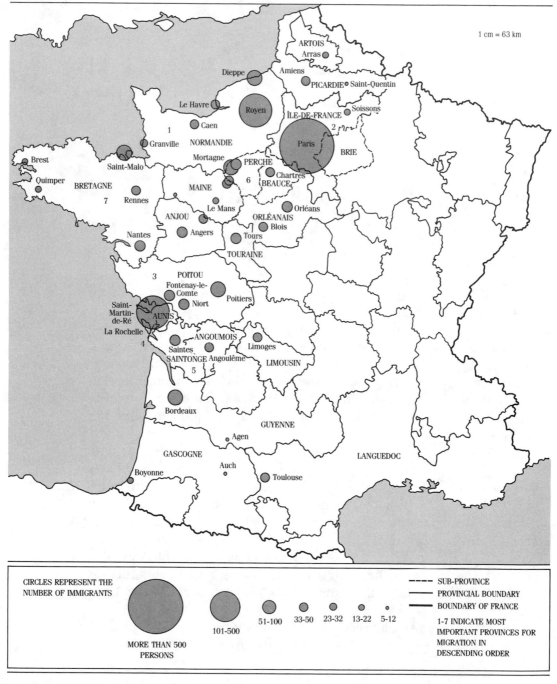

1 cm = 63 km

ARTOIS
Arras

Dieppe   Amiens
         PICARDIE ● Saint-Quentin

Le Havre   Royen   Soissons
                ÎLE-DE-FRANCE
        Caen   2
    1   Paris

Granville   NORMANDIE   BRIE
Brest   Mortagne   PERCHE
Saint-Malo   6   Chartres
Quimper   BEAUCE
BRETAGNE   MAINE
7   Rennes   Le Mans   Orléans
    ANJOU   ORLÉANAIS
Nantes   Angers   Blois
                Tours
            TOURAINE

3   POITOU
Fontenay-le-
    Comte
Saint-   Niort   Poitiers
Martin-
de-Ré   AUNIS
La Rochelle
    4   ANGOUMOIS
    Saintes   Limoges
    SAINTONGE Angoulême   LIMOUSIN
        5

    Bordeaux

            GUYENNE

        Agen

GASCOGNE   LANGUEDOC
        Auch
Boyonne   Toulouse

CIRCLES REPRESENT THE   ---- SUB-PROVINCE
NUMBER OF IMMIGRANTS   ──── PROVINCIAL BOUNDARY
                ──── BOUNDARY OF FRANCE

            51-100 33-50 23-32 13-22 5-12   1-7 INDICATE MOST
        101-500   IMPORTANT PROVINCES FOR
                            MIGRATION IN
MORE THAN 500   DESCENDING ORDER
PERSONS

FROM R. COLE HARRIS, ED. *HISTORICAL ATLAS OF CANADA I: FROM THE BEGINNING TO 1800*. REPRINTED BY
PERMISSION OF UNIVERSITY OF TORONTO PRESS.

ORIGINS OF IRISH-CATHOLIC MIGRANTS MARRIED IN TORONTO IN THE 1850s

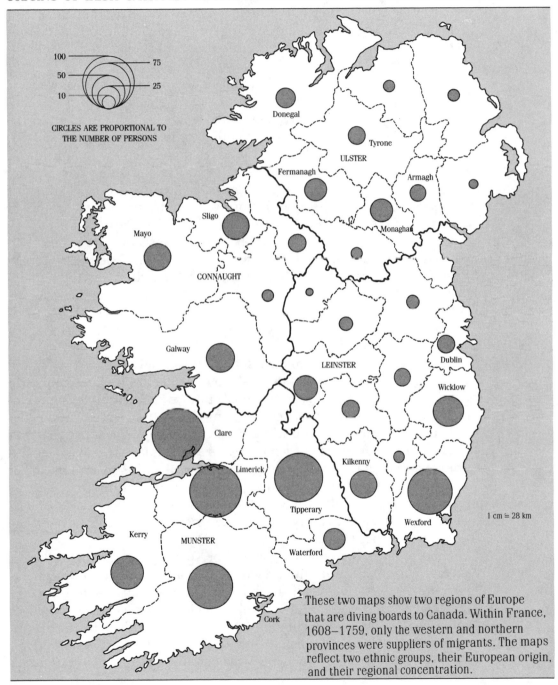

100 — — 75
50 — — 25
10

CIRCLES ARE PROPORTIONAL TO
THE NUMBER OF PERSONS

Donegal
Tyrone
ULSTER
Fermanagh
Armagh
Monaghan
Sligo
Mayo
CONNAUGHT
Galway
LEINSTER
Dublin
Wicklow
Clare
Limerick
Kilkenny
Tipperary
Wexford
Kerry
MUNSTER
Waterford
Cork

1 cm ≅ 28 km

These two maps show two regions of Europe
that are diving boards to Canada. Within France,
1608–1759, only the western and northern
provinces were suppliers of migrants. The maps
reflect two ethnic groups, their European origin,
and their regional concentration.

intriguing details of Canadian historical events that we forget that these events have to be judged within the framework of certain important general observations. The hardest thing for a student of history to do is to keep both sides of any event (or of any culture or of any nation) in mind at the same time: the unique and the general.

Canada as a nation has been vulnerable to outside pressures: we were sprung from the two largest empires of the eighteenth and nineteenth centuries (the French and the British) and since then have lived under the shadow of the great empire of the twentieth century, the United States. So, understandably, Canadian historians have emphasized the uniqueness of Canadian historical processes as one way of maintaining our identity against outside pressures. As Carl Berger has written, "One of the most persistent strands in Canadian historical literature since the First World War has been the concentration on Canadian national history and nationality...Canada's historians have all been nationalists of various hues...." An earlier commentator, Allan Smith, writing in the *Canadian Historical Review*, noted that "the nationalist uses language to define the nation's character and experience in a way that will provide a rationale for its continued existence." He adds: "In the course of fulfilling that purpose, nationalist ideology, like ideologies generally, often does violence to truth and masks reality."

One way that historians in the last two decades have tried to break away from the nationalist bias and its masking of reality has been to emphasize the reality of Canada as a set of regional cultures and, within those several regions, of local societies. There are some fascinating "micro-studies" of individual communities and it has been convincingly demonstrated that not just each province, but each township and hamlet has a character and unique history of its own. Such studies are useful, but as an antidote to the vice of excessively nation-oriented history, they are misdirected. That is, regionalist history and its stepchild, local history, can lead to a *reductio ad absurdum*—eventually, every township, every family, and every person has a unique and special history.

There is no reason why this should be so. The cure for the follies of excessive nationalism in thinking about Canadian history is the same as the cure for excessive regionalism and excessive localism—to recognize the singularity of Canada, of each of its regions, of each of its provinces and, indeed, of each local community, but to do so within the framework of European history. Our history should fit together like a nest of boxes. Each community is a distinct entity historically, but it fits within a larger box, the province. And each province nests, with other provinces, within its region; and regions within the entity that we call Canada. And the dominant tone of Canadian society in the nineteenth and twentieth centuries has been that set by European civilization.[1]

The Options

To make clear the fundamentally European character of Canadian society, imagine that it is the year 1600 and that you are one of the few non-native persons in what is today Canada. Imagine also that by some stroke of fate you are the cultural czar of this vast area and have both the knowledge and the power to introduce and perpetuate any sort of extant society that you wish. What choices, what options, do you have? There are in the world of your time, 1600, only five major sorts of cultures from which you could choose.

1. Asiatic, of which we can take Japan as an example. In 1598 Ieyasu Tokugawa came to the throne. He was able to combine the role of emperor and "shogun" (an old military title meaning literally "barbarian-subduing generalissimo"), and he created a feudal monarchy that lasted until 1868. Japanese feudal society during this period was intensely inward looking. It severely limited contracts with outsiders and did not encourage exploration of the outside world or trade with that world. Tokugawa Japan was highly stratified, in the form of six castes: the imperial family; warriors ("samurai"); farmers; artisans; merchants; and outcasts. Notice how low on the scale the merchants were. This was a militarily based hierarchy, and trade was considered a low activity, appropriate only to the servile. Certainly it was not something to be honoured. The rules of this feudal society limited people's rights to travel from one place to another and to change ways of making

---

[1] Of course this is not the only way of keeping the generalized aspects of Canadian history in mind. One developing school of international histories views Canada (along with Australia, New Zealand, and Argentina) as "countries of recent settlement" all of which share certain common characteristics. See, for example, Donald Denoon, *Settler Capitalism. The Dynamics of Dependent Development in the Southern Hemispheres* (Oxford: Clarendon Press, 1983) and "Understanding Settler Societies," *Historical Studies*, vol. 18 (Oct. 1979), pp. 511–527. See also, J.P. Fogarty, "The Comparative Method and Nineteenth-Century Regions of Settlement," *Historical Studies*, vol. 19 (Oct. 1981), pp. 412–429.

a living. Upward social mobility was very difficult, and usually it took a family several generations to move upward significantly.

2. Polynesian, (including Melanesian and Micronesian). The Polynesians were heroic explorers and travellers. They charted and settled vast areas of the Pacific long before European explorers had ventured more than a few hundred kilometres from their own shorelines. By roughly the time of the birth of Christ, they had settled not only Fiji, Samoa, and Tonga but had colonized the heart of the Polynesian triangle that embraces the Marquesas, the Society Islands, and the Cook Islands. In the succeeding millennium, they settled areas as far distant as Hawaii in the north, Easter Island in the south and east, and New Zealand in the southwest. The surface area bounded by these Polynesian settlements was several times the size of the entire continents of Europe and North America combined. To say that Magellan, Cook, and other Europeans "discovered" the Pacific is a racial conceit: the Polynesians did. The Polynesians were supported by an economy that involved agriculture, especially the cultivation of trees and root crops as well as animal keeping, and by hunting and fishing. The various Polynesian societies were extremely complicated socially and possessed highly articulated oral cultures that involved the passage of genealogies and mythologies from generation to generation. Their skills as explorers, though, were limited by lack of a written language, no system of complex mathematics, and no method of processing hard metals, most importantly, iron.

3. Sub-Saharan Africa. This included a bewildering variety of societies, some comprising no more than several families, others consisting of "tribes" that numbered members in the tens of thousands. This part of Africa included simple hunting and gathering societies but also held communities that were knowledgable about agriculture and animal keeping. Most African societies were nonliterate and only numerate at a low level, but some had developed pictographs and many had complex oral cultures. What the Sub-Saharan groups shared was a style of social and economic life that was subordinate to the natural environment and therefore was much more in consonance with the environment than are the "modern" societies with which we are familiar. The African tribal groups, in sharp contrast to the Polynesians, were not given to seaborne exploration and thus were essentially locked into their own world.

4. Amerindian. This covers the wide range of people who, it is thought, stemmed from a migration from Asia across the Bering Strait 14 000 or more years ago. The Amerindians include the Mayans, who were extraordinarily adept in mathematics and astronomy, the Incas, one of

the most architecturally accomplished cultures of any era, and, in North America, a variety of groups that ranged from settled agriculturalists to primarily hunting and gathering peoples. Most Amerindians used stone tools, although metals were employed by some.

5. European, by which is meant those nations whose dominant culture originated in the Fertile Crescent and who, after passing through the time period that was classical Greece and Rome, merged with that of the barbarian groups of continental Europe. European society was mostly Christian in religion and Indo-European in language. For the most part, European economies were agricultural, but urban centres were well developed and elementary (prefactory) manufacture was common. Trade patterns in Europe were complex, and money was used both as a storehouse of value and as a medium of exchange. Although most people in Europe in 1600 could not read, the society's major cultural traditions were stored in books. Numeracy was nearly universal, and highly complex mathematical and navigational calculations were within the reach of the society's more educated people. Europe at this time probably was the wealthiest of the world's cultures and had resources to spare for high cultural development. Nevertheless, in many ways, European society was a bit nasty. Unlike the Amerindian, African, and Polynesian societies, it did not attempt to work within the bounds of nature but rather to gain control over it. Thus, European civilization was immensely wasteful and ecologically destructive, and, simultaneously, wondrously productive of ideas and inventions (whose purpose mostly was to overcome nature). This aggressive attitude toward the natural world was parallelled by an assertiveness toward the world outside Europe. European nations financed large expeditions that sought to discover and, eventually, to conquer, previously unknown portions of this planet.

There is no question which one of these groups dominated the history of Canada: the European did. Thus, it becomes one of the central tasks in dealing with Canadian history to discover what kind of European society Canada became and why.

Language

Language is the medium in which the human mind moves. But because it is so universal, we are apt to take language and its effects upon us for granted.

One of the things that linguistic scientists have established in the last three decades is that language is not passive. That is, it is not something that we control completely—like a physical tool—for selective use. Language is active. The particular language that one is programmed with as a child helps to determine three things: what you can think, how well you can think about certain matters, and what some of your social attitudes will be. Consider the first item. The human mind can only reflect consciously and articulately upon matters for which it has concepts, either abstract symbols (such as mathematical symbols) or words. This directly affects human society. For example, when the ideals of the French Revolution—liberty, equality, and fraternity—were preached in the Celtic-speaking areas of Ireland and Scotland, they fell on deaf ears. There were no Gaelic equivalents of these concepts, or anything close, and it was literally impossible for the bulk of the Gaelic speakers to comprehend the concepts these three words signified.

Now, second, it is clear that some languages have more precise and more sophisticated ways of dealing with some matters than do others. For example, it is well known that several of the native Canadian dialects have a vocabulary for various types of snow and ice that permit several dozen degrees of shaded description. In English we have very few words for the same thing. One can think about the nature of snow or ice in the English language, but one can think about it better, and at a more sophisticated level, in several other tongues.

And, third, language may very subtly influence a person's (or an entire society's) attitudes, thought processes, and decision making. For example, linguists point out that languages that make heavy use of the passive voice ("the man was made rich") inculcate an attitude toward the world that is quite different from tongues that stay mostly in the active voice ("the man made money").

By the mid-nineteenth century, it was clear that there would be two master languages in Canada, English and French, and that every other tongue would be subordinate. Of course there were enclaves of other languages—Gaelic and German were the most common of the other European languages—and there were the languages of the native Canadian peoples. But the languages of the people who controlled the government were either English or French, and the language of commerce, the passport to doing business outside one's home community, was English or French. The mid-nineteenth century was a period of great linguistic flux, and it was all in one direction: toward people from other linguistic bases acquiring English or French as a second language. Among the children of such people, English or French usually became the first language.

No one would claim that English and French work in the same way linguistically. (Any typesetter can tell you that, as a rough rule of thumb, it takes 20 percent more words in French to say the same thing as in English, so manifestly there are functional differences). However, English and French share two important characteristics. First, they both include a range of nouns and adjectives that are extremely large as compared to most other languages. This is especially true of English, which at mid-nineteenth century probably had the largest effective vocabulary in the world. Second, each of these tongues is particularly assimilative of words that involve technology. The greatest burden that languages have had to bear in the last three centuries is the immense proliferation of technological concepts. Thus, the large operational vocabulary of English and French and their easy assimilation of technological terms meant that people who were trained in either of these languages had an automatic advantage in dealing with a world where the rapid and often confusing process of modernization was taking place. Just as it is easier to perform any task with a personal computer that has 640K memory capacity, than one with, say, a 512K, so it is easier to grapple with a rapidly changing world if one has a language that is highly flexible and has a very large vocabulary.

By mid-nineteenth century, both English and French had encapsulated into their bank of concepts a set of terms and habits of word association that has been called "the European Enlightenment vocabulary." This was a vocabulary that emphasized the role of human reason, implied a detached attitude toward received tradition, and emphasized the rights of the individual. The phrase in the United States Constitution is an Enlightenment formulation that virtually every adult speaker of English in North America was acquainted with:

That all men are created equal, that they are endowed by their Creator with certain unalienable rights, that among these are life, liberty and the pursuit of happiness and to secure these rights governments are instituted among men deriving their just powers from the consent of the governed.

Similarly, the language of commerce and economics, from Adam Smith onward, with its emphasis on the maximization of individual interest, is a direct application of the Enlightenment vocabulary. The key point about this vocabulary is that one did not have to agree with the conclusions of the Enlightenment thinkers (or even to have heard of them directly) to be influenced by their concepts. If, as so many people did, one spent time arguing about the rights of the individual, then one was implicitly accepting the fact that human beings can consciously manipulate their social environment. Social manipulation was thus embedded in the language by the Enlightenment vocabulary in the same way that manipulation of the physical environment was embedded through the wide technological vocabulary of English and French.[2]

In addition to these linguistic characteristics, it was crucial that the two languages, English and French, were tied into world-circling geopolitical networks. In the mid-nineteenth century, England was the heart of the largest empire in the world and was on its way to being, by century's end, heart of the largest empire in world history. France at mid-nineteenth century was, as it were, between empires, but even in this relatively slack period of French imperialism, French was spoken not only in the homeland but in cultivated circles throughout the world where it was used as the language of diplomacy and as the tongue of state power in places as widely dispersed as the imperial Russian court and the French-conquered islands of the Pacific, such as Tahiti.

Therefore those inhabitants of Canada who spoke either French or English were plugged into the linguistic equivalent of one of two massive computers. The main frames were located in metropolitan France and in the British Isles, but millions of people, all over the world, were joined to one of the two networks. This occurred automatically and probably most Canadians took it so much for granted that they hardly noticed.

Religion

If this book had been written, say, 20 years ago, we probably would have spent a good deal of space dealing with a simple fact: that the nature of the beliefs a culture has about the invisible world, about things that are usually called religion and magic greatly influence what that society believes about the visible world, and therefore, how it acts. That is no longer necessary. You live in a world where everyday the newspapers show how

---

[2] For a readable study, see Robert Anchor, *The Enlightenment Tradition* (New York: Harper and Row, 1967).

directly influential religion is in determining human behaviour: the rise of Islamic fundamentalism, the persistence of Catholicism in Eastern Europe, the depth of religious feelings in the Middle East are constant reminders that religion is central to human social organization. And, if anything, religion was much more important in the nineteenth century than it is today. One may not wish to go as far as Reginald Whitaker, who has asserted that "religion of one sort or another is the glue that holds Canadian history together, helping to shape everything from racism to radicalism," but important it clearly has been.

The religion that affected Canada's history so deeply was not the indigenous beliefs of the Amerindians (though such beliefs survived among the indigene more than is often recognized) and not any eastern faith (Hinduism, Confucianism, Buddhism), nor that of the then-contemporary Middle East (Islam, Judaism). It was Christianity and of a very specific sort: that which had evolved in western Europe in the sixteenth, seventeenth, and eighteenth centuries and that was sharply distinct from the eastern forms of Christianity, such as the Coptic Church and the various Orthodox faiths that had their roots in the eastern portion of the Roman Empire. The two main branches of that western European faith— Roman Catholicism and Protestantism—more than any other set of factors determined what the ethical base of the new society emerging in Canada would be. And, to a large degree, religion determined the meaning of any given event. Here it is necessary to emphasize that for religion to have been a pervasive influence upon society, not everyone had to be religious nor to be religious in the same way. Beliefs about religion are inherently individualistic (what someone believes in their heart is impossible to know, much less to standardize). And beliefs about religion shade into superstitions and into faith in magic and astrology and alchemy and all sorts of ideas that are not part of official religious dogmas.

Nevertheless, the Christian tradition laid down certain bedrock beliefs that were accepted generally throughout Canadian society: that there was an omniscient and omnipresent God; that humankind was inherently sinful; that humanity was redeemed from its inherent flaws by the death of Jesus Christ, provided that certain beliefs and practices were followed (the exact nature of these varied by denomination); and that there was both a heaven and a hell and that Christians merited eternal life, and others did not. If you had asked an average English-speaking or French-speaking Canadian of the last century if this was a Christian country, the answer certainly would have been "of course it is," although Catholics and

Protestants in those days did not always consider each other to be Christian.

Of the older of the two western European religious systems, Roman Catholicism, in theory, it was one church in Canada. But in day-to-day operation there were two major churches: the one French Canadian in ethnicity and French in its pastoral language, the other Irish in ethnicity and English speaking. Even in Quebec, Catholic congregations were either French or Irish. Irish priests served Irish congregations and they looked to Dublin (and particularly to Archbishop Paul Cullen) as their spiritual, if not their official, ecclesiastical head. French Catholics, who lived mostly in Quebec, were served almost entirely by French-speaking priests and governed by French bishops, some of whom were native-born Canadians, others came from France. Although ethnically divided, Irish and French Catholics shared a common sacramental system that emphasized the power of the priest as a channel of God's grace. And they both accepted the ultimate religious authority of the pope.

FIGURE 1

RELIGIOUS PERCENTAGES OF CANADIAN POPULATION, 1871

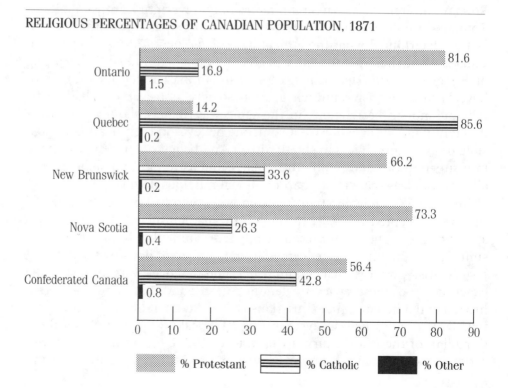

The other main branch of western European Christianity, Protestant-ism, was divided into several denominations. The most important in Canada were the Anglican, Methodist, Presbyterian, and Baptist. What they held in common was a sense of their own history. Each traced its origins to the Reformation and to the split with Rome in the sixteenth and seventeenth centuries. In contrast to the Catholic system, these denomina-tions emphasized that each person was capable of receiving grace from God directly and that the intervention of priests between God and human-kind was not necessary. (The Anglicans were somewhat less clear on this point than were the others). In their mode of organization, the Protestant churches gave a great deal more power to the laity than did the Catholic Church, and, consequently, individual congregations had a degree of autonomy (and, sometimes, of eccentricity) that was not permitted in the Catholic faith.[3]

The Christianity of Canada, a direct importation from western Europe, could scarcely lay claim to any great originality. In fact, the authorities of most denominations laid great emphasis upon their group's strict con-formity with Christian traditions that had been established long before the denomination's migration to the New World. That stated, three notewor-thy developments occurred in Canadian religious life. One of these was the appearance in Nova Scotia of a religious genius, the Reverend Henry Alline (1748–1784). Alline underwent a radical conversion experience in 1775 and became a virtual prophet. Through sermons, songs, and poetry and, most importantly, through revival services, he effected the equivalent in Maritime Canada of the Great Awakening in the United States and was instrumental in founding scores of Baptist and Congregational churches. Much of the distinctively "independent" character of Maritime religion at mid-nineteenth century was attributable to churches that traced their character to Alline.[4] A second development in Canada that went beyond precedents in the Old World occurred in the Anglican communion: the

---

[3] A discerning discussion of the interplay of Protestantism and nineteenth-century society is William Westfall, *Two Worlds: The Protestant Culture of Nineteenth-Century Ontario* (Kingston and Montreal: McGill-Queen's University Press, 1989)

[4] See J. M. Bumsted, *Henry Alline* (Toronto: University of Toronto Press, 1971); George A. Rawlyk (ed.), *Henry Alline: Selected Writings* (New York: Paulist Press, 1987); George A. Rawlyk, *Ravished by the Spirit: Religious-Revivals, Baptists, and Henry Alline* (Kingston and Montreal: McGill-Queen's University Press, 1988).

melding of Irish and English elements. The Anglican church in nineteenth-century Canada is usually referred to as the "Church of England."
This is misleading. In fact, the Anglican communion was part of what had
become in 1801 the "United Church of England and Ireland." In the British
Isles, this ecclesiastical union had influenced only the very top level of the
church, but in Canada, the Irish and English elements mixed thoroughly
at all levels. Irish Protestants, therefore, played a very strong part in the
development of the Canadian church's doctrines, liturgical style, and
administrative methods. At mid-nineteenth century, probably at least one-
fifth of the laity was of Irish background and a markedly higher proportion
of the clergy. Indeed, a significant cadre of clergy came directly from
Trinity College, Dublin. The notably "low" stance of the Anglican Church
in Canada stems largely from this Irish influence: the Irish Protestants
were energetically opposed to any rituals or beliefs that resembled those of
the Roman Catholics. The extremely "Protestant character" that was
stamped upon Canadian Anglicanism differentiated it considerably from
both the Episcopal Church in the United States and from the established
church in England. A third signal development in Canadian Christianity
occurred within Ontario, where Methodism achieved a force unequalled in
any other province. There were various forms of Methodism in Canada—
Wesleyan, Episcopal, Primitive, among others—but they were well on the
way to coalescing into a single phalanx by the time of Confederation. The
actual process of union was not completed until June 1884, but the force of
Methodism was felt long before that date. At mid-century, Methodism was
the most assertive of the major Christian denominations, and in Ontario it
seemed to be the unofficial state church.[5]

Along with their beliefs about God, heaven, hell, and right and wrong,
the various Christian denominations brought with them to Canada their
hatreds. In Western Europe, Protestants and Catholics had fought bloody
wars. As recently as 1798, a virtual civil war between Catholics and
Protestants had been waged in the south of Ireland. These were not distant
historical events, but events kept alive in the memory. Thus, one finds
religious riots in Kingston and Perth in Ontario in the 1820s, and later in
New Brunswick. In Toronto, the annual Orange Parade held in July was

[5] See, for example, Goldwin S. French, "Egerton Ryerson and the Methodist Model for Upper
Canada," in *Egerton Ryerson and his Times*, N. Mcdonald and A. Chaiton (eds.) (Toronto:
MacMillan, 1978), pp. 45–48; reprinted in J.K. Johnson and Bruce G. Wilson (eds.), *Upper
Canada. New Perspectives* (Ottawa, Carleton University Press, 1989), pp. 537–553.

the scene of regular riots, not just between Irish Protestants and Irish Catholics, but between Catholics and English-, Scots-, and Canadian-born Protestants. Because sectarian violence is so irrational and so repugnant, it is easy for us to push it out of sight. This will not do. Religious prejudice was persuasive in nineteenth-century Canada, and it was not something invented in Canada. It was imported.

Immigration

The language and the religion of Canada at mid-nineteenth century were European because the great bulk of the people had European origins. This is not a truism; it is central to an understanding of Canadian culture and politics. In 1871 the first census after Confederation was carried out, and the enumerators asked each person what his or her national origin was. In essence, this question was, "Where did your forebears come from?" a query that today would be called an "ethnicity question." The results are shown in Figure 2 and tell us very clearly what sort of Europeans the Canadians of the nineteenth century were: in background they harkened either to France or to the British Isles. Indigenous people and Europeans from other nations were significant groups in specific communities, but the Canadian polity rested upon two quite narrow ethnic bases.

These data on ethnicity tell us something else: that what is frequently called the history of "English Canada" in the nineteenth century actually involved people who were for the most part *not* English in background. The largest ethnic group in the "English Canada" of Confederation (Ontario, Nova Scotia, New Brunswick), and later Prince Edward Island and British Columbia, was the Irish. The English ethnic group (which in the census included the Welsh as well as the English) was only half the size of the combined Scottish and Irish groups. Thus, instead of referring to "English Canada," we should be referring to "English-speaking Canada," for the social, cultural, and political environment was dominated by the Scots and by the Irish.

The arrivals of the two European ethnic streams that are so clearly delineated in the 1871 census—that of French origin and that of British Isles origin—were timed differently. Direct migration from France had dropped to a trickle after 1763. The French-language culture at mid-nineteenth century was primarily (but not entirely) a Quebec culture. (The Acadians were a significant, if small, population.) Contemporaries from the English-speaking sectors of Canada frequently referred to Quebec society as "archaic," but this missed the point. What had once been New France had become a socially and culturally integrated world, a cohesive set of local communities, a fragment of continental French society that had adapted in its own way to the exigencies of North American life.

English-speaking Canada was completely different. It experienced massive immigration during the nineteenth century and was in a constant state of flux. English-speaking Canada was buoyant, expansive, and was modernizing quickly and entering the capitalist age. It was exciting, yes, mature and cohesive, no. During the nineteenth century, anglophone Canada was flooded by individuals (and, as the century passed, by their descendants, born in Canada) whose roots were in the British Isles. This dispersion began in 1815 at the end of the Napoleonic Wars and by the

FIGURE 2

ETHNIC PERCENTAGES OF CANADIAN POPULATION, 1871

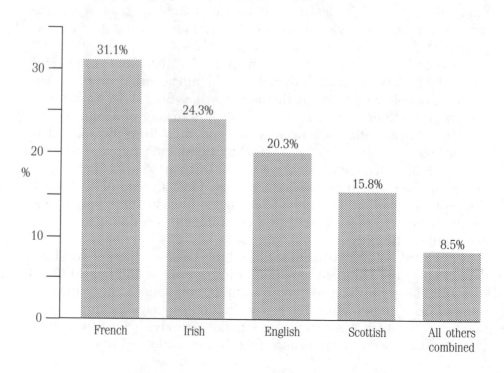

1830s had become a massive international migration, a part of the same exodus that peopled Australia, New Zealand, and significant portions of southern Africa and the United States.

Considering that this migration is so central to Canadian history, it is amazing that we do not know its precise dimensions as it affected Canada. In part this is because the records of both the "exporting" and the "importing" ends of the migration process are not trustworthy for most of the nineteenth century. And even when the records of immigrants into Canada become accurate, it is never clear whether someone getting off an immigrant ship in Montreal, for example, actually intended to stay in Canada or (as frequently was the case) to go to the United States, in which case his or her leaving Canada was not recorded. Nor were immigrants accurately recorded if they landed, say, in Philadelphia or New York and made their way from there to Canada. So, the figures for the immigration flow into Canada from 1815 until Confederation should be taken as rough indicators only. Shown on page 494 are rough figures for migration from the British Isles to Canada.

The result of this heavy in-flow to the anglophone provinces from the early 1830s until well after Confederation was that the overwhelming majority of individuals either had been born in the British Isles or were the offspring of parents who had been born in the British Isles. A conservative estimate calculated for Ontario in 1842 was that 80 percent of the population either was born in the United Kingdom or had parents who had been born there.[6] Because of the great flood of famine Irish immigrants, this proportion probably rose in the late 1840s and did not begin to drop appreciably until the late 1850s.[7]

---

[6] On migration matters see: D.H. Akenson, *Being Had: Historians, Evidence, and the Irish in North America* (Port Credit: D. Meany, 1985) and J.M. Bumsted, *The People's Clearance, Highland Emigration to British North America, 1770–1815* (Edinburgh: Edinburgh University Press, 1982).

[7] On immigrant adaptation, see "Ethnicity and Occupational Structure in Canada in 1871: The Vertical Mosaic in Historical Perspective," *Canadian Historical Review*, vol. 61 (Sept. 1980), pp. 305–333; Canadian Historical Association, "Ethnicity and Class Transitions Over a Decade: Ontario, 1861–71," *Historical Papers, 1984*, pp. 111–137; "Class in Nineteenth-Century Central Ontario: A Reassessment of the Crisis and Demise of Small Producers During Early Industrialization, 1861–1871," *Canadian Journal of Sociology*, vol. 13 (no 1–2), 1988, reprinted in Gregory S. Kealey (ed.), *Class, Gender, and Region: Essays in Canadian Historical Sociology* (St. John's: Committee on Canadian Labour History, 1980, pp. 49-72.

TABLE 1

Year	Total Migrations	Year	Total Migrations
1815	680	1842	54 123
1816	3 370	1843	23 518
1817	9 797	1844	22 924
1818	15 136	1845	31 803
1819	23 534	1846	43 439
1820	17 921	1847	109 680
1821	12 955	1848	31 065
1822	16 013	1849	41 367
1823	11 355	1850	32 961
1824	8 774	1851	42 605
1825	8 741	1852	32 873
1826	12 818	1853	31 779
1827	12 648	1854	35 679
1828	12 084	1855	16 110
1829	13 307	1856	11 299
1830	30 574	1857	16 803
1831	58 067	1858	6 504
1832	66 339	1859	2 469
1833	28 808	1860	2 765
1834	40 060	1861	3 953
1835	15 573	1862	8 328
1836	34 226	1863	9 665
1837	29 884	1864	11 371
1838	4 577	1865	14 424
1839	12 658	1866	9 988
1840	32 293	1867	12 160
1841	38 164		

Immigration and the Indigene

What term in the English language one uses to specify the people who were in Canada before the Europeans arrived is something that has been argued about heatedly.[8] Of course the individual indigenous people have

---

[8] The Canadian Historical Association publishes a series of short, informative pamphlets on the history of the various ethnic groups in Canada (in progress, 14 groups are covered as of 1989). Useful community studies of major ethnic groups are: D.H. Akenson, *The Irish in Ontario. A Study in Rural History* (Kingston and Montreal: McGill-Queen's University Press, 1984); J.M. Bumsted, *Land, Settlement and Politics on Eighteenth-Century Prince Edward Island* (Kingston

their own names for their own groups, but there is no generally accepted non-European word for these groups as a collectivity. Although there is no universally acceptable vocabulary in English, the most acceptable terms at present are: (1)"indigene," a word borrowed from anthropology that refers to all the indigenous inhabitants of this land; (2) "aboriginal," which also covers all of the pre-European inhabitants and their descendants. This has the disadvantage of not being employed much outside of North America, as it usually is used to describe the original inhabitants of Australia (the so-called "aborigine"); and (3) "first nations" and "native Canadians," phrases favoured by many of the indigenous peoples. Here the word "native" is not employed in the same way it was used, for example, by the nineteenth-century explorers of Africa to imply a primitive people, but in the same sense as "indigene" or "aboriginal," to mean those who were the original indigenous inhabitants of the northern part of the North American continent.

Whatever the name, there is no disagreement about the historical reality: from the moment that the carriers of European culture landed on this continent, a war was underway in which the indigenous cultures were under attack. This held even during eras of apparent "co-existence" such as the Micmac-Acadian détente prior to 1710. It could not have been any other way. The cultural imperatives that made the Europeans explore the world, the aggressiveness that was so characteristic of the European nation-state, the striving to conquer nature that was so central a part of European intellectual life, and the self-righteous sense of mission imparted by the Christian faith all served to guarantee that there would be no co-existence in Canada between the culture of the Europeans and that of the indigene. The European attack—in which actual military conquest was least important—was continual and unremitting on all fronts. Once the settlers had established a firm beachhead, it was inevitable who the victors would be.

---

and Montreal: McGill-Queen's University Press, 1987); Bruce S. Elliott, *Irish Migrants in the Canadas. A New Approach* (Kingston and Montreal: McGill-Queen's University Press, 1988); Marianne McLean, *The People of Glengarry: Highlanders in Transition, 1750–1820* (Montreal and Kingston: McGill-Queen's University Press, 1991). There are two recent, excellent American studies that deal with migrations and adaptation in rural communities, similar to those settled in Canada. Jon Gjerde, *From Peasants to Farmers. The Migration from Balestrand, Norway to the Upper Middle West* (Cambridge: Cambridge University Press, 1985; Walter D. Kamphoefner, *The Westfalians. From Germany to Missouri* (Princeton: Princeton University Press, 1987).

At what date the Europeans gained the upper hand is open to debate. It has been suggested by Bruce Trigger that, in French Canada, up until 1665 the native peoples had the upper hand, superior in numbers and stronger militarily. After that time, the Europeans were increasingly potent. The comparable date for Upper Canada (Ontario) would be some time in the 1790s. Until the end of the war of 1812–14, Amerindians were important military partners with the Europeans, but thereafter the respect granted them as autonomous social groups declined greatly. It is fair to say that the immigrants who flooded into Canada from 1815 onward thought of the indigenes only as impediments to land acquisition and as potential social nuisances.[9]

Of course there were some direct military conflicts between the Europeans and the indigenes, but these frequently are overemphasized. The real battles were economic, cultural, and geographic, and they took place continually, township by township, and almost family by family. Gradually the Europeans co-opted the indigene economically. How the fur trade developed is well known, but the flow of furs to Europe ultimately was of less consequence than the way the fur trade system seduced the Amerindians into desiring European goods. The same thing happened to the tribes living along the St. Lawrence, who, though not greatly involved in the fur trade, were exposed to European tastes. By the mid-seventeenth century, they were substantially involved in trading for European clothing and small manufactured goods.

This seduction of the indigene by the European market economy was not a culturally neutral phenomenon: the integrity of indigenous cultures was incompatible with the market system, for the emerging capitalist structure encapsulated everyone *within* itself. As a system, this emerging capitalism was the epitome of European culture, and those who became part of it were required to operate by European rules. As the Amerindians desired more and more European goods, they increasingly had to alter their behaviour to produce the goods or services that the Europeans wanted. As the industrial revolution of the nineteenth century took hold, mercantilism was replaced by full-blown capitalism. In that system, most

---

[9] The most important scholarly study of the Canadian native peoples is Bruce Trigger's *The Children of Aataentsic. A History of the Huron People to 1660*, 2 vols. (Kingston and Montreal: McGill-Queen's University Press, 1976, new edition, 1987).

indigenes had either of two values for Europeans: they were cheap and easily exploited unskilled rural labour, or they were reckoned to be without economic worth at all.

The European peoples' "domestic imperialism" (to use a term from British historical studies) also was cultural. The strenuous efforts of the Catholic religious orders to convert the indigene are well known. The efforts of English-speaking Protestants were less well organized, but in the nineteenth century more pervasive. The Protestant and the Catholic attempts at converting the aboriginal peoples was nothing less than the destruction of their cosmology, their view of how the world operated. This was parallelled in the nineteenth century by a leeching away of the native Canadian's linguistic independence. To deal with the capitalist economic system, to confront the government, to discuss the new religious ideas imported by European Christians required that at least some of the members of each indigenous community learn French or English. Once that happened, these individuals acquired economic and social advantages as intermediaries with European civilization, and that in turn stimulated others to learn to deal in English or French.

In stating that the expansion of European society in Canada in the nineteenth century implied a cultural and economic war against the indigene, one does not wish to give the wrong impression. Although the native peoples retreated (and in some cases, entire Amerindian cultures were destroyed), this does not mean that all indigenous cultures were broken or even that those that eventually disappeared were fragile and unresisting. Quite the opposite: considering the overwhelming odds against them and the implacable nature of European intolerance toward non-European peoples, it is impressive how well the indigene actually did. This fact invites reference to the concept of *resistance*, a major motif that is being developed in studies of indigenes not only in Canada but all over the world. Scholars are just beginning to realize in full that all over the world indigenous cultures fought effectively, though rarely with complete success, against European imperialism. The best known examples in the international literature are the Zulu kingdom in southern Africa, the Maori of New Zealand, and the Mayans in the Yucatan Peninsula of Mexico. Each of these was a culture that combined a strong social system with a considerable degree of military discipline, and thus for at least half a century all were able to keep the Europeans at bay. The Amerindians of Canada were never that strong, but some groups, such as the Six Nations of Iroquois in the Great Lakes region, made alliances with Great Britain that resulted in their being recognized as allies, not subordinates. By playing the geopolitical game shrewdly, the Six Nations preserved their own identity.

There is at present a vigorous native-rights movement in Canada. That this movement exists is the best indication that, despite a variety of attacks on native peoples, a continuous resistance has been mounted by them to preserve their indigenous cultures.

Immigration and French Canada

The European conquest of Canada involved not only a war against the indigene but intense competition between two streams of European imperialism, one originating in France and the other in the British Isles. After 1763 the confrontation between these streams was no longer military, but cultural, economic, and demographic. In many ways, the contest was uneven. Present-day Quebec was separated from France in 1763 and missed the rapid political and economic modernization that was associated with the French Revolution. In contrast, emigrants from the British Isles did not have the ties to their mother country cut. Their homeland was the most economically advanced in Europe, and further, during the nineteenth century was undergoing rapid political modernization.

There is a good deal of argument among historians about how to characterize the society of French Canada before, roughly, the 1840s, when it began to modernize quite rapidly. The argument revolves around the word "feudal." Can French Canada in the era of the great European migrations be accurately described as feudal? One answer comes from Cole Harris's classic work on the seigneurial era (the late seventeenth and early eighteenth centuries). He holds that feudal restrictions on behaviour were largely irrelevant to colonization, settlement patterns, economy, and society. In other words, Harris argues that the seigneurial form of French feudalism was very weak even at its high point. Consequently, by the early nineteenth century, French Canada cannot accurately be said to have been feudal. Against this view, other modern scholars have argued that although "feudalism" in the limited and technical sense of the term did not exist, it existed in a more fundamental sense right up to the 1840s. For instance, Alan Greer has argued that from 1740 to 1840 in certain regions of Quebec, there existed a form of exploitation and domination that was essentially feudal. The characteristics of French-Canadian society according to Greer (he is of course generalizing and there were variations on the pattern) were that the society was overwhelmingly rural, that the basic agrarian unit was the self-sufficient "peasant" household, and that over the peasantry was an ascendancy of "lay and clerical aristocracy" who controlled the political and legal system and forced the peasantry to turn over a share of their production to the upper classes.[10]

Now, whether or not the word "feudal" is appropriate cannot be settled here, but the debate points to an important fact, namely, that in the late eighteenth century and in the first half of the nineteenth, French-Canadian society was undeniably different from that of the rest of the country. In contrast to the rapidly changing settlement pattern in English-speaking Canada, the French-Canadian settlements generally were socially cohesive and were characterized by relatively low degrees of transience. (The chief exceptions were the wintertime lumbering communities.) The French-Canadian communities were not filled up with outsiders—migration from metropolitan France had come to a virtual stop in 1763—but by persons born and bred in Quebec. It is estimated that in the century and a half that Quebec was a French colony, only 10 000 persons came there as immigrants from France. Thus, the fact that by 1790 the population of Quebec was approximately 165 000 means that French-Canadian society had become demographically independent of the Old Country, something that was very different from the situation that held in English-speaking Canada. Within the boundaries of Quebec, French-Canadian society was vigorous and expanding. Birth rates were very high. By 1815 the population of Quebec had reached 300 000 of whom the overwhelming majority were francophones.

After 1815, this French-Canadian society was, first, surrounded by a flood of English speakers from the British Isles and, second, infiltrated by the settlement of anglophones. In this contest between the English-speaking and French-speaking communities in Canada, one is viewing nothing that is unique to this country. It is simply the North American facet of a fight for cultural hegemony between France and the United

[10] Richard Colebrook Harris, *The Seigneurial System in Early Canada. A Geographical Study* (Madison: University of Wisconsin Press, 1966; reprinted with a new preface, Kingston and Montreal: McGill-Queen's University Press, 1984); Allan Greer, *Peasant, Lord, and Merchant, Rural Society in Three Quebec Parishes 1740-1840* (Toronto: University of Toronto Press, 1985). For a valuable review of the historical literature see Roberta Hamilton, *Feudal Society and Colonization: The Historiography of New France* (Gananoque, Ont: Langdale Press, 1988).

Kingdom that was being fought all over the world: in Europe, in the outposts of the British and French empires in Africa, the Pacific, and the Middle East. In Canada, in the period from 1790 until Confederation, most of the victories went to the English speakers.

It is estimated that in 1790, 80 percent of the European population of British North America was French speaking. But then came the "late" Loyalists, and, after 1815, the great flood of migrants from the British Isles. If one takes the situation in 1860–1861 and looks at the four original provinces of Canada, the population was as follows:

Quebec	1 111 566
Ontario	1 396 091
New Brunswick	252 047
Nova Scotia	330 857

Despite a high degree of marital fertility, the French Canadians by 1861 had become a demographic minority within Canada and one of a distinctive sort: the overwhelming majority of francophones lived in Quebec and their society was surrounded on two sides by English-speaking Canadians, to the South by English-speaking Americans, and in the North by vast emptiness. Today's "distinct society" in Quebec owes its fundamental character, that of an embattled francophone isle in a sea of anglophones, to the demographic shifts that occurred throughout British North American as a result of heavy European immigration in the nineteenth century.

French Canada, however, was not merely surrounded; it was infiltrated. Whereas in 1790 only a tiny proportion of the inhabitants of Quebec were not francophone, by 1861 22 percent of the total population of Quebec was non-French in origin. The "invaders" were mostly persons whose family roots were in the British Isles. These incomers did not settle evenly in Quebec, but aggregated in the cities and in a few specific townships. As early as 1815, 40 percent of the inhabitants of Quebec City and nearly one-third of the population of Montreal originated in the British Isles. The urban invasion was especially significant because the newcomers were not merely from a different European language group than the French Canadians but from a different world. The British Isles was the world's first capitalist society, and the culture, attitudes, and behaviours that these emigrants brought with them would have been alien to those of the French Canadians even if these immigrants had spoken the same language and had the same religious faith. The British Isles group in the cities of Quebec ranged from the owners of banks and trading companies to individual artisans and day labourers. What they all had in common was experience in the world of money, wages, and (in the case of the rich) capital. Roberta Hamilton has argued that

the English Conquest of Quebec was just the second capitalist takeover in history. Only Ireland preceded Quebec to that particular privilege. . . . To [José] Iguarta's question, "Did the [English-speaking] newcomers gain their predominance from previous experience with the sort of political and economic conditions created in post-Conquest Quebec?" the answer would surely have to be a resounding yes! But not just their experience counted; it was also their capital and their connections.

If the English-speakers set the economic rules in the large urban areas of French-speaking Canada, they also settled heavily in certain rural areas. After 1815 the area north of the Ottawa River came to support a very mixed population: French Canadians, Scots, Irish, and English settlers who made a half-living farming the Canadian Shield and worked the other half of the year in lumber camps. More important was the settlement of the Eastern Townships of Quebec. By 1817, there were 20 000 English-speaking inhabitants of the townships. Their roots were in northern New England, although their ultimate ethnic affiliations were with the British Isles. They were soon joined by the direct migration of individuals from the United Kingdom. Interestingly, this invasion was met by a form of resistance on the part of the francophones. On a family by family basis, francophones moved into the Eastern Townships, clearing bush or buying the cheapest pieces of land from the anglophones and from these beginnings they expanded. By 1871, the northern tier of the Eastern Townships was 80 percent French Canadian and the southern tier (nearest the American border) 25 percent. This instance of rural French-Canadian resistance to anglophone invasion should not be overemphasized: but it is useful as a predictor of future developments. In the last quarter of the nineteenth century and the first quarter of the twentieth, francophones re-established their control over virtually the entire rural landscape of Quebec.[11]

---

[11] An interesting study is J.I. Little, *Nationalism, Capitalism, and Colonization in Nineteenth-Century Quebec* (Kingston and Montreal: McGill-Queen's University Press, 1989). See also Little's pamphlet, *Ethno-Cultural Transition and Regional Identity in the Eastern Townships of Quebec* (Ottawa: Canadian Historical Association, 1989).

English-Speaking Canadians: Official Culture, High Culture, Popular Culture, and Group Identity

"Culture" is an infuriating word for many people, because it can be used in so many ways. In this chapter, thus far "culture" has been employed in a very wide sense to refer to the attitudes, beliefs, and behaviourial patterns of European society as it developed outside of Canada and was eventually imported into Canada. The word also has been used to refer to all of the "soft" ways in which societies tussle with one another: thus the concept that the franco-anglo confrontation after 1763 was not military but cultural. Now, let us use some of the various narrower definitions of culture in order to shed light on some of the characteristics of English-speaking Canadians at roughly the middle of the last century.

First, consider "high culture," in the sense of artistic work that hangs in museums, music that is played in concert halls, and writing that becomes accepted as "literature." The fact is that in poetry, fiction, painting, sculpture, and chamber music (the forms most popular in high cultural circles in the last century), Canadians did nothing that in its formal elements cannot be traced back directly and easily to European roots. There was no such thing as Canadian high culture in the sense of the development of any new and quintessentially Canadian form. What was unique about the Canadian high art of the period was unique only within the established boundaries of European tradition. This does not mean that there was not some quite wonderful work being done—Mrs. Jameson's ethereal water colours and Susanna and John Weddeburn Dunbar Moodie's tart observations on Upper Canadian life come at once to mind— but all of this work was derivative from European precedents. In that sense, English-speaking Canadians' high culture was very much a European culture.[12]

Now, consider "popular" or "demotic culture," the sort of thing that genteel Victorians looked down upon: folk tales, ballads, popular verse, vernacular hymns. There was a rich popular culture in both the Maritimes and in Ontario, one that by and large is lost to us now because it was not

---

[12] For an historical survey of recent studies, see Maria Tippett, "The Writing of English-Canadian Cultural History, 1970-85," *Canadian Historical Review* vol. 67 (Dec. 1986), pp. 548–561.

recorded.[13] We know, however, that in its modes of expression this popular culture was based entirely upon traditional modes of expression imported from Europe. In fact, throughout nineteenth-century North America, one can point to only one development either in high or low culture that can be considered unique and non-European—the development of the musical form that eventually became jazz. And Canada had no part in that development.

Another use of the term culture is in the phrase "official culture," which usually refers to the beliefs and attitudes that the people who control the state and the economic system wish the general population to embrace. This official culture can be inculcated in a variety of ways, for example, by the way people are required to act when they require the state's permission to do something (remember what you had to go through to get a driver's licence?). But the main way that the official culture is maintained is through the establishment of state school systems that pass along to children the "proper" view of government and of social and economic behaviour and of class and gender ideology. Obviously, the school as an institution was not invented in Canada; that is hardly a piquant observation. But what is salient is that in the largest jurisdiction in English-speaking Canada (Ontario) and in the provinces that modelled their school system on Ontario's, we can trace the origin of the official culture as taught in the schools directly back to the Old Country. The most advanced system of popular education in the British Isles was in Ireland, founded in 1831. In Ireland there had developed a system of mass education built around a remarkable set of school books, the Irish National readers, which have been described as the best series of elementary school texts in the nineteenth century English-speaking world. When the educational reformer Egerton Ryerson took control of the Ontario school system in the 1840s, he introduced these texts into Ontario's schools. By the time of Confederation, virtually all young people of English, Scottish, and Irish ethnicity in that province acquired their ideas of political loyalty and were taught moral values through a curriculum that had been designed specifically for Ireland. The Irish National Readers were also widely used by individual schools in Quebec and the Atlantic provinces. These books

---

[13] The strength of certain aspects of the popular culture of English Canada is found in the fact that even at the present time it is possible to collect respectable bodies of folk poetry. See Pauline Greenhill, *True Poetry: Traditional and Popular Verse in Ontario* (Montreal and Kingston: McGill-Queen's University Press, 1989).

from Ireland did not include Irish history, language, or folklore; instead, they attempted to reflect and reinforce British cultural and political values.

In addition to its curriculum, Ontario's educational structure was also taken from Ireland. Ryerson adopted the Irish system of a strong central authority that controlled what was taught in schools, operated a "normal school" to train teachers, and attempted to control teacher qualifications. At the same time, Ontario followed the Irish pattern of giving local school boards day-to-day control of the schools and of teacher employment policy. As in Ireland, the Ontario structure of education combined a strong central educational authority with a good deal of local control and a virtual absence of middle management. This system was transmitted to British Columbia by John Jessop, who had studied in Ryerson's normal school in Toronto during the 1850s when that school was run by masters who themselves came directly from the central Irish normal school in Dublin. Largely through Jessop's work, British Columbia's Public School Act of 1872 was based on Ryerson's Ontario legislation of 1846–71. The Ryerson system was also followed in the Northwest Territories and in Manitoba, giving the Irish model considerable indirect influence. Of course, the overseas model was adapted to the needs of each individual province, but the genealogy of this part of Victorian Canada's official culture should not be forgotten.[14]

At this point you well may be asking, did anything genuinely new culturally develop in Canada in the last century? Yes, and this relates to the emerging sense of the collective identity of English-speaking Canadians. You probably have noticed that in this chapter we have been very careful about referring to "English-speaking Canadians" and not to "English-Canadians," and the word "British" has not been used except in two specific ways: to refer to Great Britain, which was formed by the union of England, Wales, and Scotland in 1707, and to the "British Isles," which comprises England, Wales, Scotland, and Ireland. By referring to the culture of everyone who came from the British Isles as "British" or, worse, "English" or using "English-Canadian," one totally distorts the nature of the European cultural heritage that was brought to Canada. There was no

---

[14] The Irish background on this matter is found in D.H. Akenson, *The Irish Education Experiment* (Toronto: University of Toronto Press, 1970), and the New World carryover in Akenson, *Being Had: Mass Schooling in Ontario, the Irish and "English Canadian" Popular Culture*, pp. 143–187. For a summary of these matters see David Wilson, *The Irish in Canada* (Ottawa: Canadian Historical Association, 1989), pp. 18–19.

such thing in the home islands as a single "English" or "British" culture, and that point holds not only for the nineteenth century, but right down to the present day. In the British Isles, the various factions of Anglo-Celtic cultures have yet to blend into a common homogeneity. The Welsh, English, Lowland Scots, Highlanders, Irish Catholics, and Irish Protestants share some very important cultural characteristics (most importantly, usage of English as their first language), and most of the inhabitants of the British Isles are under the suzerainty of the government of the United Kingdom to which they give varying degrees of loyalty. But the various national groups remain distinct, despite the homogenizing influence of more than a century of mass state schooling and despite the blending influences of various communications media. This is obvious to anyone who has watched an England-Scotland football match; and do not try telling a young trooper from Birmingham as he patrols the streets of Strabane in Northern Ireland that he is in the same world, much less the same culture, that he grew up in. He knows that he is not, and his staying alive depends on his not forgetting that fact. What holds true in the present day in terms of the diversity of the cultures of the British Isles was equally true in the last century.

In certain colonies—Upper Canada, the Maritimes, New Zealand, perhaps Australia, and just possibly colonial America—"British" culture was emerging in the sense that in these locales the Anglo-Celtic cultures of the British Isles lost most of their distinctive identifiers and merged. The process was distinct in each of these instances, but the fundamental course of evolution was similar. In the case of Canada, the process was quite different from the frequently depicted discussions of the emergence of the nation's sense of identity. The conventional picture is that a "British" or "English" culture, inherited from the homeland, was modified by the Canadian environment and catalyzed by the War of 1812–14 and by Canada's western expansion and became thereby the English-speaking identity. The study of the process of cultural transfer in general and of ethnicity in particular indicates that the process was more complex than that. There was no "British" or "English" culture to draw on, but, instead, several vigorous, distinct, and, in many of their details, incompatible, Anglo-Celtic cultures found in the homeland. Therefore, an integral and absolutely necessary aspect of the development of an English-speaking sense of identity was the creation of a "British" or "English" culture in the new homeland, one that did not in fact exist in the old. The melding of the several Anglo-Celtic cultures to establish a new and synthetic "British" or

"English" culture was part of the creation of the English-speaking Canadian identity. Thus, when one sees Scots, English, Welsh, and Irish accepting in many contexts the inaccurate term "British" or "English" in Canada, one is actually seeing the completion of the first step of their escape from the cultural hegemony of the Old World metropoles. It was only a short step from being "English" or "British" to being Canadian. The big step was the first one.

When the priorities of Old World sectional identities disappeared for most English-speaking Canadians is a matter of debate. For Protestants with ethnic origins in England, Scotland, Wales, and Ireland, the 1860s seem to have been crucial. In the wake of, first, the American Civil War and second, the Fenian raids, a full sense of Canadian identity seems to have crystalized. Persons of Catholic background, especially Irish Catholics, were less keen on this new identity, and they did not fully accept the English-Canadian mindset until the First World War.

So, what was new in the culture of English-speaking Canada was that out of several distinct cultures of the British Isles had emerged, in the New World of Canada, a sense of cultural identity. Of course there were (and still are) very significant regional variations, and most people think of themselves in terms of multiple identities. That is, people think of themselves as being, for example, both Canadian and, ethnically, Scottish or Irish or English. But by the time of Confederation, English-speakers in areas as widely separated as the Maritimes and Ontario recognized that they shared enough in common that they could join in the forming of a nation.

The great unspoken question is whether or not in the high Victorian era the Europeans in Canada had yet another, bigger, sense of identity—one that embraced as Canadians both anglophones and francophones? The fact of Confederation in 1867 casts no light of this. It is easy to argue that Confederation was just another instance of the use of constitutional forms imported from the British Isles to impose the will of English-speakers upon francophones. The two major constitutional precedents for Canadian Confederation came not from the United States (as it frequently is thought), but from the Old Country. In 1707, in an attempt to suffocate contumacious elements in Scotland, the English government abolished that nation as a separate national jurisdiction and merged it within the new entity, Great Britain. This worked, so following a very bloody rebellion in Ireland in 1798, the government of Great Britain subsumed that of Ireland in 1801, thus forming the new entity, the United Kingdom. This too seemed to work (although, only seemed, as the twentieth century drive for Irish independence proved). Therefore, as a means of controlling and limiting French Canada, Confederation was very attractive. A great deal is always made about the rights and privileges that Quebec maintained under Confederation. The fundamental fact, though, is that it was submerged into a larger society in which it inevitably and permanently would be a minority.

Was there a Canadian identity that encompassed both the French Canadians and the English-speakers? Such a question has not been adequately answered as yet by historians. It is a question that is the marrow of the debate in our own time, the debate on the future of the Canadian Confederation.

The Market Economy

The Europeanization of the economy of Canada was yet another aspect of the capture of British North America by external systems. In the nineteenth century, both English-speaking and French-speaking Canada were undergoing radical economy development. This can be called the first stage of "industrial capitalism." The fact that the two seminal texts on these developments, Adam Smith's *Wealth of Nations* (1776) and Karl Marx's *Capital* (1867), were written from a very broad European perspective and almost without thought of Canada should make it clear that what was happening in the nineteenth-century Canadian economy was simply a subset of an international phenomenon.

However, for a long time, Canadian historians tried to explain Canadian economic developments as unique to this country. This was attempted in a form of "staples theory" that was first fully developed by Harold Innis. In its simplest form, this theory stated that the lead sector in Canadian economic development was Ontario, and that Ontario's major cash crop, wheat, was pivotal. Wheat was said to be an export crop, and, because exports demanded transportation, it was believed that the wheat staple necessitated the development of railways and caused, in their wake, general economic development. This historical approach failed for a number of reasons (in particular, because the causal linkages between wheat and other factors, railways, for example, were never proved), but all these failings were traceable to an understandable, but self-delusory desire to prove Canada's singularity. "At the level of myth it may suit us to have a uniquely Canadian explanation for how our economy came to be," Douglas McCalla has commented, but he also points out that it is grossly misleading. In fact, Canadian economic patterns in the "staples era" follow very closely the pattern that Douglass North posited for the cotton and wheat economies of the American south and middle west. That is, in the American staples economy, wheat was not the leading export crop. For the most part, it was grown in the middle west and was shipped to the south where it was consumed. The real export crop was the south's cotton. In a similar pattern, McCalla has shown that there was a complex staples trade in Canada. Wheat was a worthwhile export crop, but from the 1830s onward, the primary market for Ontario wheat was Quebec, where, after years of attempting to grow wheat in a hostile climate, the Québécois farmers dropped out of production. The cities and lumber camps of Quebec were supplied with wheat (and its derivative, flour) by Ontario. Quebec paid for these "imports" from Ontario by exporting timber and timber by-products to the British Isles. (The timber ships frequently brought back immigrants.) The Maritime provinces, when they related to this controlled Canadian network, did so by importing Ontario wheat and paying for it by exporting fish and timber. So, what one had developing in the first two-thirds of the nineteenth century was not a simple economy that depended on sales of a commodity (wheat) overseas but an increasingly complex Canada-wide economic network, one that moved various goods around the country and collected certain items for export, that is, for sale in the world economy. In our own time, we hear a good deal about commerce being a world business; by the mid-nineteenth century, the bulk of Canadians already were part of an economy that was worldwide. And they were dealing mostly with the British Isles, the most developed of the economies of the western world.[15]

One aspect of Canada's becoming part of the world economy was the improvement in communications. The development, first, of canals, and, slightly later, of the railway system is too well known to require much comment. The important point in the development of communications was not limited to these two dramatic forms but proceeded steadily as primary roads were cut between concessions, bridges were built to replace

---

[15] For recent revisions of the "staples theory" see Douglas McCalla, "The Wheat Staple and Upper Canadian Development," *Historical Papers, 1978*, Canadian Historical Association, pp. 34–46, and "Forest Products and Upper Canadian Development, 1815–46," *Canadian Historical Review*, vol. 68 (June 1987), pp. 159–98.

fords, and heavily travelled roads were corduroyed and widened. These modest, but pervasive, improvements filled in the communications network in much the same way that tiny capillaries fill in the fine points of the human circulatory system. Not only did it become possible for goods to be transported more easily and people to move about the countryside with less difficulty, but, in the second half of the nineteenth century, most Canadians became part of an international information system: the mass postal network. Until 1851, the United Kingdom government controlled the post in the various territories in British North America and (according to a governmental report of 1846), the infrastructure was inadequate: there were too few post offices, and postal charges were too high for the ordinary colonial. This changed in 1851 when the postal service was placed under local colonial jurisdiction, and a revolution in communications began. The creation of an efficient and cheap postal service made it possible for business to open in very small towns and in remote areas and to order and pay for goods easily. The service permitted an individual in any part of confederated Canada to communicate with a person anywhere else within a ten-day period and usually in much less time. And the rates were cheap. The Canadian postal service slotted into the American and United Kingdom mail systems and formed a truly international grid. The creation of this postal system—not the invention of the telephone, the radio, or satellite television—was probably the most important communications revolution in Canada in the past 200 years.[16]

That English-speaking Canada, in both its rural and its urban sectors, had become by the time of Confederation part of the modernizing world is widely accepted, but what must here be emphasized is that Quebec, even in its rural sector, was only a trifle behind Ontario in the modernization process and was by no means backward. This bears emphasis because at one time there was what amounted to a small scholarly industry that presented French-Canadian agriculture generally as inherently backward and held more specifically that an "agricultural crisis" occurred during the first decade of the nineteenth century. Careful recent work has shown, however, that production on farms in Quebec was only slightly less than that on comparable agricultural units in Ontario and that the years 1791–1812, far from being years of economic stagnation, saw the beginning of

---

[16] See Brian Osborne and Rober Pike, "Lowering the 'Walls of Oblivion': The Revolution in Postal Communications in Central Canada, 1851–1911," *Canadian Papers in Rural History*, vol. 4 (1984), pp. 200–225.

the development of a strong market economy in rural Quebec. From 1815 until, approximately, 1840, this rural economy expanded, largely through the integration of lumbering with farming, including a shift away from wheat to crops more suitable to the Quebec climate. What can be thought of as the high period of rural modernization in Quebec began in the 1840s. It is from the 1840s onward that French Canadians began to colonize new parts of inland Quebec and also started to push out the English-speaking rural colonists in such areas as the Ottawa valley and the Eastern Townships.[17]

If the first stage of the integration of Canada into the world economic system involved the penetration of the rural world by the market system and the replacement of subsistence agriculture by a rural economy that produced and marketed livestock and crops that were surplus to local needs, it was achieved in most of Canada by approximately the early 1840s. Thereafter, a second stage occurred. This stage involved great improvement in farm efficiency. "Mixed farming" came to dominate the most productive parts of rural Canada, this being the type of farming that is most responsive to market forces. Increasingly, machinery (hay mowers, for example) boosted productivity, and improved breeds of cattle and sheep greatly increased meat output. Of even greater importance was the industrial growth of the urban cities and small towns. This growth was part of the "industrial revolution" that had begun in western Europe, especially the British Isles, and that was exported to the United States, Canada, and to parts of Latin America, Australia, and New Zealand. There are hundreds of definitions of the industrial revolution. That of David Landes, developed originally for the British Isles, fits the Canadian situation well:

The words "industrial revolution"—in small letters—usually refer to that complex of technological innovations, which, by substituting machines for human skill and inanimate power for human and animal force, brings about a shift from handicraft to manufacture and, so doing, gives birth to a modern economy.

---

[17] See R. M. McInnis, "A Reconsideration of the State of Agriculture in Lower Canada in the First Half of the Nineteenth Century," *Canadian Papers in Rural History*, vol. 3 (1982), pp. 9–49; Serge Courville and Norman Seguin, *Rural Life in Nineteenth-Century Quebec* (Ottawa: Canadian Historical Association, 1989); Gilles Paquet and Jean-Pierre Wallot, *Lower Canada at the Turn of the Nineteenth Century: Restructuring and Modernization* (Ottawa; Canadian Historical Association, 1988).

There were, Landes points out, three practical aspects:

(1) there was a substitution of mechanical devices for human skills; (2) inanimate power—in particular, steam—took the place of human and animal strength; (3) there was a marked improvement in the getting and working of raw materials, especially in what are now known as the metallurgical and chemical industries.

The traditional Canadian dating for this industrial revolution is between the mid-1840s and, roughly, 1890. That is all right, as long as one realizes that the phenomenon was a process that was both uneven and cumulative. It affected such diverse activities as shipbuilding in the Maritimes, glass making in Quebec City, and iron and steel production in Hamilton, Ontario. Many of the new industries were conducted in cities—Montreal and Toronto were the most important—but a surprising amount of the new industrial activity occurred in small towns of under 5000 people: nail making, spade manufacture, carriage making, such activities could be conducted in factories with as few as ten or twelve employees.

Thus the agricultural modernization that was occurring in the countryside and the industrialization that took place in the small towns and cities were mutually dependent. The countryside provided workers (the sons and daughters of farmers) and supplied a demand for many manufactured items (home and farm supplies). Rural modernization gave the farmers the wherewithal to buy more and more manufactured goods, and, in turn, the manufactured goods accelerated the course of agricultural modernization by improving the efficiency of the farm sector. And so on in a self-reinforcing cycle. The process was just getting up to full speed by the time of Confederation. What was happening in Victorian Canada had begun slightly earlier in England, Lowland Scotland, and northern Ireland and was occurring, as well, in the United States. All of these national industrial revolutions knitted together into an international phenomenon. Sometimes tariff barriers inhibited the passage of goods from one country to another, but no barrier could prevent the passage of ideas across national borders—the technology and the intellectual capital that is at the heart of the industrial revolution. For better or worse, Canada was part of the industrialization of the western world.

Industrialization brought major new forms of social organization, and these were generic: factories are factories no matter where they are located. Inevitably, factories imply the aggregation of people in a single place (this in contrast to the dispersed pattern on a farm), and they imply a degree of specialization. Not everyone does the same task and, frequently, the tasks are highly repetitive.

There is no reason that a factory cannot be both owned and managed by the people who work in it (as has been done in the twentieth century in several Scandinavian enterprises), but usually two distinctions arise: between management and the work-floor staff and between the people who own the enterprise ("capital") and the workers ("labour"). In the small factories that were typical of the early industrial revolution in Canada, the person who owned the firm often was also the on-site manager. However, as businesses grew, the manager frequently was no longer the owner, but a specialist who was hired for his skill in arranging production processes and for slotting workers into those processes.

The distance between owners and labourers was increased by the introduction of a new form of enterprise—the limited liability company. Until roughly the mid-nineteenth century, the almost universal forms of business were either the single-owner proprietorship of a partnership. The latter was a legal form under which every one of the owners put his entire personal worth behind the firm. Naturally this limited the total amount of capital a firm could raise (and thus the size of the factory it could run), because an investor might risk his whole fortune in concern with, say, three or four close friends, but not with 50 or 100 persons, mostly strangers, whose resources were needed to set up a big factory. However, following legal precedents set in the British Isles, from mid-century onward, it was increasingly easy for capitalists to set up what were called "joint stock, limited liability companies," the precursors of our modern corporations. The key characteristics of these new entities were twofold: an investor did not risk his or her entire personal fortune by joining in the business. Liability was limited to the amount of capital the investor originally subscribed; and, crucially, the corporation had what is called a "juridical personality." That is, in law it was like a person: it could buy and sell things, hire and fire people, sue and be sued. But, of course, a corporation really is not a person. What we have here is one of those occasional quantum jumps in the sophistication with which a society thinks about itself. The limited liability company taught the European world to conceive of economic arrangements at an abstract level, to realize that behind specific goods and services there exists an abstract set of processes, of which the heuristic personality, the corporation, is one component.

The corporation (that is, the limited liability company) placed itself between capital and labour. And, crucially, by making possible larger and larger industrial enterprises, through its ability to attract more finance capital than could mere partnerships, it hastened the arrival of the single most important social consequence of the industrial revolution: the development of a self-conscious working class and thus a class-divided society. In the British Isles, the first society to develop a self-conscious industrial working class, the emergence usually is dated in the early 1830s. In Canada, working-class consciousness was only beginning to crystallize by the time of Confederation. The most acceptable date for the existence of a working-class consciousness in Canada is the 1880s and is marked by the rise of the Knights of Labour. The further evolution of the process was slow: remember that it was not until the census of 1931 that most Canadians were urban, and fewer still were involved in heavy industry. Nevertheless, one can see the emergence of class in the figures of strikes and labour confrontations. There were between 1815 and 1859 only 59 known confrontations between labourers and capital. Between 1859 and 1889, 700 such affrays took place. Obviously, something significant was happening. Canada was beginning to adopt the pattern of class differentiation dictated by the international industrial revolution.[18]

Demography and the Position of Women

Of all the major social groups in Canadian history in the pre-Confederation era, less is known about women and their position in society than of any other group, save perhaps those bands of indigenes who were destroyed completely by the march of European culture. In the last decade,

---

[18] See Bryan Palmer, *A Culture in Conflict: Skilled Workers and Industrial Capitalism in Hamilton, Ontario, 1860–1914* (Montreal: McGill-Queen's University Press, 1979), and *Working-Class Experience: The Rise and Reconstitution of Canadian Labour, 1800–1900* (Toronto: Butterworth and Co., 1983). A useful warning against assuming that class differences developed quickly is A. Gordon Darroch, "Early Industrialization and Inequality in Toronto, 1861–1899," *Labour/le Travailleur*, vol. 11 (Spring 1983), pp. 31–61. A valuable Maritime study is Eric W. Sager, *Seafaring Labour: The Merchant Marine of Atlantic Canada. 1820–1914* (Kingston and Montreal: McGill-Queen's University Press, 1989).

there has been some admirable work published on women in early Canadian society, but it is much too early to draw up any kind of a synthesis. Instead, in the present context, it is best to stick to what is well established, namely, the basic outline of Canadian family structures and the position of women within them. It will be seen that the most influential factor influencing the lives of women was whether or not a crucial international phenomenon—the *demographic transition* of the modern European family—had occurred in each specific local Canadian community.

In order to understand Canadian development, we must turn briefly to European historical writing, for it was there that the basic analysis of the crucial demographic change was first done. Recall that during the nineteenth century, both French- and English-speaking Canadian societies underwent economic modernization. Inevitably, this affected the family structure. The classic analysis of the economic organization of the preindustrial European family was done in the 1920s by the Soviet historian A.Y. Chayanov. In what has come to be called the *Chayanovian* peasant family, the entire family operated as an economic unit. Individual members did not exist as separate economic entities but only as contributors to the collective entity, the family. While they were young, children were permitted to consume more than they produced, but they were expected to become producers the moment that they were old enough. Economic calculations were made on a family, not an individual basis. Consumption was calibrated on a family basis. This kind of Chayanovian unit predominated in Quebec before agricultural modernization and also in many of the sparsely settled bush areas of Ontario and the Maritimes in the early nineteenth century.

What the penetration of Canadian society by market forces did was to replace the Chayanovian family as an economic unit with one in which individual family members made calculations to their own best personal advantage. Children in a market economy frequently left the family in order to earn wages. The decline of the Chayanovian family as an economic unit in Canada was closely associated with the demographic transition.

What was the demographic transition? It involved a related occurrence, the switch from a society that had a high birth rate and a high death rate to one wherein a much lower birth rate and a much lower death rate prevailed. The pretransition family had a large number of children and a large number of deaths, especially child deaths. The posttransition family saw fewer children born (although families in the nineteenth century were large by today's standards), but child mortality dropped sharply.

Consider what this would mean to women. The biggest risk to the life of the adult female in the last century was death through complications of childbirth. Therefore, the reduction in the number of childbirths in the typical marriage meant that the average woman had to go through the terror of parturition less often. Consequently, she was apt to live considerably longer. Further, the demographic transition implied that at least some control was being achieved over the process of procreation. The extent to which women of the last century achieved birth control, and by what methods, is a matter of considerable historical controversy, but there is no doubt that birth control was being practised: the number of births per family dropped measurably both in French- and in English-speaking Canada.

By what methods could women be gaining control of births? In part, by the simple expedient of marrying later. If, on average, a woman enters marriage three years later, then she will have three fewer child-bearing years in her life and, if nothing else changes, one, two, or three fewer children. However, studies also clearly show that in the last century "birth spacing" became common. Whereas before the demographic transition, women typically got pregnant, gave birth, lactated, and then became pregnant soon again, after the transition, the length between pregnancies became greater: women "rested" between lactation and another pregnancy. And, clearly "birth stopping" took place. Statistically, it has been clearly demonstrated that it became common in modernized nineteenth-century Canada for couples to stop having children well before the woman was out of her child-bearing years. How couples did this (sexual abstinence, the use of home-made condoms, and the practice of coitus interruptus are all possibilities) is still unknown, but the fundamental effect is clear. By gaining at least partial control over the process of procreation, the post-transitional family for the first time freed women from being perpetual breeders.

The demographic transition occurred unevenly throughout nineteenth-century Canada, and the pattern was especially variegated in French Canada. In English-speaking Canada, the process was well underway by the 1830s and by Confederation had been accomplished in most settled farming areas and in the major cities. In Quebec, that transition seems to have begun in the modernizing areas in the 1840s, but in other locales the demographic transition did not begin until the 1860s and was not completed until the 1920s.

If one takes "patriarchy" to refer to a social and family structure in which male dominance over women is pervasive and institutionalized, then both the pre- and postdemographic transition family were patriarchal units. Yet they were very different. First, as just stated, the posttransition family greatly reduced female servility to the process of procreation. Second, since the modernized family did not operate as an integrated economic unit, but instead permitted individual family members to make their own economic calculations, the children (and sometimes the women) of post-transition families were free to leave the family unit and to take up industrial or agricultural employment for their own benefit. On occasions, this was a dubious privilege (early capitalism was very exploitative of child and female labour), but at least this was the tip of the wedge of economic independence. Third, because both boys and girls had a potential economic value outside of the home, they now usually were allowed to acquire the minimal skills (functional literacy and numeracy) that would permit their independent economic functioning. From today's perspective, the fruits of the nineteenth-century demographic transition may seem slight, but those shifts made possible the twentieth-century advances in the position of women and children.[19]

Conclusion

In common with all of the other nations that formed a "New World," the United States, Australia, New Zealand, among others, Canada was an interaction between a dominant "old world" culture with a new, and to the European settlers, very different environment. That new environment was both physical—mountains, forests, lakes, and an abundance of arable land—and social—the distinct native Canadian societies, economies, and cultures that had already existed for thousands of years.

---

[19] Nontechnical demographic material is somewhat limited. See David Gagan, *Hopeful Travellers. Families, Land, and Social Change in Mid-Victorian Peel County, Canada West* (Toronto: University of Toronto Press, 1981); Janice Potter, "Patriarchy and Paternalism: The Case of Eastern Ontario Loyalist Women," *Ontario History*, vol. 81 (March 1989), pp. 3–24; Janice Potter, *While the Women Only Wept: Loyalist Refugee Women* (Montreal and Kingston: McGill-Queen's University Press, 1992); Peter Ward, *Courtship, Love, and Marriage in Nineteenth-Century English Canada* (Montreal and Kingston: McGill-Queen's University Press, 1990).

In the mid-nineteenth century, therefore, Canada reflected its varied origins. It was overwhelmingly European in its cultural and economic configurations. It was connected to a worldwide European cultural network in language, religion, social mores, family structures, even in ways of thinking about and looking at humankind's place in the universal scheme of things. It was a product of its own historical development up to that point in time and thus was not a mere copy of British, or French, or American, or any other society. Rather it was a synthesis of its European roots and its North American experience. And it was home to rich and varied native cultures that had had a great impact on its historical development, that continued to help define its uniqueness, and that would play a role of continuing importance in the future.

CONCLUSION

Completing Confederation

As 1 July 1867 dawned across the continent, Canada was a country waiting to happen. The great diversity of peoples who lived in the British North American colonies and who had little experience in cooperating with each other virtually guaranteed that there would be strong centripetal pressures in the new dominion. The almost total lack of a central set of unifying political principles meant that there would be little incentive to work together toward the achievement of common national goals. The first generation of Canada's political leaders—John A. Macdonald and his contemporaries—would have to try to create those principles and achieve those goals. Would they be up to the task? One clue might have been that they had created a federal union out of almost nothing and that they had brought together in one new country peoples who had never expressed any real desire to work with each other. But then, much of what they had accomplished had been done with little or no grass-roots support (and much opposition), and none of it could have been accomplished without the active intervention of London.

Before Canada could be given any sort of an economic or political direction, it had to be put together. That was neither easily nor quickly done. British Columbia had played no part in the Confederation process and had not yet been invited to join, although there can be little doubt that such an invitation would have come before too long. In any case, British Columbians were to have little choice about their own future. When a new governor was dispatched to the colony from London in 1869, he carried with him instructions to bring about a union between British Columbia and Canada. Once again, British imperial designs and desires were paramount in bringing about British North American union. Before long, an agreement was negotiated with Canada that would see British Columbia enter Confederation in 1871 in return for Ottawa's guarantee of a transcontinental railway to be completed by 1881, its assumption of British Columbia's public debt, and the promise of other financial support. Once again, it was dollars and cents, not ideology or a common sense of destiny, that brought British North Americans together.

The prairie West entered Confederation under much more difficult conditions. Acquisition of the Prairies had been one of the prime objectives of the political leaders who made Confederation, especially those who represented the land-hungry farmers of Canada West. Thus, less than six months after Confederation, Canada initiated moves to acquire Rupert's Land from the Hudson's Bay Company. An agreement was arranged with the company to purchase the vast territory in return for cash, land grants, and a continued monopoly of the fur trade. The Métis and native people were completely ignored in these negotiations, not surprising given the history of European colonists' efforts to shunt aside or ignore the native peoples from the earliest days of settlement. The result was the Red River Rebellion, which broke out in the fall of 1869 and which primarily pitted the local Métis, led by Louis Riel, against the new Dominion of Canada. It ended with the creation of the province of Manitoba in 1870 and the incorporation of the remainder of Rupert's Land into Canada as the Northwest Territories at the same time. It was only after the annexation of the prairie West that Ottawa began to negotiate agreements with the native peoples of the West. Eventually, they surrendered title to much of the Prairies in return for cash and other considerations. These events are related in detail in *Nation: Canada Since Confederation*.

Although Canada had acquired a Pacific coast and all the land between that coast and Ontario by 1871, the process of Confederation moved much more slowly in the East. There had always been strong opposition to Confederation in Atlantic Canada where, unlike British Columbia, responsible government had existed for some time and where the colonists had considerable say about their future. In Newfoundland, for example, Confederation was not achieved until 1949, while in Prince Edward Island, moves to conclude a free trade agreement with the United States in

1869 signified the islanders' determination to decide their own course. Only after the collapse of an ambitious railway-building program threatened to bankrupt the government did they join Canada in 1873. In Nova Scotia, opposition to Confederation persisted even after July 1, 1867. Joseph Howe went to London in 1868 in an effort to convince the British government to repeal Confederation. The British would have none of it. Instead, better terms of union between Canada and Nova Scotia were renegotiated, and Howe entered Macdonald's cabinet as secretary of state in late 1869.

By 1873 the Confederation process had gone as far as it was going to go until Saskatchewan and Alberta were created in 1905. What had Confederation accomplished? What had it failed to accomplish? What sort of a country had emerged?

What Had Confederation Accomplished?

The union of 1867 had been designed to solve a number of very specific and very concrete problems. There had, of course, been more than a little rhetoric at the Charlottetown and Quebec conferences—much of it coming out of champagne and brandy bottles—about the great nation-building epic that British North Americans were about to embark upon. It was, however, concern about crushing debt loads, markets for trade, defence expenditures, political paralysis in the Canadas, and the need for land for the sons and daughters of Canada West farmers that had provided the impulse for union from within British North America. To that was added the great desire of Britain to withdraw from North America, but not before it had tied loose ends together by pressuring the colonists into union. There had been little popular pressure for Confederation; the peoples of the colonies were mostly strangers to each other, rivals and competitors. They had accomplished almost nothing together in the past and had no dreams to do great things together in the future.

Most of the limited goals that the Fathers of Confederation set for the new union were, in fact, achieved. A central government was created that was far better able to handle the combined public debt than had the individual colonies. That government was also able to begin, quite early, to give a consistent direction to national economic development. Within ten years of Confederation, construction of a transcontinental railway had begun, the first treaties with the native people of the West had been concluded—opening the way for western settlement—and the Dominion Lands Act had been passed (1872), which provided the legal framework for homesteading on the Prairies. Within 12 years of Confederation, the adoption of a high tariff (the National Policy tariff of 1879) signalled the federal government's intention of promoting intensive industrialization. These moves fulfilled much of the desire of the business community for a larger protected market and for an industrial policy, and of the farmers of Canada West for a government that would not only acquire the West but also promote its settlement.

Confederation solved the political deadlock in the Canadas by divorcing them. Ontario and Quebec were split asunder; French-speaking and English-speaking Canada were liberated from each other at one level, while they were united at another. Quebec was established as a province with its own government, charged with protecting the French Canadians and preserving their unique heritage. Quebecers continued to use their political leverage astutely after Confederation, as they had since the mid-1840s, and, in the tradition of Lafontaine and Cartier, they ensured that their support remained indispensable to any party wishing to form a national government. This, and the control over cultural, religious, and linguistic matters vested in the provincial governments by the BNA Act, ensured the survival of the "distinct society" within North America. At the same time, Ontario and the rest of English-speaking Canada were freed to pursue their own economic, cultural, and political aims within the larger national context.

What Had Confederation Failed To Accomplish?

With all that it did do, however, Confederation most assuredly did not create a nation, at least not for some time. The diversity of the colonists of British North America, not to mention the native peoples and Métis who lived within its boundaries, ensured that the factors dividing Canadians would remain at least as strong as those that united them. Cartier and others had hoped that the "new nationality" they were creating (the term was his), a nationality based almost exclusively on economic self-interest, would be stronger and more enduring than the European-style nationalisms based on common language, religion, and culture that were the glue of the new nation-states of Europe. But it was not. The only commonly held belief among most white Canadians was that British laws and political institutions afforded the proper balance between community cohesiveness and individual liberty to guarantee "peace, order, and good government." There was not even that to tie French Canadians to their English-speaking neighbours. The political and religious leaders of Quebec understood that British "liberty"—at least as it had evolved in the era of Victorian liberalism—had given them considerable power to guarantee their own survival. They were, thus, loyal to the Crown and its institutions. But their idea of what government was supposed to do and how it was supposed to relate to the people was quite different from that held by many English-speaking Canadians. That would become increasingly apparent in the decades following Confederation. There were, therefore, very few ties to bind a nation.

Just as Confederation did not create a nation, it also did not bring independence. The United Province of Canada, Nova Scotia, and New Brunswick were self-governing colonies on June 30, 1867, the eve of Confederation, and the Dominion of Canada was a self-governing colony on the morning of July 1, 1867. No additional power had been given Canada by Britain. The struggle for full internal self-government had almost totally been won by then in any case, but the long process of gaining self-government over Canada's relations with other countries began only in 1871 with the negotiations between Britain and the United States that brought about the Treaty of Washington and continued until the British Parliament adopted the Statute of Westminster in 1931, 63 years after Confederation!

What Sort of Country Had Emerged?

Confederation not only failed to unite British North Americans in anything other than a political sense, it also failed to address itself to the social conditions of the people. Nor did it proclaim a democratic vision for the new Canada. In the first place, the Fathers of Confederation were profoundly antidemocratic. They believed in constitutional monarchy and responsible government, not in the "mob rule" they believed they saw running rampant in the United States. In the second place, almost no one in the Canada of 1867 believed government had any direct role to play in improving the social conditions of the people. Such beliefs would not even begin to emerge in Canada until the 1880s, and, even then, it would take the better part of a century for anything significant to be put into place that could be labelled "welfare state." Of course, it is glaringly apparent that native people were virtually ignored in the BNA Act, that women still had no political rights and no equality of treatment or opportunity, that workers had no right to form trade unions or bargain collectively in an effort to achieve a higher standard of living. The Canada that emerged in 1867 was as racist, as sexist, as unconcerned about social issues as the colonies that had come together to create it. How could it have been otherwise? Confederation was designed to tackle only those issues that the Fathers of Confederation—male, white, from the business community or closely attached to it—saw as problems needing solutions. Changes in other areas were to be a long time in coming; many have not come yet.

Regionalism remained strong in the new Dominion, and the political and constitutional instruments of the day not only did not lessen it, they strengthened it. As anti-Confederate Christopher Dunkin had forecast in the Confederation debates in Canada in 1865, cabinet ministers were chosen because of religion, origin, and section of the country they represented, rather than on the basis of sheer talent. Thus the cabinet perpetuated regional division. The senate was supposed to represent regional interests, but it was also supposed to represent the wealth. It was chosen by the prime minister, guaranteeing that it would be a house of privilege and patronage and not a guardian of regional interest. Canada was thus a federation that had no effective and workable proponent of regional views as part of the federal government. By default, then, the provincial governments were bound to attempt to assume that role. Here was one of the great ironies of Canadian history; although Macdonald had wished to create a Canada without provinces—the BNA Act had tried to severely restrict provincial power and areas of responsibility—the provincial governments soon emerged as the only effective voices of Canada's regional interests. Canada was and is a diverse country; the provincial governments reflected that diversity. Provincial governments began to challenge Ottawa for greater powers within two decades after Confederation.

The story of Canadians' efforts to come to terms with the major problems that Confederation did not resolve can be found in the companion volume to this text, *Nation: Canada Since Confederation*. There, close attention has been paid to regionalism, to the rise of the labour movement, to the development and spread of industrial capitalism, and to the efforts of governments and ordinary citizens to overcome the problems that industrialization created. In that volume, too, the impact of non-French and non-British immigration on Canada is traced, and the story of the struggle of Quebecers to enter fully into twentieth-century life is told.

CREDITS
Chapter Opening Photos

Chapter 1, p.7

Wampum
Wampum consists of small cylinders or tubes about 1.9 cm long made from sea shells. These cylinders were either strung or worked up into belts. Commerce was carried on among native peoples with wampum and at an early date was declared legal tender in the British-American colonies. It ceased to be legal tender in 1670 but continued to circulate among the colonists until 1704 and among the native peoples until about 1825. Its value was reduced and destroyed by cheap imitations imported from Europe.

COURTESY OF THE NATIONAL CURRENCY COLLECTION, BANK OF CANADA.
PHOTOGRAPHER: JAMES ZAGON.

Chapter 2, p.41

Silver 15 Sol Piece
This coin was issued in accordance with an edict of Louis XIV dated February 19, 1670, in order to further the commercial transactions of La Compagnie des Indes. The "sol" had a current value in Canada of about one penny, 20 sols making one "livre." It is now one of the rarest of Canadian coins.

COURTESY OF THE NATIONAL CURRENCY COLLECTION, BANK OF CANADA.
PHOTOGRAPHER: JAMES ZAGON.

Chapter 3, p.77

Hudson's Bay Tokens
These tokens represented the unit of currency used in the fur trade for many decades. The largest—one "Made-Beaver"—was equal in value to the skin of an adult male beaver in prime condition. Smaller sizes represented one-half, one-quarter, and one-eighth Made-Beaver. Before these brass tokens came into use, a Made-Beaver was represented by a stick, a porcupine quill, an ivory disc, a musket ball, or anything else agreed upon by trader and trapper.

COURTESY OF THE NATIONAL CURRENCY COLLECTION, BANK OF CANADA.
PHOTOGRAPHER: JAMES ZAGON.

Chapter 4, p.117

Copper Company of Upper Canada One Halfpenny, 1794
Governor Simcoe of Upper Canada requested sample coinage for the new colony of Upper Canada. The Soho Mint submitted a pattern illustrating its capabilities as minters.
COURTESY OF THE CHARLTON PRESS.

Chapter 5, p.157

Card Money
First brought into use as a result of a scarcity of regular currency and as a temporary expedient, card money remained in common use for about 75 years. Full cards, half cards, quarter cards, and even portions of clipped cards were used.

COURTESY OF THE NATIONAL CURRENCY COLLECTION, BANK OF CANADA.
PHOTOGRAPHER: JAMES ZAGON.

Chapter 6, p.197

"Habitant Tokens"
In 1837 the Bank of Montreal applied for permission to import halfpennies and pennies. Permission was granted provided the City Bank, Quebec Bank, and the Bank du Peuple would also participate. The obverse design depicted a Canadian habitant standing in traditional winter costume. The reverse carried the arms of the City of Montreal with the name of the participating bank appearing on the ribbon.
COURTESY OF THE CHARLTON PRESS.

Chapter 7, p.265

"Bons"
Bons were issued by merchants to meet the need for small change. Bons, abbreviated for "bon pour" or "good for" were in wide use in the early part of the nineteenth century.

COURTESY OF THE NATIONAL CURRENCY COLLECTION, BANK OF CANADA.
PHOTOGRAPHER: JAMES ZAGON.

Chapter 8, p. 309

Province of Nova Scotia Halfpenny Token, 1856, Victoria
This denomination is represented by two obverse varieties, one with and the other without the designer's initials (L.C.W.) below the queen's bust. It seems that the variety with L.C.W. was struck only as proof.
COURTESY OF THE CHARLTON PRESS.

Chapter 9, p. 371

"Holey" Dollar and Plug of 1813

The principal coin used on Prince Edward Island in the early nineteenth century was the Spanish-American dollar. When a new governor arrived there in 1813, he found, however, that all coins were very scarce, creating something of a commercial crisis. The scarcity was due to the tendency of local businesspeople to hoard coins in order to send them abroad to pay for purchases. The governor decided to create a quantity of dollars to be perforated to form two kinds of coins. The piece punched out of the centre (the plug) was to be a shilling and the large ring that remained ("holey" dollar) was to be a five-shilling piece.

The reasoning behind the creation of the plug and holey dollar was that the coins would remain on the island, as they were overvalued some 20 percent compared to unmutilated ones. But coins would only be accepted at the inflated rate on the island. This proved correct, but problems with counterfeiting followed.

COURTESY OF THE CHARLTON PRESS.

Chapter 10, p. 419

One Penny, 1857

COURTESY OF THE CHARLTON PRESS.

Chapter 11, p. 477

1813 Trade and Navigation Copper Penny

COURTESY OF THE CHARLTON PRESS.

INDEX

Abercromby, James, 73
Abishabis (Cree leader), 361
Aboriginal peoples
  anthropological classifications, 12, 378–79
  and Atlantic colonies, 241–43
  and Confederation, 469–71
  cultures of, 175–76
  and European contact, 21, 34–35, 379–83, 495–98
  and fur trade, 95–103, 262–63, 270–72
  gender relations, 163
  land, 202–5, 216–17, 326–27
  languages, 12
  in Lower Canada, 230–31
  in Northwest, 258–60, 360–62
  origins and ancient history, 9–16
  pre-contact society, 267–70
  racism toward, 160
  and regionalism, 378–83
  religion, 14–15, 216
  social organization, 14–15, 482–83
  terms for, 494–95
  warfare, 29–31, 34, 38, 86, 360
  on West coast, 367–69
  see also Métis
Acadia, 31–32, 41, 51
  agriculture, 62–63
  as British colony, 53–54
  Catholic church in, 63–64
  cultural experience, 392
  economy, 63
  French settlements in, 48–49
  immigration to, 392
  intermarriage in, 198
  seigneurial system in, 64
  settlement of, 34, 35–36, 61–62

  social structure, 63
  trade with Massachusetts, 282–83
  see also Nova Scotia
Acadians
  culture, 175
  expulsion and return, 71–72, 183, 184–85
  on Island of Saint John, 133
  and Micmacs, 62
Achelacy (Chief), 22
Act of Union (Britain, 1707), 167
Act of Union (Canada, 1841), 328, 330–31
Act of Union (United Kingdom, 1801), 167
Alexander, Sir William, 32, 34
Allen, Ethan, 139
Alline, Henry, 146–47, 489
Allsopp, George, 304
American colonies
  on Quebec Act, 129
  regionalization of, 170–71
  see also United States
American Rebellion
  beginnings of, 137–39
  as civil war, 143–45
  and commerce, 141–43
  and Iroquois Confederacy, 145–46
  and Loyalists, 149–55, 164–65
  and Nova Scotia, 146–47
  threat to Canada, 119, 120, 139–41, 142
American Revolution: *see* American Rebellion
Amherst, Jeffrey, 73
Annand, William, 458, 472, 473
Archibald, A.G., 443
Arnold, Benedict, 139
Askin family, 208, 213
Askin, John, 208, 288
Astor, John Jacob, 95

Atlantic colonies, 240–58
  and aboriginal peoples, 241–43
  agriculture, 248–49
  crises of 1860s, 412
  cultural diversity, 240–41, 401
  economy, 244–49, 341–48, 400–403
  land acquisition, 249
  politics, 251–58, 350–56
  population, 240–43
  regional diversity within, 399–403
  religion, 348–49
  schools, 349–50
  status of women, 250–51, 349–50
  urbanization, 346–48
  and War of 1812, 253
  see also specific colonies

Baby family, 208, 213
Bagot, Sir Charles, 333
Bailey, Jacob, 187
Baillie, Thomas, 257
Baldwin, Robert, 330, 332, 333, 334–35, 336, 337
Baring, Thomas, 301
Beauharnois, Charles de, 69, 70
Bedard, Pierre, 235
Begbie, Matthew B., 366
Bering, Vitus, 93
Bidwell, Marshall Spring, 219
Bigot, François, 279–80
Black, John, 287
Blackstone, William, 172
Bodega de Quadra, Juan, 148
Bond Head, Francis, 204, 223, 224
Bourgeoys, Marguerite, 58
Bourget, Ignace, 450
Braddock, James, 71
Bradstreet, Lieutenant-Colonel, 73
Brant, Joseph, 145, 146
Brébeuf, Jean de, 38
Briand, Jean Olivier, 125, 127–28, 140

Britain
  business and politics, 303
  cultural effect on Canada, 166–74, 502–7
    immigration, 190, 491, 492–94, 499–501
    languages and dialects, 173–74, 483–86
    religion, 173, 486–91
  economy, 273–74
  and fur trade, 84–86
  imperial expansion, 49, 68–70, 119–23
  industrialization, 285–86
  legal system, 172
  political system, 167, 171–72
British North America
  anglophone culture and identity, 502–7
  Britain's policies for, 120–23, 150–55, 204–5
  Britain's relations with, 426–28
  Canada East/Canada West conflict, 412–13
  economy, 286–302, 304–5, 507–13
  extent of, 117–19, 121
  in international arena, 425–28
  legal system, 172–73
  political units of, 197
  population, 176–86, 192–95
  pre-industrial, 197–99
  religion in, 191–92
  settlement, incentives for, 12–23
  transport and communications, 291–95
  U.S. relationship with, 426–27, 428
  see also Lower Canada; Quebec; Upper Canada
British North America Act, 466
Brock, Isaac, 217
Brown, Anne Nelson, 437, 467
Brown, Ariel, 345, 347
Brown, George, 338, 339–40, 351, 364, 431, 437, 439, 444, 445, 447, 469
Buchanan, Peter, 293
Buckingham, William, 364
Bulger, Andrew, 263
Burgoyne, John, 140
Burke, Edmund, 130
Butler, Philip, 254

Cabot, John (Giovanni Caboto), 18
Caldwell, William, 364
Calvert, Sir George, 36–37
Campbell, Sir Archibald, 257
Campbell, Sir Colin, 258
Cape Breton, 400
    American takeover attempt, 69–70
    coal mining, 248
    creation as separate colony, 152
    and Loyalist resettlement, 151
    population, 179
    see also Île Royale
Carleton, Guy, 127–28, 129, 137, 139, 144,
    150
Carleton, Thomas, 152
Carnarvon, Lord, 449, 456, 472, 474; see also
    Duke of Newcastle
Carson, Dr. William, 251, 252, 411
Carter, Frederic, 453
Cartier, George-Etienne, 304, 338, 339, 340,
    431, 436, 447, 448, 449, 458, 467, 522
Cartier, Jacques, 22, 23–24, 77–79
Cartwright, Richard, 213, 288
Cathcart, Earl, 335
Chaboillez, Charles, 106
Champlain, Samuel de, 27–31, 33, 34, 82, 96
Charnisay, Charles de Menou d'Aulnay, 392
Chesnay, Aubert de la, 48
Cocking, Matthew, 92
Colbert, Jean-Baptiste, 41, 46, 47, 52, 57, 397
Colborne, Sir John, 221, 222
Coles, George, 355, 437, 452
Coles, Mercy Ann, 438, 439
Collins, Louisa, 250
Columbus, Christopher, 17
Community of Habitants of New France, 38,
    40
Compagnie de la Nouvelle-France: see
    Company of One Hundred Associates
Compagnie des Indes Occidentales, 41
Compagnie des Indies, 277–79
Compagnie-française de la Baie d'Hudson
    (Compagnie du Nord), 48

Company of One Hundred Associates, 33–36,
    37–38, 40, 41
Confederation
    accomplishments of, 521–22
    aboriginal peoples' exclusion from, 469–71
    and central/local government relationship,
        439–40
    Charlottetown conference (1864), 434,
        435–38
    and composition of federal government,
        440–42
    crises leading to, 425–34
    debates in Atlantic provinces, 451–63
    debates in Canada East and West, 443–51
    failures of, 522–23
    historians' views of, 422–25
    issues underlying, 463–71
    and language issue, 442
    London conference (1866), 471–74
    and Maritime union, 434–36
    mythologies surrounding, 419–22
    nature of country created, 523–24
    and patronage, 466
    provinces added after 1867, 520–21
    and public debt, 442
    Quebec conference (1864), 438–43
    and scientific developments, 464
    social basis of, 465–71
    and status of women, 465
    and voting rights, 465, 466
    and western expansion, 415, 464
    women's role in, 437, 467–68
    and the working class, 468–69
Connolly, Thomas Louis, 472, 473
Constitutional Act (1791), 154–55, 211–12,
    233, 234, 304
Cook, James, 93, 148
Cooper, William, 256
Corn Laws, repeal of, 311, 312
Cornwallis, Edward, 149
Corte-Real, Gaspar, 18
Corte-Real, Miguel, 18
Coureurs de bois, 84, 88–89

Craig, James, 235
Cullen, Paul, 488
Cunard, Samuel, 247
Custom of Paris, 41–44, 60, 163

Dalhousie, Lord (George Ramsay), 237
Dalrymple, George, 256
d'Aulnay, Charles de Menoir, 35
Davis, John, 24
Day, Charles Dewey, 339
De Cosmos, Amor, 367
Demographic transition, 514–16
Denys, Nicholas, 35
D'Iberville, Pierre Le Moyne, 49
Dieskau, General, 71
Dollard des Ormeaux, Adam, 40
Donnacona (Chief), 22, 23, 29
Dorchester, Lord: see Carleton, Guy
Dorion, Sir Antoine-Aimé, 428, 431, 445–47,
    449–50
Douglas, James, 362, 363, 365, 368, 369, 409
Draper, William Henry, 335
Drawback Acts (1845–46), 312
Du Quesnel (Governor of Île Royale), 69
Duncan, William, 368
Duncombe, Charles, 223
Dunkin, Christopher, 524
Duquesne (Governor of New France), 70
Durham, Lord (John Lampton), 330–31, 413

Eddy, Jonathan, 140
Egmont, Earl of, 133
Elgin, Lord, 336

Falkland, Lord, 36–37
Fanning, Edmund, 153
Fenians, 449, 462
First Nations: see Aboriginal peoples
Fisher, Charles, 352, 440
Fisher, Peter, 411

Fisheries, 18–21, 36
    and Atlantic colonies, 244–46
    and developments in Europe, 20–21
    in Île Royale, 280–82
Fitz Roy, Sir Charles Augustus, 256
Fleming, Michael, 254
"Founding peoples" concept, 157–59
France
    cultural effect on Canada
        immigration, 190–91, 491–92, 498–99
        language, 483–86
        religion, 275, 486–91
    economy in seventeenth century, 273–75
    imperial conflict with Britain, 68–70
    war with England, 49
Francklin, Michael, 132, 134
Fraser, Simon, 93
Frobisher, Martin, 24
Frontenac, Governor, 47, 49, 279, 396
Fur trade
    and aboriginal peoples, 80–82, 95–103,
        262–63, 278
    beginnings, 80–84
    by British, 84–86
    by French, 77–84, 84–86, 87–89, 191, 278
    corporate competition in, 89–92
    Hudson's Bay Company enters, 84
    and intermarriage, 88–89, 110–14
    and Métis, 108–10
    and Montreal economy, 276–79, 284
    in Northwest, 90–92, 103–5, 147, 148–49,
        260–63, 358–60
    origins of, 24–27
    on Pacific coast, 92–95
    social structure of, 103–14
    Standard of Trade, 270–71, 291
    women in, 110–14

Gage, General, 138
Galt, Alexander Tilloch, 295, 339, 436,
    444–45, 447, 449, 451, 458
Gamble, Clarke, 302

Garneau, François-Xavier, 411
Gilbert, Sir Humphrey, 18–19
Glenie, James, 153
Glyn, George Carr, 301
Gordon, Arthur Hamilton, 435, 462
Gosford, Lord, 237
Gourlay, Robert, 219–20
Graham, Andrew, 91–92
Grant, Cuthbert, 261
Gray, John Hamilton, 439
Groseilliers, Médart Chouart des, 40, 47
Groulx, Lionel-Adolphe, 87, 423–24
Guercheville, Marquise de, 32
Guy, John, 36
Guy, Pierre, 284

Haldimand, Frederick, 143
Haliburton, T.C., 411
Hamilton, Robert, 13, 288
Handrigan, James, 254
Hargrave, Letitia, 406
Harris, Robert, 293
Harvey, Frederic, 353–54
Harvey, Sir John, 257, 350
Hazen, Moses, 139, 144
Hazen, William, 144
Hearne, Samuel, 91, 92, 147, 148
Henry, Alexander, 89
Hillsborough, Lord, 128
Hincks, Francis, 332, 335, 337–38, 339
Hind, Henry Youle, 414, 464
History, as discipline, 374–76
Holton, Luther, 295
Howe, Joseph, 250–51, 258, 298, 350, 351,
    456–58, 472, 473, 474, 521
Howe, Susan Ann, 250
Hoyles, Hugh, 453
Hudson's Bay Company, 89, 90–91, 109, 230,
    260–62, 278
    and aboriginal peoples, 97, 111, 112,
        270–72
    American challenges to, 362

corporate structure, 105, 106–8, 287, 290–91
enters fur trade, 84
and Fraser River gold rush, 365–67
in Northwest, 128, 147–49, 263–64,
    405–8, 409, 413–14, 433, 470
receives royal charter, 47–48
Standard of Trade, 270–71, 291
and urban land sales, 365
and Vancouver Island colony, 362–63
on West coast, 357
Hunter, Robert, 52

Île Royale, 53–54
    cod fishery, 280–82
    see also Cape Breton
Île St Jean: see Island of Saint John; Prince
    Edward Island
Immigration
    and aboriginal peoples, 494–97
    from British Isles, 190, 491, 492–94,
        499–501
    from France, 190–91, 491–92, 498–99
Indigenous peoples: see Aboriginal peoples
Industrialization, 510–12
    in Atlantic colonies, 343
    in New Brunswick, 343
    in Nova Scotia, 343
    in Upper and Lower Canada, 316–18,
        321–23
Iroquois Confederacy, 48–51, 52, 68, 89, 216
    and American Rebellion, 145–46
Irving, Paul, 127
Irwin, Thomas, 256
Isbister, Alexander, 359
Island of Saint John, 153
    British settlement policy, 132–35
    and Loyalist resettlement, 151
    political structure, 138
    population, 179
    see also Prince Edward Island

Jarvis, Samuel P., 336
Jarvis, William, 213
Jessop, John, 504
Johnson, William, 71
Johnston, J.W., 350
Jolliet, Louis, 47

Kahkewaquonaby (Peter Jones), 204
Kane, Paul, 411
Kirke family, 33–34
Kirke, Sir David, 37
Kittson, Norman, 359, 360
Krieghoff, Cornelius, 411
Kwah (Chief), 262

La Fontaine, Louis, 332, 333, 334–35, 336,
    337, 522
La Roche-Mesgouez, Marquis de, 24, 26
La Salle, Sieur de (René-Robert Cavelier), 37,
    47
La Tour, Charles de Saint-Etienne de, 32, 35,
    63
La Vérendrye, Pierre Gaultier de Varennes et
    de, 68–69, 84–86, 96, 100
Lagimodière, Marie-Anne, 113–14
Lalemant, Gabriel, 38
Langevin, Hector, 304, 448, 449, 450
Lawrence, Charles, 71–72
Le Loutre, Jean-Louis, 64
Le Moyne brothers, 48
Legge, Francis, 137–38
Leif (son of Eric the Red), 16
Lévis, François-Gaston de, 74
Logan, Sir William, 414
London Company, 27
Longfellow, Henry Wadsworth, 64–65
Lower Canada, 224–39
    aboriginal peoples in, 230–31
    agriculture, 313
    Annexation Movement, 311–12
    Catholic church in, 324–25
    class relations, 231–32
    and Constitutional Act (1791), 233, 234
    creation of, 154–55
    economy, 225, 227–33, 276, 284, 316–18,
        321–23, 403–4
    ethnic differences, 232–36
    institutions, 324–25
    politics, 233–36, 336–41
    population, 226–27, 321
    railway construction, 314–15
    and Rebellion of 1837–38, 236–39, 329–31
    seigneurial system, 227–30
    and staples thesis, 224–25, 231
    temperance movement, 324–25
    urbanization, 313–14
    and War of 1812, 236
    work and family life, 321–23
    see also New France; Quebec
Loyalists, 149, 400
    and American Rebellion, 149–55
    cultural impact, 188–90
    migration to British North America,
        150–52, 186–90
    political impact, 153–55
    in Quebec, 154

Mabane, Adam, 127
McDermott, Andrew, 359
MacDonald, A.A., 441
Macdonald, Sir John A., 295, 302, 336, 338,
    339, 340, 373, 431–32, 436, 438, 439, 440,
    441, 444, 445, 447, 451, 462, 467, 469,
    471–72, 473, 474, 519, 521, 524
Macdonald, John Sandfield, 340, 341,
    428–31, 444, 445, 449
Macdonell, Miles, 261
MacDonnell, Richard Graves, 435
McGee, Thomas D'Arcy, 439, 471
McGill, James, 90, 288–89
MacGregor, John, 411
Mckay, J.W., 363
Mackenzie, Alexander, 93

Mackenzie, William Lyon, 222, 223, 298
McMullen, John, 411
MacNab, Allan Napier, 295, 338
McTavish, John, 114
McTavish, Simon, 106
Maisonneuve, Paul de Chomedy de, 35
Mance, Jeanne, 35
Maritime union, and Confederation, 434–36
Maritimes: see Atlantic colonies; specific
    colonies
Marquette, Jacques, 47
Martin, Calvin, 98
Matonabbee (Chief), 91
Membertou (Chief), 27
Merritt, William Hamilton, 210, 307
Metcalfe, Sir Charles, 333, 334, 335
Métis, 191, 356–57, 359–60, 360
    and fur trade, 108–10
    language, 175
    in Northwest, 109–10, 264
    women, 112–14
    see also Aboriginal peoples
Meulles, Jacques de, 390–91
Milne, Robert, 234
Mitchell, Peter, 462, 471, 472
Monck, Frances, 438
Monck, Viscount, 435
Montcalm, Marquis de (Louis-Joseph), 72, 73
Montgomery, Richard, 139, 144
Monts, Pierre du Gua de, 27, 32
Morin, Augustin-Norbert, 333, 337, 338
Morris, Patrick, 287, 411
Mullock, John, 354
Murray, James, 74, 121, 124, 125, 126–27
Murray, John, 344–45

National Policy, 373
Navigation Acts, 246, 311
New Brunswick, 400
    Confederation debates, 454–56, 458,
        460–63
    creation as separate colony, 152
    lumber industry, 345
    politics, 153–54, 253, 256–57, 351–53
    population, 179
    temperance movement, 352–53
New England Planters, 184
New France, 41–52
    Conquest of, 125–26, 283–85
    culture, 174–75
    economy, 46, 51–52, 276–85, 283–84
    extent of, 37
    the family in, 59
    and fur trade, 87–89, 276–79
    import-export merchants, 276
    military in, 56–57, 60
    regionalism in, 390–97
    seigneurial system, 55–56
    social structure, 59–61
    women's status in, 58, 60–61
    see also Lower Canada; Quebec
Newcastle, Duke of, 435; see also Carnarvon,
    Lord
Newfoundland, 49, 65–68, 152, 353–54
    in Confederation debates, 453–54
    crises of 1860s, 412
    economy, 65–66
    fishery, 136–37, 141–42, 244–46, 344
    politics, 252, 254–55
    population, 177–79
    separateness from British North America,
        398–99
    settlement of, 36–37, 65, 135–37
    social structure, 66–68
Newfoundland Act (1842), 353
North West Company, 93, 95, 97, 111,
    260–62, 407
    corporate structure, 105–6
North-West Rebellion (1885), 415
Northwest
    aboriginal peoples in, 258–60, 367–69
    cultural character, 405–7
    economic regionalism, 405–9
    exploration of, 147–49
    fur trade, 260–63

Métis in, 264
population, 356–57
settlement of, 261, 263–64, 357, 405–9,
    413–14, 433
Nova Scotia, 61–65
and American Rebellion, 146–47
British policy toward, 130–32
in Confederation debates, 452, 454–59,
    462–63
Confederation, reaction to, 474
economy, 131–32, 344–45
and Loyalists, 151, 153
politics, 130–31, 137–38, 253, 257–58,
    350–51, 400
population, 179–82
regional diversity within, 399–403
religious revivalism, 146–47

O'Connell, Daniel, 254
O'Donnell, James, 152

Pacific Fur Company, 93–95
Palliser, Hugh, 136
Palliser, John, 464
Palmer, D.B., 252
Palmer, Edward, 355–56
Papineau, Louis-Joseph, 236, 237–38
Parent, Étienne, 334
Parr, John, 150
Patterson, Walter, 138, 153
Payne, Lydia, 302
Peace of Paris (1763), 120
Pepperell, William, 69
Pérez, Juan, 79, 93
Phips, Sir William, 49
Pitt, William, 72, 73
Polk, James, 408–9
Pond, Peter, 147
Pontiac (native leader), 216
Pope, J.C., 453
Pope, W.H., 436, 452

Poutrincourt, Jean de Biencourt de, 32
Powell, Ann, 214
Prescot, Henry, 255
Prevost, Sir George, 217
Prince Edward Island
in Confederation debates, 452–53
economy, 344
entry into Confederation, 520–21
land policies, 355
politics, 252–53, 255–56, 355–56
see also Island of Saint John
Proclamation of 1763, 74–75, 121, 124, 129,
    133, 161–62, 183, 202

Quebec
as British colony, 123–30
Loyalists in, 151–52, 154
partition of, 154–55
population, 182–83
settlement patterns, 498–99
social system, 498–99
see also Lower Canada; New France
Quebec Act (1774), 128–30
and American Rebellion, 137
Quebec Revenue Act, 130

Radisson, Pierre-Esprit, 40, 47
Railways
as business organizations, 292–96
construction in Upper and Lower Canada,
    314–15
Ramezay, Louise de, 60–61
Raymond, Jean-Louis de, 394
Razilly, Isaac de, 35
Rebellion of 1837–38, 222, 223–24, 236–39,
    329–31
Reciprocity Treaty (1854), 313, 401, 426
Red River colony, 364–65
cultural characteristics, 407–8
and Hudson's Bay Company, 263–64
Métis population at, 109–10

Red River Rebellion (1869–70), 414, 520
Regionalism, 371–417
  and aboriginal peoples, 378–83
  in British North America, 398–409
  and Canadian history, 415–17
  and colonial immigration to New France,
    391–92
  components of, 383–90
  and Confederation era, 409–15
  cultural, 384–85, 409–15
  economic, 385–86
  foundations of, in Canada, 376–83
  in French regime, 390–97
  historians' view of, 374–76
  in Lower Canada, 403–4
  and natural environment, 377–78
  perceptions of, 389–90
  political, in New France, 395–97
  and political structures, 388–89
  societal, 386–88, 394–95
  in Upper Canada, 404–5
Richelieu, Cardinal (Armand-Jean du Plessis),
  33, 35
Riel, Louis, 414, 520
Riel, Louis, Sr., 359
Ritchie, William, 352
Roberval, Jean-François de La Rocque de,
  22–23, 23–24
Robinson, John Beverly, 307
Robson, John, 367
Rose, John, 302, 422
Rush-Bagot Agreement (1817), 218
Russell, Lord John, 237
Ryerson, Egerton, 223, 325, 503–4

St. Lawrence colony, 34–35, 37–41, 54–61;
  see also New France
Saint-Lusson, Daumont de, 47
Sawyer, Joseph, 204
Sayer, Pierre-Guillaume, 359
Schultz, Dr. John, 364
Scott, Richard W., 431

Sedgewick, Robert, 35
Seigneurial system, 34–35, 55–56, 64, 498
Selkirk, Earl of (Thomas Douglas), 109,
  260–61, 382–83
Semple, Robert, 261
Seven Years' War, 70–75, 119
Shea, Ambrose, 453
Shirley, William, 69–70, 71
Sicotte, Louis-Victor, 340, 428–29
Simcoe, John Graves, 202–3, 213, 305
Simonds, Charles, 251, 257
Simpson, George, 114, 359–60, 361, 362, 363
Sinclair, James, 359
Smith, Adam, 485
Smith, Albert, 460–62
Smith, C.D., 255
Smyth, D.W., 208
Staples thesis, 87, 201, 224–25, 231, 507
Stowe, Emily, 468
Strachan, John, 214, 215, 219–21, 223, 336
Stuart, John, 213–14
Sweet Grass (Chief), 360
Sydenham, Lord (Charles Poulett Thomson),
  331–32, 333

Taché, Etienne-Paschal, 431, 439, 443, 444,
  467
Talbot, Thomas, 212–13, 405
Talon, Jean, 46, 47
Tecumseh (Chief), 216, 217
Tegiac (Chief), 262
Tenskwatawa (native leader), 216
Thom, Adam, 359
Thompson, David, 93
Thomson, Charles Poulett (Lord Sydenham),
  331–32, 333
Thordarson, Thorfinnr Karlsefni, 16
Thorvaldson, Eirikr (Eric the Red), 16
Tilley, Samuel Leonard, 352, 441, 451–52,
  460, 462
Todd, Isaac, 90, 288
Tonnetuit, Pierre Chauvin de, 26–27

Tonty, Henri, 47
Tupper, Charles, 351, 456, 458, 459, 463, 471, 472, 474

United States, relationship with British North America, 426–27, 428; *see also* American colonies
Upper Canada
   aboriginal peoples, dispossession of, 202–5
   agriculture, 312–13, 320
   business in, 211, 305–7
   creation of, 154–55
   economy, 201–2, 224, 311–13, 316–18, 404–5
   Family Compact, 219, 307
   farming, 320
   immigration policy, 219, 223
   institutions, 222–23, 325–28
   land acquisition, 207–9, 319–20, 326–27
   politics, 211–24, 305–7, 336–41
   population, 200–201, 318–19
   Rebellion's aftermath, 329–31
   reform movements, 215–16, 219–24
   rural economy and society, 205–7, 209–11
   schools, 325–26
   status of women, 214–15
   urbanization, 313–14
   and War of 1812, 217–18

Vancouver, George, 148
Vancouver Island colony, 367–69
Vaudreuil, Governor, 52

Vaughan, Sir William, 36
Vialars, Daniel, 284
Viger, D.B., 335

War of 1812, 215–16
   and Atlantic colonies, 253
   and Lower Canada, 236
   and Upper Canada, 217–19
Warren, Peter, 69
Washington, George, 71, 145
West coast
   first native/white encounters, 79
   fur trade on, 92–95
   settlements on, 367–69, 408–9
Whelan, Edward, 443, 445
Whitbourne, Richard, 36
Willson, John, 221–22
Winslow, Edward, 400
Wolfe, James, 73–74
Women
   aboriginal, 163
   in Atlantic colonies, 250–51, 349–50
   and Confederation, 437, 465, 467–68
   in fur trade, 110–14
   in Lower Canada, 58, 60–61
   Loyalist, 164–65
   Métis, 112–14
   in New Brunswick politics, 353
   status of, 163–66, 513–16
   in Upper Canada, 214–15
Wood, Thomas, 368

Young, Mary, 348

STUDENT REPLY CARD

In order to improve future editions, we are seeking your comments on *Colonies: Canada to 1867* by Bercuson et al.

    After you have read this text, please answer the following questions and return this form via Business Reply Mail. *Thanks in advance for your feedback!*

1. Name of your college or university: _____

2. Major program of study: _____

3. Your instructor for this course: _____

4. Are there any sections of this text which were not assigned as course reading? ___
   If so, please specify those chapters or portions:

5. How would you rate the overall accessibility of the content? Please feel free to comment on reading level, writing style, terminology, layout and design features, and such learning aids as chapter objectives, summaries, and appendices.

6. What did you like *best* about this book?

7. What did you like *least?*

If you would like to say more, we'd love to hear from you. Please write to us at the address shown on the reverse of this card.

--CUT HERE---

--FOLD HERE---

BUSINESS
REPLY MAIL

No Postage Stamp
Necessary if Mailed
in Canada
Postage will be paid by

Attn: Sponsoring Editor, Social Sciences
The College Division
McGraw-Hill Ryerson Limited
300 Water Street
Whitby, Ontario
L1N 9Z9